TANGLED LOYALTIES

—

tangled loyalties

the life and times of Ilya Ehrenburg

JOSHUA RUBENSTEIN

BasicBooks

A Division of HarperCollins*Publishers*

Yevgeny Yevtushenko, "Babii Yar" (trans. George Reavey), from *The Collected Poems, 1952–1990* by Yevgeny Yevtushenko, edited by Albert C. Todd, Yevgeny Yevtushenko, and James Ragan. Copyright © 1991 by Henry Holt and Company, Inc. Reprinted by permission of Henry Holt and Company, Inc.

Published by BasicBooks,
A Division of HarperCollins Publishers, Inc.

Designed by Elliott Beard

Library of Congress Cataloging-in-Publication Data
   Rubenstein, Joshua.
      Tangled loyalties : the life and times of Ilya Ehrenburg / by Joshua Rubenstein.
         p.   cm.
      Includes bibliographical references and index.
      ISBN 0–465–08386–2
      1. Erenburg, Il'ia, 1891–1967—Biography.   2. Authors, Russian—20th century—
   Biography.   3. Journalists—Soviet Union—Biography.   4. Communism and
   culture—Soviet Union.   5. Soviet Union—Intellectual life—1917–1970.   I. Title.
   PG3476.E5Z794   1996
   891.73'42—dc20
   [B]   95–36588
                                                                                          CIP

---

96 97 98 99 ❖/RRD 9 8 7 6 5 4 3 2 1

This book is dedicated to the memory of my father, Bernard Rubenstein. My dad followed his youngest son's career with a mixture of wonder and anxiety. He died just as the first full draft of this book was being completed.

Contents

	Chronology	x
	Introduction	1
ONE	From the Pale to Paris	9
TWO	A Lapsed Bolshevik	23
THREE	Revolution and Civil War	44
FOUR	A Novelist in Exile	71
FIVE	A Writer in Two Worlds	82
SIX	Stalin and the First Five Year Plan	105
SEVEN	A Low, Dishonest Decade	121
EIGHT	The Spanish Civil War	156
NINE	The Second World War and the Holocaust	189

TEN   The Iron Curtain   227

ELEVEN   Anti-Semitism and the Establishment
               of Israel   253

TWELVE   The Thaw and the Politics of Culture   277

THIRTEEN   Ilya Ehrenburg and the Jewish Question   312

FOURTEEN   Illness and Old Age   327

FIFTEEN   *People, Years, Life*   334

SIXTEEN   Spring 1963 and the Fall of Khrushchev   352

SEVENTEEN   Ehrenburg and Dissent   370

EIGHTEEN   1967   385

               Epilogue   393

               Notes   399

               Bibliography   451

               Acknowledgments   461

               Index   465

In transliterating Russian words and proper names, I have relied on J. Thomas Shaw's standard work *The Transliteration of Modern Russian for English-Language Publications*, published by the University of Wisconsin Press in 1967. As all scholars on Russia know, there is no single method for rendering Russian words into English. With few exceptions I have followed Mr. Shaw's instructions, specifically, his System I, employing it throughout the text, notes, and bibliography.

Chronology

1891 Ilya Ehrenburg is born in Kiev

1895 Family moves to Moscow

1905 Ehrenburg is on the barricades during a failed revolution

1906 He joins his high school friend Nikolai Bukharin in the Bolshevik underground

1908 Ehrenburg is arrested and spends five months in jail; after release, he leaves for Paris where he meets Vladimir Lenin

1909 Ehrenburg works briefly with Leon Trotsky in Vienna; disillusioned, he quits Bolsheviks and politics altogether

1910 Ehrenburg publishes first book of poetry

1911 Begins to frequent the Rotonde Café in Montparnasse; daughter Irina is born in Nice

1914 World War I begins

1915 Ehrenburg writes articles about the war for the Moscow newspaper *Utro Rossy* (Russia's Morning)

1916 He becomes a regular correspondent on the western front for the Petrograd newspaper *Birzhevie Vedomosti* (The Stock Exchange Gazette)

1917 Czar Nicholas II abdicates in February; Ehrenburg returns to Russia in July; Bolsheviks seize power in October

1918 Russian civil war begins; Ehrenburg spends next three years in the Ukraine, Crimea, and Moscow

1919 Ehrenburg marries Lyubov Mikhailovna Kozintseva in Kiev

1921 They leave Soviet Russia for Western Europe; Ehrenburg writes *The Extraordinary Adventures of Julio Jurenito and His Disciples*

1924 Ehrenburg is visiting Moscow when Lenin dies

1928 His novel *The Stormy Life of Lasik Roitschwantz* is published in Western Europe, but banned in the Soviet Union

1929 Stalin gains absolute control of the Soviet Union

1932 Ehrenburg becomes *Izvestia* correspondent in Paris

1934 His novel *Out of Chaos* is published in Moscow. First Congress of the Union of Soviet Writers opens in Moscow; Ehrenburg accompanies André Malraux to Soviet Union

1935 Ehrenburg helps to organize the International Writers' Congress in Defense of Culture in Paris

1936 Spanish civil war breaks out; Ehrenburg goes to Spain for *Izvestia*

1937 International Writers' Congress in Defense of Culture convenes in Valencia, Madrid, and Paris; Ehrenburg is among the organizers

1938 Ehrenburg attends a session of Nikolai Bukharin's trial in Moscow

1939 Hitler–Stalin pact; Ehrenburg loses the ability to swallow solid food for eight months; World War II begins

1940 Ehrenburg returns to Moscow after Nazi Occupation of Paris

1941 Hitler invades the Soviet Union; Ehrenburg joins *Krasnaya Zvezda* (Red Star) as a regular correspondent

1942 Jewish Anti-Fascist Committee is established in Moscow; Ehrenburg receives Stalin Prize for *The Fall of Paris*

1944 Ehrenburg receives Order of Lenin for his wartime efforts; he is also made a member of the French Legion of Honor

1946 Ehrenburg makes his only visit to North America

1948 Solomon Mikhoels is murdered in Minsk; Israel is established; Jewish Anti-Fascist Committee is disbanded. Ehrenburg's novel *The Storm* receives Stalin Prize

1950 Ehrenburg meets Liselotte Mehr in Stockholm

1951 Ehrenburg travels to China with Pablo Neruda

1953 Doctors' Plot is announced in the Soviet press in January;
      Ehrenburg receives the Stalin Peace Prize; Stalin dies in March

1954 Ehrenburg publishes *The Thaw*; travels to Chile to award Stalin
      Peace Prize to Pablo Neruda

1956 Ehrenburg visits India; Khrushchev denounces Stalin in secret
      speech

1957 Ehrenburg visits Greece and Japan

1958 Boris Pasternak receives the Nobel Prize for literature to honor
      Doctor Zhivago; Pasternak is expelled from Union of Soviet
      Writers

1960 Ehrenburg begins to publish *People, Years, Life* in *Novy Mir*

1961 Ehrenburg receives Order of Lenin to honor his seventieth
      birthday; Yevgeny Yevtushenko's poem "Babii Yar" appears in
      Moscow

1962 *Novy Mir* publishes Alexander Solzhenitsyn's *One Day in the Life
      of Ivan Denisovich*

1963 Nikita Khrushchev and other party leaders publicly denounce
      Ehrenburg and his memoirs

1964 Khrushchev is removed from power

1965 The writers Andrei Sinyavsky and Yuli Daniel are arrested in
      Moscow for publishing their work abroad under pseudonyms;
      the Soviet human rights movement begins to emerge

1966 Ehrenburg signs petitions in defense of Sinyavsky and Daniel
      and against the rehabilitation of Stalin

1967 Ilya Ehrenburg dies in Moscow

His name is always mud—somewhere or other. He is Ilya Ehrenburg, the renowned Soviet writer, who has shouldered the lifelong burden of always being blamed by somebody, somewhere, for something.

—*The* Daily Mirror, *London, 1966*

Introduction

In the aftermath of communism's collapse throughout Eastern Europe and the former Soviet Union, the dual legacy of repression and complicity continues to trouble societies that have yet to overcome the trauma of Stalinist and post-Stalinist control. Under Stalin silence or at least outward conformity was required to remain alive; but the dictator commanded more than tacit compliance. He expected flattery, especially from intellectuals, and he enjoyed watching them subvert their natural talents in order to please him. By the 1930s, when the regime formally adopted "socialist realism" as the prescribed approach for all creative artists, Soviet politics came to dominate if not suffocate Russian culture. No artist or writer was immune from unrelenting pressure to conform, and few were able to survive a treacherous quarter century under Stalin and successfully retain a measure of personal and artistic integrity. Ilya Ehrenburg was one of them.

The career of Ilya Ehrenburg, the most renowned Soviet journalist of his generation, challenges our assumptions about collaboration, dissent, and survival. For half a century his life abounded in controversy and contradiction. As a teenager, he both joined and left the Bolshevik party, only to make himself useful to Stalin decades later as an emissary to European intellectuals. While other Soviet writers were disappearing, Ehrenburg carried out political assignments living in France, traveling widely and still publishing in Moscow. Such privileges, alongside his evident adaptability, raised suspicions about Ehrenburg's motives and integrity. As a Jew, he was said to have betrayed his people; as a writer, his talent; and as a man, to have kept silent about Stalin's crimes and served the dictator solely to curry and enjoy the Kremlin's favors.

But a closer, more informed examination of Ehrenburg's life reveals a determined consistency that the seismic shifts of history have always, in Ehrenburg's case, obscured. Western and Soviet detractors have ignored his acts of independence from Stalin's policies, his anguished response to the Holocaust and lifelong opposition to anti-Semitism, and his importance to millions of Soviet citizens who revered him for trying to sustain Russia's connection to European art and culture. In the confused years after the Bolshevik revolution, in the terrifying quarter century under Stalin, and the breathless, liberating, and ultimately frustrating decade under Khrushchev, Ehrenburg was courageous, at times even outspoken when *no one* of similar stature dared to voice independent views.

Such a career presents complex dilemmas to a biographer who seeks to understand and explain more than to judge or condemn. Ilya Ehrenburg lived through the greatest calamities of the twentieth century, including World War I, the Bolshevik revolution, the Spanish civil war, Stalin's purges, World War II, and the cold war. He was often on the front lines and virtually everything he wrote made someone angry. Orthodox Marxist critics hated his novels in the 1920s. The Nazis burned his books in the 1930s. His columns against the Germans were so powerful that Hitler blamed Ehrenburg for German military defeats. Then during the cold war Ehrenburg was notorious for his attacks on American culture. A public figure as much as he was a writer and a journalist, Ehrenburg's complicated, calculated, personal decisions came within crisis after crisis in European and Soviet history. He managed to survive, but in spite of his official conformity there was always a feeling about Ehrenburg that he was different. Nadezhda Mandelstam, the widow of the martyred poet Osip Mandelstam, had this in mind when she dubbed him "the odd man out" among Soviet writers.

"He was as helpless as everybody else," she recalled about the Stalin years, "but at least he tried to do something for others."[1]

Ilya Ehrenburg was not a rebellious martyr. Ironically, he began his career as a teenage activist in Moscow's Bolshevik underground. Imprisoned in 1908 at the age of seventeen, he fled czarist Russia for Paris, where he met Vladimir Lenin. Ehrenburg quickly grew bored with émigré politics and signaled his break with the Bolsheviks by ridiculing Lenin in a satirical journal he himself edited. Preferring literature to revolution, Ehrenburg published his first volume of poetry in 1910 and soon befriended such artists as Picasso, Modigliani, Chagall, Léger, and Rivera in Parisian cafés. He made a name for himself writing articles in France about World War I for a Petrograd newspaper, where he discovered how passionately he could express himself; after that, he never stopped writing, especially about politics. But it was Ehrenburg's first novel, *The Extraordinary Adventures of Julio Jurenito and His Disciples*—where a mysterious, Mephistophelean figure leads a diverse group of followers through the battlefields of the First World War and the Bolshevik seizure of power—that confirmed his reputation as a provocative presence in Soviet letters. Nothing like it had ever appeared before in Russian literature. At first glance the novel's assault on all ideological pretensions, including Western capitalism, Soviet communism, and established religious faith, reflected Ehrenburg's angry loss of innocence after the upheavals of war and revolution. Western institutions had failed and the Bolshevik revolution was turning into a dictatorship, something the novel made absolutely clear in 1921.

Julio Jurenito also revealed Ehrenburg's yearning for something to believe in, even as Jurenito and his disciples witness Europe's and Russia's collapse. Ehrenburg felt this spiritual vacuum and spent most of the 1920s bemoaning a Europe he had once adored. This disillusion and even more the threat of Nazi aggression made Ehrenburg vulnerable to the compromises and evasions that loyalty to Stalin required. Within the space of a decade, from 1921 to 1932, Ehrenburg moved from being the author of a satiric *tour de force* to being *Izvestia* correspondent in Paris; from then on he became part of Stalin's machinery in the West, establishing an intricate relationship with the regime that lasted until the end of his life.

He did not foresee, of course, all that this would entail. Ehrenburg once explained to a friend that during the purges "the Bolsheviks started by killing each other; this did not affect me. But then they began to kill people close to me, and it was too late."[2] He could not turn back. As a loyal Soviet writer and journalist, Ehrenburg had to be silent, to "live with clenched teeth."[3] This was the heart of Ehrenburg's personal tragedy. Manipulated by fear and official favors, he accepted the need to engage in heavy-handed propaganda. His articles from France and Spain, Germany, Switzerland, and England were not only directed against Fascist aggression and the illusions of Western democracies, but were often malicious attacks on Stalin's ideological opponents as well—French Surrealists and intellectuals such as André Gide, who broke with the Communists even as they shared a common hatred for fascism. For Ehrenburg it was especially necessary to write such articles in the 1930s because he needed to demonstrate his loyalty while remaining a Soviet journalist in France. Meanwhile, close friends were executed or disappeared. Ehrenburg had to mourn them in private, while survival was like a curse that haunted his life and reputation. Indeed, of all the great cultural figures to survive the Stalin era, among them the composer Dmitri Shostakovich and the poets Boris Pasternak and Anna Akhmatova, only Ilya Ehrenburg's moral standing remains in question.

Ehrenburg's leading role in the anti-Fascist movement did not make him blind or indifferent to Stalin's repression. Whenever he could, he found ways to speak his mind. In the 1930s Ehrenburg defended creative freedom even after "socialist realism" began to stifle artistic creativity. In the years 1940 and 1941, while the Soviet Union was allied with Nazi Germany, Ehrenburg continued to write and lecture against fascism, warning whoever would listen that the country could not avoid war.

Ehrenburg reached the height of his official prestige during World War II when his passionate, angry articles against the Germans helped to sustain Soviet morale; his columns were even read to Soviet troops before battle. Yet Ehrenburg still pushed the limits of Stalin's policies. He continued to write about the Holocaust until the end of the war, past the time the regime found it useful to highlight Jewish suffering.

The war reminded Ehrenburg of his Jewish origins. Faced with Hitler's Final Solution and domestic Soviet anti-Semitism, Ehrenburg was determined to document the heroism of Jewish soldiers and the destruction of Jewish communities. Under his direction dozens of Soviet writers collected testimonies from survivors of the Nazi occupation of Soviet territory and turned the material into *The Black Book*, an unprecedented account of the worst catastrophe to befall Soviet Jewry: the destruction of one and a half million Jews by German shooting units. Ehrenburg hoped to see the volume appear, but Stalin forbade its publication. For Ehrenburg this was one of the most bitter disappointments of his life. Still, he protected the original material in his apartment. After Ehrenburg's death in 1967 the original folios of *The Black Book*, including precious eyewitness accounts of Nazi massacres, were the first things his family concealed from the regime.

Ehrenburg's career under Nikita Khrushchev was equally controversial. There were writers who survived the Stalin era only to behave with no moral scruples after the dictator was gone. But Ehrenburg had the stamina and courage to challenge Khrushchev's constraints on art, literature, and historical truth. Alone among the writers of his generation, Ehrenburg strove to restore the country's historical memory. He pressed for the rehabilitation of numerous figures, insisting a new generation had the right to know the work of his friends Isaac Babel, Osip Mandelstam, and Marina Tsvetaeva. Yet even while Ehrenburg campaigned against censorship, Soviet cultural bureaucrats denounced him for "resurrecting corpses."

Khrushchev himself attacked Ehrenburg publicly. In his memoirs Ehrenburg dared to acknowledge that he had known many of Stalin's victims to be innocent, but out of fear kept silent to preserve his own life. This admission struck at the heart of the regime's legitimacy: If a journalist like Ehrenburg knew the truth behind the purges, then how could people like Khrushchev, who had worked closely with Stalin in the Kremlin, not have known? Ehrenburg's "theory of silence" had to be denounced. In March of 1963 Khrushchev and other party leaders denounced Ehrenburg, even making veiled threats to arrest him.

Nadezhda Mandelstam understood what Ehrenburg was trying to accomplish. She had first met him in Kiev in 1918 when she and his future wife, Lyubov Mikhailovna Kozintseva, were art students together. After Osip Mandelstam's arrest and death in 1938, Nadezhda Mandelstam disappeared into lonely exile, moving from town to town in the Soviet provinces to avoid detention. Ehrenburg's apartment was one of the few places she could visit during her discreet and illegal trips to Moscow. Ehrenburg never turned her away. He even kept an album of remnants and versions of Mandelstam's poetry. When Nadezhda Mandelstam regained the right to visit Moscow in the 1950s, Ehrenburg gave her the album as a gesture of loyalty to her husband's work and memory.

Nadezhda Mandelstam knew Ehrenburg for half a century, and given the circumstances of her life—her husband's martyrdom, her struggle to preserve his verse, her poverty and isolation—it would not be surprising for her to condemn Ehrenburg for the success and prestige he achieved. But she accepted Ehrenburg's friendship and offered her own.

Writing to Ehrenburg in the spring of 1963 following Khrushchev's assault on his memoirs, Nadezhda Mandelstam expressed her moral support with customary insight.

> Dear Ilya Grigorevich!
>
> I have been thinking about you a good deal (when friends think about someone he doesn't have any pain) and this is what I have finally understood.
>
> From the point of view of everyday life it is hard to live in the epicenter of an earthquake. But in a certain sense this is important and necessary. You know there is a tendency to accuse you of not reversing the direction of rivers, of not changing the course of the stars, of not breaking up the moon into honeycake and feeding us the pieces. In other words, people always wanted the impossible from you and were angry when you did the possible.
>
> Now, after the latest events, it is obvious how much you did and are doing to relax our usual ways, how great your role is in our life and how we should be grateful to you. *Everyone* understands this now. And I am happy to tell you this and to shake your hand.
>
> I kiss you affectionately and want you to be strong as always.
>
> Your Nadya
>
> Regards to Lyuba.[4]

"He was the last person I was *na ty* with," Nadezhda Mandelstam told a friend when she learned of Ehrenburg's death in August 1967.[5] (*Ty*, like the French *tu*, expresses intimacy and informality.) "There was a great crowd at his funeral," she remarked in her memoir *Hope Abandoned*, "and I noticed that the faces were decent and human ones. It was an anti-Fascist crowd, and the police spies who had been sent to the funeral in force stood out very conspicuously. It was clear, in other words, that Ehrenburg had done his work well, difficult and thankless though it was."[6]

When Ilya Ehrenburg died in 1967, his death came just as another, more outspoken generation of writers was challenging the regime's regulations and independently publishing work abroad. The careers of Alexander Solzhenitsyn, Andrei Sinyavsky, Georgy Vladimov, Vladimir Voinovich, Joseph Brodsky, Andrei Amalrik, and Vasily Aksyonov, blossoming alongside the emerging human rights movement, altered the contours of Soviet culture. All were compelled to leave the country for defying the regime's control of artistic expression. Ehrenburg's life came to an end as this new era was taking shape. He helped to prepare the ground, introducing the work of long-suppressed Soviet writers over a host of bureaucratic and ideological constraints. History will have to judge him within the framework of the years in which he lived and not by the standards that marked the epoch to follow.

ONE

From the Pale to Paris

The history of the Jews of Russia begins at the end of the eighteenth century, when large Jewish communities were annexed to the Russian Empire after the partitions of Poland. The czars wanted to minimize the "malicious influence" of these new subjects. Catherine II instituted the first regulations, defining where Jews could live and engage in trade. Further restrictions were established by her successors, Alexander I and later Nicholas I, who in 1829 designated a large area called the Pale of Settlement—comprising parts of present-day Lithuania, Poland, Belarus, and Ukraine—as the place where the czar's Jewish subjects were compelled to live.

Rights of residence outside the Pale began to be granted under Alexander II in 1859, allowing prominent merchants, university graduates, various craftsmen, army veterans, and health professionals to apply for permission to move. While the Jews hoped these changes would lead to the abolition of the Pale, they were soon disappointed. Alexander II's reforms were designed to give the "better" Jews an opportunity to gain their emancipation by assimilating "so far as the moral status of the Jews will allow it."[1]

A severe reaction against all reform followed the assassination of Alexander II in 1881. Restrictions inside the Pale were tightened: peasants could demand the expulsion of Jews from their communities, and a wave of pogroms further threatened Jewish lives. Such measures reached hysterical proportions in 1891, when a government decree ordered the expulsion of the Jews of Moscow, compelling nearly thirty thousand to leave the city. A similar decree was issued in St. Petersburg, where two thousand Jews were expelled, many of them in chains.

That same year, on January 14, Ilya Ehrenburg was born into a middle-class Jewish family in Kiev.* His parents named him Eliyahu, the Biblical name for the prophet Elijah. He was their only son, the youngest child after three sisters—Maria, Yevgeniya, and Izabella. Photographs from his early years show an alert boy with straight, cropped hair and a roundish face. By all accounts, he was spoiled and mischievous, teased his older sisters, put frogs in their clothes or tied their long braids to chairs when they were not paying attention. In a fit of anger, Ilya once tried to burn down his grandfather's dacha, and he took pride in compelling one tutor after another to quit his parents' employ. He seemed impossible to discipline. His father was rarely at home; he worked during the day as an engineer and sought enjoyment among his friends at night. Ilya's mother suffered from a lung ailment that left her delicate and weak. Her "bedroom always smelled of medicines," Ehrenburg once recalled, while doctors came to examine her frequently. Lacking parental authority, "it was only chance," Ehrenburg felt compelled to admit, "that I did not become a juvenile delinquent." Stubborn and rebellious, Ilya nonetheless was his mother's favorite, even when exile separated them for many years.

The Ehrenburg family exemplified tensions that had begun to break the pattern of traditional Jewish life in the Russian Empire. Ilya's father, Grigory, was an assimilated Jew who had no interest in Jewish ritual; he had studied in a Russian school and valued his secular education, incurring the anger of his devout father. But Ilya's mother, Anna Arnshtein, continued to observe religious customs much like her father,

---

*Until 1918, Russia adhered to the Julian calendar, which was twelve days behind the Gregorian calendar in the nineteenth century and thirteen days behind it in the twentieth. Ehrenburg was born on January 26, 1891, according to the Gregorian calendar.

who was also an Orthodox Jew. Her side of the family strongly influenced Ilya's upbringing, since as a child he spent much time in the
home of his maternal grandfather in Kiev. Boris Arnshtein was an
elderly bearded Jew. "All religious customs were strictly observed in his
home," Ehrenburg made a point of recalling in his memoirs.[2] "On Saturday, you had to rest, and this meant the grown-ups could not smoke
or the children play." Ehrenburg stressed his alienation from his grandfather's way of life, with its severe restrictions and arbitrary rules. "I did
everything wrong," he explained. "I wrote on the Sabbath, blew out the
wrong candles, and took off my cap when I should have kept it on."[3]

While Ilya felt uncomfortable with his grandfather's religious commitments, he appreciated his learning and generosity. Ilya spoke to a
family gathering after Boris Arnshtein's funeral in 1904, and based on
the eulogy that his sisters proudly preserved it is evident that he was a
sensitive, articulate adolescent.

> "An amazingly rare man, such people do not exist"—this is what was
> said about grandfather while he was alive, and the same was said over
> his remains. . . . But what made grandfather different from those
> around him? . . .
> The reason can be found in the special quality of his character.
> . . . Raised on the Old Testament, he was profoundly religious, but he
> was not fanatical. Strictly fulfilling all the customs of his religion, he
> never demanded even from his children that they do the same. For
> him, religion was not only a sea of rules, prescribing certain customs
> . . . it was a code of moral conduct for determining how a man
> should relate to himself and to others.[4]

But in spite of his grandfather's legacy and his mother's Orthodoxy,
Ilya's parents wanted him to be a well-educated, Russian-speaking Jew.
"I grew up in a family where religion was preserved only in the form
of a few superstitions," he later recalled.[5] His parents did not teach him
Yiddish, but spoke in Russian, resorting to Yiddish when they did not
want him to understand. This was quite unusual, for according to the
census of 1897 barely 25 percent of Russian Jewry could read and
write in Russian. The overwhelming majority, more than 97 percent,
considered Yiddish their mother tongue.[6]

A distant relative, Lev Arnshtein, found a different means to rebel
against life in the ghetto and still maintain a distinct interest in Jewish

learning. Although he received a secular education at Kiev University, he studied Hebrew and in 1893 translated *Not by Bread Alone*, the first story by Leo Tolstoy to appear in the holy tongue.[7] Lev Arnshtein's translation of Tolstoy reflected a mood among many Jews who wanted to bring their communities into the modern secular world and shun Yiddish culture. They were inspired by the Haskalah movement (Hebrew for "enlightenment") that had begun in Germany in the mid-eighteenth century. The followers of Haskalah believed Jews were persecuted because they differed from their non-Jewish neighbors in culture and appearance; they contended that as soon as Jews could learn the language of their respective countries and adopt the manners of the broader society, they would gain their political and social emancipation. Hebrew, which had been strictly reserved for the study of sacred texts, was only beginning to be used for nonreligious purposes in Eastern Europe and Palestine. By translating Tolstoy into Hebrew, Lev Arnshtein was helping to bring modern literature to those who until then had little access to Russian culture. At the same time, interest in Hebrew was also part of a burgeoning Zionist movement, which called on Jews to establish a homeland of their own in Palestine.

Although Ilya's family was partially assimilated into Russian society, his parents were fully aware of anti-Semitism. "I belong to those whom it is proper to persecute" was a bitter lesson he learned under the czar and repeated in his memoirs sixty years later. Kiev, where Ilya was born, was located within the Pale of Settlement, but as in many towns and cities, Jews needed special permission to live there. In 1861 the two suburbs Lebed and Podol were assigned to Jews. Ilya knew that in the 1860s his maternal grandfather had fled harassment in the small northern city of Novgorod-Seversk and moved to Kiev. Thinking of this episode, Ehrenburg wondered in his memoirs if anti-Semites had pulled his grandfather's side curls. But anti-Semitism and his own dislike for religious customs did not make him regret he was a Jew. "My father, who was an unbeliever, condemned Jews who embraced Russian Orthodoxy to make their lot easier," Ehrenburg recalled in *People, Years, Life*, "and from an early age I understood that one must not be ashamed of one's origins."[8] This attitude was common in his family. His uncle, Lazar Ehrenburg, was a talented chemist who refused to convert to Christianity when officials at Kharkov University demanded he renounce his Jewish origins; he quit the university instead.[9]

Ilya Ehrenburg grew up among these contending convictions: Orthodox ritual observance, assimilation into Russian culture, Zionism, and the miraculous revival of the Hebrew language. For the most part, Ehrenburg followed his father's lead. He became an assimilated Jew, rejecting any attachment to Jewish religious practices and never learning either Yiddish or Hebrew. Like the vast majority of Jews in the former Soviet Union, Ehrenburg lost his linguistic and cultural roots. But also like them, he felt a sense of vulnerability as a Jew. Ilya heard his parents discuss the Dreyfus affair and watched his father curse and his mother cry when they read about the death of Dreyfus's courageous defender, Émile Zola in September 1902. The following year Ilya learned about the Kishinev pogrom, when a mob killed forty-five Jews, wounded twice as many, and looted or destroyed more than five hundred homes and shops. Ehrenburg never denied his Jewish origins, and near the end of his life often repeated the defiant conviction that he would consider himself a Jew "as long as there was a single anti-Semite left on earth."[10]

TO MOSCOW

In 1895, when Ilya was four years old, his family gained permission to move to Moscow because his father became the manager of a major brewery.[11] Grigory Ehrenburg worked for the Brodsky family, who were important industrialists and philanthropists within the Jewish community. By the end of the nineteenth century, their plants were producing about one-quarter of all the refined sugar in Russia.[12] No doubt it was their intervention that gained Grigory Ehrenburg the right to live in Moscow, which was an extraordinary privilege for a Jew at that time. Most Jews had been expelled four years earlier, and by 1897 the Jewish population numbered only about eight thousand in a general population of one million.

Many of Moscow's Jews were wealthy merchants or members of the free professions—doctors, lawyers, pharmacists, and engineers like Grigory Ehrenburg. City officials remained hostile to the Jews, particularly Grand Prince Sergei Alexandrovich, who as governor of Moscow from 1891 to 1905 (when he was killed by a Russian revolutionary) wanted "to protect Moscow from Jewry."[13] The city's central synagogue was closed after the expulsion of the Jews, as were most of the smaller prayer houses; after years of petitioning, the synagogue was reopened only in 1906.

Ehrenburg's family lived in a comfortable apartment attached to the brewery in the Khamovniki section; it was mainly populated by lower-middle-class tradesmen, with a few large-estate owners. The Moscow home of Leo Tolstoy adjoined the brewery, and Ilya used to see the great man walking in the neighborhood; by then Tolstoy was over seventy, yet still a vivid presence in Russian society. Ilya saw for himself the authority a writer can command: the gates to the brewery would be locked whenever students held demonstrations—it was assumed they would march on Tolstoy's house to petition for his support. Ehrenburg met Tolstoy on one occasion when he was visiting the brewery, an encounter that left him sorely disappointed. He heard the writer explain how beer could help in the campaign against vodka. Tolstoy's attitude surprised him. Drunkenness was a scourge of Russian life, as it remains today; the young idealist expected Tolstoy to oppose alcohol altogether, not to suggest beer as a useful palliative.

Along with their fine Moscow apartment, the Ehrenburg family was prosperous enough for Ilya to travel with his mother and sisters to Germany and Switzerland on several occasions, where they vacationed at Bad Ems and other popular spas. His parents must have regarded him as unusually mature because on one trip, when he was barely a teenager, Ilya's mother allowed him to visit Berlin on his own while she returned to Russia. He stayed in a modest pension. One evening Ilya ventured out to a café that turned out to be a nightclub, which was more expensive than anticipated; he had to wire a request for money so he could make it home.

Years later, when Ehrenburg was in exile in Europe, he recalled his childhood in several poems. In "Recollections" he wrote about a family servant putting furs away for the summer and a chandelier catching sunlight in a large living room. Memories of his mother provoked longing and affection.

> If at night you could not sleep
> You would run in bare feet
> to mama
> across the great dark salon.
> Over the bed was her medicine chest—
> drops and pills.

> A flickering candle
> and linen on a chair.[14]

Servants, fur coats, a chandelier—few Jewish families escaped the Pale of Settlement into such comfortable surroundings. But their good fortune did not blind the Ehrenburg family to the misery they were able to avoid. When Ilya's school marks were poor and he was held back for a year, his father reminded him that as a Jew he would probably need a university education to stay in Moscow. As things turned out, Ilya did have to leave Moscow, but not because he was a Jew or an indifferent student; he left because he became a Bolshevik revolutionary.

IN THE UNDERGROUND

As Ilya Ehrenburg grew older, he began to see the persecution faced by Jews as part of a general crisis in czarist society. Living in Moscow made this easy to grasp. He attended one of the city's prestigious high schools, the First Gymnasium, where he was one of three Jews in his class. His classmates taunted him, calling Ilya a "damn kike" and "leaving bits of pork on [his] notebooks." Ehrenburg smacked one student in the face for insulting him.

Schools such as Moscow's First Gymnasium were also breeding grounds for young revolutionaries. By 1905, many students were beginning to discuss serious political literature and agitate against the autocracy. Ilya's rebellious nature led him in that direction. "I read only those books they prohibited me to read," he claimed. "I respected disrespect and listened to the voices of the disobedient."[15] At first, Ilya's defiance of authority involved usual adolescent behavior—collecting indecent postcards, gambling and smoking in the school lavatories, adorning walls with graffiti. But Ilya had literary pretensions, too; he became editor of a journal called *First Ray* that he refused to show to his teachers "although it contained nothing more dreadful than poems about liberty and little anecdotes describing the stupidities of school life."[16]

Larger events soon propelled Ilya to more substantial dissent. Political protests and unrest had been increasing since 1900 and became more widespread after Russia's disastrous war with Japan in 1904–5, a conflict that dramatically exposed the backwardness of czarist society. The autocracy was blamed for Russia's defeat by a small Asiatic state.

Resistance to the czar grew in the city and in the countryside. Peasants, who made up more than 80 percent of the population, increasingly turned to violence against landlords and their enormous estates.
The peasants wanted to be free of their semifeudal burdens and cultivate land of their own. Industrial workers organized frequent strikes.
Professional organizations, including lawyers, doctors, and engineers,
called publicly for constitutional reforms. But the czar dismissed such
pleas. The appeal of Russia's underground parties grew broader, particularly the Social Democratic Labor party—the Communist party—
with its Marxist propaganda, and the Socialist Revolutionary party,
with its call for radical action and terror. Only violence, it seemed,
could force the czar into granting a constitution and a parliament.

The events of 1905 played a decisive role in the history of Russia
and the life of Ilya Ehrenburg. In January, czarist troops fired on an
unarmed crowd carrying a petition of grievances to the Winter Palace
in St. Petersburg; this was Bloody Sunday, the beginning of the 1905
revolution. Anarchy seized hold of the country. Sailors mutinied on the
battleship *Potemkin;* they shot and imprisoned their officers and raised
the Red flag over one of the most powerful ships in the Black Sea fleet.
Unrest spread to other boats. Sailors refused to fire on the *Potemkin,*
while strikes disrupted the naval base of Sevastopol and the major port
at Odessa.

High school and university students responded to the revolutionary
call. Ilya, like thousands of others, stayed away from the gymnasium,
spending his time at Moscow University, where workers, students, and
professional agitators conducted mass meetings in the lecture halls.
They sang the Marseillaise, circulated pamphlets. "Huge hats inscribed
'Your contribution means arms for us' were passed from hand to
hand."[17] But by December the government overcame the rebels. The
workers' council of St. Petersburg, led by Leon Trotsky, was broken up
on December 3; the entire soviet of 190 members, including Trotsky,
was placed under arrest.

The climax came in Moscow. The news from St. Petersburg led the
Moscow committee of the Bolshevik party to call for an armed uprising. A few thousand activists erected barricades across major streets,
hoping to revive the fortunes of revolution. It was a desperate and sui-
cidal failure. They could not overcome a regiment of imperial guards
and regular troops armed with artillery. More than a thousand were
killed, including many high school and university students. Ilya had

joined the revolutionaries, helping to build barricades. "That was when I first saw blood on the snow," he recalled. "I shall never forget that Christmas: the heavy, terrible silence after the singing, the shouting, the firing."[18]

At the height of the struggle in October, Czar Nicholas II had established the Duma, the first genuine parliament in Russian history. He promised it would be a representative assembly and that its approval would be necessary for the enactment of all legislation. But after crushing the 1905 revolution, the czar reduced the Duma's powers before it even had an opportunity to assemble. In the wake of their violent defeat, the radical parties had to consider whether to participate in the new parliament. Vladimir Lenin, who was one of the leaders of the Social Democratic Labor party, feared that the Duma, in spite of its restricted powers, might genuinely challenge the czar, exert a measure of political authority, and thereby forestall the urge for revolution throughout the country. His worries were needless. The czar and the Duma failed to reach any compromise that could lead Russia away from autocratic rule. In just over two months, the first Duma was dissolved.

Czar Nicholas II survived the revolution of 1905. It was a great rehearsal nonetheless, Lenin was to observe, and it taught the Bolsheviks many lessons. It also swelled the party ranks with energetic students, an entire generation of future party leaders.[19] Ilya and his older friend Nikolai Bukharin became members at that time, in 1906. "There were no longer any meetings at the university, nor demonstrations, nor barricades. I joined the Bolshevik organization, and soon said good-bye to my schooldays," Ehrenburg later recalled.

Ilya could have joined one of several opposition groups. He rejected the Socialist Revolutionaries as too romantic, preaching terrorism and the role of the heroic individual. He was drawn to the Social Democratic Labor party, Russia's Marxist underground composed of Bolshevik and Menshevik factions. The party had first divided in 1903, when a dispute over membership arose at a party congress held in Brussels and London. When Lenin's followers gained a temporary majority of the central committee, they took the name Bolshevik (those of the majority) and dubbed the second group Menshevik (those of the minority). Other issues further separated the two factions. The Mensheviks became more conciliatory and opposed Lenin's emphasis on the dictatorial role of a heavily centralized party; they were also

willing to work with liberals to establish a new democratic order in
Russia.

Ilya preferred the Bolsheviks because they were more radical. "The
Mensheviks were moderates, more like my father," he wrote. The connection that Ehrenburg made between joining the Bolsheviks and
rejecting his father's moderation cannot be overlooked. While he wrote
very little about his father in *People, Years, Life*, the few details he provided are relevant for understanding his own upbringing and attraction
to revolution. Grigory Ehrenburg thrived in the social atmosphere of
Moscow, far from Kiev, the Podol, and the confining restrictions of the
Pale of Settlement. He belonged to the exclusive Hunt Club, where
gentlemen spent hours playing whist, and he was friends with the journalist Vladimir Gilyarovsky, a notorious man-about-town in Moscow.

Ilya shared his father's aversion to Orthodox Jewish ritual, but
though Grigory found a comfortable place for himself in Russian society, Ilya felt distant from his father and the life he fashioned for himself. Ilya was unimpressed by the fancy restaurants his father frequented, just as he looked down on his father's trivial preoccupation
with card playing. But in Paris a few years later Ehrenburg ironically
adopted some of his father's habits and even outdid him with his fondness for sitting in cafés, showing a complete lack of interest in a normal domestic life.

In spite of the Ehrenburg family's privileged position their home life
was not idyllic. Ehrenburg made only oblique references in his memoirs to his parents' difficulties, but they were separated by 1904, and
although the marriage officially endured until Anna Ehrenburg's death
in 1918, she and Grigory remained estranged from each other. It is
possible that even as a child Ilya understood that the temptations of
Moscow night life helped to undermine his parents' marriage.
Although Ehrenburg genuinely loved his mother, he disliked his father.
Grigory Ehrenburg opposed the czar in a fashionably safe manner; he
favored the Cadets (or Constitutional Democrats), a mainstream group
of Russian liberals. Ilya, though, in preferring the Bolsheviks, adopted
a political posture that rejected not only the czar but also the bourgeois
pursuits his father enjoyed.

Ilya's friendship with Nikolai Bukharin, who later became one of
the leaders of the revolution, a favorite of Lenin's, and a principal victim of Stalin's purges, was also a decisive factor in Ilya's decision to join
the Bolshevik underground. Bukharin's influence on Ehrenburg's life

and career did not end with their teenage encounters or with Ilya's exile to France in 1908; their paths would continue to cross for three more decades. Bukharin's trial and execution in 1938 marked one of Ehrenburg's most dangerous crises, when he, too, seemed vulnerable to arrest. Ehrenburg never disavowed their friendship, and when he wrote about Bukharin in his memoirs, even the brief, uncensored references to "Nikolai Ivanovich"—which everyone understood—were the first kind words about the disgraced Bolshevik leader to appear in the Soviet press for several decades. Almost everything else that Ehrenburg wrote about Bukharin was suppressed, including a chapter that was not published in Moscow until Mikhail Gorbachev's policy of *glasnost* took hold and Ehrenburg's loving memories of his childhood friend could appear:

> I would like simply to recall an eighteen-year-old youth whom we all loved and nicknamed "Bukharchik." . . . Bukharin, unlike the rest of us, was very cheerful. It seems I can still hear his infectious laughter. He would interrupt a discussion with jokes all the time, using artificial and funny words which he invented on the spot. . . . There are very gloomy people with optimistic ideas and there are cheerful pessimists. Bukharchik had a surprisingly harmonious nature—he wanted to transform life because he loved it.

Ilya was only fifteen years old when he joined the Bolsheviks. He threw himself into the work, distributing literature, working as an organizer in the same Moscow district assigned to Bukharin. Ilya composed leaflets, argued with the Mensheviks, "wrote down addresses on cigarette paper that [he] could swallow if arrested."[20]

He adapted well to Bolshevik techniques and the party entrusted him with more ambitious assignments. The year 1907 was a high point for the Social Democratic Labor party—its membership reached one hundred thousand. That spring, Ilya, Bukharin, and another student named Grigory Sokolnikov—who became a leading Bolshevik and was later executed by Stalin—were asked to edit an underground Marxist journal. By the summer, Ilya was involved with Bukharin in organizing a strike at a wallpaper factory. He spoke at meetings and collected funds from other students for the strike committee. He also established contact with soldiers from a machine-gun platoon and set up a Bolshevik cell in the barracks.

Ilya's underground work combined ideology and romantic adventure. There were chases in the night when meetings were broken up, close escapes, clandestine hiding places for party literature and material. Ehrenburg described one incident in *The Extraordinary Adventures of Julio Jurenito and His Disciples*: "There was a meeting at the Fabre paint factory . . . The police came. I ran for it. I climbed over a fence topped with spikes and left my trousers on one of them. Bang! I fell into a barrel with some paint left in it! The police did not catch me."[21]

Such political agitation was a dangerous game and Ilya was gambling with his future. The Okhrana, the czar's secret police, took note of his activity. They were planning a systematic crackdown and needed to identify key Bolshevik organizers among the students and the general population. First, Ilya was briefly detained by the police, then released on his own recognizance. His parents feared that Ilya's political activity could lead to blacklisting, which would exclude him permanently from school—where he rarely appeared—and from receiving permission as a Jewish adult to live in Moscow. With this in mind, they arranged for him to withdraw voluntarily from the gymnasium. But the police were not finished. Later that October his home was searched. "Nothing prohibited was found," the officer reported, "but a musical score of the *Russian Marseillaise* and some postcards were taken away."[22] Two months later, on January 18, 1908, a security officer filed a report on the influence of the Social Democrats on Moscow's secondary schools. Ilya was noted for his "outstanding role" and his responsibilities as a "district propagandist."[23] Two weeks later, he and his comrades were betrayed by a fellow student activist. The police came well past midnight to arrest him. "I had no chance to destroy anything. The search lasted until morning. My mother cried and an aunt from Kiev who had come to stay darted about the apartment in terror."[24] Ilya Ehrenburg had just turned seventeen.

IN AND OUT OF PRISON

A picture of Ilya from czarist police archives has been preserved that shows him standing against an oversize ruler that reaches from his knees almost to the ceiling. He is about five and a half feet tall, dressed in a jacket and heavy overcoat. His shoulders are slightly stooped, his hair thick and black, combed away from his forehead. He looks tired, as if he had not slept the previous night. Political conspiracy had been an adventure, "a mixture of Karl Marx and Fenimore Cooper," Ehrenburg once observed.[25] It was romantic to be chased by the police, but decidedly unromantic to be caught; the police treated him harshly, breaking several of his teeth.

For five months Ilya was shifted among police stations and prisons.[26] In one jail he watched police beat up drunks. In another he was not permitted to read a novel by the popular Norwegian writer Knut Hamsun because the author's name reminded the warden of the Russian word for "knout" (a leather whip for flogging); prisoners were not allowed to read about corporal punishment. Another warden charged ten rubles to admit visitors. Ilya was transferred to the Basmannaya jail, where an officer beat the prisoners regularly; they declared a hunger strike, which lasted for six days. "I asked a comrade to spit on the bread," Ehrenburg recalled. "I was hungry and did not trust myself."[27] But he held out and at seventeen felt like a hero. From there he was taken to Butyrki prison, which later held dissident activists in the post-Stalin period. In his memoirs Ehrenburg recalled seeing his comrade Grigory Sokolnikov in a prison corridor. "We said hello with our eyes. Conspiracy did not permit anything more."[28] Ilya spent two weeks in rat-infested cells "in the midst of silence and the stench of the slop-bucket."[29] Solitary confinement was particularly hard to endure and he nearly suffered a nervous breakdown.

> I lost the habit of life and little by little a kind of dull calm took possession of me. But toward evening there would be difficult moments. From a distance the singing groan of a streetcar . . . would be borne into the cell. I was seventeen then—I would turn to the wall and cry, for this sound from the free world contained everything: mamma, home, the streets in spring, life.[30]

Nonetheless, Ilya did not cave in. He refused to cooperate with the investigators or even acknowledge his underground affiliation. Meanwhile, Grigory Ehrenburg tried to gain his son's release on medical grounds, arguing that imprisonment would exacerbate Ilya's fragile, nervous condition and endanger his life. Ilya too requested release, asserting that poor prison conditions would "inevitably lead to madness or death." The police relented at the end of June. He was released pending trial and told to leave Moscow for Kiev, his place of birth, where he would be under strict police supervision.

Ilya resumed his activities in the Bolshevik underground. When the police found out, they chased him from city to city. Over the next several months he moved from Kiev to Poltava, back to Kiev, and then to Moscow illegally, where even his closest comrades could not take him in. Discouraged and exhausted, Ilya gave up. He reported to the police and asked that he be returned to prison. At that point his father intervened and gained permission for him to go abroad "for medical treatment," claiming his son suffered from tuberculosis, whereupon Ilya broke his silence and made halfhearted admissions about his Marxist activities, all the while refusing to divulge any names. This evidently satisfied the police. Grigory Ehrenburg deposited five hundred rubles (a considerable sum in those days) to guarantee Ilya's appearance in court. But by the time the case was finally heard in September 1911, Ilya was safely in Western Europe and unwilling to face a czarist judge.

His mother implored him to complete his schooling in Germany. She also feared that Paris, with its reputation for loose morals and sensuous pursuits, would corrupt her son, as Moscow had corrupted her husband. But prison had made Ilya an even more convinced Bolshevik. He insisted on Paris, as he claimed fifty years later in his memoirs, "for one reason only: to see Lenin."[31] Vladimir Lenin had just moved there from Geneva. Ilya may have had other reasons for preferring Paris to Berlin; he already knew some French and several of his Bolshevik friends had fled to France earlier that year. But writing in 1960 it certainly was politic to emphasize an adolescent reverence for Lenin. Traveling alone, Ilya arrived in Paris by train on December 7, 1908, five weeks shy of his eighteenth birthday.

TWO

A Lapsed Bolshevik

Ilya did not expect to stay long in Western Europe. He intended to return to Moscow within a year, when the czar's secret police finished assaulting the student movement and would no longer bother to pursue such a young fugitive. On his first day in Paris, Ilya found comrades from Moscow's Bolshevik underground who took him to a meeting that same night. Lenin was there, and learning that this young student had just fled Russia, invited him for a visit.

In subsequent years, Ehrenburg wrote about meeting Lenin with barely restrained awe. "[Lenin] was talking quietly with someone and drinking beer," Ehrenburg remembered. "Then he made a speech. He spoke very calmly, without melodrama and with a slightly ironic smile. . . . I was fascinated by his head. . . . It made me think not of anatomy, but of architecture."[1] Ilya visited Lenin a few days later. Lenin listened patiently as Ilya described the breakup of the Communist underground and shared his opinion on the disputes between Bolsheviks and Mensheviks. Ilya also gave Lenin addresses in Russia where party material could be sent. To his surprise, Lenin invited him to stay for dinner, then started to ask questions about the students' mood and their interest in literature. Ilya left impressed by Lenin's graciousness. "He did not make fun even of an impudent schoolboy."

There is no reason to question Ehrenburg's recollection of this one visit. Lenin felt isolated in Paris and welcomed firsthand accounts of events in Russia. But writing years later, Ehrenburg had to exaggerate his impression; after the Communist party repudiated the Stalin cult in the 1950s and replaced it with an equally inflated version of Lenin's personality and career, Ehrenburg recalled him with reverence—in contrast with Stalin, the unmentionable monster, now officially endowed with defects of character and leadership. "In life Lenin was simple, democratic, mindful of his comrades . . . ," Ehrenburg remembered. "Such simplicity is only found in great men. And often, when thinking about Lenin, I have asked myself: perhaps the cult of personality is alien, even distasteful, to genuinely great personalities."[2] Ehrenburg may have been sincere when he evaluated Lenin in his memoirs. But what happened between them in Paris in 1909 was much more complex than he could dare discuss. His encounters with Lenin and other political activists subverted his revolutionary zeal and within a year led to his break with the Bolshevik party.

THE SHOCK OF PARIS

Ilya never forgot his arrival in Paris when he walked out of the Gare du Nord into the lively streets. He went into a bar and saw cab drivers in top hats standing at the zinc counter. He sat next to the driver on the top deck of a horse-drawn bus and observed the life of the city. There were stalls on the boulevards selling meats, cheeses, hats, saucepans. Furniture stores piled cupboards and beds on the sidewalks. Singers entertained passersby. Tall, wooden roulette wheels beckoned customers. He was amazed by the numbers of *pissoirs* and the red trousers of soldiers peeking out below. Couples embraced in carriages, in bars, on street corners. Ilya suddenly understood that Christmas was nearer than he expected, since the calendar had changed; what had been December 7 in Russia was now December 20 in France, and the city had begun to celebrate. People enjoyed themselves on the streets, went for walks with no destination in mind. "My clothing was out-of-place," he recalled, "but no one paid any attention to me and within the first few hours I understood that in this city it was possible to live unnoticed; nobody cared."[3]

The émigrés, as Ilya soon found out, ignored Paris. They "led closed and severe lives. They rarely ventured outside the boundaries of their quarter" in the poorer, working-class districts and "hurriedly ate borscht and meatballs in tiny canteens."[4] Ilya joined this community initially, attending lectures, reading Russian newspapers in an attic library, and frequenting the émigrés' favorite cafés on the rue d'Orléans. But this kind of life could not sustain his interest. He saw how these émigrés were cut off from the society around them and how ideological fervor generated inflexibility, intolerance, and for him, boredom. By 1909 both the Socialist Revolutionaries and the Mensheviks had their headquarters in Paris. The émigré community found itself engulfed in arguments over how to revive the fortunes of revolution. "Endless discussions still went on at party meetings . . . I was angry with myself," Ehrenburg remembered. "Why was it that such discussions had interested me in Moscow, while here, where there were so many experienced party workers, I felt bored? I began attending meetings less and less."[5] Disillusioned with the Bolsheviks, Ilya expressed his attitude in a poem written within months of his arrival in Paris.

> I too believed in a people's dictatorship.
> I too was a Social-Democrat for an hour.
> Such fleeting, carefree dreams
> You dream only once.[6]

UP FROM POLITICS

By the spring Ilya thought of quitting the party altogether. Leaving politics behind, he was beginning to read and write poetry with the same passion previously reserved for work as a Bolshevik. This interest in poetry had an accidental awakening. He met a student from St. Petersburg at a meeting of a Bolshevik cell. Her name was Yelizaveta Polonskaya. She had a passionate love for poetry and would read verses aloud to Ilya. Yelizaveta Polonskaya later returned to Russia, where she became an accomplished and well-known poet. Her friendship with Ehrenburg endured, lasting more than half a century.

Inspired by Liza, Ilya wrote poetry for hours every day. But he was reluctant to abandon revolutionary politics altogether and made one last attempt to find a place for himself in the movement. That summer, at the recommendation of Lev Kamenev, a close associate of Lenin's, Ilya traveled to Vienna to work with Leon Trotsky. This visit gave him a unique distinction, being perhaps the only teenager in Russian history to have had personal encounters with Lenin, Trotsky, and Nikolai Bukharin.

Trotsky took an independent position within Russia's Social-Democratic movement. Although he was in close touch with Lenin, Trotsky refused to ally himself with either the Bolsheviks or the Mensheviks, a position that may account for Ehrenburg's interest in Trotsky's work, for the endless arguments over Marxist doctrine in Paris led to Ilya's political disillusion. Living in Vienna with his second wife and their two young sons, Trotsky began editing *Pravda* in November 1908, a responsibility he inherited from previous editors who had failed to make the newspaper a success.* Ilya stayed with Trotsky's family in their modest apartment, where he helped by pasting copies of *Pravda* "into a cardboard tube around which [he] packed art reproductions and then sent them to Russia by mail."[7]

Writing about this brief episode a half century later, Ehrenburg chose not to identify Trotsky. He explained to a Moscow library audience in 1966 that his publishers "would be only too happy if I were to identify this person by name. However, I consider it tactless, and even immoral, to do so, since my remarks concerning that incident in Vienna could be interpreted as assertions prompted by the subsequent activities of this individual, and the fate that befell him."[8]

> In Vienna, I lived with a prominent Social Democrat X. . . . X was kind to me and when he learned that I wrote verse, he would talk to me in the evenings about poetry and art. His ideas were not opinions which I could debate, but categorical assertions. . . . To X, the poets I admired most were "decadents," "the product of political reaction." He talked about art as something of secondary importance, a by-product. I understood that I had to leave, but I decided against telling X. I wrote a stupid, childish note and left for Paris.

*The newspaper edited by Trotsky is commonly referred to as the Viennese *Pravda* to distinguish it from the Bolshevik *Pravda*, which began in 1912.

Trotsky's "dogmatic pronouncements on the utilitarian essence of art" confirmed Ilya's suspicions about revolutionary intolerance.[9] (Ehrenburg once acknowledged to a friend that he had joined the party because of Bukharin and left because of Trotsky.[10]) He returned to Paris in November confused and distraught, not knowing what direction his life would take. He knew only that he had to renounce politics and transfer his devotion to literature.

This change in his life had overwhelming, personal consequences. With the help of Liza Polonskaya, he produced a magazine lampooning Lenin and other revolutionaries. Sources of information about this episode are few; Ehrenburg, understandably, never wrote about it himself. But a woman named Tatyana Vulikh was active in party circles in Paris at that time. She knew Ilya, Liza, and Vladimir Lenin, and recorded what happened in an unpublished memoir. "Soon after my arrival, two new members joined the cell, Ilya Ehrenburg and a young girl named Liza [Yelizaveta Polonskaya],"Vulikh recalled. "The two of them started to bring typed material to the meetings in which they mildly and ironically ridiculed members of the cell. . . . The most successful caricature was of Lenin."

> We bought up the journal and read it immediately. I remember how the mood was very boisterous. There were lots of jokes and laughter. Lenin became interested and requested a copy. He started to leaf through it and as he read, his face grew ever more grim and angry. By the end he literally flung the journal aside without saying a word. Our light mood quickly abated. Everyone quieted down and the meeting began.
>
> I heard later that Lenin did not like the journal at all and was especially outraged by the caricature of him. . . . And he did not like that Ehrenburg had printed it and apparently intended to distribute it widely.[11]

Ilya observed Lenin and other émigré leaders at close range in Paris and did not like what he saw. *Yesterday's People* ridiculed the entire spectrum of Russia's revolutionary movement with lampoons of prominent Bolsheviks, Yuly Martov (the leader of the Mensheviks), Leon Trotsky, and the Socialist Revolutionaries. Removed from the roundups that decimated the Communist underground throughout Russia, Lenin and his fellow revolutionaries appeared comic. Lenin in particular drew Ilya's scorn: he is shown standing on a tall pedestal, a broom in hand, dressed in a heavy overcoat and visored cap inscribed with the words *starshy dvornik*. (*Dvornik* commonly refers to a janitor or superintendent who carries out menial tasks and at times certain police duties within an apartment building; a *starshy dvornik* in this case is the "chief janitor," or "big nothing.") The image conveys crude power—a *dvornik* willing and able to exert control over his tenants, made even more explicit in a second journal, *The Quiet Family*, which shows Lenin with his hand curled into an enormous fist.[12]

Lenin had no patience for satire and was furious with Ilya. Exiled to Paris, his party in disarray, the prospects for revolution in Russia as hopeless as ever, Lenin was in no mood to tolerate a teenager's caricature, especially one that ridiculed his leadership and threatened to make him a laughingstock. Party leaders warned Ilya not to produce any more lampoons. Their reactions offended him and he may well have thought of the Moscow gymnasium teachers from whom he had once concealed his innocent schoolboy journal; the Bolsheviks reacted with the same nervous anxiety. Ilya's break from them was now complete. As Tatyana Vulikh recorded in her memoir, she used to see Ilya in the Latin Quarter, "but his outward appearance had totally changed." Instead of a clean-cut student, he had become "an untidy, disheveled bohemian," spending all day in cafés and always carrying a book.

> Liza said of him with pride that he lived a spartan existence, slept without sheets, but kept his copy of Balmont's verse covered with a special white parchment. In any event, he not only broke off all relations with the Bolshevik cell as a whole, but also with all its members, except for Liza; he would not even greet any of us on the street.[13]

This was the true beginning of Ilya Ehrenburg's exile from Russia and of the unique and paradoxical career he fashioned over the next half century.

A NEW FAITH

During the height of his political involvement in Moscow Ilya had been drawn to literature. He used to read novels late into the night. "Art penetrated into my underground world," he recalled. But Ilya resisted this "nonsense" and dismissed literature as "a shameful weakness."[14]

Once he quit the Bolsheviks, the romance of political conspiracy no longer restricted his instincts or his imagination. Deprived of a true home and rebelling against the Bolsheviks and the bourgeois conceits of his upbringing, Ilya abandoned himself to art and poetry. Paris was the perfect setting, its cafés, theaters, and bookstalls serving as the stage for the most unconstrained period of his life. His father sent him a monthly allowance that he supplemented with occasional odd jobs, serving as a guide to visitors from Russia, even babysitting for the children of friends. Mostly, he spent his time reading, writing poetry, and sitting in cafés.

Literature, though, was not an adequate substitute for politics. Ilya found a new faith in religion, particularly in Catholicism. "I visited a Catholic church," he wrote in *A Book for Adults*. "Everything amazed me: the stained glass windows, the whispers of the confessional, the organ. It seemed I found a certain order for my feelings. I wanted to believe in something for each morning I did not know how to live through the day."[15] He considered converting to Catholicism and entering a Benedictine monastery. Though he never converted, his poems often expressed sincere devotion to Christ and the Virgin Mary. In those years Ilya also painted small religious icons depicting Biblical parables or scenes from the life of Christ.

The French Catholic poet Francis Jammes particularly inspired Ilya. A convert to Roman Catholicism, Jammes celebrated nature with childlike simplicity, and his verses and short stories reflected newfound piety. For Ehrenburg politics meant commitment to action; art and religion offered more contemplative loyalty. "Jammes wrote about plants, about the freshness of an ordinary morning, about donkeys . . . I grew up in a city, passed nine-tenths of my life in a city, but only outside the city did I begin to move freely and lightly, to breathe without suffocating, to laugh without any particular reason." Ilya visited Jammes, hoping to clarify his spiritual confusion. But their time together disappointed him. "He greeted me kindly and served homemade liqueur. I waited to hear precepts, but he talked about ordinary things."[16] Once again, as happened with his father, Tolstoy, and Lenin, a revered older man did not measure up to Ilya's hopes. Nonetheless, Jammes's poetry sustained him. As late as 1914, in the preface to his collection of prose poems *Childhood*, Ehrenburg acknowledged his

debt to Jammes. "If in Paris my soul did not perish, I owe you thanks.
. . . When you pray on behalf of everyone, pray a little so that I, too,
will be able to pray."[17]

A POET IN BOHEMIA

Ehrenburg's interest in art and religion was not the only change in his
life. Near the end of 1909 he met a medical student named Yekaterina
Schmidt. Two years older than Ehrenburg, she was an émigré from St.
Petersburg; her parents were of German origin. Katya Schmidt was
Ehrenburg's first serious love and he always remembered her as the
woman he had loved the most passionately. They traveled to Belgium
in the summer of 1910, where he became enchanted with Bruges.
Within a year, on March 25, 1911, in Nice, Katya gave birth to his only
child, Irina. Ehrenburg was not prepared to assume his responsibilities
as a father and more than ten years would pass before he and Irina
grew closer to each other. Ehrenburg never married Katya. She wanted
more children and a more conventional life than he was willing to sustain. It was Katya who broke off their relationship and she soon married another Russian émigré. But their friendship continued. In 1913
they published an anthology of poems by Francis Jammes in Moscow,
having selected and translated the verses together.

Between 1910 and 1916 Ehrenburg published several small volumes
of poetry. Often he had to pay for the printing himself, and sent copies
to Russian poets in hope of critical response. His first collection, entitled *Verses*, contained several poems about Christ and the Virgin Mary,
Pope Innocent VI, and poems about the Middle Ages inspired by his
visit to Bruges.

Although Ehrenburg managed to print only two hundred copies—
he "fasted for several months to save two hundred francs"—*Verses* did
not go unnoticed in the Russian press.[18] The prominent poet Valery
Bryusov, who had helped to found the Symbolist movement before the
turn of the century, admired Ehrenburg's earliest work and even compared him to Nikolai Gumilyov, one of the most acclaimed poets in
Russia and the husband of Anna Akhmatova. "Among our young
poets," Bryusov wrote, "[Ehrenburg] is second only to Gumilyov in his
ability to construct verses and derive effect from rhyme and the com-

bination of sounds. . . . For now, images from the Middle Ages, the cult of Catholicism, a combination of religiosity and sensuality, gratify I. Ehrenburg, but he retells these old themes elegantly and beautifully."[19]

Gumilyov did not share Bryusov's enthusiasm. Writing in the influential St. Petersburg journal *Apollon*, Gumilyov found little to praise. "I. Ehrenburg has set himself a number of interesting goals: to reveal the face of the medieval knight who has by chance appeared amongst us; to express Catholic adoration of the Virgin Mary; to be refined; to create clear, expressive verse. But he has not even remotely accomplished a single one of these goals since he does not possess adequate resources."[20]

Encouraged by Bryusov's praise and undeterred by Gumilyov's criticism, Ehrenburg continued to write. A second collection of verses, *I am Alive*, was published in St. Petersburg in 1911. Once again, Ehrenburg included several explicitly Catholic poems, along with verses about Paris and his nostalgia for Russia. Most interesting is his poem "To the Jewish People," his first public expression of concern for his fellow Jews. Until then he had presented himself as an exiled Russian, a poet, perhaps a Catholic. This poem voiced more than despair over the historical plight of the Jews; individual verses imply a negative, condescending attitude, as if assimilation on the one hand and persecution on the other had reduced the Jews to an "impotent and sick people."[21] Despite his attraction to Catholicism, Ehrenburg still defined himself as a Jew and remained acutely aware of Jewish suffering. "Alien and persecuted, you are not needed here/Gather your exhausted children/And leave for the native fields of Jerusalem." This point of view underscores the poem's explicitly Zionist message: that Jews have no place in Europe and should return to the land of Israel. It would not be the last time Ehrenburg expressed such an acute premonition.

Nikolai Gumilyov read *I am Alive* and found encouraging improvement in Ehrenburg's abilities. "I. Ehrenburg has made great progress from the time of his first book's appearance. . . . He has passed from the ranks of imitators into the ranks of apprentices and even, sometimes, steps forth on the path of independent creativity. . . . Of course we have the right to demand still greater work from him, first of all in his language—but the most important thing is already accomplished: he knows what poetry is."[22]

Ehrenburg's commitment to art was genuine and total. "I wrote verses day and night," Ehrenburg recalled in a short autobiographical note. "I used to walk around Paris murmuring something and surprising passersby."[23] His cousin Ilya Lazarevich Ehrenburg also reached Paris in those years. He saw how Ehrenburg was changing and described him in letters to his own sister in Russia. After attending a reading in Paris, Ilya Lazarevich wrote:

> November 11 [1910]
>
> Ilya read to us more than an essay, but an artistic work. Lovely, brilliant, not worse than his best poems. You will forgive him for "burning his boats" and his exaggerations. If this was necessary for him in order to spread his wings, then let him do it. I am not sorry.

A month later, Ilya Lazarevich wrote again:

> December 14, 1910
>
> Ilya is going ever further in his views. . . . Now he values art because it is a religion. To argue with Social Democrats, who for him personify worldly progress and reason, is impossible (although he continually argues and swears at them) because art and religion are outside of life, higher than life. He has cut his hair. But he grew a beard which stands out as well as his head [Ehrenburg was well known for walking with a slight stoop].[24]

Just at that time, Ehrenburg established a daily routine centered around his favorite café. The Rotonde opened in 1911 at the corner of Boulevard de Montparnasse and Boulevard Raspail near the Latin Quarter. The warm café was a welcome alternative to Ehrenburg's unheated room. Like most cafés the Rotonde offered free writing paper to its patrons, while Victor Libion, the owner, used to give artists coffee and sandwiches on credit, helping to attract an international assortment of artists, writers, and misfits. A few were already famous, such as Pablo Picasso and the poet Guillaume Apollinaire. Others, such as Diego Rivera, Juan Gris, Jean Cocteau, Amadeo Modigliani, and Marc Chagall, were just beginning their careers and like Ehrenburg sought the warmth and companionship as well as the distractions of the Rotonde. "People wrote verses, chewed sausages, argued about art, fell in love, slept," he liked to recall. "The artist Modigliani read the prophecies of Nostradamus with the shriek of a wild bird, 'The world will soon come to an end! . . . ' Some Serb forced himself onto a

Negro woman ... People snuffed cocaine in the restroom and devoured hashish ... The model Margot would usually be disrobed by one o'clock."[25]

Ehrenburg's own appearance suited this company. He was often dirty and unkempt. One New Year's Eve his friends presented him with a comb, a toothbrush, tooth powder, soap, and eau de cologne, hoping he would put his gifts to good use.[26] The writer Alexei Tolstoy once sent a postcard to the Rotonde addressed "au monsieur mal coiffé" (to the gentleman with the messy hair) and it was immediately handed to Ehrenburg, for whom it was intended.

Marevna (Vorobyov), a Russian émigré who was Diego Rivera's second wife, came to know Ehrenburg well in those years. She preserved a sketch of her friends, eight artists and poets parading down Rue de la Gaîté in Paris.[27] (See Plate 2.) Like a snapshot, her drawing captures their cosmopolitan and bohemian mood. The Italian Jew, Amedeo Modigliani, tall and slender as one of his own paintings, smokes a dangling cigarette—or could it be a stick of hashish, his favorite addiction? The painter Chaim Soutine, who had fled a Lithuanian ghetto to pursue his art, wears a short necktie and an elegant, tailored coat. The Mexican Diego Rivera carries a stout cane, his enormous head and shoulders looming over everyone. Marevna wears an embroidered dress and a cape, while the Russian poet Max Voloshin carries a book under his arm. Ehrenburg stands between Voloshin and the Spaniard Pablo Picasso, who, in turn, is next to his close friend, the Symbolist painter and writer Max Jacob. Jacob, a Jew who converted to Catholicism in 1914, a year or two before the time of this sketch, was the only one born in France. (He would also be the only one to be killed in a Nazi concentration camp.) Jacob and Picasso wear identical caps and heavy, plaid overcoats. Only Ehrenburg looks obviously poor. His shoelaces are untied, his coat fits him poorly, while his "broad-brimmed felt hat ... towered above his head like a medieval hood," as Max Voloshin once described it.[28]

Ehrenburg found a place for himself in Paris among other émigrés, displaced artists and writers from Spain, Italy, Mexico, and Poland. He was not absorbed into French society. Although he admired Paris and French culture, Ehrenburg never resumed his education, which might have prepared him for a profession in Europe. Instead, he chose art and literature as the essential pursuits of his life. He also fulfilled a strong urge to explore Europe. Ehrenburg traveled often, to Holland, Belgium, and three times to Italy, where the work of the Renaissance captivated him, reinforcing his devotion to art and his interest in the Catholic faith.

But Ilya continued to write only in Russian. His verse was published in Moscow and St. Petersburg. Brief stories and essays appeared there as well, and occasionally in émigré publications. Ehrenburg took an active part in émigré literary affairs. In 1913 he helped to edit two issues of the journal *Helios*—it was here that Ehrenburg first wrote glowingly about the verse of Marina Tsvetaeva—and the following year helped put together two more issues of another journal, *Vechera* (Evenings).[29] Ehrenburg also enjoyed translating French verse, particularly that of Francis Jammes and the medieval poet François Villon. He published an ambitious anthology of translations in 1914, including selections from twenty-nine different poets, among them Paul Verlaine, Arthur Rimbaud, and Guillaume Apollinaire.[30]

Living in Paris, Ehrenburg was a fugitive from Russian justice. As early as July 1910 a Moscow court had asked his father for Ilya's address in Western Europe and a month later demanded that he produce his son. But Ilya was in no mood to stand trial. By September Grigory Ehrenburg forfeited his five hundred rubles, which were duly dedicated "to building prisons," as the law called for in such cases. But Ehrenburg did not relinquish all hope of returning. In 1912 he asked the wife of the poet Konstantin Balmont (who was also in exile) to intercede on his behalf, knowing that in the following year, 1913, Czar Nicholas II was likely to issue a broad amnesty decree to mark three hundred years of Romanov rule.[31] The court did permit numerous political exiles, such as Maxim Gorky, to return. By then Ehrenburg had left the Bolsheviks and had genuine hopes that the czar's amnesty would permit his return without reprisals. His parents, too, appealed for a commutation of sentence but their request was refused. That same year Ehrenburg published a cycle of poems entitled "Sighs from a Foreign Land" in a St. Petersburg journal.

> So again there are hopes about Russia—
> Only they turned into a useless dream.
> So again there are foreign roads
> And I am doomed to walk along them.[32]

WAR AND REVOLUTION

Ehrenburg was visiting Amsterdam when the First World War broke out in August 1914. He made his way quickly through Belgium to France, arriving in Paris in a train filled with French zouaves dressed in blue tunics and bright red trousers.

The war took him completely by surprise. Like most of his friends, art was Ehrenburg's overriding passion; he had no knowledge of the political maneuvers that led to the conflict. Nonetheless, Ehrenburg was overwhelmed with patriotic emotion. He volunteered for the French army but the doctors turned him down. He was too gaunt, having "preferred poetry to beef" for too many years.[33] Ehrenburg resumed his life as best he could, sharing the initial optimism of the French and then uncertainty and panic as the Germans advanced to within thirty kilometers of Paris. He saw how unprepared the French were for the fighting; when wounded soldiers first appeared people froze on the street. Because of his name Ehrenburg himself was suspected of being German and had to document his origins several times for the police.

Regulations changed; he could no longer receive his allowance from Russia. Compelled to earn a living and frustrated by his inability to enlist, he worked unloading shells and ammunition in a depot. His appearance, especially his hat with its high crown, amused other workers. But they accepted him, dubbing him "Le Chapeau." Ehrenburg worked at night, returning to his room in the morning to sleep half the day before going to the Rotonde. He was desperately poor. When he slept, he wrapped himself in newspapers to stay warm.

Ehrenburg began to write about the western front more than a year into the war. He knew that wartime censorship made it impossible to convey the reality of the fighting. The allied governments, as well as the Kaiser's regime, controlled the press completely, rendering most stories little more than pallid, abstract accounts of trench warfare. The Russian press was hardly better. Ehrenburg subscribed to *Utro Rossy* (Russia's Morning), a conservative daily; deliveries were irregular and he would often receive ten back issues at a time. Reading reports about the western front, Ehrenburg realized that the newspaper did not have a correspondent in France (as the by-line claimed) but was putting articles together in Moscow based on secondhand, outdated information. Innumerable factual errors—about the French leadership, army uniforms, and life in Paris—convinced Ehrenburg that he could do better. He went to the Rotonde and started to write. His first articles appeared in *Utro Rossy* in November 1915. Then in April of the following year, with the help of his friend, Max Voloshin (a well-known poet in the émigré community), Ehrenburg became Paris correspondent for *Birzhevie Vedomosti* (The Stock Exchange Gazette), a financial newspaper in Petrograd.*

———

Thus began one of the most remarkable journalism careers of the twentieth century. Ehrenburg was to cover two more wars and eventually become the most famous and widely read journalist in the Soviet Union. In light of his subsequent career as a Soviet correspondent, however, it is important to examine how Ehrenburg reported on the First World War when he was still an independent journalist.

In his study of war reporting, *The First Casualty*, Philip Knightley has little good to say about the press during the First World War. Fighting between the Germans and the French posed an especially severe challenge because the military leadership on both sides was committed to a grinding, massive war of attrition involving hundreds of thousands, even millions of men. "The people had to be steeled for further sacrifices, and this could not be done if the full story of what was happening on the western front was known," Knightley observes. Most correspondents, in turn, "identified themselves absolutely with the armies in the field. . . . They protected the high command from criticism, wrote jauntily about life in the trenches, kept an inspired silence about the slaughter, and allowed themselves to be absorbed by the propaganda machine."[34]

Ehrenburg did not succumb to this mood. He did not glorify the war, even though he was pro-French. A skeptic by temperament, he found it easy to resist the war's grandiose appeal. His years in the Bolshevik underground and the Rotonde Café immunized him from the allure of political authority and left him with a hatred of violence and coercion. Restrained and usually impartial, he wrote as an eyewitness, recording thoughts, feelings, and events as he observed them, with an eye for the poignant and paradoxical, able "to transform a brief dia-

---

*The name St. Petersburg was changed to Petrograd at the outset of the First World War in order to give the capital a Russian name rather than a German-sounding one. After Lenin's death in 1924, Petrograd became Leningrad.

logue or a chance encounter into an emblem of war and the human condition."[35]

To cover the war firsthand Ehrenburg crawled through mud under fire and relaxed with soldiers behind the lines, often in villages recently evacuated by the Germans. The Spanish writer Ramón Gómez de la Serna came to know Ehrenburg during this period and once observed him return from the fighting in search of Diego Rivera:

I saw [Ehrenburg] one morning just back from Verdun. He had come directly from there and without even going to his room had come to visit Rivera. "Give me a brush," he said to Rivera, "to clean off the mud of Verdun." His long greatcoat was a spectacle, and when the brush lifted the dust it seemed to me like the smoke of an explosion. . . . "The colonel who accompanied me told us, 'When you feel a sensation as if your hat were coming off, throw yourself on the ground . . . it's a shell going over your head.' But I didn't heed him because it was more frightening to throw oneself face down in the mud than to put up with the shell."[36]

Ehrenburg visited the front often and was especially impressed by the mechanization of death. "Heroism, virtue, and suffering did not decide very much. . . . A huge bakery baked two hundred thousand loaves a day. The soldiers ate the bread. The war devoured the soldiers."[37] He saw a tank for the first time in 1916.

There was something majestic and nauseating about it. Perhaps such gigantic insects once existed. It was brightly decorated for camouflage, its sides resembled futuristic paintings. It crawled very slowly, like a caterpillar, stepping across trenches and pits, sweeping away wire and bushes. Its antennae hardly moved—three-inch cannons and machine guns. It was a combination of something archaic and ultra-American, Noah's ark and a bus from the twenty-first century. There were men inside, twelve small, wretched pygmies who naively thought they were driving it.[38]

He also saw colonial troops at the front, mostly Senegalese, who had been pressed into service and taken to Europe. They were bewildered, not knowing where they were or why or whom they were fighting. The French used them in particularly exposed positions. Neither the

British nor the French press wrote stories about them; Ehrenburg did, and his dispatches so infuriated French authorities that he was almost expelled from the country.

The war had a devastating impact on Ehrenburg. Cut off from his family and his homeland, he suffered a nervous breakdown. "I am twenty-four, but look thirty-five," he wrote in *A Book for Adults* twenty years later. "Torn shoes, a fringe on my trousers. A mass of hair. . . . I eat extremely rarely. I have become neurasthenic but I am happy with my disease."[39]

Marevna, too, remembered the war's effect on Ehrenburg. "For some time," she recalled,

> Ilya had been drinking too much, much too much. In a café, in the street . . . he would utter shrill cries. We did not know if he did this as a joke or if his cries were a form of delirium tremens. Sometimes he did not sleep at night. He would write until very late and then go out to walk around Paris. In the morning, pale and wasted, he could be found editing his article in the Rotonde. I found Ehrenburg changed, without knowing why. I told myself that everyone inevitably changes little by little. It was the war, and it was difficult for us as well.[40]

Around that time, Marevna drew another sketch of her friends. Entitled "When Will the War End?" the drawing shows Ehrenburg, Modigliani, and Rivera sitting quietly in Rivera's studio (see Plate 2). All three appear grim and depressed, not looking at one another, staring blankly into space. Ehrenburg is reclining on a narrow bed, his back against the wall, a pipe to his lips. A cup of coffee sits half empty on one side of him, an open book on the other. The war, Marevna seems to be saying, was a terrible interruption, destroying the life they knew and taking them toward a destination they could not discern. Looking at this sketch we cannot help but think of her friends' fate: Modigliani would die of tuberculosis within two years after the war's conclusion, never to know the reverence or wealth attached to his paintings; Rivera would leave Paris and return to his beloved Mexico to become one of his country's most famous artists; and Ehrenburg, his hair hanging to his shoulders, could not have imagined that a year later he would return to Russia and find his destiny connected to a country he thought he had abandoned.

The war had renewed Ehrenburg's love for his homeland, bringing him into contact with ordinary Russian peasants who were sent to fight on the western front. In November 1916 he traveled to northeastern France where they were stationed. "Everywhere there were Russian faces, Russian speech," he reported to his readers. "Eight years ago, on a December evening, by the gates of the Brest station, I looked for the last time on such a workman, such cabdrivers, on Moscow, on Russia. I woke up two days later in cold, alien Berlin. Eight years have passed and today, in a small village in Champagne, a few miles from the Germans, I once again found my own unforgettable motherland."[41]

From the start the Russian brigades had a tragic fate. Their officers beat the men at will; many were then shot by their own troops. There were episodes of mutiny; nine soldiers were executed in 1916 for leading such a revolt. Relations between the French and Russian troops were tense as well. Russian leaders made the situation more complicated by trying to isolate their soldiers from France's democratic society and the numerous émigrés who had found a home there. When Russian troops arrived in a village the officers would assemble the French civilians and forbid them to sell wine to the troops. The French assumed the soldiers were savages—even children are given wine in France—and would have nothing to do with them. They laughed at the Russians for eating buckwheat kasha; the Russians, for their part, could not fathom how the French could eat snails and frogs.

Finally, in the midst of the fighting, the czar's abdication in March 1917 made the position of Russian troops in France completely untenable.* According to Ehrenburg they were not informed of the news for ten days, when they were withdrawn from the front to rest. Fearing there would be a breakdown of discipline, the French decided to send the Russian troops immediately into battle. Ehrenburg witnessed their confused exaltation. Ranks were divided between those willing to go on fighting in France and those who insisted on returning home. Arguments broke out over how to treat officers, over attitudes toward the French, over rumors that peasants back home were seizing land; as weeks went by, bringing ever more startling and troubling reports from Russia, the urge to return became universal among the troops.

The February Revolution, as it came to be called, marked the end of the czarist autocracy, but it was only the beginning of a confused

---

*Because Russia still followed the Julian calendar, the czar's abdication took place in February.

and cruel set of events that would culminate in the Bolshevik's seizure of power. The strikes and mass rallies seemed at first like a replay of 1905. On February 23, 1917, ninety thousand workers went on strike in Petrograd. The next day, their numbers grew to two hundred thousand. The most urgent demand was for bread, more food, and relief from the drastic inflation brought on by the war. When the police could not restore order the city's military garrison was called in but the soldiers refused to act against the crowds; some of them even fired on the police.

In the wake of these events the Duma, which refused the czar's order to adjourn, organized the Provisional Government. At the same time, a diverse group of Socialist leaders proclaimed the creation of the Petrograd Soviet of the Workers' Deputies. They both declared the czarist autocracy a thing of the past—and both announced their intention to govern the country.

Czar Nicholas II was at the Supreme Army Headquarters in the Ukrainian city of Mogilev. He expected the army to support him, but when his generals rejected him he abdicated, bringing the Romanov monarchy to an end. His son was not permitted to take the throne and his brother, Grand Duke Mikhail, refused. There was no central government with enough authority to continue the war with Germany effectively or begin to address the widespread demand for more food. Russia collapsed into anarchy.

Ehrenburg was unsure how to respond to news of revolution in Moscow and Petrograd. To his surprise, the émigré community was too busy arguing to celebrate the czar's downfall; whether the war effort should be continued or whether to defend the revolution, he knew he had to return. Russia was his home. He also felt orphaned by the fighting. Europe for him meant culture and civilization, the freedom to think and create, to travel, to enjoy museums, literature, art; this Europe required no visas and transcended the borders of language and frontiers. But the war destroyed that world and Ehrenburg's naive faith. After eight years of exile he had grown sentimental about Russia and desperately wanted to see his mother and his homeland. Russia, it seemed, offered the promise of renewal just when Europe was suffering a devastating collapse.

It was not easy to return. The Russian embassy offered to help, but would only arrange to send off genuine political refugees. Ehrenburg by that time had been romantically involved with the painter Chantal

Kenneville for several years and they would remain friends until Ehrenburg's death. On "my last night in Paris, I walked with Chantal along the banks of the Seine. I was already no longer in Paris and was still not in Moscow," Ehrenburg recalled in his memoirs.[42] Chantal tried to dissuade him, convinced he would never return from Russia. But Ehrenburg was adamant and waited impatiently until June, when he was able to leave.

He traveled to London, then by train to Scotland with other émigrés and five hundred Russian soldiers who had escaped from German prisoner of war camps. They embarked by troopship for Norway via the North Sea. Two English destroyers accompanied the boat, as the war was continuing and German u-boats were on patrol. After a few days in Norway Ehrenburg proceeded to Stockholm and from there by train to the Russian border with Finland. It was the beginning of July. His first exile was about to end. Someone told him the Bolsheviks had attempted to seize power in Petrograd but had been put down. The émigrés began to argue. "The atmosphere in my carriage reached boiling point," Ehrenburg wrote in *People, Years, Life*. "My heart sank. In Paris everyone talked of the 'bloodless revolution,' of freedom and brotherhood, and here we had yet to reach Petrograd and they were threatening each other with jail."[43]

Decades later Ehrenburg confessed his confusion during the years of revolution and civil war: he hated the violence, he could not understand the turmoil; but he did not divulge to his Soviet readers that he had opposed the Bolsheviks. While Ehrenburg supported Kerensky and feared the Bolsheviks, the disorder and chaos disturbed him most. He had left in 1908 and was not prepared for the hatred unleashed by the czar's abdication and the breakdown of political authority. Russia was engulfed in a full-scale social revolution. The country's factories, garrisons, and great estates were seized by workers, soldiers, and peasants. No political party directed or controlled this upheaval. The czarist regime had collapsed, but the Provisional Government failed to secure clear and unquestioned authority or the confidence of the people— and the German army still threatened large parts of the Ukraine.

Within two weeks of his arrival in Russia Ehrenburg wrote an article for *Birzhevie Vedomosti* entitled "Paris–Petrograd." This piece was among a group of articles he wrote and published in a Russia free of censorship, that fleeting period from March to November 1917 when the Provisional Government, headed by Alexander Kerensky, honored freedom of the press. These articles deserve particular attention because there is no mistaking what Ehrenburg means to say. In "Paris–Petrograd" he describes how a soldier at the border questioned him: " 'You are for whom? For Lenin or for Kerensky?' He heard my answer, then told me. 'You're a bourgeois? You already have your own house, your own factory.' "[44]

Ehrenburg arrived in Petrograd in July just after the Bolsheviks' first and unsuccessful attempt at an armed uprising. There was still shooting and corpses in the streets. "One woman said, 'It's the Jews' fault. They have to be killed," Ehrenburg reported. "Another man said, 'It's the fault of the bourgeoisie.' Everyone was looking for his own advantage." Ehrenburg did not conceal his despair. "Russia is sick," he wrote. "Russia is on the verge of death."

> For nine years I longed for Russia. In the West I understood her significance and spiritual power. But blood is already flowing from all sides. The Germans are approaching. The whole world is watching— is it possible Russia turned out to be a false-prophet, is it possible the spirit of reconciliation and love faded as rapidly as red flags?[45]

He had no time to sort out his confusion. Meanwhile, Yekaterina Schmidt also returned to Petrograd, with Ehrenburg's six-year-old daughter, Irina. Katya's father was a successful butcher, the owner of several stores and apartments in the city. He hated Ehrenburg; "on top of all my other crimes," Ehrenburg noted later, "I was a Jew." But Katya brought Irina to see him and they walked together in the city. He did not know his daughter well and it would be several more years before they grew devoted to each other.

Ehrenburg did not stay in Petrograd for long before leaving for Moscow. The city was calmer but no more reassuring. He met writers and poets, frequented cafés, and tried to write even though the waitresses, unlike those in Paris, made him order more to drink. The summer ended. His mother was in Yalta and Ehrenburg took a long train ride south to see her. "I found my mother greatly aged; she coughed, was wrapped in a knitted shawl, and lived in terror of street fighting."[46]

Ehrenburg's trip to Yalta provided the occasion for one of his last articles before the Bolshevik takeover. "In the Train Carriage" appeared in *Birzhevie Vedomosti* on October 15. Ehrenburg once again shared his despair and hopelessness over the fate of Russia. His fellow passengers were thieves or speculators, creating a pervasive atmosphere of suspicion and greed while "comrades"—Bolshevik activists—patrolled the train. As in Paris, when he admired Jammes's faith and grappled with his own confusion, Ehrenburg invoked the image of prayer to underscore Russia's spiritual collapse:

> There were many new passengers at each station. Never before in Russian history were so many people traveling; the waves were rising higher and higher in the storm. They are running to and fro, but no one had any hope, only gloomy anger and fear.
>
> It was then that an old, ragged Jew donned a silk shawl, fastened straps to his forehead, opened a book, and swaying, began to pray. A young soldier started a long, complicated, obscene phrase, but another, older one cut him short: "Keep quiet you. Can't you see the kike is praying." We all looked once again on the swaying Jew. Not comprehending his stern God, not understanding the dark words of his prayer, everyone—I could feel—was envious that even now he could not only hate or suffer, but could still remain faithful and pray.[47]

Watching that elderly Jew, Ehrenburg could well have been thinking of his mother's faith, a faith inaccessible to him but which he longed for and would continue to seek in various guises.

Ten days after his article appeared, the Bolsheviks overthrew the Provisional Government in Petrograd.

THREE

Revolution and Civil War

Ilya Ehrenburg had been in Russia four months when the turmoil of 1917 climaxed in the Bolshevik takeover. He arrived in Moscow from Petrograd just as the major battle took place. His apartment building was shelled and he witnessed violence and atrocities in the city. In his novel *Julio Jurenito*, the fictitious poet "Ilya Ehrenburg" experiences the terror of revolution:

I sat in a dark room, cursing my wretched nature.... Right then men were making history under my window, not with their brains, their imagination, or their verses, but with their bare hands.... What could be better, it seems. Just run down the stairs and act, do it quickly, while your fingers still hold clay and not granite, while you can still write it with bullets, and not read it in a scholarly German's six-volume edition! But I sat in my room, munching cold meat. ... Remember, ladies and gentlemen of so-called 'posterity,' what the

Russian poet Ilya Ehrenburg was doing during those never-to-be-repeated days.[1]

A month after Lenin's coup, Ehrenburg joined a group of writers in an unusual protest. Calling themselves the Moscow Writers' Club, figures as diverse and prestigious as Konstantin Balmont, Ivan Bunin, Max Voloshin, Vyacheslav Ivanov, Alexei Tolstoy, and Yuri Eikhenvald circulated a one-day newspaper entitled *For Freedom of Speech!* on December 10, 1917. Their action was a direct response to the Bolsheviks' initial efforts to suppress opposition journals.[2]

For Freedom of Speech! carried several outspoken slogans, among them "Long Live Cultural Democracy" and "Without Freedom of Speech and the Press There Is No Democracy." Ehrenburg contributed the poem "Divine Speech." Written as a parable about a bird whose voice is necessary to save the world, the poem expresses chagrin over Russia's fate as well as naive religious faith in its redemption.

As far as we know, neither Ehrenburg nor any of the other writers involved in *For Freedom of Speech!* faced untoward consequences for arranging the newspaper's appearance. That winter the Bolsheviks had more pressing challenges to their authority, particularly from other revolutionary parties who wanted their share of power and from the Germans who occupied parts of the Ukraine and were prepared to continue fighting on their eastern front. These professional writers could be expected to entertain a sentimental attachment to freedom of the press; in spite of their literary prestige they had no political standing, and the regime could afford to tolerate their faint protest. Some of these writers, such as Ivan Bunin, never made their peace with the Bolsheviks and left the country.* Others were too old to carry on in opposition. A few, such as Ehrenburg and Alexei Tolstoy, later moved to Western Europe, only to return under harsher conditions of censorship than those they protested in December 1917.

That winter Ehrenburg continued to denounce the revolution in his poetry. His most notable collection of verse from those years, *A Prayer for Russia*, appeared in Moscow in early 1918, a testament to the regime's short-lived tolerance for literary and political expression.

---

*Bunin became the leading writer in emigration and was awarded the Nobel Prize for literature in 1933.

Ehrenburg expressed his despair in these poems, repeatedly depicting Russia as a woman who lies vulnerable, even naked, as violent men laugh and molest her.

In his long, discursive poem, "Judgment Day," Ehrenburg surveyed the progress of revolutionary turmoil, commenting on the three crucial events of 1917: the abdication of the czar and the formation of the Provisional Government in the spring, Lenin's attempted coup in July, and the triumphant Bolshevik takeover in October. Among all the poems of this period, "Judgment Day" carries the most outspoken denunciation of the Bolsheviks. Russia is described as a dying mother, while the poem climaxes with the image of rape as a metaphor for the revolution.

> At this final hour
> Those poor small girls
> In huge military coats
> Still wanted to die
> For Russia
> When everyone had betrayed her.
> The crowd was yelling
> "Crucify her!"
> Sailors were already running up the stairs:
> . . . "Oh, grab this girl!
> Let's open her up!
> She'll fit all of us!
> Hell!
> This is really our last and decisive battle!"
> . . . .
> Tell the children, "In the fall of
> one thousand nine hundred seventeen
> We crucified her!"[3]

A battalion of women soldiers did indeed form the last line of defense in front of the Winter Palace, a famous episode immortalized in Sergei Eisenstein's *Ten Days That Shook the World*. In Ehrenburg's poem the Bolsheviks violate one of these women and celebrate their crude triumph with the exclamation "This is really our last and decisive battle!"—a line Soviet readers instantly recognized from *The Internationale*, the song of the Communist movement. Such verse could only be taken as a sign of utter contempt for the Bolsheviks and all they stood for.

Writing in 1918, the poet Vladimir Mayakovsky decried *A Prayer for Russia* as "tiresome prose printed in verses" and Ehrenburg as "a frightened intellectual."[4] But Ehrenburg's friend Max Voloshin wrote an enthusiastic review. Voloshin recognized the dimensions of Ehrenburg's life that made his work so compelling: he was a Jew, an émigré who had returned from France, an ex-Bolshevik; his status as an outsider helped to ensure a balance and spontaneity in his poetry that other writers lost in the face of their country's collapse. "All of Ehrenburg's verses are built around two ideas," Voloshin wrote,

> the idea of the motherland and the idea of the Church. . . . No Russian poet has felt the motherland's ruin with such intensity as this Jew. . . . "A Jew does not have the right to compose such verses!"—I once had to hear this exclamation about Ehrenburg's poem. It seemed to me the highest compliment to his poetry. Yes—he has no right to compose such verses about Russia, but he claimed this right for himself and exercised it with such power as not one of those who were endowed with the fullness of this right. And that is the way it always happens.[5]

Ehrenburg never disavowed these poems but tried to obscure his reaction to the Bolshevik triumph in subsequent years. Soon after his return to Western Europe in 1921 he dismissed *A Prayer for Russia* as "artistically weak and ideologically impotent."[6] By the 1930s Ehrenburg was under much greater pressure to clarify his attitude to the October Revolution because of the prevailing conditions under Stalin and because he was now an *Izvestia* correspondent in Paris. His poems and other writings still haunted him. The *Great Soviet Encyclopedia* of 1934 stated that he "greeted the 1917 revolution as an anti-Bolshevik."[7]

Ehrenburg made an initial attempt to justify his response to the October Revolution in *A Book for Adults* in 1936.

> I saw the revolution in my own fashion; I expected smiles and happiness. I wanted freedom for everyone. . . . In the October days, I believed they were taking my homeland away from me. I grew up with an understanding of freedom inherited from the last century. . . . I wrote the verses *A Prayer for Russia*. . . . With frenzy I swore by the God in whom I had never believed and mourned a world which had never been mine.[8]

Using vague and poetic language, Ehrenburg essentially pleaded confusion: he had always spoken up for the weak, and when the Bolsheviks took power he retained his sentimental instincts and failed to recognize the necessity of their methods. His explanation was also sincere;
he had attacked the revolution in the name of Russian Orthodoxy and
lamented the old order that had imprisoned and exiled him. But the
passionate conviction of *A Prayer for Russia* shows that Ehrenburg had
been less confused than he cared to admit. His explanation must have
been acceptable since *A Book for Adults* was published and Stalin never
ordered his arrest. Stalin in fact preferred people with a tainted political history to those with an unblemished pedigree within the party. His
chief prosecutor Andrei Vyshinsky, who helped to organize the notorious show trials of the 1930s, had been a Menshevik and at one point
even distributed orders for Lenin's arrest in Moscow in 1917. Vyshinsky's background made him all the more likely to be an obedient servant; Stalin expected the same from Ehrenburg.

—

Following the revolution, Ehrenburg longed to leave the country. "I
am earnestly dreaming about going abroad," he wrote to Max Voloshin
in early 1918. "As soon as it is possible, I will leave. I am doing this in
order to preserve the possibility of living in Russia spiritually. . . . I very
much want to work—here it is quite impossible."[9] But in spite of such
hopes and his anti-Bolshevik attitudes Ehrenburg remained in Moscow.
After years of exile he was not prepared to abandon Russia and was
enjoying new friendships with several leading poets, among them Boris
Pasternak and Vladimir Mayakovsky, both of whom he saw frequently.
They read verses to each other for hours at a time and frequented the
Poets' Café, where a writer could entertain an audience and receive a
modest fee.

Ehrenburg's reputation was growing. The poet Alexander Blok noted
the attitude of young people in a diary entry for January 31, 1918:
"First there were the three B's—Balmont, Bryusov, Blok. Then they
began to seem tame, and there was Mayakovsky. Now he seems tame
as well, and there's Ehrenburg (he makes the most pungent fun of himself, and that is why, very soon, we shall all like no one but Ehrenburg)."[10]

But life in Moscow was not easy. "Everyone in those days lived in a
state of emergency."[11] Ehrenburg rented a room from a professor and
made a meager living reading poetry in cafés and writing articles about
life in Paris. He did not hesitate to write about politics as well. The

Socialist Revolutionary party still existed and continued to publish newspapers such as *Vlasti Naroda* (The Power of the People) and *Novosti Dnya* (News of the Day). Ehrenburg contributed pieces to these newspapers throughout the spring and expressed himself as forthrightly as he did in his poetry. Drawing on earlier encounters with leading Bolsheviks in France, he denounced them in Moscow, often in personal, insulting terms. Lenin was "a stocky bald man" who resembled "a good-natured burgher." Followers such as Kamenev and Zinoviev were "high priests" who "prayed to the god Lenin," while all the Bolsheviks, according to Ehrenburg, argued endlessly over minute points of party dogma.

Ehrenburg did more than recall the Bolsheviks' hatred of one another in Paris; he also scorned them in prophetic terms:

> For a very long time, it has been the fate of Russia to be enthralled by foreigners. You expected the Varangians, but it was not the Varangians who arrived amongst us in sealed wagons. The spirit of the people who are in power now is alien to Russia. They do not know Russia and they do not like her. They came, they will leave, and once again in smoke-filled cafés, they will expel one another as Trotskyites or Bukharinites. They came, they will leave. You will remain, Russia, humbled and disgraced by this darling family.[12]

Writing in Moscow in the spring of 1918, Ehrenburg proved to be only partly correct. While the Bolsheviks did not resume their exile in Parisian cafés, they went on to denounce each other in the Kremlin itself, in the very terms Ehrenburg first heard in the Latin Quarter.

As his poems and articles make clear, Ehrenburg had no illusions about the Bolsheviks' intentions. He recognized their intolerance and understood that the hatred so easily expressed over minor ideological disputes was about to be extended over an entire country. Still, Ehrenburg's pieces, however prescient they seem, were characterized more by anger and an intuitive understanding of Bolshevik methods than by a systematic analysis of revolutionary politics.

Ehrenburg was not the only literary figure to take on the Bolsheviks in Moscow. Maxim Gorky, who knew Lenin far more intimately than Ehrenburg did, wrote scores of articles in 1917 and 1918, expressing his belief that Lenin was a dangerous fanatic. Gorky reached the height of his considerable powers as a political commentator during these years.

He repeatedly protested arrests and executions and tried to rally public opinion to defend freedom of speech and demonstration. Gorky's newspaper *Novaya Zhizn* (New Life) was ultimately shut down on Lenin's orders in July 1918. Like Ehrenburg, Gorky left Soviet Russia three years later and did not return for nearly a decade, when he became a champion of Stalin's regime. Gorky's articles against Lenin and the Bolsheviks were long suppressed and never referred to in official accounts of his life until Gorbachev permitted a more honest approach to Soviet history.[13]

That such writers were able to condemn the Bolsheviks so openly in Moscow in 1918 reflected the shifting political tides. Artists and writers were permitted to experiment. In *People, Years, Life*, Ehrenburg emphasized the creative freedom he and his friends enjoyed in Moscow. Futurist poets such as Mayakovsky and David Burlyuk pasted "decrees" on buildings announcing the abolition of "store-rooms and warehouses of human genius; palaces, galleries, salons, libraries and theaters" were to close and art be made available to everyone.[14]

It was no surprise for Ehrenburg when adherents of modern art supported the revolution while traditional artists and writers fled to Europe. "The Futurists, the Cubists, and the Suprematists remained," Ehrenburg recalled in his memoirs. "Like their counterparts in the West—the prewar habitués of the Rotonde—they hated bourgeois society and saw revolution as the way out."[15] Stalin would later destroy this connection between revolutionary politics and experimental art; in writing his memoirs one of Ehrenburg's goals was to restore the reputation of these Soviet artists, whose innovative work had flourished well into the 1920s.

A JEW IN THE UKRAINE

In the fall of 1918 Ehrenburg received word that his mother was gravely ill in the Ukrainian city of Poltava. He rushed there only to learn she had died on October 13; he arrived two days too late. Anna Ehrenburg was buried in Poltava, her gravestone inscribed in Hebrew and Russian. In his memoirs Ehrenburg cryptically remarked about her death that he "spent two or three weeks with [his] father. One could say a good deal about those weeks, or be silent."[16] Ehrenburg chose to be silent. But the memory of his mother remained precious to him, particularly during World War II, when she came to symbolize for him the doomed, helpless Jews wiped out by the Nazis.

In his memoirs Ehrenburg gives the misleading impression that he was still in Moscow when he heard about his mother's illness and that he rushed from there to the Ukraine to see her; in truth he had fled Moscow for Kiev in September fearing arrest, a fact too politically inconvenient for him to divulge in the 1960s. In the summer of 1918 the country's political situation was growing more complex and dangerous. In July, elements of the Socialist Revolutionary party seized control of several provincial cities and threatened a coup against Lenin. Their revolt was turned back by the Bolsheviks, leading to wholesale executions. Their newspapers, too, were closed down in Moscow, depriving Ehrenburg of the principal forum for his articles. That same month Lenin ordered the shooting of Czar Nicholas II, his family, and members of his personal entourage. They were being kept in Yekaterinburg in the Urals, not far from White forces who were also contending for control of the country. Lenin wanted to make sure the czar would never be rescued and that Russia, like England and France before her, be disposed of her monarch in such a way that the old order could never be revived.

The summer's final shock came on August 30, when a deranged woman named Fanny Kaplan attacked Lenin, shooting him twice in the chest; Lenin survived. Fanny Kaplan was executed without a trial. The Bolsheviks used this incident to increase the terror against their enemies, particularly the Socialist Revolutionaries, massacring hundreds of people in Moscow alone.

It was in this atmosphere that Ehrenburg fled Moscow for the Ukraine, fearing for his life. His poems and articles in the Socialist Revolutionary press already marked him, and with the shooting of Lenin Ehrenburg could not be sure how widely the Bolshevik net would be cast. He shared his fears with Max Voloshin in a letter written from Poltava on October 30: "I had to flee Moscow in September, because the Bolsheviks would have taken me as a hostage. It was a nightmarish trip, but I somehow managed to make it," Ehrenburg wrote to his friend. "Soon after, my parents followed me to the Ukraine. Mother came down with pneumonia along the way, and reaching Poltava, she died."[17]

Ehrenburg was still intent on leaving the country. In the same letter to Voloshin he mentioned a desire "to make [his] way to Switzerland."

Life in Moscow had become almost too terrible for words. "It was a delusion, but more real than any reality that ever existed. I am completely devastated and only inertia allows me to have thoughts and feelings." His mother's death compounded his despair over Russia's fate. "The fact is my soul is filled only with negative attitudes, and destruction is ever-present. I don't know what to do next. . . . It is loathsome here, and now and then, I even feel nostalgic for Moscow." Ehrenburg, though, could not bring himself to leave just yet; he headed for Kiev rather than Switzerland.

Ehrenburg "chose a bad time to come to Kiev." Several armies were fighting for power, including Ukrainian nationalists, White forces who wanted to restore the monarchy, and Red Army units. German soldiers still occupied the city. A Ukrainian officer named Paul Skoropadsky claimed authority over the entire region but owed his position to the Germans, and when they left in December he followed them to Berlin. Others took their place. Ehrenburg stayed in Kiev for a year under four different regimes. "Governments, regulations, flags, even shop-signs changed," he later wrote. "The city was a battlefield in the civil war. There was pillaging, murder, and execution."[18] Refugees from all over the country poured through Kiev on their way to Odessa and then to Berlin or Paris. But Ehrenburg stayed. Kiev was his birthplace, and though he had not lived there since 1895 he always thought of Kiev as his home town.

As always, he continued to give readings and lectures. For several weeks in January 1919 Ehrenburg and the writer Andrei Sobol, who was also escaping from the Bolsheviks, "traveled around the cities of the Ukraine in exchange for cereals of various kinds," Sobol remembered. "I. Ehrenburg recited his verses and I read my stories. In Berdichev there was a priest sitting in the front row (*A Prayer for Russia* appeared on the announcements)."[19] The irony is unmistakable: while he and Sobol were both Jews, Ehrenburg's poem attracted the attention of a priest who assumed the evening in Berdichev would be devoted to prayer.

Andrei Sobol had a tragic fate. The Bolsheviks arrested him in Odessa in 1921 when they took over the city, but he was soon released and later made his way to Moscow. Permitted to visit Berlin the following year, he returned to Russia and there published several statements that seemed to recant his previous opposition to Bolshevik rule before committing suicide in June 1926. Ehrenburg proved to be sturdier and more flexible.

In Kiev Ehrenburg's talent for meeting unusual people did not desert him. His friendship with the great poet Osip Mandelstam began in Kiev, where they saw each other frequently in a literary club that held its meetings in the basement of the Writers' Union. The club had the curious name of Khlam, an acronym whose letters stood for "artists, writers, actors, musicians," and was identical to the Russian word for rubbish. Khlam had a distinguished membership and played a fateful role in the history of Soviet literature. Aside from Ehrenburg and Mandelstam it included the Yiddish poet Peretz Markish, the artist and set designer Alexander Tishler, and the translator Valentin Stenich, who later introduced James Joyce and John Dos Passos to the Russian public. Markish and Tishler became Ehrenburg's lifelong friends. He also came to know a distant cousin, Lyubov Mikhailovna Kozintseva, who was studying art in Kiev with the famous designer Alexandra Exter. One of her classmates was Nadezhda Khazina. Ehrenburg married Lyubov Mikhailovna in 1919. Nadezhda Khazina married Osip Mandelstam three years later.

Eight years younger than her husband, Lyubov Mikhailovna was an educated and attractive woman. They met in her father's home, where Ehrenburg stayed when he first reached Kiev. Ehrenburg once told a friend that he fell in love with his wife when he saw her for the first time walking her dog in the street.[20] Their wedding took place on August 13 (26) over her parents' objections. They did not take Ehrenburg seriously and tried to discourage the marriage by insisting that the couple have a religious ceremony in addition to the customary civil one, but Ehrenburg agreed to this. Even so, he could not find proper clothing; during the religious ceremony he had to whisper to Lyubov Mikhailovna for a pin to hold up his trousers.

Their marriage was never conventional. At first they did not live together; Ehrenburg remained in his own apartment while Lyubov Mikhailovna continued to live with her parents. They also granted each other a broad measure of sexual and emotional independence. Ehrenburg's habits as a bohemian poet made him unsuitable for domestic life and he was never monogamous, even when deeply in love.

Several months before the wedding Ehrenburg had become involved with another woman, an eighteen-year-old student named Yadviga Sommer. Born into a Polish family in Kiev, Yadviga was studying to be a teacher at the city's pedagogical institute. She loved serious literature and was already familiar with Ehrenburg's work when she learned in

the spring of 1919 that he had just opened a school for young poets.
Yadviga immediately enrolled. Her first impression of Ehrenburg is
reminiscent of all who knew him in those years. "His clothes were
baggy, his hair dissheveled," Yadviga recalled in a memoir of her own.
One evening after class Yadviga "was the last to leave" and Ehrenburg
"politely inquired which way [she] was going." They walked out
together. "Not many people were around. The weather was spring-like.
It had just rained. The streets glittered. . . . I was wearing a beret and a
black cloth cape. We spoke about our favorite poets and quickly found
a common language. . . . Ehrenburg took me by the arm and walked
me to my dormitory where he kissed my hand," Yadviga remembered
a half century later. "I entered my room and quickly lay down, but
could not fall asleep for a long time."[21] In his memoirs, Ehrenburg
remembered her with equal tenderness. "Slim, dark-haired Yadviga,
who looked like the heroine of an Italian neo-realist film."[22]

Soon they were lovers and continued to be intimate even after
Ehrenburg announced his engagement to someone else. Yadviga was
shaken by the news and by Ehrenburg's desire to introduce her to
Lyubov Mikhailovna. "I did not know what would come of our relationship. I had no illusions," she admitted. Ehrenburg, for his part, "was
afraid of my reaction. He looked at me apprehensively, but I sat frozen
in my chair."[23] Ehrenburg brought Lyubov Mikhailovna to his school
to meet Yadviga a few days later, where they had a brief, polite, but
otherwise desultory conversation. It seems Ehrenburg was testing
Lyubov Mikhailovna. From the outset of their marriage he was brutally honest with her, as he remained throughout their forty-eight
years together. He wanted to be sure she understood the terms of his
commitment. Although he genuinely loved and cared for her, he was
not promising fidelity; she would have to accept his heartfelt attach-
ments and numerous affairs. As it turned out, Lyubov Mikhailovna was
frigid sexually and altogether passive. They did not have children and
there is even some question of their sexual intimacy once they were
married, though they remained devoted friends. Ehrenburg was always
protective of her. Upon his return to Paris in May 1921 he introduced
Lyubov Mikhailovna to Diego Rivera, who soon began to court her;
Ehrenburg cleverly distracted her. Each morning he "wrote satirical
verses about her and an infatuated artist."[24] Lyubov Mikhailovna
would not leave him, particularly once they settled in Paris where she
could enjoy a European style of living as the wife of a successful

writer far from the harsher, everyday demands of life in Russia.

In Kiev Osip Mandelstam helped Ehrenburg obtain a job under the Bolsheviks in the Department of Social Welfare, where Mandelstam was already working. (The Bolsheviks gained control of Kiev in the early spring of 1919.) Ehrenburg was put in charge of the aesthetic education of juvenile delinquents. It was an unlikely post for him, but people took all kinds of jobs in those years in order to survive. And the Bolsheviks may have preferred to hire Jews, figuring they were more sympathetic to the revolution. Kiev's large Jewish community faced much greater violence from Ukrainian nationalists or the Whites than it did when the Bolsheviks were in control of the city.

Ehrenburg took his work seriously. It gave him firsthand knowledge of Kiev's social conditions. He visited reform schools, orphanages, and run-down hotels where homeless children took refuge. Plans were discussed in his office for choral groups, theatrical performances, and a pilot colony for delinquents. After Yadviga finished her studies, most of her classmates found teaching positions in cities throughout the Ukraine. But Ehrenburg insisted that she stay in Kiev, where he found a job for her in his department organizing theatrical productions in schools and orphanages. His own investigations confirmed the need for food, clothing, and a stable environment: the girls were turning to prostitution, the boys were joining gangs and armies in the countryside. A colleague recalled how "thanks to [Ehrenburg's] persistence and responsiveness, a good deal of medical attention and a general improvement in the lives of hundreds of miserable orphans and half orphans was provided during wartime in Kiev."[25]

Ehrenburg impressed Nadezhda Mandelstam as well. "Our comradely mob was gradually infiltrated by new arrivals from the north. One of the first was Ehrenburg," she wrote years later. "He seemed to view everything with great detachment. What else could he do after his *Prayer for Russia?*—and took refuge in a kind of ironical knowingness. He had already understood that irony is the only weapon of the defenseless."[26]

Although Kiev was controlled by the Bolsheviks until the fall of 1919, the Whites shelled Kiev whenever they had the chance, and there was much random violence. Even the most sensitive people grew indifferent to the cruelty and loss of life around them. Nadezhda Mandelstam sensed that callousness in herself and recalled how Ehrenburg eloquently set her right.

The head-hunting mentality spread like a plague. I even had a slight bout of it myself, but was cured in time by a wise doctor. This happened . . . when a visitor . . . read out some couplets by Mayakovsky about how officers were thrown into the Moika canal in Petrograd to drown. This brash verse had its effect and I burst out laughing. Ehrenburg, who was also there, at once fiercely attacked me. He gave me such a talking-to that I still respect him for it, and I am proud that, silly as I was at the time, I had the sense to listen to him and remember his words forever afterward.[27]

The Bolsheviks held on to Kiev until September, when the army of General Anton Denikin gained control of large parts of the Ukraine. Denikin had been an officer in the czar's imperial army. After Lenin's coup he became a prominent leader of the counter-revolutionary White forces and posed a serious threat to the Bolsheviks. Fighting continued, and in October the Bolsheviks mounted a counteroffensive, regaining Kiev for two days before Denikin's forces drove them out once again. Ehrenburg witnessed the see-saw battle for control of Kiev. The half-year of life under the Bolsheviks had confirmed his hatred for them and he initially welcomed the triumph of Denikin's men, "greeting the Whites with hope."[28] That September and October, while the Whites held Kiev, Ehrenburg wrote sixteen articles for the newspaper *Kievskaya Zhizn* (Kiev Life) in which he recounted his contempt for Lenin and the Bolshevik cause.

In the spring of 1917, there were flags, songs, and holiday smiles. The naive virgin—Russia—. . . believed in a wonderful groom, in a night of love, in the miracle of transformation. Instead of a groom came Lenin and in the young girl's room a drunken orgy broke out. They hit each other, broke each other's bones, slaughtered one another. Foreigners tried to calm them down, but some became drunk themselves, while others squeamishly left waving their hands . . .

The stores are empty, our heads are empty. We are not only barefoot and hungry, we are ignorant and dead. . . . We gave Europe Dostoevsky and Tolstoy, Mendeleev and Mechnikov, Moussorgsky and Ivanov. Now we have neither bread nor books nor ideas. Death is wandering through an empty house.[29]

In October the Bolsheviks drove out the Whites for a couple of days before once again being expelled. Ehrenburg witnessed the flight of the city's population trying to escape the violence. He ran away from the Bolsheviks as well, together with Lyubov Mikhailovna and Yadviga Sommer, and headed east in the direction of Kharkov, where Ehrenburg's father was living. After a full day's walk with hundreds of other refugees they reached the nearby town of Svyatoshino and found refuge for the night in an empty train carriage, sleeping in the aisle as best they could alongside the others. The following morning they learned that the Whites had repulsed the Bolshevik attack on Kiev. Although they were exhausted, Ehrenburg, Lyubov Mikhailovna, and Yadviga walked back.

Within days he wrote an article entitled "Exodus" for *Kievskaya Zhizn*, one of the most candid and startling of his career. It is hard to find a similar example of such outright hatred of the Bolsheviks by any other important Soviet personality, let alone by one who later flourished as Ehrenburg did.

> The Bolsheviks are not political enemies, but rapists and conquerors. The first of October was not "a change of regime," but a marauding raid, the exodus of townspeople, and the capture of those who could not leave. . . .
>
> Once again there is death, destruction, and wild hatred. . . . It does not matter—we will build again. We fled from bolshevism, we walked away from it, and no power will compel us to live once again from decree to decree.[30]

Ehrenburg's passion for the Whites was short-lived. Regardless of his hatred for the Bolsheviks, he quickly understood that he was in much greater danger under Denikin. Once in control of Kiev Denikin's forces carried out a full-scale pogrom, raiding Jewish neighborhoods, looting shops, raping women, and killing scores of people. "With my Semitic lips and suspicious name," Ehrenburg recalled, "I might have ended my difficult earthly journey at any moment."[31] He despised the logic of reactionary anti-Semitism. "Today many people believe," Ehrenburg wrote in an article that September,

> that Jewish blood can help against the plague-like infection of bolshevism. I am not speaking about the shopkeeper who sits on the

corner of my street. She is so firm in her belief that the other day, when a dog tipped over her basket of small pies, she cried out, "We won't have order until all the kikes will be killed." . . . If Jewish blood could cure, then Russia would be a flourishing country. But blood cannot cure, it only infects the air with malice and discord.[32]

Ehrenburg never forgot the terror of those months. Nine years later, in his story "The Old Furrier," he recalled the widespread fear that enveloped the city's Jewish neighborhoods. "And the people? The people are screaming. . . . One scream is picked up by everyone, it infects an apartment, a floor, and then already it is not one person screaming, it is the house screaming."[33] The reactionary press of Kiev hurried to justify attacks on the Jews. Newspapers fabricated incidents, giving addresses where Jews were said to have fired on Denikin's troops or spied on their movements for the Bolsheviks. The notorious anti-Semite Vasily Shulgin played a prominent role in the pogrom, serving as the principal apologist for Denikin's cause. Shulgin was the editor of *Kievlyanin* (The Kievan), an influential monarchist newspaper. His article "The Torture of Fear" blamed the Jews themselves for their suffering.

Will the Jews in these nights of terror learn something, will they learn what it means to incite the classes against each other according to the recipe of the "great master, Karl Marx"? . . . Will the Jews beat their breasts, cover their heads with ashes and repent before all the world that the sons of Israel took such active part in the Bolshevik madness?[34]

Individual Jews had indeed played an inordinately prominent role within the revolutionary parties. Reactionaries like Shulgin in Eastern Europe and the former Soviet Union seized on that fact to exploit anti-Semitic feeling within broad elements of the population, a strategy that continues to this day. Ehrenburg was among those who responded to Shulgin's challenge. Writing in *Kievskaya Zhizn*, he described his own fear and the fear of his fellow Jews. "There are those who are not thinking about Zion or the Internationale," Ehrenburg wrote, "but only about a hat which would make them invisible and save them from the crazy glance of an angry passerby." But Ehrenburg could not relinquish his love for Russia. "I want to address those Jews who like me have no other motherland, except Russia," he wrote that fall, "who have received all good and bad things from her. . . . It is possible to pray and to cry. But one cannot cease to love. One cannot renounce even a brutal people, who kill officers, pillage estates, and betray their fatherland."[35]

Some Jews resented Ehrenburg's Russian patriotism, terming it "slavish," even degrading. "A Jew, the poet Ehrenburg," one man wrote, "provides a blessing, an acceptance, a justification for the whip. . . . In those days the Jew Ehrenburg forgot about everything in this world, except for love of Russia, a love in spite of anything that happens."[36] Not being able to resolve the tension between his Jewish origins and his attachment to Russia, Ehrenburg looked in vain for a way to honor both loyalties. For him the persecution of the Jews was occurring in the larger context of Russia's collapse; they could not be rescued without Russia, too, being saved. But Ehrenburg was in despair over Russia. While he had greeted Denikin with hope, he hated the pogroms and his articles more than implied—at some risk—that he blamed the Whites for attacking Jews as a means to save Russia. Such ideas placed his life in jeopardy. One night a group of officers in Denikin's army came to the offices of *Kievskaya Zhizn* looking for Ehrenburg. The printers protected him, hiding Ehrenburg under a staircase and telling the officers he had not yet arrived for work.[37]

Ehrenburg did not want to wait for the Bolsheviks' return and could not be confident about surviving under Denikin. Caught between opposing forces, he decided to leave Kiev in October and go to the Crimea, where his friend Max Voloshin had a home in Koktebel. Ehrenburg made the travel arrangements for a small group of people, including his wife and Yadviga Sommer, Osip Mandelstam and his brother Alexander, and the artist Isaak Rabinovich.

Ehrenburg did not want to leave Kiev without Yadviga. Since his marriage two months earlier Yadviga had tried to distance herself from him, missing appointments or keeping them to a minimum of time. Yet Ehrenburg remained devoted in spite of his marriage, and asked her to stay loyal to him. He also convinced her that she would be able to find work wherever she lived, "in White Guard Crimea as well as in White Guard Kiev." As for Lyubov Mikhailovna and Yadviga, their relationship was understandably "cold and alienated, but fully proper. [Lyuba] could have, she had the right to demand that our trio be disbanded," Yadviga once recalled.[38] But Lyubov Mikhailovna accepted Ehrenburg's infidelity, as she chose to do throughout their long life together.

Ehrenburg's brush with death in Kiev was not his last during the civil war. The trip to the Crimea was as dangerous as the Kiev pogrom. The train ride to Kharkov lasted a week—it normally takes ten hours. White officers and cossacks often stopped the train looking for Communists and Jews. At one stop three cossacks stormed into their carriage shouting "Kikes, get off the train!" No one moved. The cossacks grabbed Ehrenburg's friend Isaak Rabinovich, who had Semitic features, and pushed him outside. Then they began checking documents, but slowly, for only one of them could read. Ehrenburg was terrified. "He stood by, documents in hand, waiting his turn," Yadviga recalled.[39] Finally the cossacks explained they only wanted to ride on the train and were looking for places for themselves. Seats were quickly provided and Isaak Rabinovich was allowed back on. This time, at least, the cossacks did not intend to shoot anyone.

Ehrenburg and Lyubov Mikhailovna stayed in Kharkov for three weeks while their friends traveled further south to Rostov. In Kharkov Ehrenburg visited with his father. In the years before the revolution Grigory Ehrenburg had become a real-estate broker in Moscow and was involved in the last private sale of the famous Metropol Hotel before it was requisitioned by the revolutionary government. Little is known of his subsequent fate, only that he died in Kharkov on March 26, 1921. Ehrenburg all but forgot him. During his stay in the city Ehrenburg continued to write, sending articles to *Kievskaya Zhizn*, giving lectures on art and poetry, even trying to stage a play. He and his wife left Kharkov at the end of November and joined their friends in Rostov. There, too, Ehrenburg continued to denounce the Bolsheviks as he had in Kiev, writing with so much fury that the editor of the local newspaper found it necessary to "soften [his] bloody hurray-patriotism."[40] From Rostov, Ehrenburg, his wife, Yadviga Sommer, and the Mandelstam brothers traveled south to Mariupol by train, then to Feodosia by boat across the Sea of Azov and the Black Sea. "We traveled for a good (no, a bad) month, digging ourselves into the darkest corners of freight cars, hiding in ships' holds among people sick and dying of typhus; we lay there covered with a thick layer of lice. Again and again we heard the monotonous cry: 'Any Yids in there?' "[41]

On the boat from Mariupol to Feodosia Ehrenburg was attacked by a cossack, who threatened to "baptize" him by throwing him into the sea. They struggled on the deck and Ehrenburg thought they both would land in the icy waters. Yadviga heard Ehrenburg's cries for help and alerted a Jewish White officer who, brandishing his revolver, intervened and saved Ehrenburg's life.

Ehrenburg's cousin, Ilya Lazarevich, was not so fortunate. He, too, had returned to Russia from Western Europe after the February Revolution. He was in Kharkov by 1918 and resumed his work as an artist, teaching and designing costumes and stage sets for the theater. Although he was an active Menshevik, he joined a Red Army unit in July 1919 and went to the front. "Our party is being mobilized," he wrote to his wife in Geneva, "even though our Central Committee is in jail."[42] No one heard from him for more than a year and his family assumed he had been killed; but he was living in Alexandrovsk in southern Ukraine. In August the Whites drew closer to Alexandrovsk and Ilya Lazarevich was among those evacuated by train from the city. He did not have much longer to live. The train was surrounded by cossacks. They knew he was a Jew, questioned him, then took him away; his comrades never found his body or saw him again.

THE CRIMEA

Ehrenburg spent nine difficult months in Koktebel. He arrived at the height of winter with little to wear, little to eat, and hardly any money. Ehrenburg would comb the beach collecting driftwood to burn in the stove. Once he even boiled a dead seagull he had found in the sand. Lyubov Mikhailovna sold pieces of jewelry her mother had given her. Ehrenburg continued to write but it was impossible to sell his poems or essays in the Crimea.

Yadviga found work in Feodosia eighteen kilometers away tutoring children in exchange for room and board, but Ehrenburg insisted she return to Koktebel on weekends. Each Saturday after half a day's work Yadviga walked back to Voloshin's house, an arrangement that lasted for two months until Ehrenburg came up with a better way to support themselves.

With Yadviga's help he organized a playground for peasant children, hoping to earn some food from their parents. They read stories, rehearsed a play, set up a clay-modelling class. But the peasants were tight-fisted and suspicious. While there was no established fee, Ehrenburg occasionally received a bottle of milk or a few eggs. More often he went hungry, while the children would eat in front of him, taunting him with their bacon and cake. The playground closed after a few months because the parents, inspired by the village priest, grew frightened of their children's clay models; only a Jew and a Bolshevik could teach such things.

Hungry and poor, Lyubov Mikhailovna became ill with typhus. Stricken with chest pains, Ehrenburg did not have the strength to care for her. Yadviga, younger and stronger, assumed responsibility for Lyubov Mikhailovna, staying up long nights when she was delerious and looking for food during the day. Osip Mandelstam and his brother Alexander were also in Koktebel—Nadezhda Khazina had stayed in Kiev—and Alexander once rode on horseback to Feodosia to find a syringe so Lyubov Mikhailovna could receive an injection. But then Ehrenburg had to find alcohol to sterilize the needle. He approached the parents of his pupils, but they refused to help, calling him a drunkard. One night Lyubov Mikhailovna's pulse disappeared and Ehrenburg, frantic for help, made his friends give her an injection of strychnine to stimulate her heart. She survived the illness, but it left them all physically and emotionally exhausted. Yadviga fell into an unexpected depression; she threw herself into the sea one night in a halfhearted attempt at suicide and Voloshin had to drag her onto the beach to save her life.

The Crimea did not prove as peaceful a refuge as Ehrenburg had hoped. Although Denikin's forces were defeated in the Ukraine in early 1920, the Whites maintained an army in the Crimea under Pyotr Wrangel. Ehrenburg was present when White officers searched Voloshin's home. Osip Mandelstam was arrested in Feodosia and accused of being a revolutionary. Learning of Mandelstam's arrest, Ehrenburg turned to Voloshin, insisting that he go to Feodosia to help Mandelstam. "He was soon released," Ehrenburg remembered, "but it was really a lottery—he could have been shot."[43]

Gradually Ehrenburg started reassessing his country's upheaval. For three years he had denounced the revolution in his poems and articles, dismissing it as a convulsion whose only significance lay in the breadth of its destructiveness. He "was frightened by the senseless sacrifices, by the ferocity of the reprisals," but in Koktebel he began to regard the disorder and violence in a new light.[44] For a time Ehrenburg had believed the Whites could stop the Bolsheviks and restore order in the country, but after the pogroms in Kiev his faith in their cause collapsed. He understood they were a hopeless alternative to the Bolsheviks, that they would not succeed, and that Russia would never be the same again.

In Koktebel Ehrenburg and Voloshin were joined by Sergei Efron, the husband of Marina Tsvetaeva. Efron had fought alongside the Whites before abandoning their cause. He witnessed atrocities first-hand and what he shared had a decisive impact on Ehrenburg. In her memoir Yadviga Sommer recalled listening to Efron talk about his experiences:

> [Efron] sat with Ilya Grigorevich beside a table, while Lyuba and I made ourselves comfortable on a bed at the other end of the room, stretching our legs and leaning against the wall. Efron spoke for several hours about the White army, about its terrible corruption, about its cruel treatment of Red Army prisoners. . . . We had the feeling that his entire way of looking at the world had been destroyed, that this man had been devastated and did not know how he would go on living.[45]

Conversations with Osip Mandelstam in Koktebel also influenced Ehrenburg's thinking. Mandelstam helped him to understand that the revolution involved momentous change. As Ehrenburg wrote soon after,

> Poets greeted the Russian revolution with violent shrieks, hysterical tears, weeping, enthusiastic raving, and curses. But Mandelstam, poor Mandelstam, who never drank unboiled water, and who crosses the street rather than walk past a police station—only he understood the tremendous significance of events. Men wailed, but a small habitué of cafés in Petersburg and other cities, understanding the scale and the grandeur of history in the making, . . . praised the madness of our times: "Well, then, let us try a tremendous, awkward, creaking turn of the helm!"[46]

Ehrenburg was not implying that Mandelstam welcomed the revolution or supported the Bolsheviks; rather, Ehrenburg learned from him that it was pointless to denounce the revolution with "violent shrieks" or "hysterical tears," as he had done in *A Prayer for Russia*. It mattered little if he liked the revolution or not, just as one's attitude to an earthquake would be insignificant. By 1920 Ehrenburg relinquished his opposition. "The chief thing . . . was to convince myself that this was not a terrifying, bloody riot, not a gigantic Pugachev rebellion," Ehrenburg wrote in his memoirs, "but the birth of a new world, with new ideas of human values."[47] His poem "To Russia," written in Koktebel, expressed his change of heart.

> Russia, they have mistaken your birth fever for that of
>   death. . . .
> Childbirth is cruel. . . .
> But on the dark refuse heaps,
> Washed with our blood
> Another great age is born.[48]

Still, the civil war continued. Red Army units drew closer to the Crimea and would soon overwhelm the last of Wrangel's forces. Ehrenburg did not want to be there when the Red Army took over. These units came from the Ukraine. Someone might remember his articles against the Bolsheviks and want to settle accounts with him. Ehrenburg decided to travel to Georgia, an independent democratic republic governed by the Mensheviks. From there he could also return to Moscow.

Ehrenburg's two weeks in Tbilisi that September were his most carefree and relaxed during the entire civil war. He remembered them as "a lyrical intermezzo."[49] Georgia was quiet and prosperous. Thanks to Osip Mandelstam, who had reached Tbilisi before them, Ehrenburg, Lyubov Mikhailovna, and Yadviga Sommer were entertained by two leading Georgian poets, Paolo Yashvili and Tizian Tabidze. Ehrenburg had met Yashvili only briefly at the Rotonde in 1914, but in Tbilisi they greeted each other like old friends. For two weeks they enjoyed restaurants and wine gardens, sulphur baths, ancient temples, and the city's marketplace. Ehrenburg and Mandelstam also gave a poetry reading in a local café.

The visit came to a close with news from the Soviet embassy that their travel plans to Moscow were arranged. In his memoirs Ehrenburg never explains why the Soviet ambassador would trust two poets who had been living under Wrangel in the Crimea; moreover, the ambassador ordered Ehrenburg to carry a packet of mail and three bales of material adorned with ten wax seals (the material was inconsequential newspaper), turning him into a diplomatic courier, one of his more improbable occupations. He and Lyubov Mikhailovna, joined by Yadviga, traveled with Osip and Alexander Mandelstam. They sat in crowded, ordinary carriages that were attached to armored trains. As in the Ukraine, the Whites attacked several times. They once succeeded in tearing up the tracks and fired directly on the train. Mandelstam panicked and suggested to Lyubov Mikhailovna that they hide in the nearby hills until the danger had passed, but she persuaded him to stay on the train. The Red Army soldiers repulsed the Whites with machine guns and the ride continued. They all survived and reached Moscow in eight days.

A CURIOUS INCIDENT

Ehrenburg's troubles were not over. He had been in Moscow for two weeks when he was arrested by the Cheka (the Bolshevik secret police) on November 1 and taken to Lubyanka prison, accused of being an agent of Wrangel. Ehrenburg's interrogator remembered meeting him in the Rotonde, then challenged him to prove he was not a White agent. The Cheka had no real evidence against him, while friends rallied in support: Lyubov Mikhailovna alerted Ehrenburg's high school comrade, Nikolai Bukharin, now editor of *Pravda* and one of the most powerful men in the country; Ehrenburg was released after four days of interrogation, doubtless a result of Bukharin's intervention.

Forty years later Ehrenburg treated this episode lightly in his memoirs, remembering the sailors who shared his cell and how they accidentally met in a theater after their release. But Ehrenburg knew that many others were not so fortunate. He knew how the Cheka behaved in Kiev; according to Nadezhda Mandelstam, trucks carried corpses from its headquarters every day. He might also have feared that the Cheka knew of his activity in Kiev, his defense of the Whites, and his denunciation of the Bolsheviks. His poems were not taken seriously— "in those years people were killed for every reason except verses," he remarked in *A Book for Adults*—but an article like "Exodus" could have endangered him had the Cheka known of it; even Bukharin might not have been able to save him.[50]

Although Ehrenburg camouflaged his fears when he wrote about the incident in his memoirs, he revealed more of his feelings in a short story less than a year after the arrest took place. "A Curious Incident" tells the story of a Bolshevik leader who decides to inspect the jail where he had spent four years as a prisoner under the czar. Fate intervenes. He is accidentally locked up and finds himself sharing a cell with an old Menshevik friend. Their encounter undermines the Bolshevik's resolve. The jail, the guard, even the prisoners are the same. The world cannot be saved through evil. When the mistake is discovered the party chief refuses to leave and the Cheka is forced to remove him to a sanitarium, where he shouts through the window every morning, "I only want to subvert." While "A Curious Incident" is not transparently autobiographical, its irony conveys the truth of Ehrenburg's experience.[51]

ONCE MORE, FROM MOSCOW TO PARIS

After his release from the Lubyanka, Ehrenburg and Lyubov Mikhailovna resumed their careers. Lyubov Mikhailovna gained admission to an art school where she studied under the renowned artist and designer Alexander Rodchenko. Ehrenburg found opportunities to read verses. He appeared in small cafés and also joined a prestigious group of poets—Andrei Bely, Valery Bryusov, Sergei Yesenin, and Boris Pasternak—in an evening of readings entitled "Russia in the Storm," which took place in December 1920.

Ehrenburg continued to write literary criticism as well. Between 1919 and 1921 he completed a collection of brief essays on twelve of Russia's most accomplished poets, among them Anna Akhmatova, Alexander Blok, Andrei Bely, Sergei Yesenin, Osip Mandelstam, Vladimir Mayakovsky, Boris Pasternak, and Marina Tsvetaeva. These essays reveal Ehrenburg's taste and his ability to recognize poetic excellence. Many of the poets were already famous, but Tsvetaeva, for one, was not widely known and Pasternak had published very little before 1921. Nonetheless, Ehrenburg did not hesitate to call Pasternak "the most beloved of all the brothers of my craft." While he wrote about Pasternak many times, always with respect and admiration, this first sketch was especially generous and tender: "Not one of his poems could have been written before him. He had the ecstasy of surprise, the rush of new emotions, the power of freshness." Although Ehrenburg often disliked lyric poetry, he recognized that in Pasternak's verse there was "nothing of autumn, sunset, or other nice but unreassuring things. [Pasternak] showed that lyric poetry exists and can exist in the future outside the question of social environment."[52]

Ehrenburg's friendships revolved around his literary vocation. Pasternak was a neighbor and frequently stopped by. Osip Mandelstam left Moscow for St. Petersburg but before departing asked Lyubov Mikhailovna to locate Nadya Khazina; Ehrenburg's wife wrote to him in January 1921 with Nadya's new address in Kiev. Mandelstam went there in March and he and Nadya were not separated again until the 1930s when he suffered arrest, exile, and death. The Ehrenburgs were instrumental in the marriage and Lyubov Mikhailovna always referred to herself as their "matchmaker."[53]

Ehrenburg continued to write poetry but could not earn a living from his verse; he was fortunate to land another improbable job. He met the director Vsevolod Meyerhold, who hired him for the theatrical section of the Education Ministry, placing him in charge of the country's children's theaters. In his memoirs Ehrenburg referred to Meyerhold as the head of the theatrical section; he was in fact the deputy director. As often happened in *People, Years, Life*, the peculiar circumstances of Soviet historiography compelled Ehrenburg to alter the facts. The actual director was Leon Trotsky's sister, Olga Kameneva; her husband, Lev Kamenev, became a principal victim of Stalin's purge trials in 1936. Olga Kameneva disappeared then as well and is presumed to have been shot.

Ehrenburg's work in the Education Ministry was fairly routine. He spent most of his time helping to draft projects and arrange rations for actors, but it afforded him an opportunity to work closely with Meyerhold, one of the most influential directors in the history of Russian theater. Meyerhold too fell victim to Stalin in 1940, but Ehrenburg remained faithful to his memory. As he did in the cases of Babel and Mandelstam following Stalin's death, Ehrenburg helped to revive Meyerhold's place in Russian cultural history, lecturing about him in Moscow and often writing about him.

Their months together in the Education Ministry remained vivid to Ehrenburg. Meyerhold had a difficult personality, "kindness combined with a quick temper, and his complex inner world was tinged with fanaticism." Their first disagreement reveals much about Ehrenburg's responsibilities in the ministry and how he was viewed by committed Communists. One day a sailor submitted a mediocre script for a children's play about the revolution. Ehrenburg rejected it but Meyerhold read the script, then berated Ehrenburg, claiming he "was against revolutionary activity and against October in the theater." Ehrenburg defended himself, saying that such an accusation was "demagoguery." Meyerhold was ready to go even further, accusing Ehrenburg of sabotage and calling for his arrest. But then, just as suddenly, Meyerhold relented. He telephoned Ehrenburg the next day for his advice "as if yesterday's scene had never taken place."[54]

In spite of his work Ehrenburg remained desperately poor. Moscow, like all areas under Bolshevik control, lived under the policy of "war communism." In the countryside this meant the forcible expropriation of large estates, the confiscation of produce from better-off peasants, and the despatch of armed detachments from the cities to requisition grain and other staples. All business and industry was nationalized and a system of barter was introduced in place of ordinary trade. As might be expected, the results were catastrophic. Commerce and industry collapsed. Agriculture and the distribution of foodstuffs came to a virtual halt. Only the regime's brutal requisitions and widespread black marketeering prevented a famine of enormous proportions.

It became difficult to find even the most ordinary necessities. While Ehrenburg relied on rations from the Ministry of Education, his only pair of trousers was badly torn and he wore a dilapidated overcoat to conceal them. By chance, Nikolai Bukharin was able to help him. In his memoirs, as they first appeared, Ehrenburg described an accidental meeting with his "old associate from the prerevolutionary underground organization," the code language he had to use when referring to Bukharin, who gave him a note of introduction to Moscow's mayor. Lev Kamenev was chairman of the Moscow soviet at the time. He received Ehrenburg and saw to it he was clothed.[55]

Although it was not an easy process, Ehrenburg later recalled the episode with humor in a Soviet magazine published in 1927. After seeing Bukharin, Ehrenburg hesitated to approach Kamenev, too embarrassed to request trousers from a prominent official. "How could I declare to a man who was busy with international problems that my pants were worn out?" Ehrenburg asked himself. Kamenev reassured him. "You need more than a suit. You need a winter coat, too." Early the next morning Ehrenburg went to the clothing warehouse with a note from Kamenev and, to his surprise, found a long line leading from the door down the street. He did not reach the manager's office until it was nearly dark.

Kamenev's note was short, lofty, and abstract. It consisted of only three words: "To dress Ehrenburg." The manager sighed melancholically. "We have little clothing, comrade. Choose one of these two: either a coat or a suit." That was quite a choice. Never in my life have I experienced such ambivalence! It was almost like God tempting Solomon. I did not answer right away, although the rumble of the line pressed me for an answer. After a day spent in the freezing weather, I leaned toward an overcoat. I was already prepared faintheartedly to say "only a warm one." But my vanity won out. I remembered all the humiliation of being without trousers for months and finally answered, "trousers." They gave me a slip for a suit.[56]

This incident was not the last time Bukharin helped him. By the beginning of 1921 Ehrenburg was ready to leave the country. He had an idea for a novel about the prewar years and the revolution but felt that he could not begin it in Moscow. "It seemed to me that I needed to sit down in a Paris café, ask the waiter for coffee, a few sandwiches, some paper, and the book would be written." He mentioned his idea to Bukharin and a short time later was called to the Foreign Ministry, where he requested permission to go to France for an "artistic mission."[57] A few weeks later the deputy head of the Cheka, which oversaw trips abroad, granted passports to Ehrenburg and his wife but warned that the French might not receive them cordially. In 1921 Soviet Russia did not have diplomatic relations with any major Western European country.

Ehrenburg's request to travel came just as the regime's policies were shifting in a more tolerant direction. In March, after Lenin's insistence, the policy of "war communism" was abandoned in favor of the New Economic Policy (NEP). Lenin perceived the need to respond to the drastic decline in the Bolsheviks' popularity and the increased tensions in the country, represented most vividly by the Kronstadt Rebellion in Petrograd, when Red Navy sailors led by anarchists demanded the overthrow of the Bolshevik government. They were all ruthlessly suppressed in the beginning of March during the Tenth Party Congress, which debated and approved Lenin's proposals. NEP signaled the (temporary) end of class warfare in the countryside and led gradually to greater abundance of food and other material goods in the cities.

Just months before, Ehrenburg had been arrested on suspicion of being a White agent. Now, in a stark reversal of fortune, the regime granted him an extraordinary privilege. He and Lyubov Mikhailovna secured permission to leave in March 1921, a full year before other writers and intellectuals were permitted to travel. With Bukharin's help, they may have been the first citizens to leave the country legally with Soviet passports. Only the Soviet physicist and future Nobel laureate Pyotr Kapitsa received a Soviet passport for private travel as early in 1921.* Other Soviet intellectuals were treated differently. Maxim Gorky left for Italy in the fall of 1921, ostensibly for medical treatment but in reality as an expression of protest against the regime. His prestige secured him a Soviet passport. By the spring of 1922 the regime established routine procedures for writers to travel. Many (although not all) left the country intending to return; still other intellectuals were forced to leave. In September 1922 the regime expelled a group of one hundred twenty cultural figures, including the philosopher Nikolai Berdyaev, because of their anti-Bolshevik hostility; they were not issued passports and lost their Soviet citizenship.

Ilya Ehrenburg left to write *Julio Jurenito*. But there is no doubt Ehrenburg's principal reason for leaving was his disillusion with Soviet Russia. He had spent four years enduring hunger, disease, and the violence of civil war in a vain attempt to find a place for himself. He no longer wanted to live there. Ehrenburg nonetheless renewed his passion for Russia and did not want to lose her as he had in 1908, when political circumstances compelled him to flee. This time he wanted to be sure he could return. As he wrote on the train ride to Riga, "Then, Moscow, you will forget / The affront of all partings / And will answer the guilty knock / With a loving rumble."[58] Ehrenburg intended to remain a Soviet writer but he also wanted his independence; a passport and the memory of life in Paris offered a unique solution to that dilemma.

---

*Kapitsa worked for thirteen years in England, conducting research in Cambridge under Ernest Rutherford. At the time he was a young, promising student. Like Ehrenburg, he retained his Soviet citizenship and visited the Soviet Union periodically. Unlike Ehrenburg, Kapitsa's arrangement came to an abrupt halt in 1934, when the Soviet government did not allow him to return to England after one of his frequent trips to Russia. A year later, the Kremlin allocated significant funds to buy equipment from the British and reconstitute Kapitsa's Cambridge laboratory in Moscow.

FOUR

A Novelist in Exile

By 1924, three years after his return to Europe, Ilya Ehrenburg had secured a significant place in Soviet literature. Almost everything he wrote was either published in separate editions on both sides of Russia's political divide or sold openly in Western editions in Moscow without government interference. These essays, reviews, and novels, particularly his first, *The Extraordinary Adventures of Julio Jurenito and His Disciples*, provoked tremendous controversy within émigré circles and in Russia itself, where orthodox critics and government censors paid close attention to each of his books.

After Ehrenburg's collection *Unlikely Stories* appeared in Berlin in 1922, two stories, "A Curious Incident" and "Uskomchel," were left out of Soviet editions, no doubt because of their ironic treatment of life under the Bolsheviks. As mentioned earlier, "A Curious Incident" concerns a party leader who accidentally lands in jail after the revolution; "Uskomchel" has an equally sardonic message. The title is an acronym based on the Russian phrase for "an improved Communist man." The protagonist, a Kremlin bureaucrat named Vozov, is "such a pure Communist that a Socialist Revolutionary would kill him with pleasure."[1] Vozov loves to draw graphs and charts; even in his dreams he conjures up projects to regulate births. But then Vozov creates the ideal Communist agitator who turns on Vozov himself and disrupts his life so completely that Vozov goes mad and dies. The story ends with his burial and a voice from beyond the grave intoning that now Vozov truly is "an improved Communist."

Although "Uskomchel" was not published in the Soviet Union, it was mentioned by name and highly praised by no less a figure than Joseph Stalin. Stalin was already general secretary, maneuvering against Trotsky and other leaders for control of the party. In April 1924, three months after Lenin's death, Stalin delivered his lecture "The Foundations of Leninism" at Sverdlov University. This was a major statement of his views on revolutionary tactics, reformism, and factions and unity within the party, all to advance his claim as Lenin's legitimate heir. The brief, final section concerned two attributes of Lenin's approach to work, what Stalin called "Russian revolutionary zeal and American businesslike practicality." But revolutionary zeal, he explained, often succumbs to the "fatal disease" of projects "concocted in the blind belief that a decree can change everything, can bring order out of chaos." At that point Stalin praised "one of our Russian writers, I. Ehrenburg, who described in his story 'Uskomchel' a character who was overwhelmed by this disease. His goal was to devise a scheme for an ideal man, but he 'drowned' in this 'work.' The story is a great exaggeration," Stalin continued, "but Ehrenburg understood the disease correctly, that's for sure."[2]

Stalin praised only one other Soviet writer in this context, Boris Pilnyak, whose book *The Naked Year* was the country's most widely read novel on the revolution and civil war. By the late 1920s, though, Pilnyak became the object of harsh official censure and despite efforts to regain Stalin's favor he disappeared at the height of the purges in 1937.

Ehrenburg was luckier. "Uskomchel" may have offended Glavlit (the official censorship bureau), but for Stalin, who mistrusted Bolshevik idealists and whose plans led to the destruction of the party's leading cadres, there must have been something appealing in Ehrenburg's sarcasm, something equivocal, even defenseless, that might someday come in handy. Or perhaps Stalin simply liked the idea of a Communist who destroys himself.

TWO WEEKS IN PARIS

Ilya Ehrenburg's return to Paris in 1921 differed greatly from his exile in 1908, when he traveled from Moscow to Paris directly by train. A catastrophic war, the collapse of dynasties in Berlin and Vienna, and the Bolshevik triumph in Russia had irreparably transformed Europe. Now he needed visas for himself and for his wife. It was impossible to obtain a visa for Yadviga Sommer; she remained in Soviet Russia, got married, and soon gave birth to her only child, a daughter, in 1924.

Anticipating difficulties, Ehrenburg carried a passport issued by the Provisional Government in 1917 to prove he had lived in Paris, but the French consul in Riga (his initial stop outside Soviet Russia) was not impressed. Ehrenburg wrote to friends in Paris for help and then resigned himself to waiting. He and Lyubov Mikhailovna spent over four weeks in Latvia. Within days of their arrival Ehrenburg's father died in Kharkov, a fact Ehrenburg did not mention in his memoirs. In Riga he was preoccupied with obtaining a French visa. He also arranged publication of a new book of poems, *Reflections*, and gave lectures on artistic and literary developments in Soviet Russia. When the French visas finally came the Germans refused permission to travel through their country. Ehrenburg and his wife had to make their way through Danzig to Copenhagen, and from there to London. Finally, on May 8, they reached the French capital.

The Rotonde had changed hands; tourists were displacing the artists and writers. Apollinaire had died of war wounds in 1918; Modigliani succumbed to tuberculosis in 1920. "Something was wrong with Paris, something was wrong with me, and something was wrong with everything. But it was still nice to sit at the Rotonde," Ehrenburg later remarked.[3] He found friends in new cafés in Montparnasse. Picasso and Rivera embraced him. They wanted to hear about Moscow and the revolution. But Russian émigrés were suspicious of him, even hostile. "Nature has endowed Ehrenburg generously," the writer Viktor Shklovsky scoffed. "He has a passport."[4] Émigrés turned away, "some with anger, others out of fear."

If Ehrenburg was not a political refugee, what was he? The French police had their own answer. After two weeks in Paris, on May 26 Ehrenburg was brusquely deported to Belgium under police escort. He never learned the precise reason for his expulsion. One official told him, "France is the freest country in the world. If you're being expelled, there must be good reasons for it." Another official told his friends he was "pushing Bolshevik propaganda."[5] The émigré press was astonished. One daily newspaper, *Obshchee Delo* (Common Cause), carried Ehrenburg's troubles on the front page. "This expulsion, evidently, is the result of some kind of misunderstanding," the editors declared. "Ehrenburg, first of all, is not a politician but a decadent poet."[6]

It is difficult to know if Ehrenburg's deportation was provoked by anything more substantial than his Soviet passport. An émigré might have told the police about Ehrenburg's admiration for a good deal of art and literature that was still coming out in Russia, insinuating political sympathies from his aesthetic judgments. Ivan Bunin was already in Paris and saw Ehrenburg soon after his arrival. Bunin was appalled by Ehrenburg's opinions; he seemed to "accept the Bolsheviks" and "tried all the time to point out the good they were doing and avoid the scandalous through silence." Bunin was suspicious and wondered how Ehrenburg had left, how he managed to have "so much money." For Bunin, "it was all very strange."[7] The writer Nina Berberova, who arrived in Berlin the following spring, claims it was common knowledge that Alexei Tolstoy had denounced Ehrenburg.[8] Ehrenburg and Tolstoy had been friends before the revolution and worked together on a play in Moscow in 1918. But they had a falling-out in 1921—Ehrenburg asserts in his memoirs that he forgot over what—and were not reconciled for several years.

Ehrenburg's eighteen days in Paris proved to be sufficient inspiration for his novel. Once in Belgium (he and his wife managed to enter without proper visas) they settled in the seaside resort of La Panne where, "surrounded by sand dunes and breezes," Ehrenburg wrote *The Extraordinary Adventures of Julio Jurenito and His Disciples*.[9] Although his poetry and wartime articles had made him well known, *Julio Jurenito* established Ehrenburg as a provocative and unpredictable presence in Soviet literature.

Earlier, in Kiev, he had been rehearsing it. He used to sit with Nadezhda Khazina, Lyubov Mikhailovna, and Yadviga Sommer, regaling them with adventures from his years in Paris, often "telling his stories in verse form—this kind of improvisation went on for hours."[10] Some were real, many were imagined. Gradually, he understood he was composing a novel in his head. But he needed Paris to enliven his memories. Ehrenburg made it back to the Rotonde. He was thrilled to be alive, in spite of the efforts of Germans, marauding Communists, and vengeful anti-Semites to do away with him. Like the teenager who had earlier escaped to Paris, he felt intoxicated with his survival. Written in twenty-eight days, the novel reads as if it had been dictated in one breath. "It seemed to me," Ehrenburg recalled years later, "that I was not moving a pen over a sheet of paper, but leading a bayonet charge."[11] *Julio Jurenito* marked Ehrenburg's rebirth and revenge on all those who had threatened or betrayed him.

A PROPHETIC MEPHISTOPHELES

Julio Jurenito opens in the Rotonde, where an impoverished poet named Ilya Ehrenburg is "sitting as usual on the Boulevard Montparnasse before a cup long drained of its coffee, waiting in vain for someone to liberate [him] by paying the patient garçon six sous." With a touch of self-mockery Ehrenburg poked fun at his own life and habits, casting "this author of mediocre verses, a jaded journalist, a coward, an apostate, a trifling bigot" into a central figure in the novel's drama.[12]

Waiting in the Rotonde, Ehrenburg meets a mysterious gentleman who quickly enlists him in his plans to disrupt Europe. This is Julio Jurenito, a Mephistophelian character whose Mexican origin is a tribute to Diego Rivera. "He did not believe in any religious truths or ethical precepts," Ehrenburg discovers.[13] Assuming the pose of a metaphysical cheerleader for mankind's ability to destroy itself, Jurenito is "a great provocateur," out to undermine Europe's sacred myths and complacent assumptions about religion and politics, love and marriage, art, socialism, and the rules of war.

Ehrenburg becomes Jurenito's first disciple, and they are soon joined by an inspired collection of national stereotypes: a French undertaker, who cares only for gratifying his sensual desires; the American Mr. Cool, whose life is dominated by a watch, a checkbook, and his worship of the Bible; a Russian who wallows in self-pity, continually telling the story of his miserable life; an Italian who embodies mankind's "chaotic urge to Freedom," never having learned to work; an African, whose simple nature and naive faith distinguish him from the Europeans; and the most compelling portrait of all, Karl Schmidt, whose violent German patriotism and extreme commitment to socialism presage the Nazis.

Jurenito leads his disciples on a rollicking tour of Europe, Africa, and

Soviet Russia. In Rome the Pope turns out to be a senile old man, while the Vatican sells religious amulets to gullible soldiers at the front. In the Hague a committee of smug, elderly, distinguished gentlemen explain that "war was not the wild butchery it had seemed to us, but was ennobled by 1713 paragraphs of rules covering humane methods for the killing of human beings."[14] In Geneva an international array of Socialists are ensconced in a hotel they have transformed into a grotesque version of the war itself, its lobbies and grounds divided by moats, ramparts, and barbed-wire entanglements. Asked if they oppose the war, Socialists from all sides affirm its criminal nature then quickly denounce each other.

Although these bitter caricatures and the novel's cynical mood contributed greatly to Ehrenburg's reputation as a man who believed in nothing, *Julio Jurenito* is more than a collection of extravagant lampoons. The European war and Russia's revolutionary turmoil provoked grimmer fantasies in Ehrenburg, especially when Jurenito insists that his disciples confront three particular subjects: the character of Karl Schmidt, the nature of Soviet Communism, and the fate of the Jews. In these episodes Ehrenburg explores this century's most terrible crimes with startling prescience and psychological insight.

His antipathy to the German national character as he understood it began long before the rise of Nazism. On a visit to Germany as a child Ehrenburg was told by his mother that the train was scheduled to arrive at a certain hour and minute. He did not believe her. Russian train stations are disorderly places and no Russian would assume that a train could arrive precisely on time. But that day in Germany Ehrenburg anxiously regarded his mother's watch, and when the train arrived at the correct moment, he grew deeply frightened and began to cry, sensing something sinister in Germany's commitment to punctuality.[15]

Karl Schmidt embodies the worst dimensions of this thirst for order; he follows a weekly routine of work, study, eating, sleeping, and visits to a prostitute, referring to a detailed chart. During World War I Schmidt advocates the colonization of Russia and the absorption of France and England into a greater Germany to "perfect the economic organization of a single Europe and finally the happiness of mankind." Consistent with his philosophy, Schmidt is even willing to approve the "slaughter of ten thousand infants for the benefit of society." "Do you think that I, that all of us Germans enjoy killing?" Schmidt asks his fellow disciples.

I assure you that I enjoy drinking beer or cognac, or attending a concert . . . much more. To kill is an unpleasant necessity. It is a dirty business, without exalting cries or joyous bonfires. I do not think that a surgeon experiences delight when he pokes his fingers into a stomach bloated with gas and undigested food. But there is no choice. . . . To kill one lunatic for the benefit of mankind or ten million— the difference is only arithmetical. But it is necessary to kill, otherwise the world will continue its stupid, irrational life. Others will grow up to replace those who are killed. I love children no less than you do.

Schmidt's ideas disturb Ehrenburg, but Jurenito recognizes a worthy disciple. "Your hopes are fated to be rewarded sooner than you think," he says to Schmidt. "As for the rest of you," the Master tells the others, "here is someone who is destined to stand at the helm of mankind, now and for a long time to come."[16] Jurenito could not have been more accurate.

History mimicked art when Heinrich Himmler, Reichsführer SS and chief of the German police, unknowingly repeated Karl Schmidt's insane intentions in a speech about the Final Solution to Nazi officers in Poznan in 1943:

Most of you know what it means when one hundred corpses are lying side by side, when five hundred are lying there or when one thousand are lying there. To have stuck this out and at the same time—apart from exceptions due to human weaknesses—to have remained decent, that is what has made us hard. This is a page of glory in our history which has never been written and is never to be written.[17]

Ehrenburg created a Nazi in his imagination long before the world got its first glimpse of Adolf Hitler. But in 1921, when he wrote *Julio Jurenito*, Ehrenburg understood that the Nazis would not be an isolated horror and that a second European dictatorship—this time in Soviet Russia—would complement Hitler's murderous ideology with one of its own.

Jurenito leads his disciples to Moscow just as the Bolsheviks are taking over the country. Confusion, revolutionary meetings, and bureaucrats abound while freedom has few defenders. Russia has turned into "a savage ship." Jurenito and his disciples are arrested and despatched to Butyrki jail, where Ehrenburg had been imprisoned as a teenager. The experience confirms that the revolution will rely on coercion, just as the czarist autocracy had done before. The revolution had promised freedom, but individual liberty turns out to be "a fading phantom." In a climactic chapter Ehrenburg accompanies Jurenito to the Kremlin where the Master interviews an unnamed political leader; this is obviously Lenin. The party had to seize power, Lenin explains, "to direct the entire force of this wrath, the full yearning for a new life, toward one clear and defined thing." As for opponents, Lenin has nothing but pitiless contempt and vows to eliminate them all. Lenin's candid admissions remind Ehrenburg of Karl Schmidt, who has changed "from a general in the German imperial army into a grim Spartacist in a patched coat." Schmidt has become a powerful commisar in Moscow, having realized that the "Communist International was more likely to subject Europe to a single plan."[18] The proto-Nazi has found a home among the Bolsheviks, confirming the essential similarity of Schmidt's two passions: violent German nationalism and extreme socialism. Under either of these ideologies, Ehrenburg makes clear, Schmidt has the freedom to express the pathology of his nature.

Ehrenburg realized in 1921 that he was witnessing the birth of a terrible new world and surmised that the Jews would be this new Europe's favorite victim. Ehrenburg first addressed anti-Semitism in the poem "To the Jewish People" in 1911; four years later he wrote "Somewhere in Poland," a poem about a pogrom threatening a mother and child most likely inspired by reports of anti-Semitic incidents on the eastern front. "Our tribe is well-rehearsed," Ehrenburg lamented. "We have seen nine hundred captivities."[19] But neither of these poems exhibits the prophetic anxiety over the fate of the Jewish people expressed in *Julio Jurenito*, one that Ehrenburg carried with him all his life.

In the novel, to the astonishment of his disciples, the Master prepares an invitation to the "Extermination of the Jewish tribe in Budapest, Kiev, Jaffa, Algiers, and numerous other places." Jurenito foresees Jews being buried alive and other methods for "purging the land of suspicious elements. . . . Cardinals, bishops, archimandrites, English lords, Roman nobles, Russian liberals, French journalists, all members of the Hohenzollern family" are invited, and admission is free. The Russian disciple, Alexei Tishin, objects, denying that such abominations could take place. But Jurenito assures him that it "will turn out to be a boisterous and thoughtless century without any moral prejudices." He then describes how the Jews have been scapegoats throughout history, in Egypt, Spain, and Italy, blamed for droughts, epidemics, and earthquakes; these invitations were prepared for the next inevitable round of violence. Alexei Tishin is still confused and asks Jurenito, "Aren't the Jews people just like us?" In response the Master proposes to demonstrate that the Jews are not like everyone else by means of "a somewhat childish game." "Tell me," Jurenito addresses his disciples, "if you were asked to keep one word out of all human words and specifically had to choose either 'yes' or 'no,' which would you prefer?" They begin to respond. The American chooses "yes" because it is assertive while "no" is immoral and criminal; the Frenchman prefers "yes" because it implies happiness; the Russian prefers it out of spiritual faith; the German chooses it as an organizational tool; the Italian decides on "yes" because it accompanies "every pleasant occasion"; and the African says "yes" because his gods always grant his wishes. Only the Jew, the character Ilya Ehrenburg, insists on "no," and as he speaks the others move away from him. Jurenito's lesson is complete. When all the nations agree, the Jews will be ready to dissent. They are the "world's great medicine." This is their role in history and the reason for the universal hatred they endure.[20]

Ehrenburg held on to his belief that Jews were different from other people. Four years after writing *Julio Jurenito* Ehrenburg compared the role of Jewish writers in world literature to "a spoonful of tar in a barrel of honey." It was they who provided a measure of skepticism, even when skepticism "poorly fits in with society's everyday needs."[21] Ehrenburg identified himself with this tradition.

——

Julio Jurenito was initially published in Berlin in the fall of 1921. More than a year passed before it appeared in the Soviet press. During that time individual copies made it into the country. One reached Ehrenburg's old friend from Paris, Liza Polonskaya, who was now living in Petrograd. She showed it to friends while other copies circulated widely in the city. "The appearance of *Julio Jurenito* is remembered by everyone," the novelist Veniamin Kaverin wrote. "In two or three weeks, Ehrenburg became famous."[22] Even *Pravda* made note of Ehrenburg's achievement. The critic Alexander Voronsky called it "magnificent," one of those Russian books published abroad "which should have been re-published by our official press a long time ago."[23]

Nonetheless, the secret police confiscated every copy of the émigré edition they could find in Petrograd in the fall of 1922. Such news depressed Ehrenburg. "I am writing only for Russia," he wrote to a friend. "For the émigrés I am alien and hostile."[24]

Ehrenburg also shared his anxiety with Liza Polonskaya. "I know [the book] is dangerous," he wrote to her on November 25, 1922. "But they noticed this belatedly, as it were. The Government Publishing House has bought a second edition, stipulating that it will supply an introduction, which either Bukharin (I would like) or Pokrovsky is supposed to write. Perhaps [the publishers] will reconsider now. Write me in detail all that you know about the confiscation."[25] In the end Bukharin did write an introduction, assuring that the first Soviet edition could appear at the outset of 1923 in a printing of fifteen thousand copies, a large number for those years. *Julio Jurenito* was published two more times in the Soviet Union in the 1920s, always with Nikolai Bukharin's introduction. Calling the novel "a most fascinating satire," Bukharin conceded that Ehrenburg exposed "a number of comic and repulsive sides to life under all regimes." But he emphasized Ehrenburg's attitude toward the West, especially his attacks on capitalism and war.[26]

Julio Jurenito was a great literary success and it remained Ehrenburg's favorite novel. "It is my one serious book," he wrote in 1922. "It seems that neither the critics, nor readers, nor I myself, can precisely determine where the ironic smile ends."[27] Translated into French, Yiddish, Czech, Spanish, and English by 1930, it was also popular inside Russia, especially among young, idealistic party members. Even Lenin admired the novel, remarking to his wife Nadezhda Krupskaya that "our shaggy-haired Ilya [as Ehrenburg was dubbed in Paris] had done a good job."[28]

Julio Jurenito provoked other intense reactions. The writer Yevgeny Zamyatin provided especially thoughtful insight. Writing in 1923, Zamyatin admired Ehrenburg's use of irony most of all, terming it "a European weapon" that Russian writers seldom employ. He applauded Ehrenburg for not adopting a particular ideological position from which to direct his attack, preferring instead to ridicule all available targets. "He is, of course, a real heretic (and therefore—a revolutionary)," Zamyatin remarked, signifying the highest praise. "A genuine heretic has the same virtue as dynamite: the explosion (creative) takes the line of *most* resistance."[29]

More than half a century later the book's prophetic qualities have confirmed Ehrenburg's unrelenting pessimism. His portrait of Karl Schmidt, his premonition of Europeans gathering to watch multitudes of Jews consumed by fire, even his offhand remark that a weapon of mass destruction would be employed against the Japanese, make it easier for us to accept his dark portrayal of Western civilization. Ehrenburg not only witnessed and survived the initial rounds of this century's violence, but also sensed the protagonists and the direction of its future course.

Ehrenburg never disavowed *Julio Jurenito*, even in the late 1940s when the Kremlin's cultural policies reached grotesque extremes. The book by then was long out of print and could not conceivably appear. But Ehrenburg remained attached to the novel. In 1947, during an official exhibition at the Writers' Union marking the thirtieth anniversary of Soviet literature, Ehrenburg noticed that *Julio Jurenito* was not included among his works. He was furious and stalked out of the auditorium.[30] At that time in Stalin's Russia such a display of resentment took genuine courage, even with regard to an insignificant act of censorship. For Ehrenburg, who understood that the regime preferred his novels from the 1930s—such as *Out of Chaos* or *Without Taking Breath*, which suited Stalin's taste for industrial soap opera—the exclusion of *Julio Jurenito* was an insult and no doubt a poignant reminder of his literary fortune. *Julio Jurenito* was his first, his favorite, and his most honest novel. He wanted to be remembered for it. But the novel did not appear again in Moscow until 1962, when it was included in a nine-volume collection of Ehrenburg's works. Bukharin's preface had to be left out and the account of Jurenito's interview with Lenin was also suppressed.

In *Julio Jurenito* Ehrenburg did not contrast the West with an idealized Russia; he did not identify with either place. The book's fictional narrator, the disciple Ilya Ehrenburg, leaves Russia at the close of the story and returns to Europe in order to write this book. He and the other disciples (Jurenito is dead) want to leave "the purgatory of revolution" for Europe's "cozy hell." While Ehrenburg does not restrain his irony when he returns to Europe there is a measure of sincere relief when he describes the westward journey as a "single, unbroken demonstration of the triumph of peace, order, prudence, and civilization."[31] Far from perfect, Europe is where Ilya Ehrenburg chooses to settle.

FIVE

A Writer in Two Worlds

I f Paris was the political center for the Russian emigration before and after the revolution, Berlin became its literary capital in the early 1920s. While the Soviet government had yet to establish diplomatic relations with France or England, the Weimar Republic welcomed friendly relations with Moscow after the close of the civil war and the beginning of Lenin's New Economic Policy.

Bearers of Soviet passports, such as Ilya Ehrenburg and his wife, could enter Germany. Moreover, the country's high inflation and relatively low prices were favorable to the publishing industry. By 1922 there were as many as thirty Russian-language publishers in Berlin, their output rivaling the number of books published in German. These books were not restricted to an émigré audience. Several publishers had direct connections to Soviet authors and many books, although printed in the West, could be openly sold in Russia as late as 1925. At the same time Soviet writers such as Boris Pasternak, Vladimir Mayakovsky, and Sergei Yesenin traveled to Berlin, enjoyed the city's rich cultural activity, and met openly with their émigré colleagues.

Unable to live in Paris, Ehrenburg and his wife left Belgium and joined the large Russian community in Berlin in October 1921. Perhaps as many as three hundred thousand émigrés crowded into Berlin's working-class neighborhoods. Although he did not expect to like the city, Berlin's mood—its poverty, decadence, and loss—suited Ehrenburg's own and reflected the true state of Europe after the war.

> If I live in Berlin, it is because . . . during the years of revolution, I fell in love with grimy railroad junctions, with day-dreaming refugees, and unworkable timetables. . . . In Dresden, the Communists are organizing a workers' government and in Munich the Fascists are preparing a revolt. Reading about this, Berliners think that Dresden and Munich are fortunate cities. They have genuine timetables. In Berlin no one knows when and where the next train will be leaving.[1]

As he described Berlin, he could have been describing himself.

The most important émigré journal in Berlin was *Russkaya Kniga* (The Russian Book). It began in January 1921 under the editorial leadership of Alexander Yashchenko. Yashchenko had been a law professor in Perm University before leaving a Soviet trade delegation during a visit to Germany in 1919; he was among the first Soviet officials to defect. Despite his opposition to the Bolsheviks Yashchenko was sympathetic to artistic developments in Soviet Russia and wanted to help overcome the ideological division of Russian literature. To accomplish this it was necessary for *Russkaya Kniga* to "remain outside of any political struggle and outside of all political parties whatsoever."[2] *Russkaya Kniga* was unique in attempting to assume a nonpartisan editorial position. The journal carried articles and reviews, news about publishing and the arts in Russia and among the many émigré communities scattered around the world.

Ehrenburg had read the first issue of *Russkaya Kniga* in Moscow and when he reached Paris in May 1921 promptly wrote to Yashchenko expressing admiration for the journal. Ehrenburg supplied Yashchenko with details about nearly eighty literary and artistic figures whose lives had been disrupted by the civil war, a generous and unprecedented contribution to *Russkaya Kniga* that the editors quickly used. The main point of Ehrenburg's letter, though, was to correct a tendency within the émigré community to denigrate writers and other artists who remained in Russia. "Unfortunately," Ehrenburg wrote, "certain attacks, perhaps based on false information or a misunderstanding of the special quality of contemporary Russian psychology and life, have crept into your journal, which we admire for its devotion to Russian literature."[3]

By July 1921 Ehrenburg's first article appeared in *Russkaya Kniga*. Written in Belgium, where he had just completed *Julio Jurenito*, "Above the Battle" expressed Ehrenburg's unique position within émigré circles as someone who would try to create a place for himself between both halves of Russia's literary community.

> I will permit myself, while the Civil War is still raging, to remain a heretic who suggests that neither Balmont, who damns Communism, nor Bryusov, who praises it, lose any respect for their literary activities as two poets of the previous generation who founded symbolism. As a poet, I personally love neither Balmont nor Bryusov. My social sympathies are equally remote from both of them, but this cannot justify abusing or scorning them.[4]

Ehrenburg did not defend the Soviet regime in his numerous articles for *Russkaya Kniga*, but he repeatedly and eloquently asserted that art and literature were not moribund in Soviet Russia, in spite of severe paper shortages and the fact that poetry "circulates . . . mainly by word of mouth."[5] Ehrenburg defended Vladimir Mayakovsky as a poet whose work would be recited after *Pravda* and émigré newspapers would be forgotten. He championed the poetry of Yesenin, Tsvetaeva, Pasternak, and Mandelstam. These poets were not as revered as they are today, and Ehrenburg's reviews often took on a polemical tone in the face of hostility or indifference to their work. He chided émigré critics for regarding Pasternak as "an insignificant debutante."[6] His review of Tsvetaeva's verse took the form of a tender, personal letter, recalling how their first volumes of poetry were both published in 1910. "We traveled next to each other and perhaps because of this nearness, because your step became for me the sound of a cloudburst and the beating of a heart, I saw your face but did not gaze into it."[7]

Ehrenburg, in turn, could not help ridiculing the most drastic, anti-Bolshevik fantasies within the émigré community. In his review of the book *Freemasonry and the Russian Revolution* by Grigory Bostunich,

Ehrenburg hilariously describes a day in the life of a Russian émigré who takes extreme reactionary views to heart; he begins to detect signs of a great conspiracy everywhere, mixing Jews, Bolsheviks, the YMCA, and Lloyd George into his paranoia. After sending up the book, Ehrenburg signed the review:

> *Mason of the Julio Jurenito lodge,*
> *Mexican rite, thirty-second degree*
> *("prince of the royal secret")*
> *hasid and tzaddik,*
> *Chekist in the four masks*
> *(kike-magyar-latvian-chinaman)*
> *Ilya Ehrenburg*[8]

In April 1922 Nikolai Bukharin visited Berlin on official business and looked up his old high school comrade. They found a small, out-of-the-way café where they talked for three hours. Few writers had Ehrenburg's opportunity to speak privately with a leading member of the party, and the two had always been candid with each other. "I remember saying," Ehrenburg wrote, "that many things are taking place that we did not dream about. 'You were always muddleheaded,' Bukharin responded. Then he smiled and added, 'They call me muddleheaded, too. But it's easier for you. You can get confused in novels or in private conversations, but I am no less than a member of the Politburo.'"[9] After their meeting Nikolai Bukharin returned to Moscow, where he resumed his political responsibilities as well as editing *Pravda* and later *Izvestia* before he was executed in 1938.

Ehrenburg remained in Berlin for almost two more years, assuming a prominent role in the cultural life of the Russian community. Writing about that period in his memoirs Ehrenburg emphasized the respect writers held for each other. "A place existed in Berlin that recalled Noah's Ark, where the clean and the unclean met peacefully. . . . It was called the House of Arts and was an ordinary German café where Russian writers got together on Fridays."[10] The House of Arts, like *Russkaya Kniga*, served as a bridge between the two receding halves of Russian culture. Ehrenburg frequently took part in the club's debates, read from his work, and accompanied friends from Moscow, such as Pasternak and Mayakovsky, to its meetings. When Mayakovsky left for Paris in November 1922 Ehrenburg helped to arrange his visa,

then alerted friends to Mayakovsky's arrival in the French capital, urging them to show him the city.[11]

Ehrenburg also helped Marina Tsvetaeva and Boris Pasternak on
their visits to Berlin. When Ehrenburg had first reached Western
Europe in 1921 he carried out a significant favor for Tsvetaeva. She had
asked him to locate her husband, Sergei Efron; as a former White officer, Efron had fled Russia in fear of the Bolsheviks. Ehrenburg soon
learned that Efron was in Prague and contacted him with news of
Tsvetaeva's whereabouts. Efron immediately wrote to Tsvetaeva in
Moscow, thrilled to know that she was still alive. Once Tsvetaeva
arrived in Berlin in May 1922, Ehrenburg welcomed her and her ten-
year-old daughter Ariadne (Alya) to his hotel. Alya was quickly
charmed by Ehrenburg. He "is like a grey cloudy day," she wrote in her
diary. "But with such eyes, like a dog's." She was especially fascinated
by his fondness for tobacco and the two pipes he carried in different
pockets. Tsvetaeva valued Ehrenburg's generous assistance, inscribing a
book that May, "To you, whose friendship is more dear to me than any
enmity, and whose enmity is more dear than any friendship."[12]

During her three-month stay in Berlin Tsvetaeva's personal life
complicated several relationships. The Russian literary community was
riven with romantic liaisons; Tsvetaeva succumbed to the mood. While
Sergei Efron remained in Prague she fell in love with the publisher
Abram Vichniac. In those years in Berlin Ehrenburg's favorite publishing house was Helikon. Headed by Abram and Vera Vichniac—Abram
was a cousin of the photographer Roman Vishniac, who later documented East European Jewry on the eve of the Holocaust—Helikon
published a distinguished array of writers, including Tsvetaeva, Pasternak, and Andrei Bely. The Vichniacs were among Ehrenburg's closest
friends. Ehrenburg had an intense affair with Vera Vichniac, while
Abram Vichniac and Ehrenburg's wife Lyubov Mikhailovna took up
with each other in a more casual way. All this left Tsvetaeva feeling like
a "fifth wheel." By August, unable to withstand the emotional strain,
she left Berlin for Prague. Not even Pasternak's impending arrival in
Berlin was enough to keep her in Germany.[13] She adored his poetry
and their correspondence in subsequent years helped to sustain her,
but Tsvetaeva, even in Berlin, preferred to keep their friendship at a
distance.

Pasternak remained in Berlin from August 1922 until March 1923.
In a letter to friends he wrote generously about Ehrenburg: "Ehren-

burg—a wonderful man, who once fell in love with Dostoevsky. In reality, he is a confessing patriot, a man with a broad outlook on the world, and a good friend."[14] But not everyone loved Ehrenburg and he was often the target of attacks by other writers. The most notorious incident occurred on October 29, 1922, when the critic Ilya Vasilevsky, who wrote under the pseudonym Ne-Bukva (Non-Letter), attacked Ehrenburg in the prestigious émigré newspaper *Nakanune* (On the Eve), accusing him of self-promotion and base pornography. Ehrenburg had already published at least twelve books in Berlin and Vasilevsky, provoked by such fecund talent, characterized his productivity as nothing more than "wild graphomania" and wondered "if a psychiatrist is more urgently needed here than a literary reviewer? Perhaps a mentally ill man is wandering amongst us on the Kurfürstendam. He makes faces, he giggles, and showers us with his various multicalibered books." The article shocked many and there was an attempt to ban Vasilevsky and the paper's literary editor Alexei Tolsoy from the House of Arts. Ehrenburg responded with greater equanimity. In a letter to a friend on October 30, the day after the article appeared, Ehrenburg referred to "a big literary scandal. . . . The article really is rotten. But in my opinion, it is rubbish. Andrei Bely and Vladislav Khodosevich want to exclude [Vasilevsky] from the House of Arts."[15]

At the same time Ehrenburg tried not to allow politics to intrude on his personal life. He befriended the writer Roman Gul, who had fought against the Bolsheviks before reaching Berlin. Gul worked as an editor at *Russkaya Kniga* and often reviewed Ehrenburg's books with enthusiasm; he regarded Ehrenburg as a genuinely independent figure. According to Gul, Ehrenburg spoke highly of Bukharin but liked to joke about Lenin and his wife, Nadezhda Krupskaya. Babel was Ehrenburg's favorite writer and he used to compare the collection *Red Cavalry* to *War and Peace*. But Ehrenburg's friendship with Roman Gul did not outlast the 1920s. As Ehrenburg made his peace with the Soviet regime Gul found it impossible to be close to him. Years later Gul wrote scathing articles against Ehrenburg, castigating him for his service to Stalin.[16]

Another friendship also succumbed to politics. By the end of the 1920s the Ehrenburgs and the Vichniacs were all living in Paris. But as Ehrenburg became more outspokenly pro-Soviet, the Vichniacs saw him less and less, until the European crisis erupted after the Munich agreement in 1938. Their friendship revived and Ehrenburg left his personal library with them before returning to Moscow in the summer of 1940. Remnants of the library survived the war, but Abram and Vera Vichniac did not. They were captured by the Nazis in France and perished in the gas chambers of Auschwitz.[17]

—

Virtually alone within the émigré community, Ehrenburg insisted that Soviet art, literature, architecture, and theater be regarded as an integral part of European culture. He championed the experimental designs of Vladimir Tatlin and Alexander Rodchenko, and the paintings of Kazimir Malevich and Lyubov Popova, whose work was little known or appreciated outside of Soviet Russia. Ehrenburg described their accomplishments in Yashchenko's journal, in his own book *And Yet It Turns*, which appeared in 1922, and in the unique, short-lived magazine *Veshch* (The Object), which he edited with the artist and designer El Lissitzky that same year.

And Yet It Turns and *Veshch* reflected Ehrenburg's deeply held belief that art should not be constrained by political frontiers. "Nationalism, Clericalism, Classicism" were all attempts to impede progress. "Everyone knows that nationalists of various countries are similar to each other, like twins," Ehrenburg asserted. In Brussels Ehrenburg could not find a German book, except in one store where German volumes were sold under the counter to avoid attack by "heroic patriots." Russia was hardly more tolerant. Her revolutionaries were extremely reactionary when it came to art. "Russia is an example of much nonsense," he claimed in *And Yet It Turns*.[18]

The journal *Veshch* embodied his hopes. Although Ehrenburg and El Lissitzky prepared as many as six issues, they were able to publish only three in the spring of 1922. Each contained material in three languages—French, German, and Russian. A long manifesto by Ehrenburg in the first issue proclaimed the editors' intentions to unite Europe's artistic avant-garde across national frontiers:

> The blockade of Russia is coming to an end. The appearance of *Veshch* is one sign of the exchange of experiences, accomplishments, and objects between young artists of Russia and Europe. Seven years of a separate existence have demonstrated that what is common in the work and methods of art in various countries is not a coincidence, a dogma, or a passing fashion, but an inevitable quality of a mature humanity. Art today is INTERNATIONAL.[19]

Veshch, as well as *And Yet It Turns*, celebrated technology and industry as fundamental inspirations for art in the twentieth century. Ehrenburg even claimed that industry was "the only mechanism capable of bringing art to life."[20] He particularly admired Constructivism, the radical new school of design that incorporated materials and geometric shapes from familiar industrial images, producing forms expressive of the modern scientific age. Both Constructivism and a second movement, Suprematism—which combined three-dimensional and flat, abstract forms—had originated in Moscow. Ehrenburg intended to dedicate the fourth issue of the journal to artistic developments in Russia and wrote to Mayakovsky that June, imploring him to help arrange material, "poems, articles, news items. . . . Without the possibility of distribution in Russia, *Veshch* would come to an end."[21] Ehrenburg in fact was not permitted to distribute *Veshch* in Soviet Russia. The fourth issue never appeared. Ehrenburg did not explain why, but it is possible that his political and cultural attitudes also undermined the journal's fate. *Veshch* had been published by Skify, an émigré publishing house noted for its right-wing, Slavophile orientation. *Veshch* was decidedly internationalist, with two Jewish editors and the support of several of the most progressive figures in Europe, such as Fernand Léger, Le Corbusier, and Vladimir Mayakovsky, whose articles and poems appeared in the journal. Skify could not have appreciated what Ehrenburg was trying to do.

BERLIN NOVELS

Ehrenburg resumed his former habits in Germany. "I love to smoke a pipe and to watch people amusing themselves in a café. I work in cafés as well. It is difficult to work at home (a Parisian habit with economic roots—they did not heat the rooms)."[22] His unusual style of working was notorious. The novelist Veniamin Kaverin described Ehrenburg's vivid image among people in Russia.

A great deal was readily said about him: he is a bohemian, he sits all day in cafés, behind the window—Paris, Madrid, Constantinople. A heap of manuscripts hardly fits on the small table, pages fall to the ground. He patiently picks them up, puts them together, and once again disappears in puffs of smoke. He is a European, smiling from the corner of his mouth. He is the soul of indifference, sarcasm, irony. He is a traveler, a journalist, easily writing one book after another.[23]

Ehrenburg's productivity was astonishing. Over the course of a single decade he published nineteen books and scores of articles, reviews, and travel essays. "It seemed to me I had set out on my path, that I had found my themes and my language," he recalled in his memoirs.[24] The stories and novels from his two years in Berlin exemplify Ehrenburg's instincts as a writer. The short-story collection *Thirteen Pipes* and the three novels—*The Life and Death of Nikolai Kurbov, Trust, D.E.*, and *The Love of Jeanne Ney*—were all immensely popular and helped magnify Ehrenburg's reputation in Western Europe and in the Soviet Union. They were widely translated, not only owing to their charm and inventiveness but also on account of Ehrenburg's willingness to ridicule both European and Soviet institutions. He was a Soviet writer of a different sort, one who did not adopt optimistic formulas or ignore troubling aspects of the new revolutionary order. Underlying his work for most of the 1920s is a brooding sadness over the fate of his country.

In *The Life and Death of Nikolai Kurbov* Ehrenburg focuses on a dedicated Chekist who works tirelessly against opponents of the regime. Uncorrupted by power or sentimentality, Nikolai Kurbov signs death warrants without hesitation, the supreme mark of a secret policeman's devotion. But then Kurbov's faith is shaken when Lenin's conciliatory NEP initiative is announced. Kurbov cannot resolve his doubts; his revolutionary ethic offended, Kurbov shoots himself.

Although the novel did not convey a particular political line, it displeased ideological guardians in Moscow and Berlin. Writing in *Russkaya Kniga*, Roman Gul foresaw that conservative émigrés and orthodox Marxists would both "like to see the book banned."[25] As Gul predicted, Bolshevik critics struck a scornful tone. The Moscow journal *Na Postu* (On Guard) had little patience for Ehrenburg or his popularity. Writing in the journal's premiere issue in 1923, Boris Volin, who later served as head of Glavlit, considered *Kurbov* "nauseating literature [that] distorts revolutionary reality, libels, exaggerates facts and types, and without stop and without a twitch of conscience slanders, slanders, slanders the revolution, revolutionaries, Communists, and the party. . . . One has to lose all revolutionary feeling to publish . . . *The Life and Death of Nikolai Kurbov*."[26]

This kind of attack signaled more official measures. Months before,

Ehrenburg's publisher had secured the permission of Lev Kamenev to bring out the novel. Now, with orthodox critics targeting Ehrenburg, a second member of the Politburo, Grigory Zinoviev, ordered its confiscation in Petrograd, a ban that lasted several weeks and resulted in the loss of most of the printing.[27] Ehrenburg's position as a Soviet writer remained precarious.

———

Two years earlier, when he wrote *Julio Jurenito*, Ehrenburg was recovering from his sojourn in Soviet Russia and still mourning the collapse of European culture during the war. But after several months in Europe Ehrenburg began to temper his nostalgic attachment and acknowledge his disappointment over the manner of Europe's recovery.

This disillusion pervades Ehrenburg's next novel, *Trust, D.E.*, a book that recalls the themes and language of *Julio Jurenito*. *Trust, D.E.* (the initials stand for "hand over Europe") relates the adventures of Ens Boot, an international vagabond who despairs of life in Europe. Ens Boot—Ehrenburg once called him a "nephew of Jurenito"—fulfills Jurenito's fantasies.[28] Determined to destroy all of Europe, he convinces three American millionaires to finance his plans. Using viruses and poison gas he reduces the continent to a desert. "But why Europe?" Ens Boot is asked. "Because I love her," is his reply.[29]

Ehrenburg's colleague from Moscow, the director Vsevolod Meyerhold, visited Berlin in 1923 and suggested to Ehrenburg that he adapt *Trust, D.E.* for the stage. Meyerhold had an extravagant production in mind, "half circus, half propaganda pageant."[30] Ehrenburg was already at work on his next novel, *The Love of Jeanne Ney*, and expressed only halfhearted interest in adapting *Trust, D.E.* Upon learning that Meyerhold still intended to produce the play Ehrenburg insisted that he write the script himself.[31] Meyerhold went ahead without him, and as happened two years earlier, his resentment of Ehrenburg's attitude led to a sharp and this time public ideological rebuke. "In my theater, which serves and will continue to serve the cause of the Revolution," Meyerhold wrote to Ehrenburg in a letter that was published in Moscow in 1924, "tendentious plays are needed, plays which have only one goal in mind: to serve the Revolution. Let me remind you: You emphatically refuse to follow Communist tendencies in your work, invoking your lack of belief in social revolution and your innate pessimism."[32]

Ehrenburg's apostasy notwithstanding, Meyerhold and the playwright Mikhail Podgaretsky borrowed the title of Ehrenburg's novel, its story line, and its principal character, Ens Boot. But Meyerhold's intentions were different from Ehrenburg's. On stage the gallant prole-tariat intervenes to save the day, digging a tunnel from Petrograd to New York to surprise the wicked monopolists in their lair. Europe is pulled back from the brink, while the Red Army guarantees the suc-cess of revolution in decadent America. This was not what Ehrenburg had in mind.

———

The Love of Jeanne Ney marked a new stage in Ehrenburg's deft experimentation with narrative styles. The story concerns the love between Jeanne Ney, a young, innocent French bourgeois girl, and Andrei, a Russian Communist, who kills Jeanne's father for political reasons. Inspired this time by Dickens, Ehrenburg devised a colorful, tightly knit plot with many characters and coincidental encounters, leading his readers from the Crimea to Paris and Berlin. Although the story's stock characters and sentimental devices diminish the novel's impact, Ehrenburg continued to assert his independent standing as a writer. References to the Bolsheviks and the Cheka resound with irony and suspicion, even as bourgeois European characters care only for their wealth and personal comfort.

The Love of Jeanne Ney was the only work by Ehrenburg adapted for the screen. Directed by the noted German filmmaker G. W. Pabst, the movie was produced because recent films by Soviet directors Sergei Eisenstein and Vsevolod Pudovkin (*Potemkin* and *Mother*, respectively) had been the rage all over Germany in 1926 and Pabst's studio, Ufa, wanted a Russian theme for his next project.

The movie was highly regarded and much discussed among film critics, particularly for its stylistic innovations and Pabst's "unerring choice of camera angle for the expression of mood."[33] Pabst went to great lengths to evoke the portrayal of counter-revolutionary feeling in the Crimea. "For this scene," the film journal *Close Up* reported, "one hundred and twenty [White émigré] officers, including seven generals, came in their own uniforms, working for twelve marks a day. Pabst supplied vodka and women, waited, and then calmly photographed."[34]

Ehrenburg visited the set that day and was "immediately disori-ented," even frightened, by the sight of former White officers. He remembered his journey to the Crimea during the civil war when a soldier "in a similar sheepskin cap" tried to throw him into the sea. Meanwhile, Pabst got what he wanted from them. "They knew how to carouse," Ehrenburg saw for himself, "how to break dishes and tease the ladies." Ehrenburg did not dismiss them as pathetic émigrés, however; he recognized the tragedy of their fate as fellow Russians. "So among the props and the indifferent cameramen, one minor episode in a great historical film is playing itself out," he consoled himself. He was not referring only to Pabst's production. "I have seen Russian women in sailors' dens in Constantinople. Now I see these obsequious extras. Surely they consider anyone who remained in Russia 'a traitor.' They protect these uniforms from moths and indignity. Today they are depicting lewd White officers and dreaming of playing courageous Bolsheviks next week."[35] They were all Russians, even this group of men whose comrades had almost shot him several times. They were all characters in the same "great historical film." And just as he had rediscovered his homeland when he visited Russian troops in France in 1916, so too did he acknowledge on a German movie set a decade later that he and these émigrés came from the same crucible of history.

THE DEATH OF LENIN

Ehrenburg had been in Western Europe for nearly three years when he and Lyubov Mikhailovna visited the Soviet Union at the outset of 1924. He spent several months traveling, lecturing, and reading from his books. He saw Odessa for the first time and gave talks in Kharkov, Homel, and Kiev, where he spent time with his wife's family. In Kiev he attended an elaborate staging of his novels. "Ilya Ehrenburg was shown on the stage," Ehrenburg remembered. "The American Mr. Cool sat on his shoulders and shouted, 'Faster, faster, my bourgeois steed.' My father-in-law Dr. Kozintsev was outraged, but I found it funny."[36]

In fact Ehrenburg objected to the production altogether. Entitled *The Universal Necropolis*, it was based on three of his books—*Julio Jurenito, Kurbov,* and *Trust, D.E.*—and managed to misrepresent all of them. Living in Germany made it difficult if not impossible for Ehrenburg to protect the integrity of his novels. "This kind of reworking of a living author inside the Soviet Union would not be tolerated," Ehrenburg wrote to a newspaper in Kiev that February. In response to Ehrenburg's public protest the producers replaced the characters' names with new ones and moved the action of the play to different locales. Ehrenburg decided not to press his case further "out of respect for the work that had already been done by the studio collective."[37]

But Ehrenburg had more than professional reasons to visit the country. He also wanted to see his daughter Irina, who was thirteen years old and living in Moscow with her mother, Yekaterina Schmidt, and her mother's husband, Tikhon Sorokin, whom Ehrenburg had known and liked from his early years in Paris. Until then Ehrenburg had not taken responsibility for Irina's upbringing; aside from letters he could only send her crayons or children's books from Europe. Now he was determined to be a real father and plan her education; and Paris would soon be open to him. That spring the French government recognized the Bolshevik regime, making it possible for Ehrenburg to move to the French capital. Irina had been born out of wedlock, so Ehrenburg, wanting her to complete her schooling in France, formally adopted her. With Bukharin's assistance he also arranged visas for his three sisters, and they, too, along with Irina, were able to leave for Paris.[38]

Ehrenburg, though, made clear to his daughter that Russia was their homeland and that she would not stay in France. During one summer vacation Irina Ehrenburg came across a large group of Russian families. "Their children got together on the beach, they danced and played in the water," she recalled. "Learning that I was 'Soviet' and intended to return to the U.S.S.R., they started to taunt me."[39] Irina Ehrenburg did not return to Moscow until 1933, after completing high school and college in Paris.

Soon after his arrival in Moscow Ehrenburg witnessed a fateful event. He had been there barely a few weeks when Vladimir Lenin died on January 21, 1924. Instinctively, Ehrenburg thought of seeing Bukharin. "I went to Nikolai Ivanovich, my comrade in the illegal school organization. He lived in the Second House of Soviets [the Metropol Hotel]. Usually cheerful, he was silent, and suddenly I noticed tears in his eyes." Bukharin had once acknowledged to Ehrenburg that the revolution was turning out differently from what they had dreamed of. "With Ilych we will not fail," Bukharin insisted to his friend.[40] Lenin in fact had died in Bukharin's arms. Now Lenin was gone. The revolution, too, was in jeopardy.

Lenin's death compelled Ehrenburg to reevaluate the founder of the Soviet state. His earlier portraits of Lenin—the sarcastic teenage caricature in Paris in 1909, the scornful denunciations in Moscow and Kiev during the civil war, the portrayal of a ruthless Kremlin leader in

Julio Jurenito—could not be repeated; the Bolsheviks were firmly in power and Ehrenburg had to watch himself. Moreover, Bukharin revered Lenin, an attitude not to be ignored. The time had arrived for Ehrenburg to reassess Lenin and publicly demonstrate his patriotic, if not ideological, allegiance.

Political and professional necessity dictated his decision. With a handful of other writers, Ehrenburg was invited to contribute to a special one-day newspaper devoted to Lenin's memory on the day of his funeral. This was a significant honor—he was the only writer among them living abroad—that Ehrenburg used to its full advantage. "On the Usual and the Unusual" reflects a unique perspective. Writing about Lenin's apartment in Paris, Ehrenburg recounts how the landlady frequently complained about police visits to this "most ordinary man." He quickly adds that it was not her fault for reacting this way. Even "the most clever dogmatists" did not understand Lenin's stature. "Only he knew it," Ehrenburg proclaimed, "and this was his greatness. . . . Who could have thought that out of childish, romantic barricades, out of library buildings, out of long arguments among such 'awkward tenants' would be created an enormous, living pyramid, one-fifth of the planet constructed according to a plan fastened with blood?"[41]

Later that year, when he was back in Paris completing his novel *The Grabber*, Ehrenburg concluded the book with a brief, stirring account of Lenin's funeral. Lenin's death left a terrible void. "Who will be victorious?" Ehrenburg wondered after viewing Lenin's corpse. He found himself contrasting "the severe precision of the skull with the spontaneous swarming of the crowd, the smoking bonfires, the uneven speeches. Perhaps it was a useless question," he concluded, "because he and they are one . . . Russia."[42]

PARIS NOVELS

Ehrenburg's visit to the Soviet Union did not resolve his doubts about the revolution or the society that was emerging under NEP. In his next series of novels—*The Grabber, A Street in Moscow*, and, most notably, *The Stormy Life of Lasik Roitschwantz*—Ehrenburg dealt with Soviet society directly as he saw it. These books do not constitute a rejection or a lampoon of Soviet life. They are an altogether clear-eyed and sober indictment of a society in the making. Religion, commerce, politics, literature, and often language itself have been debased. No guideposts remain. There is only the grim reality of everyday existence, its poverty and crudeness, and a new, ever-growing and ever more intrusive power—the Soviet state—that all his characters acknowledge, some with exaltation but most with an anxious glance over their shoulders. Mournful, full of harsh emotion and violence, these novels evoke a difficult period of transition, when Soviet society was not sure how to resolve its confusion and sense of loss.

Together, the novels clarify Ehrenburg's mood and principal dilemma. Although he lived in Western Europe, he never considered himself an émigré, at a time when many artists were choosing either to return to the Soviet Union or settle permanently in the West. Written as late as 1927, these novels affirm his literary and psychological autonomy while also reflecting his virtues as a writer—the ability to express acute social observations in a fast-paced, engaging narrative. Veniamin Kaverin had these qualities in mind when he called *The Grabber* Ehrenburg's finest novel. "It was [his] first attempt to see the country from the inside," Kaverin noted, "and not through the wrong end of binoculars."[43]

In *The Grabber*, Mikhail Likov has no consistent beliefs to guide him through the horrors of the civil war and the opportunities of NEP. He wants more than simple survival; he wants to prosper. But the revolution and the Bolsheviks frighten him. Rejecting the Bolsheviks, Mikhail joins the Socialist Revolutionaries. Here his story begins to resemble Ehrenburg's own: in the summer of 1918, when the revolt against Lenin by the Socialist Revolutionary party fails, Mikhail, like Ehrenburg, flees Moscow for Kiev, where he works with delinquents and abandoned children. There, Mikhail witnesses the full violence of the civil war.

Ehrenburg makes clear in *The Grabber* that the Bolsheviks share responsibility for the war's cruelty. The Cheka is universally feared; an elderly neighbor of Mikhail's commits suicide when she learns she is about to be interrogated. The word "Cheka" itself assumes mythic proportions. "Children learned these two syllables . . . before they could say 'mama' because they were used to frighten babies in the cradle the way 'boogieman' had once been."[44]

Mikhail survives the civil war and makes his way back to Moscow but no longer understands society's rules. NEP has begun; goods have become plentiful alongside graft, speculation, and greed. The politics of

NEP mean an acceptance of privilege and inequality. Even at the end of *Julio Jurenito* the Master expresses despair when he realizes the revolution and the civil war are about to culminate in a new and pragmatic policy: "I cannot bear to look at this airplane that cannot fly," he complains to Ehrenburg. "It's a bore."[45] And so the Master proclaims his willingness to be killed by thieves out to steal his high-laced boots. Mikhail Likov, too, falls victim to NEP. He is arrested because of his links to a currency speculator, and unable to withstand the prison regimen, commits suicide.

———

A Street in Moscow takes place under NEP as well, in 1926, at a time when Ehrenburg and his wife were visiting the Soviet capital. They intended to stay in a hotel, but lodging was expensive, so they accepted the hospitality of Yekaterina Schmidt and Tikhon Sorokin, who were living in Protochny Lane. In those years this neighborhood was one of Moscow's most colorful and dissolute, "the favorite haunt of thieves, petty speculators, small-time peddlers," Ehrenburg recalled in *People, Years, Life*.[46]

A Street in Moscow is a portrait of an exhausted population. Almost all the characters are miserably poor, inhabitants of a social order that has no use for them. The novel's central event is drawn from an incident Ehrenburg witnessed himself: the owner of a boarding house blocks up a hole to the cellar with snow, hoping to entomb a gang of homeless children while they are asleep and thereby be rid of them.

These abandoned, homeless children who must lie, steal, and even assault people to survive occasionally find compassion from adults who recognize their essential innocence. Ehrenburg had often worked with children during the civil war and this was not the first time he recalled them in his novels. Their plight signified more to him than human cruelty. Although they manage to escape Protochny Lane, their future, like Russia's, was still uncertain. "And it seems that this is our own Russia tramping along the road," Ehrenburg wrote, "our own Russia, as young and orphaned as these abandoned children, as visionary and embittered, without a corner of her own, with never a caress, with no one to look after her."[47]

———

The following year Ehrenburg wrote the most unusual book of his career. Built around the adventures of a character from Yiddish folklore—a poor, misunderstood tailor who cannot hurt a flea but whom everyone abuses and exploits—*The Stormy Life of Lasik Roitschwantz* is Ilya Ehrenburg's only Jewish novel. None of his previous works presages the ethnic intensity of *Lasik*; his language and exploits, his stories, even his death make Ehrenburg's hero an exemplary Jewish victim. Six years earlier, in *Julio Jurenito*, Ehrenburg insisted that what set Jews apart was their willingness to say no when everyone else said yes. *Lasik* too is a subversive book that sneers at any civil, religious, or political authority; Lasik confronts them all and all mistreat him.

The novel is a series of disjointed stories and anecdotes that follow Lasik from his birthplace of Homel, a city in Byelorussia with a decidedly Jewish character, to Moscow, Warsaw, Germany, France, and finally to England, where Lasik joins a group of Jews sailing for Palestine. Nothing works out for Lasik, whether he is minding his own business or devising a harmless swindle. In Kiev he tries to join the Communist party but must first demonstrate his reliability by insuring that couples in a nightclub dance the waltz, which is politically acceptable, but not the foxtrot, which is too bourgeois. In Tula he promotes a rabbit-breeding experiment without a single rabbit to show for his trouble.

Ehrenburg exercises no restraint in these episodes, targeting industry, agriculture, and the country's intellectual life. He was not reconciled to revolutionary violence, and behind the slapstick humor lies a heartfelt cry against the indiscriminate beatings and killings Lasik barely survives. The Cheka often mistakenly takes people and executes them. "When these fanatics and hundred percenters walk down the street," Lasik explains, "there is nothing for an ordinary person to do but die politely—with an exalted look on his face." Lasik's musings on the Cheka remind him of a Hasidic legend involving the famous Berditchever Rebbe. The story takes place on Yom Kippur, when the Rebbe is summoned to Heaven to defend an unrepentant swindler. He quickly gains God's mercy for the man, then sensing the advantage, the Rebbe presses God again, only this time tries to convince Him to send the Messiah and redeem the world. The Rebbe argues and cajoles, embarrasses God, and realizes that God may soon respond. Just at that moment when the entire world could be free of its misery, the Rebbe remembers his congregation back on earth. Yom Kippur has already drawn to a close, but the Rebbe, who appears to his followers as if dozing on the pulpit, still needs to conclude the prayers so the congregation can end the solemn fast.

And suddenly the Rebbe sees old Hersh fainting and falling to the ground. No wonder—he had not eaten, nor had he drunk anything since yesterday. The Rebbe knew that old Hersh would die on the spot if the prayer would not come to an end at once. And he said to God:

"Perhaps what I am doing now is very foolish. I should try to convince you that it is impossible to wait any longer. Then you might save all mankind. But at this moment I cannot spend any more time talking to you; if I were to stay just another hour in Heaven, old Hersh who washes dirty linen in Berditchev, will surely die. But where is it written that I have the right to pay for the happiness of all mankind with the life of old Hersh?"

For Lasik, the Rebbe's message is clear and compelling. The revolution, the civil war, the unending executions—all were carried out in the name of mankind's future happiness. But if the Rebbe could not allow an old Jew to die to insure the coming of the Messiah, then who could ever have the right to order the sacrifice of another human being?[48]

In his memoirs Ehrenburg gives a brief account of how he came to write the book, recalling that in 1927 he heard many amusing stories about Hasidim and their superstitions; but this innocuous explanation is misleading. Except for a handful of Hasidic tales, *Lasik* has nothing to do with traditional Jewish life in the myriad *shtetls* throughout Poland and the Ukraine, communities Ehrenburg could only vaguely know from visits to his grandfather in Kiev. The novel is not about the life that Lasik and Ehrenburg's family left behind; it is about a Jew who rejects this traditional life and tries vainly to find a place for himself in the broader secular world. Whether he lives in Communist Moscow or bourgeois Paris he is kicked around and beaten up until finally he decides to go to Palestine, where he expects to find a society organized for his benefit.

It is neither accident nor simple literary invention that Lasik Roitschwantz seeks refuge in Palestine. Palestine is a logical refuge, yet Lasik is miserable there, too. The Jews behave like everyone else, even to one of their own; Lasik is again beaten and imprisoned—his nineteenth jail. Undaunted, he decides to organize a "Society for Return to the Home Country" and go back to Homel. Lasik's sentiments provoke such indignation that he is chased through the streets of Jerusalem until he finds himself alone at night on a country road. Losing strength, he collapses and dies on Rachel's Tomb.[49]

———

When Ehrenburg visited Moscow for the first Soviet Writers' Congress in 1934 he attended a reception at the home of Maxim Gorky, where the entire Politburo, except for Stalin, was present.[50] Several members told him they had read *The Stormy Life of Lasik Roitschwantz* (evidently the Western European edition) but feared that the depiction of such a hapless Jewish figure could encourage anti-Semitism Only Lazar Kaganovich, the sole Jew in the Politburo, disapproved of the book for the opposite reason. For Kaganovich the novel was an expression of "bourgeois Jewish nationalism," a dangerous accusation and one that Kaganovich was prone to employ whenever he sensed sympathy for Jewish suffering. *Lasik* was Ehrenburg's first novel to be refused publication outright and marked the height of his career as an independent writer; it did not appear in the Soviet Union until 1989.

THE CRITICS RESPOND
———

Ehrenburg's novels were part of a general revival of literature and culture that occurred under NEP. Many of the most prominent writers in those years were not members of the Communist party. Ehrenburg, Anna Akhmatova, Alexei Tolstoy, Boris Pilnyak, Yevgeny Zamyatin—all maintained their independence to varying degrees and their work did not conform to any strict ideology.

Ehrenburg was the only Soviet writer living abroad, however, making him particularly vulnerable to crude ideological attacks. As the decade progressed the fate of Ehrenburg's novels reflected the regime's ever more severe attitudes toward art and literature. Orthodox Marxist critics were especially unforgiving of his work. In a long article on October 1, 1923, *Izvestia* declared that Ehrenburg "sits at the juncture of two cultures, but he does not wholly belong to either. It is characteristic that the Whites consider Ehrenburg a Red, and the Reds—a White. . . . In reality," *Izvestia* went on, "he is only a splendid, anarchistic, intellectualizing philistine, that is, in the political sense of the word, neither fish nor meat;" *Izvestia* concluded that Ehrenburg was "harmful" to the working class.[51] Another critic called him the "last born child of bourgeois culture," a "literary anachronism."[52] For these critics Ehrenburg was an illegitimate outsider, a kind of interloper whose unhealthy, subversive books reflected the outlook of a writer whose imagination and loyalty belonged more to the bourgeois West than to the Bolshevik East.

The Grabber confirmed Ehrenburg's reputation as a dangerous writer. One publishing house was warned by a reviewer that an introduction to the book should "expose the bourgeois nature, at times, the hostility of Ehrenburg to Soviet power."[53] *A Street in Moscow* provoked a similar reaction. In a prominent newspaper a Leningrad critic accused Ehrenburg of describing a society so mean and corrupt that he must have been "carrying out the social commission of the émigré intelligentsia, having drawn a corner of Soviet Moscow without Communists, without Socialist construction, without the inspiration of building a new life."[54]

Ehrenburg closely followed criticism in the Soviet press, trying to gauge how such attacks would affect his standing. The fate of *The Grabber* particularly worried him. The book was written in Paris between July and November 1924, in the immediate months following his return from Moscow. By January he learned that it might not appear in a Soviet edition. The Lengiz publishing house refused to accept the book; one editor, "having acquainted himself with the contents . . . , reached the conclusion that it would be impossible to publish in the Soviet Union."[55] Meanwhile, Ehrenburg arranged for an émigré press in Paris to bring out *The Grabber* that July.

He then sent copies to friends in Russia, including Liza Polonskaya, whose judgment and friendship he relied on. Ehrenburg anxiously sought her opinion. Writing in September he confessed, "I am afraid *The Grabber* will not pass [in the Soviet Union]. What do you think? . . . Show your copy to the literary public and write me their opinion. I am very isolated and this is not ever pleasant." In the same letter Ehrenburg mentions in passing that he is "starting an 'autobiographical' novel . . . Paris, vagabondage, boredom." This was *Summer 1925*, Ehrenburg's most personal and saddest novel. (He originally considered calling it *The Despair of Ilya Ehrenburg*.) The book captured his miserable, impoverished mood. Once again a character in his own novel, Ehrenburg searches for cigarette butts on Parisian sidewalks for much of the narrative. While writing the novel that fall Ehrenburg complained to Liza Polonskaya that he "had fallen into 'black poverty.' I am living off Scandinavian translations and aesthetic fantasies," referring to short pieces he contributed to Soviet newspapers.[56] A month later he repeated his sorrows, telling Polonskaya that he longed to visit Russia but that he "did not know if [he] could manage it because of the money."[57]

Ehrenburg continued to press Polonskaya for news about the fate of
The Grabber. In October he wanted to know "if [she] had seen a single
person who would applaud it."[58] In December, still haunted by the
novel's failure in Russia, he wondered if his standing had changed during the previous year "(1) in the upper realms and (2) among readers."[59]
Osip Mandelstam knew of his friend's difficulties. In a letter to his wife
in February 1926, after visiting Lengiz publishing house, Mandelstam
mentioned that two writers, "Fedin and Gruzdev, among others, are
trying to force *The Grabber* through."[60] Ehrenburg did not succeed
until 1927, when a small cooperative publishing house in Odessa issued
an expurgated version of the book.

For all their efforts Ehrenburg's critics had little if any clout for most
of the 1920s. Under NEP the Communist party was not ready to
impose strict ideological control over literature. Ehrenburg benefited
from this official tolerance. He often published in the journal *Krasnaya
Nov* (Red Virgin Soil), which, under the guidance of Alexander Voronsky, was the most important literary magazine of its time. The party had
commissioned Voronsky to establish *Krasnaya Nov* in 1921 with the
express intent of creating what the Russians call a "thick" literary journal—a serious, high-brow forum for literature and criticism that had
been common in Russian intellectual life before the revolution. Voronsky edited *Krasnaya Nov* until 1927, and more than any other person was
responsible for reviving literature after the upheavals of revolution and
civil war. An honest and courageous editor, Voronsky was less concerned
with the class origin or ideology of his authors than he was with the literary value of their submissions. Ehrenburg contributed several stories,
essays, and travel pieces to the journal. *Krasnaya Nov* in fact was his preferred outlet in the Soviet press. Not surprisingly, Voronsky too was a
principal target of the "On Guard" critics. "Voronsky's policy," the editor of *Na Postu* contended, "is making it possible for bourgeois elements
to use our own literature against us and thus it happens that under the
seal of the Communist party, a great deal of filth is being turned out."[61]
Ehrenburg's novels were among the "filth" this critic had in mind.

A BRIDGE BETWEEN TWO WORLDS

Despite his prolific output, Ehrenburg's role in Soviet culture in the
1920s was not based on his books or articles alone. He continued to

live in Paris and act as a bridge between artistic developments in Western Europe and the new Soviet state. As long as he could, Ehrenburg tried to bring Soviet art to Europe and European art to the Soviet Union. When he left Moscow in 1921 he carried manuscripts of Pasternak, Tsvetaeva, Yesenin, and others with the hope of finding publishers for their work.[62] In Berlin between 1921 and 1923 he edited *Veshch* and produced an endless stream of essays and reviews on Soviet artistic life. Ehrenburg also published anthologies of Russian poetry in Berlin, providing European writers and the émigré community an opportunity to assess contemporary Soviet poets.[63]

Other Soviet writers relied on Ehrenburg for help and advice. When he visited Moscow in 1926 he carried new verses from Marina Tsvetaeva to Boris Pasternak. Yevgeny Zamyatin approached Ehrenburg in 1927 when excerpts from his anti-utopian novel *We*—which later directly inspired Orwell's *1984*—appeared without his permission in an émigré journal in Prague. Zamyatin learned about this in a letter from Ehrenburg, and at Zamyatin's request, Ehrenburg wrote the editors to insist that *Volya Rossy* (The Will of Russia) cease publication of the novel. Two years later *We* appeared in a French translation in Paris; there is reason to believe that Ehrenburg helped Zamyatin to arrange for its publication. Zamyatin's precarious status in the Soviet Union and the obviously anti-Soviet nature of his novel did not deter Ehrenburg from trying to assist him.[64]

He took other initiatives to sustain the Soviet Union's connection to Western culture as well. When Ehrenburg traveled to Moscow in 1926 he made a point of bringing clips from films by the most famous French directors, among them Abel Gance, René Clair, and Jean Renoir, and used them to accompany a lecture he gave on "The New French Cinema." His presentation was widely discussed in the Soviet press and he was applauded for his efforts. "For Muscovites," *Vechernaya Moskva* (Evening Moscow) commented, "few of whom are acquainted with the innovative direction of French cinematography, this was a genuine revelation."[65] The following year Ehrenburg published a small pamphlet in Moscow about developments in European film art entitled *The Materialization of the Fantastic*. Like many of his books, which were often illustrated by contemporary artists, *The Materialization of the Fantastic* carried a cover design by Alexander Rodchenko, underscoring Ehrenburg's identification with the remnants of Russia's artistic avant-garde.

There was more. In 1931 Ehrenburg and his closest friend, Ovady Savich, who also worked in Paris as a Soviet correspondent, put together a long, ambitious anthology of quotations about French life drawn from two centuries of Russian literature called *We and They*. As Ehrenburg and Savich explain, "France personified Europe, and at times under the guise of discussing the merits and vices of France, an argument would develop over the healing properties of European culture for Russia."[66] Writers as diverse as Fyodor Dostoevsky, Osip Mandelstam, Alexander Herzen, Elsa Triolet, and Nikolai Gogol were represented, and it is significant that several comments by Leon Trotsky, who had been expelled from the Soviet Union two years before the book's publication, were also included. It was probably these innocuous quotations from Trotsky that prevented *We and They* from being published in the Soviet Union; Ehrenburg and Savich were able to publish the book only in Berlin.

Ehrenburg was, however, able to publish his book of photographs of Parisian life in Moscow in 1933. *My Paris* features scores of candid images of workers, children, and that uniquely French institution, the concierge. With his Leica and a right-angle lens Ehrenburg captured numerous pictures without alerting his subjects that he was photographing them. Not a single interior scene is included in the book; even the concierges are shown on the sidewalk or in doorways, while Ehrenburg's camera catches the playful image of the Parisian *pissoir*—a French convenience unknown and unfathomable to a Soviet citizen. His book brought a vivid, loving portrait of Paris to Moscow just as the Soviet Union was becoming more isolated.

Still, Ehrenburg was careful to protect himself. When his friend, the Italian journalist Nino Frank, approached him in Paris in the late 1920s to support a new international literary journal named *Bifur*, Ehrenburg readily accepted. But he also insisted that the editorial board issue a statement affirming that he "dissociated himself in advance from any attitude or political demonstration that the journal could assume."[67] Ehrenburg wanted to join their efforts but also wanted to be sure that none of the journal's artistic or political initiatives would compromise his standing as a Soviet writer. Mindful of his vulnerability, Ehrenburg accepted the need to play an intricate game and avoid provoking his Soviet masters.

SIX

Stalin and the First Five Year Plan

NEP did not have long to last. A dramatic struggle was about to unfold, whose outcome would affect all of Soviet society. Since Lenin's death in 1924 members of the Politburo had been maneuvering for supreme leadership. By 1927 Joseph Stalin, with the help of Nikolai Bukharin, had gained the upper hand and expelled his principal rivals—Leon Trotsky, Lev Kamenev, and Grigory Zinoviev—from the Politburo. Trotsky was sent in disgrace to far-off Alma-Ata. Kamenev and Zinoviev had to be removed from their apartments in the Kremlin; Zinoviev, who had been especially close to Lenin and had served as his private secretary, was seen carrying Lenin's death mask under his arm. Although their political careers were over, he and Kamenev remained in Moscow and were permitted to work in prestigious jobs. Their final reckoning was still to come.

Bukharin benefited from this brief alliance with Stalin and some even considered him a co-leader of the country; but Bukharin could not sustain his political fortune. By 1929, the same year Trotsky was banished from the Soviet Union, Bukharin was totally eclipsed by Stalin.

Stalin's rise to supreme power marked the end of NEP and the onset of the First Five Year Plan. NEP had been a period of transition, when the party tried to accommodate the needs of the peasants and establish economic and social equilibrium. For many militants, though, NEP reflected the party's lack of nerve, its unwillingness to enforce rapid social change; Stalin put an end to this dissatisfaction. With the First Five Year Plan in 1928 he began a program of rapid industrialization and then forced collectivization of agriculture. The party went on the offensive against the population. All human resources were mobilized, including those in literature and the arts. NEP and its atmosphere of tolerance were over. The kingdom of Stalin—the kingdom of fear— began to envelop the country.

Ehrenburg's difficulties with Glavlit grew more serious. Although he was still able to publish books and articles, criticism began to come with greater and more pointed misgivings. In 1927, for example, his collection of essays on European culture and society, *White Coal, or the Tears of Werther*, carried an unusual and confusing introduction. Its author praised Ehrenburg's literary style and knowledge of the West, but "it is easy to prove," the introduction warned, "that the author of *Nikolai Kurbov* is still intimately connected to that past on which he pours the poison of his acrimonious satire and skepticism." Ehrenburg, it said, remains "on the other side of the barricades."[1] Even Nikolai Bukharin felt a need to retreat from his earlier support. Writing in *Pravda* in March 1928 Bukharin referred to *Lasik Roitschwantz* as "unprincipled, tedious, thoroughly false in its one-sided literary vomit."[2]

In the late 1920s Anatol Goldberg—a foreign student in Germany who would later become a renowned commentator on the BBC Russian Service, where his programs were avidly followed by millions of Soviet listeners—witnessed an incident in Berlin that reflected this official disregard. One evening he attended a reading by a group of Soviet and German writers; Ehrenburg too happened to be in Berlin, and was asked to take part. According to Goldberg the audience included German intellectuals, Russian émigrés, and foreign students like himself, who joined an equal number of officials from the large

Soviet embassy staff. Ehrenburg was the last to read, but as he turned to his new novel *The Conspiracy of Equals*—on the French revolutionary Gracchus Babeuf, who rejected the Terror and advocated an egalitarian democracy before his arrest and execution in 1797—the Soviet half of the audience left the auditorium.[3] Stalin, it turns out, did not like the book either. Speaking to a Soviet journalist in February 1929, Stalin dismissed *The Conspiracy of Equals* as "pulp literature," suitable for "a real bourgeois chamber theater."[4] Stalin was not a critic to be blithely ignored.

Then, on August 26, 1929, came an unexpected and devastating attack. Boris Volin, who had earlier condemned Ehrenburg in *Na Postu*, made a sinister denunciation of Yevgeny Zamyatin, Boris Pilnyak, and Ilya Ehrenburg on the front page of *Literaturnaya Gazeta* (Literary Gazette), the official journal of the Writers' Union. Volin claimed that all three writers had permitted the publication of at least one novel in the West after it had been banned or removed from circulation by Soviet censors. Pilnyak and Zamyatin lived in the Soviet Union, where Pilnyak was head of the Moscow section of the Writers' Union, while Zamyatin was chairman of the section in Leningrad. Their books, *Mahogany* and *We*, respectively, had been deemed "unacceptable." Living in France, Ehrenburg published *The Grabber* in separate editions, with a longer, fuller text appearing in Western Europe. "We call attention to this series of altogether unacceptable occurrences, which compromise Soviet literature, and we hope that all of Soviet society supports their condemnation," Volin concluded.[5]

The fate of Pilnyak and Zamyatin contrasted sharply with Ehrenburg's own. Throughout the 1920s Yevgeny Zamyatin was recognized as one of Russia's most talented and outspoken writers, and he paid dearly for this honor. He was placed in solitary confinement twice, earlier in 1905–6 for his revolutionary activity under the czar, and in 1922 under the commissars; both times he was held in the same prison block. Like Ehrenburg, Zamyatin was a principal target of the "On Guard" critics. His novel *We* was banned and viciously condemned in the Soviet Union. By 1929, following the attack in *Literaturnaya Gazeta*, Zamyatin was ostracized from Soviet literature. The denunciation of Zamyatin and Pilnyak in fact was part of the regime's plan to press all writers into the work of Socialist reconstruction and strip the All-Russian Union of Writers, whose membership was primarily non-Communist fellow travelers, of its apolitical character.

In the weeks following Volin's article Zamyatin and *We* were condemned by the Leningrad branch of the Writers' Union, but before he was expelled Zamyatin resigned as an expression of his continued defiance. Then two years later, in June 1931, in a dramatic move he wrote directly to Stalin asking for permission to leave the country. With Maxim Gorky's help permission was granted and Zamyatin moved to Paris; he was not able to resume his career and died, heartbroken, on March 10, 1937.

Boris Pilnyak had an even more tragic fate. In 1926 Pilnyak published a story that clouded his life. It concerned the death of Mikhail Frunze, the People's Commissar of the Army and Navy, who had died during surgery in 1925. According to rumors circulating in Moscow the operation was unnecessary, but Stalin, intending to arrange his murder, insisted that Frunze undergo it. Pilnyak's story, "The Murder of the Army Commander," was to appear in *Novy Mir*. He included a preface with a bland denial of any connection between his story and Frunze's death. Nonetheless, the circumstances of Frunze's demise were quite similar to Pilnyak's account. Moreover, Pilnyak wrote of "an unbending man," a cold, paranoid, political figure whose resemblance to Stalin is unmistakable. The regime took immediate measures. The issue of *Novy Mir* was hastily withdrawn and the editors confessed to a gross error in publishing it. Alexander Voronsky, to whom the story was dedicated, rejected the honor, calling the story "a malicious slander on our Party."[6] NEP, with its relative tolerance, was still official policy; Pilnyak was able to obtain a passport and tour the Far East, where he wrote vivid reports of his travels. Further reprisals would come later.

Pilnyak's *Mahogany*, the novella that Boris Volin condemned, was published in Berlin in 1929. On the surface there was nothing untoward in Pilnyak's decision to publish the book first with an émigré press; it was a common practice among many Soviet writers who wanted to protect their copyright. *Mahogany* had also been accepted by a Soviet journal, albeit with important cuts. So Pilnyak was thoroughly surprised by Volin's article and the slanderous campaign that ensued. Unlike Zamyatin, though, Pilnyak compromised himself; his behavior became an object lesson in how Soviet insistence on conformity destroyed talented writers even before they were physically annihilated. Pilnyak tried to recast *Mahogany* into a more acceptable, full-length novel, *The Volga Falls into the Caspian Sea*, but this effort and subsequent work only reflected a slow literary collapse. In 1933 he traveled to

America, then wrote a piece of anti-American propaganda. His talent stifled, his life too was coming to an end; Stalin never forgave him for the story about Frunze. Arrested in 1937 on the grounds of being a Japanese spy, Boris Pilnyak was executed forthwith.

—

It was in this atmosphere, as Stalin consolidated his authority, repudiated NEP, and imposed stricter censorship, that Ilya Ehrenburg made his peace with the regime. An ex-Bolshevik, a poet who had greeted the October Revolution with eloquent hatred, a Soviet writer who preferred life in France, a novelist who provoked angry denunciation from the country's most vigilant critics—Ehrenburg was all of this, but gradually he relinquished his independence as a writer, a process that climaxed in 1932 when he became Paris correspondent for *Izvestia*. This shift is one of the most troubling of Ilya Ehrenburg's life and marks the beginning of his career as an official Soviet journalist.

Unlike hundreds of friends and acquaintances, Ehrenburg never intended to become an émigré or renounce his Soviet citizenship. Living in Paris, he had a unique arrangement and he wanted to maintain it. Yevgeny Zamyatin referred to this unusual status in his appeal to Stalin in 1931. "Ilya Ehrenburg," Zamyatin wrote, "while he remains a Soviet writer, has long been working chiefly for European literature—for translation into foreign languages. Why, then, should I not be permitted to do what Ehrenburg has been permitted to do?"[7] But Ehrenburg could no longer sustain the privilege of being a Soviet writer on his own terms. Under severe financial pressure, he had to live off the sale of translations while Soviet publishing houses, which were supposed to pay him in hard currency, often failed to pay him at all. By 1927 he often felt desperate. "My book *The Grabber* was withdrawn," he wrote to Liza Polonskaya. "No one wants *White Coal. Lasik* was doomed in advance to a foreign life."[8] Ehrenburg was determined to avoid a similar fate for himself.

CRISIS IN THE WEST

Ehrenburg felt compelled to adapt to the harsher political and cultural atmosphere that was beginning to overwhelm Soviet society. His ideological ambivalence made this process easier. His enthusiasms had always been unstable, shifting from politics to art, to religion and mysticism, from one style of literature to another. Ehrenburg's friend, the critic Viktor Shklovsky, once referred to him as "Pavel Savlovich" or Paul son of Saul, suggesting his frequent conversions and pliant flexibility. For Shklovsky, whenever Ehrenburg seemed ready to accept a new belief he seemed equally reluctant to abandon the old one; he was a Saul who could never quite accept a full conversion.

The new requirements of Stalinism tested Ehrenburg's protean nature. By 1928 his writing began to shift in tone and emphasis as his work assumed a more tendentious, pro-Soviet posture. For the first time he made a point of writing about European peasants after visiting central regions of France and rural areas of Slovakia.[9] Ehrenburg also traveled to Poland and soon published an ambitious series of articles in *Krasnaya Nov*. "In Poland" embodies the politicized journalism that would mark Ehrenburg's work for many years. From the outset, Ehrenburg portrayed Poland as an expansionist state harboring designs over Russian lands. Visiting the Polish consulate in Paris, he spotted a wall map depicting "an enormous piece of the U.S.S.R. . . . marked Polish territory." He described Poland as politically harsh and authoritarian. Ehrenburg noticed a "tail" on his first day there and was proud to remark that students were being detained under "Article 102," the very same under which he had been prosecuted in 1908 for possessing revolutionary journals. Jews were not permitted into many church institutions, and public parks often allowed entry for people dressed "only in European clothes," an obvious ploy to segregate Hasidic Jews, whose characteristic broad-rimmed hats and long coats offended general society.[10]

Many of Ehrenburg's friends liked to blame Poland's shortcomings—anti-Semitism, police surveillance, political prisoners—on her heritage from czarist Russia. But the country's rulers, as Ehrenburg emphatically points out, were trying to suppress the use of Russian language and the attraction of Russian culture. "They have succeeded in destroying not only the Russian cathedral, but Russian schools, Russian libraries, even frequent references to Russian speech." Ehrenburg was appalled by Poland's official hostility to Russia. "Poland could have been a bridge between Russia and Europe," he wrote. But instead "she prefers to become a military ditch, . . . guardians of the West on certain barbarian frontiers." Nonetheless, Ehrenburg reassured his Soviet audience, "in spite of this (or perhaps because of it), the taste of Poles for our half-forbidden country has never been so strong as today. On this, factory owners and workers, poets and engineers, athletes and visionaries all agree." For the practiced ear Ehrenburg's words contain a typically Soviet intonation. "The politics of the government is one thing; the spirit of the people is another." Ehrenburg condemned Poland for looking to the West under the authoritarian leadership of General Jozef Pilsudski. The general cultivated obsessive veneration in his subjects while Polish writers seemed enthralled by "state power," "loud words," and "military music." One poet displayed not one but two portraits of Pilsudski in his home. "These were not documents of an epoch," Ehrenburg wrote, "but icons."[11] Ehrenburg could not have foreseen the irony in his observations; within two years Stalin would far outdo Pilsudski's modest cult of personality, but a quarter century would have to pass before Ehrenburg could write about it.

In the meantime, he frequently examined Europe's moral failings. In 1931 he wrote scathingly about the International Colonial Exhibition in Paris. The European powers boasted about their colonies. "Negroes had to work, eat, and sleep in front of everyone. . . . People crowded round them as in the zoo." Ehrenburg was disgusted and suggested in the Soviet press that a "white village" be constructed for the edification of Asians and Africans. A stockbroker could bellow prices, a member of parliament could make a speech, a beauty parlor and a brothel could receive their customers. The article's humor was not appreciated in France and Ehrenburg was almost expelled from the country.[12]

As Ehrenburg began to write from a more narrowly Soviet point of view his novels shifted in focus. He embarked on an ambitious project of research and writing, intending to document European capitalism, "a complicated machine that continued to produce plenty and crises, weapons and dreams, gold and apathy."[13] He called his project *A Chronicle of Our Times* and from 1928, a year before the American stock market crash, until 1932 when he joined *Izvestia*, he wrote several novels and stories focusing on particular industries and the greed of wealthy entrepreneurs. Like almost everything Ehrenburg wrote, these books provoked outrage and controversy. Relying on detailed economic and historical research, Ehrenburg took on several of the world's richest men. His work in fact included many of the techniques associated with the nonfiction novel. In *Life of the Automobile* Ehrenburg uses contemporary figures such as André Citroën, Pierpont Morgan, and Henry Ford; in *The Shoe King* he focuses on Tomas Bata, the legendary Czech capitalist who created the first footwear company to distribute cheap shoes throughout Europe; in *Factory of Dreams* he writes about Hollywood, George Eastman, and the Kodak camera; and in *The Single Front* he writes about Ivor Kreuger, the Swedish Match King.

These men were not amused. After Ehrenburg's articles in the German press appeared describing the harsh, authoritarian methods Tomas Bata allegedly used against his workers, Bata sued Ehrenburg in a German court, hoping to exact civil and criminal penalties. Ivor Kreuger was also provoked. After *The Single Front* appeared in 1930 Kreuger attacked Ehrenburg's book in French newspapers; Kreuger's secretary later reported finding this novel on Kreuger's bedside table after his death.

Yet these works too, in spite of their anticapitalist tone, did not gain easy acceptance in the Soviet Union. While they denounced capitalism's abuses, they failed to offer communism as the answer to the West's malaise. In 1930 Ehrenburg repeated earlier complaints to Liza Polonskaya.

> Aside from *The Conspiracy of Equals*, I have recently written *Life of the Automobile*. Fragments, ragged fragments, were published in *Krasnaya Nov*. Zif is supposed to publish the book, but whether it will or not—I do not know. After that I wrote *The Single Front*—this is a novel about the European trusts, about new kinds of sharks, in particular about Swedish matches and about Kreuger. For a writer, I am in a shameful position—I am writing . . . for translations.[14]

Life of the Automobile was published in Berlin in 1929, but subsequent Soviet editions never included the full text. *The Single Front*, Ehrenburg's longest and most ambitious novel in the series, has yet to appear in Moscow, even though it exposed a notorious capitalist swindler. *A Chronicle of Our Time* came out only in 1935 as a single volume, with many cuts in the texts of the stories. As Stalin consolidated control of the country Ehrenburg's status as a journalist and novelist remained in doubt. *The Single Front* was the last novel he dared to publish in Western Europe without the benefit of a Soviet edition—and when books of his appeared in Moscow, they carried introductions warning of Ehrenburg's dubious political credentials. Curiously enough, at the time Ehrenburg actually welcomed such introductions; without them, books such as *Life of the Automobile* or *Visa of Time* could not have been published at all.

Still, these introductions reflected his questionable status in the cultural firmament. In 1931 the prominent Bolshevik activist and diplomat Fyodor Raskolnikov—who was to defect in 1939 and write a devastating critique of Stalin's dictatorship—characterized Ehrenburg in the introduction to *Visa of Time* with a familiar rebuke: he "has shut himself into a shell of proud individualism and pessimistic skepticism." As for the struggle of the European working class, Ehrenburg "does not pay any attention to Communist parties, which, for example, in France, Germany, and Czechoslovakia, legally exist." For Raskolnikov this was "a serious omission" and reflected Ehrenburg's political unreliability.[15]

This was the official view of Ehrenburg's career. The 1931 edition of *The Small Soviet Encyclopedia* gives an authoritative formulation, consigning Ehrenburg to an ambiguous category of writers. He "ridicules Western capitalism and the bourgeoisie with genuine wit," the entry on him reads. "But he does not believe in communism or the proletariat's creative strength."[16]

Stalin required a more consistent kind of loyalty. "Up to the age of forty," Ehrenburg claimed, referring to 1931, "I never found myself. I turned and tossed this way and that." He felt confused, tired of living "by negation alone."[17] His novels had ridiculed East and West, Soviet institutions and European capitalism. Six years earlier in his novel *Summer 1925* Ehrenburg had written candidly of his adaptable nature and loss of faith.

> My life resembles vaudeville, with changes of costume, but honestly, I am not a hack, I only submit . . .
>
> I do not believe in anything. That is how I am constructed, and my calcified spine is no longer capable of straightening. But there are hours . . . when I am ready to love out of malice, to believe out of desperation, to believe in anything you like—in programs, in questionnaires, in registrations.[18]

The rise of Nazism in Germany compelled Ehrenburg to choose. In *People, Years, Life* Ehrenburg recalls the European crisis, the depression, fascism, and the imminent triumph of Nazism. He was well acquainted with Hitler's movement. On assignment, Ehrenburg visited Germany twice in 1931. His subsequent articles voiced apprehension over what he saw there.

At the train station, there is a schedule. A particular train arrives at 11 o'clock and thirty seconds. Who needs these thirty seconds? A tobacco salesman? A veterinarian? Public opinion? Philosophers? Death? This order is an order in spite of crisis, poverty, and despair, an order to the very end in spite of the end, an order by any means, a cruel order that is possible only in the heavens or in a madhouse . . .

What will happen in the not too distant future when passion prevails? . . . What will happen to the train schedule? Won't this precision to the actual second turn into colossal chaos, into just as maniacal a devastation?[19]

In Germany Ehrenburg found widespread poverty and humiliation, with ordinary, healthy-looking young people turning to petty crime and prostitution in order to earn a few marks. "Fear of the future resembles agoraphobia," he wrote about Berlin. The city reminded him of a man about to commit suicide "who, deciding to slit his own throat, first washes his cheeks and carefully shaves." The Nazis' violent anti-Semitism profoundly disturbed Ehrenburg. "In Berlin, Nazi emblems are prohibited," he wrote in late 1931, "but whole streets are covered with swastikas and posters reading 'kill the kikes.'"[20] His daughter, too, spent that summer in Germany as part of a student exchange; she saw Nazi thugs break Jewish store windows on Berlin's Kurfürstendam. As the Nazis gained in power and influence Ehrenburg understood that war was inevitable and that he would soon have to choose his place. He could no longer remain an uncommitted, ironic skeptic. "Between us and the Fascists," he believed, "there was not even a narrow strip of no-man's land."[21]

OUT OF CHAOS

Ilya Ehrenburg's first appearance in *Izvestia* as a special correspondent came in July 1932, when he covered the trial of Pavel Gorgulov, a deranged Russian émigré who had assassinated French President Paul Doumer in May.[22] The court proceedings revealed Gorgulov's extreme anti-Communist views, admiration of the Nazis, and resentment of French negotiations with the Soviet government. As a result of his crime, other Russian émigrés came under severe pressure. Many were dismissed from their jobs, and there were hysterical calls to expel them all from France. Partly out of self-defense, members of the large émigré community claimed Gorgulov was a Soviet agent trying to disrupt French political life. The assassination and political intrigue surrounding the case lent notoriety to the trial, giving Ehrenburg an opportunity to show his skills as an observer of French society.

Once his initial articles appeared in *Izvestia*, Ehrenburg returned with his wife to the Soviet Union in 1932 and spent part of the summer and fall exploring the country. It was their first visit in six years. *Izvestia* covered his expenses, making it possible for him to travel freely. Ehrenburg also must have felt confident they would be able to leave, a fact he could not have taken for granted. While he was still in the Soviet capital Ehrenburg gave a lecture about life in France and arranged meetings in schools in order to gather material from young people. He also found time to spend with his former lover Yadviga Sommer. Six years had passed since their last meeting. Yadviga saw him lecture and meet with students. Back in his hotel room Ehrenburg showed her a photograph of a young woman. This was Denise LeCache, a French actress with whom he had recently begun what was to become a prolonged, serious love affair. "By his gesture, by the look on his face," Yadviga wrote, "I guessed this was his new companion, perhaps even his favorite. I looked at it a long time . . . and burst out crying. Embarrassed, he took the photograph and without saying a word, passed his hand over my hair. There was no need to say anything. We understood each other well."[23] True to his almost heartless candor, Ehrenburg could not help but share the intimate details of his life with someone who loved him so well. Yadviga and he continued to correspond, while over the years the Ehrenburgs saw her in Moscow or in Yaroslavl, where she worked as a college professor.

In 1932 the First Five Year Plan was at the height of its campaign. Ehrenburg wanted to see how the country was developing. Lyubov Mikhailovna remained in Moscow while Ehrenburg spent weeks in Siberia, visiting construction sites in Sverdlovsk, Novosibirsk, Tomsk, and Kuznetsk. This period of rapid industrialization transformed the Soviet Union. Ehrenburg witnessed the changes and dislocations. He saw kulaks deported to Siberia and factory recruiting stations looking for peasants who had fled their farms. "I came across villages where it was hard to find any young men. There were only women, old men, and children. Many huts had been abandoned."[24] Ehrenburg was not indifferent to the suffering but was especially impressed by groups of enthusiastic young people. They responded generously to his curiosity, showing him their diaries and letters, and explaining their work.

On October 14, 1932, Ehrenburg wrote a letter to his friends Ovady and Alya Savich in Paris. Although circumspect, the letter conveyed the difficulties of his trip and Ehrenburg's passionate commitment to understand the country's transformation.

> Dear rabbits:
>   I am writing to you on a train going from Novosibirsk to Sverdlovsk. I saw the construction works in Kuznetsk, houses and students in Tomsk. A Siberian Chicago, that is, Corbusier and dust, the forest and the steppe. It was still Indian summer a week ago. I walked around Tomsk without an overcoat. Winter came suddenly—icy winds and snow. Now there is only the bare steppe and patches of white snow.
>   It is evening. (For you, it is still daylight and perhaps you are sitting in Le Dôme.) My head is stuffed to the limit. I cannot wait to see Sverdlovsk. I am so tired that I invariably sleep hard and sluggishly on the train. I reach Moscow on the nineteenth. . . . I have already spent twelve nights on a train (not counting the trip from Paris to Moscow). I eat whenever I can and smoke whatever comes to hand. The thought of literary work attracts and frightens me. It is too bad you did not come. You Sava should come here! We will see each other soon and talk about everything.[25]

Ehrenburg returned to Paris in November and within a month was hard at work on his next novel, *Out of Chaos*. (The exact translation of the Russian title is The Second Day, a deliberate reference to the Biblical week of creation.) Moved by what he had seen on his trip through Siberia, Ehrenburg intended to write a book that would establish his political credentials; to do this he had to simultaneously renounce his skeptical nature and affirm a newfound loyalty to the regime.

Writing to his Moscow secretary Valentina Milman in January 1933, Ehrenburg complained bitterly that "it is hard for an author who is located far from Herzen house to find justice." Other books continued to face difficulty with the regime, but now he was putting all his energy into a new book, "a novel—Soviet," as he referred to it.[26] *Out of Chaos* was finished by March. He wrote to Milman with the news and before he had even submitted it to publishers conceded that "everything concerning my new novel worries me."[27] Were it not to be accepted in Moscow, Ehrenburg feared he would have no future as a Soviet writer.

Ehrenburg's confidence was waning. His relationship with *Izvestia* appeared to be stalled. Their agreement called for Ehrenburg to write one feature a month in exchange for an established honorarium. Although he had returned to Paris more than a month before, the editors were neglecting him. "*Izvestia* has not written me at all. Nor are they sending me newspapers. Worst of all," Ehrenburg reported to Milman that January, "they have not sent any money."[28] This turned into a frequent complaint. When honorariums did come through, from *Izvestia*, *Vechernaya Moskva*, or *Literaturnaya Gazeta*, Ehrenburg sometimes asked Milman to send the money to his wife's mother in Leningrad or to Irina's mother in Moscow. Obligations to family members continued to burden him financially. A great deal was riding on the success of *Out of Chaos*.

Hitler's triumph in January 1933 compounded Ehrenburg's anxiety and economic vulnerability. "Events in Germany have affected me directly," he confided to Milman on March 9. "Not only have I lost my publishing house [Malik was forced to shut down], but with it five thousand marks, a payment from the American firm United Artist which is doing *Jeanne Ney* and had sent the money through Malik."[29]

Ehrenburg still had several difficult months ahead of him. His initial attempt to submit *Out of Chaos* went awry. He first sent his only clean copy of the manuscript by diplomatic pouch on March 11 to a literary bureaucrat named Sergei Gusev, the head of the Central Committee's publishing division; a word from Gusev could decide the novel's fate. But unbeknownst to Ehrenburg Gusev was relieved of his duties at that very moment and sent to Kazakhstan, where he soon died. Two weeks passed before Ehrenburg learned that Gusev was no longer in Moscow.

"I am alarmed," Ehrenburg wrote to Milman. "I do not have a copy of the manuscript. You yourself understand how important it is for me to learn about its fate immediately. I do not know who took Gusev's place. One of two things happened to the manuscript: either it was sent to Gusev in Kazakhstan or the package was unsealed and given to Gusev's deputy. Let me know by TELEGRAPH," Ehrenburg implored her.[30]

More disappointments followed. Milman located the manuscript and without Ehrenburg's instructions submitted it to the Soviet Literature publishing house. An editor there bluntly dismissed the novel. "Tell your father that he has written a bad and harmful book," the editor explained to Ehrenburg's daughter, who then had to call Paris with the news.[31] Ehrenburg could barely contain himself. "I am completely gloomy," he confessed to Milman.[32] But he was not without resources of his own. Determined to see *Out of Chaos* published in the Soviet Union, he printed several hundred numbered copies in Paris—in his memoirs he admits it was "a desperate measure," but having them numbered made clear that he was not intending to distribute the novel in France before it was published in Moscow—and sent them to members of the Politburo, leading editors, and other writers. Stalin received copy number two. "In the 1930s and 1940s the fate of a book often depended on chance, on the opinion of one man," Ehrenburg remembered. "It was a lottery, and I got lucky."[33] Within a few weeks an editor wrote to him accepting the novel.

———

At first glance *Out of Chaos* could be regarded as a conventional example of "socialist realism," the officially sanctioned theory endorsed by the party in 1932. The story concerns young workers in Kuznetsk who are building a blast furnace under terrible conditions. Ehrenburg admired their fortitude, and he wrote vivid descriptions of their squalid barracks, the harsh climate, and the workers' heroic efforts to overcome nature's resistance. It was this unvarnished portrayal of their painful life that made it hard for Soviet bureaucrats to publish *Out of Chaos*; "socialist realism" was supposed to celebrate the country's achievements and ignore the human cost, to portray life as it should be and not as it really was.

It is risky to assume that a character in a novel reflects the author's obsessions and beliefs. Yet Volodia Safronov in *Out of Chaos* so closely parallels Ehrenburg's stated views of himself that it is fair to understand Volodia's fate as emblematic of Ehrenburg's own. Volodia is a student who embodies Russia's forsaken social and cultural values. "He did not believe that a blast furnace was more beautiful than Venus. . . . When spring was in the courtyard, and lilacs blossomed in the old gardens of Tomsk, he did not quote Marx. He knew that lilacs were more ancient than Marx. He knew that spring had come even in the days before the revolution. Ergo, he knew nothing." His professor, recognizing how out of place Volodia seemed among his classmates, dubs him an "*izgoy*, . . . one struck off the list, . . . a prince without a domain, a ruined foreign merchant, a bankrupt." Volodia's devotion to literature, to Pasternak and Lermontov, to Baudelaire and Pascal, makes him an outcast, "doomed," like others who had "fled to Paris" or been "eliminated" by other means. As for his fellow students and workers, Volodia cannot reach them. Unable to establish friendships, Volodia records his thoughts in a diary. "Whether because of class instinct, or because of my blood, or, finally, because of my frame of mind, I have become attached to a dying culture." An opportunity to vent his frustration arises; a meeting has been called to discuss "cultural reconstruction," and Volodia decides to speak forthrightly and "stagger his listeners like a shot of shrapnel." "You are sure to be much surprised by my words," Volodia imagines himself saying.

> You are accustomed to silence. Some are silent because you have frightened them; others because you have bought them. Simple truths demand self-sacrifice now. As in the days of Galileo they can be spoken only at the stake. . . . You have eliminated from life the heretics, the dreamers, the philosophers, the poets. You have established universal literacy and equally universal ignorance.

But Volodia does not have the courage to rebuke his classmates as he had planned. Instead he recalls a recent conversation with a visiting French journalist who describes for him the life of young people in Paris. "They know a great deal, but are incapable of anything," Volodia reports to his classmates. "The important thing for them is to take a place in a life already made, whereas you want to create this life. . . . I want to be with all of you. . . . But some curse hangs over me."[34]

Without the strength to resolve or live with these contradictions Volodia is doomed. Inadvertently he inspires a drunken worker to commit vandalism on the construction site, an act of sabotage that leads to a trial. But Volodia is afraid to admit his complicity in the crime. Ashamed, overwhelmed by isolation and what he considers to be his own spiritual bankruptcy, he commits suicide.

Ehrenburg conceded in his memoirs that if Volodia "had had a less tender conscience and a little more stamina, he would not have hanged himself." The same could be said of many of Ehrenburg's protagonists, who often kill themselves or contribute to their own destruction: Julio

Jurenito, Nikolai Kurbov, Mikhail Likov, Lasik Roitschwantz, to name a few. But Ehrenburg had more confidence in himself and his own ability to survive.

He could not disown Russia, even if it meant accepting Stalin's regime; but he did not do this cynically or with blind illusions. Ehrenburg knew more than most people in the West. "Friends arriving from the Soviet Union told me about dekulakization, about difficulties associated with collectivization, about the famine in the Ukraine," he admitted in *People, Years, Life*. But the threat of fascism outweighed all other considerations. *Out of Chaos* signaled his capitulation. He would be loyal, he would be silent, he would earn the regime's trust. A part of him was now moribund, his artistic instincts subordinate to political constraints. "I did not renounce what I held dear, nor did I repudiate anything," he insisted. "But I knew I would have to live clenching my teeth and master one of the most difficult disciplines—silence."[35]

A Low, Dishonest Decade

After so many years in Paris Ilya Ehrenburg was a fixture of life on the Left Bank. His friend the Italian journalist Nino Frank thought of him as living not in France but in Montparnasse, "where he had the leisure to construct a portable, docile U.S.S.R., set up in a Paris that he had also built for himself."[1] Ehrenburg's apartment on the first floor of a small, elegant house on Rue du Cotentin, with its innumerable books and dozens of pipes arranged on his study wall, was a frequent gathering place for friends and colleagues. Ehrenburg even kept a key in the door so everyone would always feel welcome. It was a short walk to Le Dôme and La Coupole. Le Dôme, the preferred haunt of journalists, writers, artists, and politicians, was his favorite café. Simone de Beauvoir often came across him there or in the nearby La Coupole, "his fleshy face crowned with a shock of thick hair."[2]

Ehrenburg's appearance, how he dressed and carried himself, struck everyone who met him. The Italian journalist Luigi Barzini once described Ehrenburg as having "eyelids half shut over eyes that peered about like those of an alligator lying awake in the mud."[3] His broad, rounded shoulders supported a disproportionately large head. It was so unexpectedly big that the Red Army had to order a special cap for him during the Second World War. His hands, though, were small and weak, with long, delicate, finely shaped fingers stained yellow by nicotine. His legs too were extremely thin; when he walked, his feet moved in quick, tiny steps.

The prolific French novelist Georges Simenon became close to Ehrenburg in the early 1930s. "Ehrenburg was very pleasant and a bit strange," Simenon once recalled in an interview. "He listened more than he talked. He would sit in a corner somewhere, as if he were there and not there, and it seemed as if he were not listening at all. But he remembered everything we talked about."[4]

The American writer Samuel Putnam, who also lived in Paris for many years, was among the numerous observers who made note of Ehrenburg's enigmatic presence:

> With his powerfully set, stooping shoulders that gave him almost the appearance of a hunchback, he was one of the human landmarks of the carrefour Vavin. . . . Most often he sat alone. He would raise his eyes from time to time above the edge of his French or Russian newspaper, to let them roam over the blaring room as he observed the antics of a group of rowdy "artists," in all probability Americans; the next moment he would drop his gaze as if abashed at what he had seen.[5]

Ehrenburg began to adjust his critical sense to political considerations in December 1932, when he was back in Paris after his extended visit to Moscow and Siberia. In addition to writing *Out of Chaos* he adopted a new and harsh polemical tone in a series of articles about French culture, even denigrating experiments in contemporary French literature. "I also know that young writers write wonderful books about nothing," he wrote that winter. "This is great art—you have to write a novel of three hundred pages without characters, without a subject, and without ideas."[6] Needless to say, this was an unusual opinion for a former habitué of the Rotonde.

Throughout 1933 most of his articles—on Miguel da Unamuno, François Mauriac, the French Surrealists, André Gide, and André Malraux—appeared in *Literaturnaya Gazeta*.[7] When the articles were translated and published in France in 1934 their appearance confirmed Ehrenburg's reputation as a harsh polemicist; the Surrealists in particular, led by the poet André Breton, came to mistrust him deeply, assuming he had become an outright apologist for Stalin.

Only in 1934, when a political crisis erupted in France, did Ehrenburg's career as an *Izvestia* correspondent begin in earnest. On February 6, a violent mob stormed police lines, hoping to reach the French parliament building. Led by reactionary and monarchist organizations such as Action Française and Croix de Feu, which sympathized with Hitler's anti-Semitism, the angry crowd surged through the streets crying for a coup d'état. Riots and demonstrations engulfed Paris. "Our life now is pretty stormy," Ehrenburg wrote from Paris to Valentina Milman. "They are shooting in the street . . . so I am somewhat unsettled."[8]

Within days the forces of the left united, fearing that France, like Germany, could succumb to outright fascism. A general strike was declared for February 12. Unlike the left in Germany, Socialists and Communists united behind the banner of anti-fascism. "I have lived in Paris for many years," Ehrenburg wrote in *Izvestia*, "but I had yet to see such determination, such self-control, such emotional tension."[9] This was the beginning of the Popular Front, which gained power two years later with the election of Léon Blum, the first Socialist prime minister of France.

That February *Izvestia* had another assignment for Ehrenburg. Only a few days after the general strike in Paris he was dispatched to Vienna to cover an attempt by Austrian workers to resist Fascist influence in the country. Ehrenburg arrived in time to see "the Viennese killings fields," where artillery attacks devastated working-class neighborhoods.[10] On March 6, the first of Ehrenburg's articles on the Austrian crisis appeared in *Izvestia*.[11] As was to be expected, they reflected Soviet policy on the struggle against fascism. In Austria, as in Germany, the Social Democrats and the Communists contended for leadership of the working class. Stalin directed the international Communist movement to denounce Socialist parties, such as the Austrian Social Democrats, who could have been natural allies in the struggle against Hitler. Nowhere was this policy more fatal than in Germany, where disputes between Communists and Socialists demoralized the left and contributed to Hitler's rise to power.

In his articles Ehrenburg described how militant workers were dis-

armed throughout Austria while Socialist leaders compromised, hesitated, and utterly failed to seize the initiative. Ehrenburg tried to
express understanding for the harsh dilemmas the Social Democrats
faced. He did not denounce them in crude Stalinist language. He never
called them "Social Fascists," which was the usual practice in the Soviet
press, and he even expressed grudging respect for their arrested leaders. "Personal courage does not necessarily exclude political cowardice" was as much as he could say.[12] But on the whole his articles
condemned the Socialists for lacking confidence in the working class.

Ehrenburg, though, was disturbed by *Izvestia*'s editing of his reports.
"The problem is," he wrote to Milman on March 9, "that the Austrian
piece was published not only with cuts, but with intolerable concoc-
tions."[13] Ehrenburg evidently protested to the editors and did not easily accept Soviet constraints on his reporting.

Ehrenburg's articles were a vivid warning of what to expect from
governments that caved in to Nazi pressure. Most European leaders did
not take Hitler's aggressive rhetoric seriously and did not understand
how violent repression in Austria, which included summary executions
of disarmed leftists, could presage more terrible events. Ehrenburg documented the danger of working-class disunity and the full threat of
Nazi-inspired violence. His articles ran for more than a week in *Izvestia* and were translated into German, French, English, and Czech, then
circulated widely in Europe. Among Soviet writers Ilya Ehrenburg was
fast becoming the preeminent witness against fascism.

EHRENBURG, BUKHARIN, AND
SOVIET CULTURE

Beginning in 1934 Ehrenburg's old friend Nikolai Bukharin enjoyed
a brief political comeback. In January he addressed the Seventeenth
Party Congress, regaining a measure of official renown. Then on February 22, while Ehrenburg was on assignment in Vienna, Bukharin
was listed for the first time as editor of *Izvestia*. By that time he had
already been running the newspaper for several weeks and no doubt
it was Bukharin's intervention that broadened Ehrenburg's role.
Bukharin's work at *Izvestia* provided his last extended opportunity to
exert public influence. Like almost all newspapers, *Izvestia* had con-
centrated on political and economic questions, but Bukharin shifted

the paper's focus to cultural developments, turning it into the most thought-provoking and popular newspaper in the country. He recruited celebrated writers and poets and he emphasized the threat of fascism to social and cultural life.

In a highly significant move, Bukharin also welcomed the work of Boris Pasternak. Pasternak had rarely published in newspapers, but within two weeks of Bukharin's appointment occasional translations by Pasternak from the work of acclaimed Georgian poets began to appear in *Izvestia*.[14] It seems likely that Ehrenburg, who never missed an opportunity to praise Pasternak, encouraged Bukharin to approach the poet. Pasternak was not only grateful for this support but also followed Ehrenburg's career closely and enjoyed his "splendid articles."[15]

Ehrenburg was carving out a role for himself, one that would transcend his work as a journalist and prove invaluable to the Soviet regime. With Bukharin in charge of *Izvestia*, Ehrenburg's articles about the rise of fascism appeared with greater frequency. That spring his pieces emphasized the chaos and moral uncertainty overtaking Europe. He traveled widely, enhancing his image in Moscow as the best-connected and best-informed Soviet citizen living abroad. In England he saw Oxford students debate pacifism. They were full of illusions about Hitler. As one "student-liberal" claimed, "Only Socialists and Jews suffer under fascism, while everyone will suffer from war."[16] In a series of articles entitled "In the Jungles of Europe" Ehrenburg shared his impressions of life in Romania and Czechoslovakia, in Yugoslavia and in Italy, where Mussolini's brownshirts provided vivid examples of Fascist intimidation.[17]

Knowing almost all of Europe's leading writers, Ehrenburg used these contacts to boost Soviet prestige, particularly in the movement against fascism. He became a mediator between Communist and non-Communist intellectuals, using the necessity to oppose Hitler as a means to help the Soviet Union. The French novelist André Malraux was among Ehrenburg's closest friends and shared his belief that Stalin's Russia could be a bulwark against fascism. Ehrenburg was instrumental in convincing Malraux and his wife to visit Moscow for the First All-Union Congress of Soviet Writers, which was scheduled for early summer. Ehrenburg could not have found a better way to prove his usefulness. Malraux was already a legendary figure, a famous explorer of the Orient and author, most recently, of *Man's Fate*, a powerful account of revolutionary intrigue in China; he had just received the

Goncourt Prize, the most prestigious award in French letters. Malraux's presence at the Writers' Congress in Moscow would demonstrate that the Soviet regime, in contrast to the Nazis, treated intellectuals with genuine tolerance and respect.

In the 1930s André Malraux and Ilya Ehrenburg were inseparable allies. "During eight years in Paris and in Spain," Ehrenburg recalled, "[Malraux] was invariably at my side."[18] Ehrenburg reviewed *Man's Fate* favorably for the Soviet press, writing with a subtlety he rarely employed in the 1930s. Ehrenburg understood that *Man's Fate* was not a call for revolution. All of Malraux's books were "born of an internal necessity," Ehrenburg observed; *Man's Fate* had as much to do with Malraux's search for romantic adventure as it had to do with revolutionary events in Shanghai.[19]

For Ehrenburg Malraux's decision to attend the Writers' Congress was both a hopeful sign and a personal triumph. They traveled together with their wives on a Soviet ship, the *Dzerzhinsky* (named after the founder of the secret police), which left from London at the end of May and arrived in Leningrad on June 14. Their arrival in Leningrad was treated as a major event: *Literaturnaya Gazeta* ran photographs and interviews on the front page, where Malraux clarified his political allegiance in words that easily gratified his Soviet hosts. "If war breaks out," Malraux declared, "and I think it will be Japan that starts it, I will be the first to work for the formation of a foreign legion and, in its ranks, gun in hand, I will fight to defend the Soviet Union, the land of freedom."[20] Malraux was not making an empty boast. When the Spanish civil war began he rushed to Madrid, then arranged for delivery of French airplanes to the republic; and during World War II he played a prominent role in the French underground.

Upon arrival in Leningrad Ehrenburg also echoed Communist propaganda on the eve of the Writers' Congress. "The fate of European culture depends on the creation of a new man and a new culture in the Soviet Union," he declared. Ehrenburg then spoke in a manner befitting his image as the country's expert on Europe. He mentioned a French translation of his literary essays, a volume containing harsh attacks on conservative and anti-Stalinist writers such as François Mauriac. He proudly reported that his articles on the workers' uprising in Austria were circulating illegally in Vienna; and he boasted how well *Out of Chaos* was doing in Europe. But then he added a complaint whose audacity seems startling to this day. A month before his arrival

Out of Chaos had been severely condemned in *Literaturnaya Gazeta* as a slander on Soviet reality. Angered by the review, Ehrenburg voiced his surprise "when criticism of a Soviet novel assumes a tone that would be more suitable for a book written by one of our enemies."[21] The novel in fact still appeared to have an ambiguous status in official circles. Although it had come out in early 1934, the Soviet press was slow to respond. Throughout March and April Ehrenburg pleaded with Valentina Milman for word about reviews. As late as May 8, he could barely contain his fears. "Why is there a conspiracy of silence around the book?" he implored her.[22]

He had another ten days to wait. A long, scathing review of *Out of Chaos* finally appeared in *Literaturnaya Gazeta* on May 18. (Ehrenburg was referring to this review when he arrived in Leningrad on June 14.) In the article, entitled "The Victims of Chaos," the critic Alexei Garry accused Ehrenburg of "slander," claiming that his characters "lost themselves in the chaos of new construction and lost their way in the ditches, excavations, and cranes" of Kuznetsk.[23] Ehrenburg's only comfort was an unusual statement the editors appended to the review, noting they did not share Garry's opinions and would soon publish a discussion of the book.

Three days after his arrival in Russia Ehrenburg's confidence was reinforced by an unusually candid article in *Izvestia*. Written by Karl Radek, a prominent journalist who was reputed to receive personal directives from Stalin, it lavished praise on *Out of Chaos* and commended Ehrenburg for "finding a new principled orientation" on Soviet life. Radek reviewed Ehrenburg's career, explicitly recalling that "the October Revolution found Ehrenburg in the ranks of its enemies, although he had been a Bolshevik in his youth." Ehrenburg "rushed about between the U.S.S.R. and abroad, creating talented but vicious books devoid of understanding where the first proletarian country was headed." The novel *The Stormy Life of Lasik Roitschwantz* was for Radek "the conclusion of the first period of Ehrenburg's literary activity, because it explained better than others what prevented Ehrenburg from joining our ranks." But the country's reconstruction during the First Five Year Plan and Europe's political and economic turmoil effected a change in Ehrenburg. His reporting from Paris and Vienna embodied his newfound regard for the proletariat. "We will wait for his new works," Radek concluded, "which will show how much his *perestroika* has succeeded."[24] Radek's review marked a turning point. With

Out of Chaos now fully accepted, Ehrenburg could assume his place in the ranks of Soviet writers.

In the meantime, the opening of the Writers' Congress was postponed from the end of June to the middle of August. Ehrenburg enjoyed a leisurely summer, traveling with his daughter to the far north for most of July and meeting with other writers in Moscow. He also wrote an unusual piece for *Izvestia*. Entitled "Plainly Speaking," the article concerns his stay in Moscow's National Hotel, where the arrival of Western tourists lost him his room. Ehrenburg watched the hotel undergo a sudden transformation. Staff uniforms improved, the halls and dining room were decorated, waiters and chambermaids learned to smile and bow. While he expected to hear that "Einstein or someone similar" was about to visit, he was furious to observe obsequious behavior for ordinary foreign guests. People who run the hotel "do not know the difference between comfort and blackmail, between hospitality and toadyism." The article also touched on a broader theme:

> Were I your guide, citizen tourists, . . . I would not equivocate or conceal from you many harsh facts. I would not say to you: "Look to the right—there's a small old church there," because on the left there is a queue lined up. There is plenty of want, stupidity, ignorance in our country, for we are only beginning to live. . . . I could tell you many other unpleasant things. We hear a lot about respect for man, but not everyone has begun to learn how to respect him.[25]

"Plainly Speaking" brought Ehrenburg some difficulty. Citing his article, the *Times* of London claimed that Russia "misled foreign tourists," while Soviet bureaucrats blamed Ehrenburg for causing cancellations and hurting the country financially. Nonetheless, as Ehrenburg recalled in his memoirs, *Izvestia* (meaning Bukharin) "stood up for me" and the episode passed without further incident.[26]

Yet underneath the ceremonies and the sightseeing that summer there was another, unpublicized drama unfolding just as Ehrenburg and Malraux reached the Soviet Union: on May 14, a month before they arrived, the poet Osip Mandelstam had been arrested in Moscow.

The immediate reason for Mandelstam's arrest was a poem about Stalin he had written the previous November and recited to a small circle of friends. Eloquent and concise, the poem was among the first to say openly what everyone was beginning to sense in their hearts, as the opening lines confirm. "We live, indifferent to the land beneath us,/No one can hear our speeches ten steps away./All we can hear is the Kremlin mountaineer/The killer and peasant-slayer."[27]

This time Mandelstam was spared. His wife did all she could to save him.[28] She called upon Bukharin, who had helped Mandelstam many times before; he did not fail now. Pasternak too, alerted to the arrest by Anna Akhmatova, visited Bukharin to share his anxiety. Without hesitation Bukharin appealed directly to Stalin and mentioned Pasternak's concern in his letter. These steps proved decisive. Within weeks Nadezhda Mandelstam was allowed to see her husband in the Lubyanka. Rather than execution or imprisonment (the poem was a "terrorist act"), Mandelstam was sent into exile to Voronezh for three years, his fate aptly defined by the evocative instruction "isolate but preserve." By the time of Ehrenburg's arrival in June Mandelstam was hundreds of miles from Moscow. Then the story reached an unprecedented climax. At the end of June Stalin telephoned Pasternak to confirm that Mandelstam would be all right. Pasternak immediately shared the news with Ehrenburg, and it was Ehrenburg who made sure that word of Stalin's solicitude circulated widely.[29] Ehrenburg even traveled to Voronezh to try to find Mandelstam, but no one could provide the poet's address and after searching for a day, Ehrenburg returned to Moscow.

Stalin had his own reasons to spare Mandelstam and appear merciful. The Writers' Congress was about to take place and he wanted to lull the country's intellectuals into a sense of hopeful security. "A miracle is only a miracle, after all," Nadezhda Mandelstam commented, "if people stand in wonder before it."[30]

Stalin's call did have wide repercussions. Pasternak's status changed abruptly; even his most extreme critics had to acknowledge his prestige. Bukharin too seemed to benefit. Just after intervening on Mandelstam's behalf he was invited to deliver a major address at the Writers' Congress. Based on these events it seemed fair to believe the Congress would herald a tolerant approach to literature, a development that could presage broader tolerance throughout society; but such hopes turned out be illusory, and by the end of the year, barely four months after the Congress opened, Stalin initiated another wave of terror.

THE FIRST SOVIET WRITERS' CONGRESS

In establishing the Union of Soviet Writers Stalin found a way to turn the country's creative writers into handmaidens of the state. He used it, as he would use similar unions in other cultural spheres, to dominate the country's intellectuals, distributing privileges, apartments, summer homes, money, and trips abroad as rewards for loyalty and subservience rather than for artistic talent. But in 1934 Ehrenburg had genuine hopes that the Congress would endorse creative autonomy for the country's writers. Two years earlier Stalin had liquidated the Russian Association of Proletarian Writers, known by its acronym RAPP. This organization had epitomized the party's doctrinaire approach to litera-ture, which, under RAPP's leadership, had divided Soviet writers into two groups: acceptable "proletarian" figures and unacceptable "fellow travelers" or even enemies. Ehrenburg for several years had been con-sidered among such "fellow travelers." Now, with RAPP dissolved and a new Writers' Union being organized, which was supposed to include writers of every tendency, Ehrenburg felt optimistic. He did not exag-gerate that he prepared himself for the opening session "like a girl for her first dance."[31]

By all available accounts the Writers' Congress resembled an extrav-agant literary circus. Enormous portraits of Shakespeare, Tolstoy, Gogol, Cervantes, Heine, Pushkin, and Balzac decorated the Hall of Columns, one of Moscow's most impressive auditoriums and the site of Lenin's funeral a decade before. Almost six hundred Soviet delegates attended twenty-six sessions for fifteen days and heard more than two hundred speeches. An orchestra greeted them on the first day while crowds gathered to see their favorite writers. The official literary busi-ness of the Congress was continuously interrupted by brief remarks from collective farmers, Red Army men, and young pioneers who represented delegations in the hall. André Malraux was one of forty foreign guests, among them Oskar Maria Graff, Klaus Mann, and Gus-tav Regler of Germany, and Louis Aragon and Jean-Richard Bloch of France.[32]

Ehrenburg was one of the most prominent figures at the Congress. He chaired individual sessions and translated for several foreign speakers; his photograph appeared twice in *Izvestia* during the pro-ceedings while *Out of Chaos* received official endorsement, its cover portrayed among other Soviet "classics" on *Izvestia*'s front page.[33]

Several speakers even remarked on Ehrenburg's newfound enthusiasm for socialism.[34]

The Congress was a complicated drama. Many of the speeches were fatuous. Maxim Gorky, who chaired the Congress and was to lead the new Writers' Union, gave the opening address, an interminable, three-hour survey of literary history and the place of Soviet literature. It was also a full-scale attack on Western culture. Stalin's henchman, Andrei Zhdanov, first came to prominence at the Congress with his obtuse proclamations about literature organizing oppressed workers to "abolish . . . the yoke of wage slavery."[35] There were also moments of genuine feeling and debate. As Ehrenburg had hoped, Bukharin's speech was eagerly received; he had intervened in defense of arrested writers and his opposition to cultural regimentation was well known. Only Maxim Gorky enjoyed a more enthusiastic ovation when he appeared at the rostrum.

Although Bukharin's topic was Soviet poetry, his real subject was the party's control of literature. At the Congress Bukharin voiced his fear of "poetic work becoming departmentally alienated from life and bureaucratized." Genuine literature required "diversity and quality." Under socialism, Bukharin contended, writers needed to explore "the entire world of emotions—love, happiness, fear, anguish, anger." On occasion Bukharin adopted a sharp, polemical tone: "The poet's business is not to paraphrase a newspaper article or to show a standard knowledge of political science." Then, to the surprise of many, Bukharin praised lyrical poetry and singled out Boris Pasternak "as one of the most remarkable masters of verse in our time."[36] Such remarks enraged a number of delegates, but the great majority responded with cheers. "Many writers," one observer remarked, "literally fell into each other's arms and, breathless with delight, spoke of the prospects of a real emancipation of art."[37] For the German Communist Gustav Regler, who was to quit the party a few years later, "[Bukharin's] speech was gold in comparison with Gorky's dross."[38]

Isaac Babel spoke modestly and with unusual candor. He tried to identify his art with the Soviet cause and recommended to his fellow writers that they study Stalin's use of words, "how terse they are, how muscular." Babel also defended himself, but with a humorous and self-deprecating tone that exemplified his stories. He had published little in recent years. "Now, speaking of silence," Babel continued, "I cannot avoid talking about myself, the past master of that art. I must admit that if I lived in any self-respecting capitalist country, I would have long since croaked from starvation and no publisher would have cared whether, as Ehrenburg puts it, I was a rabbit or a she-elephant . . . I am not happy about my silence. But perhaps this is living proof how different methods of work are respected."[39]

There was more to Babel's "silence" than a meticulous style of work. As he told Clara Malraux in private, "I have the right not to write. But I am a writer. In my drawer I have two novels. If they are found, I'm a dead man."[40] These novels were confiscated at the time of Babel's arrest in 1939 and have never appeared. Ehrenburg also spoke freely with André and Clara Malraux. He let them know that Anna Akhmatova was not invited to attend the Congress and that Boris Pasternak, for all his prominence, had difficulty publishing his own verse; it was his translations of Georgian poetry that were widely hailed at the time.

Boris Pasternak was a seminal figure at the Congress. Many speakers referred to his work and his remarks from the podium were eagerly awaited. Pasternak spoke briefly without polemical references to literature or politics. Like Babel he defended a writer's prerogative to surprise and challenge the reader.

Other delegates pleaded for books that would satisfy the taste of newly literate workers and reinforce the goals of Socialist construction. The Congress, after all, endorsed the doctrine of "socialist realism." Several European writers responded, trying to defend the complexity of art. Jean-Richard Bloch, with Ehrenburg acting as translator, spoke up for diversity and tolerance. "It is inevitable and necessary that there should be writers for millions of readers, writers for a hundred thousand readers, and writers for five thousand readers." In a country such as the Soviet Union, which is trying to create the first classless, Socialist society, "literature should not be penetrated only by vulgar mass conceptions." André Malraux voiced a similar warning. Art must not be reduced to simple renderings of reality, to a photograph. "If writers are the engineers of souls, do not forget that the highest function of an engineer is to invent!" Malraux declared. "Art is not a submission, but a conquest . . . a conquest almost always over the unconscious, very often over logic."[41]

It was in this contentious atmosphere that Ehrenburg took the podium. His years in Paris, his friendship with Malraux and Bloch, identified him with European culture, and he was the only Soviet writer to express views identical to theirs. It is significant that when he pleaded for tolerance and variety, for individual taste and artistic sophistication, he was expressing views similar to those he articulated two decades later, after Stalin's death.

Little attention has been paid to Ehrenburg's willingness to challenge the conventions of Soviet artistic life under Stalin. At the Writers' Congress Ehrenburg defended the need for books that appealed only to "the intelligentsia and an elite among the workers" and may not be understandable to the broad masses. He also defended Isaac Babel and Boris Pasternak for publishing so little, and he sided with Bukharin's plea for greater tolerance of artistic expression. As he wrote in *People, Years, Life*, "Unfortunately, it looks as though I shall not live to see the day when the questions I raised at the Congress will have become out-dated."[42]

Instead of serious literary criticism we have a red and black list of authors, and what is truly fantastic is the ease with which they are transferred from one list to the other. You cannot, after all, put an author on a pedestal one moment only to throw him off the next. We are not dealing with physical culture. It is inexcusable that literary criticism should have a direct effect upon an author's position in society. The distribution of material benefits should not depend on literary criticism. In the last analysis one cannot treat an artist's lack of success or failures as crimes and his successes as a form of rehabilitation.[43]

Evidently it was still possible to conduct a dialog about Soviet culture, for Ehrenburg's outspoken views did not compromise his standing. He was selected to join fifty-one others on the presidium of the Writers' Union, and when the Congress was over he was among two dozen of its most prominent members to receive country houses—dachas—in the small village of Peredelkino just outside of Moscow; this was the start of the famous writers' colony.

In his memoirs Ehrenburg could only provide a bland summary of the Congress's proceedings—but he could still quote long sections from his own speech and insist that the values he represented under Khrushchev had survived his years under Stalin, even as many friends did not. Ehrenburg could not have saved them. He was barely able to survive himself.

THE MURDER OF SERGEI KIROV

Following the Congress Ehrenburg and Lyubov Mikhailovna returned to Paris by a roundabout route. They traveled south to Odessa, where they took a Soviet ship through the Black Sea to the Mediterranean, stopping in Athens before disembarking in Brindisi, Italy; from there they proceeded by land to France. In his memoirs Ehrenburg emphasizes how much worse the European crisis was growing: on October 9, King Alexander of Yugoslavia and French Minister of Foreign Affairs Jean-Louis Barthou were both assassinated in Marseille by a Croat Fascist who had been trained in Italy by Mussolini's hitmen. Although Barthou was a conservative, he favored a defensive alliance with the Soviet Union to check Hitler's ambitions. "Everyone understood Barthou's murder as part of the Fascist offensive," Ehrenburg remembered. The need to oppose Hitler absorbed him more and more. On October 23 he addressed a meeting in Paris on the Soviet Writers' Congress. André Malraux and André Gide were also among the speakers, joining French Communist leaders and workers on the stage. Four thousand people attended. According to *People, Years, Life* it was then, after he returned to Paris, that Ehrenburg conceived the idea of organizing a conference of intellectuals. "I sent a long letter to Moscow reporting on the mood of the Western writers and the idea of an anti-Fascist union."[44]

Ehrenburg in fact sent the letter to Stalin a month earlier, on September 13, 1934, while in Odessa on his way back to France. Writing about the episode a quarter century later, he had good reason to downplay his audacity and obscure the true circumstances surrounding his appeal to the Kremlin. During Ehrenburg's visit to Odessa on September 12 he was joined by his old friend Nikolai Bukharin for a discussion about the Writers' Congress before a local group of writers and journalists. Bukharin's trip to Odessa was not covered by any Russian-language newspaper in the city; only Odessa's Ukrainian-language newspaper mentioned his presence. In spite of his recent and widely hailed speech at the Writers' Congress, Bukharin's status was in eclipse.

Ehrenburg and Bukharin shared profound misgivings about Stalin's doctrinaire opposition to left-wing unity. Coming so soon after the Writers' Congress, where André Malraux and Jean-Richard Bloch had pleaded for a less orthodox approach to culture, it was inevitable that Ehrenburg and Bukharin would discuss the political consequences of Stalin's policies toward Western European writers and consider an appeal to the Kremlin. Nonetheless it was clear to them both that only Ehrenburg's signature should appear on the letter in order not to distract Stalin with additional suspicions. It was also suitably cautious on Ehrenburg's part to write his first appeal to Stalin on his own and not ally himself explicitly with Bukharin, although Bukharin no doubt took the letter back with him to Moscow.[45] Even a quarter century later Ehrenburg still felt compelled to deal cautiously with this episode in his memoirs, but one fact could not be obscured: Ehrenburg was willing to assume a *political* role; he did not want to remain an ordinary Soviet correspondent, however useful he was proving to be.

Ehrenburg's letter helped to encourage a fundamental shift in Soviet foreign policy. Until that time Stalin was still opposing a broad coalition against the Nazis. For several years the International Organization of Revolutionary Writers (known by its Russian acronym, MORP) had excluded non-Stalinist, left-wing writers, extending the dogmatic methods of Soviet cultural bureaucrats into European political debates. Major American figures such as Theodore Dreiser, Sherwood Anderson, and John Dos Passos, and French ones such as André Malraux and Roger Martin du Gard, all of whom Ehrenburg mentioned by name, were being discouraged from cooperating with their pro-Soviet colleagues.

Ehrenburg and Bukharin saw the need to break with this intolerance. The Writers' Congress, which had welcomed a non-Communist figure such as André Malraux and a committed Communist such as Jean-Richard Bloch—and allowed them both to voice misgivings about "socialist realism"—provided the ideal opportunity to broaden the anti-Fascist struggle.

"The situation in the West is extremely propitious," Ehrenburg wrote to Stalin,

> the majority of the greatest, most talented and most famous writers will sincerely join us in the fight against fascism. If in place of MORP there existed a broad, anti-Fascist organization of writers, writers such as Romain Rolland, Thomas Mann, and Heinrich Mann [and a long list of others] would immediately join. . . . Briefly put, such an organization, with rare exceptions, will unite all the great and uncorrupted writers.

MORP would have to change its political rigidity and adopt a broad but exact set of goals: "the struggle against fascism and an active defense of the Soviet Union."[46]

Ehrenburg's proposal impressed Stalin. On September 23, he sent a note to Lazar Kaganovich endorsing Ehrenburg's idea and assigning Kaganovich and Andrei Zhdanov to work with him. "It would be good to broaden the framework of MORP," Stalin wrote to Kaganovich, "and place Comrade Ehrenburg as head of MORP. This is an important development."[47] Within weeks the Soviet ambassador to France invited Ehrenburg to the embassy to convey a startling message: Stalin wanted to see him personally.

Ehrenburg and his wife returned to Moscow. Their friends seemed happy, convinced that the Writers' Congress confirmed a more hopeful, more "liberal" atmosphere in the country. Isaac Babel organized a big dinner party in Ehrenburg's honor. Ehrenburg saw Vsevolod Meyerhold a great deal and enjoyed hearing how well his latest productions were going. Irina Ehrenburg's career was also flourishing. Her account of life as a French schoolgirl had just appeared in a journal and would soon be published as a book.[48] And Ehrenburg was pleased with her marriage (in December 1933) to Boris Lapin. Lapin was a Jew, an accomplished linguist, and a talented writer who loved exploring remote areas of the country, where he gathered material for his books on small Asian tribes. Although the weather was foul, cold, and wet, Ehrenburg "saw everything in a rosy light"—but he never got to see Stalin.

On December 1, 1934, life in the Soviet Union turned upside down.

I stopped by *Izvestia* and dropped in on Bukharin. He looked terrible and could barely speak. "A terrible thing has happened. Kirov has been killed." Everyone was stunned. Kirov had been loved. Grief was mixed with anxiety: who, why, what would happen next? I have noticed that great ordeals are almost always preceded by weeks or months of tranquil happiness, both in the life of an individual and in the history of nations. Perhaps it seems this way later when people recall the period before the calamity. None of us could guess, of course, that a new epoch was beginning, but everyone became subdued and guarded.[49]

This was all Ehrenburg was allowed to say in the 1960s, but in 1988 an uncensored version of what happened to him that day at *Izvestia* appeared in the Soviet press.

> "Go, write about Kirov," Bukharin shouted. . . . I knew that Kirov and Orzhonikidze were friends and defenders of Nikolai Ivanovich. He pushed me into an empty room. "Write. There won't be another one like him." I had not managed to write anything when Nikolai Ivanovich came in and whispered, "You don't have to write anything. This is a very fishy business."[50]

Sergei Kirov was the Leningrad party leader, a popular and independent-minded figure, who by 1934 was emerging as the head of a moderate faction within the Politburo. Kirov and his colleagues never sought to challenge Stalin's supreme authority. They had helped Stalin defeat Bukharin in the late 1920s and had supported the drastic steps of the First Five Year Plan, which included forced collectivization and the stepped-up campaign to expand heavy industry. With collectivization largely achieved Kirov wanted to curb the most excessive aspects of Stalin's arbitrary rule, end official terror, and restore oppositionists, such as Bukharin, to the good graces of the party.

Sergei Kirov was assassinated in the corridor of his Leningrad office, the famous Smolny Institute, where Lenin had directed the Bolshevik takeover in 1917. The full story of Kirov's murder remains a mystery. Stalin may well have plotted the crime because he felt threatened by Kirov's popularity. He did use the murder as a pretext to unleash a bloody purge; Stalin took charge of the investigation, rushing to Leningrad that same evening with his closest henchmen on the Politburo, Molotov, Voroshilov, and Kaganovich.

Repression began immediately. On December 6, scores of executions were reported in Moscow and Leningrad. On December 16, Grigory Zinoviev and Lev Kamenev were arrested; they were soon convicted for complicity in Kirov's murder but not condemned to death. Stalin had special plans for them. In the next three years tens of thousands of other victims would be shot as "accomplices" to the crime.

The day after Kirov's assassination a series of tributes from the country's writers began appearing in *Izvestia*. One signed by Ehrenburg and Pasternak was the most noteworthy. Entitled "Sorrow and Wrath," it was probably written by Ehrenburg and expressed chagrin over the loss of an important party leader in typical Soviet rhetoric:

> We know that no hired killers can stop history. But today we are full of sorrow: before us is a man who was just breathing, burning, struggling. Now he lies still. Someday history will say: "They paid a high price for the happiness of mankind." But today we do not have the composure of a historian: sorrow and wrath, wrath and sorrow![51]

Kirov's murder prevented Ehrenburg from seeing Stalin in the Kremlin. In subsequent years, while he saw the dictator on ceremonial occasions, they never had a private meeting. Still, Ehrenburg had volunteered for "official" service in the struggle against fascism and his offer had been accepted. He was sent back to Paris that December, assignment in hand. From that point on Ehrenburg was no longer an ordinary Soviet correspondent; he was part of Stalin's apparatus in the West.[52]

THE EUROPEAN CRISIS

Within days of his return to Paris Ehrenburg observed Hitler's appeal at close range. *Izvestia* sent him to the Saar in December, where one of the initial dramas of Nazi aggression was playing itself out. The Saar basin was a piece of German territory nestled against the border of France. Rich in coal, it was claimed by the French following World War I. After President Woodrow Wilson objected a compromise was reached, leading to a plebiscite scheduled for January 13, 1935. This vote would permit the Saar's German residents to choose either economic union with France or outright reunification with Germany.

The vote was never in doubt until Hitler's accession to power made people hesitate. Led by the Communists, a minority of residents tried to campaign against reunification. Ehrenburg witnessed their futile efforts. The Nazis' deft use of patriotic symbols seduced the overwhelming majority of the population while thugs disrupted Communist meetings. With the help of Gustav Regler Ehrenburg visited small villages where he interviewed miners opposed to the Nazis. The vote was a foregone conclusion: 90 percent of the population voted to rejoin Germany. "The battle may be lost," Ehrenburg reported to his Soviet readers, "but the war—never."[53]

For the next half year Ehrenburg's assignments took him all over France and the Low Countries. Europe seemed unprepared to oppose Hitler. In June Ehrenburg visited Alsace, a French province with a mostly German population. Nazi sympathizers operated openly, confident of "liberation."[54] The following month, Ehrenburg traveled to Eupen, a Belgian city that had belonged to Germany until 1918; Ehrenburg felt as if he were in Germany itself. Portraits of Hitler adorned many walls, and residents greeted one another with "Heil Hitler."

The Saar, Alsace, Eupen—these areas had once been German and the Nazis knew how to incite extreme nationalist passions. Europe was mesmerized. "These last few months, I have been doing an exhausting job," Ehrenburg wrote,

> traveling from one region to another bordering on Germany. . . . One can look at a snake for a long time and retain one's sanity; if a snake swallows a rabbit, it is, when all is said and done, a dinner. But one cannot bear to look at the rabbit for long: its glassy staring eyes can infect even a human being of steel nerves with insanity.[55]

For Ehrenburg only the Soviet Union could prevent the triumph of fascism. In Geneva he visited a small café where Lenin used to write and argue with his comrades. "This is one of the places," Ehrenburg wrote, "which compels us to stop for a moment and be lost in thought. From a small underground paper to a state without which all of Europe would now turn into a chain of trenches or into one enormous concentration camp."[56]

The Nazis were not the Germans of 1914. Europe, though, was not prepared for the truth.

THE POLITICS OF ANTI-FASCISM

The triumph of Mussolini and then Hitler made clear that extreme right-wing movements commanded tremendous appeal in a period of economic and political crisis. Fascism was a mass movement and its successes could not be dismissed as a temporary shift in popular opinion. The principal organizers and writers against fascism, however, were often Communists or Communist sympathizers who earnestly denounced Hitler yet remained blind, indifferent, or willfully silent about similar brutalities in the Soviet Union.

For many left-wing European intellectuals several factors contributed to this moral and political imbalance. Hitler always used violent and racist terminology; there could be no mistaking either his methods or his goals. When Hitler threatened the Jews, vowed to avenge Germany's defeat, and claimed absolute power for himself it was clear that he would carry out his promises. Stalin, though, was a great deceiver who knew how to invoke the humanistic language of socialism. Under the czars the Russian Empire had been a corrupt and brutal autocracy, and the Bolsheviks benefited from their image as a modern, forward-looking party that trumpeted intentions to serve the people. Stalin worked hard to conceal his crimes. There were few credible reports in the West about forced collectivization or the artificial famine that killed as many as five million people in the Ukraine. As Ehrenburg remarked in his memoirs, "Many Western writers did not understand the methods of socialist realism, but everyone understood Fascist methods: they promised bonfires for books and concentration camps for authors."[57]

Hitler and Stalin were both ruthless, but in the 1930s only Hitler threatened the stability and peace of the continent; Stalin was not seeking military expansion at the expense of his European neighbors. His foreign minister Maxim Litvinov advocated collective security, vainly trying to forge an alliance with the Western European democracies to forestall German aggression.

For Ehrenburg as well as numerous other European intellectuals the military threat of Nazism overrode whatever objections they had to Stalin's domestic regime. Many intellectuals who abhorred fascism, such as the French writer Romain Rolland, had misgivings about collaborating with Communists, a dilemma that would haunt the anti-Fascist movement until the Hitler-Stalin pact of 1939. The consolidation of Fascist regimes in Japan and Germany in the early 1930s, however, compelled them to work closely with Communists and remain silent about events inside the Soviet Union.[58]

Having articulate apologists in the West—especially individuals of the stature of Romain Rolland, André Gide, and André Malraux—served Stalin's purposes. Their solidarity with the Soviet Union helped to confuse international public opinion and distract it from the tyranny of Stalin's regime. A half century later it is incredible to read comments by these subtle intellectuals about life in the Soviet Union. In October 1934 Gide declared in Paris: "What for us will remain utopian will soon become reality in the USSR."[59]

———

Events in France soon compelled warring factions on the left to cooperate. The right-wing riot on February 6, 1934, had scared liberal and left-wing workers and intellectuals. Socialists and Communists put their differences aside. Even Stalin began to reassess his policies. By 1935 the Communist International, or the Comintern as it was generally called, which was the Kremlin's vehicle for guiding foreign Communists, formally adopted a "popular front" policy with Socialist parties against fascism. In spite of Stalin's initial idea Ehrenburg was not asked to lead MORP and it is unlikely he even knew what Stalin once had in mind. Rather, the French Communist writer Henri Barbusse was installed in December 1934 as its chairman and the headquarters moved to Paris. On the face of it Barbusse seemed like a suitable choice. He had become famous during World War I for his novel *Under Fire*, about a squadron of French soldiers enduring trench warfare; the book was awarded the Goncourt Prize. Barbusse was also a committed pacifist and by the early 1930s was heavily involved with Romain Rolland in organizing enormous conferences in Amsterdam and Paris to denounce fascism and war.

In his memoirs Ehrenburg wrote respectfully about Barbusse but in reality had misgivings about him. Barbusse was too committed a Communist and, Ehrenburg feared, too old (Barbusse turned sixty-two in 1935) to attract younger, more talented writers such as Malraux or prestigious, independent figures such as Aldous Huxley and E. M. Forster. Ehrenburg sent a letter to Mikhail Koltsov, his principal contact in Moscow, voicing his fears about the manner in which Barbusse was taking charge of MORP. Ehrenburg went so far as to try to discredit Barbusse by implying that he boasted of Stalin's personal support, a transgression the dictator would not normally abide.[60] Barbusse was about to publish a biography of Stalin in France, an overblown piece of propaganda that put him in good stead with the Kremlin and no doubt reinforced his "suitability" to lead MORP. Evidently Ehrenburg's attempt to discredit him was ignored and planning for the Congress continued.

The International Writers' Congress in Defense of Culture opened in Paris that June. Ehrenburg was one of its principal organizers, along with Gide and Malraux, Communists such as Jean-Richard Bloch and Paul Nizan, and the respected novelist André Chamson, who was an aide to Edouard Daladier, the Radical Socialist leader. Meetings were often held in Ehrenburg's living room. They had no staff or full-time secretaries. Typists worked in Gide's apartment while the organizers summoned colleagues from around the world as best they could.

The political atmosphere of 1935 helped make the Congress possible. As could be expected, Gide, Malraux, Barbusse, and Louis Aragon headed the French delegation, joined by Tristan Tzara, an originator of the Dada movement, and the Surrealist writer René Crevel. The British also provided an impressive group, including the novelists Aldous Huxley and E. M. Forster. The German émigrés Heinrich Mann, Bertolt Brecht, Ernst Toller, and Anna Seghers attended as well.

In the days before the Congress opened two events took place that exposed its political agenda and shook the confidence of its organizers. On June 16, André Malraux received word that Maxim Gorky would not be able to attend. Malraux was stunned. Gorky had been expected. It now seemed that Moscow "was making fun" of the organizers.[61] While the Congress was supposed to show solidarity with the Soviet Union, Stalin was sending a delegation of writers with little, if any, following in the West. Except for Ehrenburg, the journalist Mikhail Koltsov, and the novelist Alexei Tolstoy, the other delegates were mostly literary bureaucrats, mediocrities who did not belong in the same room with Malraux or Forster. Gorky may have been too ill to travel— he died the following year; but it was Stalin who selected, or at least approved, the makeup of the delegation, and Stalin may well have decided to keep Gorky inside the country.

Malraux quickly consulted Ehrenburg and Gustav Regler. Together they decided to have Gide approach the Soviet embassy and request that Boris Pasternak and Isaac Babel be included as additional delegates. Gide agreed to the plan. "It was our contribution to the Potemkin village that we wanted to erect for the sympathetic West," Regler observed.[62] Ehrenburg had more in mind than insuring Soviet prestige; he wanted to help his old friends. By appearing at the Congress Pasternak and Babel would demonstrate their popularity in the West, which could help protect them in Moscow.[63] The Kremlin accepted the proposal, dispatching the two writers to Paris; for both of them it was their last trip outside the Soviet Union.

A second crisis was more troubling. During that same week the writer André Breton came across Ilya Ehrenburg in a tobacco shop in Montparnasse. Breton was the recognized leader of the Surrealists. They were devoted to artistic experimentation and understood that "socialist realism" meant censorship and conformity. Breton was not willing to ignore Stalin's police state tactics, nor was he afraid to voice sympathy for the exiled Leon Trotsky. This split between orthodox Communists and the Surrealists led to bad feeling in French literary circles, and the Soviet press could not ignore the dispute's political implications; Ehrenburg had to denounce the Surrealists. Writing in *Literaturnaya Gazeta* two years earlier in June 1933, he had invoked the most vulgar terms he could find, calling them "fanatics of idleness" and advocates of "onanism, pederasty, fetishism, exhibitionism, even sodomy."[64] This insulting article (which was translated and published in Paris in 1934) helped to fuel the break between the Surrealists and the Communists. Breton had read Ehrenburg's article and was looking for a means to retaliate. Unable to restrain himself he began shouting and slapping Ehrenburg in the tobacco shop. Outraged, Ehrenburg proclaimed on the spot that Breton was assaulting a delegate to the International Writers' Congress and that henceforth Breton would be barred from participating.

At that time René Crevel was the only Surrealist who had managed to maintain a working relationship with the Communists; he was helping to organize the Congress and still wrote for *Commune*, a Communist-sponsored literary magazine edited by Louis Aragon. Crevel was determined to arrange a reconciliation and restore Breton to the program, but the Soviet delegates threatened to quit the Congress if Breton were to participate. As Ehrenburg argued, "People who resolve differences of opinion with their fists are Fascists." Crevel made one last attempt to convince Ehrenburg, pleading with him to reinstate Breton. Ehrenburg remained adamant. "Breton acted like a cop," he told Crevel. "If he is allowed to speak, the Soviet delegation will walk out."[65] Disheartened, Crevel returned home and killed himself that same night. Writing in his memoirs years later Ehrenburg confessed that "quite unwittingly I had played a certain role in this tragic story."[66] René Crevel, who was suffering from depression and tuberculosis, could not sustain his political and personal anguish. His suicide haunted the Congress and thirty years later Ehrenburg could barely acknowledge his own role in the tragedy.

The International Writers' Congress in Defense of Culture opened

on Friday evening, June 21, in the large Palais de la Mutualité. It was
unusually hot but the delegates and an audience of three thousand
patiently endured five days of speeches, translations, and debates. The
Congress exemplified the political dilemmas and moral failings of the
1930s. Dominated by Communists and their allies, the Congress was
meant to show faith in the Soviet Union and revulsion against fascism.
It was the height of the popular front. With liberals, Socialists, Communists, Christian believers, and Surrealists in attendance, Ehrenburg
and his colleagues constantly mediated among the delegates, trying to
resolve personal and political differences.

The arrival of Pasternak and Babel made Ehrenburg's work easier.
As his daily reports to *Izvestia* make clear, he used every opportunity
to stress how Pasternak upheld the honor of Soviet culture. Once the
poet's trip was confirmed, Ehrenburg wrote in his first report in *Izvestia* how an ordinary Frenchman who did not know Russian longed to
hear Pasternak's poetry, "the verse of a genuine, living poet."[67] Pasternak arrived in the hall on the evening of June 24, the next to last day
of the Congress, during a speech by the Leningrad poet Nikolai
Tikhonov. Until that time the Soviet delegates had hardly distinguished themselves. "They did not understand a word, though they
excelled at boasting of their five year plans," the ex-Communist Gustav Regler recalled. "It was all most embarrassing. They were as smug
as Hitlerites."[68] Yet Pasternak was given a hero's welcome, affording
Ehrenburg the opportunity to describe how "the auditorium stood up
and welcomed [him] with prolonged applause."[69] Pasternak spent over
a week in Paris seeing old friends such as Marina Tsvetaeva and
Yevgeny Zamyatin; but at the Congress, "he stepped quickly out of
the limelight," Gustav Regler tells us. "Ehrenburg protected him
against questioners."[70]

As hard as Ehrenburg and Malraux tried to maintain control of the
Congress they could not prevent every discordant appeal. The Congress's enthusiastic feeling of solidarity was shattered on two occasions
when Socialists raised the case of Victor Serge, a writer and militant
revolutionary who had been arrested in Moscow in 1933 and was serving three years of exile in the Urals.

Victor Serge was well-known to the European left. Born in Brussels
in 1890 to Russian émigré parents—his father was a distant cousin to
one of the assassins of Czar Alexander II—Serge had already served
time in French jails and joined a workers' revolt in Barcelona by the

time he reached Petrograd at the height of the civil war in 1919. Although he became a Communist party activist, he kept his libertarian beliefs and by 1926 joined the inner-party struggle against Stalin. Expelled from the party a year later, he was compelled to earn a living as an independent writer, sending his novels and historical works to France where he soon gained a wide following. But so-called Trotskyite connections led to his arrest in 1933.

On the second day of the Congress several non-Communist delegates spoke up about Serge, including Gaetano Salvemini, a former member of the Italian parliament who had been arrested by Mussolini. He did not hesitate to question Stalinist rule or ask why Victor Serge was a prisoner in the Soviet Union. Louis Aragon objected, claiming that for Salvemini even to mention Serge was "too much consideration for a counterrevolutionary."[71] The proceedings collapsed into chaos. Then Malraux, in a dramatic intervention, declared that anyone who mentioned Victor Serge would be expelled from the hall, exposing the organizers' submission to the Stalinist line.

Serge's supporters were not finished. They again took the floor on the last day of the Congress. Magdeleine Paz, a left-wing Socialist publisher and long-time friend of Serge, tried to speak over whistles and verbal abuse. Several Russians responded, including Ehrenburg—no doubt in line with his general instructions—who asserted the Soviet government's right to defend itself against enemies.

The Soviet press ignored the controversy, reporting only that two Trotskyites tried to use the Congress "for vile anti-Soviet attacks."[72] Ehrenburg failed to mention Victor Serge in his articles from the Congress or in his memoirs a quarter century later, in spite of the deep passion surrounding the case and its prominence in every Western account of the meeting. In his report for that day, he instead described how impressed he was by the courage of a German Communist who would soon return to underground work in Berlin. "I often ask fate for one thing," Ehrenburg wrote in *Izvestia*. "Not to wipe out from my memory those rare moments when a man feels with all his being why he lives."[73] Ehrenburg did not want to think about Serge's fate, preferring to remind himself of an overriding loyalty. As long as the Soviet Union remained a bulwark against fascism, Ehrenburg was ready to accept anything. "No matter what happened," he wrote about that era, "however agonizing the doubts, . . . one had to be silent, one had to struggle, one had to win."[74]

In his *Memoirs of a Revolutionary* Serge had little patience for the Paris Congress. It was organized "from certain Communist back rooms" to "arouse the French intelligentsia and buy over a number of famous consciences." For Serge Ehrenburg was "a hack agitator-novelist" who had forgotten "his flight from Russia, his banned novels, his accusation against bolshevism of 'crucifying Russia.' "[75] Expelled from the Soviet Union in 1936, Serge settled first in Brussels, then in Paris, and barely escaped the Nazi onslaught in 1940, when he was able to find refuge in Mexico. Isolated, harassed, constantly slandered in the Communist press of North America and Europe, Victor Serge lived and wrote in Mexico until his death in 1947.

ART AND POLITICS

While Ehrenburg was defining his role as a Soviet journalist his life with Lyubov Mikhailovna remained complex. It was in 1936 that he came closest to leaving her out of love for Denise LeCache, with whom he had an intense affair for most of the 1930s. Denise came from a distinguished French family. Her great aunt, Caroline Rémy Guebhard, had been a major figure in French cultural life at the turn of the century. Known as Séverine, she wrote about the Dreyfus case; Renoir painted her portrait. Denise's husband, Bernard LeCache, was also a journalist and author. Expelled from the Communist party in 1923, he made his name as an outspoken opponent of anti-Semitism. In 1927 he helped establish the International League Against Racism and Anti-Semitism. His novel *Jacob* depicted life among Russian-Jewish immigrants in Paris; *Quand Israel Meurt* (While Israel Was Dying) described the pogroms of the Russian civil war, including Denikin's massacres in Kiev, which Ehrenburg had witnessed. Denise was involved in left-wing political activity, entertaining workers in an actors' troupe before landing a prestigious job on French radio. Ehrenburg loved her deeply, but Lyubov Mikhailovna feared she herself would be helpless without him. Her emotional turmoil was so great that by 1936 she developed a nervous disorder in her legs that often prevented her from walking. Lyubov Mikhailovna's entreaties prevailed and Ehrenburg never abandoned his wife altogether.

Lyubov Mikhailovna remained an anxious woman, who often used nervous reactions to gain her husband's attention. One example remained vivid to their friend Alya Savich. Lyubov Mikhailovna used to become visibly upset whenever a large bug alighted on her clothing, but after Ehrenburg's death this hysteria subsided. Alya Savich noticed this and asked Lyubov Mikhailovna why she was no longer afraid of insects. "I was never really afraid," she replied, "but now I don't have anyone to impress."[76]

Although Lyubov Mikhailovna was always a talented painter, she never pursued her work seriously. People in Moscow assumed that Ehrenburg discouraged her, that he did not want artistic competition from his wife. In reality Ehrenburg encouraged her to paint and their dacha outside of Moscow had many examples of her work. Lyubov Mikhailovna rarely finished these pieces, however, lacking the will to concentrate and work that creative endeavor invariably requires.

———

In spite of his political assignments, frequent travels, and responsibilities as a journalist Ehrenburg maintained his productivity as a writer. Earlier in the 1930s, in addition to *Out of Chaos* he wrote two short novels: *Moscow Does Not Believe in Tears* in 1932, about the difficulties of a Russian artist who has the opportunity to study in Paris; and *Without Taking Breath* in 1934, which centers on heroic efforts to develop a modern timber industry in the Far North. In subsequent years Ehrenburg came to dislike *Without Taking Breath*. He felt the novel repeated too many themes from *Out of Chaos*. Nonetheless, the book contains several unusual episodes that belie expectations of what to find in a conformist Soviet novel. Ehrenburg wrote the book following a visit to Archangelsk, where he was impressed by the population's attitude and behavior as the region underwent rapid industrialization, much in the way he had been impressed by the workers' determination in Kuznetsk two years earlier. Around Archangelsk, though, he also observed the wholesale destruction of wooden churches and icons from the seventeenth and eighteenth centuries, and the neglect of Russian lace making, all fundamental elements of a traditional culture that sustained provincial village life for centuries; Ehrenburg felt compelled to describe this loss in *Without Taking Breath*. Three years later he brought out a collection of fifteen brief stories, *Beyond a Truce*, which focused on the anti-Fascist movement. In 1936 Ehrenburg also completed his most impressive work of those years, *A Book for Adults*, in which he explored many themes he would later address more fully in his memoirs. The book has an unusual scheme, alternating autobiographical chapters with scenes from a fictional story. Years later he dismissed *A Book for Adults* as a "rough draft" for *People, Years, Life*. "What I had planned was entertaining though wrong-headed."[77]

Still, the book has definite charms, including a range of portraits and events that helped make Ehrenburg such an unusual Soviet writer. He wrote about his religious grandfather, joining the Bolsheviks, struggling artists in Paris, and the travails of the Russian civil war. In one paragraph Ehrenburg could contrast Geneva, Moscow, and Paris, then provide impressions of Picasso, Modigliani, and Malraux in a way no other Soviet writer could match. He recalled how Picasso used to buy hundreds of paint tubes at a time after selling an expensive picture. In the past he had often run out of money and more than anything else Picasso "feared being left without any paint." Modigliani "lived on the edge of sanity," often turning to hashish for comfort. But Modigliani could also sit for hours at a time in a café and "draw portraits of his neighbors. They were all similar to the live models and they were all similar to each other."[78] Ehrenburg loved his friends, and by sharing memories of his bohemian youth gave Soviet readers a glimpse of a world that was becoming ever more distant and alien to them.

A Book for Adults also has astonishing emotional candor. When Ehrenburg wrote about visiting the Soviet Union he did not hesitate to say how often he encountered people who "laugh loudly, but live with clenched teeth." As for his own attitudes Ehrenburg was enigmatic, even mysterious: "There are many things I can only relate to close friends," he admitted. "There are many things I would not tell myself."[79]

A Book for Adults encountered difficulties in the Soviet Union. It originally came out in a journal—a common Soviet practice—but publication as a separate volume took an inordinately long time. "Whole pages with names that had fallen into disfavor were taken out of the book," Ehrenburg wrote in his memoirs. "In the copy which I have preserved one page is whiter and shorter than the rest—it was pasted in."[80] The names of Nikolai Bukharin and Grigory Sokolnikov had been removed. In spite of pressure from the editors of *Znamya* Ehrenburg managed to include innocuous material about these two old friends who were in trouble with Stalin when *A Book for Adults* first appeared in the spring of 1936.

Sokolnikov was older than I. He seemed like a master strategist to me: he spoke very little, hardly ever smiled, and loved chess. Bukharin was happy and noisy. When he used to come to my parents' apartment, the window panes shook from his laughter, and our pug-nosed dog Bobka invariably went after him, wanting to punish the violator of order.[81]

This was the ideologically offensive paragraph that Soviet authorities could not tolerate, going so far as to paste in a new page in the book's entire edition of ten thousand copies.

In spite of such crude censorship *A Book for Adults* still appeared. Ehrenburg was less fortunate with another project that was even dearer to his heart: to republish *The Extraordinary Adventures of Julio Jurenito and His Disciples*. On January 14, 1935, Ehrenburg mentioned the idea in a letter to Valentina Milman. Within two months she let him know of editing that would be required for the book to appear. Ehrenburg held firm, refusing to accept any cuts in the novel's text or apologize for what he had written. "I can explain the difference between the epochs," he wrote her, "but 'to dissociate myself,' 'to repent,' and so forth—no."[82] With these concerns in mind Ehrenburg wrote a preposterous epilogue for the novel, describing the subsequent fate of Jurenito's disciples in light of recent Soviet history and ideology.[83]

A new epilogue could not make up for the novel's ideological shortcomings, however, and Ehrenburg refused to go along with any tinkering of his text. In June 1936, after the epilogue had appeared in a Moscow journal—with the announcement that it would be included in a new edition of the novel—Ehrenburg wrote to Milman: "This is all very lamentable and very serious . . . I simply cannot agree on corrections and if they insist, it will be necessary to obtain cancellation of the contract."[84] The full text of *Julio Jurenito* did not appear in the 1930s, as Ehrenburg wished; it did not come out again in Moscow until 1991.

—

Ehrenburg also took other unusual initiatives in those years, among them his visit to Moscow in the fall of 1935, where he originally hoped to accompany André Gide. At that time Gide was the most prestigious intellectual ally of the Communists in France if not all of Western Europe. With Ehrenburg's encouragement Gide seemed ready to see Moscow for the first time. He was unpredictable, however; at the last minute Gide abruptly changed his mind, allowing a head cold to upset their plans. Ehrenburg complained bitterly to Malraux, as Gide's friend Maria van Rysselberghe recorded in her diary.

> Ehrenburg made a real scene. He believed that a question of health should not be the main concern. Rather, duty required that [Gide] go there, as much from the party's point of view as from the point of view of the general political situation. This change of heart at this very moment when it was so important to consolidate the Franco-Russian alliance, the intellectual alliance, is disastrous. Up to what point is Ehrenburg speaking in his own interest, up to what point does he think this trip by Gide would be held to his personal account? This is what is difficult to unravel.[85]

Ehrenburg and Lyubov Mikhailovna traveled to Moscow on their own.

More than a year after the Soviet Writers' Congress Stalinist control of the arts was growing more assertive. Unbeknownst to Ehrenburg a harsh campaign against "formalism" was about to be launched in January 1936, a campaign that would begin with an attack on the composer Dmitri Shostakovich and spread quickly to all the creative arts.

Upon arriving in Moscow in November 1935 Ehrenburg was invited to lecture by various organizations. His talks defended the same views he had expressed at the Writers' Congress—an artist's right to individual expression. He continued to extol Boris Pasternak, for example, telling the editors of *Znamya* how the audience in Paris responded with standing ovations only three times: "when André Gide approached the podium, after the speech of a revolutionary German writer, and when Boris Pasternak made his brief remarks. In this way, the Congress singled out three components of a great revolutionary literature: culture, politics, poetry."[86]

Later that month, on November 26, Ehrenburg spoke to workers in the film industry with remarks that bordered on the defiant. When he defended Isaac Babel—who was under tremendous pressure to submit material suitable for publication—Ehrenburg made his own opinions clear. "Babel's silence is significantly more valuable than the appearance of a series of books," he proclaimed. "When Babel is silent, then everyone waits, and they are right to wait." Ehrenburg spoke adoringly of Picasso as well, praised Eisenstein and Dovzhenko, who were losing favor in the Kremlin, and described Vsevolod Meyerhold—soon to be roundly condemned in the official press—as "a passionate artist, not only a wonderful one."[87]

Only Ehrenburg could invoke the work of Babel, Meyerhold, Eisenstein, and Picasso as examples of genuine artistic accomplishment to counterweight the sterile creative formulas that were increasingly prevalent in Moscow. His prestige abroad gave him greater freedom at home and he did not hold back. "Here we have the notion that a writer, a film director, or an artist is a special kind of department store. He can translate everything into reality by choosing among suggested themes. . . . It is absurd," Ehrenburg continued, using a favorite metaphor, "to advise an artist how he is supposed to fall sick with a theme." The very next day Ehrenburg appeared at a conference of the Soviet Artists' Union and did not hesitate to repeat what he told the cinematographers. Recalling the advice of Leo Tolstoy, Ehrenburg cited three requirements for writing well: "(1) Never write what does not interest you; (2) never write for money; and (3) if you cannot write what you want, don't write at all." With these principles in mind Ehrenburg drew an irreverent conclusion, recognizing that if too many people took Tolstoy's advice seriously it "would severely diminish the quantity of Soviet art in various fields, but perhaps the quantitative reduction would be compensated by qualitative improvement." Not everyone was heartened by Ehrenburg's presentation. One man challenged Ehrenburg's credibility by claiming that his wife was a student of Picasso, but Ehrenburg rejected the charge and all its implications. "My wife is not a student of Picasso," Ehrenburg answered back, "although there would not be anything outrageous about it if she were, because one can learn a great deal of worthwhile things from Picasso."[88]

Ehrenburg did not confine his argument to speeches. In an article for *Izvestia* he again defended Meyerhold's genius, reminding Soviet officials of the director's recent triumph in France, where he enthralled "all of theatrical, artistic, and literary Paris: from André Gide to Malraux, from Picasso to René Clair."[89] Soon after returning to Paris Ehrenburg wrote another article on a similar theme, this time about Vladimir Mayakovsky. Writing in *Izvestia*, he emphasized Mayakovsky's innovations and willingness to experiment, qualities Ehrenburg wanted to see preserved in Soviet art.[90]

Three weeks later the regime made further debate impossible.

Stalin's campaign against formalism began in earnest. The time had come to enforce the standards of "socialist realism." That January the dictator attended a performance of Dmitri Shostakovich's opera *Lady Macbeth of Mtsensk District*, which had been enjoying critical and popular acclaim in the Soviet Union, Europe, and the United States for two years. Stalin reacted differently. On January 28, 1936, an unsigned editorial "Muddle Instead of Music" appeared in *Pravda*. Dictated by Stalin, it directly threatened Shostakovich. "The listener is flabbergasted from the first moment of the opera by an intentionally ungainly, muddled flood of sounds. Snatches of melody, embryos of musical phrases, drown, escape, and drown once more in crashing, gnashing, and screeching. Following this 'music' is difficult, remembering it is impossible."[91] In other words, Stalin was prepared to prohibit any music he could not hum.

A week later *Pravda* published a second denunciation of Shostakovich. Later that month came the architects' turn, then the painters, then the country's playwrights and theater directors. Mikhail Bulgakov's plays were withdrawn from production. Vsevolod Meyerhold was taken to task. Meetings were hastily organized so that artists, writers, musicians, and actors could approve the articles in *Pravda*, denounce one another, and disavow their previous work.

Ehrenburg was not a principal target of this campaign. He was in France. His recent novels were politically acceptable while his role as a Soviet correspondent lent him a prestige that was difficult to condemn. Ehrenburg's admiration for Pasternak made him vulnerable to criticism, however. At one meeting the writer Vera Inber denounced Ehrenburg's report about Pasternak in which he had implied that only Pasternak had a conscience among Soviet poets.[92] At a Moscow conference in March the writer Lev Nikulin criticized Ehrenburg's literary enthusiasm. "Ehrenburg does a disservice to Pasternak when he alleges that loggers in the North read Pasternak's verse. . . . This, of course, is not true. And when in this way he tries to create literary weather abroad (it is always flattering to play literary politics), he is disorienting French readers and writers."[93]

Ehrenburg did not let such criticism pass unchallenged. In a letter to the party leader Alexander Shcherbakov on April 5, 1936, he reminded the Soviet bureaucracy what he was trying to accomplish. "I cannot pass over in silence the question of which 'literary politics' I allegedly conduct abroad," he wrote to Shcherbakov. "In this 'politics,' I am led by general political considerations and not by my personal literary tastes. The issue is not whether I like Pasternak, Babel, Sholokhov, etc., but what will more easily and reliably attract the European intelligentsia to us."[94] Although Ehrenburg was under less severe attack than many others, he wanted to prevent further criticism. He insisted that he either be permitted to express his views or he would desist from speaking altogether. By connecting his activity to Western public opinion Ehrenburg was also demonstrating his ability to manipulate Soviet bureaucrats who seemed to hesitate whenever he invoked the interest of a Western audience. It was this political talent that helped to keep him alive under Stalin and proved especially useful decades later under Khrushchev.

That February, in the midst of Stalin's campaign against formalism, Ehrenburg had an unexpected opportunity to confirm his worst fears when Nikolai Bukharin came to Western Europe for two months. Accompanied by his young, pregnant wife—other relatives, including his elderly father, remained in Russia, effectively as hostages—Bukharin was part of a three-man delegation to acquire the archives of the German Social-Democratic party that included precious manuscripts of Marx himself. The archives had been smuggled out of Nazi Germany and were in the safekeeping of Boris Nicolaevsky, an émigré Menshevik historian with whom Bukharin tried to negotiate their purchase. Ehrenburg wrote cautiously about his meetings with Bukharin, hoping in vain to include the material in *People, Years, Life* in the 1960s. Once, as they walked along the Seine, Bukharin became agitated. " 'I must return to my hotel, to write to Koba [Stalin's nickname].' I asked him what he would write about. It obviously would not concern the beauty of old Paris or the canvases of Bonnard, which he admired. With a confused smile, he told me, 'That's just the trouble. I don't know about what. But I have to write. Koba loves to receive letters.' "[95]

Bukharin returned to Moscow at the end of April. Within four months his fate was sealed. Stalin was preparing the first great "show trial," involving Lenin's close associates Grigory Zinoviev and Lev Kamenev. They were already under arrest and twice had been sentenced to long prison terms. Their trial took place in August 1936. Guided by Stalin's chief prosecutor Andrei Vyshinsky, the defendants admitted conspiring to murder Sergei Kirov and other party leaders. Bukharin, the country's former premier Alexei Rykov, and the founder of the Soviet trade union movement Mikhail Tomsky were also implicated and an investigation into their crimes was announced at the trial. Tomsky committed suicide the next day, preferring to escape the abuse and humiliation suffered by Zinoviev and Kamenev, who were soon executed. Bukharin then received a brief reprieve. The investigation against him was dropped in September and he was even invited to view the anniversary celebrations on November 7 from atop Lenin's Tomb. Yet in less than a month the press resumed its attacks, linking Bukharin to other "enemies of the people."

Meanwhile the second notorious purge trial took place in January 1937. Several of the defendants, among them Yury Pyatakov and Grigory Sokolnikov, were old friends of Bukharin's while another defendant, Karl Radek, had been Bukharin's associate at *Izvestia*. Charged with murder and espionage, the defendants all gave bizarre testimony, implicating themselves in fantastic crimes against the Soviet state. Bukharin and Rykov were principal targets of their testimony and faced arrest a month later.

Ehrenburg followed this tragedy from afar. He was out of harm's way in Paris but still felt despair over his friend's downfall, a despair he would express two years later, in 1938, after Bukharin's execution: "Let me not think too much," Ehrenburg would write, ". . . Let me not watch to the end . . . Not to see, not to remember what has happened to us in our lives." He asked only for "precise, urgent work" to distract him. His responsibilities as a journalist and political activist were clear. "The struggle with fascism was on and I was on the battlefield." He could not come to Bukharin's defense. "All we could do," Ehrenburg admitted years later, "was to press the hands of our hands now and then with particular warmth, for we were all involved in a great conspiracy of silence."[96] (For this sentence alone, the regime never forgave him.)

———

In April 1936 Ehrenburg visited Spain for two weeks and saw for himself the political tensions that would lead to civil war in three short months. Back in Paris he covered the national elections that brought Léon Blum and the Popular Front to power. Both Spain and France now had left-wing governments. Europe seemed more determined to resist fascism. In July Ehrenburg's daughter came on a visit from Russia. While Irina and Lyubov Mikhailovna vacationed in Brittany Ehrenburg stayed in Paris to finish his collection *Beyond a Truce* and file a story on France's delirious Bastille Day celebrations when over one million Parisians demonstrated, many carrying effigies of Hitler and

Mussolini. July 18 arrived, "a stifling summer evening on the Rue du Cotentin."[97] Ehrenburg was sitting and writing. It was midnight. He put his work aside and turned on the radio. The announcement startled him: a crowd was storming a barracks in Madrid. There was fighting around Oviedo. General Francisco Franco and General Emilio Mola had launched a military revolt. The Spanish civil war had begun.

EIGHT

The Spanish Civil War

Ehrenburg first visited Spain in August 1926. He was traveling in southern France and "by accident," as one might happen "into a courtyard through an open gate," he crossed the frontier and entered the small Spanish town of Seo de Urgel, six miles south of Andorra. He did not show his passport, but as he wrote at the time, "the caution of a writer and a border guard's carelessness took the place of a visa." In those years Spain was ruled by General Miguel Primo de Rivera. During Ehrenburg's brief visit he had time to see a few villages before a secret policeman advised him to leave and "restrain a curiosity incompatible with international relations."[1]

Four years later the military dictatorship collapsed. Almost immediately Ehrenburg applied for a visa but had to wait four months for permission to enter Spain. Detained at the Madrid train station, he was questioned by the deputy minister of the interior who admired his books but "for security purposes" requested a list of towns he intended to visit, then placed Ehrenburg under surveillance.[2] Undeterred,

Ehrenburg set about exploring Spain. With characteristic energy he traveled throughout the peninsula, wandering into small, remote villages that could only be reached on foot or by donkey. He also saw the renowned writer Miguel da Unamuno on the floor of the Cortes speaking "against the demands of [Spain's] national minorities." Unamuno was "a wonderful poet, a sad philosopher, and a hopeless politician."[3] For Ehrenburg there were too many intellectuals in Spain whose erudition impeded their political judgment; the Spanish parliament seemed full of them and their good intentions.

In the final days of his visit Ehrenburg met the legendary anarchist Buenaventura Durruti, a man who had already been expelled from over a dozen countries and survived more than one death sentence. Ehrenburg liked Durruti and his account of his 1931 trip climaxes with their meeting in a Barcelona café. They were not alone; a sculptor and a Communist party member joined them. An argument broke out among Ehrenburg's companions. "The sculptor for beauty. Durruti for freedom. The Communist for justice."[4] Listening to their argument, Ehrenburg understood that Spain could not avoid entanglement in the general contest over ideology and ideas that was raging in the rest of Europe. History was catching up with Spain. Her poverty, her weak democracy, and floundering parliament could not endure with impunity.

Five years later, in the spring of 1936, following the February elections when the Popular Front gained a majority of seats in the Cortes, Ehrenburg spent two weeks in Spain. He met many Communists, including the poet Rafael Alberti and the party stalwart Dolores Ibarurri—La Pasionara—who was now a member of parliament. He traveled to Oviedo in the northwestern region of Asturias where a revolt by miners in 1934 had been crushed by General Francisco Franco. Now there were strikes in Madrid and Barcelona. Right-wing journals clamored for a military takeover.

Ehrenburg had no illusions about Fascist intentions. Back in Paris he used every opportunity to alert public opinion, speaking at rallies and to groups of intellectuals, warning whoever would listen that "fascism was sharpening a knife."[5] After the generals' revolt in July the Spanish republic began the first concerted fight against fascism in Europe.

Ehrenburg never doubted that his place was in Spain. He asked *Izvestia* to send him but the editors hesitated to assign a wartime correspondent. At that time the "show trial" of Kamenev and Zinoviev was about to begin, further distracting the party apparatus from dealing with Spain. Meanwhile friends such as André Malraux, Jean-Richard Bloch, and Paul Nizan hurried to Madrid; and the *Pravda* journalist Mikhail Koltsov arrived in the Spanish capital on August 8, ostensibly to cover the war but in fact to serve as Stalin's personal emissary. Ehrenburg grew frustrated but did not remain idle. He telegraphed his first reports a week into the fighting on July 25, having based his accounts on articles in the French and Spanish press and on what friends such as Malraux had described. Ehrenburg had other resources as well. Immediately he put together an album of photographs and text from his earlier visits to Spain; the volume was completed within a month and sent to Moscow on August 24. Two days later Ehrenburg left by train for Barcelona without *Izvestia's* knowledge or consent.

He spent his first weeks traveling about Catalonia. The situation there was hopelessly muddled. "In Barcelona, no one could say who controlled Cordoba, Malaga, Badajoz, or Toledo," he recalled in *People, Years, Life*. Not until September 4 did Ehrenburg send his first dispatch, a description of an air attack on the small town of Mont-Florid. He was more than a war correspondent, however. Although he wrote more than fifty articles for *Izvestia* by the year's end, he also threw himself into political work inside Spain, using contacts to reinforce unity on the left. For Ehrenburg there was no tension between his responsibilities as a reporter and his desire to help the anti-Fascist cause. Just as in Paris he used his prestige as an *Izvestia* correspondent to rally public opinion against Hitler, so too in Spain he felt a tremendous urge to be actively engaged in the struggle against Franco. He "spoke at meetings, collected material on Fascist atrocities for the western press, and wrote anonymous pamphlets."[6] Rafael Alberti told him about García Lorca's execution, and one August night Ehrenburg experienced the first air raid on the capital.

Had the war remained an internal matter, without the intervention of outside powers, the republic might have successfully defended itself; but from the outset the rebels could rely on generous help from their allies in Germany and Italy. By the end of July German and Italian transport planes carried rebel troops from Morocco to Spain—the first military airlift in history—while Italian fighters accompanied merchant ships as they ferried several thousand more across the Mediterranean. French Prime Minister Léon Blum wanted to help the republic and at first allowed military supplies to cross the border into Spain; but England pressured France to stop the export of armaments, hoping to avoid war with Germany at all cost. The democracies (including the United States) remained neutral throughout the war, leaving the Spanish republic with few if any reliable allies.

Stalin began to weigh his options. The Soviet Union accepted the nonintervention agreement on August 23. Still, within a few days a team of highly experienced Soviet diplomats led by Marcel Rosenberg arrived in Spain, formally establishing relations with the republic. At that time, during the first months of the war, Ehrenburg was the only Soviet citizen with broad connections in Spanish society, particularly in Catalonia, where Luis Companys led an unusual coalition government of Communists, Socialists, anarchists, and Catalan nationalists. Ehrenburg felt comfortable dealing with Durruti. Many anarchists were familiar with his novels from the 1920s, most notably *Julio Jurenito*, and sensed that he was a kindred spirit. Ehrenburg also met with Companys and with José Diaz, the head of the Spanish Communist party. According to his memoirs when Ehrenburg explained the situation to Marcel Rosenberg—emphasizing that the Soviet Union should nurture a better relationship with several competing political movements in Catalonia—Rosenberg suggested that Ehrenburg cable his ideas directly to the Kremlin, which he did.

Ehrenburg also had a second project in hand. He successfully secured a van, a film projector, and a small printing press with the intent to travel along the front and entertain troops with combat propaganda. Ehrenburg wanted to educate the anarchists about guerrilla tactics; although they were daring and resourceful fighters, they had little respect for military discipline. Later in the fall he showed two classic Soviet films, *Chapaev* and *We from Kronstadt*, both depicting action in the Russian civil war. His friend Stepha Gerassi, a Ukrainian émigré in Paris, became his assistant and accompanied Ehrenburg on many of his visits to the front.[7]

On September 19 Ehrenburg returned to Paris where he continued to write about Spain for *Izvestia*. His articles generally emphasize the human side of the struggle, the suffering caused by the war and the courage of the republican defenders. As a fervent partisan Ehrenburg was not trying to provide objective reports of what he witnessed. While Ehrenburg was still in Paris the long-time revolutionary Vladimir Antonov-Ovseenko, who was being sent to Barcelona as a Soviet diplomat, sought him out. They had known each other in Montparnasse before the First World War, when both had frequented the Rotonde Café. Knowing Koltsov, Rosenberg, and Antonov-Ovseenko gave Ehrenburg contact with three of Stalin's most important representatives in Spain, lending Ehrenburg confidence in the first months of the civil war that he could make a substantial contribution to the republican cause.[8]

THE RETURN OF ANDRÉ GIDE

Before returning to Spain Ehrenburg received word that André Gide's visit to the Soviet Union that summer was about to have an unexpected outcome. Ehrenburg had encouraged Gide to make this trip, hoping to solidify Gide's attachment to Moscow. As happened with prestigious visitors, Gide received special treatment. He spoke at Maxim Gorky's funeral, appearing among members of the Politburo, including Stalin. Hundreds of thousands of postcards with Gide's portrait were distributed, making him an instant celebrity. His train was met by throngs of admirers. But Gide and his traveling companions soon realized these receptions were staged; they even noticed that impressive banners greeting them at each stop were carried on the train itself.[9]

Gide had never been a "true believer," in spite of his close identification with the Communist cause. Even at the height of his pro-Soviet involvement Gide shared misgivings with his friends. He believed the left's sectarian disputes harmed the cause itself. He disagreed with Soviet intolerance of homosexuality and was disturbed by news of executions that immediately followed Sergei Kirov's assassination. Ehrenburg sensed Gide's independence when they first met and even when he wrote enthusiastically about Gide in 1933, couched his praise with a note of caution. "He is a poet, a philosopher, a psychologist, a naturalist," Ehrenburg wrote, "but by no means is he a politician."[10]

Ehrenburg's instincts about Gide were correct. Gide kept his eyes open in the Soviet Union. Upon returning to Paris in September he began writing his impressions, producing in seven weeks a slim but explosive volume, *Return from the U.S.S.R.*, that would sharply divide French intellectuals. By today's standards, with mountains of eloquent personal testimony and Kremlin admissions of Stalin's crimes, Gide's book is a modest, restrained account. Written as much in sorrow as in anger—"too often what is true about the U.S.S.R. is said with enmity, and what is false with love"—Gide made clear that the country's intellectual and political conformity masked a brutal dictatorship that could offer no hope to Western societies.[11]

Gide's friend Maria van Rysselberghe recorded what happened when Ehrenburg called Gide near the end of October to ask for a meeting. "Evidently, he is coming to scout the terrain, to alert the U.S.S.R.," she observed. Ehrenburg tried to persuade Gide to hold back publication, adding that he approved of what Gide had written and "could say more if he wanted to!" But "when Russia is making an immense effort to help Spain," Ehrenburg concluded, "this is really not the time to attack her."[12] Gide held firm and *Return from the U.S.S.R.* appeared on November 5, 1936.

A quarter century later Ehrenburg wrote kindly about Gide in his memoirs. Gide had played a major role in rallying public opinion against fascism and as Ehrenburg candidly observed, "it would be stupid cowardice on my part, in evoking these years, to ignore [Gide]."[13] In the aftermath of his book's publication and enormous success, however, the Communist press reviled Gide without mercy. Party functionaries claimed he was "worse than Franco."[14] Ehrenburg joined the attack. On New Year's Day 1937 Ehrenburg included a denunciation of Gide in his holiday article. Gide, Ehrenburg wrote in *Izvestia*, "tried to pitch a tent between the trenches. A philosophizing tourist and a thoughtless puritan, he is gambolling between people who are building culture and others who are destroying it. In these difficult times, when our thoughts and feelings go out to the heroes of the Casa de Campo, we will respectfully be able to pass by this philosophizing, which turns out to be routine, narrow feeblemindedness."[15] Such attacks reinforced Ehrenburg's reputation as an apologist for Stalin, "an old cynic," in the words of the Polish writer (and onetime Communist) Aleksandr Wat, "who had wallowed in all the gutters of Paris."[16]

Ehrenburg was also accused of being a "propagandist" for Stalin by his old friend Ramón Gómez de la Serna. They had first known each other in the Rotonde but now, twenty years later in the spring of 1936, during Ehrenburg's visit to Madrid Gómez de la Serna saw a fundamental change in him. "He was no longer the timid, mild writer, a man of flesh and blood, but a kind of propagandist, hard and implacable." Most of all, Gómez de la Serna could not reconcile the official Soviet journalist with the young, long-haired bohemian poet he had once known in Montparnasse. "One is frightened by the insight gained from following the career of such a sophisticated international type over the years," Gómez de la Serna wrote in a profile of Ehrenburg, "watching him assassinate the artist in himself through his anguish, his fears, his concerns, and his profitable missions. Of course, under the distant control of the czar, he could write what he wanted in Paris, but now he could not do so, lest one day he disappear and never be heard from again. He is held as if by electricity and cannot let go."[17]

Ehrenburg's writings and sarcastic denunciations do border on demagoguery. He was devoted to the anti-Fascist cause and was also a Soviet journalist, two commitments that compelled him to compromise both the truth and his own conscience. Writing for Soviet publications from his base in France, Ehrenburg had to prove his loyalty at every turn. At times this required engaging in gratuitous attacks on individuals such as Victor Serge or André Gide, whose own consciences dictated opposition to the Stalinist line. At other times Ehrenburg's political commitment required his silence about crimes directed against people he knew, such as Bukharin, Babel, and Mandelstam, all of whom he genuinely loved. Ehrenburg, like everyone caught in the Stalinist net, understood the price of defying Soviet policies and adjusted his behavior to remain alive.

THE FALL AND WINTER OF 1936

By the end of September Stalin decided to sell arms to the Spanish republic and dispatch military advisers. For the republic the Soviet Union was virtually the only source of heavy armaments. Although there were never more than two thousand Soviet officers in Spain at any one time (the Italians and Germans sent many thousands more), for two years the famous international brigades organized by the Comintern sent an additional forty thousand men from all over Europe and North America during the course of the fighting. Many volunteers were political refugees from Germany and Italy; most of them were also Communist party members, and their units included a political commissar to monitor their loyalties.

Ehrenburg returned to Spain near the end of September. Determined to assist the war effort, he spent much of his time alongside anarchist and Communist militias. He was particularly eager to work with Durruti, sensing his willingness to adjust or even abandon unrealistic political principles in order to oppose Franco more effectively. Ehrenburg exerted tangible influence on Durruti, encouraging him to instill greater discipline in his men. Durruti's pragmatic policies—he advocated anarchist participation in the central government—may have cost him his life. With Madrid in jeopardy he led a column of anarchists into action in the western suburbs around the university campus, where intense fighting halted the Fascist advance. Durruti was killed there on November 21, and it is possible that he was shot by a fellow anarchist who resented the agreement to take part in the national government.

———

Ehrenburg reached Madrid in December. The city was still under attack by artillery and from the air, making it the first great metropolis to suffer what so many others—London, Tokyo, Leningrad, Rotterdam—were later to endure. Ehrenburg shared the city's mood with his Soviet readers:

> A German plane dropped a bomb here today. The alley is gone: ruins, earth, garbage. Firemen. They dragged out two corpses, an old woman and a little girl. The girl has no legs. Her face is at peace, as if she were a broken doll. . . . What is there to write about? Scream into the phone again and again that the Fascists are wild beasts?[18]

The Soviet Union was now heavily involved in the conflict and Ehrenburg had become a principal spokesman for the republican cause. In January he returned to Paris where he put together a second volume about Spain, combining his pieces from 1936 with photographs and images from anti-Fascist posters by Spanish artists. Ehrenburg left France in February and spent the next six months covering the war. February was a grim month for the republic. Malaga was captured by the rebels in the south while Barcelona came under fire for the first time.

Ehrenburg stayed in Madrid or Barcelona but often traveled to Valencia, where the Spanish government had transferred its offices and where André Malraux was directing a squadron of volunteer pilots that included a Jew from Palestine named Yehezkel Fikker. Fikker saw Ehrenburg on several occasions and remembered his particular pride over meeting a Palestinian Jew among the republic's defenders. Fikker knew of Ehrenburg's strict self-control and to his surprise glimpsed Ehrenburg in a moment of unconstrained emotion, when a young boy was killed by shrapnel near the squadron's barracks. "We saw he was dead and some of us broke out crying," Fikker recalled. "All of a sudden I saw Ehrenburg. He was standing to the side looking at the dead boy in our arms. Huge tears flowed from his eyes."[19]

STALINISM AND THE SPANISH CONFLICT

Ehrenburg understood that the physical risks of serving in Spain were compounded by acute political hazards. The tragedy of the Spanish civil war involved more than the triumph of fascism; the war coincided with the years of Stalin's Great Purge, and just as Soviet society was riddled with informers, so too were the ranks of Soviet officers and diplomats in Spain permeated with security agents. Ehrenburg knew that he was being closely monitored. Many of the Soviet "volunteers" were also anxious about being in a foreign country and suspicious of Ehrenburg. For them Ehrenburg was an outsider whose loyalty to Stalin could not be assumed. "He is not quite our own," some of them told Stepha Gerassi, "spending all his time in foreign countries." Ehrenburg in turn warned Stepha to keep her opinions to herself. "Don't tell them how much you like the Russian people, but don't like Stalin," he cautioned her.[20]

Ehrenburg intensely disliked André Marty, the supreme political commissar of the International Brigades. Marty was a long-time member of the French Communist party who first gained acclaim in 1919 when as a young sailor in the French Black Sea Fleet he protested attempts to assist White Russian forces. Marty enjoyed Stalin's full confidence and repaid it with fanatical loyalty. Ehrenburg later described Marty as "imperious, short-tempered, and always suspecting everyone of treason. . . . He spoke and sometimes acted like a man suffering from paranoia."[21] Ernest Hemingway painted a devastating portrait of Marty in For Whom the Bell Tolls as a Communist who orders countless executions of loyal volunteers; "to question him was one of the most dangerous things that any man could do."[22]

When Ehrenburg returned to Spain in February 1937 his close friend Ovady Savich came with him to represent Komsomolskaya

Pravda. Within a few months Savich was asked to write for TASS, the Soviet foreign news agency, because the previous correspondent, Yelena Mirova, had been recalled to Moscow. When Ehrenburg asked his daughter Irina about Mirova over the telephone Irina discussed the weather and refused to reply. Mirova was no longer among the living.

Ehrenburg had begun the war with ambitious ideas, intending to make a broad contribution to the anti-Fascist cause, but after several months in Spain he sensed the need to protect himself; Stalin's agents were becoming more ubiquitous. Once he returned from Paris in February 1937 Ehrenburg began to withdraw from explicitly political initiatives. He put aside his work with the propaganda van and his role as an intermediary between Soviet diplomats and the anarchists.

In *For Whom the Bell Tolls* Ernest Hemingway captured the atmosphere of deception and intrigue that characterized Soviet involvement in Spain. In one famous episode the idealistic American Robert Jordan visits Gaylord's, a hotel near the Prado museum that served as headquarters for the Soviet mission. "It was at Gaylord's," Robert Jordan thinks to himself, "that you learned that Valentin Gonzalez, called El Campesino or the Peasant, had never been a peasant but was an ex-sergeant in the Spanish Foreign Legion."[23] El Campesino was a legendary figure in Spain, a daring and effective commander whose famous beard and "peasant origins" embodied the republic's determination. It was only a small lie, a helpful exercise in propaganda, to dissemble about his background. Ehrenburg was part of this charade. In *Izvestia* he dubbed El Campesino the "Chapaev of the Spanish Revolution."[24]

Ehrenburg met Ernest Hemingway for the first time in Mikhail Koltsov's hotel suite. Their initial encounter has been described often. Speaking in French, Ehrenburg asked Hemingway if he was filing news articles and feature stories in the American press, just as Ehrenburg was doing for Soviet journals. But to Ehrenburg's astonishment Hemingway reacted violently, grabbing a whiskey bottle as if to go after him with it. Others in the room restrained Hemingway and quickly cleared up the misunderstanding, for Hemingway had mistaken the French *nouvelles* (or news) for the Spanish *novelas* (or novels) and thought Ehrenburg was teasing him about his work.

They soon became friends and met in Madrid cafés or traveled to the front together. Following the battle of Guadalajara in March 1937, they watched republican forces mop up after an important victory, bringing Italian grenades "red as large strawberries" from the Fascist trenches.[25] The photographer Robert Capa caught their last meeting in Spain. It took place in December 1937 in a Barcelona hotel. Ehrenburg was sleeping deeply when Hemingway woke him. Capa captured that moment, with Ehrenburg reclining in bed, unshaven, his hair unkempt, and Hemingway standing over him. (See Plate 5.)

Hemingway provides a less than flattering glimpse of Ehrenburg in *For Whom the Bell Tolls*. The scene takes place in Gaylord's, when the Ehrenburg character (whose name is not mentioned) approaches Karkov (Koltsov) with unmistakable deference. It is Karkov who expresses the full, worldly cynicism of knowing "how it really was; not how it was supposed to be," while Ehrenburg, whose depiction as the *Izvestia* correspondent with "a pendulous under-lip" makes him unmistakable, comes off as a weak-minded cipher.[26] Ehrenburg was not offended by this appearance in Hemingway's novel. He admired *For Whom the Bell Tolls*, even though it was fashionable in left-wing circles to condemn Hemingway's portrait of André Marty and the cynical depiction of the Soviet contingent at Gaylord's. Ehrenburg knew better. He knew how close it all came to the truth.

Ehrenburg, though, could not speak the truth himself, constrained as he was by the Stalinist line. When he wrote about Durruti or other republican units he always emphasized their compassion for captured soldiers. Ehrenburg romanticized Durruti's humanity. The republican side in fact was often as brutal as the Fascist. Simone Weil, who accompanied Durruti's men on maneuvers, was a more honest observer. She wrote to George Bernanos on the execution of a fifteen-year-old Fascist soldier by Durruti himself.[27] Other omissions were equally troubling. When Ehrenburg wrote about anarchist units on the Aragon front he recalled their initial arrangements in August 1936 and how independent "columns" made it impossible to coordinate strategy; now, by the spring, greater discipline had been achieved and the anarchist fighters were better integrated into the republican army. Ehrenburg could not mention, however, that Stalin's secret police carried out arrests and assassinations of anarchist leaders in Catalonia to insure cooperation. Anti-Communist Socialists were also targeted, especially members of the United Marxist Workers Party, or the POUM (as it was universally known), who were identified as followers of Trotsky.

In March the Spanish Communist party held a conference in Valencia. Its influence was growing exponentially as Soviet aid enhanced

Communist prestige. At the conference party leaders denounced their erstwhile left-wing allies. As Ehrenburg dutifully reported, José Diaz railed against "demagogues who promise the people everything and who will lead it to defeat." His speech made clear he was referring to "sabotage and the treacherous, subversive work of Trotskyites."[28] By April a virtual civil war within the broader conflict broke out in Barcelona pitting anarchists and anti-Stalinist Socialists against the Communists. Ehrenburg was covering Madrid and the southern front in April, making it easier for him to avoid writing about the conflict in Catalonia.

THE INTERNATIONAL WRITERS' CONGRESS

The cause of republican Spain continued to evoke passionate support among liberal and left-wing writers and intellectuals. Even if Americans and Western Europeans had understood Stalin's policies in Spain, the intervention of Nazi Germany and Fascist Italy was sufficient reason to defend the republic. In spite of the conflict, or perhaps because of it, the International Writers' Congress in Defense of Culture summoned its followers to Valencia in July 1937. About eighty delegates came, including André Malraux, the British poet Stephen Spender (who had recently joined the Communist party), the Mexican writer Octavio Paz, Chile's Pablo Neruda, and the American critic Malcolm Cowley.

Just as the Congress was about to convene Ehrenburg twice came close to being killed. He and Malraux were being taken to Madrid when their car collided with a truck carrying artillery shells. Accidents were quite common on this road. Luckily they survived without a scratch. Two days later Ehrenburg got into difficulty due to recklessness of a different sort. Just after the delegates reached Madrid republican forces launched a major attack on Brunete, a small village west of the capital. Two Soviet delegates learned of the offensive and insisted on accompanying Ehrenburg to the front; they made it safely to Brunete, where the Fascists had been routed the day before. While they lingered there, however, the Fascists carried out a counterattack that brought the road back to Madrid under heavy fire. It was only good fortune that Ehrenburg avoided an assault by Franco's Moroccan troops.

Two other well-known foreigners met a different fate near Brunete.

Two weeks after Ehrenburg's close call Julian Bell, the beloved nephew of Virginia Woolf, was killed while driving an ambulance in Brunete; and on July 25 Robert Capa's companion Gerda Taro was fatally injured when a loyalist tank sideswiped her while she was riding on the running board of a car; she was badly mangled and died of her wounds the next morning.

———

The proceedings of the Congress reflected more than the violence of the civil war. A month before it opened the Great Purge in Moscow had reached a new and perplexing chapter with the trial of several leading generals, including Mikhail Tukhachevsky, Yona Yakir, and Jerome Uborevich. Condemned as traitors, they were immediately shot. Ehrenburg reacted bitterly to the news of their executions, but there was nothing he could do and hardly anyone he could talk to. Like many of the Russians in Spain Ehrenburg was in shock over the fate of Tukhachevsky.[29] Also in June, Soviet agents carried out a bloody purge of the POUM, who were falsely accused of conspiring with General Franco.* The POUM leader Andrés Nin was arrested and disappeared; he was later shot after resisting a brutal interrogation.

Two weeks later delegates to the Congress began arriving, including a large contingent of Soviet writers. Ehrenburg dubbed the Congress a "traveling circus" in his memoirs: after opening in Valencia on July 4 it continued in Madrid on July 6, moved on to Barcelona, and then ended two weeks later in Paris.[30] The conference hardly qualified as a holiday outing. In Valencia the delegates gathered in the town hall, which lay half in ruins because of a recent attack, and in Madrid an artillery bombardment roused them from their beds at night.

Much like their counterparts in Paris two years before, the Soviet delegation resorted to crude rhetoric and set the tone for much of the proceedings. Gide's friend Jef Last attended the Congress and could not help noticing that the "main object of the Russian delegation [was] to get some sort of motion carried against André Gide," an initiative Last helped to block.[31] Gide's book had proven to be a threatening success, but the vehemence of the attacks on the French writer were equally designed to divert attention from the fate of Andrés Nin.

Although Ehrenburg was a principal organizer of the Congress, once

———

*George Orwell fought in a POUM unit and described the political intrigue of that spring in *Homage to Catalonia*.

it began he kept a distance from its harsh and public Stalinist discourse. To the chagrin of his Soviet colleagues he refused to join their attacks on Gide or denounce Red Army generals such as Mikhail Tukhachevsky and Yona Yakir. Reporting on the Congress for *Izvestia*, Ehrenburg avoided mentioning assaults on the executed generals and only referred to attacks on Gide by quoting the Spanish writer José Bergamin, who had accused Gide of slander and of trying to compromise the defense of Madrid.[32]

As the political atmosphere grew more dangerous Ehrenburg guarded his privacy, knowing that every shrug or inadvertent word could be used against him. Both Soviet and Western colleagues noted his characteristic reserve. Upon returning to Moscow the journalist Vsevolod Vishnevsky spoke to the editors of *Znamya* on August 7, 1937. "Ehrenburg still has his usual style," Vishnevsky told them. "He keeps to himself. That is his nature."[33] The British journalist Alexander Werth had a similar impression. Seeing Ehrenburg in Madrid, Werth found him "cagey and uncommunicative."[34]

Ehrenburg remained in France for several months following the Congress. He wrote a book about the civil war, *What a Man Needs*, in the form of short vignettes from the front, including sketches of action on the Fascist side. He also focused on the anarchists and their intense feelings of brotherhood for each other, qualities that appealed to Ehrenburg's own romantic nature; despite Soviet propaganda and even violence against the anarchists Ehrenburg celebrated their virtues.

By the fall of 1937 the war began moving decisively against the republic, whose advances could not be sustained; at any time, it seemed, Franco had the luxury of calling in German planes or Italian troops. Stalin's strategy also was becoming clearer: he supplied enough arms to keep the republic from being defeated, but not enough to allow it to win. He did not want a direct confrontation with Germany and Italy and hoped to keep the republic going until France and England reversed their policies of nonintervention. Only then would the republic have enough heavy armaments to overcome Franco's armies.

The internal situation in republican Spain was increasingly dominated by Soviet interference and manipulation. Numerous Soviet diplomats, journalists, and officers were recalled to Moscow where they disappeared in the purges. Marcel Rosenberg, Vladimir Antonov-Ovseenko among many others, even Mikhail Koltsov, who returned to Russia in the fall of 1937 never to see Spain again, were "destroyed," as

Ehrenburg put it in his memoirs, "for no reason at all by their own people." It is impossible to know for certain if Stalin targeted them because they opposed his policies or because, as agents of his policies, they knew too much and could not be trusted to keep silent. Others came to Spain to represent Soviet interests. Too many of them were neither "diplomats nor soldiers," as Ehrenburg once put it; they were members of Stalin's secret police.[35]

Ehrenburg stayed in France. He wrote mostly about European politics, returning to earlier themes of the 1930s when the democracies were first mesmerized by Hitler. In November 1937 he also wrote his most extensive attack on André Gide in response to Gide's appeal to the Spanish republican government on behalf of political prisoners in Catalonia. Ehrenburg lost all constraint. After describing massacres of workers and women, Ehrenburg turned on Gide, denouncing him for refusing to protest "against the hangmen of Asturias," but instead criticizing the republican government "for arresting members of the POUM." In Ehrenburg's eyes Gide was now "a new ally of the Moroccans and the blackshirts, a wicked old man, a renegade with an unclean conscience, [and] the Moscow crybaby."[36]

Gide felt compelled to respond. Printed in the independent journal La Flèche (The Arrow), his answer was sharp and brief. "I take it as a matter of honor to deserve the insults which are directed at me by the Fascists. Those which come to me from my friends of yesterday," Gide wrote, pointing directly at Ehrenburg, "can at first make me extremely sad, but I stop being sensitive when they exceed a certain degree of ignominy." Gide made clear that he considered it hopeless to send humanitarian appeals to Franco while his "great love [for the cause of republican Spain] made him want to protect it from compromises that dishonor it."[37]

A month later Ehrenburg returned briefly to Spain. The republicans were preparing a major offensive at Teruel, an operation that would last two months and end in terrible defeat. In December, though, Ehrenburg was hopeful, making note of the extreme cold and its discouraging effect on Franco's Moroccan and Italian mercenaries. He was back in Paris after a couple of weeks and there made a foolhardy, near-fatal decision: to visit Moscow and Tbilisi on a short vacation. To avoid Germany he and his wife traveled by train through Italy and Austria, reaching Moscow on December 24, 1937.

THE GREAT PURGE

In spite of all he knew Ehrenburg was not prepared for the fear that engulfed the Soviet capital. One friend immediately asked how he could have allowed himself to come. Didn't he know what was going on? His naiveté startled his daughter as well. Ehrenburg and Lyubov Mikhailovna stayed with Irina and Boris Lapin on Lavrushinsky Lane in an imposing, grey stone, ten-story building constructed in the 1930s as a residence for literary figures. Boris Pasternak was one of many writers who lived there.

It was not a secure haven. That first evening Ehrenburg noticed a curious handwritten sign in the elevator. "It is prohibited to put books down the toilet. Anyone breaking this order will be traced and punished." (It seemed dangerous to own books by newly exposed "enemies of the people.") Ehrenburg later learned that residents of the building wanted the noisy elevator to be closed at night; it kept them awake as they listened, wondering anxiously where it would stop and where the next arrest would come.

Ehrenburg's account of the Great Purge has been superseded by others more vivid and detailed, but *People, Years, Life* was published less than a decade after Stalin's death and was the first to describe the atmosphere of confusion and terror that overwhelmed Moscow's intellectual community.

After we entered the apartment, Irina leaned toward me and quietly asked, "Don't you know anything?"

We stayed up half the night as she and Lapin told us what was happening: an avalanche of names and after each one a single word, "taken."

"Mikitenko? But he was just in Spain and spoke at the Congress." "So what," Irina replied. "There are people who gave speeches or had an article in *Pravda* only the day before."

I was upset and kept asking after each name, "But why him?" Lapin tried to think up reasons: Pilnyak had been to Japan, Tretyakov met often with foreign writers, Pavel Vasilev drank and talked too much, Bruno Jasenski was Polish and all the Polish Communists had been taken away . . . Irina answered each time, "How should I know? No one knows." With a rueful smile, Lapin advised, "Don't ask anyone. And if someone starts talking, just keep quiet."[38]

When Ehrenburg arrived on Christmas Eve *Literaturnaya Gazeta* announced he would be returning to Spain in two weeks.[39] But he soon learned this would not be possible. "Everything takes time now," he was told. "The big shots are very busy. I would have to wait a month or two."[40] Ehrenburg in fact had to stay more than five months.

Friends explained their fear. Mikhail Koltsov had warned Ehrenburg not to return to Moscow and was shocked to see him in Russia.[41] "He took me into the large bathroom adjoining the office and there let himself go," Ehrenburg later recalled. "Here's the latest anecdote for you. Two Muscovites meet. One says, 'Have you heard the news? They've taken Teruel.' The other asks, 'Oh, and what about his wife?' "[42] Vsevolod Meyerhold lost his theater in January; it was closed for being an "alien" element in Soviet cultural life. People Ehrenburg knew kept a suitcase with two changes of underwear on hand at all times. He hardly tried to write, but famous for his articles from Spain, he gave as many as fifty talks during his five months in the country.

Ehrenburg was especially eager to see Isaac Babel. He "found 'the wise rabbi' sorrowful, but his courage, his sense of humor, his story-teller's gift never left him."[43] Babel described a factory where prohibited books were pulped to make paper and homes for orphans whose parents were still alive. "Today a man talks frankly only with his wife, at night with the blanket pulled over his head," was how Babel described the terror.[44]

No one knew what to believe. "We thought (probably because we wanted to think that way) that Stalin did not know about the senseless violence against Communists and the Soviet intelligentsia," Ehrenburg admitted in his memoirs. A long-time Communist such as Vsevolod Meyerhold told Ehrenburg that the repression was concealed from Stalin. Boris Pasternak too shared this common illusion. Ehrenburg came across him one night while they were both walking their dogs. "[Pasternak] waved his arms as he stood among the snowdrifts: 'If only someone would tell Stalin about everything.' "[45] Of course Stalin knew, but the terror was so profound and the sense of uncertainty so intense that few could bear the truth that Stalin had initiated the terror for his own purposes; there was no one to appeal to.

For Ehrenburg the trial of Nikolai Bukharin was the preeminent event of his sojourn in Moscow. Aside from Bukharin there were twenty other defendants, including two prominent diplomats, Nikolai Krestinsky, a former ambassador to Germany, and Christian Rakovsky, who had represented the Soviet government in Paris and London. They were accused of participating in an enormous conspiracy whose right-wing members were directed inside the country by Nikolai Bukharin and whose left-wing members were led from abroad by Leon Trotsky. Bukharin was accused of ordering Kirov's assassination and even of attempting to kill Lenin in 1918 when an attack on the Bolshevik leader almost succeeded.

Ehrenburg never had any illusions about the case. He was given a pass into the courtroom at Stalin's behest. As Ehrenburg later recalled, "One important journalist, who soon perished on the direct orders of Stalin, told the editor of *Izvestia* . . . in the presence of a dozen colleagues, 'Arrange a pass for Ehrenburg to the trial. Let him see his little friend.' " The journalist was Mikhail Koltsov, who was quoting Stalin himself; only one as evil as Stalin would have wanted Ehrenburg to see Bukharin in the dock. Although Ehrenburg attended the trial's opening sessions on March 2, he did not write about what he saw until the 1960s, when he hoped to advance Bukharin's rehabilitation with a candid portrait in *People, Years, Life*.

[The accused] related monstrous things and their gestures and intonations were unusual. It was they, but I did not recognize them. I don't know how Yezhov secured such behavior. Not one Western author of pot-boiler detective novels would be able to publish such a fantasy. . . .

It was all an unbearably terrible dream for me and I was not able to say a word about it even to Lyuba and Irina. Today as well I don't understand it at all; Kafka's novel *The Trial* seems realistic to me, a thoroughly sober work of art.[46]

Ehrenburg could barely speak when he returned to Lavrushinsky Lane. He told his family it was horrible and then lay down on the sofa, his face to the wall, and could not eat for several days.[47]

Izvestia expected him to write about the court proceedings. "I virtually screamed 'no,' and after hearing my voice," Ehrenburg recalled, "no one suggested to me that I write about the trial." As Savich heard him say, "There are things that a decent person does not write about."[48]

During those months in Moscow Ehrenburg wrote only two articles about Spain and gave one published interview. The first article, entitled "To Life," appeared less than two weeks after Bukharin's execution and describes the bombing of Barcelona and Franco's reliance on German and Italian aid.[49] None of this is remarkable. Near the end of the piece, however, Ehrenburg recalls the grotesque slogan of General Millan Astray, "Muera la inteligencia! Viva la muerte!" ("Death to the intellectuals! Long live death!"), which often animated Fascist rallies. Ehrenburg wrote hundreds of eloquent, angry pieces on the Spanish civil war but it seems more than coincidental that the one article to cite General Astray's bloodcurdling cry came after Bukharin's trial, when Ehrenburg saw a close friend destroyed firsthand and had good reason to fear for his own life. Reading this article, one cannot help wondering if the "life" he intended to defend was not his own and if the title itself, coming during a *walpurgisnacht* of recrimination and death (during Bukharin's trial crowds gathered at night around large bonfires near the Kremlin and screamed for the defendants' execution) was not a veiled or at least unconscious protest against the purges and the fate of so many of his friends. Fascists cried "Death to the intellectuals! Long live death" while Soviet prosecutors screamed for the blood of "enemies of the people." Ordinary Soviet citizens would never dare compare Stalin with Franco, not even in the most remote region of their consciousness; but Ehrenburg was no ordinary Soviet citizen.

Following Bukharin's execution, which was publicly announced on March 15, Ehrenburg could no longer wait patiently to leave the country. He decided to appeal directly to Stalin, describing Spain as the place where his talents were needed most. Several weeks went by before Ehrenburg was summoned to *Izvestia* and told he would have to remain. "Comrade Stalin thinks that in the present international situation, it is better for you to stay in the Soviet Union." His wife would be permitted to bring their books and belongings from Paris. Ehrenburg had every reason to assume he was trapped. At that moment he took an unheard-of initiative. Over the objections of his family Ehrenburg appealed again to Stalin and repeated his request for permission to leave. "I realized, of course, that I was behaving foolishly. More than likely, after such a letter I would be arrested. Nevertheless, I sent it off. . . . In my nervous state, I was hardly able to eat." His gamble succeeded, as a call from *Izvestia* confirmed. On May Day Ehrenburg was in Red Square covering the pageantry, and soon after he and Lyubov Mikhailovna left by train for Helsinki. Their sense of relief was profound. Once they reached Finland, "Lyuba and I sat in silence on a bench in a public garden," Ehrenburg wrote in his memoirs. "We could not even talk to one another."[50]

It is impossible to establish why Soviet officials changed their minds and let him go. Ehrenburg offered no explanation in his memoirs other than to say that he "lived at a time when the fate of a man did not resemble a game of chess but a lottery."[51] Yet Ehrenburg's behavior at this perilous moment remains unique, and his survival, in 1938 and later, was more than a fortuitous turn of fate. Ever since 1924, when Stalin took notice of Ehrenburg in a famous lecture, Ehrenburg's life depended on the will of one man. Other figures less well-known or otherwise more vulnerable could be arrested and liquidated on the orders of scores, hundreds, or even thousands of party leaders or policemen. Tens of millions of people were picked up in the 1930s. Stalin could not have agreed to each arrest. "If he had read the lists of all his victims," Ehrenburg wrote, "he would not have been able to do anything else."[52] Once categories of victims were identified—kulaks, religious believers, nationalists of various stripes, Zionists, Trotskyites, Bukharinites—it was up to local officials to fulfill their quota of arrests. No one, however, would want responsibility for liquidating a man who had gained Stalin's personal favor. Having made note of Ehrenburg once, Stalin might ask for him at any time. While Ehrenburg could be threatened, it would require a nod from Stalin to touch him.

Ehrenburg must have sensed this, giving him confidence to call attention to himself in the terrifying weeks following Bukharin's trial. It was a desperate strategy—even a reckless one, as his wife and daughter insisted—but the system was so unpredictable that Ehrenburg decided to throw caution to the wind. Perhaps his first letter was never shown to Stalin; or perhaps Stalin asked to see Ehrenburg's dossier and then satisfied, dispatched Ehrenburg back to Europe. In any case Ehrenburg did not wait on Lavrushinsky Lane for a noisy elevator to stop in the middle of the night. He refused to be a spectator to his own tragedy. Ehrenburg by then no doubt understood how fortunate he had been in December 1934 not to have met Stalin personally; seeing the dictator face to face would have increased the likelihood of his arrest in the future. Unlike Mikhail Koltsov Ehrenburg learned to keep his distance from the Kremlin.

Only recently has the extent of Ehrenburg's vulnerability been uncovered. Many years after Bukharin's execution Ehrenburg learned from Bukharin's secretary and from his widow, Anna Mikhailovna Larina—who spent nearly two decades in labor camps and exile—that he almost became a defendant in Bukharin's trial. Kark Radek claimed under interrogation that Ehrenburg accompanied Bukharin to his dacha where, "over an omelette," Bukharin and Radek plotted a coup d'état.[53] Although Radek was condemned in February 1937, he was not executed immediately, and there is reason to believe that Bukharin's interrogators arranged for Radek to confront Bukharin personally with false testimony. By March 1938, however, Ehrenburg no longer figured in the case.

Similar events occurred a year later. This time the principal victims were Vsevolod Meyerhold and Isaac Babel.[54] Meyerhold was arrested on June 20, 1939, at the age of sixty-five. Severely beaten by his interrogators, he "confessed" to being a Japanese spy, a conspirator alongside Rykov, Bukharin, and Radek, and a member of a Trotskyite cell, having been "recruited by Ilya Ehrenburg." Only in 1955, when Meyerhold's case was reviewed and he was rehabilitated, did Ehrenburg learn of these accusations.

Isaac Babel was also arrested in 1939, about a month before Meyerhold. Under severe interrogation that included three days and nights without sleep—the notorious "conveyor belt"—Babel too was forced to accuse Ehrenburg of recruiting him into a Trotskyite cell in which André Malraux had also served as an "espionage agent." Babel was executed on January 27, 1940; Meyerhold and Mikhail Koltsov were shot five days later. All three were "tried" before Stalin's infamous "troika" courts, three-man tribunals that condemned "enemies of the people" in proceedings that might last a few minutes. Perhaps the NKVD (the new name for the secret police) had more in mind and considered staging a "show trial" involving the country's leading cultural figures. In any case Babel, Meyerhold, and Koltsov were secretly tried and executed; their families were not officially informed of their deaths for many years. Ehrenburg was fortunate enough to be in Paris when these friends were arrested and shot. He knew of their disappearance but did not know how close he came to sharing their fate.

THE FALL OF THE SPANISH REPUBLIC

Ehrenburg was back in Spain by June. The war was going badly. In April Franco's forces had succeeded in cutting the peninsula in two and blocking any direct land route between Barcelona on the northern coast and Madrid and Valencia to the south. The outcome seemed inevitable, but this did not deter Ehrenburg. After a half year in Moscow he could not describe what his own people were going through; he could, however, describe the courage and suffering of the Spanish. He wrote eight articles in June, another nine in July. These pieces form the height of his career in Spain; they are filled with poignant detail, irony, eloquent anger, and heartfelt belief that the Spanish war was only a rehearsal for a larger and more terrible conflict to come.

That July Ehrenburg also gave himself a reckless assignment, "an escapade more suited to a twenty-year-old."[55] He knew that French Basques often smuggled goods over the border into Fascist territory. One night he accompanied a smuggler into the village of Vera de Bidasoa, where he was able to see for himself how the population lived in fear. He stayed for only a few hours, then walked back to France as dawn was breaking. In his article for *Izvestia* Ehrenburg used images he would later repeat when he wrote about the Stalin era: men talked candidly only with their wives, women mourned their children, life was drained of joy and laughter. Impossible as it is to imagine, perhaps he meant to describe life in Moscow as well.[56]

By the fall Ehrenburg had to divide his time between France and Spain. As *Izvestia* correspondent in Paris he began to cover the intense parliamentary maneuvering that marked French political life in 1938 and 1939, as the country first sought to accommodate Hitler then found itself facing a war it had vainly hoped to avoid. On October 11, 1938, Ehrenburg adopted the pseudonym Paul Jocelyn for his short dispatches about France. For the next half year Ehrenburg's articles exposed the collapse of French resolve after the infamous Munich agreement of September 30 when England and France agreed to Hitler's annexation of the Sudetenland. At the same time, Ehrenburg noted, anti-Semitism grew stronger in France, infected by Hitler's example. Reports of pogroms in Germany—which Ehrenburg vividly shared with his Soviet readers—were ignored in France. French anti-Semites organized attacks on Jews in Dijon and Lille. One provincial Socialist paper declared its unwillingness to follow Léon Blum or "defend a hundred thousand Sudeten Jews."[57] French society was breaking down. Only the Soviet Union, it seemed, appeared ready to oppose Hitler. "With what pride I am thinking now," Ehrenburg wrote in early October. "I am a Soviet citizen. There is no people which wants peace more than mine. They know the meaning of motherland, loyalty, and honor."[58]

How are we to understand Ehrenburg's willingness to employ such stale rhetoric only months after the execution of Nikolai Bukharin? By then he had no illusions about the magnitude of the Great Purge. In Spain too he knew how Stalin compromised the republican cause. Ehrenburg's loyalties were tangled among his devotion to Russia, his friendships, his hatred of fascism, his will to survive—and he saw a great evil coming, greater even than Stalin's. To an outside observer Ehrenburg appeared to be a tough-minded Soviet journalist, covering Spain and the European crisis with steadfast adherence to Stalin's political line; but as his poetry reveals, he did not regard events or his own life through the eyes of a callous cynic. His poem "Let me not think too much" more than any other expresses the wrenching tensions of his career.

> Let me not think too much, cut short that voice, I pray,
> . . . .
> That drop by drop, that figures, rhymes, that something,
> Some semblance of precise, urgent work,
> That I should fight the enemy, that I should advance with
> a bayonet against bombs and bullets,
> That eye to eye, I should stand up to death.[59]

Back in France Ehrenburg kept a promise to his friend Isaac Babel. They had last seen each other in May, when Ehrenburg returned to Paris from Moscow. "Our parting was . . . inexpressibly sad," Ehrenburg remembered.[60] As a favor to Babel Ehrenburg traveled to Brussels later that year to see Babel's sister, Meri Shaposhnikova. Honored by Ehrenburg's visit, she invited friends to hear him speak about life in Moscow, which he described in glowingly optimistic terms. Only after her company departed and they were alone did Ehrenburg speak candidly. "Isaac asked me to convey to you one word, *shlecht*"—which is Yiddish for "very bad."[61]

—

Ehrenburg followed the close of the Spanish war from Paris, filing dispatches based on reports in the French and often the Italian press. He tried to sound optimistic. As late as January 20, 1939, "Paul Jocelyn," citing pro-Franco sources, claimed that more stubborn battles lay ahead; but the final weeks of resistance in Catalonia could not prevent the inevitable.

Ehrenburg was in Paris when Italian troops entered Barcelona near the end of January. He rushed to the border, anxious to observe refugees pouring into France. He found his friend Ovady Savich in Figueras—with Ehrenburg in France Savich had been writing for *Izvestia* under the pseudonym José García. Together they witnessed the closing session of the Cortes.

Madrid and Valencia held out for another month. By then the French government grew weary of the Spanish conflict and was anxious for the republic to acknowledge defeat. Observing French attitudes, Ehrenburg wrote the most bitter articles of his career. From Argelles in southern France he described the plight of Spanish refugees. Kept in concentration camps with little food, water, or medical care, they were threatened with forcible return to Spain. Ashamed of France, Ehrenburg reported on the French government's decision to relinquish Spanish property to Franco and recognize the legitimacy of his regime.

He did more than write for *Izvestia*. He also sent telegrams to the Soviet Writers' Union in March pleading for money to support the poet Rafael Alberti and other Spanish refugees. Later that spring Ehrenburg located Savich's secretary from Spain in a French internment camp and secured her release. In Paris he put together packages of clothing and shoes for refugees who were hiding out in miserable hostels. Ehrenburg's identification with the anti-Fascist cause was uncompromising and total; but the struggle was proving to be more complicated, politically and morally, than Ehrenburg had thought. Men such as André Gide refused to be silent about Soviet tyranny. Democracies such as France and England sought to appease Hitler. "I feel as if I am choking," Ehrenburg wrote in *Izvestia* in March 1939.[62]

A greater shock was still to come. Stalin was secretly negotiating with Hitler even as he continued discussions with England and France. By the middle of April Ehrenburg's eloquence and candor were no longer welcome in *Izvestia*. Although he continued to receive a salary, his articles stopped being published. (He did not appear in *Izvestia* again until June 26, 1941, after Hitler's invasion of the Soviet Union.) A few weeks later the veteran diplomat and foreign minister Maxim Litvinov was replaced by Vyacheslav Molotov. Litvinov, a Jew and dedicated anti-Fascist, could not be in charge of Soviet diplomacy. Ehrenburg too, for similar reasons, had to be consigned to cold storage.

An incident that spring reflected his growing and prescient anxiety. One evening in April 1939 while Ehrenburg was sitting with Savich and others in a café a Russian émigré related a terrible nightmare: that the two monsters, Hitler and Stalin, would conclude a treaty and between them divide up the continent. Savich laughed, dismissing the dream as an absurd invention; Ehrenburg responded angrily. The very idea provoked him so acutely that when he stood up shouting he knocked over his chair. The nightmare corresponded too closely to reality.[63]

In the middle of May a Soviet ship took many Spaniards and Russians, including Ovady Savich, from Le Havre to Moscow; Ehrenburg remained in France.[64] He accompanied Savich to the French coast but he himself was not prepared to return. Franco's triumph aside, Stalin's repression of many sincere anti-Fascists upset Ehrenburg too deeply. It was all part of the Spanish tragedy. At the end of May Ehrenburg wrote to Savich in Moscow that he had read and admired Arthur Koestler's book *Spanish Testament*, in which Koestler described the destructive work of the Communists and, in heartrending detail, his own imprisonment in Seville while awaiting execution at the hands of Franco's men. It made "a terrifying impression," Ehrenburg confided to Savich.[65] Ehrenburg's old friend Roman Jakobson saw him in Paris months later, after the Hitler-Stalin pact was signed, when Ehrenburg was cut off from numerous people. "Ehrenburg was bitter," Jakobson recalled in an interview. "He did not understand Stalin's behavior. When it came to the purge of his comrades from Spain, Ehrenburg could only say that 'Stalin kept his own accounts.' "[66]

Everyone around him was depressed by feelings of hopelessness and moral confusion. His friend the German writer Ernst Toller committed suicide in New York. "When I visited the Soviet embassy [in Paris] I saw new faces," Ehrenburg recalled in his memoirs. "Everyone I used to know had disappeared. No one dared to mention their names.' "[67]

———

Ehrenburg spent weeks alone that summer in southern France, walking in the countryside and wondering what would happen next. He stopped writing prose—no Soviet journal would publish his work—but he could at least express his anxiety in verse. The question of loyalty lay at the heart of his personal crisis.

Ravings of the heart I shall not recall or betray.

Take aim at the heart!

Loyalty to the heart and loyalty to fate will march over
you.[68]

Ehrenburg's worst fears were about to come true. When he returned
to Paris in August he learned over the radio that Nazi Germany and
the Soviet Union had concluded a nonaggression pact. It was August
23. Within ten days Germany invaded Poland. France and England
declared war while the Soviet Union, bound by its agreement and a
secret protocol to occupy the Baltic states and the eastern half of
Poland, was now an ally of Hitler.

Ehrenburg's world changed irrevocably. The pact was an evil he
could not abide. Almost immediately he lost the ability to swallow solid
food. Seeing Louis Aragon and Elsa Triolet at the home of a mutual
friend, Ehrenburg argued with them over the treaty then stormed out
of the house.[69] André Malraux was so disturbed he would drop by
Ehrenburg's apartment to shout at him and then leave, only to return
soon after to vent his disgust all over again. Few others visited as he
grew increasingly isolated and depressed. "How can you visit me?" he
asked a friend. "I am a Soviet, a traitor to France."[70]

His illness lasted for eight months. He could take liquids and chew
only on herbs and vegetables, particularly dill. Between August and
April Ehrenburg lost over forty pounds. "My clothes hung on me as
though on a coat-hanger, I looked like a scarecrow."[71] Many thought
he was near suicide.[72]

In Moscow too Ehrenburg's continuing presence in France was
taken as a protest. Rumors began to circulate that he would not
return. Ehrenburg still had the rights to his dacha in Peredelkino. In
the spring of 1940 the writer Valentin Kataev petitioned the Literary
Fund of the Writers' Union (which officially controlled the dachas) for
permission to occupy Ehrenburg's house. Kataev claimed openly that
Ehrenburg was a defector, that he had broken with the Soviet Union
and intended to stay in France. Kataev won his case. The Literary Fund
of the Writers' Union decided on May 4, 1940, that Ehrenburg's dacha
would be transferred "temporarily" to Kataev "on the condition that
it be immediately freed by him on the occasion of Comrade Ehrenburg's return." (Kataev never relinquished the dacha.) A month later
Irina Ehrenburg sent a telegram to the Literary Fund assuring its

members that her father would soon return and claiming that only the presidium of the Writers' Union could assign the dacha to Kataev.[73] Her appeal was ignored. This was a frightening moment for Irina Ehrenburg; should her father indeed choose to defect her fate would be sealed. She was already receiving threatening letters and anonymous telephone calls. While she was confident of his devotion the Literary Fund's decision confirmed the doubts of people around her, including those in authority.

Ehrenburg in fact was not sure what to do. Hitler's armies occupied Poland and neither France nor England actively opposed Germany, in spite of their declarations of war. Ehrenburg despaired of his own future. He did not believe that either France or England could withstand the Nazi onslaught. Like his creation Lasik Roitschwantz Ehrenburg seemed unable to find a safe place in Europe—and like Lasik he considered leaving for Palestine.[74] Ehrenburg actually contacted representatives of the Jewish Agency in Paris, but nothing came of this idea and he remained in France. It was not until the Germans invaded Belgium on May 10 that Ehrenburg's illness suddenly ended. He was able to resume eating and begin to regain his strength.

The German offensive that May was Hitler's long-awaited move on the western front. The "phony war" of the previous year was over. The French had watched other countries succumb to Hitler without believing their turn would come; now France would pay dearly for inaction. Ehrenburg remained in Paris as German forces advanced along a broad front, sweeping into Holland, Belgium, Luxembourg, and northeastern France. After only five days of fighting Paris itself was threatened. The collapse of France was almost complete.

Elements of the French government still hoped to resist Germany. Pierre Cot, an old friend of Ehrenburg's, was enlisted to travel to Moscow to secure aircraft; Ehrenburg too was drawn into this plan. He was summoned by Alfred de Monzie, the minister of public works, and asked to convey a similar message to the Kremlin: that all of France would quickly fall if it could not buy planes from the Soviet Union. Ehrenburg was eager to help and immediately sent a cable from the Soviet embassy.

Their plans led nowhere. On May 28, three days after meeting de Monzie, Ehrenburg was arrested in his apartment. The warrant was issued by Vice-Premier Henri Philippe Pétain, who had assumed office only ten days before and who would soon lead the Vichy government.

Ehrenburg's papers were searched, and "evidence" of a "Communist and German conspiracy" to hand over France to the Nazis was uncovered.[75] Taken to police headquarters, he was interrogated for most of the day until the Soviet embassy, having learned of his arrest by accident, contacted Georges Mandel, the minister of the interior, who was also a Jew and a convinced anti-Fascist; Mandel ordered that Ehrenburg be released. Pierre Cot was not allowed to leave for Moscow and any attempt at a rapprochement between France and the Soviet Union was dashed.

Stranded in Paris, Ehrenburg watched the city prepare for occupation. "Iron shutters were being fixed, venetian blinds and window curtains drawn, shop fronts boarded up—as though closing the eyes of a corpse."[76] Knowing that the Germans would soon reach Paris, Ehrenburg had preparations of his own to make: he burned his personal papers, among them diaries and extensive correspondence, with Nikolai Bukharin, for example, and many other Soviet figures. On June 14 he saw German soldiers enter the city. Ehrenburg instinctively "turned away and stood silently by a wall. This, too, had to be endured."[77]

He and Lyubov Mikhailovna stayed in Paris for six more weeks, living in a small room in the Soviet embassy, where they were invited to stay for their own safety. He traveled as much as he could, once with an embassy official on a long trip through northern and central France. He heard General de Gaulle appeal for resistance over the radio from London. He helped the exiled German Communist writer Anna Seghers escape Paris; she was under surveillance and feared arrest.[78]

In his memoirs twenty years later Ehrenburg hoped to describe the Soviet embassy's collaboration with the occupying Nazis. In a draft he wrote: "Friendly relations existed between the Soviet Union and the Third Reich, but not between me and the Hitlerites, the invaders of France. I hated them, and it required a lot of strength to conceal my feelings." He could not always control himself, though, and in the presence of embassy officials at times muttered the words "Fascists, murderers, butchers!" There were also French Communists who honored Stalin's pact with Hitler. In an early draft of his memoirs Ehrenburg wrote about seeing the French Communist leader Jacques Doriot dining with a German officer. "He was proposing a propaganda plan to Hitler's officer. I could not help but listen and felt so nauseous I could not finish my dinner."[79]

France formally surrendered on June 22 at a ceremony in the

woods near Compiègne, north of Paris. Ehrenburg and Lyubov Mikhailovna departed for Moscow the next day, traveling by train with a small group of embassy personnel. Ehrenburg had no choice but to return. Despite his standing as a Soviet journalist his safety in German-occupied Paris could not be assured.

Within the Russian émigré community it was said that Lyubov Mikhailovna was so frightened by the idea of returning to Moscow that her legs failed her and she had to be carried onto the train.[80] They passed through Brussels, then spent two nights in a Berlin hotel, where a sign on the door forbade Jews to enter.[81] But Ehrenburg was traveling as a Soviet official—a representative of an allied power, to his chagrin—and though he claimed in his memoirs that "his name did not appear in the documents," it is hard to believe the Germans did not know who he was.[82]

From Berlin the train proceeded eastward through Poland into Lithuania, where the poet Kostas Korsakas boarded and shared the same compartment with Ehrenburg and Lyubov Mikhailovna. "Ilya Ehrenburg turned out to be very approachable, friendly, and talkative," Korsakas later recounted. Ehrenburg told him "they had traveled practically the entire length of Europe and had not encountered one smiling face. . . . 'The map of Europe is changing every day . . . and it may continue to change.' These were the rather pessimistic and prophetic words of the old writer." Korsakas stayed with the Ehrenburgs all the way to Moscow. Upon their arrival on July 29 Korsakas "was greatly surprised that no one from the Writers' Union was at the train station to greet Ilya Ehrenburg, who was returning to Moscow after a long absence. Both he and his wife were looking around, stricken. It seemed they were expecting to be met by his colleagues." A few days later Korsakas stopped by the Lithuanian legation and asked why Ehrenburg's colleagues would ignore his arrival in Moscow. Korsakas was told "quite sharply that Ehrenburg was now persona non grata. And why? Who can figure it out."[83]

THE EVE OF WAR

For the next year Ehrenburg did all he could to alert his country to the likelihood of war with Germany—a far more difficult task that took far more courage than one would suppose. Stalin took his pact with

Hitler seriously and ingratiated himself with the Führer, at the same time making sure not to offer a pretext for hostilities. The Soviet Union exchanged information with Germany about Polish resistance units; Stalin gave the Nazis a naval base in the far north near Murmansk, where German ships could refuel and be repaired; Soviet ships reported weather conditions to the Luftwaffe while the Germans were bombarding England. Stalin also gave Germany the right to transport strategic raw materials from Japan over the Trans-Siberian railway.

Soviet propaganda shifted as well. On August 24, 1939, immediately following the signing of the nonaggression pact with Germany *Pravda* explained to its readers that "the proper conditions for the development and flourishing of friendly relations between the Soviet Union and Germany must be created." Two months later foreign minister Vyacheslav Molotov even blamed France and England for continuing the war, claiming that Germany only wanted peace. In a major address following Hitler's attack on Poland Molotov went so far as to grant a measure of legitimacy to Nazi philosophy. "One can sympathize with Hitlerism or be disgusted by it, but all intelligent people must realize that an ideology cannot be eliminated by war," Molotov told the Supreme Soviet on October 31, 1939. "A war 'for the destruction of Hitlerism' under the false slogan of a struggle for democracy is therefore nonsense and even criminal."[84] The Soviet press also grew silent about the fate of the Jews in Nazi-occupied Europe, leaving millions of Jews in Soviet-controlled territory unaware of the treatment their Polish brethren were enduring and unprepared for what was to come after Hitler's invasion in June 1941.[85]

Ehrenburg hated this new political orientation. He tried in vain to see Molotov. Although he gave frequent lectures, his articles were not always accepted by the Soviet press, while *Izvestia* would no longer accept his articles at all. "In every line," he recalled in his memoirs, "the editors discovered slanting references to the Fascists, whom our wits called our 'deadly friends.' "[86] Meanwhile Ehrenburg followed the conflict in Europe as best he could, relying on a short-wave radio for French-language broadcasts on the BBC. The parents and sister of Boris Pasternak lived in England and Pasternak, anxious for their safety, often came upstairs to Ehrenburg's apartment late at night to follow the news with him.[87]

Yet Ehrenburg, ever a master at finding ways to say as much as possible no matter what the risk, managed to find a sympathetic editor at

the official trade union newspaper *Trud* (Labor) and "after lengthy
negotiations, amendments, and cuts," a series of five articles appeared in
August and September.[88]

In spite of censorship Ehrenburg made his ideas clear, expressing a
point of view at odds with Soviet policies. He could not vent his
loathing for the Germans; he did, however, manage to condemn those
in France who failed to oppose them. He reported on how Charles de
Gaulle and other French officers were kept at arm's length for protest-
ing against the Maginot line and other strategic inadequacies. He dismissed with contempt the idea that war and its suffering could be
avoided. He wrote in vivid detail about the thousands of refugees who
fled Paris as the Germans advanced on the city. He described anti-
Semitism as well, recalling the sign on his Berlin hotel—"Pure Aryan
Establishment. No Jews allowed"—and an editorial from a French
newspaper that echoed Nazi racism: "There is a bit of the Jew in every
one of us," the collaborators proclaimed. "What we need is an internal,
intimate pogrom."[89] His articles convey an unmistakable anti-Nazi and
anti-Munich message; if appeasement on the part of the Western Europeans was wrong, as Ehrenburg made clear, then it could be understood that Stalin's arrangement with Hitler was equally unforgivable.

These articles notwithstanding, Ehrenburg's position in the country
remained suspect. One incident in particular exemplified his questionable status. On November 5, 1940, the editors of the French edition of
Internatsionalnaya Literatura (International Literature) wrote to Alexander Fadeyev, the head of the Writers' Union, for advice. It was customary to honor prominent figures on their landmark birthdays. In
Ehrenburg's case, however, the editors needed guidance "from above"
as to "whether one could or should mark Ehrenburg's fiftieth birthday."[90] In January 1941 not a single Soviet newspaper made mention
of the fact that Ilya Ehrenburg, unlike so many friends who had disappeared, had reached the age of fifty.

———

Ehrenburg's fortunes were about to change with his novel *The Fall
of Paris*. Begun in September 1940 soon after his return to Moscow, the
novel was Ehrenburg's attempt to summarize the moral confusion, partisan intrigue, and political myopia that led to France's military collapse. For Russians *The Fall of Paris* quickly became one of Ehrenburg's
most memorable books, providing a window on life in Western Europe
and the Latin Quarter where he had passed so much of his career.

The novel confirmed Ehrenburg's reputation as the country's leading anti-Fascist writer. The first part, which covers the triumph of the
Popular Front and the subsequent decision by the French government not to intervene in Spain, was published in *Znamya* in early
1941. The Germans had yet to appear in the story, which helped
make it acceptable to the censors, but the word *fascism* had to be
removed and replaced with a more innocuous-sounding reference to
"reactionaries."[91]

Ehrenburg submitted the second part to an editor only to learn that
it touched on political areas too sensitive for the Soviet press and therefore could not be published. Ehrenburg did not give in. He sent a copy
of the manuscript to Stalin, asking for his help. A few days later, on
April 24, Ehrenburg received a call late at night. He thought it was the
doorbell ringing and instinctively reached for a small valise he kept by
his bed in case "they" were coming for him.[92] It was only the telephone, however; he was told to dial a certain number where "Comrade
Stalin" was waiting to speak with him.

This was Ehrenburg's only conversation with Stalin. It was brief and
puzzling. Stalin liked *The Fall of Paris* and asked if Ehrenburg intended
to denounce the German Fascists. Ehrenburg could only describe the
novel's final section, when the Nazis attacked and occupied the French
capital. He was afraid, he told Stalin, that the rest of the novel would
not appear. "Just go on writing," Stalin told him. "You and I will try to
push the third part through."[93]

Ehrenburg understood the call was not about literature; war was
imminent. The Nazis had just occupied Yugoslavia and Greece, leaving
no doubt about their intentions in the East. Each day was precious. The
unexpected and swift defeat of France had upset Stalin's plans—he had
hoped that Hitler would get bogged down in the West, leaving the
Soviet Union additional time to build up its forces. Soviet defense
industries worked feverishly to produce weapons and armaments but
the military took no precautions at the frontier, lest Hitler seize on
such a move as a pretext for attack.

Stalin's endorsement of Ehrenburg's novel naturally was decisive.
Word of their conversation spread rapidly throughout Moscow, adding
to Ehrenburg's enigmatic stature, and the fate of the novel changed
abruptly. *Znamya* accepted the second part; other editors called to
request chapters.

That May Ehrenburg traveled to Kharkov, Kiev, and Leningrad, giving lectures and readings. Everywhere listeners asked about the likelihood of war with Germany while more "orthodox" Communists told him to denounce British imperialism in his novel. On May 31 Ehrenburg told friends the war would begin in three weeks, a prediction that proved to be uncannily precise.[94]

War and suffering was on everyone's minds. On June 5 Anna Akhmatova visited Ehrenburg in Moscow and read her poem about the fall of Paris, a city she had not seen since 1912.[95] Ehrenburg copied her verses into his notebook. The poem "In 1940" begins with a famous, sorrowful lament—"When they bury an epoch, No psalm is heard over the coffin." Then Ehrenburg copied a poem by Osip Mandelstam (evidently brought to his attention by Akhmatova) that Mandelstam had written in 1931, only to see the text confiscated three years later at the time of his first arrest. The poem, as grim and terrifying as any from that period, contains the lines, "The wolfhound age springs at my shoulders, though I'm no wolf by blood." Mandelstam, seeing all the terror around him, wanted to escape "and so not see the snivelling, nor the sickly smears, nor the bloody bones on the wheel." But Mandelstam had no means of escape. "I'm no wolf by blood," he repeats, "and only my own kind will kill me."[96] Knowing the truth of these verses, Ehrenburg was determined to save the poem, out of defiant loyalty to Mandelstam's talent and memory and courageous act of witness. Had the poem been found in Ehrenburg's possession while Stalin was alive, Ehrenburg's career, and more than likely his life, would have been in jeopardy.

—

News out of Europe continued to be unsettling. On June 13 the BBC began reporting a huge buildup of German forces on the Soviet frontier; the Kremlin gave no warnings to its people or its troops. Nonetheless, with the most massive military force ever assembled the Germans launched a surprise attack on the Soviet Union in the early morning of June 22. Ehrenburg listened to the radio as Molotov, not Stalin, announced the outbreak of war. Stalin's confidence was shaken by the German invasion. He had hoped for more time, but Adolf Hitler had his own schedule. It would require four years of fighting and the combined armies of Great Britain, the Soviet Union, and the United States to stop him.

NINE

The Second World War and the Holocaust

Ilya Ehrenburg turned fifty in Moscow on January 27, 1941. Since the age of eighteen he had lived virtually his entire adult life in Western Europe. He was a Jew and an intellectual, more European than Russian or Soviet. He was also an ex-Bolshevik, whose brief adolescent party career had been associated with the now disgraced and executed Nikolai Bukharin. For a time Ehrenburg had even been a bitter anti-Communist.

With Hitler's attack on June 22, 1941, Ehrenburg became the most widely read and most influential journalist in the Soviet Union. This was his third war. "I remembered World War I," he wrote in his memoirs, recalling visits to the western front. "I had experienced Spain, witnessed the French collapse, so I thought I was prepared. But I must confess that at times despair overwhelmed me."[1] The Soviet Union was nearly overrun by the Germans. Within six months approximately three million Soviet soldiers were killed and four million captured. The Baltic states, Byelorussia, and the Ukraine were occupied. Leningrad was besieged and Moscow itself threatened. On November 6 Stalin addressed the Moscow City Council in an underground subway station. The next day Soviet troops paraded through Red Square on the anniversary of the Bolshevik revolution, then marched to the front; the Germans were near the suburbs.

The war touched Ehrenburg's family during those initial, terrible months. His son-in-law Boris Lapin disappeared in September. Working as a journalist for *Krasnaya Zvezda* (Red Star), he was near the front lines in Kiev as the Germans furiously advanced. Staying close to Soviet troops, Lapin and his friend Zakhary Khatsrevin retreated southeast toward Borispol. They were promised room on the last airplane out of Kiev but for some reason did not make it and had to stay with the army. Khatsrevin, who had epilepsy, fell sick, immobilized; Lapin stayed with him. Armed only with their pistols, they were never heard from again.

———

Ehrenburg was summoned to the army newspaper *Krasnaya Zvezda* within days after the invasion. The editor, General David Ortenberg, who used the non-Jewish pseudonym Vadimov in the paper, had followed Ehrenburg's career closely; he also knew Boris Lapin, from whom he had heard a great deal about Ehrenburg. All this gave Ortenberg confidence that Ehrenburg was the right person to assign a regular column. It was a fateful decision; although Ehrenburg wrote for *Pravda* and other journals, it was his commentaries in *Krasnaya Zvezda* that earned him enduring recognition.

From the outset of the fighting Ehrenburg sensed that the Soviet people did not understand the nature of their adversary. "Not only did our men not feel any hatred for the enemy, they felt a certain respect for the Germans, born of esteem for the outward signs of culture." After years of propaganda many Soviet soldiers believed it was "the capitalists and landlords who had driven the [German] soldiers into battle against us, . . . that if German workers and peasants were only told the truth, they would throw down their weapons."[2] It was Ehrenburg's self-appointed task to shatter these myths and teach the Red Army how to hate.

Ehrenburg remained in Moscow throughout that first summer. His talent and energy were immediately recognized, and he was called on by many newspapers and government agencies. Ehrenburg usually reached *Krasnaya Zvezda* by 6 P.M., where he wrote and attended meetings until midnight. Ehrenburg did all his writing on a portable Corona typewriter equipped with Cyrillic and Latin letters on each key; the machine carried no capital letters. Stalin had to see the paper before it could be printed and this step often prolonged Ehrenburg's stay. "Stalin is my first reader," Ehrenburg liked to tell his friends. Then he would go home. Ehrenburg had severe insomnia during the war and he would write poetry or translate verses, usually by François Villon, when he could not sleep. He would get to bed around 4 A.M. and be up by 7, when he would start writing articles for the foreign press and continue until 5 in the afternoon. An hour later he would resume his work at *Krasnaya Zvezda*. That was a typical day for him.[3]

During the four years of fighting Ehrenburg wrote well over two thousand articles, among them almost four hundred fifty in *Krasnaya Zvezda* alone; many were reprinted in provincial newspapers, distributed abroad, and anthologized in books and pamphlets. Half of his wartime output was produced during the first year of the war, when the country was in greatest danger. In 1942 alone thirty-nine books of his were published, many of them small collections issued in pamphlet form. Ehrenburg's columns have unique and surprising qualities. Writing in the tradition of French pamphleteering, he was emotionally direct without the pompous, cliché-ridden approach of most Soviet articles. He did not flinch from acknowledging German strength or victories. Citing Soviet reversals, Ehrenburg gained credibility with his readers, as when he wrote about the capture of Kiev.

Ehrenburg was at the editorial office in September when word of the city's collapse reached Moscow. "He sat opposite me in a deep chair lost in thought," General Ortenberg remembered. "Kiev was the city of his birth and his childhood. He still had relatives there. He sat for a time, withdrawn, quiet, and then, as if shaking off his numbness," he offered to write about Kiev's fall.[4] It had been expressly prohibited to print anything about the loss of Kiev. Ehrenburg was careful; he could not describe how many troops had been killed or captured, or the details of the fighting, but he could express his resolve in the style that made him famous. "We will liberate Kiev. The enemy's blood will wash the enemy's footprints. Like the ancient Phoenix, Kiev will rise from the ashes, young and beautiful. Sorrow feeds hatred. Hatred strengthens hope."[5] Ehrenburg's "Kiev" made such an impression that *Krasnaya*

Zvezda was no longer silent when Soviet troops abandoned a city; with each new defeat either correspondents filed a dispatch from the front or Ehrenburg, in Moscow, wrote about the retreat.

By October, a few weeks after Kiev had fallen, the Germans were approaching the Soviet capital. The newspapers were vague, stating only that the enemy was trying to reach "our most important centers of life and industry."[6] Ortenberg was frustrated by the Kremlin's refusal to arouse the troops. It was up to Ehrenburg on October 12 to make the danger to Moscow absolutely clear in his article "Hold Out."

> The enemy is advancing. The enemy is threatening Moscow. Our only thought must be to hold out. They are advancing because they want to plunder and ravage. We are defending ourselves because we want to live. We want to live like human beings and not like German cattle. Reinforcements are coming from the east. Ships with war material from England and America are being unloaded. Every day piles of corpses mark Hitler's route. We must hold out. . . . Hitler shall not destroy Russia! Russia was, is, and shall be.[7]

In early December the German advance was halted outside of Moscow and the worst seemed to be over; but Hitler quickly consolidated his forces and renewed his onslaught to the south of the capital. Although Moscow remained beyond his grasp, Hitler's armies reached the Caucasus, gaining control of nearly half of Soviet territory by the summer of 1942. Ehrenburg was in despair. Fear combined with frustration over Nazi victories provoked his most extreme writing of the war.

> We are remembering everything. Now we understand the Germans are not human. Now the word "German" has become the most terrible curse. Let us not speak. Let us not be indignant. Let us kill. . . . If you do not kill a German, a German will kill you. He will carry away your family, and torture them in his damned Germany. . . . If you have killed one German, kill another. There is nothing jollier for us than German corpses.[8]

A generation earlier, in the midst of Russia's civil war, Max Voloshin had said about Ehrenburg that "no other contemporary poet felt the motherland's ruin with such intensity as this Jew."[9] After Hitler's invasion Ehrenburg responded with equal fervor. Most Soviet soldiers (who were his primary audience) would not have guessed his origins. He was "Ilyusha" or "Our Ilya," and his writing stirred feelings that no gruesome reports of Nazi atrocities could match. Ehrenburg's columns were so popular there was even a decree forbidding the paper on which they were printed to be used for rolling tobacco; his articles had to be cut out and preserved for others to read.

Alexander Werth, who covered the eastern front for Reuters and the *Sunday Times*, described the effect of Ehrenburg's pieces:

> [E]very soldier in the Army read Ehrenburg; and partisans in the enemy rear are known to have readily swapped any spare tommy gun for a bundle of Ehrenburg clippings. One may like or dislike Ehrenburg as a writer, but . . . he certainly showed a genius for putting into biting, inspiring prose the burning hatred Russia felt for the Germans; this man, with his cosmopolitan background and his French culture, had grasped by intuition what the ordinary Russian really felt. . . . One must imagine oneself in the position of a Russian in the summer of 1942 who was watching the map and seeing one town going after another, one province going after another; one must put oneself in the position of a Russian soldier retreating to Stalingrad or Nalchik, saying to himself: How much farther are we going to retreat? How much farther *can* we retreat? The Ehrenburg articles helped such a man to pull himself together.[10]

Ehrenburg often employed references to history and literature, to the Old Testament, even to Greek mythology with its stories of gods, their passions, triumphs, and tragedies. Reading his articles today ("all very similar," Ehrenburg observed in his memoirs, "which only an over-conscientious historian will bother to read") one might dismiss such references as too abstruse, far beyond the education or intellectual grasp of the typical Red Army man, who had peasant origins and was semiliterate at best.[11] Yet when *Krasnaya Zvezda* arrived they always looked for Ehrenburg's articles first, begging their officers to read them aloud, longing to hear who Wotan was or how the exploits of General Suvorov, who fought under Catherine the Great, compared with their own. Soviet soldiers did not need to understand all the details; for them the Nazis were as bestial and cruel as any villain in myth. For Ehrenburg their struggle resembled the cosmic struggle of the gods for control of human destiny. The troops responded to his inspiration—that was why Ehrenburg's articles were read before battles and found on the corpses of fallen Soviet soldiers.

At least one Soviet officer felt Ehrenburg's rhetoric went too far. In the summer of 1942 Lev Kopelev, who later became a well-known writer and dissident activist, complained to Ehrenburg about these pieces. Kopelev had been at the front and seen Soviet troops shoot German soldiers as they tried to surrender. Kopelev was convinced that with his call for hatred and revenge Ehrenburg was inciting the troops, and he advised Ehrenburg to moderate his tone. He also challenged Ehrenburg not to write how well the Soviet people had lived before the war when in fact everyone knew this was not true. "You should write we will live better than we lived before," Kopelev told him. Ehrenburg became suspicious that Kopelev was "a provocateur" and dismissed him. Kopelev continued to berate Ehrenburg to others. A convinced Marxist, he could not accept Ehrenburg's extreme Russian nationalism. A decade earlier, in 1934, while reading newspapers in a closed party archive Kopelev had come upon many of Ehrenburg's diatribes against Lenin. Kopelev often referred to these pieces in discussions at the front and even claimed that Ehrenburg wrote as scathingly about the Germans as he had once written about the Bolsheviks—a claim that was substantially true. Such outspokenness got Kopelev into trouble. He was arrested in April 1945, just as the war was ending. The main charge against him was "bourgeois propaganda" and "pity for the enemy," as Kopelev tried to stop his fellow soldiers from wanton attacks on German civilians; the original indictment included a charge of "slandering Ilya Ehrenburg." Ehrenburg was too important, too indispensable, to be criticized by a mere major.[12]

—

Ehrenburg's fame among the troops gave rise to many legends and anecdotes. One Soviet sniper who had killed one hundred forty Germans sent Ehrenburg a note to credit him with "seventy kills;" Ehrenburg's articles had helped him to kill the remainder on his own. A second soldier dubbed Ehrenburg "a literary machine gun." In Moscow recital concerts were organized with columns by Ehrenburg set to music. The Germans also understood the power of Ehrenburg's articles and tried to keep them out of the hands of the occupied population. One Soviet woman was summarily executed by the Nazis for reading a column by Ehrenburg that partisans had nailed to a tree.[13]

His prestige among the troops was unmatched. A soldier once rigged up a mannequin in the back of his car and began to shout "Let Ehrenburg through!" in order to maneuver his vehicle more quickly through the crowded roads around Moscow.[14] Other soldiers, knowing of his devotion to French culture, sent Ehrenburg bottles of Beaujolais, Bordeaux, and French champagne they had captured from the Nazis.[15] Still others apparently exploited Ehrenburg's fame. One evening he and his family were startled by a knock on their door. A young pregnant woman was looking for Ilya Ehrenburg but when she saw him, evidently for the first time, she understood that she had been deceived by a much younger imposter, who had seduced her by claiming to be the renowned Ehrenburg himself. Upset and embarrassed, she fled without entering the apartment.[16]

A popular rumor circulated during the war that General Ortenberg was said to have changed an article by Ehrenburg in a way Ehrenburg did not appreciate. His pieces then failed to appear in *Krasnaya Zvezda* for several days. Stalin noticed their absence and called to inquire. When Ortenberg explained that Ehrenburg did not like how he was being edited, Stalin rebuked him. "There is no need to edit Ehrenburg. Let him write as he pleases."[17]

KUIBYSHEV

By the middle of October 1941 German bombers began reaching Moscow regularly. Ehrenburg's top-floor apartment on Lavrushinsky Lane was severely damaged. He hardly had time to find new quarters when he and his wife were evacuated, along with many government and cultural figures and the foreign press corps, to Kuibyshev, about seven hundred miles east of the capital. Ehrenburg spent almost three months there, "his typewriter resting on a packing-case" as he sat in a corridor or a bare hotel room, before he was able to return to Moscow.[18]

Living in Kuibyshev brought Ehrenburg closer to the dislocation and confusion brought on by the war. When it was possible he tried to help people who were in trouble. Daniel Danin, an aspiring poet and literary critic, had known Ehrenburg before joining the army. During the German advance on Moscow Danin and seventeen others were trapped in a German encirclement. With luck and ingenuity they made their way back to Moscow. As an army journalist, Danin was immediately sent to Kuibyshev, where his troubles resumed. All Soviet soldiers who escaped from behind enemy lines were treated with suspicion, compelled to demonstrate they were not spies or deserters; there were even incidents of summary execution. Danin was the first of his group to reach Kuibyshev and for a week no one could corroborate his story. He was under suspicion and feared arrest, whereupon he saw Ehrenburg in the street. When Ehrenburg realized this man could be shot as a deserter he immediately called several officials and secured his standing; Danin ended the war as a captain in an artillery unit.[19]

While Ehrenburg was in Kuibyshev an escaped prisoner named Victor Zorza also sought his help. A Polish national, Zorza was detained by the Soviets when he fled the advancing German armies. Taking advantage of the war's turmoil, Zorza escaped the camp and made his way to Kuibyshev in the fall of 1941, where he found Ilya Ehrenburg. "I visited him wearing rags for clothes and galoshes made from car tires," Zorza told an *Izvestia* interviewer years later. Ehrenburg found him clean clothes, a job, and a place to stay, and helped Zorza enlist in a Polish squadron. Within months Zorza was able to leave the Soviet Union. Like Daniel Danin, Zorza came away feeling that he owed his life to Ilya Ehrenburg.[20]

Ehrenburg could push the boundaries of acceptable behavior only so far. At the beginning of December he visited General Wladyslaw Anders' army of Polish volunteers stationed in Buzuluk, southwest of Kuibyshev near Saratov. There Ehrenburg assembled a group of Jewish volunteers to hear their assessment of Anders' forces. The Jewish soldiers were eager to talk and made clear that their Polish colleagues, many of whom had spent time in Soviet prisons, "hated the Russians as much as they hated the Germans. Before leaving, Ehrenburg warned them not to have anything to do with these 'Fascists.' "[21] One of the soldiers Ehrenburg saw that day was a Polish captain named Joseph Czapski. A painter by profession, Czapski was soon commissioned by Polish leaders to inquire about the fate of thousands of Polish officers who had been taken into custody and shot by Stalin's secret police in the Katyn forest, west of Smolensk. Looking for advice, Czapski found Ehrenburg in Moscow in early 1942, but Ehrenburg could not offer the slightest encouragement. Czapski understood immediately that his concerns were too sensitive for Ehrenburg to address.

I realized at once that if [Ehrenburg] had really wanted to help me in my work, if by a look or a glance he had expressed compassion, if, by the least little phrase, he had shown himself willing to give me useful advice, he would not have occupied in contemporary Russia the position that he did. Far from living in the luxurious Hotel Moskva, he would long since have died in the Siberian wastes . . .

I can see him still, in his low, comfortable armchair, at a safe distance from mine, and hear him talking in a loud voice, as though constantly aware of the danger of being overheard. He had no personal knowledge, he said, or practically none, of the officials with whom I should have to do business.[22]

As Joseph Czapski understood, Ilya Ehrenburg, in spite of his prestige, knew the limits of his influence and never forgot he was living within Stalin's grasp.

EHRENBURG AND THE FOREIGN PRESS

During the war years Ehrenburg came to know many foreign correspondents. Unlike other Soviet journalists he felt comfortable meeting with Westerners and appreciated their importance to the war effort. Ehrenburg was especially close to Henry Shapiro, who had originally come to Moscow in 1933 to study Soviet law. Soon after, Shapiro began filing stories for the *New York Herald Tribune* and became a full-time journalist, eventually serving as bureau chief for Reuters and then for the United Press.

Shapiro was with Ehrenburg in July during the first German air raid on Moscow. The correspondents had to work in the foreign ministry, where government censors cleared their copy. When the sirens wailed Ehrenburg and Shapiro made their way to the basement and talked for several hours, mostly about Paris and the German occupation; it was the beginning of their friendship. That summer Shapiro recruited a handful of prominent Soviet writers to submit articles to the United Press. Konstantin Simonov, Valentin Kataev, Alexander Fadeyev, and Ehrenburg all agreed, but only Ehrenburg kept his word. He filed stories regularly.

Shapiro saw Ehrenburg several times a week for most of the war, either in the Hotel Moskva or at the Metropol, where the press corps lived and had its offices. The fact that Shapiro was Jewish and knew Russian made it easier for Ehrenburg to trust him. Shapiro once complained that while Stalin answered questions submitted from other correspondents—Stalin twice responded to Henry Cassidy, who worked for the Associated Press—he never responded to Shapiro's inquiries. "With your name," Ehrenburg explained, "You'll never get an answer." Ehrenburg also discussed Palestine with Shapiro, wanting "to know what life was like there and what prospects the Jews could face in the future."[23]

Ehrenburg was friendly with Leland Stowe as well, the veteran American reporter who had covered the Spanish civil war and the fighting in Norway, Greece, and China. Stowe reached Moscow in the fall of 1942, where he met Ehrenburg for the first time. With Ehrenburg's help Stowe spent over a week around Rzhev, a hundred miles northwest of Moscow, where the Red Army was attacking a strategic German position at great cost. It was "an unprecedented privilege for me as an American correspondent," Stowe wrote at the time, "because Ilya Ehrenburg is unquestionably one of the most potent two-legged passports to the Red Army that can be found anywhere in the Soviet Union."[24] He and Ehrenburg, along with a driver and a woman officer who had also served in Spain, explored the front in a beat-up car. They traveled five hundred miles in nine days. The mud from the autumn rains was so formidable that numerous roads were covered with felled tree trunks, turning their drive into a bone-rattling experience. Twice they spent the night in peasant huts and once took shelter in a field hospital. For one day, at least, Ehrenburg was able to find an American jeep they could use. "That was really a tribute to Ehrenburg's status with the Red Army, for in nearly a week," Stowe later recalled, "we saw less than twenty jeeps along this entire front."[25] Stowe watched him question captured German soldiers, an exercise from which Ehrenburg derived grim pleasure, repeatedly asking why Germany had invaded one country after another. The prisoners "either ignored, or deliberately sidestepped, all moral questions connected with Hitler's invasions or executions." Ehrenburg always asked if the Germans sang Heinrich Heine's verses, then enjoyed reminding them that Heine was a Jew.[26]

Not all correspondents enjoyed Ehrenburg's attitudes about the war. By 1944 Ehrenburg made the Americans feel particularly uncomfortable. "As far as he was concerned, the United States was not carrying its weight in the conflict. Ehrenburg was indifferent to the war in the

Pacific. All he wanted was a Second Front," Harrison Salisbury remembered. "For Ehrenburg, Americans were a naive, ignorant, uneducated colonial people who had no appreciation for European culture. All this would come out in a sharp, sardonic way, in long French monologues. Several of the Americans tried to answer back, but his temper got so bad, a couple refused to talk with him. They'd leave the room when he showed up."[27] It is hardly surprising that *Newsweek* once described Ehrenburg as "intensely emotional, very pro-French, and extremely irritating to his American friends."[28]

All the correspondents recognized Ehrenburg's "classical French contempt for anything American or British," as Henry Shapiro described it. "Ehrenburg liked to say that the only contributions Americans ever made to civilization were Hemingway and Chesterfields. He always asked me for Chesterfields. After the war, he came back from Nuremberg with a similar complaint. It seems the 'barbarian Americans,' as he called them, served coffee right away in the officers club, ruining his palate before dinner. This offended Ehrenburg's typically French attitude about food. He could be a real snob."[29]

The French regarded him differently. They adored Ehrenburg and he looked after them as best he could. He liked to visit the Normandie squadron, a unit of French pilots who flew Soviet fighters on the eastern front. Ehrenburg also explained to Soviet officials that among the German prisoners of war were men from Alsace-Lorraine who had been pressed into the *Wehrmacht* and did not deserve to be held. Ehrenburg would go to the front to help pick them out; a nod from him saved many from captivity or worse.[30]

During the war a half-joking, half-malicious canard circulated that "Ehrenburg hates the Germans so much because they had occupied Paris, forcing him to live in Russia."[31] His hotel room in fact resembled a corner of Paris. "A Dubonnet ashtray sat on the table, lovingly swiped from a café," Jean-Richard Bloch once recalled. "In the small kitchen, a bottle of vermouth, long empty, and now pathetic due to distance and unhappiness."[32] Ehrenburg even refused to wear Soviet underwear, insisting that his wife darn his French-made ones throughout the war.[33] At the height of the conflict, in May 1942, Ehrenburg dreamed of returning to France, telling the poet Semyon Gudzenko that "after the war we will return to our former life. I will travel to Paris, to Spain, and write verses and novels." Gudzenko was surprised by how "distant" Ehrenburg seemed from Russia, "although he loves

Russia and would die for it as an anti-Fascist."[34] There were moments, too, when the provincial attitudes of his fellow Russians embarrassed him. In one dispatch an American correspondent referred to Ehrenburg as a "francophile." The censor removed the phrase. "Everyone knows Ehrenburg never liked Franco" was all the censor felt obliged to say.[35]

Charles de Gaulle was well aware of Ehrenburg's devotion to France. In April 1942, after Ehrenburg received a Stalin Prize for *The Fall of Paris*, de Gaulle sent him a congratulatory telegram from London. In October Ehrenburg wrote a glowing article about de Gaulle, drawing on his prolonged stay in Paris in 1940 when he witnessed de Gaulle's vain attempt to rally the French army and then heard de Gaulle's initial broadcast from England. When de Gaulle visited Moscow in December 1942 Ehrenburg was invited to an official dinner at the French embassy, where he was seated next to the general; and in May 1944 de Gaulle again hailed Ehrenburg as "a faithful friend of France" after Ehrenburg received the prestigious Order of Lenin.[36]

Ehrenburg remained partial to the French. Even after D-Day, June 6, 1944, Ehrenburg allowed his sympathies to get the better of his judgment. Instead of writing about the landing, Ehrenburg produced a sentimental article, invoking the French resistance, the legacy of Verdun, even the image of the Unknown Soldier rising to fight the Boches. He could not put aside antipathy for Western contributions to the war effort and offered only a halfhearted compliment—"We are delighted by the valor of our Allies, the British, Canadians, Americans." Three days later, in a statement to *Pravda*, Stalin said what needed to be said, congratulating the Allies on a unique undertaking, one that both Napoleon and Hitler had threatened but never even dared to attempt: "The gigantic plan of forcing the Channel and of landing in force on the other side."[37]

THE HOLOCAUST

From the outset of his career, Ilya Ehrenburg explored Jewish themes in his writing. Even in his early twenties when he considered becoming a Catholic, he wrote poems about anti-Semitism and hope in the Zionist dream. During World War I he described a Polish pogrom in verse and the favorite among his books, *Julio Jurenito*, contained a major chapter foretelling the Holocaust; but this work only begins to suggest Ehrenburg's preoccupation with the fate of the Jews during World War II.

Two months after Hitler's invasion, on August 24, 1941, an extraordinary collection of Soviet Jewish personalities broadcast an appeal to "brother Jews" around the world. Led by Solomon Mikhoels, the renowned actor and director of the Moscow Yiddish State Theater, speaker after speaker emphasized the unity of the Jewish people and the threat of Nazi persecution. The writer Samuil Marshak described a massacre of Jewish children in Poland. Peretz Markish, the most accomplished Yiddish poet in the country, whose fame reached beyond Jewish circles, recalled historical episodes of persecution and heroism. Ehrenburg too made a substantial speech, evoking images from his childhood and the nightmare of Nazi roundups as part of his appeal for help.

> I grew up in a Russian city. My mother tongue is Russian. I am a Russian writer. Like all Russians, I am now defending my homeland. But the Hitlerites have reminded me of something else: my mother's name was Hannah. I am a Jew. I say this with pride. We hate Hitler more than anyone else . . . I am appealing now to American Jews— as a Russian writer and as a Jew. There is no ocean behind which to take cover.[38]

This international broadcast and the gathering that took place the same day in Moscow's Park of Culture, which was attended by thousands of people, marked the beginning of the Jewish Anti-Fascist Committee. The history of the JAC is troubling and complex—nearly all of its leading figures were imprisoned or executed by 1952; its origins too carry the taste of blood.

The initial idea of forming a Jewish committee against fascism was proposed by Henryk Erlich and Viktor Alter, the leaders of the Jewish Socialist Bund of Poland. They had been arrested in Lithuania by Soviet police in the fall of 1939, then released two years later after being threatened with long prison terms and execution. By that time, in the early fall of 1941, with the Soviet Union facing military catastrophe, Stalin was anxious to improve relations with the Western powers. Erlich and Alter had strong contacts with labor groups in the West as well as with Jewish organizations. By releasing them the Kremlin hoped to placate their supporters and enlist both men in Soviet plans against Hitler. At the behest of the regime Erlich and Alter outlined a proposal for a Jewish committee against fascism that would involve refugees from German-occupied countries and the Soviet Union. Their plan was international in scope and included a Jewish Legion in the Red Army made up of American volunteers.

But their ideas never went into effect. They were submitted to Lavrenti Beria, head of the secret police, who made clear that only Stalin could approve them. Stalin was not about to establish a genuinely independent Jewish organization. Moreover, by December the Red Army began its first concerted counteroffensive, relieving the pressure on Moscow and forcing the Germans out of Rostov. Stalin's confidence was restored, making Erlich and Alter expendable. For years it was assumed they were summarily executed in early December, but in fact they were arrested and kept in solitary confinement in Kuibyshev. Erlich committed suicide in his cell in May 1942; Alter was shot in February 1943.[39]

The idea of some kind of Jewish committee against Hitler, though, remained in the air. Over the winter of 1941–42 the Kremlin put together several "front" organizations for women, scientists, Ukrainians, and Slavs that were designed to encourage the war effort at home and drum up support for the Soviet Union abroad. The Jewish Anti-Fascist Committee (JAC) was established in April 1942 and fit into this mosaic of groups, all of which operated under the direct supervision of the Soviet Bureau of Information, headed first by Alexander Shcherbakov and then by Solomon Lozovsky, a vice commissar for foreign affairs.

Though the JAC failed to include foreign delegates and was closely monitored, it became a national, representative body for Soviet Jews, whose leaders included Solomon Mikhoels, Peretz Markish, David Bergelson, and Ilya Ehrenburg, individuals of genuine moral and cultural authority within Jewish circles and, in some cases, the country at large. By allowing them to speak as representatives of Soviet Jewry Stalin inadvertently created the hope for cultural revival and greater, freer contact with Jews abroad, illusions that contradicted Soviet policies of more than two decades.

From the outset JAC leaders argued over the precise nature of the committee's responsibilities. All agreed that it should work hard to support the war effort, raise funds, and issue appeals to Jews in other countries; but as the war progressed and the extent of Jewish losses became evident many members of the committee—though not all—wanted to expand its functions. Proposals were made to help resettle Jewish refugees, to reestablish Jewish collective farms, and to revive Jewish cultural life.

Ehrenburg had his own concerns. Consistent with his hatred of anti-Semitism, he wanted to document Jewish suffering and the contribution of Jewish soldiers and partisans, which came as no surprise to Ehrenburg's close friends. Ehrenburg was an assimilated Jew in the sense that he felt removed from Orthodox ritual and spoke neither Yiddish nor Hebrew; he identified himself primarily with Russian language and culture, yet his Jewish origins were a constant source of strength to him. In a letter to Liza Polonskaya in Petrograd in 1923 Ehrenburg offered her encouragement in startling, joyous phrases. "Don't give up being a heretic," he wrote to her from Berlin. "Without it, people of our nature (and we have the same nature) could not live through a single day. We are Jews. We drank up Parisian skies. We are poets. We know how to laugh things off. Aren't these four qualities enough to keep going?"[40]

His friend, the journalist and literary critic Nino Frank, a Sephardic Jew from Italy who first met Ehrenburg in Paris in the 1920s, once drew an illuminating portrait of him.

First, I saw a Soviet man, a messenger from the country of October, a man of the new age. But he dismissed my ideas. Then I figured he was a grandson of Voltaire, loyal to these sources . . . however obsolete they had become. . . . But none of this was sufficient. There was something else more fundamental, where these elements, the Revolution and culture, were intertwined, some kind of steam pot where a secret force simmered . . .

At that time, I used to make Ehrenburg laugh . . . and I laughed myself as well, if I spoke to him about Judaism. Before 1930, this kind of discussion was out-of-date for us, and we left it for archeologists and bastards. We had no idea the latter would become so legion. It is only today I understand, when I wonder about the secret of Ehrenburg's vitality and all his constant accommodations, that I recognize an inexhaustible urge for freedom, a raging and absolute sense of freedom . . .

Ehrenburg is first of all a Jew. . . . Ehrenburg had rejected his origins with all his being, disguised himself in the West, smoking Dutch tobacco and making his travel plans at Cook's. . . . But he did not erase the Jew, what was for me a new kind of Jew, the Ashkenazi.[41]

Long before Hitler's Final Solution Ehrenburg recognized an essential dilemma of contemporary Jewish life: to identify with the plight of Jews anywhere and remain loyal citizens in a particular state. In "French Jews and the War," an article written in April 1917, Ehrenburg pointed out that whether they had been mistreated workers or comfortable merchants in civilian life, Jewish soldiers fought equally hard—including Russian and Romanian Jews, whose persecuted status was well known. He went on to describe pacifist French Jews and "thousands of Algerian, Moroccan, and Tunisian Jews who responded to the call of France," and he emphasized the satisfaction of French Jewish soldiers over the decision of Russia's newly installed Provisional Government to abolish the Pale of Settlement and grant Jews equal legal status. In spite of his assimilation Ehrenburg was sensitive to this dilemma, which remains true for Jews in all societies who find themselves living in two worlds and not part of either. Anti-Semites suspect that Jews cannot be equally loyal to both their native land and to fellow Jews. Ehrenburg understood this prejudice, which explains why he began his April 1917 article with a prescient reminder: "the Greco-Roman world indicted the Jews, claiming that in a cosmopolitan society they remained nationalists, while the modern world indicts them by claiming that among nationalists, [the Jews] are cosmopolitans."[42]

Ehrenburg never forgot that he was a Jew. In 1944 he read Julian Tuwim's article "We—the Polish Jews," which captured the profound anguish Ehrenburg felt throughout his life as a Russian patriot and a Jew. Tuwim wrote about anti-Semitism and his Polish origins on the first anniversary of the Warsaw Ghetto uprising, when he learned that his mother had been killed by the Nazis. After reading it Ehrenburg recalled how he "could not speak to anyone for a long time." The essay in fact has never appeared in Russian translation, but Ehrenburg translated it himself and quoted it often, including the following principal paragraphs in People, Years, Life:

Right away, I hear the question: "Why do you say 'we'?" The question has some justification. It has been asked of me by Jews to whom I have always said I was a Pole. Now it will be asked of me by Poles for whom I remain more or less a Jew. Here is the answer to both of them. I am a Pole because I like being a Pole. This is my personal business and I am not obligated to explain it to anyone. I do not divide Poles into those who are purebred and those who are not; I leave that to foreign and native-born racists. I divide Poles, as I do Jews and people of any nationality, into intelligent and stupid ones, honest and dishonest, interesting and dull, oppressors and oppressed, worthy and unworthy. I also divide Poles into Fascists and anti-Fascists . . . I could add that, on a political level, I divide Poles into anti-Semites and anti-Fascists because anti-Semitism is the international language of Fascists . . .

I hear voices: "Very well. But if you are a Pole, why do you write 'We Jews'?" I will reply: "Because of blood." "Then is it racism?" No. On the contrary. There are two kinds of blood: the blood that flows inside the veins and the blood that flows out of them. The first is the sap of the body. . . . The other kind of blood is that which the ringleader of international fascism pumps out of humanity in order to prove the superiority of his blood over mine.[43]

As the war progressed Ehrenburg was also disheartened by increasing anti-Semitism within the Soviet Union. As early as November 1941 he heard anti-Semitic slurs in Kuibyshev from none other than the famous Soviet writer Mikhail Sholokhov. "You are fighting," Sholokhov told him, "but Abram is doing business in Tashkent." Ehrenburg was furious and shouted that he could not "sit at the same table with a pogrom-monger."[44] Sholokhov's racism was widely known. Later that month Vasily Grossman wrote a detailed letter to Ehrenburg about anti-Semitism, about the many Jewish soldiers he encountered at the front, and about Sholokhov's disreputable behavior:

I think about Sholokhov's anti-Semitic slander with pain and contempt. Here on the south-western front, there are thousands, tens of thousands of Jews. They are walking with machine-guns into the snow storms, breaking into towns held by the Germans, falling in battle. I saw all of this. I saw the illustrious commander of the First Guards Division Kogan, tank officers, and intelligence men. If Sholokhov is in Kuibyshev, be sure to let him know that comrades at the front know what he is saying. Let him be ashamed.[45]

Jews in fact earned the most disproportionate number of military awards of any Soviet nationality during the war, distinguishing themselves in every branch of the Soviet military. Ehrenburg addressed this issue with particular poignancy in February 1943 at a meeting of the Jewish Anti-Fascist Committee in Moscow just after returning from the front areas around Kursk.

> I met a Jew of advanced age, the father of a famous pilot . . . and he told me: "I spoke with a certain civilian official who said to me: 'How do you explain the fact that there are no Jews at the front? Why doesn't one see Jews in the war?' I did not answer him because I found it hard to speak. That was only four days after I had received notice of my son's death."[46]

Ehrenburg worked hard wherever he could to counteract anti-Semitic prejudice; for some it seemed as if he was the only journalist dealing with the "torment of the Jews."[47] Writing in *Krasnaya Zvezda* in November 1942, Ehrenburg described the heroic exploits of Jewish soldiers in diverse units of the Soviet armed forces: "Hitler wanted to turn the Jews into a target. The Jews of Russia showed him that a target shoots. . . . Once upon a time, the Jews dreamed of a promised land. Now a Jew has a promised land: the main line of defense. There he can take revenge against the Germans for wives, for the elderly, for children."[48]

For Ehrenburg there could be no doubt about Jewish loyalty to the Soviet war effort. Once, at a small gathering that included Mikhail Sholokhov, Ehrenburg made a toast "to the homeland." Sholokhov tried to bait him. "Which homeland?" he asked, as if Ehrenburg had a competing loyalty to Palestine. But Ehrenburg cut him down. "The homeland Vlasov betrayed" was all he needed to say.[49] (When General Andrei Vlasov, a hero of Moscow's defense, was captured by the Germans, he began recruiting Soviet prisoners of war to fight alongside Hitler's men.) There may have been Russians who sided with the Germans, but no Jew would betray Stalin for Hitler.

———

At the height of the Nazi onslaught the Soviet regime found it useful to exploit the martyrdom of Soviet Jews. This was especially true between 1941 and 1943, when Stalin was most anxious for British and American aid and needed to repair the political damage resulting from the nonaggression pact with Hitler. That was one reason why Maxim Litvinov, who was Jewish, was dispatched to Washington, D.C., to serve as ambassador. By the summer of 1943, however, following the momentous Soviet victories at Stalingrad and Kursk, the Red Army began to push the Germans out of the country; Stalin moved to diminish official concern about the Jews.

Ehrenburg sensed this change. His articles began to be heavily censored, particularly when he wrote about Jewish martyrdom and heroism. Concerned, he appealed to Alexander Shcherbakov, who supervised the press. Shcherbakov was hardly sympathetic. "The soldiers want to hear about Suvorov but you quote Heine," he told Ehrenburg.[50] That same summer other prominent Jews were replaced; Maxim Litvinov was recalled from the United States and General David Ortenberg, the editor of *Krasnaya Zvezda*, was transferred. In 1943 Irina Ehrenburg lost her job at the front-line army newspaper *Unichtozhim Vraga* (We Will Destroy the Enemy). A Soviet colonel visited the paper's office and immediately began to curse the staff; too many of them were Jews. "What is this, a synagogue?" he shouted. The newspaper was shut down and the journalists assigned separately to other posts.[51]

Around that time the regime also undermined a major project Ehrenburg had just completed. As the Red Army counterattacked, he received hundreds of letters from soldiers about the atrocities they discovered in the Germans' wake. Eager to use the material, Ehrenburg arranged with Jean-Richard Bloch to produce a volume in Russian and French called *One Hundred Letters*; it was to appear in the summer of 1943. "The book was set up, was ready for binding, then suddenly withdrawn," Ehrenburg recalled in *People, Years, Life*. "I asked for a reason and got no reply; finally someone on the editorial staff said, 'This isn't 1941.'" The French edition appeared two years later, but the original Russian text was banned—the book contained too many references to Jews and their martyrdom for it to appear in Moscow. Even in his memoirs in the 1960s Ehrenburg was not permitted to recall the following incident from the war.

In March of 1944, I received a letter from officers in a unit that had liberated Dubno. They wrote that V. I. Krassova had dug out a shelter under her house and for almost three years concealed and fed eleven Jews in there. I wrote to Mikhail Kalinin [the Soviet president, who oversaw the granting of medals] and asked if he did not consider it just to award Krassova a ribbon or a medal. Soon after, Kalinin presented me with an award. When the ceremony was over, Kalinin said: "I received your letter. You are right—it would be good to recognize [her courage]. But you see, it is impossible now . . ." Mikhail Kalinin was a man of pure heart, a genuine Communist, and I felt that it was hard for him to say this.[52]

EHRENBURG AND JEWISH PARTISANS

By 1944 Ehrenburg often followed Red Army troops as they cleaned out Germans from cities and towns. He was with them in July when they liberated Vilna. A group of Jewish partisans numbering about one hundred men and women took part. "If any Nazis escape our siege," an officer told them, "then you capture them." Shlomo Kowarski, a member of the partisan unit, recalled meeting Ehrenburg in Vilna on July 12, 1944.

> We were resting outside when a car pulled up and a man got out to approach us. "I am Ilya Ehrenburg." It was as if he had dropped out of heaven. People started screaming, running to meet him. "Ehrenburg is here, Ehrenburg is here." We knew about him from the papers. Ehrenburg was thrilled to meet Jewish partisans. He asked what we did and we explained how we blew up trains and railroad stations. He was different, not just a Soviet journalist. We accepted him as a fellow Jew.[53]

During the last years of the war Ehrenburg came to know numerous Jewish partisans. He trusted them, invited them to his home and spoke candidly with them. Each of these encounters left a deep impression on Ehrenburg and the partisans themselves. They saw a side to Ehrenburg that few others ever did. They saw how proud he was to be a Jew, how Jewish suffering mattered to him, and how angry he was over the Kremlin's indifference. For many of these partisans, who had lost their families and survived difficult, isolated months, even years, in the forests, Ehrenburg was the first "official" to treat them with the respect they deserved. In December 1944 a partisan leader from Minsk, Hirsh Smolar, came to see the Jewish Anti-Fascist Committee in Moscow and spent time with Ehrenburg. Born in Poland in 1905, Smolar became active in the Communist movement and was living in

Minsk when Hitler invaded. He soon headed a large partisan group that helped as many as ten thousand Jews to escape into the forests in October 1943. "Ehrenburg had just returned from Kiev and he was in a rotten mood," Smolar remembered. " 'This was my hometown,' he told me, 'and I will never go back there.' Ehrenburg was shocked by all the anti-Semitism he found in Kiev after the Nazi withdrawal." Smolar went on to tell Ehrenburg what happened after Minsk's liberation. The party officials were only interested in how the partisans fought the Nazis but offered no help to the Jews who survived. "Ehrenburg listened. He sat like an old Jew, like a father who was about to cry over a son who has perished," Smolar recalled. "Look at this table," Ehrenburg said. "The floor, too." There were piles of letters. "Take any of them. They are all about one thing. Anti-Semitism."[54]

Ehrenburg had just been to Kiev and visited a large ravine on the city's outskirts, where the Nazis had shot tens of thousands of Jews. In 1961 Yevgeny Yevtushenko created an international uproar with his poem "Babii Yar," which decried German and Russian anti-Semitism and the lack of a monument to memorialize Kiev's Jewish community. But it was Ehrenburg in 1944 who wrote the first poem about the massacre.

Babii Yar

What use are words or a pen,
when this stone weighs on my heart,
when I drag another's memory
like a convict dragging a chain? . . .
My countless relatives!
As if from every pit,
I hear you calling me.
With bones, we'll knock—over there,
where still living cities
breathe with bread and perfumes.
Blow out the light. Lower the flags.
To you we came. Not us, but ditches.[55]

Leaving Babii Yar, Ehrenburg did not know if he was alive or dead, a survivor or a victim buried in a mass grave. He identified intensely with his fellow Jews, recognizing that "each ravine" was also meant for him.[56] He did not know it at the time, but Maria, the oldest of his three sisters—they had all remained in Paris during the German occupation posing as Belgian spinsters—disappeared during the war, presumably deported by the Nazis. In Kiev he saw how badly his hometown community had been decimated and so he offered a poem in place of a prayer for the dead, the Kaddish, whose words he no longer remembered.

———

Of all Ehrenburg's encounters with partisans, his friendship with the Yiddish poet Abraham Sutzkever was the most telling and significant. After the German invasion, Sutzkever, like all the Jews of Vilna, was herded into a ghetto, from where "selections" were made on a daily basis. Sutzkever survived, escaping through the sewers before the ghetto's liquidation. Along with hundreds of other Jews, he soon joined a Lithuanian partisan unit.

Two years later, in the spring of 1944, Sutzkever met Ehrenburg when they both spoke to an audience of three thousand people organized by the Jewish Anti-Fascist Committee. Although it was customary to conclude speeches with Stalin's name, Sutzkever instead ended his talk with a stirring call for vengeance.[57] Ehrenburg immediately befriended him. "He became closer to me than all my acquaintances, Jewish and non-Jewish writers and artists in Moscow," Sutzkever remembered years later.[58] By the end of April Ehrenburg published a long profile of Sutzkever in Pravda, "The Triumph of a Man," which described the poet's role in the Vilna ghetto, his saving of precious Russian manuscripts, and his partisan activity. Ehrenburg concluded the piece with a summary of "Kol Nidre," Sutzkever's famous poem about an elderly Jew who kills his son to save him from torture at the hands of the Nazis.[59]

Over the next two years Sutzkever closely observed Ehrenburg's life and work. "He read me wonderful poems from a handwritten manuscript bound in green snakeskin," Sutzkever recalled. "These were the last poems of Osip Mandelstam, written in a labor camp by a campfire among the snow and the wolves. . . . A fugitive who had miraculously escaped or been freed brought the poems to Ehrenburg. Lyubov Mikhailovna told me I was among the few people to whom he read them." Ehrenburg also recited verses of Lorca and Machado in Spanish and asked Sutzkever to read Hebrew poems aloud. "How I love the prophetic sound," Ehrenburg told him. According to Sutzkever, Ehrenburg was the only Moscow writer to take any interest in the verse of Elisha Rodin, the last Hebrew poet in the Soviet Union. Rodin's son Grigory had been killed in March 1942 fighting in an armored unit north of Moscow. Rodin composed a cycle of Hebrew verses in his son's memory; thanks to Ehrenburg he was able to send his poems to Palestine in 1942, where they were published in Tel Aviv.

For Sutzkever Ehrenburg was a one-man Jewish Anti-Fascist Committee, a kind of Russian Joseph welcoming petitions from brethren who had survived a cataclysm. He saw how Ehrenburg helped scores of young Jews gain residence permits to live in Moscow; how at Sutzkever's request he helped free partisan women from Grodno who had been falsely accused of collaborating with the Nazis; how he responded to hundreds of letters from lonely people desperate to know if any of their relatives were alive; and how he sent thousands of rubles to widows who poured out their hearts to him in letters from all over the country.

Soviet officials were not always happy to hear from Ehrenburg. "One day," Abraham Sutzkever recalled, "Lyubov Mikhailovna told me that her husband was lying in bed full of anger. . . . A month earlier, a Jewish Red Army soldier had come from Kiev to Moscow and . . . told Ehrenburg about plans to build an open market in Babii Yar on the mass grave of Kiev's Jews." Ehrenburg wrote a letter to Nikita Khrushchev, the leader of the Ukraine, asking him to prevent construction of the market. Just that day, Ehrenburg had received a reply from Khrushchev's office. "I advise you," the letter said curtly, "not to intervene in matters not your own. Better write good novels instead."[60]

Ehrenburg could not easily restrain himself. His persistence in speaking about Nazi crimes wearied many people around him. Even American officials learned of this reaction. According to a secret OSS report in April 1945, "Ehrenburg's passion and sincerity were undeniable, but his single-minded devotion to his themes and his ceaseless discussion of them at parties and in conversations had begun to make him personally obnoxious."[61]

By the spring of 1945 Ehrenburg became involved in a deeply intimate way when he helped his daughter adopt a young Jewish orphan. Fanya Fishman grew up in Rovno in the Western Ukraine. After the Germans captured the city her mother and two sisters were killed while Fanya and her father escaped to the woods. Two older brothers became soldiers—the first in the Red Army and the second in the Polish army; they both fought throughout the war all the way to Berlin. Fanya's father perished in the forest, but she was cared for by a partisan unit until Ehrenburg learned of her and brought her to Moscow. Fanya initially had been placed with a Jewish engineer's family who treated her poorly, having failed to understand that after months in the woods she required patience instead of stern discipline.

Once again Ehrenburg intervened and took her to his own apartment. He arranged for her education and also helped to locate her brothers, who came to see her soon after the war. They tried unsuccessfully to convince Fanya to join them in Palestine, but Irina, who had been left childless after her husband's death, gained Fanya's love and she agreed to be adopted. Fanya stayed in Moscow, where she studied medicine and became a distinguished cardiologist. Her brothers live today in Israel.[62]

THE BLACK BOOK

Near the end of 1944 a teenage partisan named Shlomo Perlmutter visited Ehrenburg in Moscow. Ehrenburg had just been in Lithuania, where he had found an abandoned book in Hebrew. He could not read it, so he asked Perlmutter to translate the first page. Produced in the Kaunas ghetto, the volume was entitled *Orphanhood* and was dedicated to a Hebrew teacher. Listening to Perlmutter, Ehrenburg took the book in his hands and showed it to Boris Gorbatov, a non-Jewish writer who was also visiting. "You see, we really are the people of the book," Ehrenburg told him, his voice trembling. "Show me another people, who right in the slaughterhouse, on the eve of their destruction, would publish a book. There is no other people."[63]

As the war progressed, Ehrenburg's involvement with the Jewish Anti-Fascist Committee focused on one ambitious project. Under his direction more than two dozen writers worked on *The Black Book*, a record of the greatest catastrophe to befall Soviet Jewry *before it was even over*: the murder of one and a half million Jews by the *Einsatzgruppen*, four shooting units that followed the *Wehrmacht* into Soviet territory.

Such a collaborative effort was unprecedented in the Soviet Union. Ehrenburg used his connection to the Jewish Anti-Fascist Committee to create his own committee of writers without official permission or guidance "from above." *The Black Book* afforded these writers a chance to speak the truth about what was happening to them. It would be years before any Soviet writer could dare approach Stalin's crimes with similar passion and directness; they could not write about the enormous labor camps in Vorkuta or Kolyma. But Vasily Grossman did visit Maidanek and Treblinka after their liberation by the Red Army in the summer of 1944 and was among the first to interview survivors and learn how the Germans carried out mass exterminations.[64]

Other writers too produced vivid accounts based on material handed to them by Ehrenburg or collected on their own. Abraham Sutzkever prepared over two hundred pages on Nazi atrocities in Lithuania. Ovady Savich spoke with survivors in Latvia. Margarita Aliger worked on testimonies from the Brest area in Byelorussia. Ehrenburg's daughter Irina also lent a hand. She had been to Kovno in Lithuania, where French Jews had left inscriptions on prison walls before their execution. She had copied them down and once back in Moscow translated them into Russian. Ehrenburg himself prepared a great deal of material for publication: letters from children in Byelorussia, from soldiers who lost their families, and testimonies from survivors in a host of towns and villages. He relates one particular story, about a Jew who hides from the Nazis with the help of his non-Jewish wife, with almost biblical concision:

Natalya Emelyanova hid her husband in a hole under their stove. He spent more than two years there. He had to sit bent over, since there was not room to lie down or stand up. When he sometimes came up at night, he was not able to straighten out. It was concealed from the children that their father was hiding in the cellar. Once the four-year-old daughter looked in a crack and saw large black eyes. She was frightened and shouted: "Mama, who is there?" Natalya Emelyanova calmly answered: "It's a very large rat; I noticed it a long time ago."

. . . Natalya Emelyanova fell ill with typhus. She was taken away to the hospital, and a neighbor took in her children. At night Isaak Rosenberg crawled out and ate the glue from the wallpaper for two weeks. In the hospital Natalya Emelyanova worried that she might give away her husband in a delirium.

In September 1943, units of the Red Army came almost right up to the small town. Monastyrshchina is a crossroads, and the Germans resisted strongly at that point. The battles went on, and armed Germans were next to the Rosenberg house. Like the other residents of

Monastyrshchina, Natalya Emelyanova took the children and fled
into the forest. She returned when the Red Army soldiers entered
the town. She found still-smoking ashes and the stove; the house had
burned down. Isaak Rosenberg had died from asphyxiation. He had
sat out twenty-six months in the cellar and died two days before
Monastyrshchina was liberated by Soviet units.[65]

Even as Ehrenburg continued to gather material, the fate of *The
Black Book* was subjected to the shifting aims of Soviet propaganda. The
idea originated in the United States near the end of 1942 when Albert
Einstein, the writer Shalom Asch, and B. Z. Goldberg (the son-in-law
of Sholem Aleichem), who were the leaders of the pro-Soviet American Committee of Jewish Writers, Artists and Scientists, sent a telegram
to the JAC proposing a joint volume about Nazi crimes against the
Jews. Solomon Mikhoels, the chairman of the JAC, enthusiastically
endorsed this idea but the committee would not be allowed to reach a
decision by itself and instead had to rely on the Soviet Information
Bureau for permission to proceed.

It was not until the summer of 1943 that the JAC officially took up
the project. That summer Mikhoels and his deputy, the Yiddish poet
Itzik Fefer, spent several months on a tour of North America and
England, meeting with Jewish communities and drumming up money
and support for the Soviet war effort. Einstein met them in New York
and persuaded them to join *The Black Book* project, but only after the
Soviet emissaries exchanged several telegrams with their political masters in Moscow. Permission in hand, Mikhoels and Fefer reached an
agreement with several Jewish agencies: the World Jewish Congress, the
National Council in Jerusalem, and the American Committee of Jewish Writers, Artists and Scientists. Each organization was to collect
information on the Holocaust and contribute to a joint publication in
various languages.

By January 1944 the JAC roundly supported the project, with
Ehrenburg recognized as "one of the most active initiators of *The Black
Book*."[66] He became head of the JAC's literary commission. In April
Shakhno Epshteyn, a leading figure in the JAC and editor of its news-
paper *Eynikayt*, announced that the book would appear in Russian,
Yiddish, English, Hebrew, Spanish, German, and other languages.
Ehrenburg had reason to feel gratified for his efforts. For Ehrenburg all
this work coincided with his consistent efforts throughout the war to

document Jewish suffering and heroism. His readers were a constant source of information. Ehrenburg's Moscow apartment was filled with piles of letters, thousands of them, mostly from Soviet Jews who shared their anguish with him. Ehrenburg collected these letters carefully, sorted and numbered them by nationality and often corresponded with individuals asking for further details about what they had witnessed or the fate of their loved ones. Many of these letters became primary sources for *The Black Book*, particularly after July 27, 1943, when the Jewish Anti-Fascist Committee issued a public appeal for information about the Holocaust. Ehrenburg received such letters for the rest of his life and they reflected the full pathos of Jewish existence in the Soviet Union: Nazi massacres, domestic anti-Semitism, the Doctors' Plot, the dearth of Jewish themes in Soviet literature, and the effect of Israel's establishment on Soviet Jewry.

During the war one officer asked Ehrenburg to help organize a Jewish division in the Red Army. Another wanted a separate territory for Jews in the Ukraine. Still others described how their neighbors helped the Germans round up Jewish victims. In June 1944 one survivor wrote from Odessa that "a Romanian-German infection had penetrated every Soviet institution," and could only see anti-Semitism abate once property that had formerly belonged to Jews had all been taken. For these Jews Ehrenburg was the only person to whom they could send their complaints and hope for some sympathy and redress. One compared him to Moses, another to the prophet Jeremiah, while *The Black Book* would serve as a new *Book of Lamentations* for the Jewish people, "a monument . . . , a cold stone on which every Jew will be able to shed bitter tears over his murdered friends and relatives."[67]

Ehrenburg's energy and determination seemed unlimited. In the earlier aborted project *One Hundred Letters* and in numerous articles in major Soviet newspapers and in smaller papers such as the *Birobidjaner Stern*, which were addressed specifically to the country's Jews, Ehrenburg stressed Jewish suffering in particular as often as he could. With the support of the JAC Ehrenburg now had even more outlets for dissemination of material about the Holocaust. *Eynikayt* began to publish material prepared for *The Black Book*. Ehrenburg also was able to place excerpts in *Znamya* and extensive material in the Yiddish-language anthology *Merder fun Felker* (Murderers of Peoples), which appeared in two volumes published separately in 1944 and 1945.[68]

By the fall of 1944, however, Ehrenburg grew increasingly pessimistic about the book's prospects. At a meeting of the literary commission on October 13, 1944, Ehrenburg complained that "it was not
clear whether publication would be sanctioned." As he reported to his
colleagues, leaders of the JAC had told him to "Get the book ready. If
it turns out to be good, it will be published." Ehrenburg could not help
but regard such instructions with contempt: "Since it is the Germans
and not us who write this book," Ehrenburg sarcastically observed, "its
purpose is clear. I do not understand the meaning of 'if it turns out to
be good'; after all, it is not a novel whose contents are not yet known."
Still he persisted and with his friend Vasily Grossman continued to
compile and edit scores of testimonies. Ehrenburg's strategy was clear.
"It seems to me," he told the other members of the commission, "that
once the task of assembling the manuscript became possible, it would
be easier to fight for its publication."[69]

Events soon discouraged him altogether. Sometime in late 1944
over five hundred pages of The Black Book were sent to the United
States for distribution. Ehrenburg was furious. No one had asked for
his permission or even informed him of the request from America.
Ehrenburg immediately understood that once the material appeared
in the West it would be harder to publish in Moscow. He wanted the
book to appear first in the Soviet Union, where it was most needed
to combat domestic anti-Semitism. In the West chapters appeared
mainly in Jewish newspapers rather than in general circulation mag-
azines with a broader audience. Ehrenburg believed committee leaders deliberately undermined what he was trying to accomplish. Furious, he broke off with the JAC and began referring to it as the
"Judenrat" or the "anti-Jewish committee" in the presence of startled
Jewish partisans.[70]

With Ehrenburg out of the way the JAC no longer had to contend
with his stubbornness or his prestige. The Soviet Information Bureau,
now headed by Solomon Lozovsky, formed a special committee to
review the work of the literary commission and recommend how to
proceed. Meeting on February 24, 1945, the committee approved the
project. It also made one pointed criticism of Ehrenburg's manuscript.
"Too much is recounted about the vile activity of traitors among the
Ukrainians, Lithuanians and others," the committee remarked. "This
weakens the force of the principal accusation against the Germans,
which should be the fundamental and decisive purpose of the book."

(As the material was further edited and revised, reports of collaboration were removed, much to Ehrenburg's chagrin.)[71]

Based on the committee's recommendations and Lozovsky's subsequent letter to Ehrenburg it appears that the committee actually reviewed two different manuscripts: one of testimonies collected and prepared under Ehrenburg's supervision, and a second anthology of documents. Lozovsky tried to convince Ehrenburg that both volumes needed to be published, that in fact hundreds of pamphlets should be prepared, and asked Ehrenburg to continue to work on the material. Ehrenburg was too discouraged and too bitter. He confirmed his resignation from the literary commission and sent brief letters to the writers who had helped him, including Grossman and Sutzkever, to thank them and urge them to publish the documents they had prepared when the opportunity arose. "I am deeply convinced," Ehrenburg concluded, "that your work on behalf of history will not be lost."[72]

Vasily Grossman, who had worked closely with Ehrenburg for over a year on *The Black Book*, assumed editorial responsibility. Additional testimonies continued to reach the JAC, while Grossman also intended to use material relating to the allied victory and the Nuremberg trials. Ehrenburg was not completely divorced from the project. He followed events as best he could and even believed as late as 1946 that the book would appear. "The type was set up, the book reached proof stage, and we were told it would be published in 1948," Ehrenburg recalled in his memoirs.[73] But on November 26, 1946, with no further assurance from the regime, Ehrenburg co-signed an appeal with Grossman, alongside the signatures of Mikhoels and Fefer, directed to Andrei Zhdanov, who had become secretary of the Central Committee and seemed to be in a position to reach a decision. Zhdanov failed to respond and instead passed the letter to the propaganda department. It was only on October 7, 1947, that the publications division of the propaganda department explicitly responded to Zhdanov, confirmed *The Black Book*'s "grave political errors," and forbade publication.[74] Stalin now had other plans for the Jews. Solomon Mikhoels was murdered in January 1948. Later that year the Jewish Anti-Fascist Committee was officially closed, along with its Yiddish publishing house. The typeset of *The Black Book* was broken up. It did not appear in the Soviet Union, but was published in Jerusalem three decades later.

THE FINAL YEAR

Ehrenburg's renown by the final year of the war appeared to be unassailable. The Soviet regime had bestowed on him two of its highest awards: in 1942, the Stalin Prize for literature for his novel *The Fall of Paris* and on May Day 1944, the Lenin Prize for his wartime efforts. In December 1944 Vyacheslav Molotov confided to the French diplomat Georges Bidault that Ehrenburg "was worth several divisions."[75] De Gaulle as well personally acknowledged Ehrenburg's contribution. After the liberation of France de Gaulle's new government presented Ehrenburg with membership in the Legion of Honor, the country's most prestigious award.

In the United States Ehrenburg's importance was recognized in the highest circles in Washington. In 1943 Vice President Henry Wallace, who had been studying Russian, sent Ehrenburg his first letter in that language. "I want to tell you," Wallace wrote,

> that when I speak about our century as the "century of the common man," I have in mind that national spirit that saved your motherland and which you so masterfully described in your article "The Dawn." I always read your articles with great interest. They express such faith in the people's spirit. Yes, the future belongs to nations with a steadfast spirit and with a love for freedom. I wish you all the best,
>
> Henry A. Wallace[76]

No other private Soviet citizen reached such unique stature. One American commentator remarked in 1944 that Ehrenburg enjoyed "fame and position in his homeland unlike that of any writer in the world."[77] The *New York Herald Tribune* congratulated Ehrenburg in March 1945 for his reporting on the war:

> Ilya Ehrenburg, who has known how to cut through to the heart of so many bitter truths, who has spoken so passionately for the Russian people in their greatest hour of suffering and of victory, should be better known in the United States. His most recent summary of the military position is worth all the lucubrations of fifty Congressmen, twenty columnists and a dozen political experts.[78]

In Moscow a rumor circulated that Hitler had vowed to hang three men in Red Square: Stalin, Ehrenburg, and Shostakovich (for the Seventh Symphony in honor of the siege of Leningrad). Ivan Maisky, who had served as ambassador to England and returned to Moscow in 1944, voiced the opinion in a small, private meeting at the Writers' Union that there were only two people whose role in the conflict could be compared: "the name of one was Ehrenburg. He did not name the second. It was obvious that the very idea of comparing the two was frightening."[79]

Perhaps owing to such prestige, Stalin toyed with the idea of arresting Ehrenburg as a spy in January 1945. Only one source for this astonishing episode has come to light—a conversation between Alexander Fadeyev and his close friend Kornely Zelinsky. Stalin is said to have summoned Fadeyev, a leading figure in the Writers' Union, and questioned him about the presence of "two major international spies" among its members. When Fadeyev could barely respond, Stalin claimed that Alexei Tolstoy was "a British spy" and Ilya Ehrenburg "an international one."[80] It is impossible to say for sure what Stalin had in mind. Tolstoy was severely ill and died of cancer that same month. Ehrenburg, of course, was not arrested. Nonetheless, at least two plausible reasons for Stalin's behavior, however speculative, deserve to be explored. First, it is possible that German intelligence in a desperate move planted fabricated information about Ehrenburg and Tolstoy in order to confuse Soviet troops just as the Red Army was advancing into the German heartland. Talking to Fadeyev about the accusations could have been part of Stalin's attempt to verify the charges, and once to his satisfaction they proved to be false, there was no further need to raise the matter. A second, more likely explanation is that Stalin was already planning his post-war political strategy. The Red Army had liberated Eastern Europe and was about to occupy large parts of Germany itself. Four months later, in April 1945, as will be discussed, Stalin did have Ehrenburg severely rebuked in order to signal a policy shift toward Germany. Perhaps in January he wanted to alert the writers' community to stop lauding Ehrenburg, or perhaps Stalin was contemplating an even harsher way to jettison Ehrenburg but then reconsidered; the timing was premature and the method too abrupt, even by Stalin's standards.

———

By August 1944, when Soviet troops were approaching German territory, Ehrenburg knew in detail about the concentration camps and the gas chambers. Tens of thousands of Soviet troops were taken to

Maidanek and Treblinka to emotionally prepare them for the final onslaught against the Nazis. Ehrenburg was not about to moderate his voice. Writing in *Pravda* on August 7, he described how trains brought Jews from France, Holland, and Belgium to killing centers in Poland. "We are not only on the German border, we are on the threshold of a trial," Ehrenburg wrote in his piece "On the Eve." "It is not revenge that is driving us, but a longing for justice. We want to go through Germany with a sword in order to beat out of the Germans for centuries their love of the sword. We want to go to them so that they will never again come to us."[81]

Then in December, with Soviet troops poised to invade East Prussia, Ehrenburg emphasized in *Pravda* the Nazis' greatest crime, their destruction of the Jewish people. "Ask a captured German why his countrymen destroyed six million innocent people and he will answer: 'They are Jews. They are black or red-haired. They have different blood'. . . All this began with stupid jokes, with the shouts of street kids, with signposts, and it led to Maidanek, Babii Yar, Treblinka, to ditches filled with children's corpses."[82]

Articles such as these could not be ignored. Already in March 1943, in the wake of the disastrous German defeat at Stalingrad, the leading Nazi newspaper, the *Volkischer Beobachter* (National Observer), paid ironic homage to Ehrenburg on its front page. For the Nazi press Ehrenburg was "a typical intellectual, an 'asphalt Jew,' who is at home in the Moscow Kremlin, in a Paris nightclub, or in a Jewish salon in New York." But "what he is now reporting . . . is an appalling mixture, lumping sentimental caricatures of soft-hearted and magnanimous Soviet soldiers with genuine slander about the behavior of German troops on the Eastern Front. It is all a lie from beginning to end." Next to a photograph of Ehrenburg the newspaper concludes by urging its readers "to look at this negative Jewish mug. That is enough to recognize the spirit of Stalin's number one war correspondent."[83]

Now, in December 1944, with German borders about to be overrun Ehrenburg was turned into a monstrous fiend. One German commander, wishing to raise the morale of his men, warned that "Ilya Ehrenburg is urging the Asiatic peoples to drink the blood of German women." Joseph Goebbels spread a similar rumor, distributing a pamphlet among German soldiers that Ehrenburg was encouraging Soviet soldiers to rape their wives. Even Hitler joined the charade. In an order dated January 1, 1945, the Führer complained that "Stalin's court lackey, Ilya Ehrenburg, declares that the German people must be exterminated."[84]

From England a Lady Dorothy Gibb appealed to Ehrenburg to leave justice to God and stop calling for revenge against the Germans. Ehrenburg included her letter in a column in *Krasnaya Zvezda* in October 1944, provoking a deluge of mail to her English village from Soviet troops who shared his thirst for justice.[85]

———

Ehrenburg looked forward to the end of the war with optimism, firmly believing that "life will be better, sounder, more just." He expected friendly relations with the rest of Europe and more open borders. It seemed inconceivable that Stalin's dictatorship could resume with the same ruthless abandon. Speaking to Henry Shapiro, Ehrenburg often remarked how much he expected his country to change once Germany and fascism were defeated. Ehrenburg wanted to believe, as he wrote in his memoirs, that "the past could not repeat itself."[86] It is difficult to explain Ehrenburg's wishful thinking. On a personal level, he had felt greater freedom during the war, an experience millions shared, especially at the front. He also believed that the Soviet people had shown their loyalty to the regime at its gravest hour. Hoping against hope, Ehrenburg wanted the Kremlin to respond with greater confidence in the people themselves. He was not alone in this belief. Boris Pasternak as well expected significant change for the better with the end of the war. "Nonetheless," he observed, "the inertia of the past won out."[87]

Ehrenburg's naive optimism was tragically misplaced. In March 1945 Irina Ehrenburg went to Odessa as a journalist, where captured British, French, and Belgian soldiers who had been liberated by the Red Army were being repatriated by sea. She also saw how the regime treated returning Soviet prisoners of war. Irina later told her father how thousands, including men who had escaped and joined the French underground, were received like criminals and sent to labor camps; they were not the first Soviet citizens to be abused by Stalin during the war, and their mistreatment—as cynical a policy as Stalin ever devised—presaged the renewal of official repression that marked the dictator's last years.

Ehrenburg continued to write as he had before, unaware that Stalin's primary concern was no longer the defeat of Germany. On April 11 *Krasnaya Zvezda* carried Ehrenburg's article "Enough," one of his last major pieces of the war that differed little from his earlier columns. Only now, in addition to hatred of Germany (he referred to the German people as "a colossal gang" and lumped them all together as war criminals bearing collective responsibility for Nazi crimes) Ehrenburg decried that German troops were being withdrawn from the western front, where American and British forces were advancing against little resistance, while German armies were gathering to defend Berlin against a Soviet assault.[88] Germans, it seemed, preferred to surrender to the Americans but feared a final reckoning with the Red Army. Soviet troops were poised outside the German capital; two million men and 6,200 tanks were closing in.

Ehrenburg understood better than most observers why the Germans preferred to surrender to Western forces. He had seen for himself the vicious behavior of Soviet troops against German civilians during a visit to East Prussia in early 1945. Upon his return to Moscow Ehrenburg gave two lectures: to the editorial board of *Krasnaya Zvevda* on March 5, and to one hundred fifty staff officers at the Frunze military academy on March 21. He denounced scenes of pillage and rape at the front, "the unnecessary destruction of property, provisions and livestock," even how Soviet soldiers "were not refusing 'the compliments' of German women." Ehrenburg may have felt some responsibility for this urge to carry out revenge but did not hesitate to condemn the "low cultural level" of the troops and their "lack of political preparation." Such observations were unheard of in Moscow and were immediately noted at the highest levels. In a secret memorandum to Stalin on March 29, the head of Soviet military intelligence, Viktor Abakumov, described Ehrenburg's lectures based on the testimony of several informants. For Abakumov Ehrenburg's talks were "politically harmful."[89] Coming from a figure of lesser importance, remarks such as those by Ehrenburg would surely have led to arrest or execution; Ehrenburg was not touched, although Abakumov's denunciation reminded Stalin of Ehrenburg's outspoken character and unparalleled prestige, attributes that Stalin would soon seek to diminish.

Within weeks of Abakumov's denunciation Ehrenburg was harshly rebuked in *Pravda*. On April 14 a prominent article by Georgy Alexandrov accused Ehrenburg of "simplifying" the political situation and argued that the Red Army "never intended and would never have as its goal the extermination of the German people," as Ehrenburg seemed to be advocating.[90] Instigated by Stalin, Alexandrov's article was an oversimplification of Ehrenburg's harsh rhetoric. Although Ehren-burg had called for outright revenge, he had never advocated the exter-mination of the German people or the destruction of Germany as a country. After Ehrenburg had criticized the behavior of the Red Army, however, Stalin turned Ehrenburg's wartime columns and his recent speeches in Moscow against him.

Alexandrov's piece was also a clever tactic. Just as Stalin had silenced Ehrenburg and Maxim Litvinov in 1939 while negotiating the pact with Hitler, so too in April 1945 did he see Ehrenburg's anti-Nazi and anti-German reputation as a liability. By that time Soviet troops con-trolled Germany's eastern zone. Stalin had his "own" Germans now, and if he wanted to cultivate their loyalty—or at least their obedi-ence—it would be easier to do so without Ilya Ehrenburg. On the eve of victory his articles stopped appearing; his name did not appear in print until after the German surrender.

Ehrenburg was devastated. No amount of messages from friends or from front-line troops assuaged his feelings of loss and humiliation. The national radio broadcast Alexandrov's article, while *Krasnaya Zvezda* reprinted it, deepening Ehrenburg's sense of betrayal. He could neither eat nor work. He sat alone in his apartment, doing French crossword puzzles.

Allied newspapers and journals quickly grasped the significance of Alexandrov's rebuke. The *New York Times*, referring to Ehrenburg as "that master of elaborate and frequently rather theatrical sarcasm," called Alexandrov's column "one of the most interesting articles to appear [on German wartime responsibility] in many months." In a sep-arate report from Washington, the *Times* added that the piece "consti-tuted a significant political and diplomatic step" and would "likely con-tribute to Allied understanding."[91] *Newsweek* carried the headline "Slap for Ilya" and echoed Western opinion that Alexandrov was hinting at a change in Stalin's policies by removing "the sting from Ehrenburg's criticism of the Western Allies."[92] *Time* said that Ehrenburg "was soundly spanked," while the *London Times*, in typically restrained prose, made note of Alexandrov's "firm though polite corrective to that pop-ular and independent writer, Ilya Ehrenburg."[93] *Le Monde* carried the most thoughtful reaction. In a front page editorial on April 20, 1945, the French newspaper called the dispute between Alexandrov and Ehrenburg "a curious polemic."[94] For *Le Monde* Alexandrov's repri-mand marked "an abrupt change" in policy and was probably con-

nected to the Soviet occupation of Vienna, where conciliatory appeals
had been made to the Austrians and similar assurances would now
likely be offered the Germans.

Angry and depressed, Ehrenburg appealed to Stalin, sending a letter
with the illusory hope that if he expressed his feelings directly, then
Stalin would relent.

> Having read Alexandrov's article, I thought about my work during
> the war and do not see my guilt. . . . For four years, I wrote articles
> every day. I wanted to complete my work to the end, to victory. Then
> I would be able to return to the work of a novelist. I was not express-
> ing some kind of line of my own, but the feelings of our people.
> . . . No editors, no press department ever told me that I was writing
> incorrectly, and on the eve of the article's appearance which con-
> demned me, I heard from *Pravda* that they would be re-publishing my
> article "Enough!" in a mass printing. The *Pravda* article claims,
> incomprehensibly, that an anti-Fascist calls for the universal destruc-
> tion of the German people. I did not call for this. In those years,
> when the usurpers trampled upon our soil, I wrote that it was nec-
> essary to kill the German occupiers. But at the time I emphasized
> that we are not Fascists and far from reprisals. After returning from
> East Prussia, I emphasized in several articles . . . that we are approach-
> ing the civilian population with different measures than the Hitlerites
> used. In this, my conscience is clean. On the eve of victory, I saw an
> assessment of my work in *Pravda*, which profoundly disturbed me . . .
> I believe in your sense of justice and ask you to decide if I deserved
> this.[95]

Ehrenburg never received a reply from the Kremlin. He had to take
heart from a flood of letters and telegrams and from strangers who
stopped him on the street to shake his hand. Two pilots sent the following telegram from Berlin, typical of the many he received.

> Dear Ilyusha:
>   Today, May 3, 1945, we pilots had the satisfaction of being in Berlin
> near the Reichstag on which the banner of victory has been hoisted.
> . . . We are very surprised, why is your voice not heard? Who has
> offended you? We pilots have been reading your appeals since the first
> day of the war. They inspired us to give everything we had for our

beloved motherland. Don't be down dear friend. Hack away as you began.[96]

Another group of Red Army men tried to console him with a unique gift. They sent Ehrenburg an eighteenth-century hunting rifle that had once been presented to Napoleon Bonaparte. Nazi soldiers had stolen the rifle in France, part of the large booty they hoped to enjoy after the war.[97]

Other soldiers showed their respect for Ehrenburg in a different way. His old friend, the screen actor Fritz Rasp, who had starred in *Jeanne Ney*, survived the war and was in Berlin when Soviet troops entered the city. Seeing them, he went into his garden and dug up a packet of Ehrenburg's books he had concealed from the Nazis. They were in German and each had a warm inscription above Ehrenburg's signature. Impressed, the soldiers hung a sign on Fritz Rasp's door: "Here lives a friend of Ilya Ehrenburg. This house is protected by Soviet troops."[98]

The Soviet assault on Berlin proceeded against desperate resistance. On April 30, two weeks after it had begun, Adolf Hitler killed himself. On May 1 the Soviet banner of victory flew over the Reichstag. But only on May 8 in Rheims, France, and again on May 9 in Berlin did the Third Reich formally surrender. The news reached the Soviet people late that night. By 4 A.M. Red Square and its surrounding streets were filled with cheering crowds. Ehrenburg joined them outside and like a young hero was tossed in the air by a group of soldiers. He was happy, "celebrating with everyone else." But later that night Ehrenburg's mood shifted. He no longer felt optimistic. That same night he wrote his poem "Victory." "More than likely it is in the nature of poetry to feel more sharply and deeply," he explained years later. "I was not trying to be logical in verse. I was not comforting myself. I was expressing the bewilderment and alarm that lurked somewhere deep inside me."

> A poet once mourned over them;
> They had long waited for each other,
> And meeting, they did not recognize one another—
> in the heavens, which no longer know sorrow.
> But not in paradise, on this earthly space
> Where at every step there is sorrow, sorrow, sorrow,
> I waited for her, as one waits only when one loves;

I knew her as one can only know oneself;
I knew her in blood, in mud, in anguish.
The hour struck. The war ended. I made my way home.
She came to meet me, and we did not recognize each
    other.

Hitler was gone and with him the Third Reich. "Something had ended, something was beginning."[99]

TEN

The Iron Curtain

The most morally compromising episodes of Ilya Ehrenburg's career took place during the last years of Stalin's regime, from 1945 to 1953. The wartime alliance between the Western democracies and the Kremlin broke down, leaving the Soviet people increasingly isolated and subject to unrelenting propaganda against Western culture and society. Ehrenburg had to join in. He had demonstrated his loyalty to the regime when Hitler was the enemy; now that the West—and the United States in particular—was about to become the Kremlin's principal antagonist, he would have to prove his loyalty again.

To sustain a measure of integrity, Ehrenburg had to live a double life. His country was isolated yet he was permitted to travel throughout the world. Leading Jewish figures were destined for torture and execution, while he was singled out for medals and awards. Publicly Ehrenburg thrived, but privately he was in anguish. He wanted to help his friends and fellow Jews, and he wanted to survive; all this required being useful to Joseph Stalin.

Stalin's intentions in Eastern Europe were not immediately apparent at the end of the war. In December 1945 the British and Americans, still hoping to see genuinely free elections take place in Poland, Czechoslovakia, Bulgaria, and Romania, sent their foreign ministers to Moscow to negotiate with Soviet leaders. On the night of December 23 Secretary of State James Byrnes visited the Kremlin to speak personally with Stalin. Byrnes was upset with the intransigence of the Soviet foreign ministry and tried to impress Stalin with American resolve, in part by threatening to publish a report on political developments in the Balkans by Mark Ethridge, the editor of the *Louisville Courier-Journal*. President Truman had sent Ethridge to Romania and Bulgaria as his personal representative, and it was assumed that Ethridge's report would discourage U.S. recognition of either regime "under existing conditions."[1] Secretary of State Byrnes, though, decided to withhold the report until he had a chance to discuss its conclusions with Soviet officials.

Stalin listened to Byrnes but was unimpressed with his arguments. He responded that if Byrnes published the Ethridge report then "he would ask . . . Ilya Ehrenburg, who was just as impartial, to publish his views."[2] Ehrenburg had already traveled to Eastern Europe, Germany, and the Balkans, and his articles about the region were ready to appear, as Stalin must have known. Byrnes in the end withheld Ethridge's findings altogether, claiming that he "utilized the Ethridge report to obtain some improvements in the Balkan regimes," but Ehrenburg still published a series of essays on Eastern Europe.[3]

Traveling throughout the region in the summer and fall of 1945, Ehrenburg was greeted as a hero and awarded medals and honors in virtually every country he visited. In Bulgaria he "was carried shoulder-high for a long time . . . in every city."[4] Once he reached Sofia the new government presented him with the Grand Cross of the Order of St. Alexander during an intermission at the opera house. In Albania and in Yugoslavia Ehrenburg was stunned by similar popular receptions. His arrival in Romania exemplified the triumphant nature of his tour: sitting in a Bucharest restaurant, he was recognized by a Romanian journalist and ended up giving twenty consecutive interviews over the next five hours.[5]

Nonetheless Ehrenburg was witnessing the outset of a great catastrophe—the imposition of Stalinist regimes in Eastern Europe—and his reports helped to camouflage the nature of these new governments. In typical Soviet fashion Ehrenburg reported how many freight cars had been repaired in Yugoslavia, how many miles of railroad lines had been restored, how many books and newspapers were being published. In Albania Ehrenburg saw "a really new way of life, meaning schools, roads, and above all, faith in human nature and respect for the dignity of the individual." Enver Hoxha had just come to power in Albania, "a man," Ehrenburg wrote, "of cultured background and true modesty." Hoxha had been a partisan leader and helped lead Albanian resistance to Fascist occupation. Ehrenburg could not have known that this gentleman of "true modesty" would ruthlessly retain power until his death in 1985, officially ban all organized religion, and leave Albania the poorest and most isolated country in all of Europe.

Ehrenburg was no less biased when he visited Romania. Bucharest, he wrote, was "better off than any other city in liberated Europe. People live better here than in Budapest, Rome, or Paris." Ehrenburg praised Communist leaders such as Joseph Tito of Yugoslavia and Georghe Gheorghiu-Dej of Romania, predictably dismissing their opponents as "adventurers" or "speculators" inspired by "foreign trouble-makers;" it would not be possible for Ehrenburg to credit any genuinely democratic opposition parties with misgivings about Communist rule.[6]

Ehrenburg's essays suited Stalin's purposes. They were widely published in the Soviet press, with longer versions appearing in prestigious journals such as *Ogonyok* and *Izvestia* and briefer accounts appearing in obscure regional newspapers such as *Vokrug Sveta* (Around the World) and *Molod Ukrainy* (Ukrainian Youth), often illustrated with photographs by Ehrenburg himself.[7] Published in English under the title *European Crossroad*, these essays were harshly criticized by commentators in America. The *Saturday Review of Literature*, in a typical review in 1947, dismissed the book as "superficial, inaccurate, maudlin, and unenlightening." As for Ehrenburg, he had become the "Soviet Union's leading propagandist," someone Stalin could rely on when he needed worldly demagoguery.[8]

Ehrenburg ended his travels in 1945 with a brief visit to the Nuremberg trial. After months of being hailed throughout Eastern Europe his reception by the Americans, who were in charge, reinforced his long-standing prejudice against the United States. Ehrenburg was almost denied entry into both his hotel and the courtroom. Boris Efimov, a

famous Soviet caricaturist and the brother of Mikhail Koltsov, convinced the Americans to accommodate Ehrenburg in the hotel, even
though he had arrived without proper documents. The next day, however, Ehrenburg failed to obtain permission to observe the court proceedings, finding himself unable to locate "a certain elusive colonel . . .
who had the authority to hand out passes." Utterly frustrated, Ehrenburg borrowed a pass from a member of the Soviet delegation and quietly entered the courtroom under another name. "The appearance of
his tousled grey head and slightly round-shouldered figure in a coarse
brown suit with numerous awards and ribbons on his chest did not
remain unnoticed," Efimov remembered years later. "All eyes turned to
him and there was movement even in the dock. I saw how the sinister
gaze of Rosenberg turned toward [Ehrenburg], how Keitel moved his
arrogant physiognomy ever so slightly, and how even Goering looked
sideways at Ehrenburg with a swollen, blood-shot eye."[9]

Ehrenburg wrote little about the Nuremberg trial. With the Nazis
defeated men like Goering and Streicher no longer aroused his curiosity. They were "petty criminals who have committed gigantic
crimes."[10] Now they were in custody and about to be executed; Ehrenburg was indifferent to their fate. With the help of Solomon Mikhoels
he arranged for the poet Abraham Sutzkever to testify about the Vilna
ghetto. Before his testimony on February 24, 1946, Sutzkever confided
to Ehrenburg that he wanted to smuggle a gun into the courtroom to
shoot Goering. Ehrenburg dissuaded him from the attempt, knowing
that such a desperate act would result in Sutzkever's own death. The
Nazis were no longer worthy of such self-sacrifice.[11]

Ehrenburg's attention was already turning elsewhere. A new enemy
was emerging in a more complex type of conflict.

—

Later that winter, in March 1946, Winston Churchill accepted an
invitation to speak at Westminster College, a small liberal arts school in
Fulton, Missouri. Although Churchill had been voted out of office in
July 1945, he was treated as a visiting head of state. President Harry
Truman met with him in Washington and together they and an impressive entourage of aides and journalists traveled by train to Missouri
(Truman's home state) halfway across the continent. Truman himself
introduced Churchill on the afternoon of March 2; it was in this
speech that Churchill defined the Soviet occupation of Eastern Europe
in phrases that are still recalled. "From Stettin in the Baltic to Trieste in

the Adriatic, an iron curtain has descended across the continent. Behind that line lie all the capitals of the ancient states of central and eastern Europe," Churchill declared, "and all are subject . . . to a very high and in some cases increasing measure of control from Moscow."[12]

Reaction to Churchill's speech was immediate, in particular his suggestion that the United States and Great Britain form a new military alliance. His remarks shocked many in Congress. Eleanor Roosevelt criticized him. Even those who championed Churchill's ideas felt he had been wrong to make his remarks beside the President. The Soviet press lambasted the British leader; *Pravda* denounced him as "an anti-Soviet warmonger" who wanted to dissolve the United Nations.[13] In a radio interview Stalin compared Churchill to Hitler and claimed he was seeking a war with the Soviet Union. Anxious to soften the impact of Churchill's speech on the Kremlin, Truman secretly invited Stalin to deliver an address in the United States and offered to introduce Stalin as he had done for Churchill. Stalin dismissed the idea out of hand.[14]

IN NORTH AMERICA

A month later Ilya Ehrenburg made his only visit to the United States as part of the first cultural exchange with the Soviet Union. Three editors had visited Moscow the previous year "to present American free-press views to Russian officials and editors."[15] Now, at the invitation of the American Society of Newspaper Editors, the Soviet foreign ministry dispatched three journalists to America. Ehrenburg represented *Izvestia*, the poet, novelist, and playwright Konstantin Simonov represented *Krasnaya Zvezda*, while *Pravda*'s military commentator General Mikhail Galaktionov completed the delegation. Ehrenburg and Galaktionov made their way to Berlin on a Soviet airliner, where they met up with Simonov, who had been in Japan. From Berlin the new U.S. ambassador to Moscow, General Walter Bedell Smith, took them to Paris on his private airplane.

The United States embassy arranged their brief stay in the French capital. It was Ehrenburg's first visit in six years. He immediately sought out his elderly sisters. Izabella and Yevgeniya had survived the war; Maria, the oldest, had disappeared, presumably deported by the Gestapo. Ehrenburg's friends told him about hiding from the Germans, about roundups, about the resistance. Ehrenburg also held a two-hour press conference at the Soviet embassy "to speak about the war, recon-struction, and the Soviet people's attitude towards France."[16] Everyone had fought, Ehrenburg declared. "Out of thirty-two writers" at *Krasnaya Zvezda*, "seventeen had died at the front."[17] America, however, seemed not to have suffered at all. On his way there Ehrenburg already felt alienated by the "rowdy [American] officers" and "the American food" he found at his hotel.[18] He found it natural to look down on Americans with typical French condescension.

—

Ehrenburg and his colleagues landed at LaGuardia airport in New York on April 19, 1946. They were quickly shepherded to a train bound for Washington, and after stopping at the Soviet embassy, arrived late in the afternoon for a meeting with American editors. Ehrenburg, poised and alert, dominated the proceedings. He gave a passionate speech, calling on the three hundred assembled editors to continue the fight against fascism and refrain from "malice or slander" of the Soviet Union. "Fascism is not broken for good," he warned them. Ehrenburg was also defiant. As he told his audience, the true litmus test of a Fascist "is one who hates the Soviet Union."[19]

The next day Ehrenburg and his colleagues took questions from their hosts. One of them asked about visas and the long delay American correspondents faced trying to enter the Soviet Union. Ehrenburg responded quickly. "I do not give visas," he told the editors. "If I did give them, I might give them very liberally, and perhaps that is why I do not give them."[20] Another journalist asked if a Soviet newspaper could demand Stalin's resignation. Hearing the translation, General Galaktionov turned toward Ehrenburg with "horror on his face."[21] Again, only Ehrenburg dared to respond and candidly admitted it would be impossible. "Those questions weren't very hard," he told the *Christian Science Monitor.* "You might have made them much harder."[22]

While still in Washington, the three Soviet journalists were approached by Assistant Secretary of State William Benton and offered the opportunity to see the country as guests of the United States. They accepted the invitation but turned down any subsidy, insisting the Soviet government could cover their expenses, and after some discussion chose where they would like to visit. Simonov asked to see Hollywood; Galaktionov initially resisted the invitation—he was frightened throughout his stay and was actually on the verge of a nervous breakdown—but after consulting Soviet embassy officials settled on a trip to Chicago. Ehrenburg, to the consternation of his hosts, asked for a tour of the South.

While travel arrangements were formalized, Ehrenburg, Simonov, and Galaktionov stayed in New York for several weeks. Ehrenburg was the most called upon, giving lectures and interviews and meeting with friends. He was honored at receptions in the Plaza Hotel and the Waldorf-Astoria. One evening he and Simonov spoke to a crowd of eleven hundred for the American-Birobidjan Committee and helped to raise over forty thousand dollars for Jewish and non-Jewish war orphans. Four days later, on May 12, well over three thousand people heard Ehrenburg speak at the Hotel Astor; Rabbi Stephen S. Wise praised "the record of the Soviet Union against discrimination," while the crowd pledged to raise three million dollars for Russian war relief.[23]

The press followed Ehrenburg's every move. New York's left-wing daily, *PM*, devoted a full page to a description of Ehrenburg shopping in Manhattan, where he tried on a suit for a tailor, bought Havana cigars, a pipe, and a tobacco pouch.[24] Ehrenburg had no patience for this kind of reporting, especially when the press wondered why he preferred buttons to zippers for the front of his trousers. "Instead of laughing, I felt angry," Ehrenburg recalled in his memoirs. He even challenged the paper's editor about his interest "in a man's lower half."[25]

The *New York Times Book Review* took a more serious approach, running a full-page profile of the three Soviet journalists. Ehrenburg dominated this coverage as well. "Ehrenburg, who spent much of his life in Paris, is . . . a European," *Book Review* readers were informed, "acutely aware of his own role in a scene. The most experienced of the three, he remains observant, even on a junket of hospitality." Ehrenburg asked to keep critical remarks about America off the record, "as his mother had brought him up to be polite to his hosts." He did find time to praise his favorite American writers, "four men who are like trees"— Hemingway, Steinbeck, Caldwell, and Faulkner. "They are large and sound and it is wonderful that they should grow so in a nation that has suffered, by comparison, so little, that has felt the war so little, . . . and in a culture the level of which is hardly high enough to account for them."[26]

During his stay in New York Ehrenburg did his best to visit old friends. He saw Marc Chagall, Fernando and Stepha Gerassi, Roman Jakobson, Le Corbusier, and Leland Stowe. He met John Steinbeck and the former vice-president, Henry Wallace. He also visited Harlem to see Paul Robeson. Others helped to show him New York. Zina Fogelman, a Russian émigré whose sister had been married to Sergei Eisenstein, took Ehrenburg shopping for women's clothes at Bergdorf Goodman; he wanted to bring his wife and daughter especially generous presents. John "Tito" Gerassi, the teenage son of Fernando and Stepha, who accompanied Ehrenburg shopping at Saks Fifth Avenue, was impressed by Ehrenburg's unrestrained spending. He was convinced that Ehrenburg was not a "Communist" at all, but a wealthy "capitalist."[27]

Ehrenburg's personal encounters were more sober. One evening Ehrenburg visited the mother of Ovady Savich in Washington Heights. To preserve his career, Savich had lied and officially declared his mother dead because Soviet journalists were forbidden to travel if they had close relatives outside the country. In the 1930s, while Ehrenburg was living in Paris, he had regularly sent letters to Savich's mother; once in New York, he made a point of arranging a discreet visit to her apartment.[28]

Ehrenburg also shared his true feelings with trusted friends. To Stepha and Fernando Gerassi, he disclosed his anguish over Soviet anti-Semitism and the pressure Boris Pasternak was under in Moscow. Over dinner Stepha asked Ehrenburg about their comrades from Spain. When she mentioned Marcel Rosenberg, Ehrenburg looked as if he were about to cry. "Disappeared," he replied. She asked about two others, and each time Ehrenburg responded with a forlorn "disappeared." Then he went into a litany of his own, recalling ten or more friends from their days together in Spain and after each name adding the word "disappeared." Tito watched his parents as Ehrenburg spoke; he had never seen them look so unhappy or depressed.[29]

Before heading south Ehrenburg made two brief trips out of New York. He was barely in America for a week when he and Konstantin Simonov went by train to Boston to speak at a reunion of journalists in Harvard's Nieman program. According to Anthony Lewis, then an undergraduate reporter for the *Harvard Crimson*, their visit was a "high spot of the convention. . . . What started as an after-dinner speech turned gradually into a mass press conference." Lewis was particularly struck by Ehrenburg's appearance and his forthright Soviet patriotism. "Haggard and looking fully his fifty-five years, not quite right in his shiny worsted, he was rather more bitter than serious, hitting at the 'reactionary bourgeois press' (among other things) with tongue in cheek, but not for fun."[30]

A week later Ehrenburg traveled by car from New York to Princeton to see Albert Einstein. The great physicist had agreed to host all three Soviet journalists, but only Ehrenburg came. More than curiosity moved him to make the trip: Ehrenburg wanted to show Einstein sections of *The Black Book*. Einstein had been invited to contribute an introduction when it still seemed possible for the project to reach fruition; but his brief, two-page remarks, written in 1945, were rejected by the Jewish Anti-Fascist Committee in Moscow because Einstein used the occasion to endorse the idea of a Jewish state. The regime had yet to formulate a definitive policy on Palestine, making Einstein's introduction premature and unacceptable.[31] Ehrenburg knew Einstein's feelings, however. Two years later, after the establishment of Israel, he sent an enthusiastic telegram to Einstein condemning Arab aggression.

Two days after visiting Einstein Ehrenburg began his trip to the American South. William Benton tried to discourage Ehrenburg, telling him how poor accommodations were and how difficult it would be to arrange his schedule. Other observers were certain that Ehrenburg had more than ordinary curiosity about the South; the syndicated columnist Marquis Childs suspected Ehrenburg of harboring cynical intentions about "the race problem in this country," knowing "that the editors of *Pravda* would welcome stories about the squalor in which the poor whites of the Deep South live."[32]

It is hard to imagine any other official visitor to the United States having the kind of trip Ehrenburg enjoyed. Daniel Gilmore, a left-wing New York publisher, drove him around several southern states in a large Buick convertible. The official translator was William Nelson, a state department official who was the first editor of the Russian-language journal *Amerika*, which the United States embassy distributed in Moscow. Ten days into their trip Samuel Grafton, a prominent columnist for the *New York Post*, joined them in Birmingham, Alabama, and filed stories for a full week. As Grafton makes clear in his articles, Ehrenburg insisted on meeting a broad range of people, from small-town mayors to black newspaper editors and tenant farmers. Ehrenburg approached these encounters in the way "a surgeon warms up to an operation." He needed a minimum of two to three hours for each interview, sometimes keeping everyone up until two in the morning with his questions. "Ehrenburg would say to us, 'Now ask the slaveowner about this or that,'" Sam Grafton remembered with a laugh years later. "He rather baffles Americans," Grafton concluded, "who are inclined to regard him as a handful."[33]

In many cities Ehrenburg had an opportunity to meet community leaders. In Jackson, Mississippi, the *Daily News* arranged a discussion "on the South's industrialization and race problems" with a lawyer and a staff member of the city's Chamber of Commerce. Inevitably, though, their conversation turned to the Soviet Union and growing tensions with the United States. Ehrenburg was startled by talk of war with Russia. "What kind of American is it," he asked his hosts, "that can imagine that all the mothers that have lamented their children are anxious to have the thing over again?"[34]

Ehrenburg came away with impressions that confirmed his European prejudices. After many meals on the circuit, Ehrenburg often "objected to the inevitable chicken, with no wine, for lunch. . . . He pronounced it 'lynch.' He said one time, 'In America there are two kinds of lynch, the kind they do to Negroes and the kind they do to foreign guests. They're both bad.'"[35] Throughout his trip Ehrenburg was astonished by the workers' relative prosperity. Driving along a country road in Alabama, Ehrenburg and his companions came upon a factory with hundreds of cars in a nearby parking lot. Ehrenburg commented that this had to be an automobile plant. His friends assured him that it was a textile factory, and that all the cars belonged to the workers inside. Ehrenburg did not believe them and suggested they all wait in the Buick. The factory whistle sounded at 5 P.M. and the workers—black and white—headed for their cars and drove home. Ehrenburg could barely speak.[36]

By the time Ehrenburg reached Detroit, where he rejoined Simonov, he was adapting better to his capitalist surroundings. Both he and Simonov badgered their American hosts for help in purchasing a car. The automobile industry was only beginning to revive full-scale production after wartime demands and "the manufacturers were not keen about depriving American customers to favor a couple of Russians."[37] Ehrenburg pestered one state department official until the arrangements were made: he was able to send home a Buick, a refrigerator, and a washing machine, while Simonov, who had insisted on a large Chrysler, had to settle for a Cadillac. (The washing machine was improperly hooked up in Ehrenburg's Moscow apartment. The first time they used it, it started to crawl around the floor, frightening the housekeeper.)[38]

Following their visit to Detroit and another week in New York, where an enormous rally was held in their honor at Madison Square Garden, Ehrenburg and his colleagues spent six days in Canada. Cold war feelings were far more acute there because an extensive Soviet espionage ring had just been exposed. The high point of the visit came in Toronto, when all three journalists addressed a crowd of five thousand people at Maple Leaf Gardens. Ehrenburg was the principal attraction and he used his opportunity to wonder out loud about the hard feelings he was encountering. "Why are Canadians especially being 'sicked' on Russia?" Ehrenburg asked. "There are some newspapers which frighten their readers with Russia as children are frightened with the bogeyman." Ehrenburg had been asked about Russian tanks in Iran and he dismissed the issue by insisting that "Russian factories were making baby carriages."[39] This kind of demagoguery elicited a sharp rebuke from the *Globe and Mail*. In an editorial entitled "Pram Prattle," the newspaper took Ehrenburg to task: "But just what [baby carriages have] to do with the Iranian problem, certainly a just cause for suspicion among the unenlightened Powers, was one of the many things the Russians didn't bother to explain."[40]

Ehrenburg summarized his visit twice that summer. In a column that appeared widely on the day of his departure—the three journalists embarked from Boston on the liner *Ile de France* on June 26—Ehrenburg expressed his gratitude for the chance to visit the United States. "One cannot understand the world and humanity without having seen America," he readily acknowledged. He was also happy to praise American literature and music, "the fairy-like sight of New York, and the factories of Detroit, and the powerful Tennessee works, and the splendid highways, and the high material standard of life."[41] (When he returned to Moscow later that year, Ehrenburg confided to Fanya Fishman that "Europe was two hundred years behind the United States."[42])

There was one criticism, however, that Ehrenburg insisted on raising. Sam Grafton had noted "the hungry polemical quality of [Ehrenburg's] mind," a talent that Ehrenburg used to good advantage when he described American racial attitudes.[43]

I remember how the American newspapers were roused to indignation at the fact that, in the elections in Yugoslavia, people who had compromised themselves by collaboration with the occupants were deprived of their right to vote. I have been in the State of Mississippi, where half of the population were deprived of their right to vote. What is better: To deprive of the right to vote a man who has a black conscience or one who has a black complexion?[44]

Less than a month later Ehrenburg expanded these same themes in a series of six articles in *Izvestia*. Writing in Paris, he praised everything from the Tennessee Valley Authority to coin-operated luggage lockers, the Marx brothers, even Walt Disney animations. Surprisingly, even for the Soviet press, Ehrenburg did not write about race relations in America with either bitterness or cynicism. Having traveled in the Deep South, he could not help but dwell on this most urgent example of American injustice. Yet he included a sense of hope, acknowledging the existence of numerous civil rights organizations and the education afforded to black college students at Fiske University, which he visited in Nashville. "The South is on the threshold of decisive events," Ehrenburg wrote in 1946. "Either the slave-owners will yield or the negroes, yesterday's front-line soldiers, will begin a fight for equality."[45] This kind of substantial information about the United States rarely appeared in the Soviet press; it was typical of Ehrenburg's approach, even in pieces of propaganda, to include useful facts that otherwise would never reach the Soviet public.

In his final article Ehrenburg did, however, invoke a frequent Soviet lie. He blamed the American media for fabricating an "iron curtain" that "prevents the average American from seeing what is going on in [the Soviet Union]," as if the growing political and cultural isolation of Eastern Europe that the phrase *iron curtain* vividly captured did not have an independent reality.[46]

In spite of such posturing at least one American publication regarded Ehrenburg's articles as a positive account of what he had seen. *Harper's* magazine included with its full translation the following December a cautionary note: "One has an uneasy feeling that by these articles Mr. Ehrenburg may have placed himself out on a limb. We hope, for his sake, that before doing so he took the precaution to remove his neck-tie."[47] Ehrenburg in fact came away from the United States with ambivalent feelings. He saw for himself how the American economy had benefited during the war—which made him envious and resentful—and he observed a democratic republic that was unable to resolve racial injustice. Nothing irked him more than spoiled Americans, who had already forgotten what the war had signified, especially for the Soviet people.

Following one large and noisy meeting, Ehrenburg was surrounded by autograph seekers who were carrying American editions of his books. He patiently signed his name many times until one man asked for an extra inscription. After Ehrenburg complied, the same man demanded something further. Only then did Ehrenburg refuse, whereupon the fellow "began to say how he had helped Russia by donating twenty-five dollars and that Ehrenburg had to write whatever he requested." Ehrenburg cast an angry glance at him and pulled out his wallet. "Here is fifty dollars for you, so that you'll never remind us how much you did for Russia," Ehrenburg told him. "Take it and leave me alone."[48]

After departing the United States Ehrenburg did not return immediately to the Soviet Union. With the permission of Vyacheslav Molotov he remained in France for several months—Lyubov Mikhailovna was able to join him from Moscow—to gather material for a novel about the war, including the French resistance.[49] Nonetheless, Ehrenburg understood he had to maintain personal vigilance. One afternoon, when Ehrenburg and Lyubov Mikhailovna were having lunch with Jacques and Isabelle Vichniac and two enthusiastic Communists who were eager to meet him, Ehrenburg turned sullen. Only after the couple left did Ehrenburg explain that he thought "they might be informers," as Jacques Vichniac remembered. "For all he knew, they could have been asked to check on what he was saying about the Soviet Union. The fact that they were members of the French Communist party made Ehrenburg all the more suspicious of them."[50]

That August Ehrenburg and his wife were relaxing in central France in the small town of Vouvray near Tours. Ehrenburg recalled in his memoirs how he was taking a nap in their hotel when his wife woke him up with alarming news. Reading a Paris newspaper, she found a report about an official condemnation of Anna Akhmatova and Mikhail Zoshchenko. Upon returning to Paris Ehrenburg rushed to the Soviet embassy to read the Moscow press. The details were more than alarming. In a major speech, Andrei Zhdanov, the secretary of the Central Committee of the Soviet Communist party and the official in charge of ideology, had denounced Akhmatova and Zoshchenko, initiating their expulsion from the Writers' Union. His remarks about Akhmatova were especially vulgar and crude. "The range of her poetry is so limited as to seem poverty-stricken," Zhdanov claimed. "It is the portrait of a frantic little fine lady flitting between the boudoir and the chapel. . . . Half nun, half harlot, or rather a harlot-nun whose sin is mixed with prayer."[51]

Zhdanov's attack was an opening salvo against Soviet culture. Known as the "Zhdanovshchina," it came to be marked by rigid censorship and ferocious Russian chauvinism. Following the relatively relaxed cultural atmosphere of the war years, Zhdanov's crackdown came as a complete surprise to writers and artists inside the Soviet Union. Ehrenburg was dumbstruck by Zhdanov's remarks; even Lyubov Mikhailovna was surprised by his almost naive reaction.[52] As Ehrenburg would soon experience for himself, worse things were about to happen.

BACK IN MOSCOW

Ehrenburg returned to Moscow in October. He had been outside the country almost six months. The cold war had begun in earnest and he needed to find a place for himself in the evolving political circumstances. He could not sit back. Ehrenburg quickly understood the new political line and helped to convey official Soviet attitudes. He was the first to denounce the Voice of America after it began broadcasting Russian-language programs in February 1947. Attacking American journalism, Ehrenburg employed the bombastic rhetoric that characterized Soviet commentary on Western society for many years. "The Voice of America has to advertise the most unmarketable goods— American reactionary politics," he wrote in his article "A False Voice." Reporting on events in Moscow, the Voice of America was hardly different from the Nazis. "Goering and Goebbels killed themselves. Rosenberg and Ribbentrop were hanged. In this way," Ehrenburg went on to say, "they were deprived of demanding their authors' rights from the New York radio station."[53]

American response was immediate. The state department took heart, understanding that Ehrenburg's piece indicated that "the Russian people are listening to the Voice of America."[54] U.S. ambassador General Walter Bedell Smith cabled Washington: "That a top-flight commentator like Ehrenburg should be assigned the job of lambasting our broadcasts is the most encouraging reaction we have seen. It shows that the program is on the right track."[55] The embassy only regretted that "Ehrenburg had not seen fit to include the wave lengths for the program."[56]

Ehrenburg continued to write about his trip to the United States. With each article and book his portraits grew more grim and one-sided. In a small volume entitled *In America* Ehrenburg put greater emphasis on the country's racial problems and barely mentioned his previous admiration for American technology. In one extreme piece, "Deutschland-America,"—which was also the basis for a radio broadcast—Ehrenburg contrived parallels between Nazi Germany's policies and America's plans for Europe.[57] His play *The Lion in the Square* was a shameful attack on the behavior of Americans in post-war Europe. It ran briefly in Moscow in 1948 and aroused comment in Western Europe for the viciousness of its portrayal.[58]

In 1949 Ehrenburg prepared a manuscript of well over a hundred pages about the United States for the journal *Znamya* (The Banner). Entitled *Nights of America*, its bitterness far exceeded his earlier accounts. At the outset Ehrenburg claimed that he had "held himself back before;" this time he would not restrain himself. Three years after his visit took place everything he had seen in America disturbed him, from culture to politics, from personal relations to foreign policy. He recalled his impressions with tired caricatures, claiming that all Americans dress alike, live in similar houses, wear similar clothes, and drink nothing but "coke." As for the war, it had been little more than a strenuous vacation, a chance for American soldiers "to rest up from their wives, . . . land in good masculine company, and enjoy the embraces of English, French, Italian, and German women." For Ehrenburg, because the United States had hardly any direct experience of the fighting, it seemed easy and natural for war hysteria to flourish in the United States. The atomic bomb was advertised "in the same way they advertise fifty-seven sauces of Heinz." Biological weapons were being prepared to kill "millions of Reds." Ehrenburg even claimed that the American Secretary of State James Forrestal had committed suicide because he believed the "Reds" were attacking Washington, D.C.[59]

Nights of America was never published. Whether Ehrenburg decided to withdraw it or whether other Soviet officials blocked its appearance is not known. The book was consistent with Soviet propaganda and could easily have been printed; as *Nights of America* demonstrated, there were few if any limits to what Ilya Ehrenburg was prepared to say about the United States. In his memoirs Ehrenburg later voiced regret for some of his work from that period, particularly for two articles in 1949 when he dismissed the British philosopher Bertrand Russell as "an apologist for the ruling class" and denounced Jean-Paul Sartre with insulting remarks.[60]

Ehrenburg's most compromising article appeared on the occasion of Stalin's seventieth birthday in December 1949. It was an honor to be "invited" to write about Stalin's birthday and Ehrenburg's column, carried prominently in *Pravda*, was among the many adoring articles and photographs that filled the newspapers. He concludes with the image of Stalin as a great helmsman, guiding humanity through turbulent waters:

> In restless weather at sea, the captain stands by the helm. People work or rest, they gaze at the stars or read a book. But in the crosswinds, looking into the dark night, stands the helmsman. His responsibility and his exploits are very great. I often think about a man who has taken an enormous weight on himself. I think of the burden, the courage, the grandeur. There are many breezes on this earth. People go on working, plant apple trees, nurse their children, read verses, or peacefully sleep. But he stands at the helm.[61]

Through such articles Ehrenburg contributed to the "cult of personality" while sustaining his official standing. Perhaps Ehrenburg meant to describe how Stalin imagined himself to be, but the image of Stalin as a fatherly, watchful helmsman is more than absurd; it helped to disguise the terror that everyone in the country, including Stalin's colleagues on the Politburo and Ehrenburg himself, were feeling.

One close friend of Ehrenburg's, whose husband had disappeared in the purges, used his articles for her own purposes. At the factory where she worked she was expected to join fellow workers in publicly praising Stalin and the regime. Unlike Ehrenburg, however, she could not bring herself to do it. She mentioned the dilemma to his secretary Valentina Milman, who suggested she use a paragraph from one of Ehrenburg's many articles. The strategy worked and Ehrenburg's friend survived a cynical, political exercise by quoting his words. Yet she was too embarrassed for his sake to thank him for his unwitting help.[62]

Ilya with his father, Grigory Ehrenburg, an assimilated Jew. In 1895 Grigory Ehrenburg, an engineer by profession, brought his family from Kiev to Moscow, where he managed a brewery. (Archive of Irina Ehrenburg)

Ilya with his mother, Anna Arnshtein. She was an observant Jewish woman. Ilya's parents separated in 1904 and their marriage never recovered. (Archive of Irina Ehrenburg)

Ilya as a youngster in Moscow, where he was a stubborn and rebellious student. (Archive of Irina Ehrenburg)

Ilya in Paris, where he began life as a bohemian poet and journalist in the years 1908 to 1917. (Archive of Irina Ehrenburg)

Ehrenburg and the Russian poet Max Volo-shin sit at the rear table in the Rotonde Café, which opened in 1911. "People wrote verses, chewed sausages, argued about art, fell in love, slept," Ehrenburg once wrote about the Rotonde. (Drawing by Arvid Fougstedt)

Drawing by Diego Rivera. He and Ehren-burg became close friends in Paris. Rivera drew covers for several of Ehrenburg's first books of poetry. (Archive of Stefan Mehr)

"When Will the War End?" Diego Rivera, Modigliani, and Ehrenburg sit in Rivera's studio, Paris, 1916. The war had a devastating impact on Ehrenburg, cutting him off from his family and his homeland. (Drawing by Marevna Vorobyov, reprinted with the per-mission of Marika Rivera Phillips)

"Parade, Rue de la Gaîté, Paris": Modigliani, Sou-tine, Rivera, Marevna, Vo-loshin, Ehrenburg, Picasso, Jacob. Ehrenburg found a place for himself among other émigrés, displaced artists, and writers from many countries. (Drawing by Marevna Vorobyov, re-printed with the permis-sion of Marika Rivera Phillips)

Ehrenburg and his daughter Irina, Moscow, 1924. He formally adopted her that year and brought her to Paris for her education. (Archive of Boris Frezinsky)

Ehrenburg with his Leica and right-angle lens. He enjoyed walking about Paris and taking pictures without the knowledge of his subjects. (Archive of Irina Ehrenburg)

Ehrenburg and Sergei Eisenstein, Paris. Ehrenburg lived in Paris with few interruptions from 1924 to 1940. He often hosted visiting Soviet writers and artists and championed them in the Soviet press. (Archive of Irina Ehrenburg)

Ehrenburg and André Malraux on the ocean voyage to Leningrad to attend the First Soviet Writers' Congress in 1934. "During eight years in Paris and in Spain," Ehrenburg recalled, "Malraux was invariably at my side." (Archive of Irina Ehrenburg)

Waldo Frank, Ehrenburg, Henri Barbusse, and Paul Nizan at the International Writers' Congress in Defense of Culture, Paris, 1935. Ehrenburg was one of the organizers of the Congress, asserting himself as a representative of the Soviet regime among sympathetic Western intellectuals. (David Seymour/ Magnum Photos)

Ehrenburg and Boris Pasternak at the International Writers' Congress in Defense of Culture. Ehrenburg helped to arrange for Pasternak and Isaac Babel to come to Paris, hoping to increase their prestige—and thereby their safety—in Moscow. (Archive of Irina Ehrenburg)

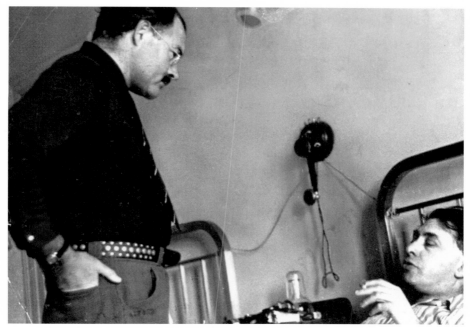

Ehrenburg and Ernest Hemingway, Barcelona, 1937. They had met in Madrid earlier in the year. Hemingway had just woken up Ehrenburg in his hotel room when Capa took this photograph. (Robert Capa/Magnum Photos)

Ehrenburg and Ovady Savich, Barcelona. Savich was Ehrenburg's closest friend for almost half a century. They both reported on the Spanish civil war for the Soviet press. (Archive of Stepha Gerassi)

Ehrenburg and other prominent Jewish cultural figures, Moscow, August 1941. The Yiddish poet Peretz Markish is sitting second from the left. The actor and director Solomon Mikhoels is standing behind the microphone. They are making a worldwide appeal to their fellow Jews to support the Soviet war effort against Nazi Germany. (Archive of Irina Ehrenburg)

Ehrenburg and Jewish partisans, Vilna, July 1944. "It was as if he had dropped out of heaven," Shlomo Kowarski remembered. He can be seen behind Ehrenburg's right shoulder. (Archive of Irina Ehrenburg)

Ehrenburg talking to liberated peasants. He followed the Red Army as it pushed back the Germans and reported on Nazi atrocities against the civilian population. (Archive of Irina Ehrenburg)

Ehrenburg and the writer Vasily Grossman at the front. They became close friends during the war and together documented Nazi massacres of Soviet Jews. (Archive of Irina Ehrenburg)

Ehrenburg, the composer Dmitri Shostakovich, and the poet Nikolai Tikhonov when they received the Stalin Prize, 1942. Hitler once threatened to hang Stalin, Ehrenburg, and Shostakovich in Red Square if he were to capture Moscow. (Archive of Irina Ehrenburg)

Ehrenburg and Albert Einstein, Princeton, May 1946. Ehrenburg was eager to show Einstein material from *The Black Book*. (Archive of Irina Ehrenburg)

Ehrenburg and U.S. Secretary of State James Byrnes, Washington, D.C., April 20, 1946. Ehrenburg had just arrived in the United States, his only visit to North America. He was part of the first cultural exchange between the United States and the Soviet Union. (AP/Wide World Photos)

Ehrenburg and Pablo Picasso, Paris, April 1949. They had met in Paris before World War I and were now delegates to the pro-Communist Partisans of Peace Congress. (AP/Wide World Photos)

Ehrenburg with the French Communist writer Louis Aragon and W. E. B. DuBois, Paris, 1949. DuBois and Paul Robeson both attended the Congress and drew the wrath of the American government. (AP/Wide World Photos)

Ehrenburg and Paul Robeson, Moscow, June 1949. Robeson visited the Soviet Union after the Paris Congress to help commemorate the 150th anniversary of the birth of Alexander Pushkin. (Archive of Irina Ehrenburg)

Ehrenburg and Pablo Neruda, Beijing, fall 1951. Ehrenburg had first met Neruda in Madrid during the Spanish civil war. They traveled together to China to present the Stalin Prize to Sun Yat Sen's widow. Ehrenburg's wife Lyubov Mikhailovna is standing behind him. (Archive of Irina Ehrenburg)

Ehrenburg in Trafalgar Square, London, July 23, 1950. Ehrenburg was among the foremost spokesmen on behalf of Soviet interests at the outset of the cold war. He rallied public opinion in the West against nuclear weapons as Stalin pushed for the development of the Kremlin's own nuclear arsenal. (AP/Wide World Photos)

Ehrenburg with the writer Konstantin Fedin and the poet Nikolai Tikhonov at Stalin's bier, March 1953. Ehrenburg was initially frightened after Stalin's death, fearing that repression would grow worse. (Archive of Irina Ehrenburg)

Ehrenburg and Nikita Khrushchev in January 1960. The others are the playwright Alexander Korneichuk, the journalist Mikhail Kotov, and Nikolai Tikhonov. Three years later Khrushchev denounced Ehrenburg over his memoirs and made veiled threats to have him arrested. (Archive of Stefan Mehr)

Irina Ilinichna Ehrenburg in Moscow. Trained as a vocational psychologist in Paris, she became a journalist and a translator upon her return to the Soviet Union in 1933. (Archive of Stefan Mehr)

Ehrenburg and Senator Hubert Humphrey, Rome, September 1961. Humphrey was attending the East/West Parliamentary Conference in Italy. (Aldo Scarmiglia, Agenzia Fotografica Corso)

Ehrenburg and John Steinbeck, Moscow, fall 1963. They had first met in New York in 1946 and saw each other again in Moscow in 1947 during Steinbeck's visit with the photographer Robert Capa. (Archive of Irina Ehrenburg)

Ehrenburg with Arthur Miller, Natalya Stolyarova, and Lyubov Mikhailovna, Moscow, winter 1965. They are in Ehrenburg's apartment, surrounded by several pieces from his collection of modern art. (Inge Morath/Magnum Photos)

Ilya Ehrenburg in Stockholm, 1961. He visited Sweden often in order to see Liselotte Mehr. (Lütfi Özkök, Älvsjö, Sweden)

Ehrenburg and Pablo Picasso, France, 1966. Ehrenburg presented Picasso with the Lenin Prize on this visit to southern France. It was the last time they saw each other. (Archive of Stefan Mehr)

Liselotte Mehr, the last great love of Ehrenburg's life. She inspired him to write his memoirs and helped to provide proper medical care when he became ill with cancer. (Archive of Stefan Mehr)

Ehrenburg in his garden outside of Moscow. He collapsed from a heart attack in the garden on August 7, 1967, and died on August 31. (Archive of Irina Ehrenburg)

Lyubov Mikhailovna, Irina Ehrenburg, and Alya Savich in Novodevichy Cemetery, September 4, 1967. Thousands of people forced their way into the cemetery through a cordon of police to honor Ilya Ehrenburg. (Archive of Irina Ehrenburg)

THE PARTISANS OF PEACE MOVEMENT

Ehrenburg's usefulness to Stalin was even greater outside the Soviet Union, where he was recognized as an adept Soviet spokesman. Following the end of World War II, the Kremlin found itself at a distinct strategic disadvantage vis à vis the United States, which not only emerged with its enormous industrial capacity intact but with sole possession of atomic weapons. To redress this imbalance, Stalin employed the country's finest physicists—among them Igor Tamm and the young Andrei Sakharov—to break the West's atomic monopoly.

In the meantime Stalin turned his country's weakness into a kind of moral advantage, sponsoring an international peace movement that played on the genuine anxieties of many that a new war could break out. Reinforcing such fear, Stalin mobilized international opinion against further development of nuclear weapons in the West. It was in this political atmosphere—while he consolidated control of Eastern Europe, renewed oppression inside the Soviet Union, and hurried to develop Soviet atomic capability—that Stalin sponsored the Partisans of Peace movement.

The Partisans of Peace had its direct origins in Poland, when the World Congress of Intellectuals gathered in Wroclaw in August 1948. Organized by French and Polish Communists, the meeting was an attempt to revive a strategy associated with the Paris Congress in Defense of Culture thirteen years earlier; only this time the target was not fascism but the West and the threat of a nuclear war in Europe. Several figures who had attended the 1935 Paris Congress came to Wroclaw, including Julian Benda and Paul Eluard. Pablo Picasso, who was a member of the French Communist party at that time, presented his famous drawing of a dove to the delegates, a symbol the peace movement immediately adopted. Also during this conference Picasso sketched Ehrenburg's portrait.

Ehrenburg and Alexander Fadeyev were the two most prominent members of the Soviet delegation at Wroclaw. Their speeches exemplied the crude anti-American tone of the proceedings. "The culture of various European nations is threatened by a dangerous barbarian invasion," Ehrenburg claimed.

Now we have bourgeois barbarianism. This barbarianism can teem with refrigerators and adult romances, automobiles and stereofilms, laboratories and psychological novels, but all of it remains barbarianism. . . . They are screaming as if they are afraid of our tanks. But in fact they are afraid of our tractors, our saucepans, our future."[63]

The Swiss writer Max Frisch attended the Congress and made note of the special treatment Ehrenburg received:

> In the discussion each speaker is allowed ten minutes. Ehrenburg speaks for twenty minutes before Julian Huxley, the chairman of the day, ventures to remind him of the time limit. Frantic applause; Ehrenburg should be allowed to go on speaking. After thirty-five minutes an American gets up, wanting to know why Ehrenburg should be allowed to go on speaking. He finishes in the fortieth minute. A clever speaker, a Danton, lively and aggressive, ironic.[64]

At the Congress, however, Ehrenburg tried to preserve a measure of integrity when it came to matters of culture. The British Communist writer Ivor Montagu first met Ehrenburg in Wroclaw. Years later he remembered how Ehrenburg made a passionate speech denying that European life and culture, "growing and influencing itself as one for centuries, could possibly be divided into East-West compartments."[65] Max Frisch as well recorded Ehrenburg's rhetorical question, "Can one visualize European music without the Russians?"[66] Frisch could only wonder what this had to do with peace, but he missed Ehrenburg's point: it was the Kremlin that was trying to cut off the Soviet people from European culture. Ehrenburg's remarks were directed, however subtly, to his political masters.

Ehrenburg demonstrated his independence in another explicit manner as well. While he was still in Poland, Andrei Zhdanov died in Moscow. *Literaturnaya Gazeta* carried a statement in memory of Zhdanov—"A Friend of Soviet Writers"—over the signatures of Soviet delegates to the Wroclaw Congress; Ehrenburg's name was conspicuously absent.[67]

Much like the anti-Fascist movement in the decade preceding World War II, the Partisans of Peace was able to enlist hundreds of prestigious artists, writers, intellectuals, and political figures—including many non-Communists—to lend an aura of respectability to what was unquestionably a vehicle for Soviet propaganda. Although the Partisans of Peace boasted that it accepted individuals of all nationalities and political convictions, its control by the Soviet government became increasingly apparent. (After Tito's break with Stalin in 1948 delegations from Yugoslavia were banned from the movement.) Most members of its executive bureau were publicly proclaimed Communists, including Frédéric Joliot-Curie, who had shared the Nobel Prize in chemistry in 1935 with his wife Irène (the daughter of Pierre and Marie Curie, the discoverers of radium), and Alexander Fadeyev, the general secretary of the Union of Soviet Writers.

Ehrenburg had been part of this movement from the beginning. He attended conferences in Paris and Vienna, in London, Berlin, and Helsinki. He was elected to leadership positions and helped to draft the movement's major statements, such as the Stockholm Appeal in 1950, which called for a halt to nuclear weapons research, and generated signatures from tens of millions of people.

Several factors contributed to Ehrenburg's passionate efforts in what Russians call the Struggle for Peace. First, he had seen how wealthy and strong the United States remained after the Second World War and he resented this prosperity. He also believed in the possibility of a nuclear war that would devastate Europe and his homeland. Anything he could do to restore military and political balance seemed worth while. Many others felt the same way, including Andrei Sakharov, who in those same years devoted himself to the Soviet nuclear weapons program. Sakharov and his colleagues were "possessed by a true war psychology;" they were determined to give the Soviet Union strategic parity and a nuclear deterrent.[68] Sakharov's job was to help Stalin catch up to the United States, while propagandists such as Ehrenburg tried to advance the principal aim of Soviet foreign policy—to restrain further Western deployment of nuclear weapons.

Political arguments aside, Ehrenburg had his own compelling agenda. By the end of the Second World War he had become an integral part of Soviet propaganda efforts and could not turn back or refuse the kind of assignments he was obliged to assume. With the founding of the peace movement Ehrenburg re-created the role he had fashioned for himself in the 1930s, becoming a unique and (he hoped) irreplaceable spokesman for Soviet interests among European intellectuals. Ehrenburg in fact was not a modest cog in this machine; he was the most widely recognized figure in any Soviet delegation abroad. His ability to handle himself, in different languages and among a wide variety of people, enhanced his image and his reputation.

The peace movement also gave Ehrenburg a chance to travel. After he returned to Moscow in June 1940 he never resumed permanent residence in Paris. His responsibilities with the peace movement made it possible to escape to Europe for weeks or even months at a time, an opportunity he could not relinquish. Later, in 1950, after he met and fell in love with Liselotte Mehr, who lived in Stockholm, he needed to travel on official assignments in order to see her.

———

During the winter of 1952–53 Yves Farge and his wife visited Ilya Ehrenburg at his dacha outside of Moscow. Farge was an independent figure in French politics, a hero of the resistance who had served a brief term as minister of food in 1946, when he distinguished himself in a vain attempt to combat black marketeers. Farge also represented France at the second atom bomb tests over Bikini Island in the Pacific, from which he returned with an abhorrence for atomic weapons. Like Ehrenburg, Farge joined the Partisans of Peace movement and it was in connection with his peace activities that Farge visited the Soviet Union.

That day they all rode together in Ehrenburg's car. There had just been a heavy snow and hundreds of men were clearing the road. When Farge asked Ehrenburg who they were, Ehrenburg responded that they were common criminals—"Every country has them." Several years later, after Stalin's death and Khrushchev's revelations about the dictator's crimes, Mme. Farge joined Ehrenburg and his companion Liselotte Mehr for dinner in Stockholm. Recalling the men shoveling snow, Mme. Farge asked Ehrenburg why he did not say those men were political prisoners. Why did he lie, she went on, when she and her husband counted on him to share the truth about his country? Quiet for a moment, Ehrenburg responded, "Do you know anyone who wants to end his life?" The next morning Liselotte told Mme. Farge that Ehrenburg had been upset during the night. He knew he had lied, he knew he had had to lie, and he hated having to deceive his friends.[69]

ODD MAN OUT
———

Ehrenburg's major writings of the post-war period reflect the preoccupations and prejudices of Soviet policy. His novel *The Storm* is a heartfelt account of the war and the enormous efforts of the Red Army to defeat Nazi Germany. A second novel, *The Ninth Wave*, published in 1951, is among the crudest books of his career and the only one he ever explicitly disavowed. Almost a parody of Soviet cold war attitudes, the novel's message is that the Soviet Union represented the best hope for world peace, while craven American politicians, generals, and journalists pursued fantastic plots to undermine Communist achievements.

Ehrenburg was richly rewarded in those years. In 1948 *The Storm* received a Stalin Prize for literature. The book was originally recommended for a second-class award before Stalin made his personal preference clear and upgraded the honor to the first rank.[70]

The following year Ehrenburg became one of the few Jewish deputies in the Soviet Congress of Nationalities. At the regime's invitation he stood for and won an uncontested election as the representative of a district in Riga. This was a signal honor and he remained a deputy until his death in 1967.[71]

A legendary story began to circulate about Ehrenburg's special status in the late 1940s. It was said that he was subjected to systematic attacks at a meeting of the Writers' Union, with speaker after speaker denouncing *The Storm* as anti-Soviet, pro-Western propaganda. According to this legend, when his turn came to respond, Ehrenburg thanked everyone for their comments then read a telegram from Stalin congratulating him for *The Storm*. Immediately the audience did an about-face, with speakers falling over themselves to express admiration for the novel.[72]

For many people in the West Ehrenburg's prestige, at a time when other Soviet writers such as Akhmatova and Zoshchenko were under severe public pressure, made him an example of all that went wrong with Russian literature under the Bolsheviks. One American observer, the writer Budd Schulberg, who had visited the Soviet Union in the 1930s and later joined the American Communist party, wrote in an article for the *Saturday Review of Literature* in 1952 how Soviet writers had two stark choices: "either to write the Zoshchenko and Akhmatova way and follow Pilnyak, Babel, . . . the poet Mandelstam . . . to some dark and dreadful oblivion, or to write the Central Committee's way, like Simonov, Alexei Tolstoy, Ehrenburg, and other members of the charmed circle of literary millionaires."[73] This was Ehrenburg's image in the West—an adept and compliant literary hireling, who had compromised his talent in order to survive and prosper.

In spite of such official acclaim Ehrenburg did not always conform to conventional Soviet attitudes. Although he continued to enjoy privileges and prestige, he sustained a degree of moral independence and helped people who were far more vulnerable to official repression. His novels, for example, conveyed views that no other Soviet writer dared to express. *The Storm* was heavily criticized in the official press before he received the Stalin Prize: the French characters seemed more human and sympathetic than the Soviet characters, and the fact that a Russian visiting Paris falls in love with a French actress broke a serious taboo of Soviet society. That same year Soviet law forbade marriages with foreigners.[74]

Other unusual episodes also caught the attention of Soviet readers. A left-wing French anthropologist invokes Galileo in a conversation, insisting on the responsibility of scientists to speak for truth even if it leads to imprisonment. A Soviet character reminds his comrades that the Germans used to be called "our mortal friends," an oblique but unmistakable jibe at the Hitler-Stalin pact. In several chapters Ehrenburg describes the massacres at Babii Yar and the deportation of French Jews to Auschwitz, conveying in plain, vivid language the terror and magnitude of the Nazi onslaught against the Jews. In such episodes Ehrenburg made clear that he preferred not to sacrifice truth in a world of power politics, that there were aspects of Soviet policy he did not admire, and that the fate of the Jews had to be part of any account of the war. Few if any Soviet writers tried to advance these ideas while Stalin was still alive.

Even *The Ninth Wave* contains several startling episodes and conversations. Foreign journalists openly mock how little they are permitted to see of real life in the Soviet Union, whether in Red Square or in an ordinary nursery school. A French journalist ridicules the lack of genuine news reporting in the Soviet press, as if droughts, divorce, and cancer are strictly phenomena of capitalist society. In the novel's most heartfelt episode, the Jewish character, Major Osip Alpert, returns to Kiev, where his family had been killed by the Nazis. Osip had fought all the way to Berlin in *The Storm*; now in *The Ninth Wave* he visits the mass grave of his relatives in Babii Yar, where he is abused by an anti-Semitic neighbor. "Why don't you go to Palestine?" the man tells Osip with disdain. "Now you've got a state of your own."[75] Appearing in 1951, at a moment of terrifying, official anti-Semitism, this passage was the only literary depiction of popular anti-Semitism to appear in a Soviet novel.

Significant portions of both *The Storm* and *The Ninth Wave* take place in Western Europe—often in the Latin Quarter of Paris—offering a glimpse of something forbidden to Soviet readers. Even when Ehrenburg deliberately lied, exaggerated, or indulged in obvious propaganda about Western political life, his novels, as the writer Vasily Aksyonov has remarked, were windows onto Europe, fascinating his Soviet audience in a manner that outweighed their literary deficiencies.[76] Moreover, Ehrenburg did not lose the respect of his fellow artists; they knew where they were living and each of them—from the most principled writer, such as Pasternak, to an outcast, such as Akhmatova, to established composers, such as Shostakovich and Prokofiev—were in touch with him, valued his presence, and understood that Ehrenburg's compromises were necessary for him to survive.[77]

Even as his career prospered Ehrenburg continued to make gestures of kindness and generosity that required unusual courage in Stalin's Russia. In 1946 Ehrenburg and Pasternak were among a group of poets to hold a reading in a large Moscow auditorium; Pasternak, whose long-awaited turn came last, was greeted with ovations as he took the podium. Audience members cried out for their favorite poems while others recited aloud from memory as Pasternak proceeded. The other poets grew nervous over such a display of admiration for a poet whose status was highly questionable and quietly left the stage, leaving Pasternak alone, except for Ehrenburg, who stayed in his seat.[78]

The following year, on a brief visit to Leningrad in 1947, Ehrenburg looked up Anna Akhmatova. They had first met in 1924 and over the years had maintained friendly but intermittent contact. Akhmatova had been among those who wrote to him during the war seeking help for friends who needed assistance. "Once again, I would like to thank you," Akhmatova had written to Ehrenburg from Tashkent on May 30, 1944, "for your readiness to do good and for your courtesy toward me."[79] Ehrenburg knew how isolated Akhmatova had become after Zhdanov's denunciation—people she had once known would cross to the other side of the street if they saw her approaching. Ehrenburg had long admired Akhmatova and tried to see her as often as he could. At that terrible time, "she was sitting in a small room," Ehrenburg recalled in *People, Years, Life*, "Sad and majestic as always, she was reading Horace."[80]

John Steinbeck and Robert Capa got a different glimpse of Ehrenburg's independence. They traveled inside the Soviet Union for two months in 1947, a trip described in their remarkably fresh account, *A Russian Journal*. At a closing banquet one of thirty Soviet writers in attendance suggested to Steinbeck that he write the truth about what he saw. Whereupon another writer "got up and said that there were several kinds of truth, and that we must tell a truth which would further good relations between the Russian and American people." Ehrenburg immediately objected and "made a savage speech," as Steinbeck recounted. "He said that to tell a writer what to write was an insult. He said that if a writer had a reputation for being truthful, then no suggestion should be offered."[81]

Later that year Ehrenburg took issue with the growing campaign against Western culture. No less a figure than the foreign minister Vyacheslav Molotov, in his speech in November 1947 on the thirtieth anniversary of the Bolshevik Revolution, condemned all forms of subservience to the West. Ehrenburg soon after firmly disagreed. Writing in the journal *Novoe Vremya* (New Times), he rejected the idea that to admire Western culture meant bowing down to the West. "It is impossible," he wrote, "to fawn upon Shakespeare or Rembrandt, because prostration before them cannot humiliate the worshipper."[82]

Still other discreet aspects to Ehrenburg's life set him apart. In 1949, after his election to the Soviet Congress of Nationalities, Ehrenburg had the need for a more efficient assistant than Valentina Milman; he hired a recent university graduate named Yelena Zonina to be his secretary, a position she held until 1955. When Ehrenburg first interviewed her Zonina explained that her father was in a labor camp, a fact she believed Ehrenburg needed to know before hiring her. Nonetheless, Ehrenburg was not afraid to take her on.[83]

Two years later, in 1952, a prisoner named Vasily Merkulov was released and went to Moscow because Osip Mandelstam, just before his death, had asked him to visit Ehrenburg and relate what had happened to him in the camp. "You are a strong person," Mandelstam told Merkulov. "You will survive. Find Ilyusha Ehrenburg! I am dying with Ilyusha on my mind. He has a golden heart. I think he will be your friend."[84] Nadezhda Mandelstam understood that her late husband "did right to ask [Merkulov] to go to Ehrenburg with his story—no other Soviet writer . . . would ever have agreed to see such a person in those years."[85]

———

The United States embassy followed Ehrenburg's career closely, filing cables to Washington, D.C., about his prominent articles and public activity. His lectures, like his novels, were windows on life in the broader world and attracted large audiences. In December 1950 Ehrenburg spoke in Moscow on the recently concluded Warsaw Congress, one of the many peace congresses he attended in those years. The embassy's observer quickly understood that an appearance by Ehrenburg was itself a significant event. "The lecture hall, which seats over a thousand persons, was filled to overflowing," the official cable began, "and outside the building you were stopped as you went in by the Muscovites asking if you had any spare tickets, just as they stop you outside a theatre when a popular ballet or play is being presented." Ehrenburg's two-hour presentation impressed the embassy's observer, who described with surprising sensitivity the nature of Ehrenburg's appeal to a Moscow audience.

> One had the impression that the large audience was interested in the lecture not because of its political topicality but because it gave them an opportunity of seeing one of their favorite authors in person and hearing personal stories about people and events in other countries. Ehrenburg's appearance, from his spectacles to his shoes, was Western rather than Soviet. The appeal of his lecture seemed to lie not in what was Soviet in it—i.e., the political propaganda—but in its Western flavour, its reflection of Ehrenburg's own Western culture, and the personal human stories with which, unlike the ordinary Soviet political propagandist, he spiced his talk.

The embassy made note of one dramatic aspect to the evening. Although Ehrenburg was reporting on the peace movement, someone in the audience referred to his comment that Pablo Picasso was "one of the greatest artists of modern times" and asked Ehrenburg to describe Picasso's work. "Ehrenburg answered," the embassy reported, "that it was very difficult to do justice to great art with mere words. 'The best thing of course would be to show them to you,'—and hastily turning to his notes he added half in an aside—'but that does not depend on me.' "[86]

Ehrenburg's official, public career, with all its prestige, honors, and gestures of independence, was not the full story of his life between the close of World War II and Stalin's death. For most of those years he was as frightened as everyone else. Harrison Salisbury returned on assignment to Moscow for the *New York Times* in May 1949 and noticed how Ehrenburg "would bow to . . . friends in the press corps but [would] not converse with them."[87] In 1954, a year after Stalin's death, when Ehrenburg ran into Henry Shapiro in Copenhagen, Ehrenburg asked for his forgiveness and on the verge of tears told him that he loved him "but had been too scared" to be seen with him. Ehrenburg indeed had compelling reasons, as an intellectual and especially as a Jew, to remember the final years of Stalin's life as the most terrible of his own.

ELEVEN

Anti-Semitism and the
Establishment of Israel

The years 1946 to 1953 are often referred to as the "Black Years of Soviet Jewry," when a systematic campaign of anti–Semitism was unleashed by the Kremlin. In 1946 the Soviet press carried severe attacks against "expressions of Jewish nationalism" in Yiddish literature. In January 1948 Solomon Mikhoels was killed in Minsk. By the end of the year the regime began an all-out assault on Jewish cultural life, arresting prominent Yiddish writers and poets and closing Yiddish cultural institutions.[1]

Ehrenburg regarded this period as "perhaps the most painful in my whole life."[2] Much of the suspicion and hostility toward him in the West arose in those years because he was one of the few members of the Jewish Anti-Fascist Committee to survive unscathed. His public activity, though, was not confined to attending peace congresses or denouncing the West. He also tried to alert the country's Jews to the danger they faced and admonish the regime indirectly for initiating anti-Semitic attacks.

———

In the spring of 1947 three former Jewish partisans, Alexander Rindzinski, Shlomo Kowarski, and Israel Kronik, invited Ehrenburg to the Vilna Jewish museum.[3] Ehrenburg accepted and came to Lithuania with his wife and their friends Ovady and Alya Savich. Alya was the daughter of Rabbi Jacob Mazeh, the famous Chief Rabbi of Moscow, who had served the Jewish community before and after the October Revolution. They traveled to Vilna in the Buick Ehrenburg had bought in America. None of them could drive, so Ehrenburg hired a soldier he knew from his days at *Krasnaya Zvezda* to act as chauffeur.[4]

As the former partisans proposed, Ehrenburg gave two talks in Vilna, the first to an overflow audience in the Jewish museum. He spoke cautiously, keeping to commonplace Soviet clichés about politics and his recent trip to the United States. But his remarks often drifted to the war and the Holocaust. A few days later a large group of former partisans from Vilna and Kovno organized a banquet for Ehrenburg in a private apartment, serving their guests traditional Jewish food, such as gefilte fish, kugel, and tsimis. Ehrenburg seemed deliberately restrained, holding his poodle on his lap throughout the dinner, but he spoke more forthrightly than he had earlier in the week. While he congratulated them on the museum he also cautioned them not to be too happy about their initial success. He had been famous and popular during the war "but look what happened to me," Ehrenburg reminded them. After the Alexandrov article in April 1945, "my telephone stopped ringing, the mail stopped, no one rang my bell. If they need you, the museum will stay open. When they don't need you, they'll close it."[5]

While in Vilna Ehrenburg offered to give the museum original documents from *The Black Book*, hundreds of letters and firsthand testimonies about German atrocities. "These letters are connected to Jewish blood," he explained. "I did everything in my power to see them appear. Unfortunately, they are impossible to publish." Ehrenburg insisted on one condition, however. If the Jewish museum were to close, they had to pledge to return the material to him in Moscow. The former partisans objected, unable to imagine why the museum could be closed. "Someone might get it into his head," Ehrenburg told them, "that such a museum belongs in Birobidjan or, for example, on the moon. If this happens, I would want the material returned to me."[6] He insisted they sign an agreement and three weeks later one of the partisans traveled to Moscow to collect the folios of documents.

THE MURDER OF MIKHOELS

Solomon Mikhoels had unique stature among Soviet Jews. After his murder a family friend said that "just as before the purges of 1937 it was necessary to have Maxim Gorky killed, so it was necessary to have Mikhoels out of the way before the regime could arrest the Jews."[7] Although Mikhoels performed only in Yiddish, he was a widely recognized personality in the theater, his performances of Tevye the Milkman and King Lear admired by Jews and non-Jews alike. As prominent members of the Jewish Anti-Fascist Committee, Mikhoels and Ehrenburg were the most prepared to help survivors of the Nazi massacres. They both received an endless stream of letters about the extent of Jewish losses and often were in touch with each other over how best to respond.

Mikhoels understood the regime had ulterior reasons for tolerating his prestige. He once explained to his daughter that the regime used him and Ehrenburg as a *shirma*, a decoy; the Kremlin could always point to them whenever someone in the West raised questions about anti-Jewish measures. Mikhoels, though, knew he was being targeted. He began receiving threatening letters as early as 1946 and so adopted a modest precaution: when he walked his dog at night he used to call Peretz Markish, who lived nearby, in order not to be alone on the street.

Mikhoels could not protect himself indefinitely. In January 1948 he was sent to Minsk as a member of the theater section of the Stalin Prize Committee, ostensibly to review a play. On the evening of January 13 he was called away from his hotel in the company of a critic named Vladimir Golubov-Potapov. Their bodies were found early the next morning; they had been assaulted or perhaps killed by a vehicle.

The regime camouflaged its complicity with a lavish funeral. Thousands of people attended and heard official speeches of praise. Promises were made to name a theater and a school after Mikhoels. His daughters were was so grief-stricken they could not imagine Mikhoels was the victim of a conspiracy nor could they respond to suggestions that their father's death was not an accident.[8]

Ehrenburg understood that Mikhoels had been assassinated. The campaign against the country's Jews was not yet explicit, however; no one could discern Stalin's ultimate intentions. Several months passed. In May the State of Israel was established. The Soviet Union was the first to recognize the new Jewish government, even as Arab armies began to attack. Stalin also approved selling Israel much-needed arms and equipment through Czechoslovakia. Although Ehrenburg did not consider himself a Zionist, he was heartened by the support Israel received from the Kremlin. In a telegram to Albert Einstein on May 19, 1948, he expressed outrage over England's ties to the Arabs and satisfaction over the creation of Israel and its efforts to defend itself.

> The birth of the Jewish state was a tragic one. The act of its creation was not written in ink, but in blood. Greedy and base gentlemen prepared the assault in a very careful way. Oh, of course, as very experienced criminals, they are covering up their tracks. They are washing their hands. They are drafting sentimental speeches. Dickens once vividly described vile hypocrites and murderers with nice, friendly smiles. But even Dickens was not able to foresee how far some of his compatriots could go . . .
>
> The Soviet government immediately recognized the new Jewish state. This recognition will inspire the heroes who are now defending Israel from mercenary legionnaires.[9]

A week later Ehrenburg had a unique opportunity to address Moscow's Jewish community. The death of Solomon Mikhoels had not been forgotten and a memorial meeting was held on May 24 in the Jewish State Theater, which now bore his name. Ehrenburg delivered one of the main speeches. He could have written a simple eulogy, recalling Mikhoels's work during the war and his talent on the stage. Instead he addressed the growing anxiety in the Jewish community, demonstrably sharing its hatred of anti-Semitism, its pride in Jewish cultural achievement, and its concern for the safety of Israel. The speech exemplified his ability to convey personal concerns and still remain within the rhetorical framework of Soviet policy. "I am convinced that in the old quarter of Jerusalem, in the catacombs, where battles rage today," Ehrenburg concluded, "the figure of Solomon

Mikhailovich Mikhoels, a great Soviet citizen, a great artist, a great man, inspires people to heroic deeds."[10]

Listeners were struck by Ehrenburg's explicit, Zionist remarks and thought they were surprisingly and dangerously outspoken.[11] His denunciation of anti-Semitism was not, however, limited to the immediate audience: by reminding Soviet authorities that anti-Semitism is a fundamental dimension of Nazism, Ehrenburg implied that the regime betrayed its own professed ideals when it adopted the racism of its implacable enemy. This was his unmistakable message; it was as far as he could go in rebuking the authorities.

THE ARRIVAL OF GOLDA MEIR

As the year progressed and the fighting in the Middle East continued, Soviet Jews were willing to express their solidarity with Israel more and more overtly. In September a young Israeli Labor party official named Golda Meir, who would later become famous as her country's prime minister, was sent to Moscow as head of the Israeli diplomatic mission to the USSR. The Israelis did not anticipate that the Jews of Moscow would dare to demonstrate their love for Israel within blocks of the Kremlin; but immediately after Golda Meir arrived on September 3 Jews began waiting in line outside the Metropol Hotel to see her. Other members of her staff were approached by individual Jews, asking about relatives or handing them notes of welcome in Hebrew.

Meir and her colleagues first attended the main Moscow synagogue on September 11 for Sabbath morning services. When they reached the building, Meir was led upstairs to the women's section while the men of the legation were seated next to the rabbi on the pulpit. Two wooden signs hung prominently above the congregation. The first read in Hebrew "The Jewish people lives" and the second announced in Russian "The State of Israel was proclaimed on May 14, 1948." At the close of the service the entire congregation began to applaud and to shout "Shalom" and "hooray," using the Hebrew expression *heidad*, which did not end until the Israelis reached the street. Even then the crowd would not let them leave quietly; many people accompanied them through the streets to their hotel.

"Exhausted from the tension, we returned to our rooms with mixed feelings," Mordechai Namir, the legation's first secretary, recalled in his memoirs, *Mission in Moscow.* "With all of our joy that fortune had granted us such a reunion with our brothers, there was also a sinking feeling in our hearts because of the suspicion that the blatant conduct of the congregation had crossed the acceptable limits of the city and that we had participated in a very tragic event."[12]

Ehrenburg shared Namir's anxiety that his fellow Moscow Jews were behaving too enthusiastically for their own good and he was determined to caution them. Ten days later his famous article "Concerning a Certain Letter" appeared in *Pravda.* This piece has long been cited as evidence of Ehrenburg's complicity in Stalin's assault on Yiddish culture. Even the veteran correspondent Harrison Salisbury, who knew Ehrenburg and who has written sympathetically about his career, believed this article signaled the beginning of the anti-cosmopolitan campaign and that Ehrenburg "savagely criticized Jews who did not place Soviet nationalism before their Jewish culture."[13] A close reading of the article, though, and the circumstances in which it was written lead to a different conclusion. As the reception for Golda Meir demonstrated, the Jews of Moscow did not restrain their euphoria and no doubt fueled Stalin's paranoia about their loyalty. Ehrenburg understood the mood of his fellow Jews. He too had witnessed Hitler's atrocities and was heartened by the establishment of Israel. But he knew that official anti-Semitism was a growing threat and that Soviet Jews needed a warning, a reminder of where they were living.

Ehrenburg's article covered a full page in *Pravda,* nearly 3,500 words. Like his speech four months earlier in memory of Mikhoels, Ehrenburg employed standard Soviet clichés while managing to convey a more subtle and complicated message. The article was written as a public response to a letter—which was probably fictitious—from a young German Jew named Alexander R., who had escaped Germany and spent the war fighting the Nazis in the French Communist underground. He returned to Munich after the war only to learn he was the sole survivor of his family. He then enrolled in a medical school where many of the students were anti-Semites and would often say to him, "Get out of here, go to Palestine." "What is to be done to prevent a repetition of [the Nazi] horrors?" Alexander R. asked Ehrenburg. "I have never been a Zionist, but I am beginning to believe in the idea of a Jewish state. I am expecting an answer from you—for you are a writer of the country in which I believe with all my heart." Ehrenburg began his reply by reminding his readers that "the Soviet government was the first to recognize the new state. . . . But though I do believe in the future of Israel," Ehrenburg continued, "my answer to my correspondent's second question—whether the establishment of Israel constitutes a solution to the so-called 'Jewish question'—must be in the negative." Here Ehrenburg pointedly reminded his readers of what was expected of them.

> I know that the solution to the "Jewish problem" does not depend on military successes in Palestine, but on the triumph of Socialism over capitalism, the triumph of the lofty internationalist principles of the working class over nationalism, fascism, and racism. . . . The October Revolution brought freedom and equality to all citizens of the Soviet land, including the Jews. Some of them regard Russian as their mother tongue, others Ukrainian, still others Yiddish, but they all regard the Soviet Union as their homeland where there is no longer the exploitation of one man by another.

This is the only mention of Yiddish in the article, making it unfair to accuse Ehrenburg of signaling the impending liquidation of the Jewish Anti-Fascist Committee and the country's Yiddish cultural institutions. Furthermore, Ehrenburg went on to denounce anti-Semitism, reserving his most passionate and eloquent remarks for a discussion of how prejudice and superstition hounded the Jews for centuries.

> If tomorrow a maniac appeared who proclaimed that all red-headed or snub-nosed people must be hounded and wiped out, we should see a natural solidarity of all red-headed or all snub-nosed people. The appalling atrocities of the German Fascists, their proclaimed policy of wholesale extermination of Jews . . . gave rise to a deep bond among the Jews of various countries. It was the solidarity of offended and indignant people.

Ehrenburg then publicly cites for the first time one of his favorite formulations, written by his friend Julian Tuwim during the war. "Blood exists in two forms; the blood that flows inside the veins and the blood that flows out of the veins . . . Why do I say, 'We Jews?' Because of blood." In the face of anti-Semitism Ehrenburg concludes that the Jews have legitimate moral and political rights to a state of their own, "an ark, a raft, holding people overtaken by the bloody flood of racism and

Fascism." This has long been an axiomatic dimension of Zionist philosophy. He even acknowledged, in answer to his correspondent, that
"it is possible that, under such circumstances, Alexander R. has no
other choice than to make his way to Israel. That may well be the solution to his personal dilemma, but it will not be the solution for all Jews
who live in many different lands under the oppression of money, lies,
and superstition."[14]

Mordechai Namir regarded Ehrenburg's article as "pro-Israeli and
anti-Zionist."[15] The article in fact expresses genuine regard for Israel
and hatred of anti-Semitism. It is not anti-Zionist about Israel's right
to exist or the need of "a raft" for persecuted Jews; it is anti-Zionist to
the extent that Ehrenburg reminds Soviet Jews that the Soviet Union
is their homeland. Ehrenburg himself, as a Russian patriot and a Jew,
also understood that life under Stalin made it too dangerous to express
overt loyalty or even support for another state.

Years later Ehrenburg divulged to his friend Menahem Flakser (who
had translated *Julio Jurenito* and *Lasik Roitschwantz* into Yiddish) how his
article came to be written.[16] According to Flakser, Ehrenburg stated
that Stalin believed a war with the United States was a genuine possibility. Although the Jews had fought heroically against Hitler, every
Soviet Jew was thought to have relatives in America and might not
remain loyal to the Soviet Union in the event of a U.S.-Soviet conflict.
Ehrenburg believed that Stalin considered deporting the Jews to
Siberia in 1948 but his colleagues on the Politburo convinced him
such an action would enrage international public opinion, especially so
soon after the Nazi massacres. Stalin then decided to decapitate the
leadership of the Jewish community—artists, poets, and scientists—in
order to intimidate the rest. Ehrenburg also told Flakser that two members of the Politburo, Lazar Kaganovich and Georgy Malenkov,
appealed to him for help, convincing him of the need to explain to
Soviet Jews that their fate was bound up with the Soviet Union.

Svetlana Alliluyeva described Stalin's mood at that time in her book
Twenty Letters to a Friend. Her recollections lend support to Flakser's
account.

A new wave of arrests got under way at the end of 1948. My two
aunts, the widows of Uncle Pavel and Redens, were sent to prison,
and so was everyone who knew them. I. G. Morozov, the father of
my first husband, was arrested, too. Next there was a campaign against

people who were called cosmopolitan. They even arrested Molotov's wife. Lozovsky was arrested and Mikhoels was killed. All of them were lumped together in a single, alleged Zionist center.

Svetlana appealed to Stalin that it made no sense to accuse her former father-in-law of Zionism, but Stalin grew even angrier. "No! You don't understand," he told his daughter. "The entire older generation is contaminated with Zionism and now they're teaching the young people, too."[17]

Ehrenburg sensed the shift in Stalin's mood, but his efforts were in vain. The Jewish community did not proceed with caution. Rosh Hashana fell within days after Ehrenburg's article; Moscow Jews responded even more enthusiastically to the Israelis than they had two weeks before.

"We had expected attention, of course," Namir recalled, "but what occurred went beyond everything we could have imagined." An enormous crowd greeted Golda Meir in front of the synagogue and waited for several hours until the service was over, when they escorted her through the streets of the capital shouting "Next Year in Jerusalem." Namir was overwhelmed. "One man . . . said to us: 'This is the answer of Moscow's Jews to Ehrenburg.'" While the capital's Jews continued to behave without restraint—another massive demonstration took place a week later on Yom Kippur—Ehrenburg remained aloof from the Israelis. A short time after the High Holidays he attended a large diplomatic reception at the Czech embassy where Meir was also present. A left-wing British journalist named Ralph Parker offered to introduce her to Ehrenburg. With her consent, Parker then approached Ehrenburg who also agreed on the condition they not discuss political matters. Their encounter was a disaster. Ehrenburg appeared to be drunk, and as soon as they met he began to berate her for not being able to speak Russian. Parker and Henry Shapiro helped to translate, trying to negotiate a truce at the same time; Shapiro did not tell her all of Ehrenburg's anti-American remarks, but nothing came of this effort. Ehrenburg and Golda Meir argued for about ten minutes before he walked away. Ehrenburg "made a severe impression on us," Namir recalled, "as someone who deliberately avoided talking about Jewish matters, an attitude that stood out even more by his being drunk."[18]

More than likely Ehrenburg was not drunk, nor was he hostile or indifferent to the Israelis' presence in Moscow. He had always been

cautious when it came to Israel.[19] That fall he began warning his
friends to keep their distance from the Israelis; he specifically did not
want to give any impression of courtesy or interest when he met Golda
Meir. Moreover, Ralph Parker was regarded as a secret police informer
by other foreign correspondents, a fact Ehrenburg would surely have
known; he would never engage in a serious conversation in Parker's
presence. So Ehrenburg feigned drunkenness and behaved crudely
enough to insure that no report to Stalin would impugn his loyalty or
his intentions.[20]

Within weeks Ehrenburg had an opportunity to talk more candidly
with Mordechai Namir near the end of November at a reception at the
Albanian embassy. Ehrenburg made his concerns explicit: Soviet Jews
would not make *aliyah* and the Israelis should stop encouraging them
to adopt Zionism. Ehrenburg insisted to Namir several times that he
was speaking "as a friend" and that his advice should be heeded. If not,
both the Soviet government and the Jews would react angrily and it
would be to the detriment of Israel.

Polina Zhemchuzhina, the wife of Vyacheslav Molotov, the Soviet
foreign minister, was not cautious enough. Zhemchuzhina had been
head of the Soviet cosmetics industry in the 1930s and later minister
of the fishing industry. When she met members of the Israeli delegation at a diplomatic reception on November 7, 1948, the anniversary
of the revolution, she could barely restrain herself. "I've heard you
attend the synagogue," Zhemchuzhina told Golda Meir, speaking in
Yiddish. "Very good. Keep going. The Jews want to see you." When
Meir asked how she knew Yiddish so well, Zhemchuzhina proudly
responded, "*Ich bin a Yiddishe tochter*" (I am a daughter of the Jewish
people), a phrase she repeated several times. Zhemchuzhina asked
about life in Israel, about the Negev and conditions on the kibbutzim.
She parted from them with tears in her eyes, saying "I wish all will go
well for you there and then it will be good for all the Jews."[21] Zhemchuzhina's enthusiasm for Israel came to Stalin's attention. She was
arrested and sent into exile within two months and did not return to
Moscow until after Stalin's death.

That fall Stalin's anti-Semitic paranoia led to even more terrible
consequences. Scores—perhaps hundreds—of Yiddish writers were
arrested, including Itzik Fefer, the vice-chairman of the Jewish Anti-
Fascist Committee, along with David Bergelson, Shmuel Halkin, and
Leib Kvitko. These arrests were accompanied by the closing of the

Emes publishing house in Moscow and Jewish professional theaters in Kiev, Minsk, Odessa, and Moscow. Then in January the theme of the assault shifted from "Jewish nationalism" to a campaign against "cosmopolitanism" and the assimilated Jewish intelligentsia.

A flood of venom engulfed the Soviet press, beginning on January 28, 1949, with an article in *Pravda* unmasking "an unpatriotic group of theater critics." Of those named, almost all were Jews. This article and the hundreds that followed employed characteristic anti-Semitic devices. They emphasized the alienation of Jews from Russian culture, asking rhetorically, "What kind of an idea can Gurvich have of the national character of Soviet Russian man?" They referred to Jews as "rootless cosmopolitans," "persons without identity," and "passportless wanderers."[22]

Peretz Markish was arrested near the end of January. Shortly after, Ehrenburg visited Esther Markish and her children—a gesture that required genuine courage. Within a few days Markish's family was exiled from Moscow to return only after Stalin's death.[23]

Ehrenburg was not immune from these developments. His work stopped appearing in February 1949 and his name removed from other published articles. The omens were familiar enough and each night he expected to be arrested. His friends too feared the worst. Many would call, then put down the receiver when they heard his voice. At the end of March a prominent party activist announced to a Moscow audience of more than a thousand people that "cosmopolitan number one and enemy of the people Ilya Ehrenburg has been exposed and arrested." Ehrenburg was informed the next day and immediately wrote a letter to Stalin, explaining his situation and asking "for the uncertainty to come to an end." Malenkov called Ehrenburg soon after and reassured him. Editors started to call again and his career resumed.

Ehrenburg survived this episode much in the way he survived before—with a direct appeal to Stalin. It is impossible to confirm if Stalin knew of Ehrenburg's predicament or if he deliberately toyed with Ehrenburg to see how he would react. Ehrenburg had been awarded a Stalin Prize for his novel *The Storm* only a year before on the dictator's own recommendation; it would have been awkward to have him arrested, yet it seemed equally surprising to have him at liberty in the midst of an "anti-cosmopolitan" campaign. The most likely reason for his survival was provided unwittingly by Ehrenburg himself. As Mikhoels understood, he and Ehrenburg were used as decoys, and

now only Ehrenburg was left; as he reminds us in his memoirs, in April
1949 the regime needed him to attend the World Peace Congress in
Paris. He was asked to write a speech and submit it for approval. "Facing a blank sheet, I began to write about what was worrying me,"
namely racism and national chauvinism. In his memoirs Ehrenburg
gives the impression that he wrote these remarks in order to admonish
the Kremlin over its anti-Semitic campaign. To his surprise, however,
he was summoned to the Kremlin and thanked for his speech, then
shown a copy "typed out on good paper" (that was how manuscripts
were usually given to Stalin) with the words "'well said' in a hand-
writing that looked painfully familiar" alongside his liberal remarks.[24]

Once in Paris Ehrenburg saw his old friends Louis Aragon and Elsa
Triolet. They asked about the "anti-cosmopolitan" campaign but
Ehrenburg could not answer their questions. He felt ill; he wanted to
go home and avoid giving his speech. He could not sleep that night
while "the image of Peretz Markish as I had last seen him rose before
me. I remembered phrases from newspaper articles and stupidly
repeated to myself 'go home'."[25] Ehrenburg, despite exhaustion and
depression, carried out his assignment. He did not reveal what had happened to Peretz Markish, to Solomon Mikhoels, or to the scores of
other friends who had already perished or were now in jail. He was not
willing to seek asylum in the West or abandon his wife and daughter
to the regime's revenge. He may have thought his remarks about racism
took courage, but once he saw Stalin's comment he understood how
much he was being used. As Esther Markish remarks in her book *The
Long Return*, "I just can't believe that a man as shrewd and experienced
as Ehrenburg could have been bamboozled by this typical Stalinist sub-
terfuge: at the height of the purges, for example, there was more talk
than ever about democracy and the rights guaranteed by the new Constitution."[26] In his memoirs Ehrenburg stresses how wretched he felt in
Paris, finally realizing "the price a man must pay for being 'true to men,
to the century, to fate.' "[27] These vague, high-sounding phrases cannot
obscure Ehrenburg's own admission; his compliance, particularly when
he traveled abroad and mingled freely with foreigners, was the price for
his survival.

Under harsh circumstances and duress Ehrenburg still found ways to
act with unusual independence. Three months after his trip to Paris the
Jewish museum in Vilna was closed, its holdings distributed to other
archives and institutions in Lithuania. The former partisans did not for-

get their obligation to Ehrenburg. Israel Kronik and a friend traveled to Moscow, carrying with them the original folios of *The Black Book* in two suitcases. Inside Ehrenburg's apartment Kronik found Ehrenburg looking pale, his hair disheveled. Only two years had passed since Ehrenburg had visited Vilna, but standing in the hallway Kronik thought Ehrenburg had aged rapidly, that something had happened to him.[28] After Kronik left Ehrenburg kept the folios hidden in his apartment in a small pantry with no outside windows. One friend remembers seeing them under his bed as late as 1965.[29] After he died the authorities asked his widow to relinquish them, but she claimed not to know where they were.[30]

———

Publicly, Ehrenburg's career proceeded as before. He continued to travel to peace congresses and to publish hard-hitting articles against the United States and its Western allies. As a newly elected member of the Supreme Soviet he took his responsibilities seriously, visiting Riga from time to time to meet with constituents and trying to help with their problems—finding an apartment, a job, an opportunity to study in Moscow.

Ehrenburg's trips to Western Europe did not go as smoothly as he would have preferred. In the spring and summer of 1950 he traveled to Sweden, Belgium, Switzerland, Germany, and England, where U.S. embassy officials followed his moves closely and tried to prevent "so notorious a spokesman against the Western democracies" from making these visits. In Brussels that April most of Ehrenburg's public appearances were in fact exercises in propaganda, "bitter and ironic denunciations of the United States based on his visit there in 1946," as the U.S. embassy was quick to note. To the embassy's chagrin, about 1,800 people showed up to hear him, a crowd "not made up of the usual wild-eyed and ragged Communist run-of-the-mill. . . . The audience was composed of the white collar classes," the embassy reported to Washington, "and the Dowager Queen of Belgium, Elizabeth, sat in the Royal Box throughout Ehrenburg's almost two-hour speech." The Queen soon became friendly with Ehrenburg. They shared a passion for flowers and over the next few years she enjoyed sending him rare bulbs and seeds for the garden he cultivated at his dacha. From Belgium Ehrenburg tried to visit France and Italy, but both countries refused him entry. At Le Bourget airport outside of Paris Ehrenburg "requested permission to remain in Paris twenty-four hours, but the Ministry of the Interior gave instructions that Ehrenburg should not leave the air-port," an unusually abrupt treatment for a recipient of the Legion of Honor.[31]

Three months later, in July, Ehrenburg experienced a different and more troublesome reception in London. His visa was granted unex-pectedly and he was able to address a large "peace" rally in Trafalgar Square; to Ehrenburg's surprise, he now found himself being ushered into a crowded press conference. Four years earlier in the United States the press had posed questions he found easy to answer. By 1950, how-ever, too much was starting to be known—or feared to be true—about events inside the Soviet Union. In his memoirs Ehrenburg acknowl-edges that "the room was packed with journalists and they behaved in such a provocative manner that it made me sweat."[32] The Korean War had recently broken out and the nearly two hundred journalists in attendance were in no mood for relaxed give-and-take. Anatol Gold-berg of the BBC was there and remembered watching Ehrenburg fight "a valiant rearguard action" for two hours, "dodging some questions and parrying others with counter-questions, seeking refuge in half-truths and veiled ambiguities, but plainly trying not to tell outright lies." One question proved impossible to dodge artfully. Ehrenburg was asked about the fate of David Bergelson and Itzik Fefer, whose arrests were suspected to have taken place. Ehrenburg reported that he had not seen either of them for two years and before that, since they were not close friends, he had seen them only rarely, a response that was more or less factually true. But then Ehrenburg added a clever lie that Goldberg understood "was deliberately decked out to sound like the truth." "If anything unpleasant had happened to them," Ehrenburg asserted in French, "I would have known about it."[33] Ehrenburg knew they had been arrested. Unless he was prepared to seek political asylum in England, he had no alternative but to help cover up the pogrom and deflate suspicions about life and death in the Soviet Union.

Such behavior assured Ehrenburg's standing with the regime and he continued to receive official honors. In January 1951 his sixtieth birth-day was publicly celebrated. *Literaturnaya Gazeta* devoted substantial space to praising him.[34] The Writers' Union held a gala reception, with an exhibition of Ehrenburg's books and posters from his career deco-rating the hall, and during the evening he was awarded the Order of the Red Banner (Civilian), one of the regime's highest honors. Addressing the assembled guests, Ehrenburg knew how to express his gratitude:

I also want to thank a man with all my heart who helped me, as he helped all of us, to write what I have already written and who will help me write what I am dreaming about. This man was with me at the front and at noisy demonstrations devoted to the defense of peace, and in the nocturnal quiet of my room, where I sit over a piece of paper. Thanking him, I am also thanking our great people.[35]

This was not the first time Ehrenburg had stooped to obsequious flattery and exploited Stalin's weakness for inflated compliments. Such behavior was common in the Soviet Union, even by people who asserted their moral independence. Osip Mandelstam, who had denounced Stalin in several poems, tried to save his own life in 1936 by writing an "Ode to Stalin." Anna Akhmatova, as well, in a desperate effort to gain her son's release from a labor camp in 1947, wrote a poem "In Praise of Peace."

In a further tribute to Ehrenburg on his birthday the Secretariat of the Writers' Union decided to publish a multivolume collection of his works. This is always significant for a Soviet writer because it invariably means substantial royalties. Ehrenburg was able to build a small dacha in the Moscow suburb of New Jerusalem, just north of the city and far removed from Peredelkino, where the country's famous writers had their country houses (and where he had lost his own in 1940). With few exceptions Ehrenburg had little respect for his professional colleagues in the Writers' Union and deliberately chose a site for his dacha away from where they lived.

Putting the collection together, though, "wore [Ehrenburg] out."[36] Critics commissioned by the Writers' Union scrutinized every page, looking for political deficiencies. *The Storm* had been written before Tito's break with Stalin; there were "positive appraisals of this spy, an enemy of the Yugoslav people," Ehrenburg was told. De Gaulle, too, was now "an Anglo-American protégé and enemy of the French people."[37] Another reviewer took issue with Ehrenburg's novel *Without Taking Breath*: the country's atmosphere in the book was "too grim;" Pasternak had not been as popular in the 1930s as Ehrenburg's text implied. Two names of writers since exposed as "enemies of the people" would have to be removed, while a paragraph about the plight of the kulaks needed correction—"it might evoke sympathy for their suffering."[38]

Nothing drew these readers' attention more than Jewish names and

Jewish themes. After reading *The Storm* one reviewer complained that Ehrenburg seemed unable "to find Ukrainian hero-patriots;" only Jews were depicted defending Kiev against the Nazis.[39] Another actually counted Jewish characters in *Out of Chaos* and in *Without Taking Breath*. "In both books, which are written about the Russian people, . . . an excessive number of names represent rootless nationalities." He then listed fourteen from the first book and nine from the other, all obviously Jewish.[40]

Ehrenburg objected strenuously to this kind of scrutiny. His books had been published in many editions, making it humiliating to re-issue them with such evident changes. As for the problem of too many Jewish names, Ehrenburg could not help but wonder what to do "about the surname on the title-page."[41]

The correspondence dragged on for two years, with Ehrenburg increasingly frustrated by his reviewers' demands. In the end the collection was issued over a three-year period between 1952 and 1954. Stalin died in March 1953 while Ehrenburg was still negotiating over the texts. Five weeks later Ehrenburg refused categorically to accept any further changes.[42] With Stalin gone it was no longer necessary to buckle under to Soviet cultural bureaucrats.

THE DOCTORS' PLOT

Ehrenburg continued to work on behalf of the Partisans of Peace, including a month-long visit to China with Pablo Neruda in the fall of 1951 to present the Stalin Peace Prize to Sun Yat Sen's widow. A year later, in December 1952, the Kremlin announced the latest winners; Ehrenburg was among them. Until then the award had been reserved for foreign Communists and fellow travelers, such as Yves Farge and Paul Robeson, whose usefulness to Soviet propaganda merited recognition. Ehrenburg was the first Soviet citizen to be so honored. Pictures of all seven recipients, including Ehrenburg, topped the front pages of *Pravda* and *Literaturnaya Gazeta*. "In his sharp pamphlets and in the novel *The Ninth Wave*," the announcement proclaimed, "Ehrenburg unmasked the vanity and internal emptiness of American contenders for global domination."[43] But the timing of the award was suspicious. Four years earlier, over the winter of 1948–49, the Kremlin had arrested leading figures in Yiddish culture. No one knew their fate, although their ranks included highly regarded writers. Lena Shtern, a distinguished biologist and the only woman member of the Academy of Sciences, was detained as well. She had served on the Jewish Anti-Fascist Committee, as had Solomon Lozovsky, a former deputy foreign minister, who was also among those arrested.

A shadow has fallen on Itzik Fefer and his role in the affair. Fefer, it turns out, was systematically tortured and forced to give testimony against his fellow Yiddish writers. The poet Shmuel Halkin reported seeing Fefer when he was brought by Halkin's interrogator for a "personal confrontation;" all Halkin could say was that Fefer resembled "a skeleton with a moustache."[44] A closed trial took place in May 1952. There were twenty-five defendants. Fefer was the only one among the defendants to testify for the prosecution. Formally, the charges revolved around an alleged plot to secure land in the Crimea for Jews displaced by the war. There had in fact been a request to Stalin, initiated by Fefer and supported by Mikhoels, Markish, and others, to consider setting aside part of the Crimea—now uninhabited due to Stalin's forced resettlement of the Crimean Tatars in 1944—for Soviet Jews who could not return to Byelorussia and the Ukraine. While the idea may well have been a provocation on the part of Fefer, there was never any intention to create a "Zionist base" in the Crimea as a means to dismember the Soviet Union, as Fefer claimed at the trial in 1952. Ehrenburg left the Jewish Anti-Fascist Committee in 1944 and was never part of any initiative for a Jewish Autonomous Region in the Crimea. According to one former KGB agent, Ehrenburg "saved his life and his position" by refusing to support such a project.[45] At the close of the trial the defendants were not all sentenced to death, but then the verdicts were reviewed by Stalin and executions imposed. Except for Lena Shtern, who received a sentence of twenty-five years, they were all secretly executed—twenty-four men on the night of August 12, 1952—a date commemorated as "The Night of the Murdered Poets."

Another atrocity was soon to come. In November 1952 fourteen leaders of the Czech Communist party, among them eleven Jews, were brought to trial accused of plotting to overthrow Communist regimes in Eastern Europe. The most prominent defendant was Rudolf Slansky, the former head of the party. Ehrenburg's old friend Vladimir Clementis, a onetime foreign minister, was also in the dock. References to "Zionist adventurers" ran through the indictment, while prosecutors emphasized the Jewish origins of most of the defendants, all of whom had been devoted Communists and thoroughly loyal to Stalin. As the trial unfolded, newspapers and radio broadcasts throughout Eastern Europe and the Soviet Union denounced Slansky and his co-defendants, invariably echoing the prosecutors' anti-Semitic ridicule. Radio Bucharest in a typical statement proclaimed: "We also have criminals among us, Zionist agents and agents of international Jewish capital. We shall expose them, and it is our duty to exterminate them."[46] A week after the Prague trial ended Slansky and ten others were hanged, their bodies cremated, and the ashes dumped along the side of a highway.

Stalin's plans were not yet over. A sinister drama was about to reach its climax.

On January 13, 1953, two lead articles on the front page of *Pravda* announced the arrests of nine doctors "who had made it their aim to cut short the lives of active public figures of the Soviet Union by means of sabotaged medical treatment." They were specifically accused of killing Andrei Zhdanov and Alexander Shcherbakov—who were thought to have died of natural causes—and conspiring to murder a list of Soviet military leaders who had been under their care. "All these homicidal doctors, who had become monsters in human form" had been recruited by a "Jewish bourgeois nationalist organization" and elements of American intelligence under the direction of "the well-known Jewish bourgeois nationalist, [Solomon] Mikhoels." The article in fact appeared exactly five years after Mikhoels's murder.[47]

In the midst of the twentieth century the Kremlin revived the medieval slander about malicious Jews who were out to poison their enemies. Overnight, panic swept over Soviet society. Doctors, especially Jewish doctors, came under suspicion. "It was like hell in the hospitals," Ehrenburg recalled in *People, Years, Life*, "many patients regarded the doctors as if they were insidious scoundrels and refused to take any medicines." A friend told Ehrenburg of a doctor who "had to swallow pills, powders, a dozen medicines for a dozen diseases;" the patients "were afraid she was a conspirator."[48]

Across the Soviet Union a full-scale anti-Semitic campaign was unleashed. Jewish students were dismissed from universities, Jewish medical students dispatched to remote areas of the country, Jewish professionals compelled to resign their positions. In the labor camps Jews were suddenly singled out for punishment. Ehrenburg felt increasingly vulnerable and afraid. Nadezhda Mandelstam saw him at that time. "I am ready for anything," he told her.[49]

Ehrenburg knew more than most about the mood of the country. He received scores of letters following the announcement of the "doctors' plot," each one expressing anguish over the growing anti-Semitic hysteria. "I am thirty-two years old," one woman wrote to him,

I was born in Moscow. I do not know a different motherland. I do not know another regime. I have never even traveled outside of Moscow.

My parents, who went to see my sister in Minsk a month before the war, were brutally killed there. My husband fell near Stalingrad. I was pregnant at the time and did not leave Moscow during the war but worked as much as I could.

I have an eleven-year-old son whom I am raising by myself. A few days ago in school, other students chased him into the bathroom and beat him up, yelling "This is how a kike should be treated!" What is going on?

Can it be you do not know about all this? Can it be you cannot relate all this to the necessary authorities?

I work . . . in a room with twelve people. I am the only Jew. Lately, no one talks with me. The charwoman gives everyone tea except for me and no one pays any attention to this.

My son was beaten. He has been in bed for two days, but no one from the school did anything or even said anything to the kids that this was or was not the right thing to do.

Who are you? Why are you silent? Are you a traitor or an honest man?

I wanted to come talk to you, but I am afraid. I do not trust you.[50]

Most of the letters asked Ehrenburg to condemn the arrested doctors as traitors. One man denounced Israel as a "military base for American imperialism" and admitted there were Soviet Jews "who could commit the most vile of crimes—an attempt on the life of Soviet government leaders—for dollars and pounds." He implored Ehrenburg "to tell the entire Soviet people, the entire world, that we, Soviet citizens, Soviet Jewish working people, have nothing in common with a group of base bourgeois nationalists."[51] It is painfully easy to understand what drove ordinary Jews to write such desperate letters. Some believed the official charges; others understood that the *Pravda* announcement was part of a broader plot. Yet they all sought some way to defend themselves.

In this atmosphere of paranoia and confusion Ehrenburg received the Stalin Peace Prize, confirming Mikhoels's stated belief that both he and Ehrenburg were used by the Kremlin to camouflage official anti-Semitism. A few days before the ceremony a high party official asked Ehrenburg to mention the "criminal doctors" in his acceptance speech. Ehrenburg refused outright, making clear that he was ready to relinquish the award. Nonetheless, the ceremony took place in the Kremlin's Sverdlov Hall on January 27, 1953, Ilya Ehrenburg's sixty-second birthday. Several friends of his, including Louis Aragon and Anna Seghers, made congratulatory speeches. Neither Stalin nor other members of the Politburo were present. The prizes were supposed to reflect humanitarian sentiments, and the presence of high government officials would have exposed the pretense.

Ehrenburg spoke briefly, but his remarks sent a chill through the hall. "On this solemn and festive occasion, . . . I want to pay tribute to those fighters for peace who are being defamed, persecuted, tortured, hounded, and killed. I want to call to mind the dark night of prisons, of interrogations, of trials, of blood, and the courage of so many."[52] Lyubov Mikhailovna was in the hall and told her husband later that when he mentioned prisons, "the people sitting near her held their breath."[53] His speech appeared the next morning on the front page of *Pravda* with a telling amendment: to Ehrenburg's words about persecutions the editors added "by the forces of reaction" should Soviet readers take Ehrenburg's inference a different way. That same day an American embassy official reported to Washington that Ehrenburg's speech "may be related to the doctors' case."[54]

The most terrifying moment was yet to come. In his memoirs Ehrenburg had to be cautious and enigmatic.

> Events were supposed to unfold further. I will omit the story of how I tried to prevent the appearance in print of a certain collective letter. Happily, the project, which was absolutely insane, did not come about. I thought at the time that I dissuaded Stalin with my letter; now it seems to me the whole business was delayed and Stalin did not succeed in doing what he wanted to do. This is history, of course, a chapter of my biography, but I believe the time has not yet come for me to say more.[55]

Toward the middle of February Ehrenburg was approached at his dacha by two important Soviet functionaries: the historian Isaac Mintz and an editor from *Pravda* named M. Marinin, whose real name was Yakov Khavinson. Both men were Jewish and they asked Ehrenburg to sign an "open letter" addressed to Stalin for publication in *Pravda*. The letter acknowledged the strong feelings aroused by the Doctors' Plot and in order to save the country's Jews from the "wrath of the people," the signatories—who were all to be Jewish—were asking Stalin to send the country's Jews to Siberia and Birobidjan, where they would be housed and protected.

Ehrenburg refused to sign and brusquely turned them away. Mintz and Marinin were not yet finished.

A few days later Mintz and Marinin came to Ehrenburg's Moscow apartment and insisted that he sign the letter to Stalin. Now Ehrenburg understood that they were not acting alone, that their actions represented a new and sinister turn in the Doctors' Plot. Once again Ehrenburg refused, but he began to consider an initiative of his own.

Ehrenburg was one of a handful of prominent Jewish figures to be approached alone. His friend, the novelist Veniamin Kaverin, was summoned to the offices of *Pravda* where Mintz and Marinin pressured him to sign the "open letter," claiming falsely that Ehrenburg agreed with its contents. Kaverin held his ground. "I cannot sign without thinking about it," he told the two men. From *Pravda* Kaverin went straight to Ehrenburg, who denied voicing any sympathy for the so-called open letter. Both understood that were their signatures to appear on such a document it would be the end of their reputations; yet they feared that their names could be included without their permission.

While Ehrenburg and Kaverin waited for the regime's next move, dozens of other Jewish writers, artists, and musicians were summoned to a hall and there instructed to sign a similar letter. The poet Margarita Aliger sat next to Vasily Grossman. Terrified, they both signed. Only two elderly men stood up to protest. Grossman left in a state of deep distress. "I have to see Ehrenburg," was all Grossman kept repeating.[56]

The regime still wanted Ehrenburg's submission. One evening, while Ovady and Alya Savich were visiting on Gorky Street, Ehrenburg was summoned to the offices of *Pravda*, where the editor-in-chief, Dmitri Shepilov, urged him to sign the "open letter." Ehrenburg firmly refused and in an act of unprecedented defiance typed his own appeal to Stalin, insisting that Shepilov deliver it to the Kremlin.

While Ehrenburg was at *Pravda*, Lyubov Mikhailovna called Irina Ehrenburg and Veniamin Kaverin to let them know what had hap-

pened. Irina, Kaverin, and his wife Lidia all immediately joined the
Saviches on Gorky Street anxiously to await Ehrenburg's return. It was
well past midnight when Ehrenburg came in the door, frightened and
depressed. Alya Savich thought he looked worse than she had ever seen
him; "shaken, ashen, beaten" were the words she used. He was holding
a copy of his letter to Stalin.[57]

Ilya Ehrenburg and Veniamin Kaverin were not the only ones to
refuse to endorse Stalin's pogrom: Major General Jacob Kreiser, a
highly decorated war hero who had led Soviet troops in the liberation
of the Crimea, and Mark Reizen, a renowned opera singer at the Bol-
shoi, also refused as a matter of principle. Only Ehrenburg, however,
attempted to reason with Stalin. He knew it would be useless to make
a moral appeal. In his letter to Stalin Ehrenburg instead invoked his
experience as an emissary to Western intellectuals and to European
Communist parties, and explained how such an action against Soviet
Jews would undermine the Kremlin's prestige and political standing.
This was the only way to approach Stalin, a step that required profound
understanding and courage.

Dear Joseph Vissarionovich!

I have decided to trouble you only because of a question which I
cannot resolve myself and which seems to me extremely important.

Comrade Mintz and Comrade Marinin today acquainted me with
the text of a letter to the editor of *Pravda* and suggested that I should
sign it. I consider it my duty to share my doubts with you and to ask
your advice.

It seems to me that the only radical solution to the Jewish question
in our Socialist State is full assimilation and the merging of individuals
of Jewish origin with the peoples among whom they live. I am afraid
that a collective statement by a number of people active in Soviet
cultural life, united only by their origin, could strengthen nationalistic
tendencies. The text of the letter speaks of a "Jewish people"; this
could encourage nationalists and others who have not yet understood
that there is no such thing as a Jewish nation.

I am particularly worried about the influence of such a "letter to
the editor" on the broadening and strengthening of the world
movement for peace. Whenever, in various commissions and press
conferences, the question has been raised as to why there are no
Jewish schools or newspapers in the Soviet Union, I have invariably

replied that after the war there no longer remained any breeding-grounds for the former "Pale of Settlement," and that new generations of Soviet citizens of Jewish descent do not wish to set themselves apart from the peoples among whom they live. The publication of this letter, signed by scientists, writers and composers, who speak of a so-called Soviet Jewish community, could fan repellent anti-Soviet propaganda which is at present being spread by Zionists, Bundists, and other enemies of our Motherland.

In the eyes of French, Italian, English and other progressive forces, the term "Jew" has no meaning as a representative of a nationality, but only a religious significance, and slanderers may use this "letter to the editor" for their own base designs.

I am convinced that it is essential to fight energetically against all attempts to revive Jewish nationalism, which inevitably leads to betrayal. It seems to me that, for this, what is essential is to have, on the one hand, explanatory articles (including some by people of Jewish origin), and on the other, an explanation in *Pravda* itself, expressing what is already so well-formulated in the text of the letter: i.e., that the overwhelming majority of Jewish-born workers are deeply devoted to the Soviet Motherland and to Russian culture. Such articles, it seems to me, would be a powerful deterrent to foreign slanderers and would provide sound arguments for our friends who are fighting for peace.

You will understand, dear Joseph Vissarionovich, that I cannot resolve these questions by myself, and that is why I have been so bold as to write to you. The letter in question represents an important political step, and therefore I decided to ask you to designate someone to inform me of your opinion on the desirability of my signing such a document. If leading comrades convey to me that the publication of this document and my signature to it may be helpful in the defence of the Motherland, and for the Peace Movement, I shall at once sign it.

With deep respect,
Ilya Ehrenburg[58]

Stalin fully intended to proceed with the plan. Barracks for exiled Jews were constructed in Siberia and Birobidjan. Lists of Jews and their addresses, district by district, were drawn up in major cities. The poet Joseph Brodsky remembers his father coming home upset and crying from his job at a Leningrad newspaper. That day he had seen the text of the "open letter" to Stalin prepared for publication with Ehrenburg's name listed among the signatories; the regime intended to invoke his prestige with or without Ehrenburg's permission.[59] The machinery was in place and only awaited the word of one man to be set in motion. Ehrenburg tried to stop it. After his letter was sent, no more signatures were collected. The organizers of the campaign understood that until Stalin made some kind of response they could not solicit further endorsements.

Then providence intervened. Stalin suffered a cerebral hemorrhage and died on March 5, 1953. Within weeks the "doctors' plot" was publicly disavowed. Seven of the nine doctors were released; two had succumbed to torture.

It is impossible to gauge the effect, if any, of Ehrenburg's letter to Stalin. Did he make the dictator hesitate or reconsider? Was a decisive move put off momentarily until, miraculously, the tyrant died and his last murderous scheme was aborted? The answer is lost to history. But there can be no question that the letter reflected Ehrenburg's genius as a diplomat and politician. He reminded Stalin of political facts, of political repercussions, and then, with respect and humility, as any vassal would approach his feudal lord, he expressed his willingness to endorse the letter if Stalin required it. But Stalin knew that Ehrenburg had refused to sign three times and that only Ehrenburg had taken the further step of writing to him. With this gesture of protest Ilya Ehrenburg made clear to Stalin and to himself that he had discovered the limit to his faithfulness; Ehrenburg could well have been shot for such defiance. But Stalin's death brought an end to the country's long nightmare. It had lasted a quarter of a century. Against so many odds and so many enemies, Ilya Ehrenburg had survived.[60]

TWELVE

The Thaw and the Politics
of Culture

With Stalin dead Ilya Ehrenburg initially feared the worst. Like many others, he had seen "the future of his country tied to what had been called everyday for twenty years— the wisdom of our leader of genius." Immense crowds in mourning passed Ehrenburg's apartment house near Red Square, and he soon learned of incidents where people crushed each other to death because of the strain and panic of the moment. "I do not think history has ever known such a funeral," he wrote in his memoirs.[1] Ehrenburg had duties to perform. During Stalin's funeral he joined several colleagues in standing by the bier in the Hall of Columns; then on March 11 he was asked to pay homage to Stalin in *Pravda*. Entitled "The Great Defender of Peace," Ehrenburg's article emphasized themes associated with his own service to the dictator—the defeat of fascism and the need for world peace and a stable balance of power—that Stalin supposedly had championed; it was Ehrenburg's last tribute to the tyrant.[2] Three weeks later, on April 4, *Pravda* carried a startling announcement: the doctors who had been accused of plotting to murder Soviet leaders were cleared of all charges, and those responsible for violating the norms of "socialist legality" were themselves arrested.

Ehrenburg's lingering fears could now be set aside. Foreigners who met him outside the country thought he remained the same harsh spokesman for Soviet interests who "goes with the wind," as the *New York Times* columnist C. L. Sulzberger observed when he saw Ehrenburg in Budapest in June 1953.[3] This was a familiar pose, particularly for Americans, that Ehrenburg also used as a cover to pursue his ultimate goal: to challenge the limits of Soviet censorship, revive Russia's connection to European culture, and restore to living memory the names and works of those whom Stalin first killed then erased from history.

———

Soviet society was changing. Over the next decade while Nikita Khrushchev remained in power the regime's defenders and the country's intellectual leaders fought for control of Soviet culture, its history and meaning. Ehrenburg's literary and political activity exemplified this struggle. His novella *The Thaw*, his essays on Tsvetaeva and Babel, Stendhal, Chekhov, and a host of other themes continuously provoked the authorities. As he observes in his memoirs, "Those years were a useful experience for me. I understood that one could write and that one had to write."[4]

Ehrenburg could not say everything he knew or believed but was determined to say as much as he could. Other writers such as Mikhail Bulgakov, Vasily Grossman, Boris Pasternak, and Nadezhda Mandelstam wrote "for the drawer," determined to wait until another generation could appreciate their works or by sending a manuscript abroad, reach an international audience. Ehrenburg never chose this path. He had to be of his time—one of the consistent weaknesses and strengths of his prose—and he had to be published in the Soviet Union for his immediate audience. Ehrenburg chose to play within the rules of the game, but always looking to challenge the limits of what was permissible. He had an uncanny ability to know what could be said and how to say it, and he was willing to stake his career each time he took on official dogmas. As the decade wore on, he combined the instincts of a journalist with the talents of a diplomat in such a way that the regime could neither ignore him nor silence him.

Virtually everything Ehrenburg wrote after Stalin's death confirmed his unique stature among the older generation of writers who had survived, a time in which Ehrenburg grew increasingly outspoken about "socialist realism" and official controls on creative freedom. His essay "On the Role of the Writer," for example, which appeared in October 1953, directly rebutted any attempt to prescribe how or what an artist should create.

An author is not a piece of machinery. An author writes a book not because he knows how to write, not because he is a member of the Union of Soviet Writers and may be asked why he has published nothing for so long. An author writes a book because he must tell people something of himself, because he is "sick" with his book, because he has seen people, things and emotions that he cannot help describing.[5]

This was the beginning of Ehrenburg's assault on the principles of "socialist realism," on the entire ideological edifice that suppressed writers and composers, painters, poets, and theater directors from exploring their own artistic compulsions.

Several weeks after the essay appeared Ehrenburg addressed the vulnerability of a writer in Soviet society. "They put him on trial," Ehrenburg explained to a Moscow library audience. "They destroy him, they direct their fire upon him." One person asked about the "generous conditions" offered to writers by publishers and the Writers Union. "They pay well?" Ehrenburg responded. "It is true, they pay. And they provide apartments? More or less, they provide. They give to some and not to others."[6] Such candor must have startled his audience.

That winter Ehrenburg rushed to complete *The Thaw*. In the ensuing months one of Ehrenburg's friends wondered if he had written an entire story solely to inject the title into the country's vocabulary. *The Thaw* in fact lent its name to an era of history.

—

It has been a peculiarity of Russian and Soviet life (at least until *glasnost* did away with enforced censorship) that a novel or a poem could provoke far-reaching political controversy. Ivan Turgenev's *Fathers and Sons*, Boris Pasternak's *Doctor Zhivago*, Yevgeny Yevtushenko's poem "Babii Yar," and Alexander Solzhenitsyn's mammoth account of Stalin's labor camp system, *The Gulag Archipelago*, each in a different way and for different reasons rattled the country's political establishment.

From a political point of view *The Thaw* belongs in the same category of literature. The story itself is simple and straightforward. It takes place in a small town in the southern Volga region. Ivan Juravliov, a generally competent factory manager, no longer has the capacity for ordinary human emotion. Like Stalin and all the cold-hearted bureaucrats he installed, Juravliov is only concerned with the factory's ability to fulfill its production quotas. Indifferent to his workers' wretched living conditions, Juravliov appropriates funds intended for the construction of new apartments in order to construct a foundry that will insure the plant's efficiency. His wife Lena, disillusioned with Juravliov, no longer understands her husband and decides to leave him.

Other characters endure similar emotional strains. The Jewish doctor Vera Sherer is a widow from the war who had lost her mother and sister to the Nazis. In relating her story Ehrenburg invokes the dread provoked by the "doctors' plot"; he was the first Soviet author even to mention this episode in a work of fiction. Losing her calm demeanor one day in the hospital, Vera apologizes to Lena Juravliov. "My nerves are on edge," Vera explains to Lena. "Sometimes people say such dreadful things. . . . It's since the announcement. . . . It's very bad—a doctor shouldn't behave like this." As Ehrenburg's story makes clear, intelligent, good-hearted people such as Lena and Vera face disheartening lives in a society that offers little comfort or reward.

The other major theme of *The Thaw* concerns the state of Soviet culture. Two characters, Volodya Pukhov and Saburov, represent two irreconcilable extremes within the country's creative community. Volodya is a naturally gifted draughtsman who has sacrificed his talent to succeed as an establishment painter; his work embodies the empty clichés of "socialist realism"—glorified portraits of workers and collective farm scenes—while in Moscow he has to "suck up to other artists, watch who was on the up-and-up and who was slipping, calculate and fight ceaselessly for [his] piece of cake."[7] Pukhov's career has become a cynical game, with no pretense of creative integrity. His childhood friend Saburov, who is equally talented, assumes an opposite kind of commitment. Devoted to painting, Saburov spends his days in a miserable apartment creating colorful landscapes and portraits of his plain, disabled wife, whose features take on genuine beauty in her husband's delicate portrayals.

Stalin's death (which is never explicitly mentioned) changes the possibilities in everyone's lives. Lena gathers the courage to leave her husband and, at the end of the story, acknowledges her love for another man she has long admired. Even Saburov receives good news. Two of his paintings are chosen for an official exhibition, lending hope that a truly gifted artist will gain recognition in his own society. As for Ivan Juravliov, he receives his just deserts. A storm destroys the workers' huts, exposing his heartless indifference for the factory's employees; he is summoned to Moscow and dismissed.

Written in haste, with a sentimental plot and listless dialogue—weaknesses common to many of Ehrenburg's novels—the book's impact can be gauged only by what Ehrenburg succeeded in conveying to the Soviet public at the time. In the cautious atmosphere of those days, one year after Stalin's death, the effect of *The Thaw* was nothing short of prodigious. The title itself is a rebuke. On February 24, 1954, members of the editorial board of *Znamya*, which was to publish the story in April, heard a predictable objection. "Is this a thaw or a spring after a cruel winter? Or is it a natural, orderly stage in our life?" one editor wondered. "[The title] gives the impression that everything has been a mistake until now. Let it be called *Nov* (Renewal) or *Novaya Stupen* (A New Stage)."[8] Ehrenburg ignored their suggestion.

Harsh and public criticism began in July from Ehrenburg's longtime colleague, Konstantin Simonov. In two long articles in *Literaturnaya Gazeta* Simonov tried to demolish *The Thaw*, arguing that it painted a dark society in which honorable people experience "a great deal of misery and little happiness." Then Ehrenburg's old nemesis Mikhail Sholokhov, speaking at a writers' conference in Kazakhstan in September, criticized Simonov's articles for "smoothing over the inadequacies of Ehrenburg's story in order to save it from more direct and sharper" condemnation. Even *Literaturnaya Gazeta* took an official position, endorsing attacks on Ehrenburg's novel expressed in dozens of letters that October.[9]

The regime never forgave Ehrenburg for posing so many subversive questions in *The Thaw*. In a discussion about the novel at a Moscow library in October 1954 Ehrenburg raised the issue of private life versus public responsibility. "I think," he told his audience, "that it is necessary to be concerned about the culture of emotions. This is the mission of literature. What do I mean by the culture of emotions? This helps an individual to understand his fellow human being."[10] For many

the political message of *The Thaw* was reinforced by the characters'
thirst for happiness. Was not this as subversive a lesson as the novel's
anti-Stalinist allusions? Ehrenburg was asserting that politics had
intruded too long and too violently into family life and personal relations. People had the right to ignore politics, to be happy, carefree, and
in love.

———

Ehrenburg's own life reflected his characters' drama. As Lyubov
Mikhailovna was aware, Ehrenburg had always pursued other women.
In 1950 he met Liselotte Mehr, the wife of Hjalmar Mehr, a prominent figure in the Swedish Social Democratic party. (Hjalmar Mehr
was a long-time city commissioner in Stockholm from 1948 to 1971
and governor of Stockholm County from 1971 to 1978. The most
prominent Jewish politician in Swedish history, Mehr was a political
mentor to Olaf Palme.) Liselotte Mehr soon became the last great love
of Ehrenburg's life. As he wrote in one of his final poems, "there is no
calendar for the heart."[11] With Stalin's death and Liselotte's devotion,
Ehrenburg's life began anew. When Liselotte saw him in May 1953, two
months after Stalin's demise, she immediately recognized a difference
in Ehrenburg's demeanor. "Liselotte told me that I had grown younger,
probably because so much in life had begun to change. Spring had
warmed a man, who was often called an incorrigible skeptic."[12] Until
Ehrenburg's death in 1967 his relationship with Liselotte Mehr played
a decisive role in sustaining his imagination, his resolve, and his health.

Both Liselotte and Hjalmar Mehr came from Jewish families with
strong connections to the international Socialist movement. Born in
Berlin in 1919, Liselotte grew up an only child in Hanover. Her father
died while still a young man; it was Liselotte's stepfather, Alfred Korach,
who determined her fate. He was a public health officer in Germany
and chairman of a group of Socialist doctors. Jailed three times for his
political activities, her stepfather fled Germany after Hitler came to
power, taking Liselotte and her mother to Paris. From there they went
to Moscow, where Alfred Korach worked on several public health projects. Her mother, who was a trained physiotherapist, had patients in
the Politburo and is said to have treated Molotov's wife. Liselotte's parents soon understood how dangerous life was becoming in Stalin's
Moscow. The Great Purge was under way; people they knew were disappearing. Three years after reaching Moscow, Liselotte's family managed to leave for Sweden.

It was Liselotte's sojourn in Moscow, where she witnessed the Great Purge as a high school student, and her familiarity with Russian language and culture, that gave her relationship with Ehrenburg its empathy and depth. She had seen families destroyed and people vanish without explanation. Born in 1919, she was almost thirty years younger than Ehrenburg and, when they met at a peace meeting in Stockholm, the mother of two small children. His nickname for her was Siam.[13] From the outset Ehrenburg and Liselotte found a common language and a common spiritual outlook; their Jewish origins too brought them closer. Both Hjalmar and Liselotte Mehr had joined Stockholm's Mosaic synagogue during the war as an act of solidarity with their fellow European Jews. After the war Liselotte volunteered for many months at a home for displaced Jewish refugees.

Ehrenburg and Liselotte were unusually candid with each other. She even asked him for a list of his important lovers and wanted to know whom he had cared for most of all. Ehrenburg surprised her. Many years earlier, when he had been with Katya Schmidt, Irina's mother, he claimed to have loved her more than anyone else; Liselotte, in this regard, had to settle for second place. (Katya, alone among Ehrenburg's serious lovers, had left him, a circumstance that no doubt affected his emotional memory of their time together.)

Throughout the 1950s and 1960s Ehrenburg would send Liselotte telegrams in French with succinct messages: "Arrive Monday via Copenhagen 11 pm," from Moscow on March 28, 1959.[14] She would drop everything and join him in Rome, Brussels, Vienna, London, or Paris. Ehrenburg rarely traveled with Lyubov Mikhailovna; like her husband, she too had lived for decades in France and wanted to visit Europe and old friends, but Ehrenburg could not travel with her and hope to see Liselotte at the same time. However unhappy his wife was over Ehrenburg's love for Liselotte, she accepted it as she had numerous other affairs.

Liselotte, in turn, not wanting to compromise her husband's career or wantonly hurt him, offered to end their marriage; but for reasons of his own Hjalmar accepted his wife's love for another man and declined her offer. He too befriended Ehrenburg. As chairman of the Round Table East-West, Hjalmar Mehr organized an ongoing, informal forum for European and Soviet intellectuals and politicians in which Ehrenburg took part. Late in the 1950s both Hjalmar and Liselotte Mehr visited Moscow on two occasions and stayed at Ehrenburg's dacha. Hjalmar Mehr was always gracious toward Ehrenburg. There was even a time when Ehrenburg and Liselotte became deathly ill with the flu while they were staying at a Paris hotel; Hjalmar Mehr rushed to France to insure proper medical treatment. Irina Ehrenburg, who became a close friend to Liselotte, always referred to this incident as the time when Hjalmar "saved their lives."

THE SECOND WRITERS' CONGRESS

Ehrenburg's essay "On the Role of the Writer" and his novella *The Thaw* turned him into a principal target of the party's Central Committee and the country's nervous literary establishment. Ehrenburg had to be reprimanded in a way that would both discredit his ideas and scare him into cowed, silent submission by means other than official "literary criticism," an effort that began with the Second Writers' Congress in December 1954.

On the eve of the opening session hundreds of delegates were invited by Nikita Khrushchev to a meeting at the Central Committee. Many writers spoke of their hopes for the Congress. The last to appear was Mikhail Sholokhov, who immediately began to attack *The Thaw*, then withdrawing a sheet of paper from his pocket read eight lines from a poem Ehrenburg had written long before, on a train from Moscow to Riga in March 1921: "But people walk with knapsacks/with bags they walked and walked/And their enormous days/they were dragging like sacks/Millstones turned/their thoughts and worries./No, Moscow, a thaw/has not touched your soul!" It was easy for Sholokhov to invoke these distant verses from a time when Ehrenburg was escaping life under the Bolsheviks as a means to discredit *The Thaw*; but the main surprise was yet to come. "[Sholokhov]," Ehrenburg wrote, "remembering my old novel *A Street in Moscow*, said that in it I depicted Russians as fools, while the hero turned out to be a Jewish musician." Nikita Khrushchev was present the whole time, making it all but certain that Sholokhov's performance was stage-managed by the Kremlin itself. At the conclusion of Sholokhov's speech Khrushchev declared the meeting over, giving no one a chance to object. Ehrenburg had been warned. The party had not forgotten his youthful (and not so youthful) indiscretions; they could be used against him at any time. Ehrenburg was outraged and threatened to boycott the Congress altogether, but a member of the Central Committee assured him that Sholokhov had been reprimanded and that his own absence "would be badly interpreted."[15]

The Second Writers' Congress pales in comparison with its predecessor. The intervening twenty years had been terrifying. Speakers memorialized those who had fallen in the war, including Ehrenburg's son-in-law Boris Lapin, but neglected to mention colleagues such as Isaac Babel, Tizian Tabidze, Boris Pilnyak, and Osip Mandelstam, who had disappeared under Stalin. Twenty years before, the Hall of Columns had been decorated with the portraits of literary giants; now the walls of the Kremlin Palace, where the Congress opened, were invisibly draped with the shadows of silenced victims.

The regime was unsure of itself, not knowing how to celebrate Soviet literature publicly and still maintain absolute control. The Congress had been twice postponed, yet there were signs of hope: Anna Akhmatova was invited to attend as a delegate from Leningrad, as was Boris Pasternak from Moscow. Neither spoke. The only reference to Pasternak, who had been a prominent figure at the 1934 Congress, was his listing among a group of twenty distinguished translators. The foreign writers in attendance, such as Pablo Neruda, Jorge Amado, Anna Seghers, and Louis Aragon (who were all close friends of Ehrenburg), did not take part in the discussions but instead confined their remarks to ceremonial greetings, choosing to remain above the fray.

While the Second Congress lacked the melodrama and pomp of its predecessor, the proceedings were alive with the tensions and recriminations of the Thaw. Alexei Surkov (who would soon replace Alexander Fadeyev as the first secretary of the Writers' Union and later distinguish himself by leading the effort to expel Boris Pasternak in 1958), in his three-hour survey of Soviet literature, congratulated Ehrenburg several times for his wartime articles and cited him as an example of a writer who had matured from the bourgeois decorativeness of the *The Love of Jeanne Ney* to the proletarian energy of *Out of Chaos*. Then, as if on cue, Surkov condemned *The Thaw* and even endorsed Stalin's campaign against "cosmopolitanism." "Our society in 1949 and 1950," he proclaimed, "acted sharply against this harmful 'tendency,' exposing its foreign and hostile essence before everyone."[16] With Sholokhov and now Surkov engaging in explicit anti-Semitic affronts, Ehrenburg at least knew who his enemies were.

Ehrenburg's only chance to speak came on the third day of the Congress. Although he was greeted warmly by the delegates, his remarks reflected a defiant unwillingness to satisfy his critics. From the outset Ehrenburg openly ridiculed his colleagues. "The Union of Writers has a section for children's literature, which has given our children many splendid books," Ehrenburg began. "But from time to time, while reading a novel in a journal, when already on the first page the author lectures the reader in a tiresome manner, you think to yourself: Isn't it about time to open a section for adult literature in the Writers' Union?" Ehrenburg then defended *The Thaw* and an individual's right to pursue personal happiness. As for criticism, Ehrenburg invoked images he had often employed in the past, describing how "the tone of certain critical articles . . . still recalls the tone of an indictment." In closing Ehrenburg made the only reference during the Congress to a fate more terrible than criticism for a Soviet writer. "One leader of the Writers' Union, speaking reasonably about the significance of 'average' writers, said that without milk, you cannot get cream," Ehrenburg recalled. "To continue this somewhat unsuccessful comparison, one could say that without cows, you will not get milk. It is useful to remember this."[17]

Four days later—the Congress lasted for twelve days altogether—Mikhail Sholokhov, not able to restrain his hatred of Ehrenburg, repeated his outrageous claim that Simonov had deliberately limited his denunciation of *The Thaw* in order "[to save] Ehrenburg from sharp criticism."[18] Sholokhov lost his credibility. Even the literary establishment agreed he had gone too far and virtually all of the final speakers publicly rebuked him. This was absurd, targeting Ehrenburg for criticism then reprimanding his critics; Ehrenburg took comfort in the foolish behavior of the Congress's organizers, whose disorderly stupidity made his own position all the more honorable.

REHABILITATION AND REVIVAL

In 1954 the regime began the enormous process of releasing Stalin's prisoners and "rehabilitating" victims. Over the next five years Khrushchev permitted as many as fourteen million people to return to their families from prisons, labor camps, and places of exile. Many relatives and survivors came to Ehrenburg for assistance. Anna Akhmatova approached Ehrenburg during the Writers' Congress and asked him to appeal on behalf of her son, Lev Gumilyov, who was still a prisoner nearly two years after Stalin's death. Ehrenburg wrote directly to Nikita Khrushchev but did not receive an answer, which Ehrenburg "took as a sign of dislike to his own person."[19] Nonetheless, Ehrenburg's appeal stirred attention to the case. Lev Gumilyov was released in May 1956 after Khrushchev's famous speech denouncing Stalin, when the process of releasing prisoners was deliberately speeded up.

Survivors of the Yiddish writers also sought Ehrenburg's support. Esther Markish, the widow of Peretz Markish, came to Ehrenburg for help in regaining permission to live in Moscow. He wrote the necessary letters and offered advice on negotiating with Soviet bureaucrats. The daughters of Solomon Mikhoels, Natalya and Nina Vovsi-Mikhoels, needed Ehrenburg's help after their father was posthumously rehabilitated. Without proper documents Nina could not gain acceptance to a university. She had no diploma and all of the teachers in her father's theater school who could vouch for her studies had been arrested. Ehrenburg wrote a letter to the Central Committee. Soon after, a special diploma arrived and Nina was able to resume her education.

Assisting survivors was not always as simple as writing a letter or dealing with the Soviet bureaucracy. One example of the moral complexity of Ehrenburg's position is his involvement with the family of Isaac Babel.

Ehrenburg had always counted Isaac Babel among his closest friends. Babel's first wife, Yevgeniya Borisovna Gronfein, had stayed with the Ehrenburgs when she first reached Paris in 1925, before Ehrenburg and Babel had even met. Over the next ten years Babel was able to visit his wife in France several times. A daughter, Nathalie, was born in Paris in 1929. By 1935, when Babel came to Paris for the International Conference in Defense of Culture, he was determined to convince Yevgeniya Borisovna to return to Moscow, but she refused to go back. By that time Babel was living with another woman in Moscow, Antonina Nikolaevna Pirozhkova, an engineer who was working on construction of the Moscow subway. After returning to the Soviet Union Babel established a common-law marriage with Antonina Nikolaevna and they had a daughter of their own named Lidia. Babel did not have long to enjoy his second family. He was arrested in 1939 and executed the following year. After his disappearance only Ehrenburg's secretary Valentina Milman offered money to Antonina Nikolaevna; everyone else avoided her. Ehrenburg saw Babel's first wife Yevgeniya Borisovna in France on two occasions after the Second World War. When he visited Paris in 1946, according to Nathalie Babel, he conveyed the message that Babel was alive and had spent the war in exile, under house arrest, not far from Moscow. If this version of what Ehrenburg said is true, it is still impossible to know if he lied on his own initiative or was instructed to pass along false information. Nevertheless, Yevgeniya Borisovna soon after learned through other, more reliable sources that Isaac Babel was dead.

When Ehrenburg saw Yevgeniya Borisovna one final time, in 1956, he informed her that Babel had been posthumously rehabilitated two years earlier. Then he made a startling request. Ehrenburg wanted her to sign a document acknowledging that she and Babel had been divorced, which was not true; Ehrenburg then explained that Babel had remarried and fathered another daughter. He insisted that she confirm their divorce. Yevgeniya Borisovna refused and collapsed in front of him. If Ehrenburg's behavior seemed awkward and disturbing, his motives, at least in 1956, were honorable: once it became clear that Babel could be published anew, Ehrenburg felt it necessary to assure Antonina Nikolaevna's rights as his widow. Yevgeniya Borisovna and Nathalie were living in Paris and could protect the rights and royalties attached to Babel's books in the West. But in Moscow, Antonina Nikolaevna and her daughter Lidia were far more vulnerable and far less secure in their claims to Babel's legacy.

In the summer of 1961 Nathalie Babel made her first trip to Moscow. She was thirty-two years old. By that time, unbeknownst to her, Babel's sister, Meri Shaposhnikova, who lived in Brussels, had begun to correspond with Antonina Nikolaevna Pirozhkova. At her aunt's insistence Nathalie called upon Antonina Nikolaevna on her first day in Moscow and there also met her half-sister, Lidia. Immediately they recognized a common love for the revered and martyred Babel. Upset and crying, "like characters in a Russian novel," as Nathalie Babel recalled, they spent hours talking about their lives and their absent husband and father. Nathalie also told them about her mother's two meetings with Ehrenburg and how he had "poisoned the last ten months of mother's life." (Yevgeniya Borisovna died in 1957.) Nathalie feared that it was Antonina Nikolaevna who had encouraged Ehrenburg to insist on the claim that Babel and her mother were divorced, but Antonina Nikolaevna explained to Nathalie that Ehrenburg and

Lyubov Mikhailovna were among her closest friends; she knew nothing about his meetings in Paris. She only knew how hard Ehrenburg worked to protect her and Lidia, and how he had pressed for publication of Babel's stories in 1957, the "rehabilitation" volume, when Babel was introduced to a new generation of readers after more than twenty years of utter oblivion.[20] It was Ehrenburg's introduction to a collection of stories by Babel that made it possible for the volume to appear at all. Ehrenburg originally wrote his essay in 1956, expecting to see the book published without delay; but as months passed and the book failed to appear, Ehrenburg wrote a letter to Pyotr Pospelov, who headed cultural affairs for the Central Committee. As he usually did in such cases, Ehrenburg used foreign connections to gain the attention of his political masters:

August 9, 1957

Dear Pyotr Nikolaevich [Pospelov]!

I have decided to trouble you about the following matter. Comrade Puzikov has told me that my introduction to the Babel collection is in your hands. The introduction was written a year ago and has been subject to several changes at the publisher's suggestion. Aragon has urgently asked for this introduction to use in a French translation of Babel's works.

I have received similar requests from Hungary and Italy. For four months I have been telling them to wait, but it is no longer possible for me to put off giving an answer to our friends abroad. I think I must either send the text of the introduction or answer that I will not be giving it to them . . . [21]

Ehrenburg's letter to Pospelov had its effect. The authorities could no longer hold back publication of the volume once foreign supporters such as Louis Aragon, an important member of the French Communist party, grew visibly anxious about its publication; Babel was too admired and too well known. In his introduction Ehrenburg expresses his love for Babel and his anguish over his friend's fate. Antonina Nikolaevna was grateful to Ehrenburg for pushing through the book's publication and securing royalties for her and her daughter.[22]

Others were not so happy. Frustrated by Ehrenburg's success, cultural bureaucrats within the Central Committee circulated an internal memorandum attacking the introduction as "written from a subjective position which can only disorient the reader"; Babel was not yet ready to be rehabilitated.[23] In line with their instructions, orthodox critics immediately targeted both Ehrenburg and Babel. In one notorious essay in 1958 Alexander Makarov used his disagreement with Ehrenburg to denigrate Babel's achievement on purely ideological grounds. According to Makarov, Babel's books would have a "greater success in the West than among Soviet readers," a not-so-subtle hint that Babel's stories would be published only in limited ways.[24] *Literaturnaya Gazeta* was equally unforgiving. Quoting extensively from Makarov's piece, an unsigned editorial condemned Ehrenburg for wanting "to amnesty any phenomenon of the past" and "illegally [*sic*] compare Babel's humanism with the humanism of all the great Russian writers."[25] Little did these critics know that in 1958 Ehrenburg was just beginning to "resurrect corpses."

Ehrenburg's devotion to Babel did not end in the 1950s. Whenever he traveled, to Europe, India, or Japan, he made a point of finding translations of Babel's stories and bringing them to Antonina Nikolaevna. (Of the fifty-three separate foreign editions she showed me in 1984, several dozen were brought by Ehrenburg.)

Then in 1964 Babel's Moscow family arranged a public celebration of his seventieth birthday. Ehrenburg and Antonina Nikolaevna wanted the commemoration to be held in a large auditorium; the Writers' Union insisted, however, that it take place in a much smaller hall in the House of Writers. When they arrived that evening, Ehrenburg and Antonina Nikolaevna saw an enormous crowd clamoring in vain to enter the building. (Loudspeakers were hastily installed on the street.) As a sign of protest, having insisted on a different space, Ehrenburg and Antonina Nikolaevna refused to join other dignitaries on the dais, preferring to sit in the audience.

The evening of speeches and readings marked a turning point in the fate of Babel's work. Presided over by Konstantin Fedin, the secretary general of the Union of Soviet Writers, the meeting signaled Babel's official acceptance. By then several of his stories, a long-suppressed interview, and even reminiscences of Babel had appeared in the Soviet press; but Ehrenburg was not satisfied. It was well past midnight when he closed the meeting with angry and loving remarks, providing the emotional high point to the whole event.

Those of us who are still alive have a duty to Babel and the reading public. Isn't it astonishing that in the country of the language in which he wrote he is published ten times less than in the other Socialist countries and in the West? This is really terrible . . . (Applause.)

If he were still alive, if he had had no talent, his collected works would have been reprinted a dozen times over. (Prolonged applause.)

Don't think that I am just letting off steam. What I want is for us writers at last to take a hand in this business, to tell the publishing houses to reissue Babel, to organize symposiums on him. . . .

And so seventy years have passed. . . . It's as though we were celebrating his birthday. I am willing to get up on my hind legs and beg like a dog in front of all the necessary organizations in order to get them to reissue his works, which have become very hard to find, though there are now no obstacles [to their republication]. Is it a question of paper? Very well, I will put off one of my own books. We cannot be indifferent to the impatience of people eager to learn about this writer who perished long ago.[26]

Such pleas by Ehrenburg and others provoked a full renaissance of interest in Babel's work. Additional memoirs and critical studies soon appeared, followed in 1966 by two separate collections of stories; Ehrenburg wrote an introduction for one of them.[27] He remained devoted to Babel's memory until the end of his life.

TRAVEL AND THE PEACE MOVEMENT

Ehrenburg's involvement in the peace movement continued throughout the 1950s and 1960s. It gave him an opportunity to travel widely, especially when he was designated to present peace prizes to foreign supporters who were often his friends. In the spring of 1954 he visited Paris for the first time in five years to give the award to his old comrade Pierre Cot. In August he traveled to Latin America (his only trip to that continent) to present a similar prize to Pablo Neruda in Santiago, Chile. In 1956 he visited India and in 1957 traveled to Greece and Japan. In 1960 alone, he crossed the Soviet frontier thirteen times on various trips to Scandinavia and Western Europe. Just as he had under Stalin, Ehrenburg made himself useful to the regime as an articulate and urbane representative in the West.

Ehrenburg's trip to Chile was particularly controversial. Traveling with Lyubov Mikhailovna, he was detained at the Santiago airport upon their arrival on August 5, 1954. Although customs and immigration officials passed them without incident, a special unit of political police arrived from the ministry of internal affairs and confiscated all of Ehrenburg's papers, including the Stalin Prize diploma, a Russian translation of a poem by Neruda, a book of French crossword puzzles, and a list in Latin of decorative plants native to Chile. Ehrenburg protested the confiscation, threatening to remain at the airport until all his material was returned to him.

The incident quickly grew troublesome. Claiming to have examined Ehrenburg's papers, the prefect of police accused him of bringing directives to the Communist parties of Latin America. The next day Chilean newspapers inflated this story, hinting at preparations for a clandestine army and a secret party congress. On the face of it the accusations sounded serious, however absurd; but within two days the melodrama turned into a farce. The police chief began compounding Ehrenburg's crimes, claiming the Soviet writer had brought instructions to Chilean Communists on plastic records. As if that were not enough, the police set off firecrackers around Neruda's house early one morning where Ehrenburg was staying. Only after four days of harassment did the president personally intervene and order the return of all of Ehrenburg's papers.[28]

Ehrenburg was not amused by such provocations. For him personally they were hardly more than an annoying inconvenience; but coming in 1954, just months after a military coup in Guatemala, where the United States conspired to overturn a democratically elected left-wing government, Ehrenburg could not help but discern American involvement in the treatment he had just endured in Chile. A few months later Ehrenburg attended a World Peace Council meeting in Stockholm, where he met a young Chilean Socialist named Salvador Allende. It is easy to imagine how Ehrenburg would have found his worst fears confirmed in Chile nineteen years later, when Allende, the democratically elected president, was either killed or committed suicide (the circumstances have never been clarified) during a successful military takeover led by General Augusto Pinochet and abetted by the United States.

Ehrenburg's visit to India in January and February 1956 was more politically tranquil and typical of his official travels. He stopped in New Delhi, Calcutta, Madras, and Bombay, meeting with writers, artists, and left-wing political activists. In New Delhi he and Lyubov Mikhailovna were invited for dinner by President Jawarahal Nehru, where they were joined by Lady Mountbatten and Nehru's daughter, Indira Gandhi. United States embassy officials followed Ehrenburg's visit closely, and in dispatches to Washington made note of his prestige and the success of his tour. With Stalin dead, Khrushchev was initiating a policy of "peaceful coexistence" and it was helpful to have a writer such as Ehrenburg, who was identified with European culture, represent the Soviet Union's benign intentions.[29]

What the Kremlin did not understand was that these tours enhanced Ehrenburg's prestige within the cultural bureaucracy, making it easier for him to challenge controls on art and literature. After Stalin's death Ehrenburg encouraged the publication of numerous books by European and Soviet writers, frequently adding introductions in which he explains how a play by Jean-Paul Sartre, the verses of Paul Eluard, or the stories of Alberto Moravia belong in the progressive heritage that Soviet culture claimed to exemplify. Ehrenburg wrote scores of such introductions in the 1950s, a time when his immense prestige as a war hero and an "elected" member of the Supreme Soviet made his support a decisive factor in a book's publication. He turned the genre of introductions into an art form, conveying in a brisk handful of pages the kind of information and opinion that few if any Soviet publications provided. While the Kremlin had its own cynical reasons for cultivating the support of prominent Western intellectuals, Ehrenburg used his contacts and prestige to broaden the Soviet public's access to Western culture, which the peace movement helped to make possible.

1956

Early in the morning of February 26 Nikita Khrushchev gave his famous speech denouncing Stalin's "cult of personality" to a closed session of the Twentieth Party Congress. Khrushchev spoke for two hours. His talk was not a general review of all of Stalin's crimes; neither anti-Semitism nor the human cost of forced collectivization was mentioned. Desperately trying to preserve the party's claims to legitimacy, Khrushchev highlighted the destruction of loyal Communists and the dread among members of the Politburo itself, who feared for their lives. Soon after, Ehrenburg was invited to the Writers' Union to read Khrushchev's speech; copies were not printed for the general public.

Khrushchev's initiative turned the Communist world upside down. For Soviet intellectuals conflicting emotions of anguish and relief were embodied in the suicide of Alexander Fadeyev. A talented writer with a love for poetry and literature, Fadeyev became an official of the Writers' Union in the 1930s and served as its general secretary from 1946 to 1953. It had been his responsibility to sign arrest warrants for writers, most of whom perished in the camps or simply disappeared. Out of shame, guilt, and fear that he might have to answer for complicity in Stalin's repressions, Fadeyev shot himself in May. Several months after Fadeyev's death Ehrenburg quietly handed Fadeyev's companion, the poet Margarita Aliger, a folder of articles and obituaries from the Western press. Ehrenburg knew Fadeyev's "ruthlessness" and the depth of his personal tragedy. His suicide was seen by many as an act of penance. As Pasternak said over Fadeyev's bier, "[He] has rehabilitated himself."[30]

———

Khrushchev's revelations about Stalin's crimes led to unrest in Poland and Hungary. Feelings in Hungary were particularly volatile and had begun to surface even before Khrushchev's attack on Stalin. Ehrenburg had a whiff of what was to come. In October 1955, during an unexpected stopover in Budapest, he was invited by the hard-line Communist leader Matyas Rakosci to spend an evening with local writers. Upon entering the hall, where a large gathering was assembled, Ehrenburg immediately sensed his colleagues' unease. The writers seemed "preoccupied," indifferent to stories about literary life in Russia. One of their questions haunted Ehrenburg. "Why in Hungary were a hundred copies of *The Thaw* printed only for the party leadership?" Ehrenburg had no reply, but he could tell from the gestures and noise in the hall how "embittered" his Hungarian colleagues were becoming.[31]

The crisis in Budapest broke out with full force in the fall of 1956. The Kremlin, at least publicly, tried to reach a political settlement, but as the insurrection grew larger and more violent, and as the new Hungarian prime minister Imre Nagy challenged Soviet arrangements— Nagy formed a coalition with non-Communists and declared Hungary's intentions to quit the Warsaw Pact and become officially neutral—Khrushchev launched a full-scale invasion. By the first week of November more than eleven Soviet divisions occupied Hungary, killing tens of thousands of people and installing a new, pro-Soviet regime led by Janos Kadar. In spite of guarantees for his safety, Imre Nagy was imprisoned in Moscow and executed.

The bloody autumn of 1956 threatened to derail the process of liberalization inside the Soviet Union and the general improvement in political and cultural relations with the rest of the world that was developing after Stalin's death. Ehrenburg had a complicated, ambiguous response to Khrushchev's intervention. As a Soviet patriot, Ehrenburg could not have wanted the balance of power disrupted in Europe. He knew that Western radio broadcasts had been encouraging revolts in Eastern Europe and promising Western aid if the local populations needed support, factors that limited his sympathies for the Hungarian uprising. Ehrenburg's overriding concern was the potential renewal of Soviet cultural isolation in the wake of repression in Poland and Hungary. The first news in the Soviet press about Hungary's political crisis appeared in *Pravda* on October 25, by coincidence the same day that Ehrenburg opened a reception in Moscow to honor an exhibit of Pablo Picasso's work. Although the exhibit remained open only until November 12, it was widely seen as a breakthrough in Soviet cultural policy, one that Ehrenburg had strenuously worked to organize. If events in Eastern Europe disrupted contacts with the West, either by the Kremlin's withdrawal of support for such initiatives or by a boycott of the country by Western intellectuals, then the result would be a return to the cultural isolation of the Stalin years, something Ehrenburg was determined to avoid.

As a prominent Soviet figure, Ehrenburg was expected to support military intervention in Hungary. He soon had several opportunities to defend Soviet aggression. On November 18 an enlarged session of the World Peace Council opened in Helsinki. By that time many supporters of the Soviet Union, such as Jean-Paul Sartre, had voiced their opposition to Soviet military action in Hungary; others, such as a delegation of Italian Socialists, came to Helsinki solely to announce their resignation from the peace movement. Ehrenburg strove to forge a compromise in Helsinki that would allow critics of Soviet intervention to feel satisfied and still remain within the movement. After a tempestuous debate a resolution was unanimously approved that blamed the cold war and "mistakes of the previous Hungarian government" for the crisis.[32] With Ehrenburg's help such a compromise kept the peace movement from completely collapsing after the Kremlin's intervention in Hungary.

Even more was expected from him by Soviet officials. When Ehrenburg returned to Moscow, he found a recent protest by French intellectuals and a response by Soviet writers reprinted in full in *Literaturnaya Gazeta*. Attempting to avoid cold war polemics, the French denounced U.S. intervention in Guatemala and condemned "hypocrites" who were not willing to see the similarity between U.S. behavior in Central America and the Soviet invasion of Hungary. The Soviet response indulged in typical cold war demogoguery, claiming that the entry of "right-wing elements" into Hungary necessitated Soviet intervention. Such Fascists "begin with burning books and end with Jewish pogroms," they wrote.[33]

Ehrenburg never liked to participate in collective statements; he knew how they were engineered by the regime. He found the letter from his Soviet colleagues to be "wordy and in places not adequately convincing."[34] But two days later Ehrenburg added his name to the statement, joining such liberal figures as Margarita Aliger, Pavel Antokolsky, and Alexander Bek, who for reasons of their own had not signed it the first time around. Ehrenburg had no choice but to sign if he wanted to maintain his official standing and accomplish what he still realistically hoped to achieve.[35]

Having demonstrated obedience to the Kremlin, Ehrenburg now undertook an initiative of his own. Earlier in the year, with the help of the France-USSR Friendship Society, he had arranged with the writer Vercors to bring reproductions of French impressionist masterpieces to Moscow. After joining protests against Soviet intervention in Hungary Vercors assumed that the project would have to be canceled; Ehrenburg was determined to save it. On December 1 he published a letter to the editor in *Literaturnaya Gazeta*, where he expressed his desire to salvage ties with the West. "It seems to me that it is necessary to know how to differentiate between our friends, who disagree with us on one question or another, and people who are urging a break with the Soviet Union and with Communists. Certain Western circles are trying to revive the climate of the Cold War and separate cultural activists, who are devoted to the business of peace and progress. I believe that it is in our interests, in the interests of peace, to do everything to prevent this." Vercors responded enthusiastically. Although he did not retract his views on the Soviet invasion, Vercors did not want to see the Soviet Union resume its isolation. In an open letter to Ehrenburg on December 18 Vercors welcomed the opportunity to bring his reproductions to Moscow, and the exhibit soon took place.[36]

PABLO PICASSO

Ehrenburg never lost faith in the power of artistic creativity to bridge the boundaries of geography and culture. His greatness as a public figure is best reflected in this consistent belief, the devotion it evoked in millions of people, and the hatred Ehrenburg invariably provoked among the same political figures who, at different times, found it necessary and proper to honor him.

The Picasso exhibit of 1956 illustrates this stubborn strategy. Ehrenburg had to overcome obstacles in the Artists' Union, where Alexander Gerasimov tried to suppress anything but the most conventional style of figurative painting, and obstacles in the Ministry of Culture, where political considerations continually intruded. On October 25, 1956, a formal reception was held at the Moscow House of Architecture in honor of Picasso's seventy-fifth birthday; an exhibit of his work was scheduled to open the next day at the Pushkin Museum. Picasso himself was supposed to attend, but the turmoil in Hungary made it impossible for him to come to Moscow. Ehrenburg entered the reception to "a great ovation," an honor reserved for him "as the most overt and prominent of Picasso's Soviet admirers."[37] That same night a long line of people gathered outside the Pushkin Museum and remained there until the morning, eager to be the first to enter the gallery. A brief ceremony had yet to take place at the entrance. As Ehrenburg was about to cut the ribbon, a restless and impatient crowd pressed forward. Ehrenburg turned to them, hoping to calm their anxiety. "You waited thirty years for this," he told them. "You can wait another ten minutes."[38]

Vladimir Slepian, a young abstract painter, recalled a few years later that "for me and for many young Soviet artists, the Picasso exhibit . . . was the most important single event of our artistic lives." As Slepian saw for himself, "During two whole weeks in the Pushkin Museum from early morning until closing time, a gigantic line . . . waited outside and the militia was compelled to admit people in small groups, because the lucky ones who got into the exhibit did not want to leave and there was no vacant space in the halls."[39]

Not everyone admired Picasso. Even among those who attended the exhibit, several left comments in the visitors' book that clearly reflected decades of propaganda. "The pictures in Ilya Ehrenburg's collection," one person wrote, "are especially abnormal and cynical."[40] When it came to Picasso's work, Ehrenburg had to contend with such attitudes all the time. He enjoyed describing the reaction of an important Soviet editor to a Picasso painting that featured the image of a toad. "At the height of one of the campaigns against formalism," the British Communist Ivor Montagu recounted,

> Ehrenburg noticed his visitor, a distinguished Soviet editor, uncomfortably taking surreptitious looks over his shoulder at this repulsive monstrosity on the wall behind him. "What do you think of it?" inquired Ehrenburg with a poker face. "A caricature against American imperialism," [he explained to his guest]. "Wonderful," exclaimed the visitor, now completely reassured. "Perfect, Ilya Grigorevich, its very essence."[41]

The writer Andrei Sinyavsky saw Ehrenburg's devotion to Picasso at first hand.[42] They met for the first time in 1959, when Sinyavsky was asked to review a section of Ehrenburg's memoirs on the novelist Andrei Bely. Later that year Sinyavsky and his friend, the art critic Igor Golomshtock, approached Ehrenburg to help them publish a small book on Picasso; until that time no book on the French artist had appeared in the Soviet Union. Ehrenburg liked their idea and offered to write a preface, an offer the editors immediately accepted, hoping it would ensure the book's appearance.

In the preface Ehrenburg introduces Picasso to the Soviet reader, emphasizing Picasso's boundless energy for work, the clutter of his Paris studios, and, naturally, his allegiance to communism. Yet several times in the text Ehrenburg recalls how Picasso ridiculed Soviet attitudes, recounting how, when Alexander Fadeyev met Picasso at the Wroclaw Conference in 1948, Fadeyev challenged him in proper Soviet style, asking why he "chose forms that were incomprehensible to people." In response Picasso reminded Fadeyev that they had both learned to read by beginning with simple sounds. "Fine," Picasso concluded, "and how were you taught to understand painting?" At which point Fadeyev gave up. "There was a time," Ehrenburg observes, "when we cultivated paintings that resembled enormous colored photographs." He describes how Picasso made fun of a young Soviet artist he had met in Paris. According to Ehrenburg, Picasso recommended that instead of having paint tubes carry the names of colors, Soviet tubes should contain mixtures marked "for the face," "for the hair," "for a dress coat." "That would make more sense for you," Picasso commented to the young man.[43]

From the time Ehrenburg first learned about the project he understood that it would be difficult to publish the book, so he took several steps to help it along. Using a familiar strategy, he contacted *L'Humanité* in Paris and encouraged them to announce that a book on Picasso would appear for the first time in Moscow. He also solicited the help of Dolores Ibarurri, hoping a word from her, the most famous Spanish Communist, would make a difference. Just as the book was to appear, however, someone "at the top" intervened to stop publication. The entire edition—a hundred thousand copies—was "arrested" on order of the Central Committee. Even Golomshtock and Sinyavsky were not allowed to receive copies. Learning of this setback, Ehrenburg appealed to the Politburo's chief ideologist, Mikhail Suslov, invoking a line of reasoning that bordered on blackmail:

June 4, 1961

Dear Mikhail Andreevich!

I am taking the liberty to disturb you about a question of minor importance, but which would have major significance for the Partisans of Peace. At the beginning of this year, Znanie publishing house printed a brochure about Picasso in an edition of one hundred thousand copies. The publishers asked for my permission to use a fragment about Picasso from my memoirs as an introduction. Being outside the country, in response to journalists' questions, I mentioned that such a book is being published, and a month ago, during my stay in Italy, I answered that the book was out—at that time, I had already received author's copies. I also saw references and articles about this book in a series of West European newspapers.

Recently the publisher let me know that it is supposed to destroy more than two-thirds of the edition. I am not concerned about whether the text or selection of illustrations is successful. I am not writing to you as a man who loves Picasso's art, but as one of the participants in the Partisans of Peace. This year, the French Communist party and progressive individuals in France and not only French organizations, will commemorate Picasso's eightieth birthday. It would be very unpleasant if news of the destruction of a large portion of books printed here were to seep out to the West, but now such things usually penetrate there. This is precisely what has compelled me to turn to you with a request, if you find it possible, to intervene in this matter.[44]

Ehrenburg was making clear, in other words, that he had already alerted Western journalists to the book's existence and that it would be an easy matter to let them know if it were destroyed by official decree. The regime had to back down. So the book, a modest effort by Western standards, with fifty pages of text and two dozen black-and-white reproductions (including Picasso's portrait of Ehrenburg and other examples from his private collection), was released for sale to the public.

Ehrenburg remained the foremost champion of Picasso's work in Moscow. In the summer of 1960 the Tate gallery approached him for help in sending several works by Picasso in Soviet museums to London for an ambitious retrospective, and again in October 1966 Ehrenburg had to intervene directly with the Minister of Culture Yekaterina Furtseva when she objected to an anniversary display of graphics to honor Picasso's eighty-fifth birthday. Ehrenburg had brought one hundred forty-two engravings to Moscow from Paris, expecting to mount an impressive show. As Ehrenburg wrote to Furtseva herself, "Not to exhibit these engravings, it seems to me, would not only be a personal insult to the artist, but politically improper in relation to our French friends."[45] His arguments won them over and despite the harsher atmosphere of the Brezhnev period, the exhibit was held.[46]

Official Soviet attitudes about his work infuriated Picasso. In spite of his Communist affiliation he refused to accept a Lenin Peace Prize in 1965. A year later, in April 1966, Ehrenburg and Liselotte Mehr visited Picasso in southern France, and only then, after Ehrenburg's insistence, did Picasso accept the award. (The Israeli newspaper Haaretz claimed it was presented in secret.[47]) In photographs taken by Picasso's wife, Jacqueline, Picasso and Ehrenburg are grinning like schoolboys, knowing that for an artist of Picasso's stature the award was hardly more than a joke. Ehrenburg, though, had serious reasons of his own to insure Picasso's acceptance: it helped to reinforce the credibility of modern art among Soviet officials.

Ehrenburg also worked hard to champion the work of his old friend, the Soviet artist Robert Falk. Falk painted urban and rural landscapes in an impressionistic style, which he had developed during years of study in Paris. His work was derided by the Artists' Union; Alexander Gerasimov, the head of the union, personally prevented Soviet museums from buying Falk's work. When Falk died in October 1958, Ehrenburg delivered the final eulogy and predicted that the time would come when museums would argue over control of Falk's paintings. When an exhibit of Falk's work opened in Moscow in the early 1960s to large and enthusiastic crowds, an informal survey confirmed that most people first learned of Falk through Ehrenburg's writings.[48]

Margarita Aliger observed the relentless energy Ehrenburg invested in these kinds of projects. In a reminiscence she wrote the following tribute:

> Remember his many years of stubborn struggle with Alexander Gerasimov for the right of truthful art, for the right of painting to be multi-imaged and original. Such a struggle seemed hopeless and senseless at the time. And if in the 1960s exhibitions took place in Moscow of Picasso and Falk, Tishler, Goncharova, and many others, if today we have already forgotten to think how long we were deprived of such possibilities—it is due in the last analysis to the struggle which Ehrenburg waged alone for many years. This is his triumph and we cannot forget about this.[49]

THE SECOND THAW

Ehrenburg was far from being the only writer willing to challenge the official limits of Soviet culture. By 1956 Vladimir Dudintsev and the young poet Yevgeny Yevtushenko (to name only two) also published work—the novel *Not by Bread Alone* and the long, discursive poem "Zima Station"—which raised ideologically awkward questions about Soviet society. These works are associated with what is remembered as the "second thaw," when a host of writers used the opportunity to explore politically charged themes in the wake of Khrushchev's secret speech.

Some writers were willing to go a step further. Ehrenburg's friend Veniamin Kaverin dreamed of establishing an independent press. In 1956 Kaverin attempted to make his idea reality. With the help of Margarita Aliger he edited and published two volumes of *Literaturnaya Moskva* (Literary Moscow), an impressive collection of stories, essays, and poetry, many of which could not have appeared in other publications. Ehrenburg joined their efforts, contributing an essay on the work of Marina Tsvetaeva, which introduced a volume of her poetry that was scheduled to appear the following year; this piece marked the first time in many years that anyone had written about Tsvetaeva. Yet both *Literaturnaya Moskva* and the Tsvetaeva collection fell victim to the regime's insecurity following the Hungarian revolt. Nikita Khrushchev personally denounced *Literaturnaya Moskva* and rebuked Kaverin and Aliger for not admitting their ideological errors with adequate submissiveness; as for the Tsvetaeva volume, it was postponed indefinitely.

Ehrenburg was also targeted for championing Tsvetaeva's verse. At a Writers' Union meeting to discuss *Literaturnaya Moskva*, his essay was cited as an unacceptable piece of writing for so important a Soviet journalist.[50] The well-known satirical magazine *Krokodil* ridiculed Ehrenburg's reverence for Tsvetaeva, insisting that she deserved only a "modest place in Russian literature."[51] Even *Pravda* weighed in with all its authority. Anxious to dismiss Ehrenburg's claims in her behalf, *Pravda* referred to Tsvetaeva as "a decadent poetess, whose name and verse did not find a response in the heart of the people and long ago sunk into oblivion."[52]

Undeterred, Ehrenburg still worked to restore Marina Tsvetaeva to her rightful place in Russian letters. For him this was as much a question of honoring her as a brilliant poet—Tsvetaeva today is universally regarded, alongside Akhmatova, Mandelstam, and Pasternak, as one of the four greatest Russian poets of the century—as it was a question of personal duty to the memory of an old friend. Their relationship was never easy or relaxed. They argued at their very first meeting in Moscow in August 1917; Max Voloshin, soon after, wrote to her that he was not surprised because they were both "capricious and provocative." By the time Ehrenburg left for Western Europe four years later she thought of him as a close friend, "kind and attentive," as she wrote to Voloshin. "I owe him all my happiness."[53] Nonetheless, after Tsvetaeva's stay in Berlin in 1922, where she saw Ehrenburg frequently, her meetings with him "became rare, accidental, and empty."[54] By the 1930s she was living in Paris with her husband and two children. Their family life was disintegrating. Sergei Efron had become a Soviet agent, urging émigrés to accept the Bolshevik government; their daughter Alya joined him in these activities and longed to move back to Moscow. But Sergei Efron also had a more discreet assignment, for he was involved in the assassination of Ignace Reiss, a former Soviet spy who defected to France. After Reiss's murder in September 1937, Efron fled to Moscow, where Alya was already living. Tsvetaeva soon felt compelled to follow him. Taking her fourteen-year-old son Moor, she joined her husband and daughter in Moscow in 1939. Their reunion was short-lived. Alya and then her father were arrested. He was executed, while she faced sixteen years of imprisonment.

Isolated and frightened, Tsvetaeva had few friends who would help her. She was under surveillance and people were too scared to be seen with her. Determined to support her son, she maintained a meager existence, writing verse translations for Soviet journals. Although Ehrenburg returned to Moscow in July 1940, they did not see each other until a year later, after the German invasion, when her life became even more precarious.

In his memoirs Ehrenburg wrote disapprovingly of his own distracted behavior during their last encounter in the summer of 1941. She came to his apartment, but he was absorbed in news from the front and could offer little advice about finding work. Unable to go on, Tsvetaeva committed suicide on August 31, 1941, in the remote village of Yelaguba, along the Kama River, in the Tatar Republic.

After her death Tsvetaeva's verse continued to face official contempt. Only in the 1950s could Ehrenburg counteract this attitude. As a member of the literary commission to review Tsvetaeva's work, he helped gain permission to publish a collection of her poetry. (Ehrenburg joined several such committees, including those for Babel, Pilnyak, and Boris Pasternak; he also offered to chair the literary commision for Vasily Grossman's work following his death in 1964, but the Writers' Union turned him down.) Learning the news, Tsvetaeva's daughter Alya Efron, who had only been released from the *gulag* the previous year, wrote to Ehrenburg on May 22, 1956: "Oh, my God, how happy I am that you will be writing the introduction! You are the only one who can do it—with heart and intelligence, and with your knowlege of her work and your clean hands."[55] A year later, on April 29, 1957, Alya wrote to a friend about the project, "Mother's book continues to hang in the air. . . . This has dragged on for two years . . . I am impatiently waiting for Ehrenburg's return from Japan. Everything is easier with him around, and he can do a great deal, even though everyone is particularly ganging up on the introduction."[56] Her hopes were disappointed. The volume did not appear until 1962, with a different combination of poems and without Ehrenburg's tribute.

That same year, on December 26, 1962, Ehrenburg presided over the first evening in Moscow devoted to Marina Tsvetaeva. Like many such occasions, a large and boisterous crowd tried to enter the hall, which was too small for everyone who hoped to attend. Ehrenburg's opening remarks demonstrated an intimate sense of Tsvetaeva's poetry, her love of life, and the tragic isolation that undermined her resolve. "First she lived, endured torment, made her mistakes, cried, was overjoyed, and only then composed her verses," Ehrenburg proclaimed. He also reminded the audience of Tsvetaeva's most famous lines: "Ghetto of the elect. A wall, a moat. Expect no mercy. In this most Christian of worlds, poets are kikes."[57] For Ehrenburg Tsvetaeva's work connected several of his own most poignant concerns: she was not a Jew, but her commitment to poetry made her an outcast, someone outside the confines of normal society. Until the end of his life Ehrenburg remained devoted to Tsvetaeva's poetry. Comparing her work to Pasternak's, he remarked in 1966: "I loved Tsvetaeva, now I worship her. I worshipped Pasternak, now I love him."[58] On the day before he died Ehrenburg commented to his friend, the poet Boris Slutsky, that he admired the poetry of Mandelstam and Tsvetaeva above all others.[59]

—

By the beginning of January 1956 Ehrenburg had already provoked enough hostility within the Central Committee that a memorandum was circulated listing his transgressions. In Budapest Ehrenburg's remarks could be invoked by "rightist anti-party elements in Hungarian literature." In Paris he had advanced a "nihilistic view of Soviet criticism and literature, not pointing to any positive or instructive dimensions." As a member of the editorial board of the new journal *Inostrannaya Literatura* (Foreign Literature), Ehrenburg had pushed for publication of Hemingway's "naturalistic and barren story *The Old Man and the Sea*" and also recommended novels by William Faulkner, "whose work is too formalistic and gloomy" for Soviet culture. The memorandum concluded that Ehrenburg should be summoned to the Central Committee and personally warned that his statements and overall behavior were "bringing harm to the influence of Soviet literature and art abroad." But Khrushchev's secret speech in February disrupted the plans of these Stalinist watchdogs. It was not until September, when they had overcome their confusion and begun to consolidate their authority once again, that Ehrenburg was called to the Central Committee and forced to listen to an official admonition.[60]

His response to this kind of pressure can best be judged by the work he continued to produce. Ehrenburg's tributes to Isaac Babel and Marina Tsvetaeva rescued their work from oblivion.[61] In 1957 and again in 1959 Ehrenburg published two long literary essays on Stendhal and Chekhov that demonstrated a deep erudition and an ability to write about one century and at the same time instruct readers about their own. This talent for scholarship, on top of his work as a poet, journalist, and novelist, compounded the hostility against him within the Writers' Union and the Central Committee; he was too literary and cultured, too *cosmopolitan,* in the true sense of the word. Who else could challenge the regime by writing two essays on nineteenth-century literature?

Ehrenburg's essay on Stendhal appeared in a summer issue of *Inostrannaya Literatura* (Foreign Literature) in 1957. Responding to renewed pressures against the literary community, Ehrenburg invoked Stendhal as a means to defend artistic freedom. Drawing on a wide range of sources, Ehrenburg showed how Stendhal's career had suffered because of his independent views on French society. He "hated despotism and despised servility," knowing how the conditions of tyranny corrupted art. An artist or a scientist needs freedom. Coercion can never lead to genuine creativity. Quoting Stendhal, Ehrenburg wrote that "Even if a king is an angel, his government destroys art: not by banning a picture on account of its subject, but by breaking the artists' souls." The most controversial aspect of Ehrenburg's essay, however, was his use of Stendhal's pointed remarks about tyranny. Khrushchev's denunciation of Stalin in February 1956 had initiated a discussion over the Soviet system as a whole, all of which made Khrushchev and his colleagues nervous; they were determined to confine any airing of Stalin's crimes to the late dictator's personal shortcomings and not permit the crimes they were willing to acknowledge to be ascribed to the system they had inherited. Ehrenburg found a quotation from Stendhal to make his own views on the dispute crystal clear:

[Stendhal] often said that what matters is not the personality of the tyrant but the nature of tyranny; a tyrant may be intelligent or stupid, kind or vicious, . . . people frighten him with conspiracies, flatter him, deceive him; the prisons overflow, the uneasy hypocrites whisper among themselves and the silence that almost makes the heart stop beating hardens.[62]

This section was sufficient to lead one American commentator to conclude that Ehrenburg's essay "is probably the strongest public condemnation of the Communist party dictatorship since Stalin's rise to
power."[63]

When Ehrenburg wrote "The Lessons of Stendhal," he anticipated
that his enemies would react harshly. The day after completing it he
sent a letter to his long-time friend Liza Polonskaya in Leningrad. "I
am fighting, but it is hard work. They fell upon me for my piece on
Tsvetaeva . . . I have been working on two essays. First I wrote on
French impressionists, and yesterday, I finished a long article on Stendhal. This is, of course, not history, but the same, ongoing struggle."[64]

Once again, in a campaign orchestrated by the Central Committee
itself, orthodox critics counterattacked, berating Ehrenburg in major
articles in *Literaturnaya Gazeta* and in *Znamya* "for his false, mediocre
and stupid judgments about Stendhal."[65] Ehrenburg's friends in Western Europe came to his defense. Louis Aragon ran a long excerpt from
Ehrenburg's essay in the Communist journal *Les Lettres Françaises* with
a ringing and detailed denunciation of Ehrenburg's Soviet critics.[66] As
was often case, Ehrenburg used his friendship with liberal-minded
Communists in the West to defend his position in Moscow.

—

Among Russian writers, Ehrenburg treasured Anton Chekhov above
all others. Writing in *Novy Mir* in the summer of 1959, Ehrenburg used
the full power of his Aesopian talent to make the great writer's career
under the czar resonate with the problems of the post-Stalin period,
particularly freedom of expression and official anti-Semitism. Con-
fronted either by the czar's tyranny or by French hostility to the Jews,
Chekhov consistently expressed outrage; "conscience was the highest
arbiter," as Ehrenburg defined his conduct. He also recalled how
Chekhov resigned from the Academy of Sciences in 1903 after the
czarist autocracy had annulled the election of Maxim Gorky. Ehrenburg's essay, appearing one year after the expulsion of Boris Pasternak
from the Writers' Union owing to *Doctor Zhivago*, was a pointed
reminder of how shamefully other writers were now behaving.

A contemporary of Zola, Chekhov followed the Dreyfus case with
intense interest and Ehrenburg was proud to recall at several points
how much Chekhov admired Zola's courage. Although it was next to
impossible for Ehrenburg to discuss contemporary anti-Semitism in
the late 1950s, it was equally difficult for Soviet censors to forbid quo-

tations from the work of Chekhov. So Ehrenburg expressed himself through Chekhov's words, citing his description of the Dreyfus affair: "Little by little a huge mess brewed up on the soil of anti-Semitism, a soil that smells of the slaughterhouse. When something is wrong inside us, we look for causes outside ourselves and soon find them."[67]

———

Over the years readers regularly responded to Ehrenburg in passionate and supportive letters. (Those who disliked him usually wrote to leading journals, to the Central Committee, or directly to the secret police, hoping to see Ehrenburg's name removed altogether from the ranks of Soviet literature.) As he grew older and his conflicts with the regime became sharper, this kind of support helped to sustain his morale and determination.

His friends were especially thrilled by his outspoken courage. On August 25, 1957, the journalist Frida Vigdorova, who would later be considered the "first dissident," sent him the following brief note: "I am taking the opportunity to tell you that you have written a splendid essay about Stendhal. Thank you very much for it. It stirs the mind and heart and makes one think about a great deal of things."[68]

Seven months later, on March 25, 1958, Nadezhda Mandelstam sent Ehrenburg a thoughtful letter reflecting not only her own curiosity about his literary plans but also a widespread interest within Moscow's intellectual community over what Ehrenburg would write next.

> Dear Ilya Grigorevich!
> I would like to see you very much. I am happy to tell you that I hear many kind and warm words about you. Do you know what is most important? To work in peace. I would of course prefer a book on poetry. I believe in it. It is curious that everyone wants to know what your next book will be about, and they often assume it will be either verses or a book about poetry. I kiss you warmly.
>
> > Nadya
> > Lyubochka, smile—I kiss you.[69]

Ehrenburg was in close touch with both Frida Vigdorova and Nadezhda Mandelstam. They followed his career closely and often wrote him letters of encouragement or sought his advice as the need arose. The most startling response to his efforts in the late 1950s, however, came from Stalin's daughter, Svetlana Alliluyeva. Born in 1926,

Svetlana became a serious student of literature and was teaching at the
Gorky Institute of World Literature in Moscow when she read Ehrenburg's essay on Stendhal in August 1957. She immediately wanted to
contact him. "For two days, I walked around with this persistent idea,"
she explained to him. In her letter she describes her love for literature,
her lifelong fascination and that of her classmates for the "process of
formulating feelings and ideas in words." But as her letter makes clear,
the reality of Soviet intellectual life compelled her and her friends to
conceal their own thinking. "The trouble is that each of us . . . has
scores of interesting notions about art, but we never pronounce them
out loud when we have the chance to express ourselves at a scholarly
conference or in a journal. Instead we chew over well-known, dried-
out dogmas with tiresome monotony. This is not hypocrisy on our
part," she points out. "It is a kind of contemporary illness. No one
regards this two-faced attitude as a vice. It has become the only way of
thinking for our intelligentsia . . . I am not knocking on an open door,"
she told him. "I am declaring all of this, unfortunately, in front of a deaf
wall." Ehrenburg's essay on Stendhal evidently assured Svetlana that she
could be candid with him, that he would understand the frustrations
of young scholars who could not express their love for literature without being smothered by strict ideological controls. But then Svetlana
in her letter grew more intimate with Ehrenburg, telling him about her
tragic romance with Alexei Kapler, who had paid for his love with ten
years of exile in the camps. She added further information about her
favorite nanny, a village girl who had spent thirty years in her family's
employ. The old woman had just died and "was buried next to our
mother" (a reference to Nadezhda Alliluyeva, Stalin's second wife, who
committed suicide in 1932) in Novodevichy cemetery. Several years
later, in the 1960s, Svetlana would write a great deal more about her
family and her friends, and even see two memoirs of her own published in the West after her stunning defection in 1967. "I have written
you all of this simply because I was incapable of not writing. Excuse
me if it is not interesting for you," she concluded. "I am very grateful
for your passionate love of art and because, alone among a select few,
you could find words of truth, proclaim them out loud, and not resort
to the two-faced attitude which has become like second nature for all
of us contemporary Soviet philistine-*intelligents*."[70]

Ehrenburg was touched by Svetlana's letter, recognizing the tragic,
human drama that lay behind her loneliness. He answered her himself,

but his response has yet to be found in a Russian archive. A decade later, after Svetlana's defection, Ehrenburg was the only major figure in Moscow to say kind words about her in public.

PASTERNAK AND THE NOBEL AWARD

The scandal surrounding Boris Pasternak's novel *Doctor Zhivago* was the most famous and closely followed confrontation between the regime and Moscow's intellectual community during the Khrushchev period. After Soviet journals turned down the manuscript Pasternak took the unprecedented step of arranging its appearance in the West through Giangiacomo Feltrinelli, a member of the Italian Communist party and a prominent publisher. The novel first appeared in Italy on November 15, 1957, and soon reached millions of readers throughout the world.

The Kremlin at first responded cautiously, with little public comment. Ehrenburg was one of the few Soviet writers to offer his opinion of the book *before* the Nobel award was announced. Speaking with the German correspondent Gerd Ruge, Ehrenburg offered an enthusiastic evaluation:

> "Boris Pasternak is a great writer. . . . He is one of the greatest living poets in the world. I have read *Doctor Zhivago*, and the description of those days is excellent . . . "
>
> Seeing my surprise at this wholly positive appraisal [Ruge continued], Ehrenburg recapitulated what he had said—but added: "As I said, I have read the novel, in manuscript. To be sure, I have not yet finished it, I have just got to the period of the revolution. Up to that time, I repeat, the description is excellent."[71]

Pasternak had given a copy of the manuscript to Ehrenburg and he remained a consistent champion of his poems, though he had sincere reservations about the novel. "There are striking pages in the book— on nature, on love, but many pages are devoted to things the author did not see and did not hear," Ehrenburg later wrote in his memoirs.[72] Yet he was not about to denounce an old friend for breaking a long-standing taboo—publishing a novel independently in the West.

The regime, however, could no longer ignore the novel's existence.

On October 23, 1958, the Swedish Academy awarded Pasternak the Nobel Prize for literature. Over the next two weeks a terrible drama played itself out. Pasternak first cabled acceptance of the award, but the regime, provoked by what it regarded as the "cold war" dimensions of the prize, unleashed its anger. On October 26 *Pravda* launched a full-scale assault, dubbing Pasternak "a lonely individualist in Soviet literature . . . who never even in his heyday was . . . regarded as a top-class writer." The character of Yuri Zhivago himself was an "infuriated moral freak," a creation of "a libeler" and "a weed."[73]

The next day a special meeting of the Writers' Union gathered to expel Pasternak from its ranks. Ehrenburg refused to attend. He had been in Stockholm on the day the Nobel Prize was announced, but was back in Moscow when his colleagues gathered to disgrace themselves. Someone kept calling him from the Writers' Union; Ehrenburg answered the phone each time with the same refrain, not bothering to disguise his voice: "Ilya Grigorevich has gone away and will not be back for some time."[74]

Ehrenburg helped to sustain Pasternak's morale. As the uproar continued, Ehrenburg followed Western press reports in Moscow and in Europe, then reported to Pasternak's son Yevgeny the reactions of people such as Hemingway and Steinbeck and of PEN clubs around the world (Poets, Essayists, Novelists, the prestigious international organization of writers). Yevgeny would pass along the news (and even an Indian edition of *Doctor Zhivago* Ehrenburg had received) to his father. Yevgeny often relied on Ehrenburg for advice and regarded him as his "rebbe." During the crisis over *Doctor Zhivago* he called on Ehrenburg many times, hoping to help his father defuse his ongoing conflict with the Kremlin. Ehrenburg defended Pasternak as well as he could in those years. "I am convinced," he wrote in his memoirs, "that Pasternak had no intention to harm our country. . . . He did not suspect that an ugly political scandal would be created out of his book and that the attack would have to be followed by a counterattack."[75]

Other than Ehrenburg, no one spoke well of Pasternak in public. In March 1960 Ehrenburg met with a group of Moscow university students and was asked his opinion of *Doctor Zhivago*. According to the *New York Times*, Ehrenburg maintained his independent judgment, although he tempered his admiration for Pasternak as a poet with an ambiguous remark about the novel.

Clearly betraying contempt for the way the Pasternak case was handled here, Mr. Ehrenburg replied he disliked discussing a novel his listeners had not had the chance to read. He said they had nothing to go on except what Moscow's *Literaturnaya Gazeta* told them of the case a few days after the Nobel Award had been made. This account, he implied, was by no means the whole story. Emphasizing that Mr. Pasternak is a "very great poet," Mr. Ehrenburg said that he finds *Doctor Zhivago* a "distressing" book. He did not say why.[76]

The final tragedy came on May 30, 1960, when Pasternak died of stomach cancer. His funeral in Peredelkino turned into one of the most memorable demonstrations of devotion ever accorded a literary figure. In spite of threats and warnings over a thousand people attended his burial, following the coffin as it was carried from his dacha to a small village cemetery. Ehrenburg was out of the country, but Lyubov Mikhailovna attended and made clear that Ehrenburg, had he been in Moscow, would have been there as well.[77]

THIRTEEN

Ilya Ehrenburg and the Jewish Question

In the initial years after Stalin's death numerous issues that had long remained taboo were brought into the open, however haltingly. Ehrenburg himself was a principal actor in this process. But as he challenged official control of the country's cultural heritage, he found himself the target of accusations concerning his survival and his relationship to Stalin. No question haunted Ehrenburg more or raised as many doubts about his integrity than his connection to the Kremlin's anti-Semitic campaigns—specifically, the execution of the Yiddish writers in August 1952.

With the official repudiation of the Doctors' Plot it was only natural that news about the fate of the Yiddish writers provoked intense interest both inside and outside the country. Khrushchev and his colleagues understood the sensitivity of this murderous episode. Coming so soon after the Second World War and the Holocaust, Stalin's systematic persecution of Jewish cultural figures raised awkward questions about the nature of the Soviet system, which is one reason why Yiddish writers were among the first to be "rehabilitated" in November 1955; but people still wondered about Ehrenburg. Only a handful of his closest friends knew about his courageous initiative, following the Doctors' Plot, to oppose the roundup and banishment of the country's Jewish citizens. Aside from Lazar Kaganovich, Ehrenburg remained the most prominent Soviet Jew to survive Stalin, a fact that was often used against him.

Few aspects of Ilya Ehrenburg's career are more complex than his relationship to his Jewish origins. An assimilated Jew, he had no attachment to religious traditions and rejected nostalgic appeals to the memory of life in the ghetto. At times Ehrenburg even expressed embarrassed disdain for the narrow, parochial customs of Orthodox Jews, whose communities he visited in Poland in 1927. In Warsaw he was impressed by the unpretentious disciples of Reb Nachman of Bratzlav, who revered their dead Rebbe with so much affection that they decided not to recognize a successor. One Sabbath morning he drove with two friends to the small town of Ger, stopping on the outskirts then walking to the Rebbe's courtyard in order to camouflage their violation of the Sabbath. In Ger Ehrenburg observed the hysterical reverence surrounding a charismatic Rebbe: followers fought each other for the opportunity to eat crumbs from his plate; it seemed as if they were worshiping a god rather than honoring a teacher. Ehrenburg understood that Hasidism began as a "mystical-revolutionary outburst," but based on what he witnessed in Poland it had turned into "a bulwark of hypocrisy." Ehrenburg had no patience for this kind of extreme religious fervor; it reinforced his own alienation from his family's religious background.[1] Nonetheless, Ehrenburg responded deeply to Jewish suffering. Though he often claimed to be an internationalist, Ehrenburg never denied his Jewish upbringing. Throughout his life, no transgression angered him more profoundly than anti-Semitism.[2]

—

After Stalin's death the regime retreated from the dictator's murderous policies against the Jews. Relations with Israel were normalized, a development that gave Soviet Jews at least some contact with their brethren outside the country. But the Soviet Union's Jewish community remained subject to numerous anti-Semitic initiatives, often within Khrushchev's broader campaign against organized religion. In the late 1950s churches as well as synagogues were closed. The number of functioning synagogues was forcibly reduced from as many as four hundred fifty in 1956 to just under a hundred in 1959, leaving the country's estimated two and a half to three million Jews with few if any institutional centers of Jewish life.

The regime's official actions encouraged anti-Semitism among the population and other elements within the country's far-flung and conservative bureaucracy. In October 1959, on Rosh Hashana, the Jewish New Year, a synagogue in the village of Malakhovka was burned by teenage arsonists. The wife of the Jewish cemetery watchman was killed, while threatening leaflets were pasted on walls, fences, and homes, expressing regret that Hitler did not finish the job of killing all the Jews. After the culprits were caught prosecutors asked Ehrenburg about the effects of a public trial on international opinion. He answered enthusiastically, knowing such a trial could also serve to warn domestic anti-Semites. The regime backed down, however, and the trial was conducted in secret.[3]

The following year a group of Mountain Jews, as they were called, who lived among a primarily Muslim population in Dagestan, came to Moscow to protest an anti-religious and anti-Semitic episode in their republic. A local party newspaper had published an editorial denouncing the existence of synagogues and the practice of circumcision among Muslims and Jews. The Jews felt especially vulnerable and sent a delegation to Moscow to expose the editorial. They visited government offices and then saw Ehrenburg, who offered his help. Adopting his usual tactic, Ehrenburg wrote to Mikhail Suslov and informed him that foreign correspondents had learned of the incident in Dagestan; Ehrenburg wanted to know how best to answer their concerns. Suslov could not ignore the possibility of an embarrassing scandal in the West. The editor of the Dagestan journal was reassigned.[4]

Worse propaganda soon followed. In October 1963 the Ukrainian Academy of Sciences published *Judaism Without Embellishment* by Trofim Kichko, a book that repeated crude canards about Jews, their love of money, and control of Western capitalism. Even more striking, the book featured cartoons showing Jews with hooked noses and other vulgar caricatures. Within a few months of its publication the Kremlin was forced to disavow Kichko's book, although it did so with only a halfhearted statement of regret. Another anti-Semitic book in 1964, directed against Ehrenburg, was *The Plant-Louse*, a novel that attacked modern artists and Jews, as if together they were conspiring to subvert Soviet culture. A *roman à clef*, the characters were based on easily recognizable figures, none more so than the principal villain, Lev Barcelonsky, whose work as an artist parallels Ehrenburg's career as a journalist.[5]

The Plant-Louse was not the first novel to attack Ehrenburg so pointedly. In the late 1950s Vsevolod Kochetov wrote his infamous book *The Brothers Yershov*, a crude defense of Stalinism in the aftermath of Khruschev's speech denouncing the tyrant. Here too Ehrenburg was the principal *bête noire*, the personification of all the Jewish and liberal values that so enraged the regime's most narrow-minded supporters. He was the quintessential Jew, a man so worldly and cosmopolitan that his loyalty to Soviet society was always in question. Seen through the eyes of such people as Kochetov, Ehrenburg was a deeply threatening figure who carried all the viruses of Western culture that Soviet power was pledged to destroy.

At the same time it is painful to recognize that there were Jews ready to assume the worst about Ehrenburg, particularly over the fate of the Yiddish writers whom Stalin had destroyed. The most serious allegations came from the Israeli journalist Bernard Turner, who in 1956 claimed to have been in a Siberian labor camp with Itzik Fefer and David Bergelson before their executions. According to Turner's account of their meeting, Peretz Markish had also been held in the camp but was then in solitary confinement, while another of the famous defendants in the group, Solomon Lozovsky, was said to have possibly committed suicide in the Lubyanka prison after severe torture. "The chief witness against those arrested, accused of Jewish nationalism and Zionism, was none other than Ilya Ehrenburg," Turner asserted. "He also had a hand in the arrest of many other Jews, including his relatives, doubtless in the attempt to save his own skin. He didn't even hesitate to turn Lozovsky, his closest friend, over to the NKVD."[6]

Turner's account is a complete fabrication. The Yiddish writers were held in secret until May 1952, when they were convicted in a closed trial. Lena Shtern was the only defendant to survive; all the others were executed. In November 1955 Lena Shtern saw Esther Markish and confirmed that Itzik Fefer had been the sole defendant to plead guilty and give testimony against the others. Solomon Lozovsky expressed contempt for Fefer as "a witness for the prosecution," while Peretz

Markish denounced the court in an eloquent final statement. There were no other witnesses and no hint that Ehrenburg or anyone else had "turned them over."[7] After Turner's story appeared in *Le Monde* on August 22, 1957, Ehrenburg angrily protested the newspaper's willingness to print outright slander. "To make accusations against someone based on the fictitious words of dead people, words which the dead cannot refute, is not a new device," Ehrenburg insisted. "But I cannot conceal my surprise that *Le Monde*, which ordinarily provides serious information, found it possible to grant space to insinuations drawn from a disreputable source."[8]

Two years later a French-Jewish journalist of Polish origin, Léon Leneman, embroidered Turner's original charges. Citing unsubstantiated testimony, Leneman describes how Ehrenburg "came to the trial [of the Yiddish writers] in his own car. After testifying against the accused, he calmly returned home."[9] According to this account, Ehrenburg was nothing less than a cold-blooded accomplice; there seemed no limit to the accusations directed against him. Ehrenburg believed that "he was the victim of a campaign of calumny launched in the Jewish world."[10] When he arrived at the Vienna airport in 1955, he was accosted by Bernard Turner, demanding to know about his role in the breakup of the Jewish Anti-Fascist Committee.[11] According to Turner (hardly a reliable witness), "Ehrenburg turned pale as chalk. His lips began to tremble, foaming at the mouth. A lost soul, he began to back away, and fled from me."[12] When Ehrenburg attended a Chagall exhibit in Paris in April 1962, the Israeli Yiddish novelist Mendel Mann challenged him to speak about "the anti-Jewish terror in Russia."[13] Even Israel's legendary Prime Minister David Ben-Gurion once denounced Ehrenburg as "the lowest Jew in the world."[14] "In those days," Ehrenburg responded, "there was no need for witnesses, star or otherwise. I defy anyone to show me one man, one solitary man, who was ever a witness at those trials. What is really held against me," he continued, "is my survival when so many others died. In the lottery of an arbitrary regime, my number—for death—never came up. It was the same with Pasternak who after all died in his bed."[15] As Ehrenburg observed, he had become different things to different people; for some, "a foreign element, a creature, if not possessed with a long nose, then nonetheless busy with dark shady matters [*gesheft*, in Yiddish], while for others, I was a man who had destroyed Markish, Bergelson, Zuskin."[16]

Other misunderstandings were attached to Ehrenburg's name. The following year, when Ehrenburg learned that his early novel *The Stormy Life of Lasik Roitschwantz* was going to be published in Great Britain in a new English translation, he protested and tried in vain to stop publication. The *Jerusalem Post* claimed that "Ehrenburg is sorry that in the twenties he wrote a work entitled *Lazar Roitschwantz* [sic], whose main protagonist embodied various negative traits."[17] Writing in his memoirs a few years later Ehrenburg explains that he did not include the novel in his collected works, "not because I think badly of it or repudiate it, but because, since the Nazi atrocities, I think it premature to republish some of its comical passages."[18] Ehrenburg had a more serious reason to oppose the book's appearance. By the late 1950s Ehrenburg endured an ongoing series of run-ins with Soviet officials. Virtually everything he wrote, from *The Thaw* to his essays on Tsvetaeva and Stendhal, provoked official rebuke, which sometimes included references to his earlier, tendentious prose and verse. *Lasik* is not only a Jewish book but also patently anti-Soviet, and its republication would not go unnoticed by Ehrenburg's enemies. His premonitions were correct. In March 1963, when the party leadership organized a concerted effort against him, *Lasik* and its recent appearance in the West "among anti-Communist circles" was included among the reasons for denouncing him.[19]

The regime understood that when it came to "the Jewish question," there were limits to Ehrenburg's cooperation. In early November 1956 Pyotr Pospelov, a prominent member of the Central Committee, summoned Ehrenburg urgently from his dacha. Ehrenburg assumed Pospelov wanted to talk with him about Hungary, where Soviet troops were mopping up armed resistance. But at the time of the Hungarian uprising an equally dangerous crisis was taking place between Israel and Egypt. To Ehrenburg's surprise Pospelov focused on the Middle East. Responding to armed incursions, the Israelis had taken control of Gaza and the Sinai peninsula, while French and British paratroopers seized the Suez Canal, which Gamal Abdul Nasser had recently nationalized. According to Pospelov, Lazar Kaganovich, who was still a member of the Politburo, wanted Ehrenburg, along with other prominent Soviet Jews, to denounce Israeli aggression. As Ehrenburg saw from the proposed statement, the French and British were barely mentioned. The whole exercise reminded Ehrenburg of 1953, when Stalin expected major Jewish figures to endorse a pogrom. "I told Pospelov," Ehrenburg wrote in *People, Years, Life*, "that I do not answer for Ben-

Gurion any more then he does and would willingly sign this text if he, a Soviet citizen of Russian origin, would sign it."[20] Four days later, on November 6, the statement appeared in *Pravda* with thirty-two signatories, including the journalist David Zaslavsky, the historian Isaac Mintz, and the film director Mikhail Romm. Ilya Ehrenburg's name was not among them.[21]

Following the crisis in Hungary, the Kremlin was eager to distract attention from its own actions by arousing public opinion over events in the Middle East. The Moscow petition Ehrenburg failed to endorse was not the only one to appear. At end of November *Izvestia* published two additional open letters signed by Jewish religious leaders that condemned Israeli aggression.[22] The Kremlin was obviously anxious to warn Soviet Jews not to identify with Israel at a moment of military and political confrontation. Ilya Ehrenburg refused to take part.

"BABII YAR"
—

By the fall of 1961 Western attention had begun to focus on the plight of Soviet Jewry. International conferences were being held in France, England, Italy, and Brazil. Prominent intellectuals and parliamentarians gathered to hear from refugees, scholars, and diplomats with firsthand knowledge of the conditions and aspirations of Jews in the Soviet Union, initial efforts that did not mobilize massive demonstrations or bring headlines to the world's press. But on September 19, 1961, Yevgeny Yevtushenko provoked a literary and political sensation with his poem "Babii Yar." Yevtushenko had recently visited the ravine in Kiev where over thirty thousand Jews had been slaughtered by the Nazis in two days of continuous shooting. The poem appeared on the twentieth anniversary of the massacre. While its immediate subject is the shameful lack of a monument to the victims, the poem is also an outspoken indictment of Soviet anti-Semitism. Its opening and closing stanzas voice an identification with Jewish suffering that was virtually unheard of in the Soviet press, especially from a non-Jewish writer.

> No monument stands over Babii Yar.
> A drop sheer as a crude gravestone.
> I am afraid.
>> Today I am as old in years

> As all the Jewish people.
> . . . .
> In my blood there is no Jewish blood.
> In their callous rage, all anti-Semites
> must hate me now as a Jew.
> For that reason
> I am a true Russian![23]

Yevtushenko was lionized by the Soviet public. In his autobiography he claims to have received twenty thousand letters, almost all expressing heartfelt gratitude. At poetry readings, audiences recited stanzas in unison.[24]

The regime reacted differently. Within days of the poem's appearance *Literatura i Zhizn* (Literature and Life) issued a long, insidious attack on Yevtushenko by the literary critic Dmitri Starikov. While Starikov did not deny Nazi atrocities against the Jews, he wondered why Yevtushenko focused on them when so many other nationalities had also suffered. To buttress his argument Starikov quotes selectively from Ehrenburg's 1944 poem "Babii Yar" and from Ehrenburg's wartime articles to demonstrate that the Jews were just one of many groups to be persecuted. The only responsible way to respond, as Ehrenburg is said to have done, is through a consistent internationalism, which excludes highlighting the misery of one people over another.[25]

Ehrenburg was furious and prepared an immediate and extensive response to Starikov's article. But *Literaturnaya Gazeta*, under substantial pressure for printing "Babii Yar" in the first place, refused to run Ehrenburg's letter. Determined to have his say and dissociate himself publicly from Starikov, Ehrenburg, with his usual cagey flexibility, appealed to Mikhail Suslov. He explained to Suslov that he was being approached by Western newspapers for his true opinion of Yevtushenko's poem and the controversy surrounding its appearance; while *Literaturnaya Gazeta* had refused to carry his lengthy response, he still preferred to express his views in the Soviet press rather than in a European journal that would exploit his position for "anti-Soviet" purposes. Suslov gave in. In the end Ehrenburg's letter to the editor, dated October 3, appeared in *Literaturnaya Gazeta* only on October 14. With barely restrained anger Ehrenburg made his position obvious: "Being abroad, I somewhat belatedly received the issue of *Literatura i Zhizn* of September 27, 1961, which contained D. Starikov's article 'About a

Certain Poem.' I deem it necessary to declare that D. Starikov quotes
from my articles and poems arbitrarily, breaking them off in such a way
as to have them correspond to his thoughts and contradict mine."[26] To
explain the two and a half weeks that passed between the appearance
of Starikov's article and his response, Ehrenburg wrote that he had been
on a trip. He had indeed been to Europe, but the claim was invoked to
conceal the regime's perfidy. Nonetheless, Ehrenburg had his say.

Over a year later, in the first of several difficult meetings with intellectuals that took place between December 1962 and March 1963,
Nikita Khrushchev remembered the "Babii Yar" incident. He accused
Yevtushenko of singling out by nationality the residents of Kiev who
had been murdered by the Nazis and added, "that Ehrenburg was guilty
of the same thing." Neither Ehrenburg nor Yevtushenko deserved such
condemnation. "Yevtushenko is a young Russian, I am an old Jew,"
Ehrenburg later wrote. "N. S. Khrushchev suspected me of nationalism.
Each reader can judge for himself if this is true."[27]

———

Ehrenburg's public statements on the fate of Soviet Jewry present an
inconsistent record of his beliefs. He was always cautious in his public
statements about Israel, not wanting to offend the Kremlin on the one
hand or say anything against Israel's legitimacy on the other. So it is difficult to evaluate his role in the revival of Jewish national feeling that
erupted after the Six Day War in June 1967. Ehrenburg, after all, died
in August, before the emigration movement gained the world's attention and before tens of thousands of Soviet Jews began clamoring for
the right to emigrate; Ehrenburg did not foresee this surge of desire to
actually live in Israel.

In May of 1959 Ehrenburg was reported to have said in France that
he "did not believe that great masses of Jews in the Soviet Union
wanted to leave their country. He estimated the number of would-be
emigrants at about 100,000." Even this level of emigration could have
a troublesome effect, he believed, and lead to the growth of anti-
Semitism in the USSR.[28]

That same year a young Jewish student wrote to him about the fate
of Soviet Jewry. Ehrenburg's response was a sincere statement of his
beliefs. He made it clear that he supported the publication of "books,
journals and newspapers in Yiddish for those who consider this language their mother tongue," although he recognized that most centers
of Yiddish culture had been destroyed by the Nazis and could not be

revived. He concluded his letter with a piece of personal advice, telling his young correspondent "not to be proud and not to be ashamed of your national origins. Pride and shame are both equally incomprehensible to me: I do not like it when people are treated as if for a lesson in pedigree. Of all nationalities, I prefer internationalism." Even so, Ehrenburg was not willing to dismiss all forms of national pride with equal disdain. As he explained to another person who wrote to him in early 1967, "Nationalism and racism are the same crude phenomenon among Russians, among Ukrainians, and among Jews. But the racism of cats is more dangerous than the racism of mice."[29]

Outside the country Ehrenburg was careful not to contradict the official Soviet line. In 1960 he was dispatched to ask André Blumel, the head of the France-USSR Society and an activist in the Jewish community, to try to stop a conference on Soviet Jewry that was about to take place in Paris.[30] If Ehrenburg made a real effort to prevent the conference, his discreet intervention failed. In 1962 he was asked by a French reporter about his attitudes toward his own Jewish origins. "You cannot love humanity," Ehrenburg responded, "unless you love the nation to which you belong." When asked about Israel directly, Ehrenburg was more cautious. "I have sympathy for several people who were forced by persecutions to go there, but I do not like the policy of this state."[31]

If Ehrenburg was sincere in asserting his internationalist beliefs, however, he did not behave like an ordinary, assimilated Jew. In his famous article in *Pravda* in September 1948 Ehrenburg claimed that "there is very little in common between a Tunisian Jew and a Jew living in Chicago who speaks American and thinks American. If there is a bond between them, . . . it is a bond created by anti-Semitism."[32] Ehrenburg felt this connection himself, and he often behaved as if whatever happened to Jews happened to him. In the face of anti-Semitism, Ehrenburg always experienced a stubborn reassertion of his Jewish identity. Such feelings could not have emerged from barren soil.

On March 16, 1959, a gala celebration of Sholem Aleichem's centenary was held in Moscow. Ehrenburg was chairman of the evening; it was his initiative and prestige that made it possible for the evening to take place. The event was held in the modest auditorium of the Literary Museum on Dmitrova Street; the hall could hold only about two hundred people. As Esther Markish recalls in her memoirs, *The Long Return*, "It was a very special occasion, indeed, for it had been many years since an evening devoted to the works of a Jewish writer had been organized." A handful of Israelis from the embassy staff attended the evening, "the insignia of the State of Israel displayed prominently on their lapels."[33] Several speakers addressed the crowd; some recited verses. One described the life and work of Sholem Aleichem. Another discussed Sholem Aleichem's relationship to Maxim Gorky. Finally, in a highlight of the evening, David Markish, the son of the martyred Peretz Markish, read a poem of his own in honor of the occasion.

Ehrenburg did not hesitate to make his sympathies clear. When he opened the celebration, he complained that the hall was too small, that a larger one should have been permitted. He also expressed his admiration for Sholem Aleichem in explicitly ethnic phrases, reporting on a decision by the World Peace Council to mark the writer's anniversary.

> And what great joy and what great pride I experienced. Pride because I am a Jew by nationality and pride because I am a writer, and pride because I am a Russian writer who knows the connection between Sholem Aleichem and great, genuine Russian literature, and pride as a Soviet man because I nevertheless remember and know that no one defended authentic internationalism more than Lenin.[34]

It was one thing to honor Sholem Aleichem, a genuine classic, who had died in New York in 1916; it was quite another to honor someone who had perished under Stalin. As the Khrushchev period matured, the regime became more relaxed about permitting public gatherings in honor of those who had disappeared. Peretz Markish had been one of the country's most famous writers in the 1930s and 1940s. On November 25, 1960, Markish's family succeeded in marking his sixty-fifth birthday with a large and enthusiastic gathering at the Writers' Union. The celebration included a prominent exhibit about Markish's career with Anna Akhmatova as one of the speakers, who had begun to translate poems by Markish with the help of interlinear translations from Yiddish. Esther Markish considered Ehrenburg's message "the high point of the evening"—though he was too ill to attend, he sent the following letter, which was read to the audience:

> I deeply regret that I cannot be with my friends tonight who have gathered to honor the unknown grave of the well-known poet,

Peretz Markish. I would like to remember him as the young and uncompromising man he was in Kiev, where sadness and hope hung like a cloud over his handsome face and narrowed the pupils of his dreamy eyes. . . . I would like, too, to tell about our last meeting, our last brief talk, the last time we shook hands—also in the corridors of the building on Vorovsky Street [the headquarters of the Writers' Union], where many of us cast a final parting glance at each other. . . . Then Peretz Markish was no more. . . . Can there be anything more senseless than such a death in spite of its profound and tragic sense? His poems remain with their vibrant ring. The image of a pure, courageous and good man remains. It uplifts multitudes, it radiates warmth in moments of solitude, it rejuvenates those in the twilight of life. Yes, it was worth writing like that, and a life like that was worth living.[35]

Ehrenburg was still defending Markish's memory five years later. In 1965 he wrote a letter to the Writers' Union reminding them of Markish's birthday and insisting that a plaque in honor of Markish be mounted on the apartment building where he had last lived in Moscow.[36]

———

The ceremonial occasions in honor of Sholem Aleichem and Peretz Markish were significant events in the life of Moscow's Jews. They marked, however modestly, the contribution of Jewish writers to Russian cultural history and the ongoing presence of a large Jewish community in Soviet society, a presence the regime only acknowledged in the most begrudging manner. Ehrenburg was happy to help arrange this kind of event; there would be others before he died in 1967.

Fifteen years after the close of World War II Ehrenburg understood that Soviet political and historical propaganda often denied or obscured the extent of Jewish losses during the war and the fundamental importance of the Final Solution to Hitler's overall plans. Ehrenburg used whatever opportunity he had to remind Soviet audiences of the Holocaust. One book in particular stirred Ehrenburg's interest, and it was only in 1960, after several years of effort, that he succeeded in pushing through a Russian translation of *The Diary of Anne Frank*. His introduction to the Anne Frank volume embodies his profound loyalty to the millions who had been destroyed. Like *The Black Book* project, Ehrenburg used his unique access to material as a means to instruct Soviet society in general and inspire Soviet Jewry in particular. "Everyone knows that the Hitlerites murdered six million Jews," Ehrenburg writes,

> citizens of twenty countries, rich and poor, the famous and the unknown. The atom bomb fell on Hiroshima suddenly; it was impossible to take cover. For several years, the Hitlerites organized raids on millions of people just as hunters chase wolves. Jews tried to conceal themselves, to hide in pits, in abandoned mines, in the crevices of cities. . . . Six million were asphyxiated in the gas chambers, shot in ravines or in forts, condemned to a slow death from hunger. . . . One voice speaks for these six million. It is not the voice of a wise man or a poet, but of an ordinary young girl.[37]

There was a Soviet equivalent to the Anne Frank volume. In 1962 Ehrenburg learned of the existence of a diary by a Jewish woman in Lithuania who had survived the Nazi onslaught. Masha Rolnikaite, a journalist and a professional musician, had kept a journal during the war describing her life as a teenage girl in the Vilna ghetto. Now she wanted to publish her account and sent a copy to Ehrenburg for his advice. He responded warmly and over the next five years they remained in close touch. Following Ehrenburg's suggestion, she published her book first in Lithuanian, which made it possible for the book to appear in other languages. She was especially happy to keep Ehrenburg informed of her success with publishers, sending him letters as she learned of translations into Russian, Hebrew, French, and German.[38]

———

In 1966 Ehrenburg was invited to mark the anniversary of Émile Zola's death at the writer's home outside of Paris. His lecture turned into a denunciation of anti-Semitism. "I remember one distant autumn morning from my childhood," Ehrenburg told his audience. "My father was reading the newspaper over breakfast. Suddenly he threw the page down. 'Zola has died.' My mother burst out crying. I was eleven years old. I often heard the adults discussing the Dreyfus case so I understood that a great misfortune had occurred."[39] More than half of Ehrenburg's lecture was devoted to anti-Semitism at the turn of the century, with particular emphasis on how closely Chekhov followed the Dreyfus case while he was living in Nice.

Ehrenburg did not expect to publish his lecture in Moscow until a young, ambitious editor from *Izvestia* named Yury Oklyansky approached him. Oklyansky had heard about the Zola piece and wanted to see it appear in Russia. Ehrenburg cautioned him to be careful. As soon as Oklyansky read the lecture, he understood Ehrenburg's warning that "publishing it would not be simple. . . . The article really did break the elusive and secretly observed norms and ideas about what is acceptable and what is not acceptable . . . in the pages of our press," Oklyansky recalled in a memoir of his own. "It threw down the gauntlet before the editorial code of . . . silence." Oklyansky was determined to see it published. A week before Ehrenburg was to deliver his lecture Oklyansky began to prepare the piece for *Izvestia*, adding a brief introduction to help it clear the censors. A Russian translation of Zola's *Collected Works* in twenty-six volumes was being published at that time, an event that Oklyansky used as a pretext to run Ehrenburg's article; but it was not printed, not the next day, as Oklyansky had expected, nor any time that week. As he later learned, the censors wondered who he was and why he was pushing Ehrenburg's article when it was so obviously "seditious." The editors themselves were in a quandary. Ehrenburg was "an old bird, with connections at the top, and even more the business involved foreigners!" Apparently, the foreign connection proved to be decisive. The text appeared in the paper's literary supplement *Nedelya* (The Week) on October 9, a week after Ehrenburg's lecture took place in France.[40]

Ehrenburg had equally good luck with the republication of his memoirs. His nine-volume *Collected Works* had begun to appear in 1962, bringing at least some of his long out-of-print and suppressed books to a new generation of readers. Ehrenburg had planned to include *People, Years, Life* in volumes 8 and 9, which were scheduled for publication in 1966 and 1967. The editor of the collection was a courageous, liberal-minded woman named Irina Chekhovskaya, who liked Ehrenburg and wanted to accommodate him. Moreover, her husband worked for the Central Committee, giving her increased authority. With her cooperation Ehrenburg was able to restore at least some of the material that the censors had earlier blocked.[41]

One major addition is a long chapter on *The Black Book* that Ehrenburg had been compelled to omit in 1963. Ehrenburg also wrote a chapter on Vasily Grossman in 1965—a year after the writer's death— that he then succeeded in placing in the new edition of the memoirs.[42] These two chapters substantially contributed to the Jewish character of Ehrenburg's memoirs at a time when few if any other works in the Soviet press explored or even acknowledged Jewish suffering under the Nazis. In the years leading up to the Six Day War in June 1967, when Soviet Jews experienced an unprecedented surge of identification with Israel and Zionism, *People, Years, Life* did as much as any other book to provide historical information and pride in Jewish cultural achievements.

———

Both Esther Markish and Nina Vovsi-Mikhoels compared Ehrenburg in their own minds to an earlier figure in Jewish history, the general Josephus Flavius, who commanded an army in the Galilee at the outset of Judea's revolt against the Roman Empire in the first century. After a terrible defeat he surrendered to Vespasian's legions. Josephus later retired to Rome, where he wrote his famous chronicle, *The Jewish Wars*. For Esther Markish and Nina Vovsi-Mikhoels, Ehrenburg adopted a similar strategy for survival in the face of overwhelming authority: to record what he knew and hope that another generation of Jews and non-Jews, under better conditions, would live happier, more secure lives. Sholem Aleichem, Peretz Markish, Anne Frank—all were part of Ehrenburg's historical and cultural memory. They inspired him, but he never wanted such knowledge for himself alone. After Ehrenburg read Julian Tuwim's essay "We—the Polish Jews" in 1944 he translated and then quoted its lines as often as he could, not simply because they moved him, helping him to define his own Jewish self-consciousness, but also because the essay was not published on its own in Russian.

In an early novel Ehrenburg wrote about Lasik Roitschwantz, who first gets into trouble when he "heaved a deep sigh, loud and doleful" during the speech of a Bolshevik functionary in Homel.[43] Ehrenburg learned to conceal his sigh beneath a veneer of silence and obedience; but he felt the pain nonetheless, which accounts for the sadness that lies at the center of so much of his work. Neither his fame, his official stature, his talent, nor his survival ever exempted him from feeling part of Russian Jewry's tragic fate.

FOURTEEN

Illness and Old Age

Ehrenburg began experiencing symptoms of prostate cancer in the late 1950s. He had been afraid of doctors and dentists all his life, permitting his gums to deteriorate to the point where he lost most of his teeth, excepting a few molars. Beginning in 1958, Ehrenburg did not consult a physician when he first had difficulty urinating, foolishly allowing months to go by. He finally went to see a specialist in Moscow, Dr. Yelena Nekhamkina, who worked at the Municipal Clinical Hospital no. 6 (or the Basmannaya, as it is affectionately known, named after the street where it is located); although not the most advanced facility in the capital, it had a reputation for good doctors, and many members of the intelligentsia went there for treatment. Dr. Nekhamkina arranged for Ehrenburg to enter the hospital discreetly through a side door. He wore a dark beret, in part to guard against the chilly weather and in part to obscure his identity. As an experienced physician, Dr. Nekhamkina immediately recognized the severity of Ehrenburg's condition. His face looked pinched and pale, and he was urinating frequently, with painful difficulty, often passing blood. The examination and subsequent tests confirmed her suspicions: prostate cancer, which had spread to the bladder. By the late 1950s chemotherapy existed and could have prevented metastasis had the doctors seen him when his symptoms first appeared, yet even after Dr. Nekhamkina's examination Ehrenburg continued to be stubborn, refusing to enter a hospital for further tests and treatment. The doctor did not tell Ehrenburg the full extent of his illness, suggesting instead that he suffered from a benign, low-grade tumor; but she explained everything to Irina Ehrenburg's adopted daughter, Fanya Fishman (who was a doctor herself), even recommending that Ehrenburg see another urologist to confirm her diagnosis and impress on him the need to begin treatments.

Months went by before Ehrenburg even asked for the names of the medicines he needed. Liselotte Mehr finally prevailed upon him to see a specialist in Stockholm, who fully confirmed Dr. Nekhamkina's diagnosis and prescribed a full course of chemotherapy. Ehrenburg rejected outright any surgery that might have immobilized him. In Moscow Irina and Fanya would call Dr. Nekhamkina from time to time, but she did not see Ehrenburg again. He would call her, though, to discuss new drugs or a flare-up of his symptoms; he specifically asked her not to tell anyone about these calls. After Ehrenburg's death in August 1967 his daughter found blood-stained underwear that he had hidden away at the dacha.[1]

In spite of his illness Ehrenburg continued to demonstrate the kind of energy and ability to work that had characterized his career for decades. Under Khrushchev there was no longer any need to restrain himself in the public arena, and he could openly respond to critics; but not all of his public interventions challenged fundamental political sensitivities. In 1959 Ehrenburg engaged in a protracted debate in the Soviet press over the long-standing tension between humanists and scientists (in Russian, *liriki* versus *phisiki*) concerning the role of art and the emotions in modern life. The dispute began innocuously when Ehrenburg responded to a letter from a young student about her cold-hearted fiancé. Soon a series of exchanges in *Komsomolskaya Pravda* caught the attention of a broad audience and generated even more letters to Ehrenburg himself.[2] Ehrenburg also conducted a campaign to introduce the Belgian endive to Soviet agriculture, convinced that its capacity to be cultivated as a winter vegetable could provide economic and nutritional advantages to his country. He went so far as to attract Khrushchev's personal attention to the proposal.

———

Ilya Ehrenburg turned seventy on January 27, 1961. For nearly eight years, ever since Stalin's death, he had been engaged in a running skirmish with the country's literary and political establishments. In spite of his many awards and service to the regime, the cultural bureaucrats at the Writers' Union looked on him with barely disguised suspicion and envy. In the early 1960s Ehrenburg was riding in Moscow with his friend Zhenya Naiditch, who was visiting from Paris, when his chauffeur was stopped for speeding by a policeman. Hoping to avoid a fine, the chauffeur explained that his boss Ilya Ehrenburg was in the back seat; the policeman let the car go without so much as a warning. "If he had been from the Writers' Union," Ehrenburg told Mme. Naiditch, "he would have given us the ticket."[3]

Nonetheless, from the regime's point of view Ehrenburg's literary stature and his contributions to the peace movement outweighed his ongoing challenge to orthodox beliefs: his birthday would have to be publicly celebrated. Now the regime was presented with a dilemma of its own making. The Soviet Peace Committee wanted to hold a lavish ceremony in Moscow's Hall of Columns, perhaps the most prestigious and among the largest auditoriums in the capital; but the Central Committee turned down the request, leaving it up to the Writers' Union to determine how to pay homage to Ehrenburg "in this complicated situation."[4]

As expected, Ehrenburg was officially honored that January. Leonid Brezhnev, at that time chairman of the presidium of the Supreme Soviet, personally presented him with his second Order of Lenin in a ceremony at the Kremlin. The Writers' Union planned a major celebration. He was also invited to read a speech over the radio, while newspapers carried laudatory accounts of Ehrenburg's career. Under the predictable headline, "A Writer—A Fighter for Peace," *Pravda*'s column struck an unusual tone for a tribute to a state prizewinner. "The creative path of I. Ehrenburg," the article suggested, "has been complicated and at different times contradictory." *Pravda* then summarized Ehrenburg's career in typical Soviet fashion, referring to his conformist novels, his heroic work against the Fascists, and his ongoing efforts for peace, but not bothering to substantiate what made Ehrenburg's career so "complicated" and "contradictory."[5] *Moskovskie Novosti* (Moscow

News) was even more paradoxical; it referred to Ehrenburg's career as "checkered."[6]

That same morning, on January 26, a tape of Ehrenburg reading his seventieth birthday speech was broadcast at ten minutes past ten—an awkward hour, chosen to minimize the potential number of listeners. Ehrenburg repeated his speech that night at the House of Writers, however, and his remarks justified the regime's instinctive wariness of what he would have to say.

The birthday celebration at the Writers' Union reflected Ehrenburg's ambiguous status. The veteran diplomat Ivan Maisky, who had known Ehrenburg for forty years, acknowledged "his profound, unwavering adherence to principle." For Maisky, Ehrenburg was continuing "the role of Herzen," the great nineteenth-century Russian writer and political exile whose journal *The Bell* helped to sustain Russia's liberal traditions during decades of czarist reaction. The writer Konstantin Paustovsky, with whom Ehrenburg had grown closer in recent years, called Ehrenburg "our present-day conscience . . . who has struggled against anti-Semitism. There is no greater vice for a nation than anti-Semitism." With that said, Ehrenburg rose to embrace and kiss Paustovsky.[7]

The journalist Mikhail Kotov, who also served as secretary of the Partisans of Peace in Moscow, handed Ehrenburg a gold medal, then announced a host of congratulatory telegrams from such figures as the British scientist and peace activist John Bernal, Dolores Ibarurri (La Pasionara), Marshall Konstantin Rokossovsky (who had led the Victory Parade through Red Square in 1945), Dmitri Shostakovich, Nazim Hikmet, and the one name that drew applause from the crowd, Anna Akhmatova. Like all her notes to Ehrenburg, this one too expressed her deep respect. "A strong thinker, an alert writer, always a poet, congratulations on today. Your contemporary, Anna Akhmatova."[8] No one besides Ehrenburg could possibly have heard from such a diverse assortment of well-wishers.

Listening to the speeches, Ehrenburg looked "gloomy, pale, thin, and old." Called to the podium, his initial remarks made clear that he was not pleased with everything about his birthday. He began by mentioning the radio program that morning. "For whom did they broadcast?" Ehrenburg complained. "For housewives, perhaps? Writers generally do not listen to the radio and other readers of mine work at that hour." Articles in the press also disappointed him. "They all claimed that I began to write at age forty, they all, as if on command, began with *Without Taking Breath* and end with *The Ninth Wave*. This means that I already died ten years ago. I do not consider my essay on Stendhal . . . or *The Thaw* to be mistakes and time has proven me correct." After these spontaneous comments Ehrenburg repeated his radio address, which included the following provocative statements:

> I hear kind words about my newspaper articles. About my books mostly silence. Perhaps this is because I write better articles than books. I do not know. Or perhaps it is because certain critics find it easier to agree with me when I write about the struggle against fascism or about the struggle for peace. A newspaper article addresses the question of how to live through one day, but a book addresses how to live an entire life. Everyone, of course, understands that peace is a necessity. But when we were completing a house, when we are figuring out how people should live inside it—this business is not less complicated. . . .
>
> Sometimes we call writers "engineers of the human soul," but in the nineteenth century they said "teachers of life." I like this more. It is closer to an educator than an engineer.
>
> We were all brought up on nineteenth-century literature. A writer should see what his contemporaries still do not see. But if he describes things that are understandable to everyone, if he copies what was written before him, if he prescribes the same medicine that is supplied in a neighboring pharmacy, then he is expressing what is fashionable, he becomes an authentic parasite, even if he writes from morning until night. . . .
>
> There has never been a more humanistic literature than Russian literature, and I am proud that I am an ordinary Russian writer. In my passport, it says not Russian, but Jew. So why do I call myself a Russian writer?

Ehrenburg then reminded his audience that "anti-Semitism is the international language of fascism." "Yes," Ehrenburg repeated, "I am a Russian writer. But as long as a single anti-Semite remains on earth, I will answer the question of nationality with pride: a Jew."[9]

Hearing these defiant words, many Jews in the audience began to applaud wildly, recognizing Ehrenburg's courageous ability to say publicly what everyone else could only keep to themselves. But their enthusiasm disturbed Ehrenburg, to the point that he began to strike the podium to silence their applause. For Ehrenburg such a demonstration of emotion was unnecessary; it reflected a ghetto mentality that needed to celebrate what to him was an ordinary but necessary affirmation.[10]

At the end of his speech Ehrenburg could not help but to refer to his own mortality and the determination that drove his spirit. "While the heart beats, you must love with passion and the blindness of youth, stand up for what is dear to you, struggle, work, and live, live while the heart beats."[11] The audience leapt to its feet, saluting Ehrenburg with long, emotional applause. Officials in the first four rows sat in stone-faced silence; they did not like what Ehrenburg had to say, nor did the Central Committee. Five days later an internal party memorandum made note of numerous ideological deviations during the celebration. Ivan Maisky and Konstantin Paustovsky were singled out for "exaggerating Ehrenburg's role and significance in our literature and social life." Two members of the Central Committee with responsibility over literature and the arts, Dmitri Polikarpov and Igor Chernoutsan, described Ehrenburg's remarks about anti-Semitism in detail and complained that too many Jews were in the audience. "Apparently," they concluded, "Ehrenburg needed the jubilee evening to state his tendentious, mistaken views under circumstances where no one could dispute them."[12]

In his speech Ehrenburg grudgingly acknowledged that "according to my age, I am a pensioner with a long record. . . . A man turns seventy, there is nothing amusing about this." For the past decade Ehrenburg had been spending more time at his dacha in New Jerusalem; he had a large garden there with an enclosed greenhouse where he could cultivate seeds and cuttings through the winter. Fanya Fishman had married young and by this time had a daughter who was nearly ten years old. Irisha was like a great-grandchild to Ehrenburg. When he was too ill to work he would lie on his bed and not allow anyone to approach him except for Irisha, who would talk and play with him.[13]

Other men his age with similar comforts and similar pains might be expected to slow down, retire, or enjoy relaxing pursuits; Ehrenburg, though, old and sickly, was neither tired nor resigned. He was not finished. He was planning one final, prolonged act before the curtain came down. Five months earlier Novy Mir had begun to carry his memoirs, *People, Years, Life*; by the end of 1960 the first thirty chapters had appeared. At least publicly, Book One (on his childhood and exile to Paris) had not aroused controversy. But Ehrenburg had a great deal more to say. The memoirs—whose entire text would not be published until long past Ehrenburg's death—would mark the crowning glory of his career.

FIFTEEN

People, Years, Life

Nearly two thousand years ago the Roman historian Tacitus described the dangers of writing history too close to one's own time. "An ancient historian has but few disparagers," Tacitus wrote, "and no one cares whether you praise more heartily the armies of Carthage or Rome. But of many people who endured punishment or disgrace under Tiberius, the descendants yet survive; or even though the families themselves may be now extinct, you will find those who, from a resemblance of character, imagine that the evil deeds of others are a reproach to themselves."[1] When Ilya Ehrenburg began to write his memoirs in 1958, Stalin had been dead for only five years, and when they began to appear in *Novy Mir* in 1960, Stalin's body still lay next to Lenin's in Red Square. Although Khrushchev had denounced the tyrant, Stalin's earthly remains haunted his heirs and the country his heirs continued to rule.

Ehrenburg had considered writing his memoirs for some time, before his love for Liselotte Mehr proved the final inspiration. Telling her stories about the people he had known, Ehrenburg understood that he was composing a memoir, much as he had written *Julio Jurenito* four decades earlier, entertaining friends in a Kiev café with his adventures in Paris; but this time he would need more than twenty-eight days. As he told the agronomist Nikolai Vasilenko, who helped him regularly in his garden, "I will begin working on a book that I will write until the end of my life."[2]

Ehrenburg's initial notes for *People, Years, Life* reflect intentions that consistently guided him. The memoirs were to focus on distinct personalities, most of whom had already been killed in the war, suffered a natural death, or perished at Stalin's hands. His notes in French consist of copious lists of people by nationality and profession.[3] Ehrenburg made a promise to himself not to write about anyone who was still alive—Pablo Picasso and Ovady Savich were exceptions—and to write only about those he had liked or admired. *People, Years, Life* has many passionate pages yet relatively few angry or bitter ones; he did not use the memoirs to settle any scores.

Ehrenburg prepared himself carefully, looking over notebooks and ordering old newspapers from the Lenin Library. Most of the work was accomplished at his dacha, where he had more room in his study and fewer visitors. To write the memoirs Ehrenburg became especially industrious, beginning the day with breakfast and spending as much as an hour with his flowers and vegetables, planting seeds or cuttings, pruning, all the while gathering his thoughts. He would then work over a typewriter for several hours, take lunch, relax with a book or a magazine— he never took naps—and resume typing in the afternoon. Ehrenburg often stayed up past midnight, drawing on the same reserves of strength and vitality he had shown during the war, only now age and the effects of cancer were taking their toll. But Ehrenburg was not discouraged. Overcoming his physical ailments seemed to add energy to his writing.

By April 1960 Ehrenburg was ready to offer the manuscript to *Novy Mir*, a natural and inevitable choice. Under Alexander Tvardovsky the journal had achieved a reputation for courageous publishing that would grow even broader as Ehrenburg's memoirs, the work of Viktor Nekrasov, Vladimir Voinovich, and Alexander Solzhenitsyn graced its pages in the 1960s. Ehrenburg wrote to Tvardovsky about the memoirs on April 25, 1960, sending him a portion of Book One.[4] As soon as the journal's editors began to read the opening chapters, Ehrenburg saw the outright taboos and hesitation that would consistently confront

his memoirs. One of Tvardovsky's first letters to Ehrenburg foreshad-
owed all of the difficulties ahead. In standard editorial fashion Tvardovsky listed several places in the manuscript where he wanted Ehrenburg to reconsider his original draft. Two points in particular became
issues of contention: the portrait of Nikolai Bukharin, and any mention of anti-Semitism.[5]

Over the next five years the editors closely examined Ehrenburg's
manuscript for how it portrayed Jewish life in the Soviet Union, compelling him to accept numerous deletions. As Ehrenburg complained
in Book Six, he "was accused of writing about Jews and keeping silent
about Icelanders."[6] The editors also suppressed inconvenient facts and
subtle allusions: Tvardovsky asked Ehrenburg to remove Kafka's name
from a list of prominent personalities who were alive in 1891, the year
of Ehrenburg's birth; Ehrenburg complied. (Kafka had yet to be published in the Soviet Union.) A few pages later in Book One Ehrenburg
begins a discussion of his Jewish origins with the following sentence:
"The intelligentsia at that time was ashamed of anti-Semitism as if it
were an infectious disease." Tvardovsky asked if the phrase "at that
time" was "not superfluous." Ehrenburg insisted that it was necessary
and the sentence remained as a rebuke to many of his contemporaries
who neglected the legacy of Chekhov and Tolstoy, who had both
denounced the persecution of Jews.[7]

When it came to Nikolai Bukharin, Tvardovsky and the censors
were even more adamant. Chapter 6 of Book One describes Ehrenburg's short-lived career in the Bolshevik underground, where he
includes a loving portrait of his high school comrades, Nikolai
Bukharin and Grigory Sokolnikov, both of whom had been condemned during the Great Purge and were not yet rehabilitated. By
writing about their youthful escapades Ehrenburg was pressing for a
review of their cases. Tvardovsky understood that the time had not yet
arrived. Ehrenburg had to back down, but only after appealing in vain
to Nikita Khrushchev. His letter is dated May 8, 1960, just two weeks
after Book One had been submitted to *Novy Mir*.

Dear Nikita Sergeyevich!

I am embarrassed to take several minutes of your time, especially at
this tense moment, but I do not see an alternative. [An American U–2
airplane, piloted by Gary Powers, had been shot down by the Russians
a week before.]

The journal *Novy Mir* is beginning to print my memoirs. At the outset I relate my modest activity in the revolutionary movement between 1906 and 1908. There I speak about the Bukharin and Sokolnikov of that time—about high school students and immature youths. I have decided to send you this chapter and mark off the two pages that, without your permission, will not be able to be printed. I especially want to mention Bukharin, who was my school comrade. But of course if this is politically inconvenient at the moment, I will omit these two pages.[8]

At the same time Ehrenburg wrote a less formal note to Khrushchev's adviser on cultural affairs, Vladimir Lebedev: "From the letter to Nikita Sergeyevich, you will understand what my request is about. Perhaps it is useless to show him the two pages—I am thinking now about his time. Perhaps you could ask him at a free moment if I could mention eighteen-year-old Bukharin in my memoirs (for me, this is of the most importance)." Ehrenburg's secretary Natalya Stolyarova personally delivered both letters to Lebedev in the Kremlin. From what Lebedev told her, Ehrenburg understood that he would not be permitted to write about his friends:

> Lebedev read the letter and said that perhaps Nikita Sergeyevich has his own opinion, which he did not know, but it seemed to [Lebedev] that it should not be published. Bukharin had not been rehabilitated, the people knew him as an enemy and then suddenly they would read how warmly and sincerely Ilya Grigorevich writes about him— all the big wigs would attack him. In the interest of preserving Ilya Grigorevich's peace of mind, it would be best not to publish the material now. Of course, if Ilya Grigorevich will insist, they can publish it. We do not have censorship, but it would not be in the interests of Ilya Grigorevich. [As she left], Lebedev said that he would, of course, pass the letter to [Khrushchev].[9]

Khrushchev and the Central Committee could not accept Ehrenburg's portrayal of Bukharin and even insisted, in vain, that all mention of "Nikolai Ivanovich" be removed from the text. Here Ehrenburg was able to forge a useful compromise. In chapter 6 he substituted the forbidden material with the following suggestive sentence: "The time has not yet come to speak about all my comrades in the high school orga-

nization." Then quoting a report from czarist secret police files, Ehrenburg was able to list Bukharin's name alongside his own as "a district
propagandist" among the Bolsheviks.[10] In addition there are a handful
of references to "Nikolai Ivanovich," a common name and patronymic,
but an unmistakable allusion to Bukharin.

That fall the widow of Nikolai Bukharin, Anna Larina, wrote him a
note of gratitude "for the first human words to appear in print" about
her late husband; she wanted "to shake his hand and kiss him." Three
years later they met and he handed her the pages he had wanted to
include in the published text.[11]

———

Ehrenburg also had difficulty publishing his portrait of Boris Pasternak, which was supposed to appear in *Novy Mir* in January 1961. Suddenly, without warning, the material was removed. Glavlit in fact had
intervened. In a letter to the Central Committee in December 1960
the head of the censorship bureau accused Ehrenburg of "trying to
rehabilitate [Pasternak] in the eyes of society" and ignore Pasternak's
isolation "from the Soviet people, from Socialist construction."[12] The
chief censor had his way; Ehrenburg's portrait of Pasternak was left out
of *Novy Mir*'s next issue. The first sixteen chapters of Book Two, among
which it belonged, were published without it.

Ehrenburg had shown his portrait of Pasternak to the poet's son,
Yevgeny, who believed that Ehrenburg had written "the chapter as he
had to;" the family was hoping to see it published.[13] When the chapter failed to appear, Ehrenburg had no choice but to appeal directly to
the Kremlin. His letter, dated January 19, 1961, was addressed to
Khrushchev's adviser, Vladimir Lebedev. As always in such circumstances, Ehrenburg found a way to manipulate the system by adopting
an argument that would make political sense to the people in charge:

> It seems to me that since a commission on the literary heritage of
> Pasternak has recently been formed, in which I am included, we will
> be publishing a collection of his verse. After everything that has hap-
> pened around *Doctor Zhivago*, a new edition of his verse will be more
> understandable to a reader who has already read my chapter devoted
> to Pasternak the poet. . . . Publication of the chapter would, in my
> opinion, be politically advisable and not "criminal." Tvardovsky and
> the entire editorial staff of *Novy Mir* share this point of view. The edi-
> tors, however, cannot overcome the difficulties that have arisen and I

decided to ask you, if you find it possible, to learn the opinion of Nikita Sergeyevich Khrushchev.[14]

Ehrenburg's letter had its effect. The chapter on Pasternak appeared in the February issue of *Novy Mir*.

Ehrenburg's memoirs, as they first appeared in Moscow and then in translation in the West, were hailed for their unique contribution to Soviet letters. But the historian Isaac Deutscher criticized him for not divulging more. "Far from lifting any iron curtain over the past," Deutscher wrote in *The Nation*, "Ehrenburg lifts only that corner of it that others, those in office, have already raised. . . . His capacity for remembering the past corresponds to the twists and turns and the tempo of the official de-Stalinization with startling precision."[15] Deutscher obviously did not know of Ehrenburg's relentless efforts to publish as much as he could or the regime's equally relentless pressure to control what Ehrenburg wanted to say. Deutscher failed to recognize what Ehrenburg was striving to do against formidable odds.

With the publication of Book Two the scope of Ehrenburg's memoirs became obvious. The memoir was already four hundred pages long—it would reach nearly fourteen hundred pages before Ehrenburg died—and was nothing less than an attempt to restore the country's cultural history. As he wrote in Book One, "History abounds with gorges and abysses, and people need fragile little bridges to connect one epoch with another." *People, Years, Life* was meant to serve as one such bridge, reviving the work of creative artists and episodes of Soviet culture that had vanished into the Stalinist "memory hole." As the Czech poet Zbignief Herbert once wrote, "Forgetting the names of the disappeared undermines the reality of the world."[16] Ehrenburg understood his obligation before history. On the first page of his memoir, he wrote that "many of my contemporaries found themselves beneath the wheel of time."[17] He had survived and as a witness insisted on helping a new generation learn what the regime wanted them to ignore.

In their moral and historical sweep Ehrenburg's memoirs have no equal in Soviet literature. In some cases, his portraits—of Tsvetaeva, Mandelstam, Tairov, Falk, and Mikhoels—were the first examples of their kind to appear in the post-Stalin era. Written in the "warm and sincere" style that so concerned the Kremlin, these chapters impressed many readers with the love that Ehrenburg showed toward friends who had either perished or seen their careers destroyed. "Mediocrity sees nothing higher than itself," Tolstoy once observed, "but talent recognizes genius instantly." Ehrenburg understood that many of these friends were more gifted than he and his portraits were as much a celebration of their work as they were heartfelt evocations of an epoch. He quoted poems of Tsvetaeva and Mandelstam that had never before appeared in the Soviet press. He described Falk's paintings; how Babel wrote a story; how Mandelstam composed verses in his head; how Meyerhold and Tairov, each in his own way, performed theatrical miracles; and he made clear how they had died and who had destroyed them.

Ehrenburg also wrote about Western figures who were little known in the Soviet Union. Modigliani, Apollinaire, Picasso, Max Jacob, Robert Desnos, Julius Pascin, Diego Rivera, and Marc Chagall had all been his friends in Paris. He summoned up their work and personalities and detailed their connection to Russian culture. Modigliani, an Italian Jew, had met Anna Akhmatova in Paris and in 1911 drew her portrait—a trivial fact that nonetheless made absolutely clear that before the revolution a young poet such as Akhmatova was free to travel, enjoy Paris, and return to her country without political or bureaucratic impediments.

In *People, Years, Life* Ehrenburg presented European culture as a whole, decrying artificial barriers that prevented Soviet art and literature from claiming their rightful place. His readers responded. Poring over the memoirs, students kept lists of names they were seeing for the first time. Literary *samizdat* grew in popularity as individuals circulated collections of verse on their own, typing copies from old editions and passing them along to friends.

Until Alexander Solzhenitsyn's novella *One Day in the Life of Ivan Denisovich* no other contribution to *Novy Mir* evoked so much passion and controversy. On August 17, 1961, Tvardovsky sent Ehrenburg the following tribute as he was editing Book Three for publication that fall: "This is a book of duty, a book of conscience, of courageous confession of one's own errors, . . . In a word, you are the only writer from your generation who crossed a certain forbidden limit. . . . You have succeeded in doing what others did not dare to try."[18]

Nadezhda Mandelstam recognized Ehrenburg's influence and in her memoir *Hope Abandoned* acknowledges his contribution in her uniquely acerbic, inconsistent manner:

He was always the odd man out among the Soviet writers, and the only one I maintained relations with all through the years. He was as helpless as everybody else, but at least he tried to do something for others. *People, Years, Life* is in effect the only one of his books to have played a positive part in this country. His readers—mostly members of the minor technical intelligentsia—first learned dozens of names quite new to them from this book. Once they had read it, their further evolution proceeded rapidly, but with the usual ingratitude of people, they were quick to disown the man who had first opened their eyes.[19]

Ehrenburg's most grateful readers were the relatives of those who had perished. Their letters to him were the most eloquent testimony to his achievement. One of the first to write was Ariadne (Alya) Efron, the daughter of Marina Tsvetaeva. Ehrenburg's chapter on Tsvetaeva, which came out in January 1961, was the true beginning of her rehabilitation into the recognized pantheon of Russian poets. Her daughter acknowledged all this in her letter of May 5, 1961.

I have a great deal of wonderful things to say to you and I should be accursed if I do not do it! But for now I will only say thank you on behalf of the resurrected people, years, and cities. . . . What difficult work these memoirs must be . . . when an entire generation of those times—that time—is only swaddled with conventional interpretations. . . . When your generosity, penetrating all the shells, reaches the unprotected essence of people, actions, events, landscapes, to the soul of everything and even to the readers'—this is a miracle.[20]

Lidia Clementis sent Ehrenburg a postcard from Prague. Ehrenburg had written about her late husband, Vladimir Clementis, whom he had first known as a literary journalist in Slovakia in the 1920s before Clementis became a Communist functionary, a career that ended tragically in the Slansky trial of 1952. "Your words will forever remain in my memory and heart," she wrote to Ehrenburg.[21] The chapter was reprinted in the path-breaking Slovak weekly *Kulturny Zivot* (Cultural Life) in September 1963 and signaled Clementis's rehabilitation in Czechoslovakia.[22] The U.S. embassy in Moscow was stirred by the appearance of Ehrenburg's essay. "This is the first intervention known to the Embassy of a prominent Soviet personality in the problem of the unjust treatment meted out to Slovak Communists in Stalinist times," the embassy cabled to Washington, D.C. "While these Slovaks of course recognize that Ehrenburg is not Khrushchev, it is of interest that a liberal Communist writer in the Soviet Union is able to stretch a hand across the border in a greeting to Slovak writers and political personalities of the same persuasion."[23]

Ehrenburg's efforts to revive the work of long-suppressed artists and writers was part of his continuous campaign against "socialist realism." Throughout the 1950s he had argued that it was harmful for writers to make their work conform to arbitrary rules of form and content. In *People, Years, Life* Ehrenburg contended that taste could not be imposed on creative artists or their audiences. "It is impossible to prescribe, instill, or impose tastes," he wrote in 1962. "The deities of ancient Greece consumed nectar . . . But if anyone had started to pump nectar down a tube into the stomachs of Athenian citizens, the matter undoubtedly would have ended with vomiting throughout Athens." His argument went even further. Writing about the poets Sergei Yesenin, Marina Tsvetaeva, and Boris Pasternak, Ehrenburg conceded that many artists had not welcomed the October Revolution with enthusiasm—himself included. Reared on nineteenth-century notions of art, politics, and personal freedom, they were troubled by the revolutionary violence, "by the senseless sacrifices, by the ferocity of the reprisals."[24] It was perfectly natural, Ehrenburg insisted, for him and others like him to react skeptically to the revolution's utopian claims. An artist's political views were irrelevant to his or her poetic genius.

Such a startling argument had far-reaching implications: If it was legitimate to question the October Revolution—whose image remained officially unblemished within the ruins of Soviet ideology after the unmasking of Stalin's crimes—then what political or cultural dogma could not be challenged? Ehrenburg, Tvardovsky, and the other *Novy Mir* writers who rallied behind the call for artistic freedom were not so naive as to expect the regime to give up censorship; they did, however, want to reassure the party that opposition to censorship of the arts did not mean hostility to its political supremacy. None of these writers was willing to up the ante so far, at least not yet. The human rights movement was still several years away.

Nikita Khrushchev, the general secretary of the Communist party, and the country's liberal-minded writers appeared to be working in tacit alliance. Tvardovsky himself was widely honored, having received the Order of Lenin in June 1960 and then the more prestigious Lenin Prize in October 1961. That same month, invited to address the Twenty-second Party Congress, Tvardovsky used the opportunity to defend *Novy Mir* and its contributors before the party elite. Writers, he declared, had the right to explore the full truth as they saw it, while readers did not need literary censorship to protect them from harmful ideas. At the end of the Congress—which condemned Stalin even more explicitly than the Twentieth Party Congress in 1956 and led to the removal of his embalmed remains from the Lenin Mausoleum to a grave beneath a concrete slab near the Kremlin Wall—Tvardovsky was selected to join the party's Central Committee as a Candidate Member, an unexpected but auspicious honor for the editor of a liberal journal.[25]

COUNTERATTACK

Moscow's conservative sentries were infuriated by Ehrenburg's and Tvardovsky's success. In June 1961 the critic Alexander Dymshits launched the opening round of their counterattack. Writing in *Oktyabr*, whose editor, Vsevolod Kochetov, was a notorious reactionary, Dymshits took issue with Ehrenburg's portraits of Osip Mandelstam and Marina Tsvetaeva. For Dymshits, Ehrenburg's efforts amounted to an "unjustified idealization of second rate artistic phenomena that were far from revolutionary approaches to art." As for Boris Pasternak, Ehrenburg's portrait was too solicitous. Ehrenburg, it seemed, "even tried to justify [Pasternak's novel]," an unpardonable transgression at a time when Pasternak was still being denounced as a traitor and a renegade.[26]

Two days after Tvardovsky's talk to the Party Congress in October, Vsevolod Kochetov weighed in as well. Without mentioning Ehrenburg by name Kochetov decried "morose compilers of memoirs . . . who rake around in their confused memories in order to drag out mouldering literary corpses into the light of day and present them as something still capable of living."[27] Kochetov's remarks were among the most obnoxious denunciations by a neo-Stalinist, and it is an indication of the mood in those years that at least some delegates to the Party Congress repeatedly interrupted his speech and heckled him with shouts of "Enough!" and "Shut up!"

The fate of *People, Years, Life* was linked to the fate of Khrushchev and his program. So long as Khrushchev remained firmly in power and able to pursue de-Stalinization, Ehrenburg's position seemed secure and his memoirs continued to appear. But as the narrative reached the anti-Fascist struggle of the 1930s, the Spanish civil war, and the Great Purge, the censors began to object more strenuously. Even Tvardovsky pressed Ehrenburg to rework whole sections, while mention of individuals such as André Gide and Paul Nizan, who had parted from the Communist line, had to be either removed or more negative assessments attached to their names.

Nonetheless, what struck readers most in these chapters was not Ehrenburg's specific memories but the candid disclosure of his fear. Without apology or elaboration, Ehrenburg recalled 1937 and 1938. "I understood that terrible crimes were being ascribed to people which they had not committed and could not have committed," he wrote. "We could not divulge a great many things, even to our loved ones. Only now and then, we shook our friends' hands with particular warmth—we were all participants in a great conspiracy of silence."[28]

Ehrenburg could not be forgiven, for if a journalist such as he, who had lived in France for many of those years, knew that innocent men and women were being persecuted, then how could Khrushchev and others like him, who were already in leadership positions by the late 1930s, not have known? Ehrenburg's "theory of silence," as it was called, struck at the heart of Khrushchev's and the party's legitimacy. By exposing the "cult of personality" and stressing the persecution endured by the party, Khrushchev sought to portray himself as a victim rather than a comrade of Stalin's who had reached high office over the corpses of countless other Communists. Ehrenburg's contention would have to be rebutted. What Khrushchev failed to understand was that by the time he rebuked Ehrenburg his own vulnerability would be exposed as well.

———

The conservatives found their opportunity in the fall of 1962. The Cuban Missile Crisis, which ended with the withdrawal of Soviet nuclear weapons from the Caribbean, severely undermined Khrushchev's authority and prestige.[29] His opponents felt emboldened to move against some of his policies. Ideological control of the arts was the easiest and most natural place to begin. From the conservatives' point of view freedom of artistic expression could not be separated from criticism of the Stalin period, a discussion that could only lead to questions over the party's supremacy.

The reactionaries began to take their revenge. At a special Central Committee plenum in November 1962 to discuss economic reform a petition from a large group of conservative artists was presented to the party leadership; their appeal urged the party to intervene against growing "formalist trends," code language for any innovation in content or creative style that would distinguish a work of art, literature, or music from the stultifying forms of "socialist realism." Two weeks later, Khrushchev, with a delegation of party leaders and cultural bureaucrats, visited a small exhibit of contemporary art at the Manezh gallery near Red Square. This incident, one of the most colorful, crude, and widely discussed of his regime, was probably set up to provoke Khrushchev's wrath against some of the very people who supported him and needed him the most.

The episode began innocently enough. On November 26 the students of a Moscow artist named Eli Belyutin opened a small exhibit of seventy-five paintings in their teacher's studio. By Moscow standards the work was considered avant-garde because most of it employed an abstract style. Several sculptures by Ernst Neizvestny were also displayed. Western correspondents, Soviet cultural officials, and hundreds of guests walked through the exhibit, while hundreds of others waited in vain outside. After a few hours the exhibit closed and was not scheduled to reopen. Then, out of the blue, Belyutin and his students were invited to hang their exhibit in three separate rooms in Manezh Hall near the Kremlin, where an enormous retrospective of conventional Soviet art was already under way. Khrushchev was brought there on Saturday afternoon, December 1. Upon viewing the work he launched into a series of vulgar denunciations. Before a still-life painting by Robert Falk, Khrushchev asked aloud, "What is this supposed to represent?" He compared the painting to the work of a "child [who] had done his business on the canvas when his mother was away and then spread it around with his hands."[30] Only Ernst Neizvestny stood up to Khrushchev. When the premier threatened to send artists out of the country, Neizvestny opened his shirt to reveal scars from his wartime wounds. "This is my country, too," he told Khrushchev, "and you can't take it away from me."[31]

The liberals reacted quickly, hoping to prevent a full-scale conservative rout and sustain Khrushchev's liberal policies. Several petitions were addressed to the party leadership, including a direct appeal to Khrushchev from seventeen prominent artists and scientists, among them two Nobel laureates in science, Igor Tamm and Nikolai Semyonov; the composer Dmitri Shostakovich; the director Mikhail Romm; and the writers Konstantin Simonov, Kornei Chukovsky, and Veniamin Kaverin. Ilya Ehrenburg signed this appeal as well, and took an active role in its composition.

Dear Nikita Sergeyevich!

We are turning to you, as a man who has done more than anyone else to uproot Stalinist tyranny from the life of our country.

We, people of different generations, work in various fields of art. We each have our own tastes, our own artistic convictions. Our concern for the future of Soviet art and Soviet culture unites us in this appeal.

If we are all appealing to you in this letter, it is only because we want to say with all sincerity that without the possibility of various artistic trends to exist, art is destined for oblivion. . . .

We are appealing to you with a request to stop the swing in the figurative arts to previous methods, which are alien to the whole spirit of our times.[32]

Although Khrushchev did not respond, several of the signatories, including Ehrenburg, soon had an opportunity to defend their views in person.

On December 17, 1962, four hundred writers, artists, and intellectuals gathered in the Pioneer Palace in Moscow's Lenin Hills, where they had been summoned to meet with Nikita Khrushchev. Their mood was hopeful. One incident in particular seemed to portend greater artistic tolerance: Khrushchev introduced Alexander Solzhenitsyn to the audience. Solzhenitsyn at that time was a schoolteacher from Ryazan, and few if any of the assembled writers had met him personally or knew anything about him besides his story *One Day in the Life of Ivan Denisovich*, which had just appeared in *Novy Mir*. Honoring Solzhenitsyn in this way reflected Khrushchev's continuing opposition to Stalinism, always an encouraging sign for the liberals.

The meeting, though, turned into a confounding exchange of opinions. The principal speaker was not Khrushchev but Leonid Ilyichev, the chairman of a new ideological commission in the party. Ilyichev reportedly spoke for ten hours, vowing to resist pressure, from the West or from within the country, for greater freedom of creative expression. When he finished, Ilyichev did not take questions from the floor; Khrushchev, however, had several candid and startling exhanges of his own. Yevgeny Yevtushenko defended abstract artists. "I am convinced," he told Khrushchev, "that formalist tendencies in their work will be straightened out in time." Khrushchev's reply stunned the audience. "The grave straightens out the hunchbacked." Yevtushenko, to his ever-lasting credit, answered Khrushchev with an admonition of his own. "Nikita Sergeyevich, we have come a long way since the time when only the grave straightened out hunchbacks. Really, there are other ways."[33] The audience burst into applause. Even Khrushchev felt compelled to join in. Ehrenburg too spoke up. He pointed to Picasso and Mayakovsky as examples of modern artists who were not political reactionaries, as the party claimed that all modern artists must be.

Neither Ehrenburg nor any of his colleagues was prepared for what followed. His conservative antagonists, no doubt with Khrushchev's connivance, had arranged a surprise. They did not stick to literary criticism, but raised the sinister question of Ehrenburg's involvement in Stalin's crimes. The charges came from Galina Serebryakova, a conservative writer and the widow of two of Stalin's victims, including Ehrenburg's high-school comrade Grigory Sokolnikov. According to Serebryakova, Ehrenburg had betrayed his colleagues on the Jewish Anti-Fascist Committee. While this was not a new charge, Serebryakova startled the audience by announcing that she had learned about Ehrenburg's complicity from Stalin's private secretary, Alexander Poskrebyshev, whom everyone in the hall assumed was no longer alive. She claimed to have met Poskrebyshev at a rest home, where he was writing his memoirs. Although the regime encouraged Serebryakova to make her accusations, her remarks were never published and no other figure publicly accused Ehrenburg of such charges. As for his fellow writers, there is no evidence that any of them took Serebryakova's indictment seriously. Even Mikhail Sholokhov approached Ehrenburg to shake his hand, an unnecessary but thoughtful gesture on the part of Ehrenburg's long-standing antagonist.

Still, the conservatives extended their attacks. On January 4 Alexander Laktionov issued a blistering denunciation of Ehrenburg and the younger writer Yury Nagibin for their support of contemporary art. Ehrenburg, according to Laktionov, had been infecting Soviet culture for too long with his devotion to European painting.[34] Five days later

Alexander Gerasimov reiterated Laktionov's rebukes in *Trud* (Labor), attacking Ehrenburg and Paustovsky for their support of modern artistic trends.[35]

This was only the beginning. On January 30, 1963, *Izvestia*, which seemed to be leading the charge against *Novy Mir*, carried a long, extensive review of *People, Years, Life* by the literary critic Viktor Yermilov, who was known to have denounced fellow writers to the secret police under Stalin. The opening sections of Yermilov's piece praised Alexander Solzhenitsyn and expressed gratitude to Ehrenburg for writing about friends who had disappeared. Then, in typical fashion, Yermilov denied Ehrenburg's claim that he and others understood that Stalin's victims were innocent but out of fear had to be silent and live with "clenched teeth." "The tragedy lay in the prevailing certainty that Stalin was right," Yermilov asserted, "that everything done in his name was unimpeachable."[36]

Yermilov's attack reflected a long-simmering resentment among the political elite for Ehrenburg's candid admission. Ehrenburg responded immediately by insisting that no one had publicly protested the persecution of innocent victims. *Izvestia* and Yermilov answered in turn, this time implying that Ehrenburg was either lying or had enjoyed "special insight" during the purges, an "advantage" that could only have been granted by Stalin himself. Such an insinuation was designed to stir doubts about Ehrenburg's past among his liberal colleagues, especially among the younger generation, who no doubt wondered how Ehrenburg had managed to survive.[37] Finally, it seemed, Ehrenburg would be compelled to repudiate his views.

But he was not cowed by this malicious assault. He had even been alerted to Yermilov's piece by *Izvestia*'s editor, Alexei Adzhubei, who was also Khrushchev's son-in-law. "Ilya Grigorevich, we are going to come out against you, but we will try to find a critic who is a little more liberal," Adzhubei told Ehrenburg. "Absolutely not," Ehrenburg said. "Otherwise you will be offending me. It's necessary for the critic to be the most sinister. Then everything will be clearer." "Could it be Yermilov?" Adzhubei asked. "That's it. Let it be Yermilov," Ehrenburg replied.[38] Ehrenburg was clever enough to understand that Yermilov's moral standing was so low that an article from such a dubious source would enhance his own stature and discredit other critics.

Following Yermilov's article, Ehrenburg ran into difficulty with the publication of Book Five of his memoirs. These chapters covered the

Second World War, a time Ehrenburg could look back on with unadulterated pride. Once again he was compelled to accept changes in the manuscript. A long chapter on *The Black Book*, with significant excerpts from the text, was reduced to a few paragraphs, while other material on the Holocaust and anti-Semitism was removed altogether.

Although the first chapters of Book Five had appeared in *Novy Mir* in January, the journal received instructions to halt further installments. On February 13, 1963, Ehrenburg appealed personally to Khrushchev for assistance:

Dear Nikita Sergeyevich!

. . . The editor of *Novy Mir*, A. T. Tvardovsky, has informed me that he has been instructed to drop the continuation of Book Five of my memoirs from the journal's February issue. When the preceding parts were being published, Glavlit and other departments informed the journal of certain cuts and changes that had to be made. I met most of their demands and the memoirs continued to appear. But on this occasion, the instruction that a series of chapters must be removed from the February issue was not accompanied by any suggestions for corrections or changes in the text.

I am appealing to you, Nikita Sergeyevich, not as an author struggling to get his work into print, but as a Soviet citizen who is concerned about the possible political repercussions of the decision conveyed to me by A. T. Tvardovsky. I would not be troubling you except for the fact that the initial installment of Book Five appeared in the January issue of *Novy Mir* with the words: "To be continued." In our literary journals, there has never been a single example in which a work already in the process of publication was broken off with the phrase: "To be continued."

I am afraid that this will not only surprise the readers, but will be used by anti-Soviet circles abroad, all the more since translations of my memoirs have appeared in many foreign countries. This puts me, as a public figure, in a false situation.

In my view, if *Novy Mir* announces in its February issue that the publication of *People, Years, Life* will be continued in a particular issue to come, that may prevent the development of a regular anti-Soviet campaign. I am sure you will understand the motives which guide me.

With deep respect.
Ilya Ehrenburg[39]

As happened so often before, Ehrenburg was able to find the right tone and argument to reach Khrushchev. Book Five resumed publication in the February issue of *Novy Mir*, whose appearance had been postponed for several weeks, just as Ehrenburg had hoped.

Ehrenburg felt confident in his own ability to handle Khrushchev's contradictory behavior. He was also willing to look out for others who were less experienced or more foolhardy. Ehrenburg visited Paris that January and made a point of seeing the young poet Andrei Voznesensky. Voznesensky, like Yevgeny Yevtushenko, had become the darling of the Western press, representatives of a new generation of Soviet poets who were challenging the shibboleths of Soviet life. That winter Voznesensky was enjoying his first visit to the West. Ehrenburg came unannounced to Voznesensky's hotel near the Louvre and invited him outside for a walk. (Voznesensky took this suggestion to mean that the room was bugged.) Once they were on the sidewalk, Ehrenburg made his intentions clear. "I've read your interviews, what you've been saying," Ehrenburg said to him. "I cannot decide whether you are daring or crazy. I cannot advise you what to do, but be cautious in your behavior and watch what you say."[40] But the advice came too late. In Paris Voznesensky was anything but cautious. Encouraged by the enthusiasm of his French admirers (the famous *New Yorker* correspondent Janet Flanner reported that "such a throng of poetry lovers assembled to hear [him] that many auditors had to stand at the back for the two hours of the performance, while others sat on the floor in the aisles"[41]) Voznesensky thumbed his nose at one Soviet dogma after another from the stage of the Vieux Colombier, the venerable avantgarde theater on the Left Bank. The audience included many students, members of the French Communist party, Russian émigrés, and even two arch-enemies, the Surrealist André Breton and the Communist writer Louis Aragon. To a crowd hanging on his every word, Voznesensky spoke warmly of Boris Pasternak and described the influence of the late poet's work on his own. In response to a question from the floor, Voznesensky defended surrealism, insisting that the "real question is not the ism but the quality of the work." The American Socialist Michael Harrington attended the reading and was struck by Voznesensky's outspoken, almost brazen demeanor. He came away from the theater thinking of Voznesensky as a "sort of politician of poetry" and concluded that he had witnessed something "momentous" and "revolutionary."[42]

The Kremlin was not equally enthralled; Voznesensky had to be disciplined. In March Voznesensky and several others, Ehrenburg among them, faced withering criticism for their writings and statements. Voznesensky was compelled to issue a public apology for his behavior, a severe setback for any rebel. It was this humiliation that Ehrenburg tried to help the young poet avoid.

SIXTEEN

Spring 1963 and the Fall of Khrushchev

No one anticipated the storm that was about to break. Ehrenburg was in Sweden at the beginning of March when he received a message requiring his return to Moscow. Yevtushenko too was ordered home from Paris. Nearly six hundred writers and artists gathered in the Kremlin's Sverdlov Hall to listen to party leaders. Like a group of rowdy schoolchildren, they were summoned for a lecture on their misbehavior.

Leonid Ilyichev was the first to scold them. His remarks reflected the regime's profound lack of sophistication when it came to the creative arts: Ilyichev was out to defend the integrity of "socialist realism" against "formalist tricks and abstractionist daubing, [and] decadent doggerel accompanied by the hysterical twanging of guitars." Some writers and artists had heeded the party's urgings and Ilyichev, in an attempt to seem generous and paternal, acknowledged the apologies of Eli

Belyutin and Yevgeny Yevtushenko, whose recent public statements showed they had "felt the loving concern of the party."[1]

Ilyichev saved his venom for Ehrenburg. That day and the next, when Khrushchev underscored Ilyichev's attack, were among the most extraordinary and difficult in Ehrenburg's life. Soviet critics had lambasted his work for forty years, ever since *Julio Jurenito* and *Nikolai Kurbov* first offended orthodox Marxist taste, but never before had the leadership of the country—including the premier—decried his work so thoroughly and categorically. "Who amongst us, who sat for two long days at this meeting," Margarita Aliger recalled, "can really recollect what they criticized Ilya Ehrenburg for? But who amongst us can forget how monstrously and disgracefully it all sounded?"[2]

In keeping with the ostensible theme of the meeting Ilyichev began discussing creative freedom and singled out Ehrenburg for daring to use Lenin's words to support tolerance for artistic experimentation; this was not, however, his greatest transgression. Ehrenburg's memoirs had raised too many thorny issues for the Kremlin and his "theory of silence" still stuck in their throats. "It is impossible, comrades," Ilyichev told the assembly, "to agree with such a false, incorrect 'theory.'"

> First of all, it casts a shadow on the Soviet people who were enthusiastically building socialism and who believed in the correctness of Stalin's actions. Yet according to I. Ehrenburg, one might think that they all, knowing about the deviations from Leninism, were merely saving their own skins and thereby helping the evil to grow stronger. . . . It is necessary only to state clearly: *The Communists, our Party, never made silence a principle.*

Ilyichev further attempted to embarrass Ehrenburg with his own words. Sitting in the audience, Ehrenburg had to listen as Ilyichev read his paeans to Stalin back to him before six hundred colleagues:

> Incidentally, the "theory of silence" is not true even in regard to I. Ehrenburg himself. After all, you were not silent then, Ilya Grigorevich, but eulogized, and eulogized with all your talent as a publicist.
>   Does what you said about Stalin in 1951 really look like silence? You said literally the following: He "helped me, as all of us, to write much of what I have written, and he will help me to write what I am dreaming about." And after Stalin's death you—expressing your

personal sentiments, and not somebody's will—wrote of him as a person who "loved people, knew their weaknesses and strength, understood the tears of the mother who had lost her son in the war, understood the labor of the miner and the stonemason," one who "knew the thoughts and feelings of hundreds of millions of people, expressed their hopes, their will to happiness, their thirst for peace."

If I quote your words, it is not in order to single you out from among the many and blame you for the words quoted. We all spoke and wrote thus at the time, without being hypocritical. We believed and wrote. And you, it turns out, did not believe but wrote! These are different positions!

This was the heart of the party's response to Ehrenburg's challenge: the party's sincerity and its belief in Stalin's genius prevented those closest to Stalin from understanding that innocent people were among his victims. Now Ehrenburg acknowledged that he had known and still chose to praise the dictator. According to Ilyichev's logic, it was Ehrenburg, not the party, who had indulged in cynical and obsequious flattery.

Ehrenburg sat quietly through Ilyichev's long tirade "with his eyes lowered, his lips set," one witness later remembered. "I don't think he moved a muscle for nearly an hour. For the first time, all of us in the auditorium felt the chill of the axe on our necks."[3] When Ilyichev finished, Ehrenburg left the hall. On his way out, he did not hesitate to acknowlege the end of his hopes. "I shall never see the flowering of Soviet art," he grimly admitted to a friend. "But you will see it—in twenty years."[4]

Ilyichev's speech was published in *Pravda* the next day, at the same time that Khrushchev delivered an even longer and more fulsome assault on the creative community. Once again, Ehrenburg was at the center of the Soviet leader's scorn.

The tenor of Khrushchev's long speech—it took up nearly fifteen thousand words in *Pravda* on March 10—embodied the party's dogmatic approach to the arts and Khrushchev's own provincial, boorish suspicions. Art was nothing more than one of "the party's ideological weapons" that needed to be maintained in proper "combat order" to be effective "in the battle for communism." The party could not "allow dirty daubs to be presented as works of art, dirty daubs which can be made by any donkey with its tail." Absolute freedom could never be recognized. The "outbursts of lunatics" had to be controlled and

Khrushchev reminded his audience that "there is the straitjacket . . . to restrain them in their wildness and stop them [from] doing harm to themselves and others."[5]

In this context of crude language and outright threats Khrushchev addressed Ehrenburg; the memoirs had to be explicitly condemned. Khrushchev reminded the audience that Ehrenburg had once

> joined the party and then left it. He evidently took no direct part in the Socialist revolution, but assumed the attitude of an onlooker. I think we shall not be distorting the truth if we say that it is from that same position that Comrade Ehrenburg appraises our revolution and the entire subsequent period of Socialist construction in his memoirs, *People, Years, Life.*

For the fourth time the party leadership refuted Ehrenburg's "theory of silence." Khrushchev himself issued a definitive statement of the party's position. "The question arises whether the leading cadres of the party knew about, let us say, the arrests of people in that period," he declared. "Yes, they did. But did they know that absolutely innocent people were arrested? No, they did not. They believed in Stalin and could not even imagine that repression could be used against honest people devoted to our cause."

Khrushchev even admitted his own devotion to the dictator. "At Stalin's funeral, many, including myself, were in tears. These were sincere tears. Although we knew about some of Stalin's personal shortcomings, we believed in him." Coming directly from Khrushchev, whose courageous initiative had led to the denunciations at the Twentieth and Twenty-second Party Congresses, this renewed evaluation of Stalin marked a tragic retreat for Khrushchev himself. The conservatives achieved what they sought: a partial rehabilitation of Stalin and a halt to Khrushchev's efforts to extend de-Stalinization deeper within the party.

Ehrenburg was no longer important. Following the March meetings, he continued to be rebuked in the press but was not threatened again in a serious way. Ehrenburg also made it manifestly clear that he would neither recant nor apologize. Further attacks against him would only make the regime look more foolish, especially in the eyes of left-wing, Western intellectuals, many of whom knew and admired Ehrenburg.

Nevertheless, Ehrenburg was devastated by this official onslaught.

His memoirs were not yet complete and he worried that he would not be able to resume publication. Friends tried to console him. His previous secretary, Yelena Zonina, suggested he write "for the drawer" and not bother with Khrushchev and the censors. Ehrenburg could not accept her advice. "I've been dragging the cart for so long," he told her, "that I can't live without it."[6] He was still tied to the regime, however tenuously. Unlike Pasternak and others, he was not prepared to send his manuscript abroad and thereby cut himself off from the Kremlin.

Andrei Sinyavsky and Igor Golomshtock, who had worked with Ehrenburg on the Picasso volume, stopped by his apartment on Gorky Street and were shocked by his outspoken anger. "Ehrenburg was lying in bed, swearing at the top of his voice. He kept calling them scoundrels and bandits. I knew he would be upset," Sinyavsky recalled in an interview, "but I could not understand why he was so morose and depressed, why he was reacting so deeply to Khrushchev's attack."[7] The main reason was far more simple than Sinyavsky knew, but only Ehrenburg's closest friends understood. Ehrenburg was afraid he would not be permitted to travel, making it impossible to see Liselotte Mehr. He remained secluded in his Moscow apartment, not wanting to appear on the street for fear that he would be recognized and subjected to a spontaneous demonstration of support "that would not have been helpful at the time," as the U.S. embassy noted. "Therefore, he . . . preferred to live very quietly until the clouds had passed."[8] After a few days his friend Nikolai Vasilenko came by and talked Ehrenburg into going to the dacha, where work in the greenhouse and garden revived his spirits.

Gardening was not Ehrenburg's only comfort. In the days following Ilyichev's and Khrushchev's speeches he received hundreds of telegrams and letters from all over the Soviet Union. Nadezhda Mandelstam wrote him a moving letter (reproduced in full in the introduction to this volume). "Now, after the latest events," she consoled him, "it is obvious how much you did and are doing to relax our usual ways, how great your role is in our life and how we should be grateful to you. *Everyone* [sic] understands this now."[9]

The dissident Frida Vigdorova wrote to him on March 8.

Many times, upon returning from different business trips, I have wanted to write to you or describe what I have had occasion to hear. But I did not get to it. Or a certain thought got in my way: Ilya Grigorevich knows all this himself.

But now I would like to say there has not been a time, when far from Moscow I have not heard the question, "Do you see Ehrenburg? You know him? There is someone whose hand I would like to shake."

And just recently in a Byelorussian village a kolkhoz chairman . . . told me what I have already heard more than once: "At the front, with any newspaper, let it wrap tobacco. But with an article by Ehrenburg, never!"

From myself, I would also like to say: I love you very much. And I am very grateful to you for everything that you are saying to people—in your articles and books.

Perhaps all of this is unnecessary for you to hear. If so, please forgive me.

I wish you peace and good health with all my soul.

> With profound respect,
> F. Vigdorova[10]

At the end of April Ehrenburg's old friend Anna Seghers sent him the following note (in French) after visiting him in Moscow.

I was terribly sad to see you so sad and not be able to find the words to make you feel happier. I was especially sad to see a man like you, who has done so many great things in peace and in war for everyone, have to endure so many attacks. But how can they be avoided in our long, difficult, packed, dense, passionate, useful lives?[11]

These voices of comfort only partly compensated for the abuse Ehrenburg continued to endure. Khrushchev's speech was reprinted in the March issue of *Novy Mir*, the same issue that carried the final installment of Book Five of *People, Years, Life*. (The March issue was actually delayed until well into April.) Where else but in the Soviet Union could a government leader's denunciation appear alongside the literary work it sought to condemn? The situation also reflected how much had changed for the better since Stalin's death: Ehrenburg was not arrested and chapters of his memoirs continued to appear. Nevertheless, Alexander Tvardovsky had to endorse Khrushchev's attack. In an interview with Henry Shapiro that ran in the West and in *Pravda* in May, Tvardovsky commented that "We take [Khrushchev's] criticism of Ehrenburg's memoirs very seriously and responsibly, and we are confident that Ilya Grigorevich will draw the necessary conclusions from it."[12]

BOOK SIX

Ehrenburg had begun work on Book Six of his memoirs in the late fall of 1962. This was supposed to be the concluding section covering 1945 to 1953, the final, terrifying years of Stalin's life when foreign policy was dominated by the onset of the cold war and domestic life was dominated by Stalin's last episodes of repression.

The events of March 1963 made it impossible for Ehrenburg to write and he put off finishing these chapters. "I have not answered you for a long time," he wrote to Yelizaveta Polonskaya on April 10, 1963. "My mood and my organism have ceased to work, reminding me of the limits of age. In the third issue of *Novy Mir*, you will soon see the abbreviated ending of Book Five. The Sixth, which I had been writing, I have put off for a better time."[13]

As the spring progressed, Ehrenburg waited for a change in his situation, yet nothing happened. Editors stopped calling him for articles. Publication of a second separate volume of memoirs, with Books Three and Four, was stalled. He had to deflect invitations to attend conferences in Europe. Frustrated and impatient, Ehrenburg sent a long letter to the Kremlin. As always in such appeals, Ehrenburg searched for an approach that could touch the understanding of the Soviet premier.

April 27, 1963

Dear Nikita Sergeyevich!

Comrade Lebedev has informed me that you have agreed to see me, but that at the moment you have a great deal of urgent work. I well understand this and would like to ask you to spare a few minutes for my letter in which I will try to set forth the most important points.

It is already two months that I am in a very difficult situation. I am appealing to you as the leader of the party, as the head of state, and as a man, with a request to determine what work I can count on in the future. In regional newspapers they are calling me "an internal émigré." The foreign press is using my name as they conduct a recurrent campaign against our ideas, our Motherland. I cannot live this way. For more than thirty years, all my work has been connected with the Soviet people, with the ideas of communism. I never betrayed them under the most excruciating conditions—among our enemies.

Although I am seventy-two years old, I do not want to move on to the status of a pensioner. I want and can continue to work. But I am looked upon with caution.

Let me provide several examples relating to my public activity. An agreement has been reached on cooperation between the France-USSR Friendship Society . . . and the Soviet Society of Friendship, along with the USSR-France Society, whose president I happen to be. . . . One of the presidents of the French society who was in Moscow asked me why my signature would not be on the document. I wriggled out of answering as well as I could, but saw that my explanations did not seem persuasive to him. Branting called me from Stockholm and asked about the scheduled session of the "Round Table." It seems to me that the support of such people as Noel-Baker and Jules Moch, who are otherwise far from us, for our proposals on the abolition of [nuclear] testing could be useful. But I had to reply to Branting that I was ill, and again I understood that my answer did not satisfy him. Professor Bernal visited me and posed questions connected to the forthcoming session of the World Peace Council. Lack of confidence that I will remain in the Partisans of Peace tied my hands. The France-USSR Society, together with the mayor of Nice, wants to put up a memorial plaque on the house where Chekhov lived. They have asked me to give a speech about Chekhov. I have not put this question before the Central Committee while the relationship of leading comrades toward me has not been clarified . . .

At my age, it is hard to change my artistic tastes, but I am a disciplined man and will neither speak nor write here or abroad in a way that would contradict the decisions of the party.

Regarding my literary work, the situation is not well-defined. Goslitizdat, which brought out the first volume of my collected works on subscription, does not know what will happen in the future. The editor says that the management is "awaiting instructions." At Sovietsky Pisatel publishing house, my own book—parts three and four of the memoirs—has been waiting since December; Glavlit has approved it, but they are also awaiting instructions.

If an article could appear in our press on an international theme, about the struggle for peace with my signature, this would help various organizations define their relationship to my subsequent work. It seems to me that such a statement or mention somewhere of my civic work would cut the wings off the anti-Soviet campaign connected to my name.[14]

Khrushchev did not respond. Not until August, when a conference of European writers gathered to discuss the modern novel, was Ehrenburg summoned to see him. The conference, which had begun on August 5, was not going well. Held under the auspices of UNESCO, the Soviets had agreed to host the conference as a means to bolster Soviet prestige without having to make any significant change in policy. This kind of closed discussion with well-known Western writers (almost all of whom were considered left-wing figures in their own countries) fit easily into the Soviet way of doing things, but the cultural bureaucrats miscalculated. Jean-Paul Sartre and Simone de Beauvoir, Nathalie Sarraute and Alain Robbe-Grillet, Hans Magnus Enzenberger, William Golding, Angus Wilson—all were sophisticated writers devoted to the liberal tradition of artistic experimentation. When veteran Soviet writers began to ridicule Western art and literature, the proceedings quickly turned into "a dialogue of the deaf," as Nathalie Sarraute described it. Konstantin Fedin went so far as to claim that Marcel Proust, James Joyce, Franz Kafka, and Samuel Beckett were infected with the virus of decadence, and in a telling admission connected Soviet unwillingness to publish these modern classics with the ban on some of Russian literature's own twentieth-century innovators. "If Soviet novelists were to follow the intuitive techniques of Proust," Fedin explained, "it would then be logical to revive some of our native-born modernists as well." Fedin compounded the atmosphere of ill-will by comparing a writer's responsibility with that of an airplane pilot: neither has the right "to be himself at the expense of others." The French novelist Alain Robbe-Grillet immediately objected. Literature "is not a means of transport," he insisted. Soviet attacks on the "new" French novel were "a scandal for a country that calls itself the cradle of revolution."[15]

The proceedings reached an impasse and might have broken up in complete disarray if Ehrenburg had not been dispatched to mediate matters. He originally had refused to attend and was in no mood to make the regime look good by attending the conference "in order to show the European writers that he was healthy and alive," as the *Novy Mir* critic Vladimir Lakshin noted in his diary. "[Ehrenburg] sent an angry letter to Surkov, that he was on the brink of death, that he did not know who he was or what he was in his own country." According to Lakshin, Tvardovsky asked Khrushchev's adviser Vladimir Lebedev to consider Ehrenburg's letter; this led to a personal appeal from Khrushchev to assuage Ehrenburg's anger and pride.[16]

Khrushchev summoned Ehrenburg to the Kremlin, where the two men had a long, private discussion. Khrushchev apologized to Ehrenburg, explaining that he had been given misleading quotations from *People, Years, Life*. Now that he had had a chance to read the book, he found nothing objectionable. For a writer of Ehrenburg's stature and experience, Khrushchev added, there was no need of censorship; Ehrenburg was free to continue his work.

Ehrenburg left soon after for Leningrad. Alexander Tvardovsky understood that no leaders of the Writers' Union would take the trouble to meet Ehrenburg at the airport, a customary courtesy whose absence could so offend Ehrenburg that he might take the next flight back to Moscow. Determined to treat Ehrenburg with respect, Tvardovsky and Lakshin traveled to the airport on their own and accompanied him to the hotel.

Ehrenburg appeared on the second day of the conference. Rumors preceded his arrival—that he had either met personally with Khrushchev or talked with the premier over the phone, in either case a dramatic sign of his rehabilitation. For this reason, "his speech was awarded with particular excitement by the young Soviet writers," the German novelist Hans Werner Richter wrote later that summer, "and this excitement infected the Western conferees." Ehrenburg "spoke with the wisdom of a man who has endured many ordeals" and he did not hesitate to rebuke his Soviet colleagues.[17] "For a person to speak of books he has not read, or of pictures he has not seen," Ehrenburg began, "inevitably means for him to fall into scholastic and dogmatic arguments. . . . It would be better for us writers to renounce it." Ehrenburg was probably the only Soviet writer of his generation to have met James Joyce or personally known Kafka's close friend Max Brod. In his comments Ehrenburg tried to define their work in such a way that it would be acceptable to the heavily didactic Soviet approach to literature.

> Can one reject Joyce and Kafka, two great writers who do not resemble one another? To me this is the past, they are historical phenomena. I do not make banners of them, but neither do I make targets of them . . .

Joyce found the most minute psychological details, the mastery of the interior monologue . . . Joyce is a writer for writers.

As for Kafka, he foresaw the terrible world of fascism. His works, diaries, and letters show that he was a seismographic station that because of the sensitivity of the apparatus registered the first tremors. They are up in arms against him, as if he were our contemporary and ought to be an optimist, but he was a major historical phenomenon.

Finally, Ehrenburg could not help but include a swipe at his shameless Soviet colleagues for their provincial and ignorant remarks. Who else but Ehrenburg, among all the assembled writers, could refer without embarrassment to his speech at the 1934 Writers' Congress?

It seems to me that it is unnecessary to be afraid of experiments. In my book I have quoted the words of Jean-Richard Bloch at the First Congress of Soviet Writers. He said that there must be writers for the millions and writers for five thousand readers, as there must be pilots "who work on already tested models" and test pilots. Charlatanism can and should be swept aside, but the right of experiment to exist in literature must not be denied.[18]

Ehrenburg's speech saved the entire conference. "The applause for Ehrenburg," Hans Werner Richter recalled, "was more than a sign of simple approval. . . . It seems as if in one instant, the ears of the deaf were opened."[19] For the European writers, who knew that Ehrenburg had been living under a cloud, his presence and his balanced observations calmed their worst fears about Soviet culture. The West German critic Hans Magnus Enzenberger had earlier observed that German writers such as Günter Grass could not deal with the country's Fascist experience using a straightforward realistic style; they had to find new methods to portray life in Germany. Enzenberger's comment provoked a stirring response among the more liberal Soviet writers, who understood that modernist methods might well be useful to evoke the Stalin era. Tvardovsky, Vasily Aksyonov, and the Leningrad writer Daniel Granin spoke up with thoughtful remarks, giving their Western counterparts hope that a dialogue with Soviet writers could lead to a fruitful exchange of experience and ideas.

Ehrenburg felt newly confident and vindicated. That September he contributed his first piece in many months to the central press. Writing in *Pravda* on September 6, he described the recently signed Test Ban Treaty in glowing, optimistic terms. For Ehrenburg the treaty, which eliminated nuclear testing in the air, on land, and in the oceans, justified his years of effort in the peace movement. China, however, was hostile to the treaty and Ehrenburg urged its leaders to reconsider. His column was both a personal expression of hope and a reflection of official Soviet policy.[20]

Two days later Ehrenburg took another important step. In spite of a resurgence in his prestige, his memoirs continued to meet resistance at Sovietsky Pisatel publishers. His *Collected Works*, the first volume of which appeared in 1962 (containing *Julio Jurenito*, *Trust*, *D.E.*, and *Thirteen Pipes*, none of which had appeared in the Soviet Union since the 1920s), were being held up as well. This time Ehrenburg appealed to Leonid Ilyichev with an explanation of his difficulties. Given Khrushchev's recent blessing, Ehrenburg had every reason to believe that Ilyichev—who had pilloried him twice—would now have to resolve Ehrenburg's concerns. Ehrenburg in fact regarded Ilyichev as "a typical *zhidomor* [Jew-baiter]" and must have gained more than a measure of satisfaction in appealing to him now.[21]

September 8, 1963

Dear Leonid Fyodorovich [Ilyichev]!

I am writing to you for the following reason. Books Three and Four of my memoirs *People, Years, Life* were supposed to come out last year as a separate volume . . . Glavlit had already passed the proofs. This year, at the beginning of August, the publishers asked me to make a major revision of these two sections in order to meet certain objections.

During my meeting with N. S. Khrushchev, I informed him about this, and added that, in my opinion, to revise a book which has already been published in a journal and in translations in a number of foreign countries was not only unacceptable to me personally, but also politically harmful. Nikita Sergeyevich agreed with me. Subsequently, Comrade Lesyuchevsky sent me a letter confirming his earlier proposal. I sent Comrade Lesyuchevsky's letter to Comrade Khrushchev's office, but I fully understand that N. S. Khrushchev cannot be concerned with the publication of one volume or another. I hope that you can help because I am now finishing Book Six, the concluding section, about which I spoke with N. S. Khrushchev.

I have one additional request. The second volume of my *Collected Works* has been submitted by Goslitizdat to Glavlit, but the latter has yet to respond.

Many thanks in advance. I am writing rather than calling in order not to take up your time.

Sincerely yours,
Ilya Ehrenburg[22]

Ilyichev evidently complied with all of Ehrenburg's requests; the separate volume of memoirs was published and the subsequent volumes of his *Collected Works* soon began to reach subscribers. But even here Khrushchev's recent endorsement did not smooth over all of Ehrenburg's difficulties. Sovietsky Pisatel publishers required him to add an apology for the memoirs; this note "from the author" appeared at the front of the volume:

My book *People, Years, Life* has provoked many arguments and rebukes. In connection with this, I would like to emphasize once again that this book is the story of my life, about searchings, confusions, and the fortunes of one man. It is, to be sure, extremely subjective, and I do not pretend by any means to give the history of an epoch or even the history of a narrow circle within the Soviet intelligentsia. I have written about people whom fate has brought my way, about books and pictures which played a role in my life. There are many great artists and writers about whom I have not written because I did not know them personally or did not know them well enough. This book is closer to a confession than a chronicle, and I believe that the readers will understand it correctly. I am presently working on the sixth, concluding section, in which I will try to connect my personal path with the events of the epoch in which I lived.

What Ehrenburg submitted was so unlike the recantation the editors were seeking that they inserted an introduction of their own in front of his. Apparently the memoirs had become so politically sensitive that they needed a warning label. Under the heading "from the publisher," readers were cautioned that the book "has deviations from historical truth."

In the author's preface to this edition, I. Ehrenburg writes that his book is "extremely subjective." Unfortunately, this extreme subjectivity appears not only in particular sections, in the characteristics of one or another person, in the appraisal of individual events and facts, but in the interpretation of important sides and processes of social life—there, where I. Ehrenburg appears in the role of a witness and judge of history. This is what leads to violations of historical truth.

Just like Ilyichev, Yermilov, and Khrushchev before them, the publishers warned the reader to beware of Ehrenburg's "theory of silence," which was said to present a "false" picture of how the population behaved under Stalin.[23]

That fall Ehrenburg resumed work on Book Six. As in each of the previous sections, this one had particular themes that he knew would provoke consternation and editorial demands. The last years of Stalin's life included Zhdanov's onslaught against the arts and the anti-cosmopolitan campaign against the country's Jewish community. Ehrenburg's text treated these subjects more candidly than any previous Soviet account. Once the manuscript reached *Novy Mir* in March 1964, however, Ehrenburg understood that the journal was under tremendous pressure to edit these chapters in such a way that their historical effectiveness would be seriously compromised.

Ehrenburg managed as best he could. The list of corrections he received in April 1964 was long and difficult, often involving changes that struck at the heart of what he was trying to say. In dealing with *Novy Mir* it became increasingly obvious to Ehrenburg that Khrushchev's assurances in August were having no influence and that if he wanted to see these chapters appear at all it would be necessary to accept many changes he would prefer to resist. He was still revising at the end of May, hoping the material could be published that summer; then on June 24 Tvardovsky himself sent Ehrenburg an unusually sharp letter. From its timing—the chapters were ready to be printed—it is evident that the Central Committee was leaning on Tvardovsky to impede publication.

Dear Ilya Grigorevich!
I have read through Book Six of your memoirs, this time in proof form. As editor, I will have to delete certain passages which we have already talked about at length, "haggled over," and discussed in letters.

This is my final decision, and I must inform you that, unless these cuts are accepted, I cannot pass the proof for publication.

1. Your explanation for the missing chapter on Fadeyev, which puts our editorial board in a curious and equivocal position. . . .

3. The next-to-last paragraph of Chapter 6, concerning the coming generation, which seems like an attack on the development of the individual under Communism.

4. The addition of the renegade [Howard] Fast among the names of the most famous writers who have joined in the struggle for peace . . .

5. The reference to a certain "unidentifiable" Nikolai Ivanovich (Bukharin).

Please be sure to let me know what you intend to do about these points.

> Respectfully,
> A. Tvardovsky

Ehrenburg responded to Tvardovsky the next day and partially gave in. Although he agreed to remove Fast's name, he challenged Tvardovsky to explain why the memoir should not contain more information on Alexander Fadeyev when further recollections had been promised. As for his reference to Bukharin, Ehrenburg offered a compromise that was eventually accepted.

> I cannot agree that Nikolai Ivanovich is not to be mentioned. But if this widely used name and patronymic strike you as politically unacceptable, I am ready to add Semyon Borisovich [a childhood friend Semyon Chlenov, who was arrested in 1937] and Grigory Mikhailovich [Commander Shtern, who was executed in October 1941; Ehrenburg had known him in Spain].
>
> I am annoyed by the tone of your letter. It is so unlike the tone of our conversation in your office. I ascribe this to your feeling upset, and not to your attitude towards me personally.[24]

This exchange with Tvardovsky had its effect, for the material was prepared for publication that summer. But then an explicit prohibition to publish Book Six reached *Novy Mir*. Ehrenburg realized that Khrushchev himself would not have issued this instruction and tried one last time on August 14, 1964, to appeal directly to the premier. By then Ehrenburg had reason to believe that hard-line elements within the regime were interfering with his life in other ways; just as in 1963, he was not being asked for articles, while opportunities to meet with students and even with his own electoral constituents were being denied him. All of this he shared with Khrushchev, desperately hoping to salvage his own work and, indirectly, to alert Khrushchev to what this harassment must mean for Khrushchev's own political authority.

Dear Nikita Sergeyevich!

You agreed to see me a year ago. I remember our talk with a feeling of sincere gratitude. If I am disturbing you once again, it is only because my present circumstances have become complicated and extremely unpleasant. We were able to talk with each other as one man to another, and no one else was present. I trust that the present letter will reach you.

I left our last meeting feeling encouraged. We discussed the need for me to finish my volume of memoirs. I have now done this. A. T. Tvardovsky and the editorial board of *Novy Mir*, after receiving the manuscript, asked me to make several changes, which I duly did. The editorial board publicly announced that publication would be completed in 1964.

The opening section of the sixth and final part of the memoirs was due to appear in the July issue of the journal. Recently, the editorial board told me they had been obliged to omit Book Six because of instructions from above, and they were powerless to resolve the question. This part of my book covers the period from the end of the war to the end of 1953.

I believe that in describing this period, I maintained correct political proportions, and so does the editorial board. At the close of the book, I write about the period following Stalin's death, when our country entered a new phase. The book ends with some reflections on those same issues which we discussed together. The book has no political sensations, nor anything that might be exploited by our adversaries.

I spent more than five years working on these memoirs. So for me, they are a very important work. You will, I am sure, understand how painful it is for a writer, especially for one who is no longer young, to see his work suddenly cut short. There is the additional point that the readers, both in our country and abroad, will not fail to realize that publication of the final section of the work has been prohibited.

Personally, Nikita Sergeyevich, I find all this distressing. For more than thirty years, I regularly worked for the Soviet press. This year is the first in the whole of that time during which not one newspaper has approached me with a request for any kind of article. Let me provide just one small example. A group of Moscow physics students asked me to talk with them about my meetings with Joliot-Curie and Einstein. At the last moment, the meeting was cancelled. I have even found it difficult to arrange meetings with my constituents. I am willing and able to continue my work as a writer and as a journalist, and to participate in the Struggle for Peace. But the banning of my memoirs sets me back to where I was before our meeting.

Neither of us is young anymore. I am sure you will understand me and issue an instruction authorizing the journal to publish this work.[25]

Khrushchev did not respond, but five days after Ehrenburg sent this letter Alexander Tvardovsky met with Vladimir Lebedev. Lebedev was growing impatient with Ehrenburg's persistence and blamed Tvardovsky "for forcing the memoirs" upon the regime. Tvardovsky did not back down. "Who made Ehrenburg a deputy, a laureate, and a famous European writer?" Tvardovsky challenged Lebedev. "As for the latter," Tvardovsky made clear, "Ehrenburg achieved this on his own."[26]

In September the Presidium itself reviewed Book Six and decided it could be published only if further changes were made in its treatment of the "Jewish question" and the country's artistic life. Ehrenburg refused to give in. The situation looked hopeless.

Then in October Khrushchev was removed from office by conservative forces who were fed up with his reforms and his failed domestic and foreign policy ventures. Suddenly, paradoxically, the opportunity to complete publication of *People, Years, Life* began to improve, despite the fact that the new regime, led by Leonid Brezhnev and Alexei Kosygin, was hostile to liberal initiatives of any kind, as events would soon make clear. Nonetheless, during their initial months in power they were anxious to reassure the country's intellectuals that they did not share Khrushchev's crude prejudices. Their policies even seemed encouraging. The country's scientists were pleased when the charlatan biologist Trofim Lysenko, whom Khrushchev had supported and whose false genetic theories had disrupted scientific life and agricultural research for decades, was removed from positions of administrative authority. *Pravda*'s new editor, Alexei Rumyantsev, even called for greater creative freedom, while the intellectual community was assured that censorship would not be tightened.

Khrushchev had publicly castigated Ehrenburg and the suppression of Book Six of his memoirs was perceived as connected to Khrushchev's shallow and inconsistent regard for culture. Ehrenburg looked as if he had been a victim of Khrushchev's policies rather than the target of those who were working to undermine Khrushchev, as was actually the case. Ehrenburg evidently exploited this perception to his advantage. In January 1965 Book Six began a four-month series of installments; Ehrenburg was able to see what he believed would be the concluding portion of his memoir in *Novy Mir*.

"It has not been easy for me to write this book," he confessed. "I knew when I started that I would be criticized, by some who would say that I kept silent about too many things and by others, who would say that I spoke about too much." In a memoir devoted to so many people, Ehrenburg ended with a quiet tribute to those who had not survived. "When I wrote about friends who are no more," he recalled, "I sometimes stopped working, went up to the window, and stood there as people stand at meetings to honor the dead. I did not look at the leaves or at the snow drifts. I saw only the face dear to me. Many pages of this book were dictated by love. I love life, I do not repent, I do not regret what I have lived through and what I have experienced. I only regret," he concluded, "how much I have not done and not written, how much I have not grieved and not loved." He thought he was finished. "Today I have too many desires and, I fear, not enough strength."[27]

Ehrenburg was not finished. A year and a half later he would begin a further series of chapters. The initial Brezhnev years embittered him, fueling his energy and willingness to speak out. With Book Seven he wanted to chronicle the Khrushchev period as a challenge to the reactionary policies of his successors; but Ehrenburg was almost seventy-five and though he charted another mountain, he did not live long enough to climb it.

SEVENTEEN

Ehrenburg and Dissent

Ilya Ehrenburg was not a Soviet dissident. A long-time member of the Supreme Soviet, an honored writer, a frequent traveler to Europe on official assignments—Ehrenburg enjoyed a privileged status until the end of his life. Even at the height of his struggle over the memoirs he did not consider publishing chapters independently in the West in order to thwart the censors.

Ehrenburg did, however, have numerous contacts with writers and activists whose work helped to inspire the human rights movement. As early as 1957, he was in touch with the journalist Frida Vigdorova; they worked together on behalf of students who got into trouble with the authorities on political grounds and helped to defend a teacher in Grodno who had been unjustly dismissed from her job. Frida Vigdorova is sometimes referred to as "the first dissident" owing to her efforts on behalf of the young poet Joseph Brodsky.[1]

Arrested as a "parasite" in December 1963, Brodsky was a twenty-three-year-old poet with an established reputation for the quality of his verse and translations.* Although he had quit secondary school, he had learned Polish and English on his own and was especially admired for translations of the metaphysical poets, particularly John Donne.

Frida Vigdorova understood that the regime wanted to punish Brodsky for his independent life and use his case to intimidate other young people. At his trial in March 1964, Vigdorova sat in the courtroom and brazenly compiled a transcript of the proceedings, an account that reached the West and alerted international public opinion to the outrageous character of the case. Vigdorova showed Ehrenburg the transcript and sought his advice on how best to proceed. Through her efforts, three Lenin Prize winners came to Brodsky's defense: Dmitri Shostakovich, Samuil Marshak, and Kornei Chukovsky. All wrote to Khrushchev. Ehrenburg signed an appeal as well. Although such protests did not prevent Brodsky's conviction and sentence of five years in Archangelsk in the Arctic north, he was permitted to return to Leningrad after two years. International and domestic attention to his case made the difference.[2]

Ehrenburg also helped Kiril Ouspensky, who was the first member of the Writers' Union to be arrested after Stalin's death. Ouspensky befriended a group of younger people (including Joseph Brodsky) who would gather at his home to discuss politics. As the author of several books and a veteran—Ouspensky had served in army intelligence in Vienna after the war—he had a great influence on this circle of artists and poets, sharing hard-to-find literature and encouraging them to look critically at government and society. An informer in the group exposed Ouspensky to the authorities and he was arrested in Leningrad on July 19, 1960. Ehrenburg learned about the case and together with Alexander Tvardovsky and another writer, Yury Dombrovsky, intervened on Ouspensky's behalf; he was eventually released on July 31, 1964, a full year before his sentence was due to expire. Ouspensky credited the discreet help of these writers for gaining his freedom.

---

*Under Soviet law, "parasitism" referred to people "who evade socially useful work;" the Supreme Soviet had issued a decree against parasitism in 1961 as a means to curb numerous idlers who practiced petty theft and conspicuously consumed liquor in public. The same law could also be used to punish people with nonconformist beliefs by first depriving them of their work and then using this lack of employment as a pretext to send them into exile.

—

In the early 1960s the character of *samizdat* began to broaden as individuals circulated politically charged literature. With the release of millions of political prisoners it was inevitable that writers such as Alexander Solzhenitsyn, Eugeniya Ginzburg, and Varlam Shalamov, among many others, would recount their experiences in memoirs and stories. Solzhenitsyn succeeded in publishing *One Day in the Life of Ivan Denisovich* in Moscow. Eugeniya Ginzburg chose to send her memoirs *Into the Whirlwind* and later, *Out of the Whirlwind*, to the West, where their publication stirred great interest in the fate of Soviet women political prisoners. Ehrenburg's last private secretary, Natalya Stolyarova, who worked with him from 1956 until the end of his life, had also been a long-time inmate. Born in France in 1912, she was the daughter of a famous Socialist Revolutionary, Natalya Klimova, who had tried unsuccessfully to assassinate the czar's prime minister, Pyotr Stolypin, in 1906. Stolyarova befriended Irina Ehrenburg in Paris, where they were in high school together. Although she was a French citizen, Stolyarova had once vowed to live in the Soviet Union out of love for Russia, a process she initiated in 1935. The Soviet consulate, however, refused to help until Ehrenburg wrote her a letter of reference. She was arrested in 1938 during the Great Purge and spent eighteen years in confinement and exile. Stolyarova knew Eugeniya Ginzburg from the camps and when she completed her memoirs, Stolyarova arranged for Ginzburg to meet Ehrenburg and to have him read her account, which he greatly admired. On subsequent trips to Europe Ehrenburg found foreign editions of Ginzburg's memoirs and brought them back to Moscow for her.

Eugeniya Ginzburg was among those who read *People, Years, Life* in *Novy Mir*. She had not yet finished her own memoirs or met Ehrenburg personally when she wrote to him on March 20, 1961.

I have just read Book II of *People, Years, Life* and I wanted to thank you . . .

I am fifteen years younger than you. But it does not matter. The end will come soon, especially when you consider the special character of my biography. Here by the final frontier, in a city alien to me, where fate has brought me after the North, how sweet was this accidental happiness—to open *Novy Mir* and suddenly read something so true and genuine.

When I was seventeen or eighteen, I knew whole pages of *Julio
Jurenito* by heart. . . . Now once again I am bowled over and want to
thank you for this work, for writing as you did about Mandelstam,
about Meyerhold, about Tabidze and Yashvili, and many others. I
hope that God will make everything good for you and that you will
be able to finish this book.[3]

Natalya Stolyarova felt especially comfortable as Ehrenburg's secretary
owing to all the appeals he would receive from ex-prisoners. They
needed help finding an apartment, gaining permission to live in a
major city, or resuming their education. Just as she arranged for Ehrenburg to read Eugeniya Ginzburg's memoirs, she managed to obtain an
advance copy of *One Day In the Life of Ivan Denisovich* and to show it
to Ehrenburg months before the novella hit Soviet newsstands.
(According to Solzhenitsyn, Ehrenburg "hated" the book, but in fact
he mentions Solzhenitsyn and his work on several occasions in his
memoirs, always in positive and admiring ways.[4]) Working with Stolyarova every day gave Ehrenburg access to *samizdat*, to news of ex-
prisoners, and to news of political dissent as it broadened and matured,
first under Khrushchev and then under Brezhnev.

Stolyarova became an intimate and important friend to Alexander
Solzhenitsyn. Using her many contacts with foreign visitors to Moscow,
she helped Solzhenitsyn smuggle out microfilm copies of much of his
work, including *The First Circle* and *The Gulag Archipelago*. Stolyarova
also appeared in *The Gulag Archipelago*, where she provided information
about Moscow's Butyrki prison and Siberian labor camps.[5] Even after
Solzhenitsyn's forced exile in 1974 she remained one of his principal
assistants in Moscow, helping to distribute support to the families of
political prisoners from funds Solzhenitsyn contributed.

Of all the dissident authors of the 1960s, however, Ehrenburg's closest relationship was with Nadezhda Mandelstam. Her two memoirs,
Hope Against Hope and *Hope Abandoned*, are among the most eloquent
volumes about the Stalin years. Nadezhda Mandelstam showed Ehrenburg an early draft and he was one of the few if not the only person
to challenge her judgment. Nadezhda Mandelstam was famous for her
acerbic tongue and Ehrenburg, like everyone else, was wary of her
anger; but after reading the manuscript Ehrenburg argued with her,
even shouted, trying to convince her to delete accusations against
"people who were considered informers, but who did not betray any-

one. You cannot make such accusations against people who are no longer alive and cannot defend themselves," Ehrenburg insisted. His arguments convinced Mandelstam and she revised her text.[6]

Ehrenburg also played a decisive role in the staging of a public gathering to honor both Osip and Nadezhda Mandelstam on May 13, 1965. With Ehrenburg's help an auditorium was secured at Moscow State University, where several hundred people gathered, many of them sitting on the floor and on windowsills. Ehrenburg was chairman of the evening and his opening remarks reflect how outspoken he had become, just as Brezhnev's new regime was making it more difficult to explore the Stalin period or express nonconformist views about art and politics. In his talk Ehrenburg observes how "students are looking for extra tickets, as people ask for a glass of water. This is a thirst for genuine poetry." Ehrenburg had been actively trying for years to publish a volume of Mandelstam's verse. As early as 1956, the authorities had said they were considering such a book. Part of the problem was that Mandelstam's verse was so apolitical that the authorities could not decide which poems to censor. "[The volume] will continue to wait, perhaps for a year, perhaps for five years—nothing can surprise me—but it will come out. Today everyone already understands this," Ehrenburg proclaimed.[7]

At the close of his remarks Ehrenburg introduced Nadezhda Mandelstam. The audience rose to their feet, loudly applauding her presence. Modestly, she asked they forget she was there and allow the program to proceed. The other highlight of the evening was the appearance of Varlam Shalamov, a long-time labor camp inmate, whose stories about Kolyma were among the most extraordinary accounts of Stalin's *gulag*. Although Shalamov did not publish his work until 1969 and then only in Paris, his stories were widely read in *samizdat* throughout the late 1960s.

That evening in Moscow Shalamov read his story "Cherry Brandy," about the death of Mandelstam in the frozen wastes of the Far North; Shalamov had written it twelve years earlier while still a prisoner in Kolyma. At one point in the program "someone from the school administration tactfully asked to have [Shalamov's] presentation stopped." Ehrenburg ignored the admonition and put the note into his pocket. Meeting for the first time that evening, Ehrenburg and Shalamov soon developed a warm correspondence.[8] Shalamov had followed Ehrenburg's career closely. He trusted Ehrenburg and understood how

Ehrenburg was trying to broaden the boundaries of Soviet culture in the tumultuous years following Stalin's death. As Shalamov once mentioned to his friend, the dissident activist Julius Telesin, "Ehrenburg has no blood on his hands."[9]

EHRENBURG AND THE STALIN QUESTION

That same year, in 1965, the veteran journalist Ernst Henry circulated "An Open Letter to I. Ehrenburg" in which he strongly criticizes Ehrenburg's portrayal of Stalin in the final chapters of Book Six. Henry objected to Ehrenburg's assertion that Stalin was politically intelligent, citing mistakes Stalin had made in the years leading up to Hitler's invasion. In particular Henry describes how the German Communists, acting under Stalin's instructions, refused to cooperate with the Social Democrats, dividing the left and thereby helping Hitler to gain power. But Henry insulted Ehrenburg by not sending him a copy of the letter before circulating it in *samizdat*, where it was widely read.[10]

By all accounts Ehrenburg did have tremendous difficulty composing his portrait of Stalin for the memoirs. At that time he often discussed Stalin for hours, wanting to fathom Stalin's appeal and the blind devotion he received from people around the world. Boris Zaks, the managing editor of *Novy Mir*, witnessed Ehrenburg's internal struggle. Zaks, the journal's principal contact with Ehrenburg, once talked with him about Stalin for two hours. Ehrenburg, it seemed to Zaks, was trying to figure out if Stalin had been "a conscious evildoer or did he think he was really doing something good for the country?"[11]

In an early draft of Book Six Ehrenburg wrote: "I have had the chance to speak on several occasions with [Stalin's] closest comrades-in-arms: Zhdanov, Molotov, Kaganovich, Shcherbakov, Malenkov. Their words were more cruel than Stalin's speeches (this is natural, of course; they were all afraid). Like all my contemporaries, I thought for a long time that Stalin was being deceived, that he did not know how the people lived, that he was being intimidated by imaginary conspiracies." Ehrenburg at one point surmised that although Stalin had "dealt with the old Bolsheviks because he was cruel, undoubtedly he thought he was protecting the party and the people from internal dissension, from people who would not be obedient, would argue, from people who were politically thoughtful and therefore unreliable." Ehrenburg's old friend Ovady Savich was his first reader throughout the writing of the memoirs and he was dissatisfied with this initial portrait of Stalin. Savich believed that Ehrenburg was groping to understand something that was either far more complicated or far more simple. As Savich wrote next to Ehrenburg's text: "Maybe [Stalin] was acting against those who knew his past?"[12]

For Ehrenburg Stalin could not be dismissed as a simple brute. Another friend, Daniel Danin, recalled how Ehrenburg launched into a four-hour monologue about Stalin one night in 1964.

> Ehrenburg could not stop . . . for he was seeking a wordy justifica-tion for decades of his life. He himself would have been happy if Stalin had never existed. But Stalin did exist. And he, Ehrenburg, had existed at the same time. And he had not only been an antagonist, but an eloquent and caressing flatterer. At the time, this had been an internal drama for him. Now it had become more external.[13]

Ehrenburg, in the end, decided against trying to provide a full portrait of Stalin in the memoirs. He lacked hard information, and having served Stalin so faithfully, Ehrenburg found it too difficult to sort out the reasons for Stalin's appeal and his own consistent loyalty.

The question continued to haunt him. Invited to speak about his memoirs in a Moscow library in April 1966, Ehrenburg again addressed Ernst Henry's criticism of his chapters on Stalin.

> I am reproached for messing up the conclusion of my book. People contend that I was obligated to denounce [Stalin] to the nth degree and so forth . . . I do not agree with this. In a letter to me that is cir-culating about Moscow, I am reproached for calling Stalin intelligent. How is it possible to consider him a stupid person when he decisively outsmarted all his indisputably smart comrades? This was an intelli-gence of a special kind, in which the most important part was treach-ery. This was an amoral intelligence. It was this that I wrote about. I do not think the book would have benefited if I had added several abusive epithets about Stalin.
>
> I did all that I was capable of doing within the framework, as I understood it, of giving a psychological portrait with economical means. This is the limit of my understanding. I acknowledge this now and acknowledged it with candor [in my book]. Is it not true that the

historical question lies not in Stalin's personality, but in what [the Italian Communist leader] Togliatti spoke about: "how could Stalin come to power? How could he hold on to power for so many years?" This is what I do not understand. Millions believed in him without ever seeing him, went to their deaths with his name on their lips. How could this have happened?

I see a rooster in a chalk circle or a rabbit before the jaws of a boa constrictor and I do not understand. References to lack of culture or the backwardness of our people do not convince me. Such arguments are not persuasive for me. Is it not true that we saw something analogous in another country [Nazi Germany], where such reasons did not exist? I am yearning for an answer to this fundamental question, fundamental for preventing such horrors in the future. I invite anyone who can answer this question to call and visit me, but I will not be doing the speaking, my visitor will.[14]

An account of Ehrenburg's remarks was compiled by someone in the audience and then circulated widely throughout the capital. Varlam Shalamov read the transcript and immediately wrote to thank Ehrenburg for his observations. Shalamov appreciated Ehrenburg's contention "that the problem is not with Stalin," as the regime wanted everyone to believe. "The question is far, far more serious than the bloody rivers of 1937." For Shalamov as for Ehrenburg, Stalin's Terror could not be explained away by references to the dictator's treacherous intelligence or paranoia. A more comprehensive explanation was necessary, one that "would take decades to search for." As for Ernst Henry, Shalamov dismissed him as "among those who do not have the right to correct [Ehrenburg]."[15]

A year later, as Ehrenburg began to extend his memoirs into a seventh book, the enigma of Stalin's power and appeal continued to obsess him. In Book Seven Ehrenburg discusses the diary of Roger Vaillon, a French Communist who had sincerely believed in Stalin only to have his faith destroyed by Khrushchev's revelations.[16] For Ehrenburg this was the crux of the dilemma: how honest and sincere people, including foreigners, could believe so fully in Stalin's benign genius. Ehrenburg had seen the phenomenon for himself—in Spain, in France, in Latin America. By invoking Vaillon's diary Ehrenburg wanted his Soviet readers to recognize the widespread character of the "personality cult" and understand that it could not be explained (or explained away) by referring to Russia's autocratic past or the methods of terror and coercion Stalin exerted inside the country. Ehrenburg himself had succumbed to its appeal. "Not believing," he wrote in *People, Years, Life*, "I still gave in to the general faith."[17] This is not a satisfying formulation. Ehrenburg himself remained confused. Knowing how much he had feared Stalin and how deeply he had mourned the disappearance of so many innocent friends, Ehrenburg was candid enough to pose the question of Stalin's appeal and then admit his own inadequate understanding.

THE CASE OF SINYAVSKY AND DANIEL

By 1965 individuals were willing to assert their consciences against the power of the state. In reaction to the arrest of two Moscow writers, Andrei Sinyavsky and Yuly Daniel, groups of people began to emerge who made the connection between freedom of artistic expression and the right under law to be protected from arbitrary arrest. The case against Sinyavsky and Daniel, who had published their stories abroad under the pseudonyms Abram Tertz and Nikolai Arzhak, raised significant fears in Moscow's intellectual community. Now, in the aftermath of Khrushchev's removal, friends and supporters of Sinyavsky and Daniel were prepared to defend them publicly; their initiatives, which included a demonstration in Moscow's Pushkin Square and the circulation of petitions and other appeals, set an example for the ensuing human rights movement.

Sinyavsky and Daniel were convicted of "anti-Soviet agitation and propaganda" in February 1966. Although Ehrenburg was among prominent figures asked to sign an appeal in their behalf, he hesitated to protest the case before the trial opened. He was about to leave for France and was afraid that if he raised his voice he would not be permitted to travel. Viktoria Schweitzer, who was a friend of Sinyavsky's and had approached Ehrenburg with the appeal, knew about Liselotte Mehr and understood that for Ehrenburg, "this was his only joy." Although Ehrenburg promised to help the defendants while in Paris, to Viktoria Schweitzer's disappointment he failed to do anything publicly. Even after their conviction Ehrenburg initially refused to sign a petition.[18]

Ehrenburg eventually did sign one of the most prominent appeals in defense of Sinyavsky and Daniel. Following the trial, Viktoria Schweitzer composed the initial draft that was to be signed by Moscow writers and would ask the authorities to release the two defendants "on bail" into the custody of the literary community. Ehrenburg, due to earlier hesitations, worried that he would not be asked to sign; he did not want to be regarded as cowardly or indifferent to the defendants' fate. When Raisa Orlova, a prominent critic and the wife of Lev Kopelev, approached him, he agreed to add his name.[19]

That same February Ehrenburg signed an even more startling petition. He joined a group of eminent scientists, artists, and writers in a direct appeal to Brezhnev against the possible rehabilitation of Stalin at the forthcoming Twenty-third Party Congress. In a warning to party officials the signatories predicted that neither the Soviet public nor Western Communist parties would support Stalin's rehabilitation. Among the names that appeared beside Ehrenburg's were the dancer Maya Plisetskaya, the veteran diplomat Ivan Maisky, and three prominent physicists—Igor Tamm, Pyotr Kapitsa, and Andrei Sakharov. This petition was Sakharov's first public expression of political dissent.[20]

Ehrenburg's stature and his support of these two petitions drew the attention of other Moscow dissidents. At that time General Petro Grigorenko was one of the most visible figures among the human rights activists. He was first arrested in 1964 for circulating pamphlets on the shooting of workers in Novocherkaask during a strike two years earlier and about the shortage of bread in many parts of the country. Accused of "anti-Soviet propaganda," Grigorenko spent a year in a Leningrad mental hospital. After gaining his release he sought Ehrenburg's advice, anxious to understand why so few people took up his call to defy the regime. Ehrenburg's response was not encouraging. He assumed "it would take three generations before people would listen."[21]

Ehrenburg shared Grigorenko's frustration. In a lecture at a Moscow library on April 9, 1966, Ehrenburg explained that Stalin's terrible legacy

> will only come to an end when people who were raised during those years will physically disappear from our society. I am speaking not only about individuals my age, but also about those who are younger than I by twenty years. My hope lies with the young who did not go through such an upbringing. . . . They undoubtedly do foolish things, but they have a critical spirit, a spirit of independent thought.

They do not look to directives but seek for themselves and they will find it.

In response to questions, Ehrenburg went on to express his opinion on several sensitive topics, including the fate of Leon Trotsky and the Stalin cult. Here Ehrenburg issued a virtual call for moral resistance and reform. "What do we urgently need at this time?" Ehrenburg asked his listeners.

We need to rehabilitate conscience. After the denial of religion, only art can do this. But art does not have a completely defined appeal: art is varied because people are varied. Some people perceive the world visually, others through sound. . . . For some, art affects them through the work of Picasso, to others through Rembrandt, on a third group through Pushkin and Gogol, on a fourth through Beethoven. Art affects some people through conventional forms; on others, through unusual and new forms. It is only necessary for this to be genuine art, and not a forgery . . .

A person who has only knowledge but no consciousness (and by consciousness I mean conscience), this is not a person, but a half-finished thing. Even if we are talking about a talented physicist . . . Our misfortune is that our world has become a world of such half-products . . . who construct not only their ideas and social feelings, but their relationships with people on the latest instructions or directives from such and such a date.[22]

That March the Twenty-third Party Congress convened in Moscow. Contrary to the fears of many people, the Congress did not explicitly retreat from earlier condemnations of Stalin. But two ominous incidents took place. Brezhnev himself dismissed any protests against the just-completed trial of Sinyavsky and Daniel, condemning "hack artists who specialize in smearing our regime."[23] And Mikhail Sholokhov, who had received the Nobel Prize in literature in December, made one of the most shameful speeches in the history of Russian letters. He too referred to the recent trial, expressing nostalgia for Stalin's summary methods. Sholokhov regretted the court's leniency—Sinyavsky had received seven years of labor camp and Daniel five years, all for publishing satirical stories in the West. Sholokhov reminded his audience that "had these rascals with black consciences been caught in the memorable 1920s, when judgment was not by strictly defined articles of the Criminal Code but was guided by a revolutionary sense of justice, the punishment meted out to those turncoats would have been quite different."[24] After this speech hundreds of Sholokhov's readers spontaneously responded with a trenchant rebuke: they dumped copies of his novels in front of his door.

———

Efforts on behalf of Sinyavsky and Daniel did not end that spring. With the help of their wives, Maria Sinyavskaya and Larisa Bogoraz, who had taken notes throughout the trial, a transcript was produced, including the defiant testimony of the defendants themselves. Another activist, Alexander Ginzburg, put the transcript and additional material, including articles denouncing the defendants and Western appeals in their behalf, into a comprehensive anthology about the case. Ginzburg called his collection *The White Book* and intended to send copies to Soviet and Western newspapers, to deputies in the Supreme Soviet, and even to the KGB, hoping to provoke a review of their convictions. Ginzburg also appealed to Ehrenburg for advice.

Alexander Ginzburg had first met Ehrenburg in 1962, when he returned to Moscow after two years in a labor camp; Ginzburg had been compiling *samizdat* collections of verse, an activity the regime tried to suppress. Back in Moscow Ginzburg needed permission to resume living in the capital and arranged a meeting with Ehrenburg to ask for his help. After some deliberation Ehrenburg decided to send a signed copy of a recent book of his to a high official in the ministry of internal affairs. A week later he sent the same official a letter asking that Ginzburg be given a residence permit for Moscow. As Ehrenburg explained to Ginzburg, if he had initially written such a request as a deputy to the Supreme Soviet, he would have been turned down. The more patient strategy worked and Ginzburg was able to remain legally in the capital.

Ginzburg saw Ehrenburg for the last time in November 1966, when he brought him a copy of *The White Book*. "Why didn't you ask for my advice before you put the material in this form?" Ehrenburg asked Ginzburg. He explained that it would have been better if Ginzburg had not included the names of such Western sovietologists as Leo Labedz and Robert Conquest. "Just have Aragon and it would have been sufficient." Ginzburg was not convinced and told Ehrenburg he preferred having these people than someone like Aragon. "You'll be the one arrested," Ehrenburg told him. "Not me."[25]

Ginzburg in fact was arrested in January 1967 and brought to trial a year later. During the investigation Ehrenburg was asked to give testimony against Ginzburg. Ehrenburg made clear that he was interested in Ginzburg's fate, that he liked the young man and would do nothing to harm him. Ehrenburg died that August, but Natalya Stolyarova was called to testify by the prosecution at Ginzburg's trial in January 1968. Under duress she confirmed Ginzburg's visit to Ehrenburg and Ehrenburg's advice that he not use "excerpts from the bourgeois right-wing press" but include "the well-known letter by Aragon and the statements of the left-wing intelligentsia, which in Ehrenburg's opinion, would have more influence on our society."[26] In a famous trial Ginzburg was convicted alongside three other defendants and sentenced to five years in a labor camp.

BOOK SEVEN

When Ehrenburg began outlining his memoirs, he intended to conclude the narrative with the events of 1953. Stalin's death marked the boundary line between two eras and a natural place to conclude. Ehrenburg also understood that it would be impossible to discuss the 1950s and early 1960s with Khrushchev still in power. But after Khrushchev's removal Ehrenburg realized that a less hopeful era was taking shape, and he wanted to describe Soviet life under Khrushchev with all of its confounding inconsistencies before Brezhnev's *apparat* succeeded in burying all that Khrushchev had managed to achieve.

The new regime was making Ehrenburg's life more difficult. In April 1965 he was scheduled to appear at a Moscow library to discuss literature. At the last minute the meeting was canceled in a manner that infuriated him, as he wrote to Dmitri Polikarpov of the Central Committee, the same official who had tried to disrupt publication of his memoirs:

On April 15, I was supposed to participate in a literary evening in one of the libraries in the Bauman district. A few hours before it was to begin, the director of the library telephoned to tell me that the evening could not take place because the cloakroom was filled. I soon learned that the evening was canceled on the instructions of the Bauman district committee [of the party]. This decision was reaffirmed by comrades in the Moscow City Council. It was stated that at previous meetings with readers, where I read chapters of my memoirs (the final part of this book is being printed in *Novy Mir* right now), I would say unacceptable things. The principal argument for the prohibition of my meetings with readers was that I had allegedly advised people to burn the Tretyakov museum.

Our correspondent in Cuba, Comrade Alexeev, has sent me via A. Surkov, the text of an interview which I gave to a Cuban correspondent. He considers a series of assertions cited in this interview to be unlikely. Last week, I responded to A. Surkov with a letter, where I indicate that I am not a Fascist, I do not intend to burn either books or paintings, and that the Tretyakov museum has many canvases which I love and consider the greatest treasures of Russian culture. I wrote that our ambassador can use my letter as he finds necessary.

It extremely surprises me to have similar rubbish repeated as an explanation for the prohibition of my meetings with readers. I will be very grateful if you could help me clear up this misunderstanding and remove this prohibition.[27]

Ehrenburg's letter to Polikarpov had some effect and he was able to resume at least some literary meetings.

Ehrenburg began to write Book Seven at the end of 1966. From his notes he clearly intended to continue in the vein of his earlier sections, basing his chapters on people and events that highlighted the years 1954 to 1964: the Second Writers' Congress, his trips to India and Japan, Khrushchev's speech to the Twentieth Party Congress, events in Hungary, Jewish affairs—these were among the first twenty chapters he finished before his death. Subsequent chapters were to discuss his difficulties under Khrushchev, including the events of 1963 and the publication of *People, Years, Life* in *Novy Mir*. Ehrenburg also intended to write about old friends such as Samuil Marshak and Anna Akhmatova, who had died in 1964 and 1966, respectively.

In May of 1967 Ehrenburg wrote to Tvardovsky about Book Seven and also submitted several chapters to *Nauka i Zhizn* (Science and Life) and to *Literaturnaya Gazeta*. He did not survive the summer and was only able to finish just over half of the chapters he had planned. On September 7, 1967, a week after Ehrenburg's death, Alexander Tvardovsky wrote the following letter to Lyubov Mikhailovna:

I understand the awkwardness of approaching you on a matter of business . . . but I think Ilya Grigorevich would not have censured me. Not long before his illness, I received . . . notification from him that sixteen chapters of Book Seven of *People, Years, Life* were written and that he could give them to me to read. . . . This permits me to ask you, Lyubov Mikhailovna, not to postpone but if possible to allow me to read what had been written before that fatal day.[28]

The manuscript of Book Seven, together with an essay on Marc Chagall that had already appeared in *Dekorativnoe Iskusstvo* (Decorative Art), was sent to *Novy Mir*. With brazen confidence the journal prepared to run them in the spring of 1968; then the censors intervened, removing chapters on the Twentieth Party Congress, the Hungarian revolt, and the Jewish question. This censored version was challenged in turn by higher authorities and *Novy Mir* was told to make further cuts. Learning about these difficulties, Ehrenburg's family decided to take the material back, not wanting to publish a disfigured set of chapters that Ehrenburg himself would never have accepted.[29] In 1969 Lyubov Mikhailovna gave the dissident Marxist historian Roy Medvedev permission to publish excerpts from Book Seven in his *samizdat* journal *Political Diary*.[30]

For nearly twenty years afterward Ehrenburg's memoirs were not republished or even mentioned in the Soviet press. The foremost student of Ehrenburg's life and career, Boris Frezinsky of St. Petersburg, who prepared scores of articles about Ehrenburg for Soviet publications throughout the 1970s and 1980s, was explicitly instructed not to mention the memoirs by a series of editors. Only in the summer of 1987, under the conditions of *glasnost*, did the Moscow journal *Ogonyok* undertake to publish Book Seven in several installments; in spite of assurances, *Ogonyok* did not publish the full text. That milestone occurred only in 1990, when Frezinsky was able to publish a fully restored version of all seven parts of *People, Years, Life* together with a detailed and comprehensive commentary.

EIGHTEEN

1967

Ehrenburg grew increasingly outspoken during the final months of his life. Already in 1966 Angelina Shchekin-Krotova, the widow of Robert Falk, had asked Ehrenburg not to speak at an opening exhibit of Falk's paintings; she feared that Ehrenburg would not restrain his anger with the Kremlin, thereby jeopardizing the exhibit. Ehrenburg knew the regime was trying to stifle him and used every opportunity to share what was on his mind. In April 1967 he responded to questions before a select audience at the Medical Library near Rebellion Square. Many concerned "the ferment presently in progress among Soviet intellectuals," as the U.S. embassy reported to Washington. One question concerned Sinyavsky and Daniel. "I don't like their works," Ehrenburg answered, referring to the stories they had sent abroad, "but I don't like their sentence either." Still another person asked about recent criticism of *Novy Mir*—Tvardovsky's journal had come under withering pressure to abandon its anti-Stalinist stance. "Whom do you take me for?" Ehrenburg curtly answered back. "Why do you think I came to you here? It seems to you that the criticism of *Novy Mir* was unjust? Glory to God, that's the way it seems to me." His most controversial remarks, however, proved to be about Stalin's daughter, Svetlana Alliluyeva, who had recently defected during a trip to India. Ehrenburg evidently had not forgotten her generous letter to him in 1957, when he was asked his opinion about a new philosophy of life she claimed to be adopting. "I don't know this philosophy and it doesn't interest me," he answered. "But I would read with interest a novel about the home in which she was born, about her childhood, about how she lived."[1]

Such public remarks were unusual, for Soviet citizens were expected to denounce any defector and leave no room for ordinary human emotion. In June the U.S. embassy sent the following enigmatic note to Washington: "We have report assertedly coming from 'Swiss Special Service' to effect that prominent Soviet intellectual Ehrenburg is in trouble with regime for supporting Svetlana Stalin both before she went abroad and after."[2]

Nonetheless, Ehrenburg had one more important trip to make. He was invited to present a lecture at an international conference on Stendhal to be held in Parma, Italy, from May 22 to May 24. Ehrenburg wrote to the Writers' Union asking for help in arranging a visa and permission "to rest in Italy on the honorarium" following the meeting.[3] His attendance was the principal highlight of the conference and he was besieged with journalists seeking interviews.[4] In Moscow, though, his triumph abroad had an unprecedented consequence.

During the time he was in Italy the Fourth Writers' Congress opened in Moscow. Ehrenburg had little regard for the Writers' Union and was probably happy to be out of the country, yet Mikhail Sholokhov used Ehrenburg's absence as the pretext for a baseless denunciation. Sholokhov's speech "shattered" the tranquility of the Congress, which was commemorating the fiftieth anniversary of the revolution. In an inflammatory set of remarks, Sholokhov identified Svetlana Alliluyeva as a "defector" with links to the CIA, to "inveterate White Guardists," even to the "political corpse [Alexander] Kerensky," who was still alive in New York. Sholokhov then went on to denounce any call for creative freedom, demagogically invoking the Vietnam War as a reason for stifling freedom of the press. As for Ehrenburg, Sholokhov accused him of putting himself above the collective by going to Italy.[5] Sholokhov was under obvious instructions to lump Svetlana Alliluyeva's defection with Ehrenburg's ongoing defiance and notable absence from the Congress. Sholokhov even claimed that Ehrenburg's "individualism and contempt for the norms of society was [*sic*] encouraging some 'grown up youngsters' to take liberties for which they would be ashamed when they grew up properly."[6]

Soon after Ehrenburg expressed his disgust with official Soviet culture to the British journalist Alexander Werth, who visited Moscow in June 1967. According to Werth, Ehrenburg voiced support for Alexander Solzhenitsyn, who had recently challenged the Writers' Union with an open letter against censorship. He voiced support as well for Sinyavsky and Daniel, and doubted that they would benefit from a rumored amnesty for political prisoners. Ehrenburg also described how *samizdat* was organized and its relation to the regime's control of literature. "Our literature is in a very strange condition," Ehrenburg explained to Werth.

> Here we have, on the one hand, the immense literary genius of the Russian people and, on the other, a hideous bureaucratic machine which continues to encourage the mediocrities by printing them in our "best" magazines, while the others—well, the others have to depend on *samizdat*. But it can't go on forever. The terrible thing is that the Writers' Union, founded in 1934, was a Stalinist institution for the regimentation of thought. . . . Nobody wants it any longer now, except the Writers' Union profiteers—those who hold the fat jobs in the union itself or in their editorial chairs, and the small hacks who live on the union's charity and get themselves published in preference to real writers.[7]

That June the world was shaken by the Six Day War in the Middle East. The Soviet media launched a scurrilous anti-Zionist campaign, employing cartoons that recalled the anti-Semitic caricatures of Nazi propaganda. Ehrenburg was asked to sign a petition condemning Israeli aggression, a proposal he absolutely refused to do.[8] As Alexander Werth heard for himself, Ehrenburg was thrilled with Israel's victory:

> Well, it's just as well they didn't allow themselves to be exterminated by the Arabs, as they were in the Hitler days. Although there were plenty of excellent Jewish soldiers in the Red Army, and many of them were even made Heroes of the Soviet Union, there is still this

unpleasant feeling that it's "natural" for Jews to be massacred. If, following in Hitler's footsteps, the Arabs had started massacring all the
Jews in Israel, the infection would have spread: we would have had
here a wave of anti-Semitism. Now, for once, the Jews have shown
that *they* [*sic*] can also kick you hard in the teeth; so there is now a
certain respect for the Jews as soldiers. . . . And in Russia we always
have a great respect for highly efficient soldiers and airmen, which
the Jews—sorry, I mean the Israelis—certainly proved to be.[9]

JULY AND AUGUST

Among Ehrenburg's family and friends it was tacitly believed that as
Ehrenburg and Lyubov Mikhailovna grew older, her death was likely
to precede his. Although she was eight years younger, she suffered
from a heart condition that recently had grown more serious. In 1965
she had spent several months in a rest home recuperating from a
severe heart attack. Ehrenburg, despite his ongoing bout with prostate
and bladder cancer, continued to write and travel. A friend described
him as "severely changed . . . Wizened, balding, a yellow stain had broken out on his head, while his feet shuffled when he walked."[10] His
voice, once robust and clear, had shrunk to a barely audible whisper.
The final blow may have been more psychological than physical: on
July 19, 1967, Ehrenburg's closest friend, Ovady Savich, died in a
Moscow hospital.

Ehrenburg broke down at Savich's funeral. "I think there can hardly
be a single person who knew Ehrenburg and his tenacious self-control
and inability to open himself to people, who could have imagined him
crying," the writer Vladimir Lidin observed. "But he did not only cry,
he was bidding farewell, as it were, to a part of his own life and with a
friendship that had consecrated it. With Savich's death . . . something
gave way in Ehrenburg, a kind of doom touched him."[11]

Ehrenburg did not have the strength to tell Liselotte Mehr about
Savich's death over the telephone. He wrote to her instead. Liselotte's
response two weeks later expressed her own disquiet. "Only today did
I receive your letter," she wrote to him. "I cannot tell you how the
news about Savich has saddened me. . . . When I spoke to you last time
it was impossible to hear you. I understood that something was wrong
. . . I thought someone was sick amongst you."[12]

Soon after, on Monday, August 7, Ehrenburg suffered his first and only heart attack. He was walking through his garden when he fell down. Irina was called immediately and rushed out to the dacha by taxi. She found her father weak and terribly pale, his face practically white. They called Ehrenburg's physician, Dr. Viktor Kanevsky, and when he learned that Ehrenburg had a severe pain in one finger, he knew before reaching the house that his patient had suffered a heart attack.

Ehrenburg was an uncooperative patient. The next day, Tuesday, August 8, he forced himself out of bed and spent several hours at the typewriter, trying to finish Chapter 21 of Book Seven of his memoirs. He began to describe a dispute that took place in 1959 over the need for scientists to have a stronger education in the humanities and greater regard for human emotion—the famous "physicists versus lyricists" controversy that engulfed Ehrenburg for several months that year—when he had to stop and return to bed. It was the last page of the memoirs Ehrenburg would write.[13]

Nurses were posted to the house on round-the-clock duty. According to their notes, the doctors tried conventional and unconventional means to relieve Ehrenburg's suffering. Narcotics were administered. "Cupping" was attempted along his spine. His pulse and blood pressure remained stable, but there was still blood in his urine.[14]

On August 13, five days after he first became ill, Ehrenburg wrote to Liselotte. "I have fallen sick and since Wednesday I am lying down and cannot move. Maybe [Irina] will tell you something. They are all lying to me. I live with the hope of seeing you again. Be strong. Ilya."[15]

Ehrenburg refused to listen to his doctors. Irina called Liselotte on August 14—the telephone in the dacha was not equipped to make or receive international calls, so Irina had to place calls from Moscow and then rush back to be with her father—and Liselotte quickly responded by letter, urging Ehrenburg to be a better patient.

> The most important thing is to get well. Be wise. . . . You know your work, your responsibilities. If it is better to go to the hospital, and if it is possible for you, for your spirits, then do it. . . . Speak openly with your doctor, Kanevsky, who needs all the information so he can give you the best advice for taking care of you. . . . How I would like to come to help you. I promise to take care of myself as well. Irina told me she was a bit annoyed that I cried. But it is hard to hear such things and be so removed.[16]

Liselotte wrote to Irina the same day and was more candid about her anxieties. She knew Ehrenburg well and understood how difficult it had to be for his daughter to manage him.

> I do not know what to do, with myself, with everything, with any-thing . . . I hope you will forgive my tears. I know that you are doing everything and that you have too much to do . . .
>
>   Was the heart attack very bad? Is he sleeping and has he stopped smoking? How have you determined what really happened? . . . Did he disparage everything at first? . . . He has this vitality which he must protect. When he knows that after he recovers the prospects are good, he will be more calm and wiser. But if he cannot believe in the possibility of working, writing, travelling—then it will be very bad. . . . For him, the fact that he could be an invalid is much more worse than having another attack.[17]

Liselotte wrote again on August 15, this time to Ehrenburg himself. "Do not be so hard on your doctors. There are times when they must be supported. . . . You will be better off in the hospital, take care of yourself more comfortably. With the telephone you would not be iso-lated. . . . We can keep you up-to-date about everything. It is never easy for sick people even in the midst of their families."[18] On August 19 Ehrenburg sent Liselotte a hopeful note: "The doctors and the women who surround me say that objectively everything is going fine. They were afraid of more serious damage. So I am waiting. I think that by September 1, I will move to Moscow. As soon as I can, I will pose the question of Zurich."[19] But Ehrenburg was not recovering. He con-tinued to feel weak and complained to his nurse: "I have not been able to eat for a month."[20] On Tuesday, August 22, Liselotte wrote to Ehren-burg again. She had received a note from him but still felt it necessary to admonish his behavior with the cardiologist:

> Thank you for your words which I received with Irina's letter. I see the effort you have been making. One thing: I cannot understand how one can lie. . . . Speak to him in a normal way, only do not talk nonsense to the doctor. I attach all my hope to your will and respon-sibility . . . and to Kanevsky who is a great doctor, as you told me . . .
>
>   Irina has written to me how everything developed day by day. I

understand that you concealed everything at first. This was probably not very wise. Don't do this any more, I implore you. I am going through an excessively difficult time, the worst of my life. . . . I think about you all the time. You consider all that you are going through right now as humiliating. After each procedure [she was undergoing treatment for a severe neurological disorder], I had to rest immobile like you . . .

Concerning the hospital. If you have your own room, a *telephone* [sic], visitors when you have the strength, the kind of attention you need to have at home, newspapers and books, answer letters when you have the strength, I think it would be more peaceful and you could recover more quickly. That's how it was for me.[21]

Although Ehrenburg continued to have internal bleeding, he could not receive a transfusion at the dacha and was growing increasingly anemic. Liselotte wrote to him on August 24.

I received your second letter. Thank you. This morning I visited a friend of ours who is a cardiologist. I asked him a lot of questions and took notes. . . . He said there is no reason not to live a normal life with work, trips, etc. Everything as it was . . .

Irina told me—touch wood—that you are getting better every day. Your mental attitude is very important . . .

Be wise and courageous. Irina has told me that you are surrounded by women. . . . Perhaps in Moscow you can speak on the telephone . . .[22]

It was the final letter from her that Ehrenburg was to read. The doctors had been urging that he be moved to a hospital or at minimum to his apartment, where it would be easier to monitor his treatment. Still, he resisted. Over the next few days Ehrenburg's condition remained the same. He had little appetite and slept fitfully. His breathing remained short and difficult. On Wednesday morning, August 30, he was moved to his Moscow apartment.

Being in the ambulance frightened Ehrenburg. He protested angrily, especially when his wife did not sit with him as he lay strapped to a stretcher (the attendants would not permit it) and accused her of "never loving him." But back in his apartment, Ehrenburg calmed down and slept through the night. "All day [on August 31] the patient felt well," one of the nurses noted. "He ate boullion twice, drank juice." His cardiogram looked promising. A telephone call was booked to Stockholm for the next day, while arrangements were made for Lyubov Mikhailovna to be out of the apartment so he could speak privately with Liselotte; but Ehrenburg did not live through the evening. At 8:25 P.M., while a nurse was checking his pulse, his heart stopped beating. Injections were immediately administered. Fifteen minutes later a medical team arrived to try to revive him. "The efforts of the doctors to restore Ilya Grigorevich Ehrenburg did not succeed," the nurse dryly noted. He was gone.

Epilogue

I lya Ehrenburg died at an awkward moment for the regime. That same Thursday, August 31, 1967, the trial of the young dissident Vladimir Bukovsky had just completed its second day. Bukovsky would be convicted the following afternoon of organizing an illegal demonstration and sentenced to three years in a labor camp. In the wake of Bukovsky's trial Soviet authorities were afraid that the crowds expected to gather in central Moscow might turn their grief over Ehrenburg's death into a demonstration against censorship. Official precautions immediately were devised. No announcements appeared in the press about the state funeral, which took place on Monday, September 4, inside the House of Writers, an impressive compound of buildings and gardens near Rebellion Square, in a neighborhood filled with embassies, including the American. That morning, U.S. officials were startled to see a crowd of fifteen thousand people—along with ten water trucks deployed nearby in case of trouble.[1]

Inside the Writers' Union building Ehrenburg's wife and daughter were joined by several close friends as they quietly watched the crowd enter and leave the hall. Babel's widow, Antonina Pirozhkova, sat with them, as did Savich's widow Alya, the poet Margarita Aliger, and Ehrenburg's former secretary, Valentina Milman. Tatyana Litvinova also joined them; an active dissident in Moscow, she testified in defense of Bukovsky hours before Ehrenburg died.[2]

From ten in the morning until half past one in the afternoon a surprisingly diverse number of people walked in long lines past the open casket. Thirty people passed Ehrenburg's bier each minute, more than six thousand in all, with many more waiting patiently along Vorovsky Street. A full array of senior military officers, veterans of the Second World War, with ribbons and medals adorning their chests, paid tribute to Ehrenburg's role in the struggle against Hitler. Elderly Jews formed a conspicuous presence alongside multitudes of young people. Many shouted expressions of gratitude. One group of students made an especially poignant impression: each carried a single flower and placed it quietly by the bier.[3]

This procession was interrupted by the officially scheduled speakers—several writers, the head of the Soviet peace committee, and a member of the Spanish Communist party. As might have been expected, they did not address "difficult" aspects of Ehrenburg's career. Among the speakers only André Blumel, the president of the France–USSR Society and a sincere Zionist, took the risk of speaking up, recalling Ehrenburg's many years in Paris, his hatred of anti-Semitism, and his devotion to European art and culture. This was the sole reference to Ehrenburg's Jewish origins during the funeral.[4]

At the close of the ceremony, uniformed police, acting on cue, hurried the casket from the building. A group of prominent writers, expecting to form an honor guard, waited at the main entrance on Herzen Street. But officials tricked them and directed the casket toward Vorovsky Street, on the other side of the wide city block. Ehrenburg's family and close friends followed the casket through the garden in the center of the Writers' Union, but as they reached Vorovsky Street they heard a peculiar, persistent drumming sound that took them a moment to identify. The crowd was throwing flowers at the casket over the policemen, and the bouquets created an eerie, drumlike cadence as they struck the red wood. The crowd, the flowers, the uniformed police jostling for room—the funeral threatened to collapse into pandemonium until officials regained control and quickly shepherded the hearse away. One friend of the family had to punch a policeman so that Ehrenburg's widow could enter her car before it drove off.

Several miles away there was a near riot at Novodevichy cemetery, where the police refused to permit a second, even larger, crowd of twenty thousand to follow the casket to the grave. "On two occasions," The *Manchester Guardian* reported, "the crowd burst through a double line of soldiers standing with arms linked in front of the cemetery gates."[5] Even Alexander Tvardovsky had difficulty entering the cemetery; he had to shout at the policemen and remind them that he was a member of the Central Committee before they would let him in.[6] Tvardovsky aside, "no prominent government or party officials were seen at the Writers' Club or the cemetery," according to the *New York Times*.[7] The authorities rushed the ceremonies along so quickly that neither Boris Slutsky nor Margarita Aliger had the opportunity to address the crowd as they had expected to.[8]

For several months Ehrenburg's grave was decorated with his photograph attached to a large bough of flowers and leaves. A handsome granite monument was erected within a year. Designed by Ehrenburg's long-time friend Natan Altman, the stone carried a metal reproduction of Picasso's portrait of Ehrenburg by the sculptor Lev Slonim, the husband of Tatyana Litvinova. Within a few years allies and adversaries joined Ehrenburg in Novodevichy. Both Khrushchev and Tvardovsky died in 1971 and each was buried within sight of Ehrenburg's grave.

Learning of Ehrenburg's death, many people wrote directly to Lyubov Mikhailovna. André Malraux, Pablo Picasso, Louis Aragon, and Pablo Neruda all sent telegrams to Moscow. A handwritten letter from the linguist Roman Jakobson was among the most thoughtful and affecting. Jakobson had been in Moscow that August and tried to visit Ehrenburg. "I knew he meant to bid me farewell and then suddenly the road was closed to me [Ehrenburg's dacha was outside the radius from Moscow that foreigners were permitted to travel] and the weight of helpless sadness fell on me," Jakobson wrote to Lyubov Mikhailovna. "Now I would simply like to sit with you Lyuba, hand in hand and eye to eye, be silent together and together remember."[9]

The year before Ehrenburg died, when he turned seventy-five, the *Daily Mirror* observed that "his name is always mud—somewhere or other. He is Ilya Ehrenburg, the renowned Soviet writer, who has shouldered the lifelong burden of always being blamed by somebody,

somewhere, for something."[10] After Ehrenburg's death Alexander Tvardovsky echoed a similar grievance in *Novy Mir*. Tvardovsky recalled
how Ehrenburg's opponents "scolded, lectured, and berated him, but
they also admired him and even praised him to the skies when the circumstances allowed it. They did everything, in fact," Tvardovsky concluded, "except they were never able to be silent about him."[11]

In a poem written in 1966 Ehrenburg expressed the poignant complexity of his life with remarkable candor:

> Time to admit—even to howl or to cry,
> I lived my life like a dog,
> I cannot say it was bad, only different,
> Not like other people or dolls
> Or a respectable man . . .
> I guarded the closed chambers
> Not for awards, but for abuse,
> When the moon was angry
> I howled and even barked,
> Not because I was an animal,
> But because I was loyal—
> Not to the kennel and not to the stick,
> And not to the fighters in the brawl,
> Not to scuffles and not to nice lies
> And not to nasty watchdogs,
> But only to weeping in a darkened house
> And to warm straw that smells like sorrow.[12]

Ehrenburg here acknowledges the circumstances that repelled him: the
stick, the brawls, the nice lies. With Brezhnev in charge and
Khrushchev's reforms under attack, Ehrenburg was in no mood to
recall the positive loyalties that had held him to his country, among
them Russian culture, the struggle against fascism, and the need for
cultural interchange and peace throughout Europe and the world.

After Ehrenburg died the regime ignored his moral complexity;
Pravda lamely remarked that "his path had been complicated and sometimes contradictory."[13] There was never any hint, of course, that he had
both joined and quit the Bolsheviks as a teenager, or that his novel *The
Thaw* helped to launch the entire process of de-Stalinization, lending
its title to a fateful period of Soviet history; *The Thaw* in fact was not

even mentioned. As for Ehrenburg's Jewish background, only *Literaturnaya Gazeta* made a fleeting reference to "the sad, sly intonations of Sholem Aleichem" that appeared in his books.[14] No other Soviet publication even suggested that Ehrenburg was Jewish.

Newspapers around the world tried to evaluate Ehrenburg's career more honestly. In a front-page article the *New York Times* summarized his "long, agile, and stormy life." For the *Times*, "Few Soviet writers were so bemedaled, few so criticized for transgressing the policy line." And in an editorial that same day the *Times* called him a "master of Aesopian writing" and acknowledged that the essays and memoirs of his last years "will continue to have a political and moral importance long after most of his literary works have been properly forgotten."[15] *Newsweek* said "he could not escape being one of the most conspicuous anomalies of Soviet society."[16] The *Manchester Guardian* dubbed him a "bridge builder between East and West."[17] *Le Monde* called him "the doubting Thomas of Soviet letters" and acknowledged "a moral courage which was rare among his contemporaries."[18] The *London Times* struck an informed and cautious balance, calling Ehrenburg "not only one of the most prolific and fluent writers of his time, but also an extremely effective Russian and French speaker with a brilliant gift of repartée." He was not "a rebel in any real sense," the *Times* concluded, but "a man who had often shown courage—though not reckless courage—in his advocacy of 'wider horizons.'"[19]

Still other journals revived unfounded allegations. Writing in the *London Observer*, Edward Crankshaw asserted that Ehrenburg "actively joined in [Stalin's] witch hunt" against the Jews and "assisted in Zhdanov's hounding of . . . all Russians who showed an interest in foreign ideas."[20] Such an article prompted Ehrenburg's friend Ivor Montagu to comment that "cold warriors of the cheaper sort, who never forgave him for surviving the years of storm, denounced him even in obituaries for misdeeds for which there is not a shred of evidence, the refuse of professional imaginations."[21]

Today, beyond the reach of rumor and accusation, it is easier to see how Ehrenburg's courage and good deeds far outweigh the compromises of a career played out under terror and dictatorship. Despite decades of enforced hypocrisy, of "howling and barking like a dog," that warped as many souls as it destroyed, Ehrenburg had the conviction and stamina to revive the memories of a doomed generation. His enemies could not forgive him. Confused by Ehrenburg's unanticipated and persistent defiance throughout the 1950s and 1960s, one of Khrushchev's advisers remarked that "he was not the same Ehrenburg they had known during the war."[22] But Ehrenburg was a man of greater consistency than his detractors, Western or Soviet, cared to acknowledge. "If within a lifetime a man changes his skin an infinite number of times, almost as often as his suits," Ehrenburg wrote in his memoirs, "he still does not change his heart; he has but one."[23]

His admirers throughout Eastern Europe and the Soviet Union looked to him for counsel and direction. Even on September 4, the day of Ehrenburg's funeral, the *New York Times* carried a front-page article with news of a startling appeal from three hundred Czech writers. Fed up with neo-Stalinist repression, they denounced "a witchhunt of pronounced Fascist character" against the entire Czechoslovak writers' community and called on a host of prominent figures, among them Arthur Miller, John Steinbeck, Alberto Moravia, Jean-Paul Sartre, Bertrand Russell, Günter Grass, and Heinrich Boll, to help them. As for Soviet writers, the Czechs could think of only four who seemed famous enough and sympathetic enough to respond: Alexander Solzhenitsyn, Yevgeny Yevtushenko, Andrei Voznesensky, and Ilya Ehrenburg. This appeal was a harbinger of the ill-fated "Prague Spring" of 1968, a cause Ehrenburg surely would have supported.[24]

Watching the Bolsheviks take over the Russian Empire, Ehrenburg observed in 1918 that "I am not sad that the monument to Alexander III or to Skobelev will be 'evacuated to storage,' but alas they are being replaced by monuments to the revolution. Evidently," he continued, "neither Russian thrones nor Moscow squares can be vacant for long. It is hard to imagine, though, that the revolutionary idols will be better than those of the czar."[25]

It was not until Gorbachev's reforms and the failure of an attempted coup by the remnants of Stalin's apparatus in August 1991 that Bolshevik monuments followed the destiny of the czarist ones they had replaced. Ehrenburg would not have been surprised. Always the Jew, the outsider, Ilya Ehrenburg was not confined by his contradictions. He was larger than all of them.

Notes

Unless otherwise noted all quotations from Ehrenburg's memoirs have been translated from the three-volume 1990 edition of *Lyudi, Gody, Zhizn (People, Years, Life)* (Moscow: Sovietsky Pisatel) edited by his daughter, Irina Ehrenburg, and Boris Frezinsky, with the help of Vyacheslav Popov. Boris Frezinsky added a commentary to each volume. In the notes this edition is designated with the abbreviation *PYL*. TSGALI refers to The Central Government Archive of Literature and Art in Moscow, the principal repository of Ehrenburg's papers.

INTRODUCTION

1. Nadezhda Mandelstam, *Hope Abandoned* (New York, 1974), p. 16.
2. Boris Birger, interview with author, Moscow, 1984.
3. *PYL,* vol. 1, p. 544.
4. Nadezhda Mandelstam to Ehrenburg, following a public attack on him by Nikita Khrushchev in the spring of 1963. Archive of Natalya Stolyarova, Moscow.
5. Viktoria Schweitzer, interview with author, Amherst, Mass., 1983.
6. Mandelstam, *Hope Abandoned,* p. 16.

CHAPTER 1. FROM THE PALE TO PARIS

1. Cited in Lionel Kochan, ed., *The Jews in Soviet Russia Since 1917* (Oxford, 1978), p. 1.
2. *PYL,* vol. 1, p. 55.
3. Ilya Ehrenburg, *Kniga dlya Vzroslikh* (A Book for Adults) (Moscow, 1936), pp. 182–83.
4. Archive of Irina Ehrenburg, Moscow. The eulogy was given in Kiev on Iyar 27, 5664, according to the Hebrew calendar, which corresponds to May

12, 1904. Other sources claim that Ehrenburg's grandfather died in 1903; see the commentary to *PYL*, vol. 1, p. 567. (The eulogy was preserved with only the Hebrew date attached.) Professor Dov Sadan of Hebrew University reported in a telephone interview in 1983 that Ben-Zion Dinur, the famous Zionist historian who served as Minister of Education and Culture in Israel from 1951 to 1955 and President of Yad Vashem in Jerusalem from 1953 to 1959, had once tutored Jewish boys in Poltava for their Bar Mitzvah. Dinur claimed that Ehrenburg had been among his students, but that he decided not to mention this fact in his memoirs because Ehrenburg turned out to be "a son of a bitch." Dinur's memoirs are entitled *Ba-Olam She-Shakah* (In the World That Set) (Jerusalem, 1958). Professor Sadan edited these memoirs.

5. Ehrenburg, *Kniga dlya Vzroslikh,* p. 173.

6. See S. Ettinger, "The Jews in Russia at the Outbreak of the Revolution," in *The Jews in Soviet Russia Since 1917,* ed. L. Kochan (Oxford, 1978), p. 16.

7. Yehuda Leib Arnshtein, *Al Mah Yichye Ha-Adam* (Cracow, 1893). This rare volume can be found in the National Library in Jerusalem. It is dedicated "to the son of my sister Eliyahu ben Zechariah Ehrenburg." Ilya Grigorevich Ehrenburg had cousins with the same first name but different patronymics.

8. *PYL*, vol. 1, pp. 56, 282. In early 1944 Ehrenburg received a letter from a Jewish Red Army officer asking why he had not changed his German-sounding name. "I do not love Germans (not only Nazis, but the nation). But I would not change my name today," he wrote back. "Under our conditions, it is not a German name but a Jewish one and changing it would be a denial not of its German intonation but of its Jewish origin." See Mordechai Altshuler, Yitshak Arad, Shmuel Krakovsky, eds., *Sovietskie Yevrei Pishut Ilye Ehrenburgu 1943–1966* (Soviet Jews Write to Ilya Ehrenburg) (Jerusalem, 1993), pp. 134–35.

9. A short biographical account of Ehrenburg's cousin Ilya Lazarevich Ehrenburg is located in the Hoover Institution Archives, Stanford, Calif., B. I. Nicolaevsky Collection, box 244, folder 2. Mention of Ehrenburg's uncle Lazar can be found here.

10. *PYL*, vol. 3, p. 101. In a brief autobiographical sketch dated May 5, 1958, Ehrenburg formulated his belief this way: "As long as there are racists walking on this earth, I, to the question of nationality will answer, a Jew." (See TSGALI, fund 1204, catalog 1, item 18.) He changed "racists" to "anti-Semites" when he delivered his radio address on the occasion of his seventieth birthday on January 26, 1961.

11. In his memoirs Ehrenburg writes that his family moved to Moscow in 1896. Based on research in Russian archives, Boris Frezinsky has confirmed that the family moved in September 1895. See Boris Frezinsky and Vyacheslav Popov, *Ilya Ehrenburg, Chronika Zhizni i Tvorchestva* (Ilya Ehrenburg, A Chronicle of His Life and Work), vol. 1, *1891–1923* (St. Petersburg, 1993), p. 12.

12. Israel Brodsky (1823–1888) was famous throughout Russia, as were his two sons Eliezer (1848–1904) and Aryeh (1852–1923), who expanded the

family business after their father's death. The Visotzky family, another group of Jewish businessmen, was known for its control of the tea industry. At the height of the revolution in 1917 anti-Semites circulated the following lyric: "Sugar is Brodsky's, tea is Visotzky's, Russia is Trotsky's."

13. "Moscow," *Encyclopedia Judaica,* vol. 12 (Jerusalem, 1978), p. 364.

14. Ehrenburg, "O Mame" (About Mother), in *Sobranie Sochinenie* (Collected Works), vol. 1 (Moscow, 1990), p. 30.

15. Ehrenburg, *Kniga dlya Vzroslikh,* p. 183.

16. *PYL,* vol. 1, p. 67. In his memoirs Ehrenburg mistakenly called this journal *Novy Luch* (New Ray). See TSAGLI, fund 1204, catalog 2, item 371.

17. *PYL,* vol. 1, p. 69.

18. Ibid., p. 70.

19. Out of 171 delegates who responded to a questionnaire at the party Congress in the summer of 1917, 58 had joined Bolshevik organizations between 1904 and 1906. Cited in Stephen F. Cohen, *Bukharin and the Bolshevik Revolution* (New York, 1975), p. 10.

20. *PYL,* vol. 1, pp. 71, 70, 73, 77. An abridged version of the chapter on Bukharin and the high school Bolshevik organization can be found in *Nedelya* (The Week), no. 20, May 16–22, 1988, p. 10.

21. Ehrenburg, *The Extraordinary Adventures of Julio Jurenito and His Disciples* (New York, 1930), p. 226. Quotations cited from this translation have sometimes been altered for greater accuracy.

22. Cited from czarist police files in *PYL,* vol. 1, p. 78. See also Frezinsky and Popov, *Ilya Ehrenburg, Chronika,* pp. 31–55. The authors have examined scores of documents relating to Ehrenburg's underground career as a teenager.

23. *Literaturnoe Nasledstvo* (Literary Heritage), vol. 65 (Moscow, 1958), p. 444.

24. *PYL,* vol. 1, p. 82.

25. Ehrenburg, *Kniga dlya Vzroslikh,* p. 42.

26. The arrest of teenagers and students for political crimes was commonplace under the czarist regime. Ehrenburg's first cousin, Ilya Lazarevich Ehrenburg, was arrested in Kiev in November 1907. He was twenty years old—four years older than his Moscow cousin—and an active Menshevik. Several letters to his family from prison have been preserved and convey a sturdy optimism. He could receive food and clothing from home and when he was ill with mange (a contagious skin disease) he was allowed to spend a month in the prison hospital, which, he assured his parents, was clean and comfortable. But Ilya Lazarevich did not burden his family with the full horror of prison life. The prisoners were kept in extremely crowded conditions. An outbreak of typhus killed many of them. Ilya Lazarevich also witnessed the murder of a cellmate; standing by the window reading a book, the fellow was shot without warning by a soldier. He did not tell his parents any of this but instead tried to comfort them. "Have you accepted the idea that every student will have to be imprisoned at some point?" he asked them a month after his arrest. "There are so many people 'sitting' now . . . that it can be considered the most ordinary thing." (Hoover Institution Archives, B. I. Nicolaevsky Collection, box 244, folders 2 and 3.)

27. Ehrenburg, *Kniga dlya Vzroslikh,* p. 50.

28. *PYL,* vol. 1, p. 74.

29. Ehrenburg, *Kniga dlya Vzroslikh,* p. 50.

30. Ehrenburg, *Lik Voyny* (The Face of War) (Berlin, 1923), pp. 165–66.

31. *PYL,* vol. 1, pp. 90, 95. As he was preparing his memoirs Ehrenburg requested documents about his revolutionary youth from old czarist archives; the police files demonstrated how closely his every move was followed.

CHAPTER 2. A LAPSED BOLSHEVIK

1. Ilya Ehrenburg, *Kniga dlya Vzroslikh* (A Book for Adults) (Moscow, 1936), pp. 110–11.

2. *PYL,* vol. 1, p. 97.

3. Ibid., p. 91.

4. Ehrenburg, *Kniga dlya Vzroslikh,* pp. 111–12.

5. *PYL,* vol. 1, p. 101.

6. Boris Frezinsky, ed., "Iz Vospominanie M. Kireeva" (From the Reminiscences of M. Kireeva), *Voprosy Literatury* (Problems of Literature), no. 9 (1982): 153.

7. *PYL,* vol. 1, p. 105.

8. Ehrenburg's remarks about Trotsky were circulated in *samizdat* in 1966 and cited in *Sovietskaya Kultura* (Soviet Culture), January 26, 1991, p. 15.

9. *PYL,* vol. 1, p. 105; vol. 3, p. 250.

10. Alexei Aisner, interview with author, Moscow, 1982.

11. Hoover Institution Archives, Stanford, Calif., B. I. Nicolaevsky Collection, box 207, folder 8. At the time Yelizaveta Polonskaya still used her maiden name of Movshenson.

12. A rare original copy of *Byvshie Lyudi* (Yesterday's People) is located in the library of the Hoover Institution. Roman Gul, in his memoirs *Ya Unyos Rossiyu* (I Took Russia with Me) discusses both this journal and *Tikhoe Semeystvo* (The Quiet Family). See Gul, *Ya Unyos Rossiyu,* vol. 1 (New York, 1981), pp. 73–74 and vol. 2 (New York, 1984), pp. 239–40 for illustrations from both journals. See also Aline, *Lénine à Paris* (Paris, 1929), p. 73, and Boris Frezinsky and Vyacheslav Popov, *Ilya Ehrenburg, Chronika Zhizni i Tvorchestva* (Ilya Ehrenburg, A Chronicle of His Life and Work), vol. 1, *1891–1923* (St. Petersburg, 1993), p. 62, about the reaction of Grigory Zinoviev.

13. Hoover Institution Archives, B. I. Nicolaevsky Collection, box 207, folder 8.

14. *PYL,* vol. 1, p. 81; Ehrenburg, *Kniga dlya Vzroslikh,* p. 169.

15. Ehrenburg, *Kniga dlya Vzroslikh,* p. 173.

16. Ibid., pp. 173, 174.

17. Ilya Ehrenburg, *Detskoe* (Childhood) (Paris, 1914), p. 5.

18. TSGALI, fund 1204, catalog 1, item 18.

19. From *Russkaya Mysl* (Russian Thought), no. 2, 1911, pp. 232–33, cited in the commentary to *Sobranie Sochinenie* (Collected Works), vol. 1 (Moscow, 1990), p. 589.

20. *Apollon,* no. 5 (1911): 78. Gumilyov then wrote to Bryusov objecting to the latter's praise of Ehrenburg. "I found nothing in [his work] except for ungrammatical and unpleasant snobbism," as cited in Frezinsky and Popov, *Ilya Ehrenburg, Chronika,* p. 76.

21. A full English translation of "To the Jewish People" can be found in *Midstream* (April 1971): 56–57.

22. *Apollon,* no. 10 (1911): 74.

23. TSGALI, fund 1204, catalog 1, item 18.

24. Hoover Institution Archives, B. I. Nicolaevsky Collection, box 244, folder 3.

25. Ehrenburg, *Kniga dlya Vzroslikh,* pp. 107–8.

26. Mrs. Alexandra Pregel, interview with author, New York, 1983.

27. Marevna (Vorobyov), *Memoirs d'une Nomade* (Paris, 1979).

28. *PYL,* vol. 1, p. 160.

29. Ilya Ehrenburg, "New Women Poets," *Helios,* no. 2 (December 1913): 45–46.

30. Ilya Ehrenburg, ed., *Poety Frantsy* (The Poets of France) (Paris, 1914).

31. Frezinsky and Popov, *Ilya Ehrenburg, Chronika,* p. 82.

32. Ehrenburg, *Sobranie Sochinenie,* vol. 1, p. 31.

33. *PYL,* vol. 1, pp. 175–76.

34. Philip Knightley, *The First Casualty* (New York, 1975), p. 80.

35. John Roger Shaw, *Ilya Ehrenburg: The Career of a Soviet Writer* (Ph.D. diss., University of Washington, 1960), p. 25.

36. Ramón Gómez de la Serna, *Retratos Contemporáneos* (Contemporary Portraits) (Buenos Aires, 1941), pp. 342–43.

37. *PYL,* vol. 1, p. 192.

38. Ilya Ehrenburg, *Lik Voyny* (The Face of War) (Berlin, 1923), p. 16.

39. Ehrenburg, *Kniga dlya Vzroslikh,* pp. 169–70.

40. Marevna, *Memoires,* p. 207.

41. Ilya Ehrenburg, "Russian Champagne," *Birzhevie Vedomosti* (The Stock Exchange Gazette), December 6, 1916, morning ed., p. 3.

42. *PYL,* vol. 1, p. 221.

43. Ibid., p. 225. In an article for *Commentary* in August 1947 a Russian émigré journalist, writing under the pen name Martin Thomas, claimed that Ehrenburg returned to Russia with Lenin's help aboard a "sealed train" from Zurich. This is an absurd invention that casts doubt on other unsubstantiated claims by Thomas. Ehrenburg's cousin Ilya Lazarevich did return to Russia on such a train; see Hoover Institution Archives, B. I. Nicolaevsky Collection, box 244, folder 2.

44. *Birzhevie Vedomosti,* July 21, 1917, morning ed., p. 5.

45. Ibid.

46. *PYL,* vol. 1, pp. 230, 247.

47. *Birzhevie Vedomosti,* October 15, 1917, morning ed., p. 7.

CHAPTER 3. REVOLUTION AND CIVIL WAR

1. Ilya Ehrenburg, *The Extraordinary Adventures of Julio Jurenito and His Disciples* (New York, 1930), pp. 278–79.

2. *Slovy-Svoboda!* (For Freedom of Speech!). I was shown an original copy of this newspaper by friends in Moscow.

3. Ilya Ehrenburg, *Molitva o Rossy* (A Prayer for Russia) (Moscow, 1918), p. 15.

4. Cited in the commentary to *Sobranie Sochinenie* (Collected Works), vol. 1 (Moscow, 1990), p. 595.

5. Max Voloshin, *Russkaya Mysl* (Russian Thought), no. 3430, September 16, 1982, p. 9.

6. Letter to the editor, *Russkaya Kniga* (The Russian Book), no. 9 (September 1921): 6.

7. *Bolshaya Sovietskaya Entsiklopediya* (The Great Soviet Encyclopedia), vol. 64 (Moscow, 1934), p. 583.

8. Ehrenburg, *Kniga dlya Vzroslikh* (A Book for Adults) (Moscow, 1936), pp. 183–84.

9. Cited in the commentary to *PYL,* vol. 1, p. 599.

10. Alexander Blok, *Sobranie Sochinenie,* vol. 7 (Moscow, 1963), p. 324.

11. *PYL,* vol. 1, p. 239.

12. *Novosti Dnya* (News of the Day), "Tikhoe Semeystvo" (The Quiet Family), Moscow, March 27 (14), 1918, p. 3. Several issues of this newspaper are located in Moscow's Lenin Library. Until recent years they were strictly held in a special closed archive.

13. See Maxim Gorky, *Untimely Thoughts* (New York, 1968).

14. *PYL,* vol. 1, p. 268.

15. Ibid., p. 269.

16. Ibid., p. 281.

17. Cited in the commentary to *PYL,* vol. 1, p. 599.

18. *PYL,* vol. 1, pp. 282, 286.

19. *Novaya Russkaya Kniga* (The New Russian Book), no. 6 (June 1922): 39.

20. Stepha Gerassi, interview with author, Putney, Vt., 1981. Although Lyubov Mikhailovna always claimed to have been born in 1900, in fact she was born in 1899; her vanity precluded her from admitting that she had been born in the nineteenth century. I am grateful to Boris Frezinsky for this information.

21. Yadviga Sommer, "Zapiski" (Notes), prepared by Boris Frezinsky, in *Minuvshee* (The Past), vol. 17 (Moscow, 1994), pp. 129–30.

22. *PYL,* vol. 1, p. 306.

23. Sommer, "Zapiski," p. 133.

24. Alexander Gladkov, "Pozdnie Vechera" (Late Nights), in *Vospominaniye ob Ilye Erenburge* (Reminiscences About Ilya Ehrenburg), ed. Galina Belaya and Lazar Lazarev (Moscow, 1975), p. 265.

25. TSGALI, fund 1204, catalog 2, item 3664.

26. Nadezhda Mandelstam, *Hope Abandoned* (New York, 1974), p. 15.

27. Nadezhda Mandelstam, *Hope Against Hope* (New York, 1979), p. 107.

28. *Novaya Russkaya Kniga,* no. 4 (April 1922): 44.

29. "Ponedelnik" (Monday), *Kievskaya Zhizn* (Kiev Life), no. 14, September 11 (24), 1919, p. 1. Several issues of this newspaper are located in Moscow's Lenin Library. Until recent years they were closely held in a special archive.

30. Ibid., October 6 (19), 1919, p. 1. An original copy of this issue is located at the School of International Affairs, Columbia University, New York.

31. Ehrenburg, *Julio Jurenito,* p. 355. In the spring of 1934 Ehrenburg again suspected that his Jewish looks could get him into trouble, this time with the Nazis. Visiting Prague, he wondered how he could best return to Paris. A diplomat suggested he take a scheduled airline flight that would stop in Nuremberg. My "face could give me away," Ehrenburg wrote in *Izvestia,* April 18, 1934, p. 6.

32. "Yevreskaya Krov" (Jewish Blood), *Kievskaya Zhizn,* no. 20, September 19 (October 2), 1919.

33. "Stary Skornyak" (The Old Furrier), *Krasnaya Nov* (Red Virgin Soil), no. 6 (June 1928): 116–19.

34. Cited in Elias Heifetz, *The Slaughter of the Jews in the Ukraine in 1919* (New York, 1921), pp. 113–14.

35. *Kievskaya Zhizn,* no. 33, October 9 (22), 1919.

36. Cited in S. Mstislavsky, "Pogromy" (The Pogroms), in *Byloe* (The Past), vol. 29 (1925), p. 193.

37. S. L. Shneiderman, "Ilya Ehrenburg Reconsidered," *Midstream* (October 1968): 57.

38. Sommer, "Zapiski," pp. 137–38.

39. Ibid., pp. 148, 167*n*.

40. Boris Frezinsky and Vyacheslav Popov, *Ilya Ehrenburg, Chronika Zhizni i Tvorchestva* (Ilya Ehrenburg, A Chronicle of His Life and Work), vol. 1, *1891–1923* (St. Petersburg, 1993), pp. 174, 176.

41. *PYL,* vol. 1, p. 298.

42. Hoover Institution Archives, B. I. Nicolaevsky Collection, box 244, folder 2.

43. *PYL,* vol. 1, p. 307.

44. Ibid.

45. Sommer, "Zapiski," pp. 145–46.

46. Ilya Ehrenburg, *Portrety Russkikh Poetov* (Portraits of Russian Poets) (Berlin, 1922), pp. 104–5.

47. *PYL,* vol. 1, p. 306.

48. Ilya Ehrenburg, *Razdumiya* (Reflections) (Riga, 1921), p. 18.

49. *PYL,* vol. 1, p. 317.

50. Ehrenburg, *Kniga dlya Vzroslikh,* p. 81.

51. "Lyubopitnoe Proisshestvie" (A Curious Incident) was included in the collection *Nepravdopodobnie Istory* (Unlikely Stories) (Berlin, 1922). This collection was republished in full in Moscow in 1991. "A Curious Incident" appeared in the Moscow journal *Ogonyok,* no. 21 (May 20–27, 1989): 26–29.

52. Ehrenburg, *Portrety Russkikh Poetov,* pp. 127, 128, 130.

53. N. Mandelstam, *Hope Abandoned,* p. 22.

54. *PYL,* vol. 1, pp. 328, 329.

55. Ibid., p. 337.

56. Ilya Ehrenburg, "O Shtanakh, O Polushubke, O Dusheestom Goroshke" (On Pants, An Overcoat, and Canned Peas), *Prozhektor* (Projector), no. 2 (1928): 10–12.

57. *PYL,* vol. 1, p. 363.

58. Ehrenburg, *Razdumiya,* pp. 29–30.

CHAPTER 4. A NOVELIST IN EXILE

1. Ilya Ehrenburg, "Uskomchel," *Nepravdopodobnie Istory* (Unlikely Stories) (Berlin, 1922), p. 123.
2. Joseph Stalin, *Voprosy Leninizma* (Problems of Leninism) (Moscow, 1931), pp. 100–101.
3. *Novaya Russkaya Kniga,* no. 4 (April 1922): 45.
4. Viktor Shklovsky, *Zoo, or Letters Not About Love* (Ithaca, 1971), p. 91.
5. *PYL,* vol. 1, pp. 371, 373.
6. *Obshchee Delo* (Common Cause), Paris, May 27, 1921, p. 1. Several issues of this émigré newspaper are located in Moscow's Lenin Library.
7. Ivan and Vera Bunin, *Ustamy Buninikh* (In the Bunins' Own Words) (Frankfurt am Main, 1981), pp. 37–38.
8. Nina Berberova, interview with author, Princeton, N.J., 1984. See also a reference to her opinion in Shklovsky, *Zoo,* p. 155. In her recent biography of Ehrenburg Lilly Marcou confirms, based on unique research in French police and government archives, that he was suspected of propagating bolshevism. He and his wife were placed under surveillance on the fifth day after their return to Paris. Despite initial confusion on the part of the police they soon understood that Ehrenburg was the same "Elie Ehrenbourg" who had lived in Paris before the Russian Revolution. According to the police memorandums, the government believed that Ehrenburg was a supporter of Kerensky and that only his opinions about the vitality of Soviet art made him suspicious, an indication that Ehrenburg indeed had been denounced by a fellow émigré. See Lilly Marcou, *Ilya Ehrenbourg* (Paris, 1992), pp. 70–73.
9. Ilya Ehrenburg, *Kniga dlya Vzroslikh* (A Book for Adults) (Moscow, 1936), p. 186.
10. Cited in the commentary to *PYL,* vol. 1, p. 601.
11. *PYL,* vol. 1, p. 377.
12. Ilya Ehrenburg, *The Extraordinary Adventures of Julio Jurenito and His Disciples: Monsieur Delhaie, Alexei Tishin, Karl Schmidt, Ercole Bambucci, Mister Cool, Ilya Ehrenburg, and Negro Aisha, in the Days of Peace, War and Revolution in Paris, in Mexico, in Rome, in Senegal, in Kineshma, in Moscow, and in Many Other Places: and also Various Opinions of the Master, on Pipes, on Death, on Love, on Liberty, on Playing Chess, on the Tribes of Israel, on Constructivism and Other Topics* (New York, 1930), pp. 3, 374.
13. Ilya Ehrenburg, *Sobranie Sochinenie* (Collected Works), vol. 1 (Moscow, 1962), p. 9 of the introduction to *Julio Jurenito.*
14. Ehrenburg, *Julio Jurenito,* pp. 18, 97, 221–22.
15. Ilya Ehrenburg, *Bely Ugol, ili Slezy Vertera* (White Coal, or the Tears of Werther) (Leningrad, 1928), p. 153.
16. Ehrenburg, *Julio Jurenito,* pp. 251, 127, 251–52, 132.
17. Cited in Gerhard Schoenberner, *The Yellow Star* (New York, 1973), p. 121.
18. Ehrenburg, *Julio Jurenito,* pp. 315, 292, 319, 334, 335.
19. The full text of this poem can be found in Alexander Donat's anthology

of Russian poetry on Jewish subjects, *Neopalimaya Kupina* (The Burning Bush) (New York, 1973), p. 320.

20. Ehrenburg, *Julio Jurenito,* ch. 11, pp. 133–42.
21. Ehrenburg, *Bely Ugol,* pp. 86–91. The essay is dated 1925.
22. Cited in the commentary to *Julio Jurenito* in *Sobranie Sochinenie* (Collected Works), vol. 1 (Moscow, 1990), p. 612.
23. *Pravda,* June 28, 1922, p. 2. Voronsky had not always been a champion of Ehrenburg's work. In 1918 he derided Ehrenburg and other writers for not appreciating the new Soviet reality, accusing them of living on an "absolutely different planet." See *Literaturnoe Nasledstvo* (Literary Heritage), vol. 93 (Moscow, 1983), p. 630.
24. Cited in the commentary to *Julio Jurenito* in *Sobranie Sochinenie,* vol. 1 (1990), p. 613.
25. Cited in the commentary to *PYL,* vol. 2, p. 414.
26. Nikolai Bukharin's introduction to *Julio Jurenito* (Moscow, 1928).
27. *Novaya Russkaya Kniga,* no. 4 (April 1922): 45.
28. Nadezhda Krupskaya, *O Lenine* (About Lenin) (Moscow, 1965), p. 95. Lenin asked the Russian embassy in Germany to send him the book. See Boris Frezinsky and Vyacheslav Popov, *Ilya Ehrenburg, Chronika Zhizni i Tvorchestva* (Ilya Ehrenburg, A Chronicle of His Life and Work), vol. 1, *1891–1923* (St. Petersburg, 1993), p. 243.
29. Yevgeny Zamyatin, "Ehrenburg," *Rossiya,* no. 8 (1923): 28. Ehrenburg valued Zamyatin's opinion above all others. He thought of him as the "only European" writer among his Russian colleagues and sent him a warm letter of gratitude on May 16, 1923. "My perception of you as the supreme master made me anxiously await your judgment. For that reason, your good words so pleased and encouraged me." See Frezinsky and Popov, *Ilya Ehrenburg, Chronika,* pp. 257 and 315.
30. Andrei Sinyavsky, interview with author, Paris, 1983.
31. Ehrenburg, *Julio Jurenito,* pp. 384, 387.

CHAPTER 5. A WRITER IN TWO WORLDS

1. Ehrenburg, *Viza Vremeni* (Visa of Time) (Berlin, [1929]), pp. 6, 10–11.
2. *Russkaya Kniga,* no. 1 (January 1921): 1–2. *Russkaya Kniga* (The Russian Book) changed its name to *Novaya Russkaya Kniga* (The New Russian Book) in January 1922. Ehrenburg contributed six articles and twelve reviews during the course of the journal's brief existence.
3. See *Russkaya Kniga,* no. 5 (May 1921). See also Lazar Fleishman et al., *Russky Berlin 1921–1923* (Russian Berlin 1921–1923) (Paris, 1983), p. 137.
4. "Au-dessus de la mêlée" (Above the Battle), *Russkaya Kniga,* no. 7–8 (July-August 1921): 1–2.
5. *Russkaya Kniga,* no. 9 (September 1921): 2.
6. *Novaya Russkaya Kniga,* no. 6 (June 1922): 10–11, in a review by Ehrenburg of Pasternak's collection of verse, *Sestra, Maya Zhizn* (Sister, My Life).
7. Ibid., no. 2 (February 1922): 17.
8. Ibid., no. 3 (March 1922): 10. Bostunich was born in Kiev. He later became

an SS officer and a confidant of Hitler. See Walter Laqueur, *Russia and Germany* (London, 1965), pp. 134–37.

9. *PYL,* vol. 2, p. 164.

10. Ibid., vol. 1, p. 391.

11. TSGALI, fund 2712, catalog 1, item 163. Letter to Galina Izdebskaya, November 18, 1922.

12. Boris Frezinsky and Vyacheslav Popov, *Ilya Ehrenburg, Chronika Zhizni i Tvorchestva* (Ilya Ehrenburg, A Chronicle of His Life and Work), vol. 1, *1891–1923* (St. Petersburg, 1993), pp. 131, 228, 255.

13. For further details on Tsvetaeva's stay in Berlin see Viktoria Schweitzer, *Byt i Bytie Mariny Tsvetaevoy* (The Life of Marina Tsvetaeva) (Paris, 1988), pp. 286–97.

14. Cited in *Vstrechi s Proshlim* (Encounters with the Past), vol. 4 (Moscow, 1987), p. 158. Following Pasternak's arrival in Berlin, Ehrenburg wrote to Liza Polonskaya that Pasternak "is the only poet with whom I could fall in love with a genuine humane love (of a man)." See Frezinsky and Popov, *Ilya Ehrenburg, Chronika,* p. 273. Ehrenburg so admired Pasternak that the great poet once inscribed a book to Ehrenburg with the phrase: "Your stupid love will ruin me."

15. *Nakanune* (On the Eve), October 29, 1922, pp. 4–7. Also discussed in Lazar Fleishman et al., *Russky Berlin,* pp. 46–47.

16. Roman Gul, interview with author, New York, 1984. For his harsh criticism of Ehrenburg see *Narodnaya Pravda* (The People's Truth), January 1951, pp. 15–16, where Gul accused Ehrenburg of accepting the role of "lying to the West about Russia, and in Russia of lying to the Soviet people about the West." See also Gul's review of *The Thaw* in *Novy Zhurnal* (The New Journal), no. 40 (1955): 295–301.

17. Jacques and Isabelle Vichniac, interviews with author, Geneva, 1984; and their son Gerard, interview with author, Newton, Mass., 1985.

18. Ilya Ehrenburg, *Vsyo-Taki Ona Vertitsa* (And Yet It Turns) (Moscow-Berlin, 1922), pp. 37, 34, 46.

19. *Veshch* (The Object), no. 1–2 (March-April 1922): 1.

20. Ehrenburg, *Vsyo-Taki Ona Vertitsa,* p. 23.

21. In the commentary to *PYL,* vol. 1, p. 614, citing a letter of June 3, 1922.

22. *Novaya Russkaya Kniga,* no. 4 (April 1922): 45.

23. Veniamin Kaverin, *Sobesednik* (Interlocutor) (Moscow, 1973), p. 23.

24. *PYL,* vol. 1, p. 393.

25. *Novaya Russkaya Kniga,* no. 5–6 (May-June 1922): 16.

26. *Na Postu* (On Guard), Moscow, no. 1 (June 1923): 10. The article was entitled "Slanderers: Ehrenburg, Nikitin, Brik." Two months later Alexander Voronsky responded to Volin's attack with a stinging rebuke of orthodox Marxist critics and a determined defense of Ehrenburg and other independent-minded writers. See *Krasnaya Nov,* no. 5 (August-September 1923): 347–84.

27. See the commentary to *Nikolai Kurbov* in *Sobranie Sochinenie,* vol. 2 (Moscow, 1991), pp. 704–5.

28. Frezinsky and Popov, *Ilya Ehrenburg, Chronika,* p. 308.

29. Ilya Ehrenburg, *Trust, D.E.* in *Sobranie Sochinenie,* vol. 1 (Moscow, 1962), p. 271.

30. *PYL,* vol. 1, p. 330.

31. TSGALI, fund 998, catalog 1, item 2667, in a letter from Ehrenburg to Meyerhold on March 5, 1924 from Leningrad.

32. Cited in Konstantin Rudnitzky, *Rezhissyor Meyerhold* (The Director Meyerhold) (Moscow, 1969), p. 281. For further details about the production see S. Frederick Starr, *Red and Hot: The Fate of Jazz in the Soviet Union, 1917–1980* (New York, 1983).

33. Paul Rotha, *The Film Till Now* (London, 1967), p. 263.

34. *Close-Up,* no. 6 (December 1927): 21. To Ehrenburg's chagrin the producers removed aspects of the story that appeared to be morally troubling. The film does not allow Jeanne and Andrei to sleep together, as the novel had done; instead, the fastidious producers have them spend the night on separate chairs. In Ehrenburg's novel Jeanne gives herself to the villain in a vain attempt to save Andrei from the guillotine; in the movie, not only does Jeanne avoid Khalibiev's embrace, Andrei is spared execution altogether while Khalibiev is dragged away by the police, changing Ehrenburg's tragic ending to a happy, optimistic conclusion. This shameless bowdlerizing infuriated Ehrenburg, who was not a puritan in his life or in his imagination. In a letter to the *Frankfurter Zeitung* that appeared on the front page on February 29, 1928, Ehrenburg protested that Ufa did not film the novel as it had promised. Ehrenburg reminded his German readers that the novel was about a love so overwhelming that it leads the heroine to forgive her father's killer, then prostitute herself to save him from the gallows. Ehrenburg was especially annoyed by the movie's "false morality." When the lovers seek to consummate their passion they go to a hotel; but as Ehrenburg noted in his letter, "there is a crucifix in the room, but no bed in a place where prostitutes take their clients. Let us assume this generally common piece of furniture was swallowed by a well-meaning censor." Ehrenburg imagined audiences would foresee an idyllic bourgeois future for Andrei the Bolshevik and his bride: "a *gemütliche* apartment, a cradle, an electric vacuum cleaner, de-caffeinated coffee, and sensational Ufa films once a week. Long live the lovely newlyweds! Long live the protective, solicitous matchmaker, Mrs. Ufa!" *Frankfurther Zeitung,* February 1928, pp. 1–2. (I would like to thank Andrei Markovits and Marc Rubenstein for helping me translate the German text.) It was only natural for Ehrenburg to blame the film's producers for the changes he deplored. What Ehrenburg did not realize was that Ufa wanted a film in the (then) Hollywood manner, to "Americanize" the story for the export market. Evidently, this required a happy ending and the removal of morally ambiguous episodes.

35. Ilya Ehrenburg, *Bely Ugol, ili Slezy Vertera* (White Coal, or the Tears of Werther) (Leningrad, 1928), pp. 105, 107.

36. *PYL,* vol. 1, p. 379.

37. *Proletarskaya Pravda* (Proletarian Pravda), Kiev, February 24, 1924, p. 5.

38. Irina Ehrenburg, interview with author, Moscow, 1986. She visited Bukharin to obtain her visa.

39. Irina Ehrenburg, *Lotaringskaya Shkola, Zametki Frantsuzskoy Shkolnitsy* (The Loteringskaya School, Notes of a French Schoolgirl) (Moscow, 1935), p. 82.

40. *Nedelya* (The Week), no. 20, May 16–22, 1988, p. 10. See *PYL*, vol. 2, pp. 164–65, for a slightly different version.

41. *Lenin* was issued with the participation of literary figures and groups. Profits were to help needy writers. An original copy of this newspaper can be found in Harvard's Widener Library.

42. Ilya Ehrenburg, *Rvach* (The Grabber) (Paris, 1925), p. 446. Ehrenburg's account of Lenin's funeral in *Rvach* was left out of the 1964 Moscow edition of the novel that was included in vol. 2 of his *Collected Works*.

43. Kaverin, *Sobesednik,* pp. 26–27.

44. Ehrenburg, *Rvach,* p. 98.

45. Ilya Ehrenburg, *The Extraordinary Adventures of Julio Jurenito and His Disciples* (New York, 1930), p. 371.

46. *PYL,* vol. 1, pp. 459–60.

47. Ilya Ehrenburg, *A Street in Moscow* (New York, 1932), p. 250.

48. Ilya Ehrenburg, *The Stormy Life of Lasik Roitschwantz* (New York, 1960), pp. 77, 84–85. The author has made slight changes in the text of this translation.

49. Ibid., p. 298.

50. *PYL,* vol. 2, p. 38. This incident was left out of earlier editions of the memoirs.

51. See *Izvestia,* October 1, 1923, p. 4.

52. Ivan Yevdokimov, "Ilya Ehrenburg," *Novy Mir* (New World), August–September, 1926, pp. 225–26. The previous year a Leningrad critic named N. Tereshchenko published a tendentious pamphlet entitled *A Contemporary Nihilist* (Leningrad, 1925) expressing ideological criticism of six works of fiction by Ehrenburg, and was probably the first book written about him.

53. TSGALI, fund 1204, catalog 1, item 114. This is a handwritten note to an unnamed publisher dated November 12, 1926. A second critic warned a prospective publisher not to give Ehrenburg "enthusiastic comments" in an introduction; the publishers could harm themselves if they were not careful. See TSGALI, fund 613, catalog 1, item 4409.

54. *Krasnaya Gazeta* (Red Newspaper), Leningrad, evening ed., October 26, 1927.

55. Cited in the commentary to *PYL,* vol. 1, p. 622.

56. Letter to Yelizaveta Polonskaya, September 9, 1925. I would like to thank the Swiss scholar Joy Brett-Harrison for sharing her copies of these letters with me. I would also like to thank Ewa Bérard of Paris for sharing material on Ehrenburg's career in the 1920s and for our discussions.

57. Letter to Polonskaya, October 5, 1925.

58. Ibid., October 25, 1925.

59. Ibid., December 30, 1925.

60. Osip Mandelstam, *Sobranie Sochinenie,* vol. 3 (New York, 1969), p. 224.

61. Cited in Edward J. Brown, *The Proletarian Episode in Russian Literature* (New York, 1953), p. 29.

62. See Frezinsky and Popov, *Ilya Ehrenburg, Chronika,* p. 204.

63. The German poet Rainer Maria Rilke acknowledged in a letter to Boris Pasternak's father that he had read several of his son's poems in "a small anthology edited by Ilya Ehrenburg." See Rilke, Pasternak, Tsvetaeva, *Pisma 1926* (Letters 1926) (Moscow, 1990), p. 48. The letter was dated March 14, 1926.

64. Max Eastman, *Artists in Uniform* (New York, 1934), p. 88. Eastman wrote a chapter on Zamyatin's difficulties with the Soviet censors. Zamyatin responded to an attack by Boris Volin in *Literaturnaya Gazeta* in a letter of his own to the newspaper on October 7, 1929, in which he described Ehrenburg's help. Several years earlier, on December 1, 1924, Ehrenburg wrote to Zamyatin in Leningrad with the news that he was trying to arrange French translations of his works. See *Voprosy Literatury* (Problems of Literature), no. 9 (1973): 203.

65. *Vechernaya Moskva* (Evening Moscow), June 11, 1926, p. 3.

66. Ehrenburg and Ovady Savich, *Myi i Oni* (We and They) (Berlin, 1931), p. 5. Born in 1897, Ovady Savich attended a Moscow gymnasium and then entered law school, but was drawn to literature and the arts. His first poems were published in 1915. He also worked as an actor in spite of his parents' opposition. Savich first met Ehrenburg in 1923 during a visit to Germany to see his mother, who had emigrated from Soviet Russia. He soon became *Komsomolskaya Pravda* correspondent in Berlin and then Paris; like the Ehrenburgs, Savich and his wife lived for many years in France.

67. Nino Frank, *Memoire Brisée* (A Broken Memoir), vol. 2 (Paris, 1968), p. 14. The journal *Bifur* enjoyed a short but distinguished life. Published between 1929 and 1931, its foreign editorial advisers included James Joyce, William Carlos Williams, Boris Pilnyak, and Ehrenburg's old friend from the Rotonde, Ramón Gómez de la Serna. Nino Frank served as editorial secretary. A French translation of Ehrenburg's novel *The Conspiracy of Equals* appeared in the first issue in May 1929. Three stories by Isaac Babel also appeared, as well as photographs by André Kertész and Laszlo Moholy-Nagy.

    When Lilly Marcou examined French police archives from the late 1920s she found that they had no misgivings about Ehrenburg's presence in France. Close surveillance continued—the police made note of his voluminous correspondence and receipt of many foreign journals; but they believed he was a "sincere anti-Bolshevik" and concluded that within the émigré community Ehrenburg "is not the object of any criticism from a political point of view." See Lilly Marcou, *Ilya Ehrenbourg* (Paris, 1992) p. 96.

CHAPTER 6. STALIN AND THE FIRST FIVE YEAR PLAN

1. Introduction to Ilya Ehrenburg, *Bely Ugol, ili Slezy Vertera* (White Coal, or the Tears of Werther) (Leningrad, 1928), p. 4.

2. *Pravda,* March 29, 1928, p. 2.

3. Anatol Goldberg, *Ilya Ehrenburg: Writing, Politics, and the Art of Survival* (London, 1984), p. 10.

4. Joseph Stalin, *Sobranie Sochinenie*, vol. 11 (Moscow, 1952), p. 329, in an interview dated February 2, 1929, with the journalist Bil-Belotserkovsky.

5. *Literaturnaya Gazeta*, August 26, 1929, p. 1.

6. Boris Pilnyak, *Mother Earth and Other Stories*, trans. and ed. Vera T. Reck and Michael Green (New York, 1968), p. xvi. The story "The Murder of the Army Commander" is also known as "The Tale of the Unextinguished Moon."

7. Yevgeny Zamyatin, *A Soviet Heretic*, ed. Mirra Ginsburg (Chicago, 1970), p. 309.

8. Letter to Polonskaya, July 25, 1927. Archive of Joy Brett-Harrison, Zurich.

9. "In Slovakia" and "In the Center of France," in Ilya Ehrenburg, *Viza Vremeni* (Visa of Time) (Berlin, [1929]), pp. 239–71, 97–108; both essays are dated 1928.

10. *Krasnaya Nov* (Red Virgin Soil), no. 3 (1928): 182, 183, 207.

11. Ibid., pp. 183, 191, 185, 186, 190.

12. *PYL*, vol. 1, p. 521.

13. Ibid., p. 492.

14. Ehrenburg to Polonskaya, November 21, 1930.

15. Fyodor Raskolnikov in his introduction to Ehrenburg, *Viza Vremeni* (Moscow, 1931), pp. 3–8. This introduction notwithstanding, Raskolnikov valued Ehrenburg's friendship. They had first met in the 1920s when Raskolnikov was an editor at *Krasnaya Nov*. On February 13, 1934, while he was in Copenhagen, Raskolnikov sent Ehrenburg a new book with a warm, personal inscription. (The volume is among a handful from Ehrenburg's Paris library that were preserved by the Vichniac family in Geneva.) Then in 1939, when Raskolnikov decided to defect rather than return to Moscow, he sought Ehrenburg's advice in Paris.

16. *Malaya Sovietskaya Entsiklopediya* (The Small Soviet Encyclopedia), vol. 10 (Moscow, 1931), p. 312.

17. *PYL*, vol. 1, pp. 541, 543.

18. Ilya Ehrenburg, *Lyeto 1925 Goda*, in *Sobranie Sochinenie*, vol. 2 (Moscow, 1964), pp. 368–69, 374.

19. "V Predchustvy Kontsa" (Foreboding of the End), *Krasnaya Gazeta* (Red Newspaper), February 25, 1931, evening ed., p. 3.

20. "Pered Zimoy" (Before Winter), *Prozhektor*, no. 31–33 (1931): 10–11.

21. *PYL*, vol. 1, p. 541.

22. Ehrenburg's articles on the trial of Gorgulov appeared in the following issues of *Izvestia* in 1932: July 26, 27, 28, and 29.

23. Yadviga Sommer, "Zapiski" (Notes), prepared by Boris Frezinsky, in *Minuvshee* (The Past), vol. 17 (Moscow, 1994), p. 156.

24. *PYL*, vol. 1, p. 552.

25. Archive of Irina Ehrenburg, Moscow.

26. Ehrenburg to Valentina Milman, January 14, 1933. Archive of Irina Ehrenburg.

27. Ibid., March 3, 1933. Archive of Irina Ehrenburg.

28. Ibid., January 6, 1933. Archive of Irina Ehrenburg.

29. Ibid., March 9, 1933. Archive of Irina Ehrenburg.

30. Ibid., March 27, 1933. Archive of Irina Ehrenburg.

31. *PYL,* vol. 1, p. 561.

32. Ehrenburg to Milman, April 22, 1933. Archive of Irina Ehrenburg.

33. *PYL,* vol. 1, p. 561–62; and Boris Frezinsky, interview with author, Moscow, 1990.

34. Ilya Ehrenburg, *Out of Chaos* (New York, 1934), pp. 66, 65, 69, 68, 150–51, 215, 218–19, 224–25.

35. *PYL,* vol. 1, pp. 560, 541, 544.

CHAPTER 7. A LOW, DISHONEST DECADE

1. Nino Frank, *Memoire Brisée,* vol. 2 (Paris, 1968), p. 20.

2. Simone de Beauvoir, *The Prime of Life* (Cleveland, 1962), p. 224.

3. Luigi Barzini, *Memories of Mistresses, Reflections from a Life* (New York, 1986), p. 80.

4. Interview with Georges Simenon, *Inostrannaya Literatura* (Foreign Literature), no. 10 (1971), reprinted in Georges Simenon, *Novie Parizhskie Sekrety* (New Secrets of Paris) (Moscow, 1988), p. 303.

5. Samuel Putnam, *Paris Was Our Mistress* (New York, 1947), pp. 93–95.

6. *Izvestia,* December 16, 1932, p. 2.

7. Ehrenburg's major articles on European culture for *Literaturnaya Gazeta* appeared in the following issues of 1933: "Miguel Unamuno and No Man's Land," May 29; review of Malraux's *La Condition Humaine,* June 11; "The Surrealists," June 17; on François Mauriac, July 5; on Georges Duhamel, July 29. These essays and others were later collected and published by Gallimard under the title *Duhamel, Gide, Malraux, Mauriac, Morand, Romains, Unamuno vus par un Écrivain d'U.R.S.S.* on June 6, 1934, just as Ehrenburg was arriving in Moscow to attend the First Soviet Writers' Congress.

8. Ehrenburg to Milman, February 7, 1934. Archive of Irina Ehrenburg, Moscow.

9. *Izvestia,* February 15, 1934, p. 2.

10. Ehrenburg to Milman, March 3, 1934, from Prague. Archive of Irina Ehrenburg.

11. Ehrenburg's articles on the Austrian crisis appeared in the following issues of *Izvestia* in 1934: March 6, 9, 12, and 15. They were translated that same year into English by Ivor Montagu under the title *A Soviet Writer Looks at Vienna* and published in London.

12. Ehrenburg, *A Soviet Writer Looks at Vienna,* p. 4.

13. Ehrenburg to Milman, March 9, 1934. The previous year, on September 5, 1933, Ehrenburg referred to his arrangements with *Izvestia* in another letter to Milman: "The usual conditions," he stipulated. "The article should be printed without any cuts." Archive of Irina Ehrenburg.

14. Translations by Pasternak appeared in the following issues of *Izvestia* in 1934: March 3, April 6, May 6, and November 21.

15. *Harvard Library Bulletin* 15, 4 (October 1967): 324; the letter is dated March 6, 1933.

16. *Izvestia,* February 24, 1934, p. 2.

17. Ehrenburg's series of articles entitled "In The Jungles of Europe" appeared in the following issues of *Izvestia* in 1934: April 18, May 6, and May 11.

18. *PYL,* vol. 2, p. 8.

19. *Literaturnaya Gazeta,* June 11, 1933, p. 2.

20. Ibid., June 16, 1934, p. 1.

21. Ibid.

22. Ehrenburg to Milman, May 8, 1934. Archive of Irina Ehrenburg.

23. *Literaturnaya Gazeta,* May 18, 1934, p. 2.

24. *Izvestia,* June 18, 1934, p. 2.

25. Ibid., July 26, 1934, pp. 3–4.

26. *PYL,* vol. 2, p. 28. When Book Four of his memoirs first appeared in *Novy Mir* in 1962 Ehrenburg was not permitted to mention Bukharin by name. When these memoirs were republished a few years later, however, in the last two volumes of his *Collected Works* Ehrenburg was able to invoke Bukharin's name; see vol. 9 (Moscow, 1967), p. 33.

27. Osip Mandelstam, *Sobranie Sochinenie,* vol. 1 (Munich, 1967), pp. 202 and 511.

28. In her memoir *Hope Against Hope* (New York, 1979), Nadezhda Mandelstam described the events surrounding the arrest of her husband.

29. See Lazar Fleishman, *Boris Pasternak v Tritsatie Gody* (Boris Pasternak in the 1930s) (Jerusalem, 1984), pp. 185–87, for Ehrenburg's role in this episode.

30. Mandelstam, *Hope Against Hope,* p. 146.

31. *PYL,* vol. 2, p. 7. Ehrenburg was criticized for his initial hopes in 1934 by the writer Vadim Kozhenov in a review of Anatoly Rybakov's anti-Stalinist novel *Children of the Arbat*; the review has a subtle anti-Semitic edge to its criticism of Ehrenburg. See *Nash Sovremmenik* (Our Contemporary), no. 4 (1988): 160–75.

32. A stenographic transcript of the proceedings was published the same year in Moscow. See *Pervy Vsesoyuzny Sezd Sovietskikh Pisateley* (The First All-Union Congress of Soviet Writers) (Moscow, 1934).

33. *Izvestia,* August 12, 1934, p. 1; See *Izvestia,* August 23 and 25 for photographs of Ehrenburg, while a drawing of him among a host of other writers appeared on August 12.

34. For example, A. Selivanovsky remarked how Ehrenburg used to be skeptical but now is "optimistic and understands that capitalism is crumbling, while socialism means the blossoming of humanity." See *Izvestia,* August 12, 1934, p. 3.

35. An English translation of Gorky's and Zhdanov's speeches and others by principal Soviet functionaries can be found in H. G. Scott, ed., *Problems of Soviet Literature* (New York, 1935). The citation from Zhdanov's speech is on p. 17.

36. Citations from Bukharin's speech can be found in Scott, ed., *Problems of Soviet Literature,* pp. 185–258.

37. Cited in Stephen F. Cohen, *Bukharin and the Bolshevik Revolution* (New

York, 1975), p. 356, from Gleb Glinka, "Na Putyakh v Nebytie" (On the Road to Oblivion), *Novy Zhurnal* 35 (1953): 136.

38. Gustav Regler, *The Owl of Minerva* (London, 1959), p. 208.

39. *Pervy Vsesoyuzny Sezd Sovietskikh Pisateley*, pp. 279–80.

40. Clara Malraux, *Le Bruit de Nos Pas* (The Sound of Our Steps), vol. 4 (Paris, 1973), p. 287.

41. *Pervy Vsesoyuzny Sezd Sovietskikh Pisateley*, pp. 191, 286–87.

42. *PYL*, vol. 2, p. 38. In a letter to a Moscow editor in 1936 Ehrenburg wrote that as much as he respects "literature intended for millions [of readers], [he] cannot renounce literature that demands certain qualifications from the reader." See *Voprosy Literatury* (Problems of Literature), no. 9 (1973): 210.

43. The full text of Ehrenburg's speech at the Congress can be found in *Pervy Vsesoyuzny Sezd Sovietskikh Pisateley*, pp. 182–86.

44. *PYL*, vol. 2, pp. 44, 45.

45. Boris Frezinsky, "Paris Started in Odessa," *Nevskoe Vremya* (Nevsky Times), June 27, 1995, p. 4. Frezinsky and his colleague Vyacheslav Popov pieced together the circumstances surrounding this episode by finding a reference to Bukharin's visit to Odessa in the Ukrainian-language newspaper *Moloda Gvardiya* (Young Guard)in September 1934.

46. Commentary to *PYL*, vol. 2, p. 401; and Natalya Gorbanevskaya in her review of Ewa Bérard, *La Vie Tumultueuse d'Ilya Ehrenbourg* (Paris, 1991) in *Russkaya Mysl* (Russian Thought), no. 3875, April 19, 1991, p. 13.

47. Ibid.

48. Irina Ehrenburg, *Loteringskaia Shkola, Zametki Frantsuzskoy Shkolnitsy* (The Loteringskaya School, Notes of a French Schoolgirl) (Moscow, 1935). The book was first published in the journal *God 17* (The Year 17), no. 4 (1934).

49. *PYL*, vol. 2, p. 47. A similar text already appeared in 1967; see Ehrenburg, *Sobranie Sochinenie*, vol. 9 (Moscow, 1967), p. 53.

50. *Nedelya* (The Week), no. 20, May 16–22, 1988, p. 10; and *PYL*, vol. 2, p. 166.

51. *Izvestia,* December 2, 1934, p. 2.

52. Lyubov Mikhailovna once observed to the artist Boris Birger: "I married a good poet, then I turned into the wife of a political activist." Boris Birger, interview with author, Moscow, 1984.

53. Ehrenburg's articles on the Saar crisis appeared in *Izvestia,* December 24, 28, and 29, 1934.

54. *Izvestia,* June 15, 1935, p. 2.

55. Ibid., July 23, 1935, p. 2.

56. Ibid., April 24, 1935, p. 2.

57. *PYL*, vol. 2, p. 44.

58. See David James Fisher, *Romain Rolland and the Politics of Intellectual Engagement* (Los Angeles, 1988).

59. *Izvestia,* October 26, 1934, p. 1, when Gide presided at a meeting of French writers to discuss the Soviet Writers' Congress.

60. Frezinsky, "Paris Started in Odessa," p. 4.

61. Herbert R. Lottman, *The Left Bank* (Boston, 1982), p. 84.

62. Regler, *Owl of Minerva,* p. 231.

63. Yevgeny Pasternak, interview with author, Moscow, 1984.

64. *Literaturnaya Gazeta,* June 17, 1933, p. 2. Years later the French writer and Communist party activist Pierre Daix asked Ehrenburg how as a friend of Picasso's and the author of *Julio Jurenito* he could have denounced the Surrealists so mercilessly. Ehrenburg said: "I did not write what I believed. I was told to write it because Breton had become an enemy. I had no choice. I was convinced it was a question of life or death." Pierre Daix, interview with author, Paris, 1984.

65. Lottman, *The Left Bank,* pp. 3–4. See also André Thirion, *Revolutionaries Without Revolution,* trans. Joachim Neugroschel (New York, 1975), p. 380, where he quotes Breton as saying, "This well-deserved reproof delighted me, for I had always hated [Ehrenburg]."

66. *PYL,* vol. 2, p. 60.

67. *Izvestia,* June 22, 1935, p. 3.

68. Regler, *Owl of Minerva,* p. 231.

69. *Izvestia,* June 26, 1935, p. 2.

70. Regler, *Owl of Minerva,* p. 231.

71. Cited in Lottman, *The Left Bank,* p. 93.

72. *Izvestia,* June 26, 1935, p. 1.

73. Ibid., p. 2.

74. *PYL,* vol. 2, p. 78.

75. Victor Serge, *Memoirs of a Revolutionary* (Oxford, 1980), p. 103.

76. Alya Savich, interview with author, Moscow, 1990.

77. *PYL,* vol. 2, p. 77.

78. Ehrenburg, *Kniga dlya Vzroslikh* (A Book for Adults) (Moscow, 1936), pp. 143, 144. Anna Akhmatova once acknowledged this unique quality of Ehrenburg's career. In a memoir about Modigliani, who drew a famous portrait of her in Paris in 1911, she had occasion to comment: "It seemed to me that I would never hear anything more about [Modigliani]. . . . Then, in the 1930s, Ehrenburg told me a great deal about him." See Akhmatova, *Stikhi i Proza* (Verses and Prose) (Leningrad, 1976), pp. 570–71.

79. Ehrenburg, *Kniga dlya Vzroslikh,* pp. 64, 16.

80. *PYL,* vol. 2, p. 78.

81. See *Znamya,* no. 5 (1936): 21, and compare with pp. 45–46, which were pasted into the published edition of *A Book for Adults* (Moscow, 1936).

82. Ehrenburg to Milman, August 9, 1935. Archive of Irina Ehrenburg.

83. The epilogue was published in the Moscow journal *Krokodil,* no. 6 (1936): 5–6.

84. Ehrenburg to Milman, June 9, 1936, cited in the commentary to *PYL,* vol. 2, p. 406.

85. Maria van Rysselberghe, *Les Cahiers de la Petite Dame,* in *Cahiers André Gide,* vol. 5 (Paris, 1975), pp. 478–79.

86. V. Tonin, "Vstrechi s Ilye Ehrenburgom" (Meetings with Ilya Ehrenburg), *Literaturnaya Gazeta,* November 11, 1935, p. 6.

87. TSGALI, fund 1204, catalog 2, item 155.

88. TSGALI, fund 990, catalog 2, item 4(3).

89. *Izvestia,* November 24, 1935, p. 4.

90. Ehrenburg, "The Traditions of Mayakovsky," *Izvestia,* January 6, 1936, p. 3.

91. *Pravda,* January 28, 1936, p. 3.

92. See "Literatura i Destvitelnost, Rech tov. V. Inber" (Literature and Reality, the Speech of Comrade V. Inber), *Literaturnaya Gazeta,* February 29, 1936, p. 4.

93. *Literaturnaya Gazeta,* March 27, 1936, p. 2.

94. Commentary to *PYL,* vol. 2, pp. 403–4. The letter was dated April 5, 1936.

95. *Nedelya* (The Week), no. 20, May 16–22, 1988, p. 10; and *PYL,* vol. 2, p. 166.

96. *PYL,* vol. 2, pp. 182, 77, 180.

97. Ibid., p. 84.

CHAPTER 8. THE SPANISH CIVIL WAR

1. Ilya Ehrenburg, *Bely Ugol, ili Slezy Vertera* (Leningrad, 1928), pp. 223–24.

2. Ilya Ehrenburg, "In Spain," *Krasnaya Nov,* no. 3 (1932): 58. Ehrenburg's account of his trip to Spain in 1931 appeared in the first three issues of *Krasnaya Nov* in 1932.

3. *Literaturnaya Gazeta,* May 29, 1933, p. 2.

4. *Krasnaya Nov,* no. 3 (1932): 67.

5. See the memoir of Alexei Aisner in *Internatsionalnaya Literatura,* no. 6 (1957): 251–52.

6. *PYL,* vol. 2, pp. 87, 93.

7. See Simone de Beauvoir, *Memoirs of a Dutiful Daughter* (Cleveland, 1959), p. 293; Stepha Gerassi befriended de Beauvoir when de Beauvoir was beginning her studies at the Sorbonne, and it was Stepha who played a decisive role in introducing her to the sophisticated life of Paris. De Beauvoir also wrote about Fernando Gerassi; see ibid., p. 303.

8. *PYL,* vol. 2, pp. 97–103. Other letters that fall to Marcel Rosenberg and Vladimir Antonov-Ovseenko can be found in the archive of Irina Ehrenburg, Moscow. Although Ehrenburg and Koltsov worked together on many projects involving Western European intellectuals, their careers were indelibly joined in Spain. In an inscription to his book *Spanish Spring* Koltsov wrote to Ehrenburg in November 1933, three years before the outbreak of the civil war: "We are all Spaniards in our hearts." Archive of Jacques and Isabelle Vichniac, Geneva.

9. See Jean Guéhenno, *Journal d'Une Revolution, 1937–1938* (Paris, 1939); and Louis Guilloux, "D'Un Voyage en U.R.S.S.," in *Hommage à André Gide, 1869–1951, La Nouvelle Revue Française* (Paris, November 1951), pp. 244–51.

10. Ilya Ehrenburg, *Duhamel, Gide, Malraux, Mauriac, Morand, Romain, Unamuno vus par un écrivain sovietique* (Paris, 1934), p. 209.

11. André Gide, *Return from the U.S.S.R.* (New York, 1937), p. xiv.

12. Maria van Rysselberghe, *Les Cahiers de la Petite Dame,* in *Cahiers André Gide,* vol. 5 (Paris, 1975), p. 565.

13. *PYL,* vol. 2, p. 56.

14. Gustav Regler, *The Owl of Minerva* (London, 1959), p. 313.
15. *Izvestia,* January 1, 1937, p. 2.
16. Aleksandr Wat, *My Century: The Odyssey of a Polish Intellectual* (Berkeley, 1988), p. 253.
17. Ramón Gómez de la Serna, *Retratos Contemporáneos* (Contemporary Portraits) (Buenos Aires, 1941), pp. 353–56.
18. *Izvestia,* December 20, 1936, p. 2.
19. *Maariv* (Evening), July 23, 1971, p. 13.
20. Stepha Gerassi, interview with author, Putney, Vt., 1981.
21. *PYL,* vol. 2, p. 136.
22. Ernest Hemingway, *For Whom the Bell Tolls* (New York, 1940), p. 417.
23. Ibid., p. 229.
24. *Izvestia,* April 4, 1937, p. 2.
25. *PYL,* vol. 2, p. 127.
26. Hemingway, *For Whom the Bell Tolls,* p. 237.
27. Simone Petrement, *Simone Weil* (New York, 1976), pp. 277–78.
28. *Izvestia,* March 8, 1937, p. 2.
29. Stepha Gerassi, interview with author, Putney, Vt., 1981.
30. *PYL,* vol. 2, p. 145.
31. Jef Last, "Noble Pages in History's Book," in *Spanish Front, Writers on the Civil War,* ed. Valentine Cunningham (Oxford, 1986), p. 96.
32. *Izvestia,* July 9, 1937, p. 3.
33. TSGALI, fund 1204, catalog 2, item 3626.
34. Alexander Werth, "Do Svidaniye, Ilya," *Nation,* October 9, 1967, p. 344. This was Werth's personal obituary to his old friend.
35. *PYL,* vol. 2, pp. 294, 124.
36. *Izvestia,* November 3, 1937, p. 4.
37. André Gide's letter in *La Flèche,* November 20, 1937, cited in Jean Guéhenno, *Journal d'Une Revolution,* pp. 213–17.
38. *PYL,* vol. 2, pp. 154–55.
39. *Literaturnaya Gazeta,* December 26, 1937, p. 6.
40. *PYL,* vol. 2, p. 156.
41. Irina Ehrenburg, interview with author, Moscow, 1984.
42. Ilya Ehrenburg, *Memoirs: 1921–1941* (Cleveland, 1964), p. 421.
43. *PYL,* vol. 1, p. 471.
44. *PYL,* vol. 2, p. 158.
45. Ibid., p. 159.
46. *PYL,* vol. 2, pp. 166–67; and *Nedelya* (The Week), no. 20, May 16–22, 1988, p. 10. Boris Yefimov, the Soviet caricaturist and brother of Mikhail Koltsov, sat next to Ehrenburg at Bukharin's trial. "Now, perplexed, [Ehrenburg] listened to the testimony of his former classmate and, gripping my hand at every moment, muttered, 'What is he saying? What does this mean?' I responded to him with a similar look of confusion." See *Ogonyok,* no. 43 (1988): 3.
47. Irina Ehrenburg, interview with author, Moscow, 1986.
48. *PYL,* vol. 2, pp. 167–68.
49. *Izvestia,* March 30, 1938, p. 2.

50. *PYL,* vol. 2, p. 161.

51. *PYL,* vol. 1, p. 46.

52. *PYL,* vol. 3, p. 233.

53. *Nedelya* (The Week), no. 20, May 16–22, 1988, p. 10.

54. See two articles in the Soviet press on the case of Meyerhold, Babel, and Koltsov: *Ogonyok,* no. 39 (September 1989): 6–7; on Isaac Babel, see pp. 22–23; and *Literaturnaya Gazeta,* May 4, 1988, p. 12, on the case against all three of them.

55. *PYL,* vol. 2, p. 173.

56. *Izvestia,* July 18, 1938, p. 3.

57. Ibid., October 10, 1938, p. 2. Two weeks later, on October 26, Ehrenburg again reported in *Izvestia* on incidents of stark anti-Semitism and threats to Jews in the central German town of Muhlhausen. This came within weeks of Kristallnacht.

58. *Izvestia,* October 2, 1938, p. 2.

59. *PYL,* vol. 2, p. 182.

60. *PYL,* vol. 1, p. 471.

61. *Al-Hamishmar* (On Guard), September 3, 1967, p. 3.

62. *Izvestia,* March 6, 1939, p. 4. Beginning in December 1938 and ending in April 1939, Ehrenburg wrote a series of bitter articles for *Izvestia.* On December 18 he described how German anti-Semitism was infecting France, compromising France's fabled liberty. On January 25 he reported on calls to stop Spanish refugees at the border. On January 28 he urged the need for France to recognize the Fascist threat. On February 2 he described French threats to return refugees to Spain by force. On February 10 he reported on the French government's desire for the Spanish republic to surrender. On February 12 he described the wounded in Spanish refugee camps and the long lines for water. On February 22, in an article entitled "Shameful," Ehrenburg again described the camps and expressed his "shame for the country he loves." And on March 1, in an article entitled "This Is Not France," he described how the French government turned over property of the Spanish republic to Franco.

63. Zhenya Naiditch, interview with author, Paris, 1984.

64. The Spanish loyalist commander Valentin Gonzalez, who was known as El Campesino, was apparently aboard this ship and claimed to have traveled with Ehrenburg, who warned him to remain loyal to Stalin and not be "shocked" when he sees "how things are really like." See El Campesino (Valentin Gonzalez) and Julian Gorkin, *Life and Death in Soviet Russia* (New York, 1952), pp. 40–41. Ehrenburg was not aboard this ship and neither was Mikhail Koltsov, the only other Soviet journalist in Spain of comparable renown. While it is not inconceivable that El Campesino met Savich on the ship and later confused him with Ehrenburg, it would have been out of character for Savich (or for Ehrenburg) to behave as El Campesino claimed. The encounter as described is a fabrication.

65. See commentary to *PYL,* vol. 2, p. 418; the letter is dated May 26, 1939. Boris Frezinsky was not permitted to mention Ehrenburg's admiration for Koestler's book in the Soviet press until the 1990s.

66. Roman Jakobson, interview with author, Cambridge, Mass., 1981.

67. *PYL*, vol. 2, p. 199.

68. Ibid., p. 200.

69. Jacques Vichniac, interview with author, Geneva, 1984.

70. Zhenya Naiditch, interview with author, Paris, 1984. According to Simone de Beauvoir, at least some of Ehrenburg's friends were afraid to visit him because of the obvious police surveillance. See de Beauvoir, *The Prime of Life* (Cleveland, 1962), p. 322.

71. *PYL*, vol. 2, p. 202.

72. De Beauvoir, *The Prime of Life*, p. 304. She believed Ehrenburg was near suicide.

73. TSGALI, fund 631, catalog 15, item 511(1). In the original version of the memoirs in the 1960s Alexander Tvardovsky did not permit Ehrenburg to describe how Kataev engineered the expropriation of Ehrenburg's dacha. See the commentary to *PYL*, vol. 2, p. 420.

74. Roman Jakobson, interview with author, Cambridge, Mass., 1981; and Henry Shapiro, interview with author, Madison, Wis., 1984.

75. *PYL*, vol. 2, pp. 212–13. Mme. Luce Hilsum, who was Ehrenburg's upstairs neighbor on Rue du Cotentin throughout the 1930s, witnessed his physical collapse after the pact and his arrest by French police in May 1940. She kept a diary in May and June, which she shared with me during an interview in Paris, December 1984. According to French police archives, Ehrenburg was considered "pro-Stalinist" in January 1940 and by April 22, 1940, an order was issued for his immediate expulsion. The police actually came for him on May 12 and ordered him to leave by May 22. Ehrenburg had in fact already requested a visa, but a confusing dispute over taxes (he did not owe) prolonged his stay in France, which was then further complicated by the aborted attempt to secure airplanes from Stalin. See Lilly Marcou, *Ilya Ehrenbourg* (Paris, 1992), p. 191.

Foreseeing a German victory, Ehrenburg certainly would have preferred to avoid being in Paris when the Nazis reached the capital; his reputation as an anti-Fascist might well outweigh his status as a Soviet journalist. The police records, as reported by Lilly Marcou, are ambiguous, for it is not altogether clear how early that fateful spring Ehrenburg tried to obtain a visa or how serious French officials were in trying to expel him; after all, in 1921, under far more relaxed circumstances, they had moved with alacrity. Finally, there were at least some French officials, such as Georges Mandel, who admired Ehrenburg and were prepared to protect him and even to enlist him in their last-ditch efforts to resist Hitler's onslaught. Louis Aragon, in his novel *Les Communistes* (Paris, 1951), provides a dramatic reconstruction of Ehrenburg's arrest by the forces that would soon create the collaborationist government in Vichy.

76. Ehrenburg, *The Fall of France Seen Through Soviet Eyes* (London, 1941), p. 16.

77. *PYL*, vol. 2, p. 217.

78. Lev Kopelev, interview with author, New York, 1984. See also TSGALI, fund 1204, catalog 2, item 1586.

79. Commentary to *PYL*, vol. 2, pp. 422, 427. Ehrenburg did not include the incident in his memoirs. Referring to Doriot as a "scoundrel" made it impossible for the paragraph to appear in the Soviet press in the 1960s. Ehrenburg too had promised himself not to write about people he truly hated. Doriot did not seem worth making an exception.

80. Nathalie Babel, interview with author, Washington, D.C., 1984.

81. Ehrenburg, *Fall of France,* p. 25.

82. *PYL,* vol. 2, p. 221.

83. *Pergale,* no. 10 (1989): 119. I would like to thank Jura Strimaitis for translating this text from the Lithuanian.

84. *Pravda,* November 1, 1939, pp. 1–2.

85. See Ben-Cion Pinchuk, "Soviet Media on the Fate of Jews in Nazi-Occupied Territory (1939–1941)," in Livia Rothkirchen, ed., *Yad Vashem Studies,* vol. 11 (Jerusalem, 1976), pp. 221–33.

86. *PYL,* vol. 2, p. 226.

87. Yevgeny Pasternak interview with author, Moscow, 1984.

88. *PYL,* vol. 2, p. 224. The articles appeared in *Trud* on August 31, September 4, September 7, September 11, and September 19, 1940.

89. Ehrenburg, *Fall of France,* p. 25.

90. TSGALI, fund 631, catalog 15, item 511(2). There was another striking omission of Ehrenburg. The bibliographer Nikolai Matsuev edited comprehensive lists of Soviet literary works for several decades. In 1939 he submitted his manuscript for the years 1933 to 1937 to the censors. Although Ehrenburg published at least ten books during that period, his name does not appear, a telltale sign that must have left him wondering where he stood with the regime. See Nikolai Matsuev, *Khudozhestvennaya Literatura* (Artistic Literature) *1933–1937* (Moscow, 1940).

91. *Znamya,* no. 3 (1941). Publication was then resumed in *Znamya,* no. 6 (1941).

92. Annette Lotte, interview with author, Paris, 1984.

93. *PYL,* vol. 2, p. 228.

94. Commentary to *PYL,* vol. 2, p. 436.

95. *PYL,* vol. 2, pp. 218 and 229, and the commentary to vol. 2 on pp. 421 and 424. The full text of Akhmatova's poem can be found in Akhmatova, *Stikhotvoreniya i Poemy* (Verses and Poems) (Leningrad, 1976), p. 208; the poem is dated August 5, 1940.

96. The full text of Mandelstam's poem can be found in Mandelstam, *Sobranie Sochinenie,* vol. 1 (Munich, 1967), p. 162.

CHAPTER 9. THE SECOND WORLD WAR AND THE HOLOCAUST

1. *PYL,* vol. 2, p. 233.

2. Ibid., pp. 246–47.

3. Jean Cathala, interview with author, Paris, 1984.

4. David Ortenberg, "Gody Voennie" (War Years), in *Vospominanie ob Ilye Ehrenburge* (Reminiscences About Ilya Ehrenburg), ed. Galina Belaya and Lazar Lazarev (Moscow, 1975), p. 85.

5. *Krasnaya Zvezda,* September 27, 1941, p. 3.

6. Ortenberg, "Gody Voennie," p. 86.

7. *Krasnaya Zvezda,* October 12, 1941, p. 2.

8. Ibid., "Kill," July 24, 1942, p. 4. Ehrenburg was not alone in expressing such sentiments, particularly in the summer of 1942. Konstantin Simonov published a poem entitled "Kill Him" in *Krasnaya Zvezda,* July 18, 1942, p. 3.

9. Max Voloshin, *Russkaya Mysl* (Russian Thought), no. 3430, September 16, 1982, p. 9.

10. Alexander Werth, *Russia at War, 1941–1945* (New York, 1964), pp. 411–12.

11. *PYL,* vol. 2, p. 397.

12. Lev Kopelev and Raisa Orlova, interview with author, New York, 1984. See also Lev Kopelev, *To Be Preserved Forever* (Philadelphia, 1977), pp. 10 and 160. After Alexandrov's article appeared in April 1945, references to Ehrenburg were removed from the indictment against Kopelev.

13. TSGALI, fund 1204, catalog 2, item 223. Ehrenburg cited these incidents in a speech to the War-Time Commission of the Union of Soviet Writers on January 11, 1943.

14. Jean-Richard Bloch in the introduction to Ilya Ehrenburg, *Cent Lettres* (Paris, 1945), pp. 8–9.

15. Cyrus Sulzberger, interview with author, Paris, 1984. Sulzberger also recalled how Ehrenburg traded vodka for bottles of vintage French wine that were found by Soviet soldiers among the captured booty of defeated Nazi troops.

16. Irina Ehrenburg, interview with author, Moscow, 1984.

17. Lev Kopelev, interview with author, New York, 1984.

18. *PYL,* vol. 2, p. 240.

19. Daniel Danin, interview with author, Moscow, 1982.

20. *Izvestia,* September 6, 1990, p. 3. Zorza later became a highly regarded columnist at the *Washington Post.*

21. Alexander Zvieli, interview with author, Jerusalem, 1983, and his article, "Jews of the Koltubianka," *Jerusalem Post Magazine,* August 18, 1978, p. 18.

22. Joseph Czapski, *The Inhuman Land* (London, 1951), pp. 116–17.

23. Henry Shapiro, interview with author, Madison, Wis., 1984.

24. Leland Stowe, "Off to the Soviet Front with Stowe," *Evening Bulletin,* October 13, 1942, pp. 1 and 4; this was the first of twenty-two dispatches. I am grateful to the State Historical Society of Wisconsin for providing numerous clippings.

25. Stowe, *They Shall Not Sleep* (New York, 1944), pp. 256–57.

26. Stowe, *Evening Bulletin,* October 28, 1942, p. 19.

27. Harrison Salisbury, interview with author, New York, 1982.

28. *Newsweek,* April 23, 1945, p. 65.

29. Henry Shapiro, interview with author, Madison, Wis., 1984.

30. Jean Cathala, interview with author, Paris, 1984. See also the introduction by Jean-Richard Bloch to a speech by Ehrenburg on October 4, 1946, in

Paris. Reprinted in Ilya Ehrenburg, *L'U.R.S.S. et la Civilization* (Paris, 1946), p. 16.

31. Lev Kopelev, interview with author, New York, 1984.
32. Jean-Richard Bloch in the introduction to Ehrenburg, *L'U.R.S.S. et la Civilization,* pp. 16–17.
33. Tatyana Litvinova, interview with author, Brighton, England, 1985.
34. Semyon Gudzenko, *Armeyskie Zapisnie Knizhki* (Army Notebooks) (Moscow, 1962), p. 35.
35. Harrison Salisbury, interview with author, New York, 1982.
36. *New York Times,* May 13, 1944, p. 5. In his wartime memoirs de Gaulle commented that Ehrenburg was full of talent, "though determined to use [it] only in the direction and tone prescribed." See *The War Memoirs of Charles de Gaulle, 1944–1946* (New York, 1960), p. 72. In August 1944 Andrei Vyshinsky publicly criticized Ehrenburg for flattering de Gaulle too much; see Arkady Vaksberg, *The Prosecutor and the Prey* (London, 1990), p. 248.
37. *Pravda,* June 11, 1944, p. 3, and ibid., June 14, 1944, p. 1.
38. All the speeches, including Ehrenburg's, were widely quoted in the Soviet press. See *Pravda,* August 25, 1941, pp. 3–4; *Izvestia,* August 26, 1941, p. 3.
39. Victor Erlich, interview with author, New Haven, Conn., 1984. He only recently received documents from Soviet archives about the fate of his father and Viktor Alter. For further information see Shimon Redlich, *Propaganda and Nationalism in War-Time Russia* (Boulder, Colo., 1982), p. 21.
40. Cited in Boris Frezinsky and Vyacheslav Popov, *Ilya Ehrenburg, Chronika Zhizni i Tvorchestva* (Ilya Ehrenburg, A Chronicle of His Life and Work), vol. 1, *1891–1923* (St. Petersburg, 1993), p. 321.
41. Nino Frank, *Memoire Brisée,* vol. 2, pp. 22–23.
42. *Birzhevie Vedomosti,* April 15, 1917 (April 28), morning ed., p. 59.
43. *PYL,* vol. 1, pp. 402–3. The Polish-Jewish actress Ida Kaminska related to Shimon Redlich in an interview that Ehrenburg was determined "to use Tuwim's article somehow in [his] writings whether 'they' allow it or not."
44. Commentary to *PYL,* vol. 3, p. 403.
45. Letter of Vasily Grossman to Ehrenburg near the end of November, 1941. From the archive of Irina Ehrenburg.
46. Cited in Nora Levin, *Jews in the Soviet Union Since 1917,* vol. 1 (New York, 1988), p. 415.
47. Commentary to *PYL,* vol. 2, p. 433.
48. *Krasnaya Zvezda,* November 1, 1942, p. 3.
49. David Fishman, interview with author, Haifa, Israel, 1985.
50. *PYL,* vol. 2, p. 322.
51. Irina Ehrenburg, interview with author, Moscow, 1991.
52. *PYL,* vol. 2, pp. 323, 356–57. See also Ehrenburg, *Cent Lettres* (Paris, 1945).
53. Shlomo Kowarski, interview with author, New York, 1984.
54. Hirsh Smolar, interview with author, Tel Aviv, 1982. Leib Kunyahovsky was another partisan hero who brought his concerns to Ehrenburg. In April 1945, just as Berlin was about to fall, Kunyahovsky came to Ehrenburg's apartment at the suggestion of the Yiddish writer David Bergelson.

Kunyahovsky was a civil engineer and had the opportunity to return to his native Lithuania. "What should I do?" he asked Ehrenburg. "Work for them? They killed my family," Kunyahovsky said, referring to Lithuanian collaborators. Listening to Kunyahovsky, Ehrenburg began to shiver with emotion and stood up from his chair. "I am also a Jew," he said to Kunyahovsky. "What can be done?" Before Kunyahovsky walked out, Ehrenburg confided to him that he had personally rebuked the veteran Lithuanian Communist leader Antanas Snechkus. "I told him the hands of his people are wet with the blood of my people. I told him more, but I cannot share this with you." Leib Kunyahovsky, telephone interview with author, 1983. His partisan exploits are discussed in Yehuda Bauer, *They Fought Back* (New York, 1978), p. 160.

55. The text of the poem first appeared in Ilya Ehrenburg, *Derevo* (Moscow, 1946), pp. 45–46. At the same time Ehrenburg wrote "Babii Yar" he wrote a second poem about a similar theme entitled "In the Ghetto":

> People will not enter this ghetto.
> People used to be somewhere. There are ditches here.
> Somewhere, even now, days pass by.
> Do not request an answer. We are alone,
> Because you are in trouble,
> Because you wear a star,
> Because your father is different,
> Because only others know peace.

The poem originally appeared in Ehrenburg, *Derevo*, p. 47.

56. *PYL*, vol. 2, p. 351.

57. *Yevreysky Narod v Borbe Protiv Fashizma* (The Jewish People in the Struggle Against Fascism) (Moscow, 1945), p. 56. The volume was published by the *Emes* publishing house, which was attached to the Jewish Anti-Fascist Committee.

58. Abraham Sutzkever, *Moznayim* (Balance), May-June, 1985, p. 53.

59. *Pravda,* April 29, 1944, p. 4.

60. Sutzkever, *Moznayim,* May-June, 1985, p. 56; and Elisha Rodin, *La-Ben* (To a Son) (Tel Aviv, 1943).

61. National Archives, Report No. EES/21445/2/12 USSR Political Information, April 19, 1945.

62. Fanya Fishman, interview with author, Moscow, 1986; Joseph Fishman, interview with author, Haifa, Israel, 1985; and Ephraim Fishman, interview with author, Tel Aviv, 1985. See also Ilya Ehrenburg and Vasily Grossman, *The Black Book* (New York, 1980), pp. 357–58. In the spring of 1958, on his way from Teheran to Paris, Ehrenburg's flight made a one-hour stopover at Lydda Airport outside of Tel Aviv. It was around midnight and, according to the Israeli newspaper *Haaretz,* Ehrenburg spent the hour in a buffet surrounded by four other men. (*Haaretz,* April 1, 1958, p. 5.) The *Jerusalem Post* had a more imaginative account of his visit. Under the prominent headline "Ilya Ehrenburg's Daughter Waited In Vain," the

Jerusalem Post claimed that Ehrenburg refused to leave the airport or to contact a daughter, who was said to have "arrived in Israel under an assumed name to avoid publicity." To add further confusion, the article conceded that Ehrenburg might not have a daughter of his own in the country, but an adopted child whom he found severely wounded on a battlefield near Moscow during the war. He took the little girl to a hospital and later adopted her legally. In 1948 the girl learned that one of her brothers was alive and had settled in Israel. With Ehrenburg's help she managed to leave Russia and join her brother. Ehrenburg is said to have been very fond of his adopted daughter and the reason why he did not try to contact her was because he was accompanied by two bodyguards who were probably secret police agents.

The *Jerusalem Post* inflated a single fact into a malicious legend. Ehrenburg had helped Fanya Fishman, but she remained in Moscow. Ehrenburg had no daughter in Israel. This article can be found in the archives of the *Jerusalem Post*; however, the author has not been able to find the article in an actual issue of the newspaper. It is possible that a sensible editor killed the story.

63. Shlomo Perlmutter, interview with author, Tel Aviv, 1983. See also his diary entries in the Hebrew journal *Yalkut Moreshet* (Anthology of Our Heritage), June 1982, pp. 7–45, and December 1982, pp. 37–62.

64. See Grossman's essay on Treblinka in *The Black Book,* pp. 399–429. It was also published as a separate volume in the Soviet Union. See also Jean Cathala, *Sans Fleur Ni Fusil* (Paris, 1981), p. 371. The French journalist Jean Cathala was urgently summoned by Ehrenburg in August to hear firsthand accounts of what the soldiers had found. Grossman was supposed to join them, but after returning from the camps he suffered uncontrollable nausea and was forced to stay in bed.

65. Ehrenburg and Grossman, *The Black Book,* pp. 256–57. See also *PYL,* vol. 2, pp. 357–58. This episode, which Ehrenburg included in his long chapter on *The Black Book,* was left out of the *Novy Mir* edition of his memoirs and was only restored in the 1966 edition as part of his *Collected Works.*

66. Cited in Redlich, *Propaganda and Nationalism,* p. 67, from *Eynikayt,* January 27, 1944.

67. Mordechai Altshuler, Yitshak Arad, Shmuel Krakowski, eds., *Sovietskie Yevrei Pishut Ilye Ehrenburgu* (Soviet Jews Write to Ilya Ehrenburg) (Jerusalem, 1993), pp. 140, 159–60.

68. *Znamya,* no. 1–2 (1944): 185–96.

69. Ilya Altman, "Toward the History of *The Black Book,*" in *Yad Vashem Studies,* vol. 21 (Jerusalem, 1991), pp. 225–30.

70. Hirsh Smolar, interview with author, Tel Aviv, 1983.

71. A further collection of material that Ehrenburg compiled during the war has been jointly published by Yad Vashem in Jerusalem and by the Government Archive of the Russian Federation. Entitled *Neizvestnaya Chyornaya Kniga* (The Unknown Black Book), ed. Yitshak Arad (1993), it contains additional reports of atrocities, including information about collaboration by Soviet citizens.

72. Sutzkever, *Moznayim,* no. 5–6 (1986): 56. Ehrenburg sent a similar note to Vasily Grossman; see TSGALI, fund 1710, catalog 1, item 123.

73. Ilya Ehrenburg, *Post-War Years* (Cleveland, 1967), p. 130.

74. Mordechai Altshuler and Sima Ycikas, "Were There Two Black Books About the Holocaust in the Soviet Union?," *Jews and Jewish Topics in the Soviet Union and Eastern Europe,* vol. 1, no. 17 (Spring 1992): 48–49.

75. Jean-Richard Bloch in Ehrenburg, *L'U.R.S.S. et la Civilization,* p. 18.

76. TSGALI, fund 1204, catalog 2, item 2162.

77. See the *Saturday Review of Literature,* August 8, 1944, p. 7, for William White's review of Ehrenburg's *The Tempering of Russia.* A portrait of Ehrenburg appeared on the magazine's cover.

78. *New York Herald Tribune,* March 15, 1945, p. 22.

79. Commentary to *PYL,* vol. 2, p. 434.

80. See Kornely Zelinsky, *Voprosy Literatury,* no. 6 (1989): 172–73.

81. *Pravda,* August 7, 1944, p. 3. Ehrenburg received numerous letters in response to this article, particularly from Jews whose relatives had been killed by the Germans. "I read your words out loud in the presence of my comrades," a man wrote to him from a Moscow suburb, "but I did not have the strength to finish it because my tears choked me." See Altshuler et al., eds., *Sovietskie Yevrei Pishut Ilye Ehrenburgu,* p. 148.

82. *Pravda,* December 17, 1944, p. 3. Many other articles on the Nazi death camps appeared in the Soviet press and described how Soviet troops were taken there before entering German territory. See *Pravda,* August 11, 1944, p. 2, and ibid., August 12, 1944, p. 3, for reports on Maidanek. Another full-page article on Maidanek appeared in *Pravda* on September 16, 1944, p. 2, while on October 27, 1944, p. 4, *Pravda* reported on Auschwitz with specific mention of its Jewish victims.

83. *Volkischer Beobachter* (National Observer), March 25, 1943, p. 1. I am grateful to Gisela Koester for translating this article for me.

84. *PYL,* vol. 2, pp. 251–52. This was not the first time the Führer took note of Ehrenburg. In April 1943 he referred to Ehrenburg as an adviser to Roosevelt and responsible for a plan to destroy Europe altogether. Hitler blamed the Jews for the Wehrmacht's difficulties on the Eastern front; he identified Ehrenburg as the principal agent of this disaster. On January 1, 1945, Hitler lumped Ehrenburg, de Gaulle, and Morgenthau together as part of a giant conspiracy of Western Judeo-Capitalism and Eastern Judeo-Bolshevism. See Lilly Marcou, *Ilya Ehrenbourg* (Paris, 1992), p. 213. It is worth noting that Austin J. App, one of the first American academics to advocate denial of the Holocaust, also blamed Ehrenburg and Henry Morgenthau for the rape of German women by Red Army troops. See Deborah E. Lipstadt, *Denying the Holocaust: The Growing Assault on Truth and Memory* (New York, 1994), p. 97.

85. See *Krasnaya Zvezda,* October 15, 1944, p. 4, and the pamphlet *Soviet Russia Today* (December 1944), pp. 9–10.

86. *PYL,* vol. 2, pp. 275, 395–96.

87. Veniamin Kaverin, *Epilogue* (Moscow, 1989), p. 365.

88. *Krasnaya Zvezda,* April 11, 1945, p. 3.

89. Leonid Reshin, "'Comrade Ehrenburg Oversimplifies': The Real Story of the Famous *Pravda* Article," *Novoe Vremya* (New Times), no. 8 (1994): 50–51.

90. *Pravda,* April 14, 1945, p. 2. The article was reprinted the next day in *Krasnaya Zvezda,* April 15, 1945, p. 2.
91. *New York Times,* April 15, 1945, p. 8.
92. *Newsweek,* April 23, 1945, pp. 265–66.
93. *Time,* April 23, 1945, p. 57; *London Times,* April 17, 1945, p. 3.
94. *Le Monde,* April 20, 1945, p. 1. The *New York Times* made note of this article on April 20, 1945, p. 5.
95. Commentary to *PYL,* vol. 2, pp. 443–44. Writing in 1990, Boris Frezinsky was convinced that Ehrenburg did not send this letter to Stalin. But subsequent material found in Kremlin archives has convinced him that Ehrenburg did send the letter and that Stalin read it. See Boris Frezinsky, *Nevskoe Vremya,* April 14, 1995, p. 6, for his article on the fiftieth anniversary of this incident.
96. From the archive of Irina Ehrenburg.
97. *PYL,* vol. 2, p. 385. Ehrenburg arranged for return of the rifle to a French museum in 1966 through André Malraux, who had become de Gaulle's minister of culture.
98. Alexander Dymshits, "Trudnaya Lyubov" (A Difficult Love), in *Vospominanie ob Ilye Ehrenburge,* ed. Galina Belaya and Lazar Lazarev, pp. 57–58.
99. *PYL,* vol. 2, pp. 394–96.

CHAPTER 10. THE IRON CURTAIN

1. *New York Times,* December 12, 1945, p. 5. Ethridge visited Bulgaria and Romania in October and November as a personal representative of President Truman.
2. W. Averell Harriman and Elie Abel, *Special Envoy to Churchill and Stalin, 1941–1946* (New York, 1975), p. 524.
3. *New York Times,* January 1, 1946, p. 16.
4. *PYL,* vol. 3, pp. 17–18.
5. See Savva Dangulov, "Dva Portrety," *Oktyabr,* no. 6 (1985): 187, for an account of Ehrenburg's visit to Romania in 1945 by a former Soviet diplomat.
6. Ilya Ehrenburg, *European Crossroad* (New York, 1947), pp. 123, 120, 6, and 75. His articles were collected and published in English in this volume.
7. See the following journals and newspapers: *Ogonyok:* "On Bulgaria," no. 3 (1946); "In Macedonia," no. 4 (1946); "In Albania," no. 12 (1946); "In Prague," no. 14–15 (1946). *Izvestia:* "Crossroads of Europe," January 1, 1946. *Vokrug Sveta:* "In Bulgaria," no. 2 (February 1946). *Molod Ukrainy:* "Roads of Europe," no. 19 (1946).
8. Leigh White, *Saturday Review of Literature,* March 29, 1947, p. 28.
9. Boris Yefimov, *Rabota, Vospominanie* (Moscow, 1963), pp. 174–76.
10. Ehrenburg, *European Crossroad,* p. 148.
11. On Sutzkever, see *PYL,* vol. 3, p. 31. See also Joseph Leftwich, *Abraham Sutzkever: Partisan Poet* (New York, 1971), pp. 10 and 51.
12. *New York Times,* March 3, 1946, p. 1. Churchill's speech is entitled "The Sinews of Peace."
13. Cited in *New York Times,* March 12, 1946, p. 1.

14. Interview with Clark Clifford on "The MacNeil-Lehrer News Hour," March 5, 1990.
15. *New York Herald Tribune,* March 11, 1945, p. I-9.
16. *PYL,* vol. 3, p. 39.
17. *Liberation,* April 16, 1946, p. 1.
18. *PYL,* vol. 3, p. 38.
19. *New York Times,* April 20, 1946, p. 5.
20. Ibid., April 21, 1946, p. 4.
21. *PYL,* vol. 3, p. 40.
22. *Christian Science Monitor,* April 23, 1946, p. 4.
23. *New York Times,* May 13, 1946, p. 18. The *Times* covered almost all of Ehrenburg's public appearances in New York.
24. *PM,* May 2, 1946, p. 11.
25. *PYL,* vol. 3, p. 60.
26. *New York Times Book Review,* May 19, 1946, p. 3.
27. John Gerassi, interview with author, New York, 1990.
28. Zhenya Naiditch, interview with author, Paris, 1984.
29. Stepha Gerassi, interview with author, Putney, Vt., 1984; John Gerassi, interview with author, New York, 1990. On another occasion Ehrenburg attended a small dinner party for the conductor Serge Koussevitzky, where he saw the American correspondent William Shirer. Shirer and Ehrenburg had come across each other in Paris after the German Occupation. In New York Shirer heard Ehrenburg speak in public about the freedom Soviet writers enjoyed. But over dinner Ehrenburg spoke more candidly, making clear to Shirer and to Koussevitzky how terrible things really were. William Shirer, telephone interview with author, 1989.
30. *Harvard Crimson,* May 7, 1946, pp. 1 and 4. See also the *Harvard Alumni Bulletin,* vol. 48, no. 16 (May 25, 1946): 649–50.
31. See Albert Einstein, "Unpublished Preface to a Black Book," in *Out of My Later Years* (New York, 1950), pp. 258–59.
32. *St. Louis Post-Dispatch,* April 30, 1946, final 2★★ ed., p. 3B.
33. *New York Post,* May 23, 1946, p. 32; Sam Grafton, interview with author, New York, 1990.
34. *Jackson Daily News,* May 22, 1946, p. 1. I would like to thank Angelina Snodgrass for finding this material.
35. Fred Warner Neal, "I Escorted the Soviet Big Shots," *Saturday Evening Post,* January 6, 1951, p. 82.
36. Samuel Grafton, interview with author, New York, 1990.
37. Neal, "I Escorted the Soviet Big Shots," p. 27.
38. Fanya Fishman, interview with author, Moscow, 1991.
39. *Globe and Mail,* June 15, 1946, p. 5. At the end of the war Stalin had occupied a portion of northern Iran and his troops were still there in the spring of 1946, raising concern in the West that the Soviets intended to remain.
40. *Globe and Mail,* June 18, 1946, p. 6.
41. *New York Times,* June 26, 1946, p. 11.
42. Fanya Fishman, interview with author, Moscow, 1986.
43. *New York Post,* May 23, 1946, p. 32.

44. *New York Times,* June 26, 1946, p. 11.

45. *Izvestia,* August 7, 1946, p. 4.

46. Ibid., August 9, 1946, p. 4.

47. "Tovarich," *Harper's,* December 1946, p. 582.

48. Konstantin Simonov, "He Was a Fighter," in *Vospominanie ob Ilye Ehrenburge* (Reminiscences About Ilya Ehrenburg), ed. Galina Belaya and Lazar Lazarev (Moscow, 1975), pp. 133–34.

49. Ehrenburg also met Henri Matisse and at the artist's invitation posed three times while Matisse sketched a series of fifteen portraits. The drawings were unique and surprising, portraying Ehrenburg with a lively and youthful expression; see Louis Aragon, *Matisse* (Moscow, 1978), p. 28. Matisse later explained to Aragon that just before Ehrenburg came to pose, he (Matisse) had been viewing a documentary film about young Soviet athletes parading in Red Square. The spectacle had so moved him that he could not help but reproduce their expression in his portraits of Ehrenburg.

50. Jacques and Isabelle Vichniac, interview with author, Geneva, 1984. Ehrenburg always behaved cautiously around Western Communists, not only because some may have been informers but also because their own naiveté or willful ignorance about Stalin's Russia put them in jeopardy. Ehrenburg once told Nina Cot, the wife of his old friend Pierre Cot, that he was amazed at how easily French Communists were taken in by Soviet propaganda. One young French couple repeatedly asked him for help in finding an apartment in Moscow but he waited until after Stalin's death before responding; he did not want to help anyone move from the West to the Soviet Union. (Nina Cot, interview with author, Paris, 1984.) There was one important exception, however. Ehrenburg's two sisters, Yevgeniya and Izabella, remained in Paris after the war. With advancing age—they reached their mid-60s in 1950—it was growing harder for them to manage on their own; Ehrenburg heard reports they were picking through garbage for food. Just as in 1924 he understood that they would be better off under his protection in Paris, so too in 1952, even though Stalin was still alive, he began to arrange their return to Moscow. They arrived after Stalin's death and lived in a room at Ehrenburg's dacha until their own deaths in 1965. See TSGALI, fund 1204, catalog 2, item 1172.

51. Cited in Amanda Haight, *Anna Akhmatova* (New York, 1976), pp. 143–45. It seems the Zhdanov family had similar views about Ehrenburg. Zhdanov's wife once complained that "Ilya Ehrenburg loves Paris because there are naked women there," as cited in Svetlana Alliluyeva, *Only One Year* (New York, 1969), p. 418.

52. *PYL,* vol. 3, p. 34. Several of Ehrenburg's paragraphs on Zhdanov were removed from the initial editions of his memoirs and restored only in 1990.

53. *Kultura i Zhizn* (Culture and Life), April 10, 1947, p. 4. See also Ehrenburg's second article, "A Reply to David Lawrence," in *Kultura i Zhizn,* April 20, 1947, p. 4.

54. *New York Times,* April 12, 1947, p. 4.

55. Walter Bedell Smith, *My Three Years in Moscow* (Philadelphia, 1950), p. 180.

56. *New York Times,* April 12, 1947, p. 4.

57. TSGALI, fund 1204, catalog 2, item 279. The radio address was dated August 12, 1949.

58. See cable of March 30, 1948, from the American Consulate in Marseille to the Department of State, National Archives, Washington, D.C. It is also possible that part of Ehrenburg's motivation for writing this play was to help Alexander Tairov and Robert Falk. Tairov staged the production and Falk designed and painted the sets. Ehrenburg's play gave them an opportunity to be associated with an ideologically acceptable work.

59. TSGALI, fund 618, catalog 14, item 854, pp. 3, 10, 95, 96, 103, 106.

60. Ehrenburg denounced Russell in *Kultura i Zhizn,* December 11, 1949, p. 4, and Sartre in *Bolshevik,* no. 2 (1949): 62–63. A few years earlier Ehrenburg had told a Moscow audience that he had read Sartre's play *Huis Clos* (No Exit) during his flight to the United States. See TSGALI, fund 631, catalog 14, item 839.

61. *Pravda,* December 13, 1949, p. 2. Ehrenburg's obsequious praise of Stalin was typical for the Soviet press in those years. Peretz Markish wrote the following in *Literaturnaya Gazeta* on February 10, 1946, p. 3: "Every word of Comrade Stalin's speech breathed with wisdom and tranquility. All over again, we saw how he furthered science, labor, the people's enthusiasm in the pre-war years and during the war; how he made fate itself serve the interests of the nation; how he commanded fronts on the boundless spaces of the earth." Such accolades did not save Markish.

62. Interview with a friend of Ehrenburg's who prefers to remain anonymous, Moscow, 1984.

63. TSGALI, fund 1204, catalog 2, item 278. It is unlikely that anyone in the audience knew that Ehrenburg had sent home a Buick and a refrigerator from America two years earlier.

64. Max Frisch, *Sketchbook 1946–1949,* trans. Geoffrey Skelton (New York, 1977), p. 209.

65. Ivor Montagu, "Ilya Ehrenburg, Peacemonger, 1891–1967," *Anglo-Soviet Journal,* vol. 28, no. 2 (January 1968): 29 (from TSGALI, fund 1816, catalog 2, item 303).

66. Frisch, *Sketchbook,* p. 209.

67. *Literaturnaya Gazeta,* September 1, 1948, p. 2.

68. Andrei Sakharov, *Memoirs* (New York, 1990), p. 97.

69. Mme. Yves Farge, interview with author, Paris, 1984.

70. See *Znamya,* no. 4 (1988): 58–59.

71. Ehrenburg took his responsibilities as a deputy seriously. See *PYL,* vol. 3, pp. 337–43, for a chapter about his duties; see also TSGALI, fund 1204, catalog 2, item 3271, for documents about his work. My interviews with Natalya Stolyarova in Moscow, 1984, confirmed this attitude on his part.

72. Mr. and Mrs. Henry Shapiro, interview with author, Madison, Wis., 1984; and *Newsweek,* April 18, 1949, pp. 39–40.

73. Budd Schulberg, "Collision with the Party Line," *Saturday Review of Literature,* August 30, 1952, p. 34. Schulberg had been to the First Soviet Writers' Congress in 1934.

74. For examples of criticism of *The Storm*, see *Zvezda*, no. 6 (1948): 174–80; *Izvestia*, January 30, 1948, p. 3; and *Oktyabr*, no. 1 (1948): 183–91.
75. Ilya Ehrenburg, *The Ninth Wave* (London, 1955), p. 366.
76. Vasily Aksyonov, interview with author, Washington, D.C., 1983.
77. Letters from Shostakovich to Ehrenburg can be found in TSGALI, fund 1204, catalog 2, item 2391; Shostakovich also attended Ehrenburg's funeral in 1967. Prokofiev and Ehrenburg often exchanged letters and telegrams; see TSGALI, fund 1929, catalog 2, item 509 and item 763. On January 3, 1953, Ehrenburg dropped Prokofiev a brief note saying he was "touched" by Prokofiev's attention.
78. Larisa Bogoraz, interview with author, Moscow, 1982.
79. Two letters from Anna Akhmatova to Ehrenburg during the Second World War can be found in TSGALI, fund 1204, catalog 2, item 1243.
80. *PYL*, vol. 3, p. 35.
81. John Steinbeck and Robert Capa, *A Russian Journal* (New York, 1948), p. 217.
82. Ehrenburg, "Zashchitniki Kultury" (The Defenders of Culture), *Novoe Vremya*, no. 46 (1947): 5–10.
83. Yelena Zonina, interview with author, Moscow, 1982.
84. O. G. Lazunsky, ed., *Zhizn i Tvorchestvo O. E. Mandelshtama* (The Life and Work of O. E. Mandelstam) (Voronezh, 1990), p. 50.
85. Nadezhda Mandelstam, *Hope Against Hope* (New York, 1979), p. 384. There is a short, handwritten note from Nadezhda Mandelstam to Ehrenburg about his portrait by Picasso. Undated, it was probably written in the late 1950s. "What Picasso saw, was you. This is what Osya understood in you and therefore I. You had proof of this. If it were not for this, Osya would not have called out your name before his death. It is a startling portrait. In her fifties, an old woman can be sentimental. I cannot get it out of my mind. I kiss you, old friend. Nadya." From the archive of Irina Ehrenburg.
86. "Public Lecture on the Warsaw Congress by Ilya Ehrenburg," January 15, 1951, 700.001/1–1551, pp. 1–2, Department of State, National Archives, Washington, D.C. The Dutch documentary filmmaker Joris Ivens was in Warsaw for the conference to produce his film *Peace Over War*. He was told to be sure to include applause for Ehrenburg and Fadeyev on the soundtrack. Joris Ivens, interview with author, Paris, 1984. Ehrenburg tried to bring Picasso to the attention of the Soviet public whenever he could. During World War II he mentioned Picasso twice in his columns; see *Krasnaya Zvezda*, November 16, 1944, p. 4, and *Sovietskoe Iskusstvo* (Soviet Art), November 7, 1944, p.3.
87. Harrison Salisbury, *Moscow Journal* (Chicago, 1961), pp. 33–34.

CHAPTER 11. ANTI-SEMITISM AND THE ESTABLISHMENT OF ISRAEL

1. For detailed accounts of this period, see Benjamin Pinkus, ed., *The Soviet Government and the Jews, 1948–1967* (Cambridge, 1984); Louis Rapoport, *Stalin's War Against the Jews* (New York, 1990); Yehoshua Gilboa, *The Black*

Years of Soviet Jewry (Boston, 1971); and Arkady Vaksberg, *Stalin Against the Jews* (New York, 1994).

2. *PYL,* vol. 3, p. 95.

3. Alexander Rindzinski, interview with author, Beersheva, Israel, 1983; Israel Kronik, interview with author, New York, 1984; and Shlomo Kowarski, interview with author, Bronx, New York, 1984.

4. Alya Savich, interview with author, Moscow, 1984. Rabbi Mazeh testified in defense of Mendel Beilis at the notorious blood libel trial in Kiev in 1913. A street in Tel Aviv is named for him.

5. Alexander Rindzinski, interview with author, Beersheva, Israel, 1983.

6. Ibid.

7. Natalya Vovsi-Mikhoels, interview with author, Tel Aviv, 1983.

8. Ibid. See also Svetlana Alliluyeva, *Only One Year* (New York, 1969), p. 153, where she describes how she "almost became a witness to an intentional murder." She overheard Stalin saying over the telephone that Mikhoels's death should be termed an "automobile accident."

9. Archive of Irina Ehrenburg.

10. Archive of Irina Ehrenburg. The full text of the speech was published in *Teatr,* no. 4 (1990): 8–35. The journal also provides an account of Mikhoels's funeral and the texts of other speeches.

11. Natalya Vovsi-Mikhoels, interview with author, Tel Aviv, 1983; and Esther Markish, interview with author, Tel Aviv, 1983.

12. Mordechai Namir, *Shlihut bi-Moskva* (Mission in Moscow) (Tel Aviv, 1971), p. 49.

13. Harrison Salisbury, *To Moscow and Beyond* (New York, 1960), p. 74.

14. *Pravda,* September 21, 1948, p. 3. The translation can be found in Pinkus, ed., *Soviet Government and the Jews,* pp. 39–42.

15. Namir, *Shlihut bi-Moskva,* p. 60.

16. See S. L. Shneiderman, "Ilya Ehrenburg Reconsidered," *Midstream* (October 1968): 47–67.

17. Alliluyeva, *Twenty Letters to a Friend* (New York, 1967), p. 196.

18. Namir, *Shlihut bi-Moskva,* pp. 65–68. Additional information was provided by Henry Shapiro, interview with author, Madison, Wis., 1984; and the Israeli diplomat Aryeh Levavi, interview with author, Jerusalem, Israel, 1985.

19. In 1946 Fanya Fishman's two brothers Joseph and Ephraim stayed with the Ehrenburgs in the Gorky Street apartment. They often spoke about their interest in leaving for Palestine. One day Lyubov Mikhailovna reminded them that they "were in the home of a Soviet writer and asked them not to speak so openly about Palestine." Joseph Fishman, interview with author, Haifa, Israel, 1985; and Ephraim Fishman, interview with author, Tel Aviv, 1985.

20. Harrison Salisbury, in his memoir *A Journey for Our Times* (New York, 1983), p. 252, voiced suspicion that Parker was a KGB informer. Parker's book *Moscow Correspondent* (London, 1949) could only have been written by a conscious dupe of the regime.

21. Namir, *Shlihut bi-Moskva,* pp. 83–91.

22. *Pravda,* January 28, 1949, p. 3.

23. Esther Markish, interview with author, Tel Aviv, 1983.

24. *PYL*, vol. 3, pp. 102–5.

25. Ibid.

26. Esther Markish, *The Long Return* (New York, 1978), p. 238.

27. *PYL*, vol. 3, p. 105.

28. Israel Kronik, interview with author, New York, 1984.

29. Anonymous, interview with author, Moscow, 1984.

30. Irina Ehrenburg, interview with author, Moscow, 1986. The folios were among the first things the family concealed from the authorities after Ehrenburg's death.

31. See "Visit of Ilya Ehrenburg," Dispatch 650 from the U.S. embassy in Belgium to the Department of State, May 12, 1950, pp. 1–2. Similar telegrams from U.S. embassies in Moscow, Paris, and other European capitals kept the state department informed of Ehrenburg's comings and goings from the late 1940s until his death in 1967. National Archives, Washington, D.C.

32. *PYL*, vol. 3, p. 164.

33. Anatol Goldberg, *Ilya Ehrenburg: Writing, Politics, and the Art of Survival* (London, 1984), pp. 11, 240.

34. See *Literaturnaya Gazeta,* January 27, 1951, p. 1.

35. Ibid., January 30, 1951, p. 2.

36. *PYL*, vol. 3, p. 179.

37. TSGALI, fund 613, catalog 7, item 433 (internal review of *The Storm* by B. Novikov, October 28, 1951).

38. TSGALI, fund 613, catalog 7, item 433 (internal review of *Without Taking Breath* by a critic named Plantonova, April 24, 1952).

39. TSGALI, fund 613, catalog 7, item 433 (Novikov's internal review of *The Storm,* October 28, 1951. He went on to admit that he "could not make these remarks openly.")

40. TSGALI, fund 613, catalog 7, item 433 (internal review of *Out of Chaos* and *Without Taking Breath* by V. Akshinsky, June 13, 1952).

41. *PYL*, vol. 3, p. 180.

42. TSGALI, fund 613, catalog 7, item 433, April 11, 1953.

43. *Pravda,* December 21, 1952, p. 1.

44. Hirsh Osherovich, interview with author, Tel Aviv, 1983.

45. Ilya Dzhirkvelov, *Secret Servant: My Life with the KGB* (New York, 1987), p. 250. It is also worth noting a section of the memoirs of Efim Dolitsky, who wrote about a meeting between Mikhail Suslov and leaders of the Jewish Anti-Fascist Committee over an official proposal to resettle all of the country's Jews in a new Jewish autonomous republic based on the already existing region of Birobidjan. Ehrenburg did not attend this meeting. The others were soon arrested, perhaps for objecting to Suslov's idea. See the historical almanac *Zvenya* (Links), vol. 1 (Moscow, 1991), pp. 535–59. The series is published by the Memorial movement.

46. Meir Cotic, *The Prague Trial: The First Anti-Zionist Show Trial in the Communist Bloc* (New York, 1987), p. 144.

47. *Pravda,* January 13, 1953, p. 1, carried a lead editorial, while a TASS dispatch on p. 4 carried further details.

48. *PYL*, vol. 3, p. 227.

49. Nadezhda Mandelstam, *Hope Against Hope* (New York, 1979), p. 115.
50. Archive of Irina Ehrenburg.
51. Mordechai Altshuler, Yitshak Arad, and Shmuel Krakowski, eds., *Sovietskie Yevrei Pishut Ilye Ehrenburgu* (Soviet Jews Write to Ilya Ehrenburg) (Jerusalem, 1993), pp. 315–19.
52. *Pravda,* January 28, 1953, p. 1.
53. *PYL,* vol. 3, pp. 226–27.
54. USSR, Telegram no. 1089, from Beam to Secretary of State, January 28, 1953. National Archives, Washington, D.C. Cited in Louis Rapoport, *Stalin's War Against the Jews* (New York, 1990), p. 184.
55. *PYL,* vol. 3, p. 228. In the 1960s Ehrenburg was permitted to relate even less about what happened:

> Things continued to develop. February proved very difficult for me, but it is premature to describe what I went through. In the eyes of millions of readers I was a writer who could go to Stalin and tell him that I disagreed with him on this or that question. But in actual fact I was the same "cog" or "screw" like any of my readers. I tried to protest, but fate, not my letter resolved the case.

Ehrenburg, *Sobranie Sochinenie,* vol. 9 (Moscow, 1967), p. 730.
56. Margarita Aliger, interview with author, Moscow, 1988; and Semyon Lipkin, interview with author, Moscow, 1982.
57. Irina Ehrenburg, interview with author, Moscow, 1984; Alya Savich, interview with author, Moscow, 1984; Veniamin Kaverin, and his wife, Lidia Tynyanova, interview with author, Peredelkino, 1982.
58. The text of the letter is based on the translation from Goldberg, *Ilya Ehrenburg,* p. 281, and *PYL,* vol. 1, pp. 36–37.
59. Joseph Brodsky, interview with author, New York, 1981.
60. Alexander Yakovlev, the liberal adviser to Mikhail Gorbachev, has advanced the opinion, based on his research in secret Kremlin archives, that Stalin was not directly behind the plan to exile the country's Jews. Yakovlev believes that Stalin put an end to the scheme before he died and that Ehrenburg, "who wrote to Stalin, played a certain role." See Lilly Marcou, *Ilya Ehrenbourg* (Paris, 1992), p. 289; and Alexander Iakovlev, *Ce Que Nous Voulons Faire de l'Union Sovietique,* Entretien avec Lilly Marcou (Paris, 1991), pp. 147–48. Nikita Khrushchev once provided a completely different view of what happened. He claimed that Mikoyan and Molotov objected to the deportation plan and that even Voroshilov said it would be criminal and resemble the acts of Hitler. Khrushchev claimed that Stalin grew furious in the face of their objections and that he suffered his fatal stroke a few days later; see *Le Monde,* April 17, 1956, p. 3.

CHAPTER 12. THE THAW AND THE POLITICS OF CULTURE

1. *PYL,* vol. 3, pp. 230, 229.
2. *Pravda,* March 11, 1953, p. 4.

3. C. L. Sulzberger, *A Long Row of Candles* (New York, 1969), p. 885.

4. *PYL,* vol. 3, p. 317.

5. *Znamya,* no. 10 (1953): 165.

6. The text of Ehrenburg's discussion in a Moscow library on December 17, 1953, can be found in TSGALI, fund 618, catalog 16, item 11.

7. Ilya Ehrenburg, *The Thaw* (Chicago, 1955), pp. 28, 120.

8. TSGALI, fund 618, catalog 16, item 143.

9. Simonov's articles appeared in *Literaturnaya Gazeta* on July 17, 1954, pp. 2–3, and July 20, 1954, pp. 2–3. Ehrenburg's response came on August 3, 1954, p. 3. Sholokhov's remarks were reported on September 18, 1954, p. 2. Simonov's response to Sholokhov's attack appeared on September 23, 1954, p. 3. The letters to the editor, along with the editors' own rebuke, came on October 5, 1954, pp. 3–4.

10. The text of Ehrenburg's discussion on October 15, 1954, can be found in TSGALI, fund 618, catalog 16, item 88.

11. Ehrenburg, *Sobranie Sochinenie,* vol. 1 (Moscow, 1990), p. 201. The poem is entitled "Last Love" and dated 1965.

12. *PYL,* vol. 3, p. 245.

13. When I described the details of their relationship to Boris Frezinsky, he asked me what Siam meant. "The old name for Thailand," I explained. "Then it was systematic," he responded, his finger jabbing the air, "he called another companion Japan!" Boris Frezinsky, interview with author, Moscow, 1990.

14. Archive of Stefan Mehr, Stockholm. There are scores of such telegrams among his late mother's papers.

15. *PYL,* vol. 3, p. 267. Alexander Tvardovsky was present and thought Sholokhov behaved "shamefully." See his diary notes in *Znamya,* no. 7 (1989): 150.

16. *Vtoroi Vsesoyuzny Sezd Sovietskikh Pisateley* (The Second All-Union Congress of Soviet Writers) (Moscow, 1956), p. 32. The little-known novelist Galina Nikolaeva took time during her remarks to say that "Ehrenburg has populated *The Thaw* with nothing but petty, passive, untypical people and created what for us is an alien atmosphere of inactivity." See ibid., p. 386.

17. See ibid., pp. 142–45, for the text of Ehrenburg's speech. See also Thomas Whitney, "Ehrenburg Lifts the Iron Curtain a Bit," *New York Times Magazine,* December 26, 1954, p. 9.

18. *Vtoroi Vsesoyuzny Sezd Sovietskikh Pisateley,* p. 377.

19. Emma Gerstein, "Memoirs and Facts," in Ellendea Proffer, ed., *Anna Akhmatova: Poems, Correspondence, Reminiscences, Ikonography* (Ann Arbor, 1977), pp. 103–14.

20. Nathalie Babel, interview with author, Washington, D.C., 1984.

21. Archive of Irina Ehrenburg, Moscow.

22. Ehrenburg's introduction appeared in the volume *Izbrannoe* (Selections) (Moscow, 1957), pp. 5–10. Antonina Nikolaevna Pirozhkova, interview with author, Moscow, 1984; and Nathalie Babel, interview with author, Washington, D.C., 1984.

23. See *Voprosy Literatury* (Problems of Literature), no. 4 (1993): 286–87; the

memorandum was written on December 27, 1957. This issue of *Voprosy Literatury* contains several documents from Central Committee archives about Ehrenburg's career. They reflect how closely the regime examined all of his writing and public appearances and how anxious he made the authorities.

24. *Znamya,* no. 4 (1958): 194–202.

25. *Literaturnaya Gazeta,* April 24, 1958, p. 3.

26. The full, translated text of Ehrenburg's speech and an account of the circumstances can be found in Isaac Babel, *You Must Know Everything* (New York, 1969), pp. 223–37.

27. Isaac Babel, *Izbrannoe* (Kemerovo, 1966), pp. 5–14, for Ehrenburg's introduction.

28. *Pravda,* September 3, 1954, p. 3.

29. See "Visit of Ilya Ehrenburg to India, January-February, 1956." Despatch No. 894, February 15, 1956, from the U.S. embassy in New Delhi to Department of State. National Archives, Washington, D.C. See also Ehrenburg's brief essay in K. Natwar-Singh, ed., *The Legacy of Nehru* (New York, 1965), pp. 53–55.

30. Olga Ivinskaya, *A Captive of Time* (New York, 1978), p. 141.

31. *PYL,* vol. 3, pp. 284–85.

32. Ibid., p. 311.

33. *Literaturnaya Gazeta,* November 22, 1956, p. 1.

34. *PYL,* vol. 3, p. 312.

35. *Literaturnaya Gazeta,* November 24, 1956, p. 1.

36. Ibid., December 1, 1956, p. 4; ibid., December 18, 1956, p. 4; and Vercors, interview with author, Coulommier, France, 1983. Ehrenburg and Vercors had an unusual friendship. It began inauspiciously during the war when Ehrenburg reviewed Vercors' famous novel *The Silence of the Sea,* the first literary work of the French Resistance. Written during the initial months of the German Occupation of Paris, *The Silence of the Sea* was an understated denunciation of the Nazis. Ehrenburg denounced the book and called Vercors a virtual collaborator; the French experience with the Germans did not compare to the Germans' behavior on the eastern front. Ehrenburg and Vercors met after the war and became good friends. Ehrenburg's secretary, Natalya Stolyarova, translated the novel into Russian in the late 1950s.

37. Vladimir Slepian, "The Young vs. the Old," *Problems of Communism,* vol. 11, no. 3 (1962): 55.

38. Natalya Stolyarova, interview with author, Moscow, 1984.

39. Slepian, "The Young vs. the Old," pp. 56–57.

40. TSGALI, fund 1204, catalog 2, item 3208. Ehrenburg's friend, the Turkish poet Nazim Hikmet, also attended the exhibit and recorded a reaction of his own in the guest book: "[Picasso], like a genuine Communist and poet, is not a sectarian, not a fanatic."

41. Ivor Montagu, "Ilya Ehrenburg, Peacemonger, 1891–1967," *Anglo-Soviet Journal,* vol. 28, no. 2 (January 1968): 32. TSGALI, fund 1816, vol. 2, p. 303.

42. Andrei Sinyavsky, interview with author, Paris, 1983.

43. Introduction by Ehrenburg to Igor Golomshtok and Andrei Sinyavsky, *Picasso* (Moscow, 1960), pp. 4–9.

44. Archive of Irina Ehrenburg.

45. TSGALI, fund 1204, catalog 2, item 1180. The letter was dated October 24, 1966.

46. Another Picasso exhibit was held in Akademgorodok in 1967. The organizer was Mikhail Makarenko, an activist within the human rights and artistic community. He had had several contacts with Ehrenburg concerning the work of Marc Chagall and Robert Falk. Makarenko was arrested in 1968 and sentenced to eight years in a labor camp for organizing an unauthorized art show. Makarenko lives in the Washington, D.C., area today. Mikhail Makarenko, telephone interview with author, 1991.

47. *Haaretz,* April 28, 1966, p. 3.

48. Angelina Shchekin-Krotova (the widow of Robert Falk), interview with author, Moscow, 1988; and her article "Stanovlenie Khudozhnika" (The Formation of an Artist), *Novy Mir,* no. 10 (1983): 227.

49. Margarita Aliger intended to include this paragraph in her essay for the volume of reminiscences about Ehrenburg in 1975, but it was removed by the censors along with other sensitive material. Archive of Margarita Aliger, Moscow.

50. Sarah Babyonysheva, interview with author, Brookline, Mass., 1991.

51. *Krokodil,* February 20, 1957, pp. 10–11.

52. *Pravda,* February 20, 1957, p. 5.

53. Boris Frezinsky and Vyacheslav Popov, *Ilya Ehrenburg, Chronika Zhizni i Tvorchestva* (Ilya Ehrenburg: A Chronicle of His Life and Work), vol. 1, *1891–1923* (St. Petersburg, 1993), pp. 131, 228.

54. *PYL,* vol. 1, p. 243.

55. See the commentary to *PYL,* vol. 1, p. 592.

56. *Literaturnoe Obozrenie* (Literary Survey), no. 4 (1990): 16.

57. Archive of Irina Ehrenburg.

58. Boris Frezinsky, interview with author, Moscow, 1990.

59. *Ogonyok,* no. 3 (January 1991): 21.

60. Unpublished article by Boris Frezinsky, which features a letter from Svetlana Alliluyeva to Ehrenburg in August 1957. The article is scheduled for publication in *Voprosy Literatury,* no. 3 (1995).

61. Two additional episodes of official public carping with Ehrenburg deserve to be recalled. In the summer of 1956 Ehrenburg managed to place a favorable article about the poetry of Boris Slutsky in *Literaturnaya Gazeta* (July 28, 1956, p. 3); within weeks both he and Slutsky were denounced in the same newspaper (August 14, 1956, p. 3). In 1957 Ehrenburg contributed a brief essay to a volume in memory of Lidia Seyfullina, a Soviet novelist who had been a close friend of Isaac Babel. Ehrenburg emphasized her integrity and hatred of Russian chauvinism; his essay was removed from the volume when it was republished in 1958; see Afanasy Koptelov, ed., *Seyfullina v Zhizni i v Tvorchestve* (Seyfullina in Her Life and Work) (Novosibirsk, 1957), pp. 88–91. It is worth noting that Babel, dur-

ing his forced confession in 1939, implicated Seyfullina. She was said to be part of his "Trotskyite" circle and connected to espionage on behalf of Austria. Seyfullina, like Ehrenburg, was not arrested. She also helped Ehrenburg with *The Black Book* during the Second World War.

62. Ilya Ehrenburg, *Chekhov, Stendhal, and Other Essays* (London, 1962), pp. 154, 156. The essay on Stendhal first appeared in the journal *Inostrannaya Literatura*, no. 6 (1957): 199–212. All quotations are from the English translation.

63. James Critchlow, *The New Leader*, October 16, 1959, pp. 11–12.

64. Cited in an unpublished article by Boris Frezinsky, to appear in *Voprosy Literatury*, no. 3 (1995).

65. *Znamya*, no. 10 (1957): 224, and *Literaturnaya Gazeta*, August 22, 1957, p. 3. The *New York Times* also made note of these attacks on Ehrenburg. Citing a recent article in *Literaturnaya Gazeta*, the *Times* reported that Ehrenburg "was taken to task for glorifying the concept of 'emotional self-expression.' He was called down also for daring to regard a writer's personal experiences as a more vital influence on his work than the demands of society." See the *New York Times*, September 8, 1957, p. 28. The *Times* in those years did not know what to make of Ehrenburg. On March 24, 1957, the newspaper carried a front-page article describing an effort by Ehrenburg, in the pages of *Literaturnaya Gazeta*, to defend the accomplishments of American culture. But two days later the *Times* editorial page had second thoughts, questioning his moral authority because he was a man "who has long amazed people in and out of Russia with his unerring ability to detect which side his bread is buttered on." See "No Thanks, Ilya," *New York Times*, March 26, 1957, p. 32.

66. *Les Lettres Françaises*, no. 688 (September 19–25, 1957): 1 and 5.

67. Ehrenburg, *Chekhov, Stendhal*, pp. 24, 25.

68. TSGALI, fund 1204, catalog 2, item 1370.

69. Archive of Irina Ehrenburg.

70. The letter from Svetlana Alliluyeva to Ehrenburg was only recently discovered. It is scheduled for publication in Boris Frezinsky's article in *Voprosy Literatury*, no. 3 (1995).

71. Gerd Ruge, "Conversations in Moscow," *Encounter* (October 1958): 25.

72. *PYL*, vol. 1, p. 256.

73. *Pravda*, October 26, 1958, p. 4, as cited in Robert Conquest, *The Pasternak Affair* (Philadelphia, 1962), pp. 164–71 (for a translation of the full article).

74. Natalya Stolyarova, interview with author, Moscow, 1984. In response to one of his readers on November 18, 1965, Ehrenburg wrote: "I did not agree with [Pasternak's] expulsion from the Union of Writers and did not participate in the voting." Archive of Irina Ehrenburg.

75. *PYL*, vol. 1, p. 256.

76. *New York Times*, March 10, 1960, p. 2.

77. *Haaretz*, June 10, 1960, p. 3.

CHAPTER 13. ILYA EHRENBURG AND THE JEWISH QUESTION

1. *Krasnaya Nov* (Red Virgin Soil), no. 4 (April 1928): 165.
2. For a comprehensive review of Ehrenburg's relationship to his Jewish origins see the introductory essay by Mordechai Altshuler in Altshuler et al., eds., *Sovietskie Yevrei Pishut Ilye Ehrenburgu* (Soviet Jews Write to Ilya Ehrenburg) (Jerusalem, 1993), pp. 9–105.
3. For an anonymous letter to Ehrenburg about the events in Malakhovka see *PYL,* vol. 3, p. 324, and Altshuler et al., eds., *Sovietskie Yevrei Pishut Ilye Ehrenburgu,* pp. 420–21.
4. Natalya Stolyarova, interview with author, Moscow, 1984. See also the newspaper *Kommunist* (in the Buinaksk region of Dagestan), July 14, July 30, August 6, August 13, and August 16, 1960. On page 1 of the September 6 issue the Regional Party Committee disavowed earlier articles that had denounced circumcision among the Jewish and Muslim populations and the presence of a synagogue in Dagestan. Ehrenburg also appealed to the Central Committee on behalf of a Jewish man in Georgia accused of drawing blood from a Christian child in the summer of 1962; the man was later released. See Ehrenburg's correspondence in Altshuler et al., eds., *Sovietskie Yevrei Pishut Ilye Ehrenburgu,* pp. 431–40.
5. See *PYL,* vol. 3, p. 325.
6. Bernard Turner's article originally appeared in the Israeli Yiddish journal *Die Goldene Keyt,* no. 25 (1956): 3–37. Portions were reprinted in *Dissent* (Winter 1957): 88–91, and in *Le Monde,* August 22, 1957, p. 3. It was ludicrous for Turner to describe Solomon Lozovsky as Ehrenburg's "closest friend." They had first met in 1909, when Lozovsky was the editor of a Communist party journal in Paris. During World War II Ehrenburg had a good deal of contact with Lozovsky, who served as a deputy foreign minister and head of the Soviet Information Bureau. In this latter capacity Lozovsky supervised reporting on the war and the activities of the Jewish Anti-Fascist Committee. But he and Ehrenburg were not close friends.
7. Esther Markish, *The Long Return* (New York, 1978), pp. 241–45.
8. *Le Monde,* September 26, 1957, p. 10.
9. Léon Leneman, *La Tragédie des Juifs en U.R.S.S.* (Paris, 1959), p. 95.
10. *Jerusalem Post,* January 27, 1963, p. 3.
11. Bernard Turner, "With the Yiddish Writers in Siberia," *Dissent,* vol. 4, no. 1 (Winter 1957): 91.
12. Ibid.
13. *Jerusalem Post,* June 24, 1962, p. 1.
14. Cited in Tom Segev, *Ha-Milyon Hashviyi* (The Seventh Million) (Jerusalem, 1991), p. 192.
15. *Jerusalem Post,* January 27, 1963, p. 3.
16. *PYL,* vol. 3, p. 326.
17. *Jerusalem Post,* August 15, 1965, p. 3.
18. *PYL,* vol. 3, p. 100.

19. See the speech by Leonid Ilyichev on March 7, 1963. A full translation of Ilyichev's speech can be found in Priscilla Johnson and Leopold Labedz, eds., *Khrushchev and the Arts: The Politics of Soviet Culture, 1962–1964* (Cambridge, Mass., 1965), pp. 137–47.

20. *PYL*, vol. 3, p. 310.

21. *Pravda,* November 6, 1956, p. 5.

22. See *Izvestia,* November 28, 1956, p. 4, for a petition from religious Jews in Tashkent, and *Izvestia,* November 29, p. 4, for a petition from Jewish religious leaders from different cities.

23. As translated by George Reavey in *Yevgeny Yevtushenko: The Collected Poems 1952–1990,* ed. Albert C. Todd with the author and James Ragan (New York, 1991), pp. 102–4. The poem first appeared in *Literatunaya Gazeta,* September 19, 1961, p. 4. Two years earlier, on October 10, 1959, Viktor Nekrasov, in a long letter in *Literaturnaya Gazeta,* had protested a proposal to build a park and an athletic stadium at Babii Yar. Ehrenburg shared Nekrasov's outrage. In a letter dated November 30, 1959, Ehrenburg wrote to a woman named Shargorodskaya: "I entirely share the views of V. Nekrasov—I have repeatedly approached a series of cities which have their own 'Babii Yars,' pointing out the necessity of protecting the graves of fascism's victims." Archive of Irina Ehrenburg.

24. Yevgeny Yevtushenko, *A Precocious Autobiography* (New York, 1963), pp. 121–22.

25. Dmitri Starikov, *Literatura i Zhizn,* September 27, 1961, p. 3.

26. *Literaturnaya Gazeta,* October 14, 1961, p. 4; and Boris Frezinsky, interview with author, Moscow, 1990.

27. *PYL*, vol. 3, p. 325.

28. *Jerusalem Post,* May 11, 1959, p. 1.

29. Both letters are from the archive of Irina Ehrenburg.

30. Yaakov Ro'i, *The Struggle for Soviet Jewish Emigration, 1948–1967* (Cambridge, 1991), pp. 138–39.

31. *Jerusalem Post,* January 26, 1962, p. 1.

32. *Pravda,* September 21, 1948, p. 3.

33. Markish, *The Long Return,* pp. 254–55.

34. A copy of Ehrenburg's speech and other details of the program are contained in the archive of the Literary Museum in Moscow. In 1959 a six-volume collection of the works of Sholem Aleichem in Russian was published in Moscow in a printing of 225,000 copies.

35. Markish, *The Long Return,* pp. 256–57.

36. TSGALI, fund 1204, catalog 2, item 1168. The letter was dated October 12, 1965; Markish's birthday came on November 25, 1965.

37. Anne Frank, *Dnevnik Anny Frank* (Moscow, 1960), pp. 5–6. That same year Ehrenburg also tried, this time unsuccessfully, to publish a book about the Warsaw Ghetto Uprising; see Altshuler et al., eds., *Sovietskie Yevrei Pishut Ilye Ehrenburgu,* pp. 445–46.

38. TSGALI, fund 1204, catalog 2, item 2116, contains the letters of Masha Rolnikaite to Ehrenburg. Her book was published in *Zvezda,* no. 2 (1965): 132–71, and no. 3 (1965): 102–30. Ehrenburg wrote the introduction to

the French edition in 1966. Masha Rolnikaite, interview with author, St. Petersburg, 1994.

39. Ilya Ehrenburg, *Hommage à Zola,* October 2, 1966. An extract from *Cahiers Naturalistes,* no. 2 (1966). The lecture appeared in Russian in *Nedelya* (The Week), no. 42, October 9–15, 1966, p. 16.

40. Yury Oklyansky, *Schastlivie Neudachniki* (Lucky Failures) (Moscow, 1990), pp. 380–89.

41. Boris Frezinsky, interview with author, Moscow, 1990. Her husband was Igor Chernoutsan, who signed several internal memorandums critical of Ehrenburg in the 1950s and 1960s, at least one of which concerned the memoirs. It was an irony of life in Moscow at the time that his wife was helping to publish a fuller version of *People, Years, Life* than her husband in his role at the Central Committee would have approved. After her death Chernoutsan married Ehrenburg's close friend, the poet Margarita Aliger.

42. The additional material on Vasily Grossman and the fate of *The Black Book* appeared as chaps. 20 and 21 in Book Five of vol. 9 of Ehrenburg's *Sobranie Sochinenie* (Moscow 1967), pp. 407–18. According to Shimon Markish (the son of the martyred poet), *People, Years, Life* had an enormous influence on young Soviet Jews. "No one, besides Ehrenburg, could have openly, with a full voice and in millions of copies, taught our youth this first lesson in their national upbringing. . . . No other book in Russian Soviet literature during the fifteen years following Stalin's death did as much for Jewish awakening." Cited in Altshuler et al., eds., *Sovietskie Yevrei Pishut Ilye Ehren-burgu,* p. 491.

43. Ilya Ehrenburg, *The Stormy Life of Lasik Roitschwantz* (New York, 1960), p. 10.

CHAPTER 14. ILLNESS AND OLD AGE

1. Irina Ehrenburg, Fanya Fishman, and Dr. Yelena Nekhamkina, interviews with author, Moscow, 1991, provided information about Ehrenburg's illness.

2. Ehrenburg's initial letter can be found in *Komsomolskaya Pravda,* September 2, 1959, p. 3. The newspaper ran subsequent letters from readers throughout October and November. Ehrenburg closed the discussion with an article on December 24, 1959.

3. Zhenya Naiditch, interview with author, Paris, 1984.

4. See *Voprosy Literatury,* no. 4 (1993): 288–94, for internal party memorandums about Ehrenburg's seventieth birthday celebration.

5. *Pravda,* January 25, 1961, p. 4; the radio listings on the same page announced Ehrenburg's speech for 10:10 A.M. On the front page of *Pravda,* January 26, 1961, an announcement awarding the Order of Lenin to Ehrenburg appeared over the signature of Leonid Brezhnev.

6. *Moskovskie Novosti,* January 28, 1961, as cited in Incoming Telegram, American embassy to Department of State, January 27, 1961. National Archives, Washington, D.C.

7. Archive of Irina Ehrenburg. See also *PYL,* vol. 3, p. 101.

8. TSGALI, fund 1204, catalog 2, item 1243.

9. Archive of Irina Ehrenburg, Moscow. See also *PYL,* vol. 3, p. 101.

10. Ehrenburg had little patience for special pleading on the part of his fellow Jews. In July 1962 a Russian-Jewish émigré in Miami wrote Ehrenburg a letter in which he asked if Jews should be offended by Shakespeare's portrait of Shylock in *The Merchant of Venice.* "It seems to me," Ehrenburg responded on November 9, "that the Jews have as much reason to be angry with Shakespeare as the British have because of Lady Macbeth and the moors have because of Othello." Both letters can be found in the archive of Irina Ehrenburg.

11. Archive of Irina Ehrenburg.

12. *Voprosy Literatury,* no. 4 (1993): 291.

13. Fanya Fishman, interview with author, Moscow, 1986.

CHAPTER 15. *PEOPLE, YEARS, LIFE*

1. Moses Hadas, ed., *Complete Works of Tacitus* (New York, 1970), p. 126.

2. Nikolai Vasilenko, interview with author, Moscow, 1991.

3. TSGALI, fund 1204, catalog 2, item 134.

4. TSGALI, fund 1702, catalog 9, item 38. Ehrenburg respected Tvardovsky. He once told the Polish-Jewish critic Arthur Sandauer that "Tvardovsky looks like a hooligan, but he is a decent man." Arthur Sandauer, interview with author, Brookline, Mass., 1985.

5. TSGALI, fund 1702, catalog 9, item 47 (part 2).

6. *PYL,* vol. 3, p. 8. Internal party memorandums from the head of Glavlit and other cultural bureaucrats repeatedly focused on Ehrenburg's "tendentious" views about anti-Semitism. As one note complained in February 1963, Ehrenburg "again and again artificially raises the question of national discrimination against Jews in our country." See *Voprosy Literatury,* no. 4 (1993): 302.

7. TSGALI, fund 1702, catalog 9, item 47 (part 2).

8. Archive of Irina Ehrenburg.

9. Commentary to *PYL,* vol. 1, p. 569. Also, Natalya Stolyarova, interview with author, Moscow, 1984.

10. See *Novy Mir* (August 1960): 43.

11. Anna Larina, interview with author, Moscow, 1982.

12. *Voprosy Literatury,* no. 4 (1993): 425.

13. Yevgeny Pasternak, interview with author, Moscow, 1984. In his careful approach to the memoirs Ehrenburg typically would ask people to review individual chapters; he showed his portrait of Isaac Babel to Antonina Pirozhkova and his chapter on Maxim Litvinov to the diplomat's daughter, Tatyana. (Interviews with Antonina Pirozhkova, Moscow, 1984, and with Tatyana Litvinova, Brighton, England, 1985; the latter's detailed and lively response to Ehrenburg can be found in TSGALI, fund 1204, catalog 2, item 1820.)

14. Commentary to *PYL,* vol. 1, p. 594.

15. Isaac Deutscher, "Survival's Favorite Son," *Nation,* December 21, 1964, p. 495.

16. Zbignief Herbert, from the poem "Mr. Cognito on the Need for Precision," in *Report from the Besieged City and Other Poems,* trans. John and Bogdana Carpenter (New York, Ecco), p. 67.

17. *PYL,* vol. 1, pp. 191, 46.

18. TSGALI, fund 1204, catalog 2, item 2218.

19. Nadezhda Mandelstam, *Hope Abandoned* (New York, 1974), p. 16.

20. Commentary to *PYL,* vol. 1, p. 590.

21. TSGALI, fund 1204, catalog 2, item 1683.

22. See *Kulturny Zivot,* September 14, 1963, pp. 1 and 8. The editors informed their readers in a footnote that Ehrenburg had supplied the material to them in manuscript form. The correspondent Anatole Shub, in his book *An Empire Loses Hope* (New York, 1970), p. 126, observes that this was a striking example of "Bratislava rebels [summoning] Soviet liberals to their aid." In the early 1960s Shub also followed the efforts of Hungarian reformers to translate and publish the poetry and prose of Soviet writers, such as Ehrenburg, Yevtushenko, and Akhmadulina, as a way to challenge the limits of Hungarian censors. See ibid., p. 181.

23. Airgram from the American embassy in Prague to the Department of State, October 4, 1963. National Archives, Washington, D.C.

24. *PYL,* vol. 1, pp. 270, 307.

25. I would like to acknowledge the work of Dina Spechler, who explored the evolution of dissent in the work of Alexander Tvardovsky at *Novy Mir.* See Dina Spechler, *Permitted Dissent in the USSR* (New York, 1982).

26. Alexander Dymshits, "Memuary i Istoriya," *Oktyabr,* no. 6 (1961): 194–98.

27. Vsevolod Kochetov, speech to the Twenty-second Party Congress, *Pravda,* October 31, 1961, p. 8. Outside the country the harshest criticism of Ehrenburg's memoirs came in West Germany. With their publication in German translation, right-wing elements revived Nazi claims against him. The *Deutsche Soldaten Zeitung* called Ehrenburg "the greatest inciter to murder of all time." Bookstores were warned not to carry the memoirs, and there was even a threat of an organized boycott. See *Der Spiegel,* "Kill, Kill, Kill," September 5, 1962, pp. 71–76, and *Sonntag,* September 30, 1962, p. 6, for a discussion of the controversy.

28. *PYL,* vol. 3, p. 180.

29. Ehrenburg was called on during the crisis to write an article denying that Soviet missiles were in Cuba. He refused, telling an official at the Kremlin that "I have an international reputation. If I write such an article today, the missiles could be exposed a week later. Then I will look foolish." With that he slammed down the phone. Boris Birger, interview with author, Moscow, 1984.

30. Priscilla Johnson and Leopold Labedz, eds., *Khrushchev and the Arts: The Politics of Soviet Culture, 1962–1964* (Cambridge, Mass., 1965), pp. 101–2. I would like to acknowledge this anthology and Priscilla Johnson's essay as particularly helpful sources of information about this period.

31. Ernst Neizvestny, interview with author, New York, 1981.

32. Archive of Irina Ehrenburg, Moscow.
33. Priscilla Johnson and Leopold Labedz, eds., *Khrushchev and the Arts* (Cambridge, Mass., 1965), p. 11.
34. Alexander Laktionov, *Pravda,* January 4, 1963, p. 4.
35. Alexander Gerasimov, *Trud* (Labor), January 9, 1961, p. 3.
36. *Izvestia,* January 30, 1963, pp. 3–4.
37. *Izvestia,* February 6, 1963, p. 4.
38. *Molodyozh Estony* (The Youth of Estonia), no. 88, May 6, 1989, p. 2. One long-time admirer, Alexander Barenboim, whose tank unit had "adopted" Ehrenburg during the war, wrote to him from Odessa on February 6, 1963. Barenboim's letter exemplified the passionate support Ehrenburg was receiving throughout the country, particularly among veterans of the war, Jews, and young people:

> Dear Ilya Grigorevich!
> I have just read your letter in *Izvestia* and the response by this scum. I cannot understand why you enter into an argument with such a scoundrel. . . . What you explained to him in your letter was clear to every decent person. And the ten people with whom I had occasion to speak after [Yermilov's] first belch very precisely and unequivocally understood the kind of concoction this bigot and hypocrite cooked up against you. I would be happy to share the opinion of these people with you if I were sure that your secretary were not a woman . . .
> Be healthy in order to outlive all your and our enemies.
> Sincerely yours,
> Alexander Mendeleevich Barenboim

From TSGALI, fund 1204, catalog 2, item 1258. Many years later Barenboim published a series of five articles about his wartime contacts with Ehrenburg in *Svet Oktibrya* (The Light of October), a Communist party newspaper in Tatsinsk in the Rostov region. The articles appeared in the following issues in 1982: November 20, November 23, November 25, November 27, December 2, and December 4.

39. Archive of Irina Ehrenburg.
40. Andrei Voznesensky, interview with author, Peredelkino, 1984.
41. Janet Flanner, "Letter from Paris," *The New Yorker,* January 26, 1963, p. 102.
42. Michael Harrington, "The New Parabolist," *The Reporter,* February 14, 1963, p. 52.

CHAPTER 16. SPRING 1963 AND THE FALL OF KHRUSHCHEV

1. A full translation of Ilyichev's speech can be found in Priscilla Johnson and Leopold Labedz, eds., *Khrushchev and the Arts: The Politics of Soviet Culture, 1962–1964* (Cambridge, Mass., 1965), pp. 137–47.
2. Archive of Margarita Aliger, Moscow.
3. Ralph Blum, "Reporter at Large," *The New Yorker,* August 28, 1965, p. 96.
4. Johnson and Labedz, eds., *Khrushchev and the Arts,* p. 23.

5. A full translation of Khrushchev's speech can be found in Johnson and Labedz, eds., *Khrushchev and the Arts,* pp. 147–86.

6. Yelena Zonina, interview with author, Moscow, 1982.

7. Andrei Sinyavsky, interview with author, Paris, 1983.

8. Airgram from the American embassy in Moscow to the Department of State, September 9, 1963. National Archives, Washington, D.C.

9. Archive of Natalya Stolyarova, Moscow.

10. TSGALI, fund 1204, catalog 2, item 1370. Ehrenburg also received a telegram from a group of Italian writers, including Italo Calvino, Alberto Moravia, Giorgio Bassani, and Pier Pasolini; they offered their firm support. See TSGALI, fund 1204, catalog 2, item 1930.

11. TSGALI, fund 1204, catalog 2, item 1586.

12. *Pravda,* May 12, 1963, pp. 4–5. A translation of Tvardovsky's interview with Henry Shapiro can be found in Johnson and Labedz, eds., *Khrushchev and the Arts,* pp. 210–16.

13. Cited in *Pamyatnie Knizhnie Daty* (Memorable Book Dates), 1990, p. 138, in an article by Boris Frezinsky marking the twenty-fifth anniversary of the publication of Book Six of Ehrenburg's memoirs.

14. Archive of Irina Ehrenburg. Ehrenburg once handed the Soviet editor and official peace activist Yury Zhukov the following handwritten note on the back of an envelope: "Ten years after my death, they will understand that in 1963 I was not twenty-nine years old, but seventy-two, and that I defended the good name of our country abroad for thirty-two years." Archive of Irina Ehrenburg.

15. Johnson and Labedz, eds., *Khrushchev and the Arts,* p. 65.

16. Vladimir Lakshin, "Novy Mir Vo Vremya Khrushcheva (1961–1964)," *Znamya* (July 1990): 90.

17. Hans Werner Richter, "Pisateli na Beregakh Nevy" (Writers on the Banks of the Neva), *Novoe Russkoe Slovo,* September 22, 1963, pp. 7–8.

18. A full translation of Ehrenburg's remarks can be found in Johnson and Labedz, eds., *Khrushchev and the Arts,* pp. 240–45. The *Manchester Guardian,* among many Western observers, was impressed by Ehrenburg's resolve. "For [Ehrenburg]," the *Manchester Guardian* commented, "old age is neither crabbed nor cautious; criticised by Khrushchev for gross ideological errors, he has not quailed as lesser writers might do, but has hit back with a vigour which must have pleased the young liberal intelligentsia who have always looked upon him as their spokesman." *Manchester Guardian,* August 14, 1963, p. 6.

19. Richter, "Pisateli na Beregakh Nevy," pp. 7–8.

20. *Pravda,* September 6, 1963, p. 6.

21. Alexander Werth, *Russia: Hopes and Fears* (New York, 1970), p. 182.

22. Archive of Irina Ehrenburg.

23. Ilya Ehrenburg, *Lyudi, Gody, Zhizn* (People, Years, Life) (Moscow, 1963), pp. 5–9.

24. *Pamyatnie Knizhnie Daty,* 1990, p. 139.

25. Archive of Irina Ehrenburg.

26. Lakshin, "Novy Mir Vo Vremya Khrushcheva (1961–1964)," *Znamya* (July 1990): 133.

27. *PYL,* vol. 3, pp. 259, 260.

CHAPTER 17. EHRENBURG AND DISSENT

1. See two letters from Frida Vigdorova to Ehrenburg in TSGALI, fund 1204, catalog 2, item 1370, and letters from Ehrenburg to Vigdorova in TSGALI, fund 1204, catalog 2, item 518. There is also a letter dated October 2, 1962, from Vigdorova to Ehrenburg, in which she seeks his help for Pasternak's companion, Olga Ivinskaya, who was still incarcerated in a labor camp. From the letter it is clear that Ehrenburg had already helped to secure better conditions for Ivinskaya. In 1991 Alexander Daniel delivered a series of lectures on the history of the Soviet human rights movement to students in Moscow. The son of Yuly Daniel and Larisa Bogoraz, he was among the most active dissidents and firsthand witnesses to events in Moscow from the inception of the movement in 1965 to the onset of *perestroika* and *glasnost* under Mikhail Gorbachev. In his lectures Daniel described Frida Vigdorova as "the first dissident."

2. See *The New Leader,* August 31, 1964, pp. 6–17, for a transcript of Brodsky's trial. According to Simone de Beauvoir, Ehrenburg encouraged Jean-Paul Sartre to send an appeal on Brodsky's behalf to Soviet President Anastas Mikoyan in 1965; Brodsky was released soon after. See de Beauvoir, *All Said and Done* (London, 1974), pp. 314–15.

3. Archive of Irina Ehrenburg, Moscow. Eugeniya Ginzburg acknowledged Ehrenburg's help in the epilogue to the Soviet edition of her memoirs, *Krutoy Marshrut* (Moscow, 1990), pp. 595–96.

4. See Aleksandr Solzhenitsyn, *Invisible Allies* (Washington, D.C., 1995), p. 147.

5. Natalya Stolyarova, interview with author, Moscow, 1984. See also Alexander Solzhenitsyn, *The Gulag Archipelago,* vol. 1 (New York, 1974), p. 131, and vol. 2 (New York, 1975), pp. 239 and 561, where Solzhenitsyn cites Stolyarova as a source of information about political imprisonment under Stalin. According to Michael Scammell, a rumor circulated in Moscow that Ehrenburg photocopied Solzhenitsyn's novella and passed copies to friends; see Scammell, *Solzhenitsyn* (New York, 1984), p. 425. Ehrenburg is also believed to have written a letter to the Soviet Writers' Union supporting the award of the Lenin Prize for literature to Solzhenitsyn; see Priscilla Johnson and Leopold Labedz, eds., *Khrushchev and the Arts* (Cambridge, Mass., 1965), p. 75. In addition, see the article by Solzhenitsyn about his relationship with Natalya Stolyarova in *Literaturnaya Gazeta,* August 28, 1991, p. 12.

6. Boris Birger, interview with author, Moscow, 1984. Birger witnessed their argument.

7. An account of the evening in honor of Osip Mandelstam can be found in TSGALI, fund 1893, catalog 2, item 9, and *Grani,* no. 77 (1970): 82–88.

8. The letters of Varlam Shalamov to Ehrenburg can be found in TSGALI, fund 1204, catalog 2, item 2116, and *Sovietskaya Kultura,* January 26, 1991, p. 15, in an article prepared by Boris Frezinsky marking the centenary of Ehrenburg's birth.

9. Julius Telesin, interview with author, Jerusalem, 1983. Telesin was a well-known dissident activist in Moscow in the late 1960s. He was called "the king of *samizdat*" because he was always carrying forbidden literature in his pockets. Shalamov's attitude toward Ehrenburg carries enormous weight. Solzhenitsyn regarded Shalamov as a model for his own career. See *The Gulag Archipelago,* vol. 2, p. 7, where Solzhenitsyn praises him: "In the *Kolyma Stories* of Shalamov the reader will perhaps feel more truly and surely the pitilessness of the spirit of the Archipelago and the limits of human despair."

10. Ernst Henry's open letter to Ehrenburg was published in *Druzhba Narodov* (Friendship of the Peoples), no. 3 (1988): 231–39.

11. Boris Zaks, interview with author, Jersey City, 1981.

12. Commentary to *PYL,* vol. 3, p. 397.

13. Daniel Danin, interview with author, Moscow, 1982, and material from Danin's archive. See *Kultura i Zhizn,* October 31, 1948, p. 4, for an article denouncing Danin during the anti-cosmopolitan campaign.

14. *Sovietskaya Kultura,* January 26, 1991, p. 15.

15. TSGALI, fund 1204, catalog 2, item 2116.

16. *PYL,* vol. 3, pp. 296–301.

17. *PYL,* vol. 3, p. 345.

18. Viktoria Schweitzer, interview with author, Amherst, Mass., 1983.

19. Raisa Orlova and Lev Kopelev, *Myi Zhili v Moskve* (We Lived in Moscow) (Ann Arbor, 1988), p. 185. The text of the appeal with the names of the signatories can be found in the *Archiv Samidata,* no. 4, AC 219–301, no. 220.

20. See Andrei Sakharov, *Memoirs* (New York, 1990), pp. 268–69, for Sakharov's account of how he came to sign the petition.

21. Zinaida Grigorenko, telephone interview with author, New York, 1992.

22. *Sovietskaya Kultura,* January 26, 1991, p. 15. The émigré writer Nina Berberova admired Ehrenburg's efforts from afar. Reading *People, Years, Life* in the 1960s, she described their impact in her memoir *The Italics Are Mine* (New York, 1969), pp. 526–28:

    > I cannot tear myself away from his pages; for me his book means more than all the rest for forty years. I know the majority of his readers condemn him. But I do not. I am grateful to him. I thank him for every word. . . . Only in the awakening of consciousness lies the answer to everything that was, and only one out of all—Ehrenburg—inaudibly mooing and gesturing in that direction, shows us (and future generations) the way to this consciousness.

23. *New York Times,* April 4, 1966, p. 13.

24. Ibid., April 2, 1966, p. 4. Ehrenburg always loathed Sholokhov, having regarded him a Fascist.

25. Alexander Ginzburg, interview with author, Newton, Mass., 1981. Ginzburg's book on the Sinyavsky–Daniel case appeared in English as *On Trial,* trans., ed., and with an introduction by Max Hayward (New York, 1966).

26. Pavel Litvinov, comp., and Peter Reddaway, ed., *Trial of the Four* (New York, 1972), pp. 168–70, for the text of Stolyarova's testimony.

27. TSGALI, fund 1204, catalog 2, item 1174. Later that same year Ehrenburg was harshly attacked in *Literaturnaya Gazeta* for calling the 1920s the "golden age" of Soviet literature, as compared with the Stalinist 1930s, when "poets penned verse for the occasion." The article was part of Brezhnev's campaign to reverse the more candid discussion of Soviet cultural history that had been tolerated under Khrushchev. See *New York Times,* December 29, 1965, p. 10.

28. Commentary to *PYL,* vol. 3, p. 401.

29. Ibid., p. 402.

30. Roy Medvedev, *Politichesky Dnevnik (1964–1970)* (Political Diary) (Amsterdam, 1972), pp. 603–8. Roy Medvedev, interview with author, Moscow, 1982.

CHAPTER 18. 1967

1. Airgram from the American embassy in Moscow to Department of State, May 9, 1967. National Archives, Washington, D.C.

2. Incoming telegram from the American embassy in Moscow to Department of State, June 2, 1967. National Archives, Washington, D.C.

3. TSGALI, fund 1204, catalog 2, item 1168. Ehrenburg's letter to officials at the Writers' Union was dated April 12, 1967.

4. *Le Monde* described Ehrenburg's remarks as the "most moving" of the conference. See *Le Monde,* May 31, 1967, suppl. p. II.

5. Incoming telegram from American embassy in Moscow to Department of State, May 26, 1967. National Archives, Washington, D.C.

6. *London Times,* May 25, 1967, p. 1.

7. Alexander Werth, *Russia: Hopes and Fears* (New York, 1969), pp. 186–87. Ehrenburg also explained how *samizdat* worked to Simone de Beauvoir and Jean-Paul Sartre. See Simone de Beauvoir, *All Said and Done* (Great Britain, 1974), pp. 319–20.

8. Natalya Stolyarova, interview with author, Moscow, 1984.

9. Werth, *Hopes and Fears,* pp. 218–19.

10. Yury Oklyanski, *Schastlivie Neudachniki* (Lucky Failures) (Moscow, 1990), p. 365.

11. Commentary to *PYL,* vol. 3, p. 401.

12. This letter and others from Liselotte Mehr to Ehrenburg and to his daughter Irina can be found in TSGALI, fund 1204, catalog 2, item 1889.

13. Irina Ehrenburg, Fanya Fishman, Alya Savich, separate interviews with author, Moscow, 1991, and Natalya Stolyarova, interview with author, Moscow, 1984, about Ehrenburg's death.

14. TSGALI, fund 1204, catalog 2, item 3772. These are handwritten notes by Ehrenburg's nurses.

15. Archive of Stefan Mehr, Stockholm. I am especially grateful to Stefan Mehr for sharing with me Ehrenburg's last handwritten notes to his mother.

16. TSGALI, fund 1204, catalog 2, item 1889.
17. Ibid.
18. Ibid.
19. Archive of Stefan Mehr.
20. TSGALI, fund 1204, catalog 2, item 3772.
21. Ibid., item 1889.
22. Ibid.

EPILOGUE

1. Telegram from American embassy to Department of State, Washington, D.C., September 5, 1967. National Archives, Washington, D.C. Also, private communication (April 18, 1983) to author from Yale Richmond, a foreign service officer who worked in the American embassy in 1967.

2. Testimony of Tatyana Litvinova in defense of Vladimir Bukovsky can be found in Pavel Litvinov, *The Demonstration in Pushkin Square* (Boston, 1969), pp. 87–90. Tatyana Litvinova felt especially close to Ehrenburg. He showed her an initial draft of his chapter about her father and she responded with a long, detailed, and loving letter, including material that Ehrenburg added to his portrait. The letter is dated February 3, 1964. See TSGALI, fund 1204, catalog 2, item 1820.

3. Interviews with Irina Ehrenburg (Moscow, 1986), Alya Savich (Moscow, 1986), Boris Birger (Moscow, 1984), Daniel Danin (Moscow, 1984), and Boris Frezinsky (Moscow, 1986), contributed to this account of Ehrenburg's funeral. See also Margarita Aliger's essay in the collection *Vospominanie ob Ilye Ehrenburge* (Reminiscences About Ilya Ehrenburg), ed. Galina Belaya and Lazar Lazarev (Moscow, 1975), pp. 210–11.

4. *Haaretz* (The Land), September 5, 1967, p. 3.

5. *Manchester Guardian,* September 5, 1967, p. 7.

6. Vladimir Voinovich, interview with author, Brookline, Mass., 1984.

7. *New York Times,* September 5, 1967, p. 43.

8. See the anthology *An End to Silence,* ed. and with an introduction by Stephen F. Cohen (New York, 1982), p. 271. This volume contains material from Roy Medvedev's *samizdat* journal *Political Diary.*

9. TSGALI, fund 1204, catalog 2, item 3829.

10. *Daily Mirror,* January 27, 1966, p. 11.

11. *Novy Mir,* no. 9 (1967): 286.

12. Ehrenburg, *Sobranie Sochinenie,* vol. 1 (Moscow, 1990), pp. 204–5.

13. *Pravda,* September 3, 1967, p. 3.

14. Mikola Bazhan, "The Pen of a Humanist," *Literaturnaya Gazeta,* September 6, 1967, p. 8.

15. *New York Times,* September 2, 1967, pp. 25, 24.

16. *Newsweek,* September 18, 1967, p. 48.

17. *Manchester Guardian,* September 2, 1967, p. 7.

18. *Le Monde,* September 2, 1967, p. 20.

19. *London Times,* September 2, 1967, p. 12.

20. *London Observer,* September 3, 1967, p. 4.

21. Ivor Montagu, "Ilya Ehrenburg, Peacemonger, 1891–1967," *Anglo-Soviet Journal,* vol. 28, no. 2 (January 1968): 34. (From TSGALI, fund 1816, catalog 2, item 303.)
22. Natalya Stolyarova, interview with author, Moscow, 1984.
23. *PYL,* vol. 1, p. 52.
24. *New York Times,* September 4, 1967, p. 1. It is worth noting in this context that Ehrenburg was also approached by the British lawyer Peter Benenson in 1961, when Benenson founded Amnesty International. He wrote to a number of well-known people around the world to enlist their support. Benenson's aunt, Manya Harari, was a distinguished Russian translator in London (she had translated Ehrenburg's novella *The Thaw* and, with Max Hayward, *Doctor Zhivago*) and provided him with Ehrenburg's address. Ehrenburg's reply has been lost. Benenson, in a letter to the author on January 7, 1992, recalled "that it was favourable, although wrapped in the mysterious cloak which his character and position seemed to require." Benenson's original letter to Ehrenburg can be found in TSGALI, fund 1204, catalog 2, item 1272.
25. Ehrenburg, "Le Roi S'Amuse," *Novosti Dnya,* April 22 (9), 1918, p. 3.

Bibliography

Ilya Ehrenburg's memoirs *Lyudi, Gody, Zhizn*, or *People, Years, Life*, are an indispensable resource for any student of his career. The memoirs have appeared in different versions in Moscow, compelling the attentive biographer to examine each edition for obvious and subtle changes.

The memoirs (specifically, Books One through Six) first appeared in serial form in the journal *Novy Mir*, nos. 8–10 (1960); 1–2, 9–11 (1961); 4–6 (1962); 1–3 (1963); 1–4 (1965). They were then collected and published in three separate volumes by Sovietsky Pisatel publishing house in 1961, 1963, and 1966. Vols. 8 (1966) and 9 (1967) of Ehrenburg's *Collected Works* (the last published during his lifetime) carried the fullest text up to that point. In 1987 the journal *Ogonyok* published a nearly complete version of Book Seven in nos. 22–25, the first time this section appeared as a whole. Finally, Boris Frezinsky, working with Ehrenburg's daughter Irina and his colleague Vyacheslav Popov, brought out a three-volume edition of *People, Years, Life* in 1990 with as much of the text restored as it was possible to reconstruct, and with a full-scale commentary.

In the United States the memoirs were published in four volumes: *People and Life, 1891–1921*, trans. Anna Bostock and Yvonne Kapp (New York: Knopf, 1962); *Memoirs: 1921–1941*, trans. Tatiana Shebunina and Yvonne Kapp (Cleveland: World, 1964); *The War 1941–1945*, trans. Tatiana Shebunina and Yvonne Kapp (Cleveland: World, 1964); and *Post-War Years: 1945–1954*, trans. Tatiana Shebunina and Yvonne Kapp (Cleveland: World, 1967).

During his lifetime Ehrenburg helped to prepare three separate editions of *Collected Works*: an eight-volume edition in 1927–1928; a five-volume edition in 1952–1954; and a nine-volume edition in 1962–1967. Each of these editions includes novels, stories, poems, and articles, as well as introductions and commentaries. Beginning in 1990, a new *Collected Works* in eight volumes began to appear. As of this writing, the first four volumes have been published under the editorial direction of Irina Ehrenburg and Boris Frezinsky.

The following books and articles by Ilya Ehrenburg were also consulted for this biography:

———

Angliya (England). Moscow: Federatsiya, 1931.

A Vsyo-Taki Ona Vertitsa (And Yet It Turns). Moscow: Helikon, 1922.

Bely Ugol, ili Slezy Vertera (White Coal, or the Tears of Werther). Leningrad: Priboy, 1928.

The Black Book. Edited with Vasily Grossman. Translated by John Glad and James S. Levine. New York: Holocaust Library, 1981.

Cent Lettres (One Hundred Letters). Translated by A. Roudnikov. Paris: Hier et Aujourd'hui, 1945.

Chekhov, Stendhal and Other Essays. Translated by Anna Bostock and Yvonne Kapp. London: MacGibbon & Kee, 1962.

Chto Cheloveku Nado (What a Man Needs). Moscow: Khudozhestvennaya Literatura, 1937.

Derevo. Stikhi (The Tree. Verses). Moscow: Sovietsky Pisatel, 1946.

Duhamel, Gide, Malraux, Mauriac, Morand, Romain, Unamuno vus par un écrivain sovietique. Translated by Madeleine Etard. Paris: Gallimard, 1934.

European Crossroad: A Soviet Journalist in the Balkans. Translated by Anya Markov. New York: Knopf, 1947.

The Extraordinary Adventures of Julio Jurenito and His Disciples. Translated by Usick Vanzler. New York: Covici Friede, 1930.

The Fall of France Seen Through Soviet Eyes. London: Modern Books, 1941.

The Fall of Paris. Translated by Gerard Shelley. New York: Knopf, 1944.

Frantsuzskie Tetrady (French Notebooks). Moscow: Sovietsky Pisatel, 1958.

Ispanskie Reportazhi (Spanish Reports). Edited by Boris Frezinsky and Vyacheslav Popov. Moscow: Novosti Press, 1986.

Ispansky Zakal (The Spanish Temper). Moscow: Goslitizdat, 1938.

Kanuny (Eves). Berlin: Mysl, 1921.

Kniga dlya Vzroslikh (A Book for Adults). Moscow: Sovietsky Pisatel, 1936.

Letopis Muzhestva (A Chronicle of Courage). Edited by Lazar Lazarev. Moscow: Sovietsky Pisatel, 1983.

The Life of the Automobile. Translated by Joachim Neugroschel. New York: Urizen Books, 1976.

Lik Voyny (The Face of War). 2d ed. Berlin: Helikon, 1923.

The Love of Jeanne Ney. Translated by Helen Chrouschoff Matheson. New York: Doubleday, Doran, 1930.

Molitva o Rossy (A Prayer for Russia). Moscow: Severnie Dny, 1918.

Moy Parizh (My Paris). Moscow: Izogiz, 1933.

Myi i Oni (We and They). With Ovady Savich. Berlin: Petropolis, 1931.

Neizvestnaya Chyornaya Kniga (The Unknown Black Book). Edited by Yitshak Arad. Jerusalem: Yad Vashem and Moscow: Government Archive of the Russian Federation, 1993.

Nepravdopodobnie Istory (Improbable Stories). Berlin: S. Efron, 1922.

The Ninth Wave. Translated by Tatiana Shebunina and J. Castle. London: Lawrence and Wishart, 1955.

Ogon (Fire). Homel: Veka i Dni, 1919.

Out of Chaos. Translated by Alexander Bakshy. New York: Henry Holt, 1934.

Portrety Russkikh Poetov (Portraits of Russian Poets). Berlin: Argonavty, 1922.

Razdumiya (Reflections). Riga: Dzintars, 1921.

Russia at War. London: Hamish Hamilton, 1943.

Rvach (The Go-Getter). Paris: Navarre, 1925.

Shest Povestey o Lyogkikh Kontsakh (Six Stories About Easy Endings). Moscow and Berlin: Helikon, 1922.

Sovest Narodov (The Conscience of the Peoples). Moscow: Sovietsky Pisatel, 1956.

A Soviet Writer Looks at Vienna. Translated by Ivor Montagu. London: Martin-Lawrence, 1934.

The Storm. Edited by Isidor Schneider and Anne Terry White and translated by J. Fineberg. New York: Gaer Associates, 1949.

The Stormy Life of Lasik Roitschwantz. Translated by Leonid Borochowicz and Gertrude Flor. New York: Polyglot Press, 1960.

A Street in Moscow. Translated by Sonia Volochova. New York: Covici Friede, 1932.

The Tempering of Russia. Translated by Alexander Kaun. New York: Knopf, 1944.

Ten Derevev (The Shadow of Trees). Edited by Yelena Zonina. Moscow: Progress, 1969.

The Thaw. Translated by Manya Harari. Chicago: Henry Regnery, 1955.

Uslovnie Stradaniya Zavsegtadaya Kafe (The Relative Sufferings of a Café Habitué). Moscow: Novaya Zhizn, 1926.

Viza Vremeni (Visa of Time). Berlin: Petropolis, [1929].

Voyna: June 1941–April 1942 (War). Moscow: Goslitizdat, 1942.

Voyna: April 1942–March 1943. Moscow: Goslitizdat, 1943.

Voyna: April 1943–March 1944. Moscow: Goslitizdat, 1944.

V Smertny Chas (At the Fatal Hour). Kiev: Letopis, 1919.

We Come as Judges. London: Soviet War News, 1945.

"What I Have Learned," *The Saturday Review,* September 30, 1967, pp. 28–31.

Yaponiya, Gretsiya, Indiya (Japan, Greece, India). Moscow: Iskusstvo, 1960.

Ya Zhivu (I am Alive). Petersburg: 1911.

Zatyanuvshayas Razvyazka (The Drawn-out Dénouement). Moscow: Sovietsky Pisatel, 1934.

Selected Bibliography

Alexandrova, Vera. *A History of Soviet Literature.* Translated by Mirra Ginsburg. New York: Doubleday, 1963.

Aline [pseud.]. *Lénine á Paris.* 2d ed. Paris: Les Revues, 1929.

Alliluyeva, Svetlana. *Only One Year.* Translated by Paul Chavchavadze. New York: Harper & Row, 1969.

———. *Twenty Letters to a Friend.* Translated by Priscilla Johnson McMillan. New York: Harper & Row, 1967.

Altman, Ilya. "Toward the History of *The Black Book,*" *Yad Vashem Studies* 21, edited by Aharon Weiss. Jerusalem, 1991.

Altshuler, Mordechai; and Ycikas, Sima. "Were There Two Black Books About the Holocaust in the Soviet Union?" *Jews and Jewish Topics in the Soviet Union and Eastern Europe* 1, no. 17 (Spring 1992): 37–55.

Altshuler, Mordechai; Arad, Yitshak; and Krakowski, Shmuel (Eds.). *Sovietskie Yevrei Pishut Ilye Ehrenburgu, 1943–1966* (Soviet Jews Write to Ilya Ehrenburg). Jerusalem: Yad Vashem, 1993.

Antonov-Ovseenko, Anton. *The Time of Stalin.* Translated by George Saunders. New York: Harper & Row, 1981.

Aragon, Louis. *Les Communistes* (Mai 1940). Paris: La Bibliothèque Française, 1951.

Avins, Carol. *Border Crossings: The West and Russian Identity, 1917–1934.* Berkeley: University of California Press, 1983.

Babel, Isaac. *You Must Know Everything.* Edited by Nathalie Babel. New York: Farrar, Straus & Giroux, 1969.

Baron, Salo W. *The Russian Jew Under Tsars and Soviets.* New York: Macmillan, 1964.

Barzini, Luigi. *Memories of Mistresses, Reflections from a Life.* New York: Macmillan, 1986.

Bazanov, V. G. *Literaturnoe Nasledstvo* (Literary Heritage). Vol. 81. Moscow: Nauka, 1969.

———. *Literaturnoe Nasledstvo.* Vol. 82. Moscow: Nauka, 1970.

Beauvoir, Simone de. *All Said and Done.* Translated by Patrick O'Brian. London: Andre Deutsch, 1974.

———. *Force of Circumstance.* Translated by Richard Howard. New York: G. P. Putnam's Sons, 1965.

———. *Memoirs of a Dutiful Daughter.* Translated by James Kirkup. Cleveland: World Publishing, 1959.

———. *The Prime of Life.* Translated by Peter Green. Cleveland: World Publishing, 1962.

Belaya, G., and L. Lazarev (Eds.). *Vospominanie ob Ilye Ehrenburge* (Reminiscences About Ilya Ehrenburg). Moscow: Sovietsky Pisatel, 1975.

Bell, Daniel. "The Erosion of Soviet Ideology." *The New Leader,* April 15, 1963, pp. 18–23.

Berberova, Nina. *The Italics Are Mine.* Translated by Philippe Radley. New York: Harcourt, Brace and World, 1969.

Berdnikov, G. P. (Ed.). *Literaturnoe Nasledstvo.* Vol. 93. Moscow: Nauka, 1983.

Bloch, Jean-Richard. *L'Homme du Communisme* (The Man of Communism). Paris: Éditions Sociales, 1949.

Blot, Jean. "Ehrenbourg entre Montparnasse et Moscou." *Preuves* (January 1962): 69–74.

Brachfeld, Georges I. *André Gide and the Communist Temptation.* Geneva: Librarie E. Droz, 1959.

Brown, Clarence. *Mandelstam*. Cambridge, Eng.: Cambridge University Press, 1973.

Brown, Edward J. *The Proletarian Episode in Russian Literature, 1928–1932*. New York: Columbia University Press, 1953.

———. *Russian Literature Since the Revolution*. Cambridge, Mass.: Harvard University Press, 1982.

Brumberg, Abraham. "The Screws Are Tightened Again." *The Reporter*, May 9, 1963, pp. 21–23.

Bunin, Ivan, and Bunin, Vera. *Ustamy Buninikh* (In the Bunins' Own Words). Frankfurt: Possev, 1981.

Cathala, Jean. *Sans Fleurs Ni Fusil* (Without Flowers or a Gun). Paris: Albin Michel, 1981.

Cattell, David T. *Communism and the Spanish Civil War*. Berkeley: University of California Press, 1955.

———. *Soviet Diplomacy and the Spanish Civil War*. Berkeley: University of California Press, 1957.

Caute, David. *The Fellow Travellers: Intellectual Friends of Communism*. New Haven: Yale University Press, 1988.

Cohen, Stephen F. *Bukharin and the Bolshevik Revolution*. New York: Vintage, 1975.

Cohen, Stephen F. (Ed.). *An End to Silence*. New York: Norton, 1982.

Conquest, Robert. *The Pasternak Affair: Courage of Genius*. Philadelphia: Lippincott, 1962.

Cunningham, Valentine. (Ed.). *Spanish Front: Writers on the Civil War*. Oxford: Oxford University Press, 1986.

Czapski, Joseph. *The Inhuman Land*. Translated by Gerard Hopkins. London: Chatto & Windus, 1951.

Dabit, Eugene. *Journal Intime (1928–1936)* (Intimate Journal). Paris: Gallimard, 1939.

Dementiev, Alexander. *V. I. Lenin i Sovietskaya Literatura* (V. I. Lenin and Soviet Literature). Moscow: Khudozhestvennaya Literatura, 1977.

———. *Vtoroi Vsesoyuzny Sezd Pisateley—Vazhneishaya Vekha v Istory Sovietskoy Literatury* (The Second All-Union Congress of Soviet Writers—The Most Important Landmark in the History of Soviet Literature). Moscow: Znanie, 1955.

Drug, Stefan. (Ed.). *DAV a davisti* (DAV and Its Followers). Bratislava: Obzor, 1965.

Dubnow, S. M. *History of the Jews in Russia and Poland*. Vols. 2 and 3. Philadelphia: Jewish Publication Society, 1918 and 1920.

Duhamel, Georges. *The French Position*. Translated by Basil Collier. London: Basil Collier Dent, 1940.

Dzhirkvelov, Ilya. *Secret Servant: My Life with the KGB and the Soviet Elite*. New York: Harper & Row, 1987.

Eastman, Max. *Artists in Uniform*. New York: Knopf, 1934.

Ehrenburg, Irina. *Lotaringskaya Shkola: Zametki Frantsuzskoy Shkolnitsy* (The Lotaringskaya School: Notes of a French Schoolgirl). Moscow: Khudozhestvennaya Literatura, 1935.

Einstein, Albert. *Out of My Later Years*. New York: Philosophical Library, 1950.

Eizenstadt, Yakov. "Nasledstvennoe Delo Ilyi Ehrenburga" (The Estate of Ilya Ehrenburg). *Vremya i Myi* (Time and We), no. 79 (1984): 153–58.

Erdman, Nikolai. *Pesyi. Intermedy. Dokumenty. Vospominanie Sovremmenikov* (Plays. Interludes. Documents. Reminiscences of Contemporaries). Moscow: Iskusstvo, 1990.

Erlich, Victor. "Ilya Ehrenburg Takes a Bow." *Problems of Communism* (Sept.-Oct. 1965): 72–74.

———. "The Metamorphoses of Ilya Ehrenburg." *Problems of Communism* (July-August 1965): 15–24.

Fast, Howard. *Being Red*. Boston: Houghton Mifflin, 1990.

Fisher, David James. *Romain Rolland and the Politics of Intellectual Engagement*. Berkeley: University of California Press, 1988.

Fleishman, Lazar. *Boris Pasternak v Dvatsatie Gody* (Boris Pasternak in the 1920s). Munich: Wilhelm Fink Verlag, 1981.

———. *Boris Pasternak v Tritsatie Gody* (Boris Pasternak in the 1930s). Jerusalem: Magnes Press, 1984.

Fleishman, Lazar; Raeff, Marc; Raevsky-Hughes, Olga; Struve, Nikita (Eds.). *Russky Berlin, 1921–1923* (Russian Berlin). Paris: YMCA Press, 1983.

Frank, Anne. *Dnevnik Anny Frank*. Edited by I. Karintseva and translated by I. R. Rait-Kovalyovoy. Moscow: Inostrannaya Literatura, 1960.

Frank, Nino. *Memoire Brisée* (Broken Memory). Vols. 1 and 2. Paris: Calmann-Levy, 1967 and 1968.

Frezinsky, Boris; and Popov, Vyacheslav. *Ilya Ehrenburg, Chronika Zhizni i Tvorchestva*. (Ilya Ehrenburg, A Chronicle of His Life and Work). Vol. 1. *1891–1923*. St. Petersburg: Lina, 1993.

Friche, V. *Zametky Sovremennoy Literature* (Notes on Contemporary Literature). Moscow: Moskovsky Rabochy, 1928.

Fyvel, T. R. "The Stormy Life of Ilya Ehrenburg." *Encounter* (December 1961): 82–90.

Gide, André. *Literature Engagée*. Paris: Gallimard, 1950.

———. *Return from the U.S.S.R.* New York: Knopf, 1937.

Gilboa, Yehoshua. *The Black Years of Soviet Jewry*. Boston: Little, Brown, 1971.

Ginzburg, Eugeniya. *Krutoy Marshrut* (Journey into the Whirlwind). Milano: Arnoldo Mondadori Editore, 1979.

Goldberg, Anatol. *Ilya Ehrenburg: Writing, Politics, and the Art of Survival*. With Erik de Mauny. London: Weidenfeld and Nicolson, 1984.

———. "Ilya Ehrenburg." In *Jews in Soviet Culture*. Edited by Jack Miller. New Brunswick: Transaction, 1984.

Gómez de la Serna, Ramón. *Retratos Contemporáneos* (Contemporary Portraits). Buenos Aires: Editorial Sudamericana, 1941.

Gorbachev, Georgy. *Sovremennaya Russkaya Literatura* (Contemporary Russian Literature). Leningrad: Priboy, 1928.

Gorkin, Julian; and El Campesino (Valentin Gonzalez). *Life and Death in Soviet Russia*. Translated by I. Barea. New York: G. P. Putnam's Sons, 1952.

Gouzenko, Igor. *This Was My Choice*. Montreal: Palm Publishers, 1968.

Graebner, Walter. *Round Trip to Russia*. Philadelphia: Lippincott, 1943.

Graf, Oskar Maria. *Reise in die Sowjetunion* (Trip to the Soviet Union). Luchterhand, 1974.

Guéhenno, Jean. *Journal d'Une Révolution, 1937–1938*. Paris: Grasset, 1939.

Gul, Roman. *Ya Unyos Rossiyu* (I Took Russia with Me). Vols. 1 and 2. New York: Most, 1981 and 1984.

Haight, Amanda. *Anna Akhmatova*. New York: Oxford, 1976.

Harriman, Averell W.; and Abel, Elie. *Special Envoy to Churchill and Stalin, 1941–1946*. New York: 1975.

Hayman, Ronald. *Sartre*. New York: Simon & Schuster, 1987.

Hayward, Max; and Labedz, Leopold (Eds.). *Literature and Revolution in Soviet Russia 1917–1962*. London: Oxford, 1963.

Hayward, Max. *Writers in Russia, 1917–1978*. Edited by Patricia Blake. San Diego: Harcourt, Brace, Jovanovich, 1983.

Heifetz, Elias. *The Slaughter of the Jews in 1919*. New York: T. Seltzer, 1921.

Hemingway, Ernest. *For Whom the Bell Tolls*. New York: Charles Scribner's Sons, 1940.

Ivinskaya, Olga. *A Captive of Time*. Translated by Max Hayward. New York: Doubleday, 1978.

Johnson, Priscilla; and Labedz, Leopold (Eds.). *Khrushchev and the Arts: The Politics of Soviet Culture, 1962–1964*. Cambridge, Mass.: MIT Press, 1965.

Knightley, Phillip. *The First Casualty*. New York: Harcourt, Brace, Jovanovich, 1975.

Kochan, Lionel (Ed.). *The Jews in Soviet Russia Since 1917*. New York: Oxford, 1978.

Koestler, Arthur. *Spanish Testament*. London: Victor Gollancz, 1937.

Kopelev, Lev. *To Be Preserved Forever*. Translated and edited by Anthony Austin. Philadelphia: Lippincott, 1977.

Korey, William. "Ehrenburg: His Inner Jewish Conflict." *Jewish Frontier* (March 1968): 25–31.

_____. *The Soviet Cage*. New York: Viking, 1973.

Labedz, Leopold. "A Chronicle of the Chill." *Partisan Review* (Spring 1963): 99–108.

Lacouture, Jean. *André Malraux*. Translated by Alan Sheridan. New York: Pantheon, 1975.

Landau, Efim. "Memoiry, Istory, i Sovremennost." *Prostor* (June 1962): 98–103.

Laqueur, Walter Z.; and Lichtheim, George (Eds.). *The Soviet Cultural Scene, 1956–1957*. London: Atlantic Books, 1958.

Lauterbach, Richard E. *These Are the Russians*. New York: Book Find Club, 1945.

Laychuk, Julian. "The Evolution of I. G. Ehrenburg's *Weltanschaung* During the Period 1928–1934." *Canadian Slavonic Papers* 12, no. 4 (1970): 395–416.

_____. *Ilya Ehrenburg: An Idealist in an Age of Realism*. Bern: Peter Lang, 1991.

Leftwich, Joseph. *Abraham Sutzkever: Partisan Poet*. New York: Thomas Yoseloff, 1971.

Leneman, Léon. *La Tragédie des Juifs en U.R.S.S.* Paris: Desclee de Brouwer, 1959.

Lenormand, Henri-René. *Les Confessions d'un Auteur Dramatique*. Vol. 2. Paris: Albin Michel, 1953.

Levin, Nora. *The Jews in the Soviet Union Since 1917: Paradox of Survival*. Vols. 1 and 2. New York: New York University Press, 1988.

Lottman, Herbert R. *The Left Bank*. Boston: Houghton Mifflin, 1982.

Lundberg, Yevgeny. *Zapiski Pisatelya* (Notes of a Writer), *1920–1924*. Vol. 1. Leningrad: Pisateley, 1930.

Malraux, Clara. *Le Bruit de Nos Pas* (The Sound of Our Steps). Vol. 4. Paris: Bernard Grasset, 1973.

Mandelstam, Nadezhda. *Hope Abandoned*. Translated by Max Hayward. New York: Atheneum, 1974.

———. *Hope Against Hope*. Translated by Max Hayward. New York: Atheneum, 1979.

Mandelstam, Osip. *The Prose of Osip Mandelstam*. Translated by Clarence Brown. Princeton: Princeton University Press, 1965.

Marcou, Lilly. *Ilya Ehrenbourg*. Paris: Plon, 1992.

———. *Ce Que Nous Voulons Faire de l'Union Sovietique*. An interview with Alexander Yakovlev. Paris: Seuil, 1991.

Markish, Esther. *The Long Return*. Translated by D. I. Goldstein. New York: Ballantine, 1978.

Mathewson, Rufus. "Ehrenburg as Hero." *Partisan Review* (Spring 1963): 117–22.

Medvedev, Roy. *Nikolai Bukharin: The Last Years*. Translated by A. D. P. Briggs. New York: Norton, 1980.

Mirsky, Dmitry S. *Contemporary Russian Literature, 1881–1925*. New York: Knopf, 1926.

Morath, Inge; and Miller, Arthur. *In Russia*. New York: Viking, 1969.

Nekrasov, Viktor. "Chasy Dobra i Nedobra" (A Time of Good and Evil). *Novoe Russkoe Slovo*, January 19, 1986, p. 5.

Oklyansky, Yury. *Schastlivie Neudachniki* (Lucky Failures). Moscow: 1990.

Orlova, Raisa. *Hemingway v Rossy* (Hemingway in Russia). Ann Arbor: Ardis, 1985.

Orlova, Raisa; and Kopelev, Lev. *Myi Zhili v Moskve* (We Lived in Moscow). Ann Arbor: Ardis, 1988.

Parker, Ralph. *Moscow Correspondent*. London: Frederick Muller, 1949.

Pasternak, Boris. *I Remember: Sketch for an Autobiography*. Translated by David Magarshack. New York: Pantheon, 1959.

Paz, Abel. *Durruti: The People, Armed*. Translated by Nancy Macdonald. Montreal: Black Rose Books, 1976.

Pervy Vsesoyuzny Sezd Sovietskikh Pisatley 1934 (The First All-Union Congress of Soviet Writers 1934). Stenographic Record. Moscow: Khudozhestvennaya Literatura, 1934.

Pinkus, Benjamin. *The Jews of the Soviet Union: The History of a National Minority*. Cambridge: Cambridge University Press, 1988.

———. *The Soviet Government and the Jews, 1948–1967*. Cambridge: Cambridge University Press, 1984.

Putnam, Samuel. *Paris Was Our Mistress*. New York: Viking, 1947.

Rapoport, Yakov. *The Doctors' Plot of 1953*. Translated by N. A. Perova and R. S. Bobrova. Cambridge, Mass.: Harvard, 1991.

Redlich, Shimon. *Propaganda and Nationalism in Wartime Russia: The Jewish Antifascist Committee in the U.S.S.R., 1941–1948*. East European Monographs, no. 108. Boulder: East European Quarterly, 1982.

————."The Crimean Affair." *Jews and Jewish Topics* 2, no. 12 (Fall 1990): 55–65.

Regler, Gustav. *The Owl of Minerva.* Translated by N. Denny. London: Rupert Hart-Davis, 1959.

Rilke, Rainer Maria; Pasternak, Boris; Tsvetaeva, Marina. *Pisma 1926* (Letters 1926). Moscow: Kniga, 1990.

Rodin, Elisha. *La-Ben* (To a Son). Tel Aviv: Am-Oved, 1942.

Ro'i, Yaacov. *The Struggle for Soviet Jewish Emigration 1948–1967.* Cambridge: Cambridge University Press, 1991.

Rotha, Paul. *The Film Till Now.* London: Spring Books, 1967.

Rothberg, Abraham. *The Heirs of Stalin: Dissidence and the Soviet Regime, 1953–1970.* Ithaca: Cornell University Press, 1972.

Rubashkin, Alexander. "Pisma" (Letters). *Voprosy Literatury*, no. 12 (1987): 160–82.

Rudnitsky, Konstantin. *Rezhissyor Meyerhold* (The Director Meyerhold). Mosow: Nauka, 1969.

Rysselberghe, Maria van. *Les Cahiers de la Petite Dame* (The Notebooks of the Little Lady). Vols. 5 and 6 in the *Cahiers André Gide.* Paris: Gallimard, 1974 and 1975.

Salisbury, Harrison E. *To Mosow—And Beyond: A Reporter's Narrative.* New York: Harper & Brothers, 1960.

————. *A Journey for Our Times.* New York: Carrol & Graf, 1984.

Savich, Ovady. *Dva Gody v Ispany* (Two Years in Spain). Moscow: Sovietsky Pisatel, 1961.

Schweitzer, Viktoria. *Byt i Bytie Mariny Tsvetaevoy* (The Life of Marina Tsvetaeva). Paris: Syntaxis, 1988.

Scott, H. G. (Ed.). *Problems of Soviet Literature: Reports and Speeches at the First Soviet Writers' Congress.* Moscow: Cooperative Publishing Society of Foreign Workers in the U.S.S.R., 1935.

Serge, Victor. *Memoirs of a Revolutionary.* Translated by Peter Sedgwick. Oxford: Oxford University Press, 1980.

Shaplen, Robert. *Kreuger: Genius and Swindler.* New York: Knopf, 1960.

Shaw, John Roger. *Ilya Ehrenburg: The Career of a Soviet Writer.* Ph.D. diss. University of Washington, 1960.

Shklovsky, Viktor. *Zoo, or Letters Not About Love.* Translated and edited by Richard Sheldon. Ithaca: Cornell University Press, 1971.

Shub, Anatole. *An Empire Loses Hope.* New York: Norton, 1970.

Sinyavsky, Andrei; and Golomshtok, Igor. *Picasso.* Moscow: Znanie, 1960.

Slobazhin, I. I. (Ed.). *Ob Anne Akhmatovoy* (On Anna Akhmatova). Leningrad: Lenizdat, 1990.

Solzhenitsyn, Alexander. *The Oak and the Calf.* Translated by Harry Willetts. New York: Harper & Row, 1980.

Souvarine, Boris. "Les Memoires d'Ehrenbourg." *Preuves* (December 1962): 76–81.

Stalin, Joseph. *Leninism.* Vol. 1. Translated by Eden and Cedar Paul. New York: International Publishers, 1932.

Starr, Frederick. *Red and Hot: The Fate of Jazz in the Soviet Union, 1917–1980.* New York: Oxford University Press, 1983.

Steinbeck, John. *A Russian Journal.* With pictures by Robert Capa. New York: Viking, 1948.

Stevens, Leslie C. *Russian Assignment*. Boston: Little, Brown, 1953.

Stowe, Leland. *They Shall Not Sleep*. New York: Knopf, 1944.

Sulzberger, C. L. *A Long Row of Candles*. New York: Macmillan, 1969.

Tereshchenko, N. *Sovremenny Nigilist* (A Contemporary Nihilist). Leningrad: Priboy, 1925.

Thomas, Hugh. *The Spanish Civil War*. 3d ed. London: Hamish Hamilton, 1977.

Ulam, Adam B. *The Bolsheviks*. New York: Macmillan, 1974.

Vaksberg, Arkady. *The Prosecutor and the Prey*. Translated by Jan Butler. London: Weidenfeld and Nicolson, 1990.

Vercors [Jean Bruller]. *The Silence of the Sea*. Translated by Cyril Connolly. New York: Macmillan, 1944.

———. *The Battle of Silence*. Translated by Rita Barisse. New York: Holt, Rinehart & Winston, 1968.

Vinogradov, V. V. (Ed.). *Literaturnoe Nasledstvo*. Vol. 65. Moscow: Academy of Sciences, 1958.

Vorobyov, Marevna. *Memoires d'une Nomade*. Paris: Encre, 1979.

Vovsi-Mikhoels, Natalya. *Avi Shlomo Mikhoels* (My Father Shlomo Mikhoels). Translated by Menahem Ben-Iyyar. Tel Aviv: Hakibbutz Hameuchad, 1982.

Wat, Aleksandr. *My Century: The Odyssey of a Polish Intellectual*. Translated and edited by Richard Lourie. Berkeley: University of California Press, 1988.

Werth, Alexander. *The Khrushchev Phase*. London: Robert Hale, 1961.

———. *Russia at War*. New York: Dutton, 1964.

———. *Russia: Hopes and Fears*. New York: Simon & Schuster, 1970.

Wurmser, André. *Fidèlement Votre* (Yours Faithfully). Paris: Bernard Grasset, 1979.

Yemelchenkovoy, M.; and Nikiforova, Y. (Eds.). "Dokumenty Svideltsvuyut" (The Documents Testify). *Voprosy Literatury*, no. 4 (1993): 262–325.

Yevtushenko, Yevgeny. *A Precocious Autobiography*. Translated by Andrew R. MacAndrew. New York: Dutton, 1963.

Zamyatin, Yevgeny. *A Soviet Heretic*. Edited by Mirra Ginsburg. Chicago: University of Chicago Press, 1970.

———

The following newspapers and journals were frequently consulted for articles by and about Ilya Ehrenburg:

———

Birzhevie Vedomosti

Haaretz

Izvestia

Krasnaya Zvezda

Maariv

L'Humanité

Le Monde

Literaturnaya Gazeta

New York Times

Pravda

Yediot Ahronot

Acknowledgments

Many people helped me to complete this book and I would like to acknowledge their support.

Mark Kuchment first encouraged me to take on this project in the summer of 1980 and must have been amazed to observe how quickly I transformed his fascination for Ehrenburg into an obsession of my own.

During eight research trips to Moscow, from 1982 to 1994, Irina Ehrenburg welcomed me to her home, entertained endless questions about her father, and shared memories and documents with me. Alya Savich, who died shortly after my visit to Moscow in April 1991, had been a long-time friend of Ehrenburg's; she greeted me as a grandchild and also helped me to understand what it means to survive a regime of terror. I also would like to give special thanks to the St. Petersburg scholar Boris Frezinsky, a student of Ehrenburg's life, for his time and attention; no one could ask for a more thorough, thoughtful, or fair-minded chronicler. Valya Morderer lent me her bibliographic skills in

Moscow, while Martin Sherwin helped to arrange two month-long stays in the Soviet capital. With his assistance I was able to spend long hours at TSGALI, the Central Government Archive of Literature and Art, where the bulk of Ehrenburg's papers are kept; the staff of TSGALI was particularly helpful.

As I began writing, Boris Katz, Susanna Kaysen, Susan Quinn, Will Watson, and Mark Kuchment read long portions of the manuscript and offered helpful comments of their own. David and Kay Ariel, Michael Berenbaum, Napua Davoy, Ellen Hume, Natalya Katz, Fern Miller, Howard Norman, John Shattuck, Richard Sobol, Katy Moss Warner, Ronnie Mae Weiss, and Shomer Zwelling were always encouraging, as were my mother, Ruth Rubenstein, and my brother, Marc. I am also grateful to staff members of Harvard's Widener Library, the New York Public Library, the Columbia University Library, the Hoover Institution Archives, the National Archives, the British Museum Library, the National Library of Israel, and Moscow's Lenin Library for their patient assistance. In addition, I would like to express my gratitude to Harvard's Russian Research Center, where I enjoy the privileges of a Fellow, and to the American Council of Learned Societies for the fellowship I received in 1985 that permitted me to take a leave of absence from my work with Amnesty International. My colleagues at Amnesty shared my astonishment when I discovered that Ehrenburg had been among the prominent figures approached at the moment of our founding.

I would like to thank the scores of people I interviewed, some only by telephone, who made my work a particular pleasure: Alexei Aisner; Vasily Aksyonov; Rafael Alberti; Margarita Aliger; Nathalie Babel; Sarah Babyonysheva; Rita Barisse; Nina Berberova; Boris Birger; Larisa Bogoraz; Joseph Brodsky; Abraham Brumberg; Jean Cassou; Jean Cathala; Nina Cot; Daniel Danin; Irina Ehrenburg; Victor Erlich; Mme. Yves Farge; Ephraim Fishman; Fanya Fishman; Joseph Fishman; Zina Fogelman; Boris Frezinsky; Daria Gamsaragan; John Gerassi; Stepha Gerassi; Alexander Ginzburg; Yevgeny Gnedin; Eduard Goldstücker; Samuel Grafton; Zinaida Grigorenko; Roman Gul; Luce Hilsum; Joris Ivens; Roman Jakobson; Lou Kadar; Jack Kamaiko; Veniamin Kaverin; Bronka Klebansky; Lev Kopelev; Naum Korzhavin; Shlomo Kowarski; Israel Kronik; Leib Kunyahovsky; Anna Larina; Aryeh Levavi; Anthony Liehm; Semyon Lipkin; Pavel Litvinov; Maya Litvinova; Tatyana Litvinova; Annette Lotte; Mikhail Makarenko; Esther Markish; Roy Medvedev; Stefan Mehr; Arthur Miller; Zhenya Naiditch; Fred Warner

Neal; Yelena Nekhamkina; Raisa Orlova; Hirsh Osherovich; Kiril Ous-pensky; Helene Parmelin; Yevgeny Pasternak; Shlomo Perlmutter; Antonina Pirozhkova; Vladimir Pozner; Alexandra Pregel; Alexander Rindzinski; Masha Rolnikaite; Abraham Sabrin; Dov Sadan; Harrison Salisbury; Arthur Sandauer; Alya Savich; Viktoria Schweitzer; Mr. and Mrs. Henry Shapiro; Angelina Shchekin-Krotova; Alexander Shedrin-sky; William Shirer; S. L. Shneiderman; Andrei Sinyavsky; Hirsh Smolar; Natalya Stolyarova; Cyrus Sulzberger; Julius Telesin; Lidia Tynyanova; Nikolai Vasilenko; Vercors (Jean Bruller); Mme. Astier de la Vigerie; Isabelle Vichniac; Gerard Vichniac; Jacques Vichniac; Vladimir Voinovich; Andrei Voznesensky; Natalya Vovsi-Mikhoels; Nina Vovsi-Mikhoels; Yevgeny Yevtushenko; Boris Zaks; Yelena Zonina; and Alexander Zvieli. I saw them during trips to England, France, Sweden, and Spain; to Israel, Moscow, and Leningrad (St. Petersburg); to New York, Washington, Madison, and San Francisco. Stefan Mehr of Stock-holm was especially gracious to share his mother's papers with me.

I also would like to add heartfelt thanks to my agent, Robin Straus, for her steady enthusiasm; to Andrew Nurnberg for his invaluable assis-tance in London; to Lelia Ruckenstein for her careful and persistent attention; to Steve Fraser, my editor at Basic Books, for his discerning commitment, and to Michael Wilde, for his unstinting efforts. My wife Jill Janows, who joined me for the final, difficult laps, exhibited grace-ful fortitude, literary insight, support, and devotion in the face of my prolonged efforts to finish the manuscript.

Index

Abakumov, Viktor, 222
"Above the Battle," 84
Action Française, 123
Adzhubei, Alexei, 348
Akhmatova, Anna, 4, 30, 66, 100, 129, 132, 188, 239–40, 247, 249, 267, 285, 286–87, 302, 322, 330, 340, 383, 416n78
Aksyonov, Vasily, 7, 249, 362
Albania, 228, 229
Alberti, Rafael, 157, 158, 179
Aleichem, Sholem, 214, 321–22, 323, 326, 397
Alexander I, 9
Alexander II, 9–10
Alexander, King of Yugoslavia, 134
Alexandrov, Georgy, 222–24, 254
Alexandrovich, Sergei, Grand Prince, 13
Aliger, Margarita, 213, 273, 294, 296, 301, 302, 353, 394, 395, 441n42
Allende, Salvador, 292
Alliluyeva, Nadezhda, 308
Alliluyeva, Svetlana, 260–61, 307–9, 386–89
All-Russian Union of Writers, 107
All-Union Congress of Soviet Writers. *See* Soviet Writers' Congress
Alter, Viktor, 201–2
Altman, Natan, 395

Amado, Jorge, 285
Amalrik, Andrei, 7
American-Birobidjan Committee, 233
American Committee of Jewish Writers, Artists and Scientists, 214
American Society of Newspaper Editors, 231
Amnesty International, 450n24
Anders, Wladyslaw, 196
Anderson, Sherwood, 135
And Yet It Turns, 88, 89
Anti-Semitism, 2, 278, 349, 384, 442n6; Babii Yar and, 209, 211, 220, 240n23, 248; cossacks and, 60–61; czars and, 15, *see also* Pogroms; fascism and, 123, *see also* Jewish Anti-Fascist Committee; France and, 123, 177, 204; Germany and, 114, 140, 177, 184, 186, *see also Black Book, The*; Holocaust; Israel and, 387–88; Khrushchev and, 285, 306–7, 313–26, 368; LeCache and, 146; pogroms, 10, 13, 57–59, 62; Poland and, 110–11; Soviet Union and, 208–10, 217, 234; Stalin and, 5, 198, 201–2, 206–7, 217, 248, 253–76, 312–13, 322, 434n60; White Army and, 60–61; World War II and, 4–5,

Anti-Semitism (*cont.*)
  192–93, 200–217, 219–221, 248;
  Zionism and, 12, 13, 157, 256, 260,
  261, 262, 269–70, 315, 326, 387,
  394. *See also* Holocaust; Jew,
  Ehrenburg as a; Yiddish
Antokolsky, Pavel, 296
Antonov-Ovseenko, Vladimir,
  159–60, 169
Apollinaire, Guillaume, 32, 34, 73,
  340
Apollon, 31
App, Austin J., 426n84
Arabs, 235, 256, 317
Aragon, Louis, 130, 142, 143, 145,
  181, 264, 272, 285, 289, 306, 350,
  381, 382, 395, 420n75, *pl. 9*
Arnshtein, Boris, 11
Arnshtein, Lev, 11–12
Arrest. *See* Imprisonment
Artists' Union, 297, 300–301
Asch, Shalom, 214
Astray, Millan, 174
Atomic bomb. *See* Nuclear
  weapons/war
Austria, fascism and, 123–24

Babel, Isaac, 5, 67, 87, 131–32, 133,
  136, 142, 144, 150, 151, 172, 176,
  178, 278, 285, 287–91, 303, 305,
  340, 411n67, 437n46, 442n13, *pl. 4*
Babel, Nathalie, 287, 288–89
Babii Yar, 209–10, 211, 220, 248,
  440n23
"Babii Yar" (Ehrenburg), 209–10, 319
"Babii Yar" (Yevtushenko), 209, 279,
  318–20
Balmont, Konstantin, 34, 45
Barbusse, Henri, 141, 142, *pl. 4*
Barenboim, Alexander, 444n38
Barthou, Jean-Louis, 134
Barzini, Luigi, 121–22
Basmannaya jail, 21
Bata, Tomas, 111–12
BBC Russian Service, 106
Beckett, Samuel, 360
Bek, Alexander, 296
Belgian endive, to Soviet agriculture,
  328–29
Belgium, 73–74
Bell, Julian, 168

Bell, The, 330
Bely, Andrei, 66, 86, 87, 298
Belyutin, Eli, 345, 353
Benda, Julian, 243
Benenson, Peter, 450n24
Ben-Gurion, David, 316, 317–18
Benton, William, 232, 235
Berberova, Nina, 74, 447n22
Berdyaev, Nikolai, 70
Bergamin, José, 169
Bergelson, David, 202, 262, 266, 315
Beria, Lavrenti, 202
Berlin, 82–93
Bernal, John, 330
Bernanos, George, 166
Beyond a Truce, 147, 154
Bidault, Georges, 218
Bifur, 104, 411n67
Birger, Boris, 415n52
Birobidjaner Stern, 215
Birth, of Ehrenburg, 10
Birzhevie Vedomosti (The Stock
  Exchange Gazette), 36, 41–43
Black Book, The, 5, 212–17, 235,
  254–55, 265, 323, 325, 349,
  425n64, 441n42, *pl. 8*
Bloch, Jean-Richard, 130, 132, 134,
  135, 142, 158, 199, 207
Blok, Alexander, 48, 66
Bloody Sunday, 16
Blum, Léon, 123, 154, 158–59, 177
Blumel, André, 321, 394
Bogoraz, Larisa, 381, 446n1
Bolshevik Revolution, 2, 3, 41, 42,
  43–50, 62, 63–64, 342
Bolsheviks, 2, 3, 16–17, 18, 19–20, 22,
  23, 25, 26, 27, 28, 29, 34, 36, 40, 46,
  47, 48, 49, 50, 51, 55, 56, 57, 59, 60,
  62, 63, 64, 65, 68, 69, 73, 83, 87, 95,
  96, 140, 396, 398, 406n8
Book for Adults, A, 29, 38, 47, 48, 65,
  147–49
Borisovna, Yevgeniya, 287
Bostunich, Gregory, 84–85
Brecht, Bertolt, 142
Breton, André, 123, 143, 350, 416n64
Brezhnev, Leonid, 300, 329, 368, 369,
  373, 374, 379, 380, 382, 396
Brod, Max, 361
Brodsky, Joseph, 7, 275, 370–71,
  446n2

Brodsky family, 13, 400*n*12
Brothers Yershov, The (Kochetov), 315
Bryusov, Valery, 30–31, 66
Bukharin, Nikolai, 17, 18–19, 26, 27,
 65, 68–69, 70, 80, 81, 85, 87, 94,
 95, 105–6, 124–25, 128, 129, 131,
 134, 135, 137, 148, 153, 154,
 172–74, 175–76, 178, 183, 189,
 336–38, 366, 414*n*26
Bukovsky, Vladimir, 393, 394
Bulgakov, Mikhail, 152, 278
Bulgaria, 228
Bunin, Ivan, 45, 74
Burlyuk, David, 50
Butyrki prison, 21, 78, 373
Byrnes, James, 228, *pl. 8*

Cadets (Constitutional Democrats),
 18
Canada, 237
Capa, Robert, 166, 168, 249–50, *pls.
 5, 12*
Cassidy, Henry, 198
Catherine II, 9
Catholicism, 29–30, 31, 34
Central Committee, 304, 305, 306,
 307, 317, 325, 329, 332, 338, 382
Chagall, Marc, 3, 32, 233, 316, 340,
 384, 437*n*46
Chamson, André, 142
Chapaev, 159
Cheka, 65, 69, 96, 98
Chekhov, Anton, 305, 306–7, 324, 336
Chekhovskaya, Irina, 325
Chernoutsan, Igor, 332, 441*n*41
"Cherry Brandy" (Shalamov), 374
Childhood, 30
Childs, Marquis, 235
Chile, 291–92
China, 363, *pl. 10*
Chronicle of Our Times, The, 111–12
Chukovsky, Kornei, 346, 371
Churchill, Winston, 230–31
Civil war, in Soviet Union, 51–61,
 62–63, 64, 83. *See also* Spanish civil
 war
Clair, René, 103, 151
Clementis, Lidia, 341
Clementis, Vladimir, 269, 341–42
Close Up, 92
Cocteau, Jean, 32

Cold war, 2, 227, 237, 240–41,
 243–44, 247, 295, 296, 310, *pl. 10.*
 See also Iron curtain
Collected Works, 325, 363–65, 414*n*26
Collected Works (Zola), 325
Collectivization, 137
Comintern. *See* Communist Interna-
 tional
Commune, 143
Communist International (Com-
 intern), 141, 162
Communist party, 100, 102. *See also*
 Social Democratic Labor party
Companys, Luis, 159
Concentration camps, 213, 220. *See
 also* Holocaust
"Concerning a Certain Letter,"
 258–60
Conquest, Robert, 381
Conspiracy of Equals, The, 107, 112,
 411*n*67
Constitutional Democrats. *See* Cadets
Constructivism, 89
Contemporary Nihilist, A
 (Tereshchenko), 410*n*52
Cossacks, 60, 61
Cot, Nina, 429*n*50
Cot, Pierre, 182, 183, 291
Coupole, La, 121
Crankshaw, Edward, 397
Crevel, René, 142, 143
Crimea, 61–65, 269
Croix de Feu, 123
Cuban Missile Crisis, 344, 443*n*29
Cubists, 50
"Curious Incident, A," 65–66, 71
Czapski, Joseph, 196–97
Czechoslovakia, 228
Czechoslovak writers' community,
 398

Dada movement, 142
Daix, Pierre, 416*n*64
Daladier, Edouard, 142
Daniel, Alexander, 446*n*1
Daniel, Yuly, 378–79, 380–81, 385,
 387, 446*n*1
Danin, Daniel, 195–96, 376
Death, of Ehrenburg, 6–7, 282, 320,
 382, 383, 388–98, 445*n*14, 445*n*18,
 pl. 16

De Beauvoir, Simone, 121, 360, 417*n*7, 446*n*2

De Gaulle, Charles, 183, 186, 200, 267, 423*n*36

Dekorativnoe Iskusstvo (Decorative Art), 384

De Monzie, Alfred, 182

Denikin, Anton, 56, 57, 58, 59, 62, 146

Desnos, Robert, 340

Deutscher, Isaac, 339

"Deutschland-America," 241

Diary of Anne Frank, The, 323–24

Diaz, José, 159, 167

Diplomatic courier, Ehrenburg as, 64–65

Dissidents, 307, 356, 370–75, 378–82, 384, 385–87, 393, 394, 446*n*1, 447*n*9. *See also* Human rights movement

"Divine Speech," 45

Doctors' Plot, 215, 268–76, 278, 312, 313

Doctor Zhivago (Pasternak), 279, 306, 309–11

Dolitsky, Efim, 433*n*45

Dombrovsky, Yury, 371

Dôme, Le, 121

Doriot, Jacques, 183

Dos Passos, John, 53, 135

Dostoevsky, Fyodor, 104

Doumer, Paul, 114

Dovzhenko, 150

Dreiser, Theodore, 135

Dreyfus affair, 13, 306–7, 324

DuBois, W. E. B., *pl. 9*

Dudintsev, Vladimir, 301

Duhamel, Gide, Malraux, Mauriac, Morand, Romains, Unamuno vus par un Écrivain d'U.S.S.R., 413*n*7

Duma, 17, 40

Durruti, Buenaventura, 157, 159, 163, 166

Dymshits, Alexander, 343

Dzerzhinsky, 126

Eastern Europe, Stalin and, 228–29, 230–31

Education, of Ehrenburg, 15, 20, 22, 33

Education Ministry, theatrical section of, 67–68

Efimov, Boris, 229–30

Efron, Ariadne (Alya), 302, 303, 341

Efron, Sergei, 63, 86, 302–3

Ehrenburg, Anna Arnshtein, 10–11, 18, 22, 42, 43, 50–51, 52, *pl. 1*

Ehrenburg, Grigory, 10, 13, 18, 21, 22, 29, 34, 60, 73, *pl. 1*

Ehrenburg, Ilya Lazarevich (Ehrenburg's first cousin), 32, 61, 401*n*26, 403*n*43

Ehrenburg, Irina Ilinichna, 30, 42, 94, 114, 117, 118, 128, 136, 154, 165, 171, 181–82, 207, 211–12, 213, 221, 273–74, 284, 328, 372, 389, 390, *pls. 3, 12, 16*

Ehrenburg, Izabella, 429*n*50

Ehrenburg, Lazar, 12

Ehrenburg, Lyubov Mikhailovna, 5, 53, 54–55, 57, 59, 60, 61, 62, 64, 65, 66, 67, 70, 73, 74, 86, 93, 115, 134, 146–47, 150, 154, 171, 174, 183, 184, 210, 211, 239, 240, 272, 273–74, 282, 283, 289, 292–93, 311, 383–84, 384, 388, 391, 392, 395, 404*n*20, 415*n*52, 432*n*19, *pls. 10, 13, 16*

Ehrenburg, Yevgeniya, 429*n*50

Eikhenvald, Yuri, 45

Einsatzgruppen, 212

Einstein, Albert, 214, 235, 256, *pl. 8*

Eisenstein, Sergei, 46, 92, 150, 151, 234, *pl. 3*

Elizabeth, Queen of Belgium, 265

Eluard, Paul, 243, 293

Emes publishing house, 263

Émigrés, 3, 25, 27, 32–33, 34, 39, 40, 41, 73, 74, 83, 87

England, 177, 231, 256; Hitler and, 179; World War II and, 181, 182, 185

"Enough," 221–22

Enzenberger, Hans Magnus, 360, 362

Epshteyn, Shakhno, 214

Erlich, Henryk, 201–2

Ethridge, Mark, 228

European Crossroad, 229

"Exodus," 57, 65

Experimental art, 50

Exter, Alexandra, 53

Extraordinary Adventures of Julio Jurenito and His Disciples, The, 3, 20,

44–45, 70, 74–81, 91, 93, 95, 97, 98, 149, 159, 200–201, 335, 353, 363
Eynikayt, 214, 215

Factory of Dreams, 112
Fadeyev, Alexander, 186, 197, 219, 243, 245, 285, 294, 298, 366, 431*n*86
Falk, Robert, 300–301, 339, 340, 345, 385, 430*n*58, 437*n*46
Fall of Paris, The, 186–87, 200, 218
"False Voice, A," 240
Farge, Yves, 246
Fascism, 4, 114, 120, 123–24, 125, 134–36, 138, 139–41, 154, 161, 162, 178, 179, 180, 185, 187, 232, 420*n*75; Austria and, 123–24; France and, 123, 154–55; International Writers' Congress in Defense of Culture and, 141–46; Italy and, 134; Spain and, 154, *see also* Spanish civil war. *See also* Hitler, Adolf; Nazis
Fathers and Sons (Turgenev), 279
Faulkner, William, 304
February Revolution, 39–40
Fedin, Konstantin, 102, 290, 360, *pl. 11*
Fefer, Itzik, 214, 217, 262, 266, 269, 315
Feltrinelli, Giangiacomo, 309
Fikker, Yehezkel, 163–64
Film: Ehrenburg lecturing on, 103; *The Love of Jeanne Ney* and, 92–93, 117, 409*n*34
First Casualty, The (Knightley), 36
First Circle, The (Solzhenitsyn), 373
First Five Year Plan, 106, 115–16, 127, 137
First Gymnasium, 15, 20
First Ray, 15
Fishman, Ephraim, 432*n*19
Fishman, Fanya, 211–12, 237, 328, 332, 424*n*62, 432*n*19
Fishman, Joseph, 432*n*19
Flakser, Menahem, 260
Flanner, Janet, 350
Flèche, La (The Arrow), 170
Fogelman, Zina, 234
For Freedom of Speech!, 45

Formalism, campaign against, 150, 151, 152–53, 298, 345, 347, 352
Forrestal, James, 241
Forster, E. M., 141, 142
For Whom the Bell Tolls (Hemingway), 164, 165–66
"Foundations of Leninism, The," 72
France, 179, 199–200, 204, 218, 232, 265–66; fascism and, 154–55; Hitler and Nazis and, 177–78, 179; Popular Front and, 123, 154–55; Vichy, 182–84, 420*n*75; World War II and, 181, 182–84, 185, 186, 187. *See also* Paris, France
France–USSR Friendship Society, 296
France–USSR Society, 321, 394
Franco, Francisco, 155, 157, 163, 168, 169, 170, 174, 176, 179, 180, 200
Frank, Anne, 323–24, 326
Frank, Nino, 104, 121, 203–4, 411*n*67
Frank, Waldo, *pl. 4*
Freemasonry and the Russian Revolution (Bostunich), 84–85
"French Jews and the War," 204
Frezinsky, Boris, 384
Frisch, Max, 244
Frunze, Mikhail, 108, 109
Furtseva, Yekaterina, 300
Futurists, 50

Galaktionov, Mikhail, 231, 232–33
Gance, Abel, 103
Gandhi, Indira, 293
Garry, Alexei, 127
Gerasimov, Alexander, 297, 300–301, 348
Gerassi, Fernando, 233, 234
Gerassi, John "Tito," 234
Gerassi, Stepha, 159, 164, 233, 234, 417*n*7
Germany: anti-Semitism and, 177, 184, 186, *see also* Black Book, The; Holocaust; *The Extraordinary Adventures of Julio Jurenito and His Disciples* and, 76–77, 78; World War II and, 181, 182–86, 187–200, 202, 219–23. *See also* Hitler, Adolf; Nazis
Gheorghiu-Dej, Georghe, 229
Gibb, Dorothy, 221

Gide, André, 4, 122, 134, 140, 142, 149–50, 151, 160–61, 162, 168, 169, 170, 179, 344

Gilmore, Daniel, 235

Gilyarovsky, Vladimir, 18

Ginzburg, Alexander, 381–82

Ginzburg, Eugeniya, 372–73

Glasnost, 19, 279, 384

Glavlit, 72, 90, 106, 338, 442*n*6

Goebbels, Joseph, 220

Gogol, Nikolai, 104

Goldberg, Anatol, 106–7, 266

Goldberg, B. Z., 214

Golding, William, 360

Golomshtock, Igor, 298, 299, 356

Golubov-Potapov, Vladimir, 255

Gómez de la Serna, Ramón, 37, 161–62, 411*n*67

Gonzalez, Valentin, 419*n*64

Gorbachev, Mikhail, 19, 50, 398, 434*n*60

Gorbatov, Boris, 212

Gorgulov, Pavel, 114–15

Gorky, Maxim, 34, 49–50, 70, 100, 108, 131, 142, 160, 255, 306, 322

Government Publishing House, 80

Grabber, The, 95–97, 101, 102, 107, 109

Graff, Oskar Maria, 130

Grafton, Samuel, 235–36, 237–38

Granin, Daniel, 362

Grass, Günter, 362

"Great Defender of Peace, The," 277–78

Great Purge, 164, 168, 171–76, 178, 282–83, 336, 372

Grigorenko, Petro, 379

Gris, Juan, 32

Grodno, 211

Gronfein, Yevgeniya Borisovna, 287, 288

Grossman, Vasily, 205, 213, 216, 217, 273, 278, 303, 325, 441*n*42, *pl. 7*

Gruzdev, 102

Guatemala, 292, 296

Gudzenko, Semyon, 199–200

Guebhard, Caroline Rémy, 146

Gul, Roman, 87, 90, 408*n*16

Gulag Archipelago, The (Solzhenitsyn), 279–80, 373, 447*n*9

Gumilyov, Lev, 287

Gumilyov, Nikolai, 30–31

Gusev, Sergei, 117

Halkin, Shmuel, 262, 269

Hall of Columns, 130

Hamsun, Knut, 21

Harrington, Michael, 350

Haskalah movement, 12

Hebrew language, 12, 13

Heine, Heinrich, 198, 207

Helikon, 86

Helios, 34

Hemingway, Ernest, 164, 165–66, 304, *pl. 5*

Henry, Ernst, 375, 376–77

Herbert, Zbignief, 339

Herzen, Alexander, 104

Hikmet, Nazim, 330

Hilsum, Luce, 420*n*75

Himmler, Heinrich, 77

Hitler, Adolf, 2, 4, 77, 113, 117, 123, 124, 125, 134, 139, 140, 154, 170, 177–78, 179, 180, 181, 182, 183, 184–85, 188, 189, 192, 201, 202, 206, 209, 218–19, 220–21, 225, 375, 426*n*84, *pl. 7*

Hitler–Stalin pact of 1939, 140

Holocaust, 2, 4–5, 51, 86, 185, 201, 207, 208–10, 211, 219–20, 230, 231, 254, 323–24, 349, 425*n*64, 426*n*81, 426*n*84

Honors: Legion of Honor, French (1944), 218, 266; Order of Lenin (1944), 200, 218; Order of Lenin (1961), 329; Order of the Red Banner (Civilian) (1951), 266–67; seventieth birthday, 329–32; sixtieth birthday, 266–67; Stalin Peace Prize (1953), 272; Stalin Prize (1942), 200, 218, *pl. 7*; Stalin Prize (1948), 247, 248, 263

Hope Abandoned (Mandelstam, N.), 6, 340–41, 373

Hope Against Hope (Mandelstam, N.), 373

House of Arts, 85, 87

Hoxha, Enver, 229

Human rights movement, 370–71, 379, 437*n*46, 446*n*1. *See also* Dissidents

Humphrey, Hubert, *pl. 12*

Hungary, 294–95, 296, 297, 302, 304, 317, 443*n*22
Hunt Club, 18
Huxley, Aldous, 141, 142

I am Alive, 31
Ibarurri, Dolores, 157, 299, 330
Illness, of Ehrenburg, 327–28, 335, 388–92
Ilyichev, Leonid, 346–47, 352–54, 356, 363–64
Impressionist masterpieces, 296
Imprisonment: 1908, 3, 20–22; 1920, 65–66; 1921, 69; of teenagers and students against regime, 401*n*26. *See also* Labor camps
In America, 241
Inber, Vera, 152
India, 292–93
"In 1940," 188
Inostrannaya Literatura (Foreign Literature), 304, 305
"In Poland," 110
International Brigades, Spanish civil war and, 162, 164
International Colonial Exhibition, 111
Internationale, The, 46
International League Against Racism and Anti-Semitism, 146
International Organization of Revolutionary Writers (MORP), 135–36, 141
International Writers' Congress in Defense of Culture, 141–46, 167–69, 243, 287, *pl. 4*
Internatsionalnaya Literatura (International Literature), 186
"In the Ghetto," 423*n*55
"In the Jungles of Europe," 125
"In the Train Carriage," 42–43
Into the Whirlwind (Ginzburg), 372
Introductions, Ehrenburg writing, 293, 298–99
Iran, 237
Irisha, 332
Iron curtain, 230–31, 238. *See also* Cold war
Israel, 157, 235, 256, 258–60, 261–62, 313, 317–18, 320, 322, 326, 387–88

Italy, Mussolini and, 125, 134, 139, 145
Ivanov, Vyacheslav, 45
Ivens, Joris, 431*n*86
Ivinskaya, Olga, 446*n*1
Izvestia, 3, 47, 85, 100, 109, 114–15, 117, 123–25, 127, 128, 130, 137–39, 144, 145, 146, 151, 154, 157–60, 161, 165, 169, 173, 174, 176–79, 185, 229, 231, 318, 348, 419*n*62

Jacob (LeCache), 146
Jacob, Max, 33, 340, *pl. 2*
Jakobson, Roman, 180, 233, 395
Jammes, Francis, 29–30, 34, 43
Jew, Ehrenburg as a, 2, 52, 198, 203–5, 227, 247, 252, 313, 321, 330, 331–32, 398, 400*n*8, 400*n*10, 414*n*31, 439*n*4, 442*n*6, 442*n*10; anti-Semitism toward, 60–61, 62; childhood and, 9–15; "Concerning a Certain Letter" and, 258–60; in death, 394, 397; *The Extraordinary Adventures of Julio Jurenito and His Disciples* and, 76, 77, 78–79, 81; Jewish Anti-Fascist Committee and, 201–3, 206, 208, 212, 214, 215, 216, 217; Jewish partisans and, 208–12, 423*n*54, *pl. 6*; journalistic writings and, 43; Khrushchev and, 313–26; in Kiev, 55; Nazis and, 405*n*31, 426*n*81, 426*n*84, *see also* World War II; New York visit and, 233; *People, Years, Life* and, 336; poetry and, 31, 47; pogroms and, 57–59; Stalin and, 253–76; *The Stormy Life of Lasik Roitschwantz* and, 95–96, 97–99, 100; works and, 31, 43, 47, 76, 77, 78–79, 81, 95–96, 97–99, 100, 200–201, 248, 336, *see also Black Book, The*; World War II and, 4–5, 192–93, 201, 205–8, 212–17, 219–21. *See also* Anti-Semitism
Jewish Anti-Fascist Committee (JAC), 201–3, 206, 208, 210, 214, 215, 216, 217, 253, 255, 259, 262, 269, 316, 347, 433*n*45; *The Black Book* and, 212–17, 235
Jewish Autonomous Region, in the Crimea, 269

Jewish partisans, 208–12, 423n54, pl. 6
Jewish Socialist Bund of Poland, 201
Jocelyn, Paul, 177, 178–79
Joliot-Curie, Frédéric and Irene, 245
Journalism career, 35–36, 161–62; *Birzhevie Vedomosti*, 36, 41–43; Eastern Europe and, 228–29; *Izvestia*, 47, 109, 111, 114–15, 117, 123–25, 128, 137–39, 144, 145, 146, 151, 157–60, 161, 169, 173, 174, 176–79, 419n62; *Kievskaya Zhizn*, 56, 57, 58–59, 60; *Krasnaya Gazeta*, 114; *Krasnaya Zvezda*, 190–95, 206, 221–22; *Novosti Dnya*, 49; *Pravda*, 258–60, 277–78, 321; Spanish civil war and, 166–67, 173–74, 176–77, 419n62; United States trip and, 231–39; *Utro Rossy* and, 35–36; *Vlasti Naroda*, 49; World War I and, 36–38; World War II and, 190–200, 218, 220, 221–22. *See also* Literary criticism
Joyce, James, 53, 360, 361, 411n67
Judaism Without Embellishment (Kichko), 314
"Judgment Day," 46
Julio Jurenito. See Extraordinary Adventures of Julio Jurenito and His Disciples, The

Kadar, Janos, 294
Kafka, Franz, 336, 360, 361
Kaganovich, Lazar, 100, 136, 137, 260, 317, 375
Kameneva, Olga, 67
Kamenev, Lev, 26, 49, 67, 68–69, 91, 105, 137, 153, 154
Kanevsky, Viktor, 389
Kapitsa, Pyotr, 70, 379
Kaplan, Fanny, 51
Kapler, Alexei, 308
Kataev, Valentin, 181, 197
Kaverin, Veniamin, 79, 89–90, 96, 273–74, 301, 302, 346
Kenneville, Chantal, 40–41
Kerensky, Alexander, 41, 386, 406n8
Khatsrevin, Zakhary, 190
Khavinson, Yakov, 273
Khazina, Nadezhda (Nadya), 53, 62, 67, 74

Khlam, 53
Khodosevich, Vladislav, 87
Khrushchev, Nikita, 2, 5–6, 133, 211, 246, 278, 284, 328, 329, 334, 336–37, 342, 344, 345–46, 347, 348, 349–50, 353, 354–55, 356, 357, 369, 377, 378, 382, 383, 395, 396, pl. 11; anti-Semitism and, 285, 306, 307, 313–26; culture under, 278–311; dissidents and, 371, 373; Ehrenburg and, 5, 287, 320, 352–55, 357, 358–60, 361, 363, 364, 365–68, 369, 398; Hungary and, 294; peace movement and, 291, 293; rehabilitation under, 286–91, 313; Stalin and, 286, 287, 293, 294, 305, 315, 365
Kichko, Trofim, 314
Kiev, 12, 18; Babii Yar, 209–210, 211, 220, 248, 440n23, *see also* "Babii Yar"; Ehrenburg in, 51–59; Jewish community of, 209–10, 211
Kievlyanin (The Kievan), 58
Kievskaya Zhizn (Kiev Life), 56, 57, 58–59, 60
Kirov, Sergei, 136–38, 153, 160, 173
Kishinev pogrom, 13
Klimova, Natalya, 372
Knightley, Philip, 36
Koba, 153
Kochetov, Vsevolod, 315, 343
Koestler, Arthur, 180
"Kol Nidre" (Sutzkever), 210
Koltsov, Mikhail, 141, 142, 158, 160, 165, 169, 172, 173, 175, 176, 230, 417n8, 419n64
Kolyma prison, 374
Komsomolskaya Pravda, 164–65, 328
Kopelev, Lev, 194, 379
Korach, Alfred, 282
Korean War, 266
Korneichuk, Alexander, pl. 11
Korsakas, Kostas, 184
Kosygin, Alexei, 368
Kotov, Mikhail, 330, pl. 11
Koussevitzky, Serge, 428n29
Kowarski, Shlomo, 208, 254, pl. 6
Kozhenov, Vadim, 414n31
Kozintseva, Lyubov Mikhailovna, 53. *See also* Ehrenburg, Lyubov Mikhailovna

Kozintsev, Dr., 93
Krasnaya Gazeta, 114
Krasnaya Nov (Red Virgin Soil), 102, 110
Krasnaya Zvezda (Red Star), 190–95, 206, 207, 221–22, 223, 231, 232
Kreiser, Jacob, 274
Krestinsky, Nikolai, 172–73
Kreuger, Ivor, 112
Krokodil, 302
Kronik, Israel, 254, 265
Kronstadt Rebellion, 69
Krupskaya, Nadezhda, 80, 87
Kulturny Zivot (Cultural Life), 341
Kunyahovsky, Leib, 423n54
Kvitko, Leib, 262

Labedz, Leo, 381
Labor camps, 250, 270, 279–80, 373, 374, 381, 382, 393, 437n46, 446n1
Lady Macbeth of Mtsensk District (Shostakovich), 152
Lakshin, Vladimir, 360–61
Laktionov, Alexander, 347–48
Lapin, Boris, 136, 171, 190, 285
Larina, Anna Mikhailovna, 175–76, 338
Last, Jef, 168
Lazarevich, Ilya. *See* Ehrenburg, Ilya Lazarevich
Lebed, 12
Lebedev, Vladimir, 337, 338–39, 361, 368
LeCache, Bernard, 146
LeCache, Denise, 115, 146
Le Corbusier, 89, 233
Léger, Fernand, 3, 89
Legion of Honor, French (1944), 218, 266
Leneman, Léon, 316
Lengiz publishing house, 101, 102
Lenin, Vladimir, 3, 17, 18, 22, 23–24, 26, 27–28, 29, 45, 48, 49, 50, 51, 56, 69, 72, 78, 80, 81, 82, 87, 96, 105, 130, 153, 173, 194, 353; death of, 94–95; evaluation of, 24, 94–95; lampooning, 27–28
Lenin Peace Prize, to Picasso, 300
Lenin Prize. *See* Order of Lenin
"Lessons of Stendhal, The," 278, 305–6, 307, 308

"Let me not think too much," 178
Lewis, Anthony, 234–35
Libion, Victor, 32
Lidin, Vladimir, 388
Life and Death of Nikolai Kurbov, The, 90–91, 93, 353
Life of the Automobile, 111–12
Lion in the Square, The, 241
Lissitsky, El, 88
Literary criticism, 66–67, 122–23, 278, 413n7; on Chekhov, 278, 305, 306–7; *Krasnaya Nov*, 102, 110–11; "The Lessons of Stendhal," 278, 305–6, 307, 308, 317, 331; on Tsvetaeva, 278 Literary Fund of the Writers' Union, 181–82
Literatura i Zhizn (Literature and Life), 319–20
Literature, Ehrenburg's devotion to, 27–34. *See also* Poetry; Works
Literaturnaya Gazeta (Literary Gazette), 107, 117, 122–23, 126, 127, 143, 172, 244, 266, 281, 290, 296, 306, 319, 383, 397
Literaturnaya Moskva (Literary Moscow), 301–2
Litvinov, Maxim, 140, 179, 206–7, 223, 442n13
Litvinova, Tatyana, 394, 395, 442n13, 449n2
Long Return, The (Markish), 264, 321–22
Lorca, García, 158
Love of Jeanne Ney, The, 90, 91, 92–93, 117, 285, 409n34
Lozovsky, Solomon, 202, 216–17, 269, 315, 439n6
Lubyanka prison, 65, 66, 129, 315
Lysenko, Tofim, 368

Mahogony (Pilnyak), 107, 108–9
Maidanek, 213, 220
Maisky, Ivan, 219, 330, 332, 379
Makarenko, Mikhail, 437n46
Makarov, Alexander, 290
Malenkov, Georgy, 260, 263, 375
Malevich, Kazimir, 88
Malik, 117
Malraux, André, 122, 125–26, 128, 130, 132, 134, 135, 140, 141, 142,

Malraux, André (*cont.*)
144, 145, 148, 150, 151, 158, 163,
167, 176, 181, 395, *pl. 4*
Malraux, Clara, 132
Mandel, Georges, 183, 420*n*75
Mandelstam, Alexander, 59, 60, 62, 65
Mandelstam, Nadezhda, 2–3, 5–6,
55–56, 65, 129, 250, 270, 278, 307,
340–41, 356, 373–74, 431*n*85
Mandelstam, Osip, 2, 5–6, 53, 55, 59,
60, 62, 63, 64, 65, 66, 67, 84, 102,
104, 128–29, 188, 210, 250, 267,
285, 302, 304, 339, 340, 343, 374
Manezh gallery, 345
Mann, Heinrich, 142
Mann, Klaus, 130
Mann, Mendel, 316
Man's Fate (Malraux), 125–26
Markish, David, 322
Markish, Esther, 263, 264, 287, 315,
321–23, 326
Markish, Peretz, 53, 201, 202, 255,
263, 264, 269, 287, 315–16,
322–23, 326, 430*n*61, *pl. 6*
Marriage. *See* Ehrenburg, Lyubov
Mikhailovna
Marshak, Samuil, 201, 371, 383
Martin du Gard, Roger, 135
Martov, Yuly, 27
Marty, André, 164, 166
Marx, Karl, 153
Marxists, on Ehrenburg's works, 2,
100–101
Materialization of the Fantastic, The,
103
Matisse, Henri, 429*n*29
Matsuev, Nikolai, 421*n*90
Mauriac, François, 122, 126
Mayakovsky, Vladimir, 47, 48, 50, 66,
82, 84, 85–86, 89, 151, 347
Mazeh, Jacob, 254
Medvedev, Roy, 384
Mehr, Hjalmar, 282, 283–84
Mehr, Liselotte, 246, 282–84, 300,
328, 334–35, 356, 378, 388, 389,
391, 392, *pls. 14, 15*
Meir, Golda, 157, 258, 261–62
Memoirs of a Revolutionary (Serge),
146
Mensheviks, 17–18, 19, 23, 25, 26,
27, 48, 61, 64

Merder fun Felker (Murderers of Peo-
ples), 215
Merkulov, Vasily, 250
Metropol Hotel, 60, 197–98
Meyerhold, Vsevolod, 67–68, 91, 136,
151, 152, 172, 176, 340
Mikhail, Grand Duke, 40
Mikhailovna, Lyubov. *See* Ehrenburg,
Lyubov Mikhailovna.
Mikhoels, Solomon, 201, 202, 214,
217, 230, 253, 255–57, 264, 269,
270, 272, 287, 339, *pl. 6*
Mikoyan, Anastas, 446*n*2
Miller, Arthur, *pl. 13*
Milman, Valentina, 116–18, 123, 124,
127, 149, 242, 250, 287, 394
Ministry of Culture, 297, 300
Mintz, Isaac, 272–73, 318
Mirova, Yelena, 165
Mission in Moscow (Namir), 258
Modigliani, Amedeo, 3, 32, 33, 38,
73, 148, 340, 416*n*78, *pl. 2*
Mola, Emilio, 155
Molod Ukrainy (Ukrainian Youth), 229
Molotov, Vyacheslav, 137, 179, 185,
188, 218, 239, 250, 262, 375
Montagu, Ivor, 244, 298, 397
Moravia, Alberto, 293
MORP. *See* International Organiza-
tion of Revolutionary Writers
Moscow: Ehrenburg family in,
13–15, 18; Jews expelled from, 10,
13–14
Moscow Does Not Believe in Tears, 147
Moscow University, 16
Moscow Writers' Club, 45
Moskovskie Novosti (Moscow News),
329–30
Mountain Jews, 314
Mountbatten, Lady, 293
Munich agreement, 177
"Murder of the Army Commander,
The," 108, 109
Mussolini, Benito, 125, 134, 139, 145,
155
My Paris, 104

Nachman, Reb, 313
Nagibin, Yury, 347
Nagy, Imre, 294
Naiditch, Zhenya, 329

Nakanune (On the Eve), 87
Naked Year, The (Pilnyak), 72
Namir, Mordechai, 257–58, 260, 261, 262
Na Postu (On Guard), 90, 102, 107
Nasser, Gamal Abdul, 317
National Council, 214
National Hotel (Moscow), 128
Nauka i Zhizn (Science and Life), 383
Nazis, 2, 3, 76, 77, 113–14, 124, 135, 138–39, 140, 182, 183, 185, 187, 326, 405*n*31, 420*n*75, 443*n*27, *pls.* 6, 7; Jews and, 4–5, *see also Black Book, The*; Holocaust. *See also* Hitler, Adolf
Nedelya (The Week), 325
Nehru, Jawarahal, 293
Neizvestny, Ernst, 345
Nekhamkina, Yelena, 327–28
Nekrasov, Viktor, 335, 440*n*23
Nelson, William, 235
NEP. *See* New Economic Policy
Neruda, Pablo, 167, 268, 285, 291–92, 395, *pl. 10*
New Economic Policy (NEP), 69, 82, 95, 96–97, 100, 102, 105, 106, 108, 109
"New French Cinema, The," 103
New York Times, 438*n*65
Nicholas I, 9
Nicholas II, 17, 34, 39–40, 41, 51
Nicolaevsky, Boris, 153
"Night of the Murdered Poets, The," 269
Nights of America, 241–42
Nikolaeva, Galina, 435*n*16
Nikulin, Lev, 152
Nin, Andrés, 168
Ninth Wave, The, 247, 248, 268, 331
Nizan, Paul, 142, 158, 344, *pl. 4*
NKVD, 176, 315
Nobel Prize, to Pasternak, 309–11
Not by Bread Alone (Dudintsev), 301
Not by Bread Alone (Tolstoy), 12
Novaya Zhizn (New Life), 50
Novgorod-Seversk, 12
Novoe Vremya (New Times), 250
Novosti Dnya (News of the Day), 49
Novy Mir, 108, 306, 332–33, 334, 335, 336–37, 338, 339, 342–43,

348, 349, 350, 357, 358, 360, 365, 369, 375, 383, 384, 385–86
Nuclear weapons/war, 241, 243, 245, 246, 363, *pl. 10*
Nuremberg trial, 217, 229–30

Obshchee Delo (Common Cause), 74
October Revolution. *See* Bolshevik Revolution
Ogonyok, 229, 384
Okhrana, 20
Oklyansky, Yury, 325
Oktyabr, 343
"Old Furrier, The," 58
Old Man and the Sea, The (Hemingway), 304
One Day in the Life of Ivan Denisovich (Solzhenitsyn), 340, 346, 372, 373
One Hundred Letters, 207, 215
"On Guard" critics, 102, 107
"On the Role of the Writer," 279, 284
"On the Usual and the Unusual," 95
Order of Lenin: (1944), 200, 218; (1961), 329
Order of the Red Banner (Civilian), 266–67
Orlova, Raisa, 379
Orphanhood, 212
Ortenberg, David, 190, 191, 192, 195, 207
Ouspensky, Kiril, 371
Out of Chaos, 81, 116–20, 122, 126–28, 130, 147, 268, 285
Out of the Whirlwind (Ginzburg), 372

Pabst, G. W., 92–93
Pale of Settlement, 9–10, 12, 15, 18, 204
Palestine, 12, 198, 206, 211, 212, 235, 432*n*19
Palme, Olaf, 282
"Parade, Rue de la Gaîté, Paris" (Vorobyov), *pl. 2*
Paris, France, 3, 4, 18, 19, 22–41, 69–70, 71, 73–74, 94, 121–24; Rotonde Café, 32–33, 35, 36, 64, 65, 73, 74, 122, 160, 161, *pl. 2*
"Paris-Petrograd," 41–42
Parker, Ralph, 261, 262
Partisans of Peace, 243–46, 268, 330, *pl. 9*

Pascin, Julius, 340
Pasternak, Boris, 4, 48, 66–67,82, 84, 85, 86–87, 103, 125, 129, 131, 132, 133, 137, 142, 144, 150, 152, 171, 172, 185, 221, 234, 249, 267, 278, 279, 285, 294, 302, 303, 304, 306, 309–11, 316, 338–39, 342, 343, 350, 356, 408n14, 438n74, *pl. 4*
Pasternak, Yevgeny, 310, 338
Paustovsky, Konstantin, 330, 332
Paz, Magdeleine, 145
Paz, Octavio, 167
Peace movement, 253, 265, 266, 329; Hungary and, 295; Khrushchev and, 291–93; Partisans of Peace, 243–46, 268, 330, *pl. 9*; Picasso's dove as symbol of, 243; Stalin Peace Prize, 268, 272; Warsaw Congress, 251; World Peace Council, 292, 295
Peace Over War (Ivens), 431n86
People, Years, Life, 12, 18, 41, 50, 67, 97, 113, 120, 133, 134, 148, 153, 158, 171, 173, 204–5, 207, 249, 270, 317–18, 325–26, 333, 334–51, 372–73, 375–78, 382–84, 389, 414n26, 441n42, 447n22
Perlmutter, Shlomo, 212
Pétain, Henri Philippe, 201
Petrograd Soviet of the Workers' Deputies, 40
Picasso, Pablo, 3, 32, 33, 73, 148, 150, 151, 243, 251, 295, 297–300, 335, 340, 347, 356, 395, 431n85, 431n86, 437n46, *pls. 2, 9, 15*
Pilnyak, Boris, 72, 100, 107, 108–9, 285, 303, 411n67
Pilsudski, Jozef, 111
Pinochet, Augusto, 292
Pirozhkova, Antonina Nikolaevna, 287, 288–89, 290, 394, 442n13
Pirozhkova, Lidia, 287, 288, 289
"Plainly Speaking," 128
Plant-Louse, The, 314–15
Plisetskaya, Maya, 379
Podgaretsky, Mikhail, 91
Podol, 12, 18
Poetry, 25–26, 29, 30, 31–32, 48, 178, 180–81, 188, 249, 284, 396; "Babii Yar," 209–10, 319; *Childhood*, 30; "Divine Speech," 45; first volume

of (1910), 3; *I am Alive*, 31; "In the Ghetto," 423n55; *A Prayer for Russia*, 45–48, 52, 55; "Recollections," 14–15; *Reflections*, 73; school for, 53–54; "Sighs from a Foreign Land," 34; "Somewhere in Poland," 78; "To the Jewish People," "To Russia," 64; 78; translations, 34; *Verses*, 30–31; "Victory," 225–26
Poets' Café, 48
Poets, Essayists, Novelists (PEN), 310
Pogroms, 10, 13, 57–59, 62
Pokrovsky, 80
Poland, 110–11, 181–82, 185, 228, 294, 295
Polikarpov, Dmitri, 332, 382–83
Politburo, 91, 100, 105, 118, 137, 160, 293
Political Diary, 384
Polonskaya, Liza (Yelizaveta), 25–26, 27, 79, 80, 101, 102, 109, 112, 203, 306, 358, 408n14
Popova, Lyubov, 88
Popular Front, 123; France and, 123, 154–55; Spain and, 157
Poskrebyshev, Alexander, 347
Pospelov, Pyotr, 289, 317
Potemkin, 16
POUM, 168, 170
"Prague Spring," 398
Pravda, 26, 65, 79, 84, 85, 106, 152, 158, 185, 190, 200, 210, 220, 222, 231, 242, 258–60, 263, 270, 271, 272, 273, 277–78, 295, 302, 310, 318, 321, 329, 354, 357, 363, 368, 396
Prayer for Russia, A, 45–48, 52, 55, 63
Presidium, 368
Primo de Rivera, Miguel, 156
Prison. *See* Imprisonment
Prokofiev, Sergei, 249
Prostate cancer, and Ehrenburg, 327–28, 335
Proust, Marcel, 360
Provisional Government, 40, 41–42, 43, 73
Pudovkin, Vsevolod, 92
Purges, Stalin and, 2, 3–4, 5, 18, 19, 67, 137–38, 153–54, 169–70, 242, 264, 348; anti-Semitism and, 253–76; Great Purge, 164, 168, 171–76, 178, 282–83, 336, 372

Pushkin, Alexander, *pl. 10*

Pushkin Museum, Picasso exhibit at, 297

Putnam, Samuel, 122

Pyatakov, Yury, 154

Quand Israel Meurt (While Israel Was Dying) (LeCache), 146

Quiet Family, The, 28

Rabinovich, Isaak, 59, 60

Race relations, American South and, 235–36, 237–38, 241

Radek, Karl, 127–28, 154, 176

Rakosci, Matyas, 294

Rakovsky, Christian, 172–73

Raskolnikov, Fyodor, 113, 412*n*14

Rasp, Fritz, 225

"Recollections," 14–15

Red Army, 52, 61, 64, 65, 122, 130, 169

Red Cavalry (Babel), 87

Red Navy, 69

Reflections, 73

Regler, Gustav, 130, 131, 138, 142, 144

Rehabilitation, under Khrushchev, 286–91, 313

Reiss, Ignace, 302

Reizen, Mark, 274

Relationships: with Chantal Kenneville, 40–41; with Denise LeCache, 115, 146; with Katya Schmidt, 283; with Liselotte Mehr, 246, 282–84, 328, 334–35, 356, 378, 388, 389–91, 392; nature of, 53–54; wife, *see* Ehrenburg, Lyubov Mikhailovna; with Yadviga Sommer, 53–54, 55, 57, 59, 60–61, 62, 63, 64, 65, 73, 74, 115; with Yekaterina Schmidt, 30, 42

Religion. *See* Catholicism; Jew, Ehrenburg as a

Renoir, Jean, 103

Return from the U.S.S.R. (Gide), 160–61

Revolution: Bolshevik, 41, 42, 43–50, 62, 63–64, 342; February, 39–40; of 1905, 15–17

Richter, Hans Werner, 361, 362

Rimbaud, Arthur, 34

Rindzinski, Alexander, 254

Rivera, Diego, 3, 32, 33, 37, 38, 54, 73, 75, 340, *pl. 2*

Robbe-Grillet, Alain, 360

Robeson, Paul, 234, *pls. 9, 10*

Rodchenko, Alexander, 66, 88, 103

Rodin, Elisha, 211

Rodin, Grigory, 211

Rokossovsky, Marshall Konstantin, 330

Rolland, Romain, 140, 141

Rolnikaite, Masha, 324

Romania, 228, 229

Romm, Mikhail, 318, 346

Roosevelt, Eleanor, 231

Rosenberg, Marcel, 159, 160, 169, 234

Rotonde Café, 32–33, 35, 36, 64, 65, 73, 74, 122, 160, 161, *pl. 2*

Round Table East-West, 283

Ruge, Gerd, 309

Rumyantsev, Alexei, 368–69

Russell, Bertrand, 242

"Russia in the Storm," 66

Russian Association of Proletarian Writers (RAPP), 130

Russian Journal, A (Steinbeck and Capa), 249–50

Russkaya Kniga (The Russian Book), 83–84, 87, 90

Russo-Japanese War, 15

Rykov, Alexei, 153, 154, 176

Rysselberghe, Maria van, 150, 161

Saar, 138

St. Petersburg: Jews expelled from, 10; workers' council of, 16

Sakharov, Andrei, 243, 245, 379

Salisbury, Harrison, 199, 251–52, 258

Salvemini, Gaetano, 145

Samizdat, 372–73, 374, 375, 381, 384, 387, 447*n*9

Sarraute, Nathalie, 360

Sartre, Jean-Paul, 242, 293, 295, 360, 446*n*2

Savich, Alya, 116, 147, 254, 273, 274, 394, *pl. 16*

Savich, Ovady, 104, 116, 164–65, 179, 180, 213, 254, 273, 274, 335, 376, 388, 411*n*66, *pl. 5;* mother of, 234

Schmidt, Yekaterina (Katya), 30, 42, 94, 283

Schulberg, Budd, 247

Schweitzer, Viktoria, 378, 379

Seghers, Anna, 142, 183, 272, 285, 357

Selivanovsky, A., 414n34

Semyonov, Nikolai, 346

Serebryakova, Galina, 347

Serge, Victor, 144–46, 162

Seyfullina, Lidia, 437n46

Shalamov, Varlam, 372, 374–75, 377, 447n9

Shapiro, Henry, 197–98, 199, 221, 252, 261, 357

Shaposhnikova, Meri, 178, 288

Shchekin-Krotova, Angelina, 385

Shcherbakov, Alexander, 152, 202, 207, 270, 375

Shepilov, Dmitri, 273

Shirer, William, 428n29

Shklovsky, Viktor, 73, 110

Shoe King, The, 111–12

Sholokhov, Mikhail, 205, 206, 281, 284–85, 286, 347, 380–81, 386–87

Shostakovich, Dmitri, 4, 150, 152, 218–19, 249, 330, 346, 371, *pl. 7*

Shtern, Lena, 269, 315

Shulgin, Vasily, 58

"Sighs from a Foreign Land," 34

Silence of the Sea, The (Vercors), 436n36

Simenon, Georges, 122

Simonov, Konstantin, 197, 231, 233, 234, 236, 281, 286, 346

Single Front, The, 112

Sinyavskaya, Maria, 381

Sinyavsky, Andrei, 7, 298, 299, 356, 378–79, 380–81, 385, 387

Six Day War, 387–88

Skify, 89

Skoropadsky, Paul, 52

Slansky, Rudolf, 269, 270, 341

Slepian, Vladimir, 297

Slonim, Lev, 395

Slutsky, Boris, 304, 395, 437n46

Small Soviet Encyclopedia, The, 113

Smith, Walter Bedell, 231, 240–41

Smolar, Hirsh, 205–9

Smolny Institute, 137

Snechkus, Antanas, 423n54

Sobol, Andrei, 52

Social Democratic Labor party, 16, 17, 19, 20, 26

"Socialist realism," 1, 4, 118, 132, 135, 140, 143, 152, 279, 342, 345, 352

Socialist Revolutionary party, 16, 25, 27, 49, 51, 96

Socialist Revolutionary press, 51

Sokolnikov, Grigory, 19, 21, 148, 154, 336–37, 347

Solzhenitsyn, Alexander, 7, 279–80, 335, 340, 346, 348, 372, 373, 387, 446n5, 447n9

"Somewhere in Poland," 78

Sommer, Yadviga, 53–54, 55, 57, 59, 60–61, 62, 63, 64, 65, 73, 74, 115

Sorokin, Tikhon, 94

Soutine, Chaim, 33, *pl. 2*

Soviet Artists' Union, 151

Soviet Congress of Nationalities, 247, 250

Soviet Information Bureau, 214, 216

Soviet Literature publishing house, 118

Soviet passport, Ehrenburg receiving, 70

Soviet Peace Committee, 329

Sovietsky Pisatel publishers, 363, 364–65

Soviet Writer Looks at Vienna, A, 413n11

Soviet Writers' Congress: First (1934), 100, 125–26, 128, 129, 130–33, 134, 135, 136, 150, 285, 362, 413n7, *pl. 4*; Second (1954), 284–87; Fourth (1967), 386–87

Spanish civil war, 2, 126, 154, 155, 156–60, 162–67, 168, 169, 170, 173–74, 176–77, 178, 180, 419n62, 419n64, *pl. 5*

Spanish Testament (Koestler), 180

Spender, Stephen, 167

Stalin, Joseph, 1, 2, 3, 24, 47, 48, 50, 72, 81, 87, 100, 105–6, 109, 111, 118, 123, 125, 131, 133, 134, 135, 140, 141, 142, 143, 145, 148, 154, 158, 159, 160, 190, 200, 213, 218, 221, 246, 252, 334, 335, 343, 344, 345, 346, 347, 348, 358, 365, 382, *pls. 7, 10*; anti-Semitism and, 5,

198, 201–2, 206–7, 217, 248, 253–76, 312–13, 322, 434*n*60; Brezhnev and, 374, 379–80; censorship under, 106–9, 128–129, 150, 151, 152–53, 240, *see also* "Socialist realism"; Churchill and, 231; death of, 268, 276, 277–78, *pl. 11*; Eastern Europe and, 228–29, 230–31; Ehrenburg and, 2, 109, 112, 113, 120, 123, 127, 131, 134–36, 138, 152–53, 154, 161–62, 165, 174–75, 178, 180, 187, 188, 191, 195, 196–97, 219, 222–23, 224, 227, 229, 242, 247, 252, 262, 263–64, 266–67, 272–73, 274, 277–78, 375–78, 379–80, 430*n*61; First Five Year Plan, 106, 115–16, 127, 137; Hitler and, 179, 180, 181, 183, 184–85, 186, 187, 223; Khrushchev and, 286, 287, 293, 294, 305, 315, 352–55, 357; labor camps, 250, 270, 279–80, 373, 374, 381, 382, 393, 437*n*46, 446*n*1; Partisans of Peace movement, 243–46; repression under, 221; "socialist realism" and, 4, 118, 132, 135, 140, 143, 152, 279, 342, 352; Spanish civil war and, 163, 164–67, 169, 178, 180. *See also* Purges, Stalin and
Stalin Peace Prize: to Ehrenburg (1953), 272; to Sun Yat Sen's widow (1951), 268
Stalin Prize: (1942), 200, 218, *pl. 7*; (1948), 247, 248, 263
Starikov, Dmitri, 319
Steinbeck, John, 233, 249–50, *pl. 13*
Stendhal, 278, 305–6, 307, 308, 317, 331, 386
Stenich, Valentin, 53
Stolyarova, Natalya, 337, 372, 373, 382, 436*n*36, *pl. 13*
Stolypin, Pyotr, 372
Storm, The, 246–47, 248, 263, 267, 268
Stormy Life of Lasik Roitschwantz, The, 95–96, 97–99, 100, 106, 109, 127, 317
Stowe, Leland, 198, 233
Street in Moscow, A, 95–96, 97, 101, 284
Struggle for Peace, 245

Sudetenland, 177
Sulzberger, C. L., 278
Summer 1925, 101, 113
Suprematists, 50, 89
Supreme Soviet, 265, 293, 370, 381
Surkov, Alexei, 285, 360
Surrealism, 4, 122, 123, 142, 143, 144, 350, 416*n*64
Suslov, Mikhail, 299, 314, 319, 433*n*45
Sutzkever, Abraham, 210–11, 213, 217, 230
Suvorov, 207
Symbolist movement, 30

Tabidze, Tizian, 64, 285
Tacitus, 334
Tairov, Alexander, 339, 340, 430*n*58
Tamm, Igor, 243, 346, 379
Taro, Gerda, 168
TASS, 165
Tatlin, Vladimir, 88
Telesin, Julius, 375, 447*n*9
Ten Days That Shook the World (Eisenstein), 46
Tereshchenko, N., 410*n*52
Test Ban Treaty, 363
Thaw, The, 278, 279–82, 285, 286, 294, 317, 331, 396–97, 435*n*16
Thirteen Pipes, 90, 363
Thomas, Martin, 403*n*43
Tikhonov, Nikolai, 144, *pls. 7, 11*
Tishler, Alexander, 53
Tito, Joseph, 229, 245
"To the Jewish People," 31, 78
"To Life," 173–74
Toller, Ernst, 142, 180
Tolstoy, Alexei, 33, 45, 74, 87, 100, 142, 219
Tolstoy, Leo, 12, 14, 29, 151, 336, 340
Tomsky, Mikhail, 153–54
"To Russia," 64
Treblinka, 213, 220
Triolet, Elsa, 104, 181, 264
"Triumph of a Man, The," 210
"Troika" courts, 176
Trotsky, Leon, 16, 26–27, 72, 104, 105, 106, 143, 173, 380
Trud (Labor), 186, 348
Truman, Harry, 228, 230, 231
Trust, D.E., 90, 91–92, 93, 363

Tsvetaeva, Ariadne (Alya), 86
Tsvetaeva, Marina, 5, 34, 63, 66, 84, 86, 103, 144, 278, 302–4, 305, 306, 317, 339, 340, 341, 342, 343
Tukhachevsky, Mikhail, 168, 169
Turgenev, Ivan, 279
Turner, Bernard, 315–16
Tuwim, Julian, 204–5, 259, 326
Tvardovsky, Alexander, 335, 336, 340, 342–43, 344, 357, 361, 362, 365–66, 368, 371, 383–84, 385, 395, 396
Twenty Letters to a Friend (Alliluyeva), 260–61
Tzara, Tristan, 142

Uborevich, Jerome, 168
Ufa, 92
Ukraine, 50. *See also* Kiev
Unamuno, Miguel da, 157
Under Fire (Barbusse), 141
Underground parties, 16. *See also* Bolsheviks
UNESCO conference, 360–62
Unichtozhim Vraga (We Will Destroy the Enemy), 207
Union of Soviet Writers. *See* Writers' Union
United States, 198–99, 218, 231–39, 240–42, 243–44, 245, 247, 250–51, 265, 292, 296; cold war and, 240
Universal Necropolis, The, 93–94
Unlikely Stories, 71
"Uskomchel," 71–72
Utro Rossy (Russia's Morning), 35–36

Vaillon, Roger, 377–78
Vasilenko, Nikolai, 335, 356
Vasilevsky, Ilya, 87
Vechera, 34
Vechernaya Moskva (Evening Moscow), 103, 117
Vercors, 296, 436n36
Verlaine, Paul, 34
Verses, 30–31
Veshch (The Object), 88–89, 103
Vichniac, Abram, 86, 87, 88
Vichniac, Jacques and Isabelle, 239
Vichniac, Vera, 86, 87, 88
Vichy France, 182–84, 420n75
"Victory," 225–26

Vigdorova, Frida, 307, 356–57, 370–71, 446n1
Villon, François, 34, 191
Vilna, 208, 210, 230, 324, *pl. 6*
Vilna Jewish museum, 254–55, 264–65
Visa of Time, 112, 113
Vishnevsky, Vsevolod, 169
Vishniac, Roman, 86
Visotsky family, 400n12
Vladimov, Georgy, 7
Vlasov, Andrei, 206
Vlasti Naroda (The Power of the People), 49
Voice of America, 240–41
Voinovich, Vladimir, 7, 335
Vokrug Sveta (Around the World), 229
Volga Falls into the Caspian Sea, The (Pilnyak), 108
Volin, Boris, 90, 107, 108, 411n64
Volkischer Beobachter (National Observer), 220
Voloshin, Max, 33, 36, 45, 47, 48, 51, 59, 61, 62, 63, 192, 302, *pl. 2*
Volya Rossy (The Will of Russia), 103
Vorobyov, Marevna, 33, 38, *pl. 2*
Voronsky, Alexander, 79, 102, 108, 407n23
Voroshilov, 137
Vovsi-Mikhoels, Natalya, 287
Vovsi-Mikhoels, Nina, 287, 326
Voznesensky, Andrei, 350–51
Vulikh, Tatyana, 27, 28
Vyshinsky, Andrei, 48, 153, 423n36

Wallace, Henry, 218, 234
"War communism," 68, 69
Warsaw Congress, 251
Warsaw Pact, 294
Wat, Aleksandr, 161
We from Kronstadt, 159
Weil, Simone, 166
Weimar Republic, 82
"We—the Polish Jews" (Tuwim), 204–5, 326
Werth, Alexander, 169, 193, 387–88
Western Communists, 429n50
West Germany, 443n27
We and They (Savich), 104
We (Zamyatin), 103, 107–8
What a Man Needs, 169

"When Will the War End?"
(Vorobyov), 38, *pl. 2*
White Army, 51, 52, 55, 56, 57, 59,
60, 61, 62–63, 65
White Book, The (Ginzburg), 381
White Coal, or the Tears of Werther, 106,
109
Williams, William Carlos, 411*n*67
Wilson, Angus, 360
Wilson, Woodrow, 138
Without Taking Breath, 81, 147, 267,
268, 331
Woolf, Virginia, 168
Workers' council of St. Petersburg, 16
Works: *And Yet It Turns*, 88, 89; *Beyond
a Truce*, 147, 154; *The Black Book*, 5,
212–17, 235, 254–55, 265, 323,
325, 349, 425*n*64, 441*n*42, *pl. 8*; *A
Book for Adults*, 29, 38, 47, 48, 65,
147–49; *The Chronicle of Our Times*,
111–12; *Collected Works*, 325,
363–65, 414*n*26; *The Conspiracy of
Equals*, 107, 112, 411*n*67; "A Curious Incident," 65–66, 71;
"Deutschland-America," 241;
devotion to literature and, 27–34;
*Duhamel, Gide, Malraux, Mauriac,
Morand, Romains, Unamuno vus par
un Écrivain d'U.S.S.R.*, 413*n*7;
European Crossroad, 229; *The Extraordinary Adventures of Julio Jurenito
and His Disciples*, 3, 44–45, 70, 71,
74–81, 91, 93, 95, 97, 98, 149, 159,
200–201, 335, 353, 363; *Factory of
Dreams*, 112; *The Fall of Paris*,
186–87, 200, 218; *The Grabber*,
95–97, 101, 102, 107, 109; *In America*, 241; "In the Jungles of Europe,"
125; introductions, 293, 298–99;
*The Life and Death of Nikolai Kur-
bov*, 90–91, 93, 353; *Life of the Automobile*, 111, 112; *The Lion in the
Square*, 241; *The Love of Jeanne Ney*,
90, 91, 92–93, 117, 285, 409*n*34;
The Materialization of the Fantastic,
103; *Moscow Does Not Believe in
Tears*, 147; *My Paris*, 104; *Nights of
America*, 241–42; *The Ninth Wave*,
247, 248, 268, 331; "The Old Furrier," 58; *One Hundred Letters*, 207,
215; "On the Role of the Writer,"
279, 284; "On the Usual and the
Unusual," 95; *Out of Chaos*, 81,
116–20, 122, 126–28, 130, 147,
268, 285; *People, Years, Life*, 12, 18,
41, 50, 67, 97, 113, 120, 133, 134,
148, 153, 158, 171, 173, 204–5,
207, 249, 270, 317–18, 325–26,
333, 334–51, 372–73, 375–78,
382–84, 389, 414*n*26, 441*n*42,
447*n*22; *A Prayer for Russia*, 63;
Russkaya Kniga, 83–84; *The Shoe
King*, 111–12; *The Single Front*, 112;
A Soviet Writer Looks at Vienna,
413*n*11; *The Storm*, 246–47, 248,
263, 267, 268; *The Stormy Life of
Lasik Roitschwantz*, 95–96, 97–99,
100, 106, 109, 127, 317; *A Street in
Moscow*, 95, 97, 101, 284; *Summer
1925*, 101, 113; *The Thaw*, 278,
279–82, 284, 285, 286, 294, 317,
331, 396–97, 435*n*16; *Thirteen
Pipes*, 90, 363; *Trust, D.E.*, 90,
91–92, 93, 363; *Unlikely Stories*, 71;
"Uskomchel," 71–72; *Veshch*,
88–89, 103; *Visa of Time*, 112, 113;
What a Man Needs, 169; *White
Coal, or the Tears of Werther*, 106,
107; *Without Taking Breath*, 81, 147,
267, 268, 331; Writers' Union collection, 267–68; *Yesterday's People*,
27–28. *See also* Journalism career;
Literary criticism; Poetry
World Congress of Intellectuals, 243
World Jewish Congress, 214
World Peace Congress, 264
World Peace Council, 292, 295, 322
World War I, 2, 3, 35–39, 41, 45
World War II, 2, 4–5, 51, 122, 126,
181, 189–226; anti-Semitism and,
1, 4–5, 192–193, 200–217,
219–221, 248, 426*n*84, *see also*
Holocaust; Jewish partisans and,
208–12, 423*n*54; journalism career
during, 190–200, 218, 220, 221–22;
Nuremberg trial and, 230
Wrangel, Pyotr, 62, 64, 65
Writers' Congress. *See* Soviet Writers'
Congress
Writers' Union, 53, 81, 107, 108,
179, 184, 186, 219, 239–40, 245,
247, 266, 267–68, 279, 285, 286,

Writers' Union (*cont.*)
290, 293, 294, 302, 303, 305, 306, 310, 322, 323, 329, 330, 361, 371, 386, 387, 393–94; Literary Fund of, 181–82
Wroclaw Conference, 298

Yakir, Yona, 168, 169
Yakovlev, Alexander, 434*n*60
Yashchenko, Alexander, 83, 88
Yashvili, Paolo, 64
Yefimov, Boris, 418*n*46
Yermilov, Viktor, 348
Yesenin, Sergei, 66, 82, 84, 103, 342
Yesterday's People, 27–28
Yevtushenko, Yevgeny, 209, 279, 301, 318–20, 347, 350, 352, 353
Yiddish, 11, 12; attack against, 253, 255–57, 258, 259, 260, 262–63, 268–69, 287, 312–13, 315–16, *see also* Anti-Semitism; Ehrenburg on, 320–21
Yugoslavia, 228, 229, 245

Zaks, Boris, 375
Zamyatin, Yevgeny, 80, 100, 103, 107–8, 109, 144, 407*n*29, 411*n*64
Zaslavsky, David, 318
Zelinsky, Kornely, 219
Zhdanov, Andrei, 131, 136, 217, 239–40, 244, 249, 270, 365, 375, 397
"Zhdanovshchina," 240
Zhemchuzhina, Polina, 262
Zhukov, Yury, 445*n*14
"Zima Station" (Yevtushenko), 301
Zinoviev, Grigory, 49, 91, 105, 137, 153, 154
Zionism, 12, 13, 157, 256, 260, 261, 262, 269–70, 315, 326, 387, 394
Znamya (The Banner), 148, 150, 169, 187, 215, 241, 281, 306
Zola, Émile, 13, 324–25
Zonina, Yelena, 250, 356
Zorza, Victor, 196
Zoshchenko, Mikhail, 239, 247

DATE DUE
